The New World Power

The New World Power

American Foreign Policy, 1898–1917

ROBERT E. HANNIGAN

PENN

University of Pennsylvania Press

Philadelphia

10   9   8   7   6   5   4   3   2   1

Published by
University of Pennsylvania Press
Philadelphia, Pennsylvania 19104-4011

Library of Congress Cataloging-in-Publication Data

The new world power : American foreign policy, 1898–1917 /
Robert E. Hannigan.
    p.   c.m.
  ISBN 0-8122-3666-1 (acid-free paper)
  Includes bibliographical references and index.
  1. United States—Foreign relations—1865–1921. I. Title
E744 .H353   2002
327.73 21   2002020424

For Irene and Ted

Contents

Preface

My principal purpose in this book is to try to explain the trajectory (or fundamental course, objectives, and methods) of American foreign policy in the era running from the late 1890s to 1917 (the year the United States became a military participant in World War I). Although commonly referred to, and accorded significance, as the age of America's "emergence as a world power"—a label correctly connoting that it was in this period that Washington began to involve itself as never before in developments beyond the continent of North America—most studies of American diplomacy in the early twentieth century have either been organized around the boundaries of particular presidential administrations or focused on one particular geographical region of U.S. external activity (normally the Caribbean or the Far East, the two regions of highest profile activity).[1]

Historians have now attained sufficient distance from, as well as knowledge of, the turn-of-the-century era, however, to enable us to probe beyond these boundaries and to try to reveal more about the direction and methods of this extra-continental involvement. The potential exists to identify and discuss in detail more fundamental patterns running both through this whole period and through the different U.S. global engagements. Some useful efforts to go beyond the basic theme of "emergence" have been undertaken in essay form, especially in several articles that have tried to find a correspondence between "progressivism" and early twentieth-century foreign policy.[2] But this marks the first systematic, book-length effort to do that for this period.[3]

Attempts to discern patterns and continuities (without denying that each administration in this era had its own distinctive qualities and style) must also contend with the commonly held idea that Woodrow Wilson's foreign policy constituted a rejection in substance of the diplomacy of his predecessors. That notion stems mostly, I think, from the simple fact that scholars have tended to be far too accepting of Wilson's own descriptions of what he and the Republicans who came before him were all about.[4] Its adoption, nevertheless, undoubtedly helps to explain why historians have tended not to accord sufficient importance to whole areas of pre-1913 diplomacy that do not seem to fit into this framework (such as Pan-Americanism and the Hague system) and why the sophistication and complexity of pre-1913 diplomacy has tended to be neglected in favor of crude and simplistic stereotypes.[5] The result, inevitably, has been for Wilson, who is so often considered the fount of America's subsequent twentieth-century diplomacy, to be inadequately understood himself. I would contend that even Wilson's rhetoric, which clearly *was* more sophisticated than that of his predecessors, can be better comprehended against the backdrop of debates and dialogues that had been going on within domestic American politics since at least 1898.

Precisely in order to bring such patterns to light, I have avoided a strict chronological organization and have instead (at least in Chapters 2–7) structured the book around discussions of the development of policy in each of the era's most significant areas of (essentially regional) American involvement and interest. My object throughout, however, has been to use these separate studies as a way of both identifying and illuminating themes and approaches that are fundamental to U.S. foreign policy as a whole in these years.

Chapter 1 serves as an introduction, but not only to the book's discussion of concrete strategies and engagements. It is also designed to introduce important ideological concepts that informed the thought and behavior of virtually all of the policy makers in this era—not least because of their similar backgrounds—and to elucidate certain recurring "key words" and terms that are best understood within this ideological context.

The following three chapters discuss in turn the areas of the extracontinental underdeveloped world that were of most concern to Washington. Although Caribbean and China policies have been discussed extensively elsewhere, our understanding of American activity in both regions is, I think, enhanced by examining those involvements side by side and by trying to view them within the framework of U.S. policy overall. This is especially the case with the Caribbean, whose enormous significance in the minds of policy makers cannot be understood except by reference to the strategic ideas of Alfred Thayer Mahan and others who held that U.S. control there would be absolutely pivotal to the country's international posture in the future. Similarly important initiatives toward South America, as suggested, have heretofore received little systematic attention at all.

As the United States assumed a higher profile in such more distant regions at the turn of the twentieth century, that inevitably also had an impact on its relations with its immediate neighbors in North America. Canadian-American relations in this period (or any other) have constituted another area of scholarly neglect (at least from the U.S. side), but they were clearly accorded importance then. At different times, developments in both Canada and Mexico came to be seen as central to the working out of Washington's relations with other powers (especially Britain) or regions (the Caribbean). The resources of both countries came increasingly to be appreciated for their potential impact on the global U.S.

economic position. And all North America came to be viewed strategically as a kind of giant analog of the British Isles. From both a strategic and an economic standpoint, Canada and Mexico appear increasingly to have come to be thought of as part of an extended home base for this new global power. These issues are addressed in Chapter 5.

The last two chapters take up the issue of "world order." Chapter 6 contains a more wide-ranging discussion of the U.S. relationship to British power in the period up to 1914. While Washington was eager to reduce Britain's political and military role in the Western Hemisphere, a theme addressed in several of the early chapters, it wanted to see that power upheld in other regions. This chapter also analyzes American efforts (often in conjunction with London) in these same years to promote new mechanisms for the settlement of international disputes.

Chapter 7 deals with the years after the outbreak of World War I. Our understanding of American diplomacy in that time frame has been limited, I believe, by the tendency of historians to focus too narrowly on the question of how Washington eventually became a military participant in that conflict, to look backwards, in other words, from 1917. I have instead tried to examine more broadly the objectives and concerns of American foreign policy and to explore how these were seen as threatened by the disruptions of the war and by the activities and ambitions of the other powers.

Briefly put, what I argue American leaders were seeking to do throughout this era was to ensure a framework within which, as they saw it, the U.S. might successfully realize "wealth and greatness" in the coming twentieth-century world. This seemed to them not only desirable, but, given America's growing economic might (the U.S. had already become the globe's leading industrial, though not as yet financial, power by the turn of the century), well nigh inevitable, so long that is as the U.S. was able to neutralize current worrisome developments in the international system.

Policy makers were particularly concerned that the political-military expansion of other great powers not be allowed to infringe upon areas where they felt that the U.S. would otherwise be able to extend its commercial and political influence. Taking note of the recent Scramble for Africa, they fretted that what they saw as "greed"—especially on the part of other great powers—and "irresponsibility"—especially on the part of people in the underdeveloped world—might lead to the spread of this dangerous trend elsewhere.

In the middle decades of the nineteenth century, the U.S. had itself rearranged the boundaries of much of an entire continent, expanding across the whole midsection of North America. As policy makers sought to prepare the way for the role that they wanted the U.S. to play in the 1900s, however, they assumed somewhat the opposite posture, becoming in key ways defenders of an international status quo that they saw operating in their favor.

U.S. leaders focused above all on ways by which they might be able to shore up and institutionalize nineteenth-century political boundaries and frameworks for trade throughout the rest of the Western Hemisphere and in East Asia. These arrangements had to a large extent been established and upheld by Great Britain during the nineteenth century, but if they could be sustained, it was believed, America would ultimately succeed to the position of political and economic leadership that England had occupied throughout those sectors of the globe and emerge on the world stage as a power at least equal in stature to London. That such an international role would be in the interest of the entire world was, as shall be seen, simply axiomatic to these men, since they had already become used to making similar arguments for the positions that people like themselves occupied within their society at home.

The Western Hemisphere and East Asia were the areas of greatest interest, but even in this period American policy makers were not unconcerned with broader Old World-Eastern Hemisphere issues and developments. As much as they prized the geographic distance of the United States from Europe and the advantages throughout the Americas and (if to a lesser extent) in East Asia they thought their location gave them, leaders wanted trade access to other areas. They also worried about war and other forms of disruption, which might both disturb commercial and other exchanges with the Old World and lead to new assemblages of power there. These considerations were what lent emphasis to their desire, at least throughout most of this period, to see British power remain strong in other regions of the globe. They are also critical to understanding Washington's growing interest in arbitration and other potential instrumentalities of stabilization and order.

Such concerns inevitably conditioned the response of American policy makers to the outbreak of war in Europe in 1914. Accounts of the U.S. reaction to that conflict have typically treated it as having little to do with preexisting American policies, especially with regard to non-European countries.[6] But the war—right from its beginning—was seen as posing a challenge to the kind of world order that policy makers had been trying to secure, and their commitment to that project fundamentally influenced their diplomacy throughout the period of "neutrality."

Not only were the goals of American policy makers relatively consistent throughout this period, there were also important continuities, or at least broad similarities, in terms of approach. These are apparent, I argue, both in the methods by which the different administrations sought to regulate how countries in the underdeveloped world would be governed and in the means by which they sought to regulate and contain the behavior of other great powers.

In the less developed areas deemed most important to them, policy makers sought to promote regimes that would act on their own, as the great powers defined it, "responsibly," this so as to stave off partition and to secure the conditions under which the United States' trade and influence would continue to expand into those countries. Officials sought to cultivate and strengthen elements within such nations that they thought they might rely on. They created inducements and pressures designed to ensure that such governments accepted their "international obligations." And, if all else failed, and the stakes were deemed high enough, they were prepared to move still further and to extend what they defined as a "guardianship" over these nominally independent states.

With regard to their direct dealings with the other major powers, every administration in this period committed itself to a policy of forcefully defending the Monroe Doctrine throughout the Americas. Further away, where such a prohibition on other great power political and military activity could not plausibly be enforced, they returned again and again to the idea that unwanted activity on the part of rivals might be contained by the substitution, in some fashion, of collective and cooperative for unilateral approaches. This idea, I argue, was ultimately central to the promotion of such schemes as the League of Nations.

Chapter 1

Ideology and Interest

Despite their differences, all the major policy makers in this period are exploring shared certain key fundamental assumptions about how the world worked and what their responsibilities in it were, assumptions that—it will be argued here and in subsequent chapters—had a great impact on diplomacy. These ideas, and the attitudes that they helped to engender and reinforce, influenced how policy makers read and responded to foreign developments. They also offered justifications for the posture that, under their leadership, the U.S. government assumed toward the world.[1]

Social evolutionary thought, in particular, was central. This is hardly unfamiliar terrain. The racialist hierarchies and ideas about "stages of development" that were fundamental elements of that outlook have certainly been noted by diplomatic historians, especially to explain the condescension toward nonwhite peoples that was characteristic of policy in this era. But what has been insufficiently appreciated is just how broadly influential this thought was and what its central dynamics were.

Social evolutionism has occupied its most important place in the historiography of American diplomacy in connection with the overseas territorial expansion of the late 1890s. Pride of place belongs to historian Julius Pratt, who in the 1930s argued that not business interests but Social Darwinian ideas took the lead in bringing on that imperialism (especially with regard to America's acquisition of the Philippines).[2] The need to enter the struggle for survival, the need to grow or fall behind, that in his view was the motivation behind U.S. policy. And, indeed, this explanation has continued to be employed often by historians studying America's turn-of-the-century colonial acquisitions.

Since it was seen to be connected to military conflict and territorial expansion, however, Social Darwinism, as Pratt employed the concept, has never been accorded quite the same relevance for the years beyond the late 1890s.[3] In much the same way, historians of domestic American politics have tended to see Social Darwinism as tied to the nineteenth-century rise, and turn-of-the-century fall, of unadulterated laissez-faire.

Part of the problem stems from a collapsing of social evolutionism into Social Darwinism, which was in fact merely one social prescription based on evolutionary premises. But it undoubtedly stems as well from a misunderstanding of the appeal that social evolutionism, including Social Darwinism, had in late nineteenth-century America. As several studies of the popular philosopher Herbert Spencer have shown, his message had much less to do with a celebration of militarism and military conquest than it did with a vision of progress that in fact saw a so-called military stage of human evolution passing away before a more orderly industrial age of individual, marketplace competition.[4]

The social evolutionary ideas discussed below were in fact virtually all-pervasive among comfortable, propertied, old-stock Americans during the late nineteenth and early twentieth centuries. In an era of great domestic socioeconomic change and social conflict, they provided such Americans with reassurance that there was a definite order to life, that there were indeed discernible laws governing societal development. Moreover, there was also a widespread belief that if the laws of evolution, as they supposedly related to society, were properly understood and followed, the results would be highly beneficial (Woodrow Wilson captured the spirit of this when he remarked that America was in the process of seeing a Newtonian constitution replaced by a Darwinian one). As it had done for the middle class throughout the nineteenth century, science would continue to show the way. A teleology was built into social evolutionism that was absent from Darwin's own formulations about biology. Social evolutionism put on new foundations the nineteenth century middle-class belief in "progress," while it played simultaneously to a growing concern among the propertied about order and security.[5]

Perhaps most important, social evolutionary ideas also provided the core around which was shaped an updated ideology of the self-made man in America.[6] In the mid-nineteenth century, heralds of the new industrial capitalist order then taking shape in the North had proclaimed what they saw as that society's advantages over the slave system of the South. The North, they argued, was creating a society where all men could be whatever they would make of themselves and where the best interests of society at large would be furthered under conditions that allowed individuals the maximum leeway to pursue their own economic interest. Hard work was the key. By observing the work ethic, any man could, and it was assumed most men would, rise from the ranks of wage laborer to self-employed entrepreneur during the course of his lifetime. If he failed to do so, the fault was to be found in his own moral shortcomings.[7]

In the decades after the Civil War, however, even as the U.S. developed into a great industrial giant, American society became much more, not less, stratified socially. Moreover, this condition increasingly became the target of farm and labor critics who argued that the organization of society actually worked to perpetuate such disparity and inequality.[8] In their most popular formulation, social evolutionary ideas provided a supposedly scientific and objective rejoinder to such criticisms and protest and a reassuring explanation of the workings of American society. They did so basically by reasserting the notion that where people were in the society was by and large a reflection of themselves and by accounting for the growth of inequality by seeing it as a reflection of an inequitable distribution of capabilities throughout humanity.

From the late eighteenth century through the Civil War, a relatively favorable view of human nature, at least by Western standards, plus a theoretical, if not always practical, commitment to the notion that "all men are created equal" had predominated in the rising commercial and industrial centers of America. It is probably in these two spheres that the thought being investigated here broke most clearly with the past. The social groups that dominated American society at the turn of the twentieth century continued to have a quite positive view of themselves and their kind, and if anything an increasingly optimistic view of their capabilities. Yet at the same time, they generally held that the great Western liberal thinkers of the Age of Revolutions had been much too naive and positive in their appraisal of humanity at large.[9]

Meanwhile, such "respectable" Americans—and, as scientist and historian Stephen Jay Gould (among others) has shown, none more so for a while than academics and intellectuals—were almost obsessively preoccupied with identifying, describing, sometimes measuring, and always categorizing what they saw as significant differences within humanity.[10] The notion that "all men are created equal" now came formally to be replaced by an emphasis on different races with different capabilities.[11]

There are several distinguishing characteristics of this new evolutionary racism. First of all, reflecting fears of social and labor unrest in the industrial North and West, the threat of which was attributed especially to new immigration, this racism made sharp, prejudicial distinctions *within* the population of Americans of European background as well as between old stocks and non-Europeans. Second, while there had been hierarchical classifications of race employed before, the racialist thought of this era held that there was a particular dynamic and pattern to the development of races, and to their relationship to one another, and this specific framework was new. Third, outside frontier-colonial areas and the Old South, openly espoused racialist thinking had probably never achieved such a high degree of social respectability as it did at this time, in part because of the scientific and academic support that could be claimed for these ideas. Deemed to be scientific, such racial notions were held to be progressive.

This "biological," social evolutionary worldview was meanwhile also one that was highly gendered.[12] Visions of social order in this period were closely related to ideas about appropriate domestic, family relationships. And for the people of most interest to this study, notions of what was appropriate, even though they were under challenge from other quarters, still revolved very much around the idea that women were profoundly weak and passive and that there should be sharp distinctions made between men's and women's roles. It is critical to note as well that the comparisons of races that were so central to the social views of this time were in fact generally comparisons of the supposed attributes of the men of various ethnic backgrounds. As such, they reflected the preoccupation with masculinity and definitions of manhood that historians have noted among upper- and upper-middle-class men in America during these years.[13]

Within important intellectual and academic circles, as historian Carl Degler shows, scientific racism was already coming under attack by World War I.[14] But this certainly did not affect the views of the individuals of principal concern to this study. Likewise, it seems clear that *some* of those associated with progressivism were also coming to see many of these evolutionary categories as irrelevant. Philosopher John Dewey is a good example, although he valued Darwinism on quite different grounds, for what he saw as its challenge to fixity.[15] It has to be emphasized, however, that this set of ideas was by no means at odds with either state interventionism or with environmentalist approaches per se. Indeed, on the latter count, as numerous scholars have made clear, social evolutionism in America was from its inception framed more along the lines of Jean Baptiste Lamarck's ideas than those of Charles Darwin, especially in its discussions of the mechanisms of evolution, and it remained so even after Lamarck's ideas (centering on the inheritability of acquired characteristics) were discredited in the field of biology.[16] Moreover, although Social Darwinism was closely tied to the notion of laissez-faire, social evolutionary ideas could and did coexist with and provide support for more interventionist approaches on the part of those people who were deemed by it to be the "responsible" members of society.[17]

In Julius Pratt's day, American historians commonly viewed ideas and interests as historical explanations that were at variance with one another, with "Progressive-school" historians often visualizing the former as propaganda to be understood as a smoke screen masking other, usually direct economic desires. It was in part as an effort to get around the resultant economic determinism that, in the field of diplomatic history, William A. Williams subsequently focused on an "open door ideology" which, he argued, led American policy makers to seek to realize and sustain their vision of the good society at home through open door marketplace expansion abroad after 1890.[18] The great success of this approach was Williams's ability to establish the vital importance of economics in U.S. foreign policy. Yet this resolution of the problem also tended to restrict the explanatory power of his interpretation. By treating the "open door ideology" as *the* ideology of policy makers and then assigning to it control over U.S. diplomacy, Williams ultimately worked at cross purposes to the interest he showed elsewhere in studying foreign policy as the product of an entire social, rather than just economic, order.

More recently, historian Michael H. Hunt has sought to promote the study of this general topic in his work *Ideology and U.S. Foreign Policy*.[19] There he seeks also to describe what he terms "America's twentieth century foreign policy ideology." Hunt identifies, and provides a valuable discussion of, three prominent and long-standing American cultural attitudes (racism, the desire for national greatness, and a hostility to revolutions) and argues that by the early 1900s these had become fused together into "an informal but potent ideology that would point the direction for subsequent foreign policy."[20] For any given point in time, however, Hunt's approach seems able to provide only a fragmented and incomplete picture of the outlook of an era, and then only at a fairly high level of generalization.[21] His yield does not appear to be comparable to the increases in understanding that have come from studies of the ideologies of specific groups of people within specific historical contexts done by a number of American historians in recent decades.[22]

The ideology of American policy makers in this era was based on the premise that the world was inhabited by many quite different kinds of people. What differentiated them, as well as most other socially secure, old-stock Americans like themselves, from the rest—and what both explained and justified their leadership status in society—had to do at bottom with a strength that they believed they possessed in greater measure than anyone else. This was a strength of character that was both their special legacy from their forefathers, as they saw it, and a product of their own achievements.

"Character" had always been central to middle-class thought, but in the mid-nineteenth century a good character had been held to be something that almost any man could have.[23] By the late nineteenth century, a good character required not only conducting oneself in accordance with an ethic of hard work, abstinence, and the like. It also required a mastery of oneself. "There is no prohibition ... so potent as the prohibition which each individual puts upon himself," asserted McKinley.[24]

"Self-mastery" too was not a new term or concept at the turn of the twentieth century. But earlier it had referred to the Protestant religious injunction to avoid sin and temptation.[25] Now it was a condition or state, and while it was believed that the individual had some control over it, it was also felt to be a biological inheritance from one's forebears. This dual explanation for "self-mastery" was important. Those who held these ideas were anxious not to be considered merely lucky. They also wanted to be able to hold those old stocks who did not fare well, or who simply did not comport themselves in ways considered proper, personally responsible. Thus the gravitation toward Larmarckian notions of inheritance. What such people saw as their strong character, stemming from their "self-mastery," was seen to be the product both of inheritance and of generations of continued accomplishment on the part of their "race," alternately termed

Anglo-Saxons, Teutons, or simply "real Americans." Their strong character was the product of centuries of development on the part of people
who had been special to begin with, but who had also developed themselves again and again by rising to numerous challenges and by training
each successive generation to be stronger than the last.[26]

Chief among their race's accomplishments had literally been the taming
of the basic human nature they shared with all other men. By contrast with
views common during the Enlightenment, and now pointedly described as
naive, all the people of interest to this study held that human beings were
at bottom essentially "brutish," "cruel," and "beastly." It was this original
animal nature that their ancestors had gradually become strong enough to
hold in check. Yet each generation still had to tend to the task. "The truth,"
said Theodore Roosevelt, "is that each one of us has in him certain passions and instincts which if they gained the upper hand in his soul would
mean that the wild beast had come uppermost in him."[27]

"Self-mastery" had enabled these peoples of northern European background to control and tame the "lower passions" of man so that they could
be directed toward productive ends. It had also enabled them increasingly
to respect and protect the rewards of each man's industry. It had enabled
them, as they saw it, to discover and pioneer the one and only "path of
progress," eventually to become that path's principal custodians in the modern world. It had also made it possible for them to become the builders
and leaders of societies like America, the masters of natural resources and
other men, the custodians of civilization and its future.[28]

Since it was viewed as the most important quality in their lives and in the
world, these men constantly sought to obey and to conduct themselves in
accordance with what they saw as the dictates of "self-mastery." It was seen
as providing the key perspective on all the problems that they faced, and
also as key to their own fate. As a result, references to this condition—as
this study will show—are ubiquitous in the documentary literature of that
time. Again and again one finds, if not that term itself, then others that
reflect the same concern: "self-control," "self-command," "self-restraint," "self-
possession," and "self-discipline," among others. Implicit in this emphasis, of course, was the idea that the essential self in themselves and in all
human beings was something dangerous, something that ought to, and
perhaps for the sake of civilization had to, be controlled, disciplined, and
ordered.

Viewing their own social circumstances at home in the U.S., and America's technological advantages over the rest of the world, and evaluating
the relative merits of different societies on these grounds, American leaders of this time also explained what they described as the "backwardness"
of other peoples in America and in the world in terms of this calculus
of "self-mastery." Most other people were where they were in terms of
their wealth and technology because they were deemed to be less capable

people. Not only did they not work hard enough, or behave properly, they also did not have the capacity to master tasks, to direct men and resources to the same degree.

Social evolutionary thought supported the notion that the different races of human beings it identified could be ranked and compared in terms of how far they had evolved or advanced biologically down the "path of progress." Working backward from the "evidence" and drawing liberally on long-standing stereotypes of other nations and ethnicities, those who held these ideas defined non-old-stock members of their own society as well as the rest of the peoples of the world as lacking—to greater or lesser degrees—the same inherent capabilities, the same character, that they had. Other peoples were defined as failing to possess the same capacity to master and channel the "lower passions." Thus the adjectives used to describe them invariably indicated that they were less disciplined, more emotional or sensuous, less independent (because less strong), and less intelligent and rational (because both were likewise seen to depend upon control). This bid to classify all the rest of humanity was one more manifestation of a late Victorian urge to name and categorize, and thereby presumably know and master the world and what it contained. Intellectually equipped in this way, American leaders could, with supposed scientific authority, claim to speak of what they saw as the deficiencies of the Irish, Italians, and Eastern Europeans, or about what they saw as the still weaker characters of non-European people.[29]

These others were said by their very nature to be less civilized races compared to comfortable old-stock Americans, whose culture, lifestyle, and deportment were taken to define the essence of civilization. But they were also frequently said to be less mature and less adult as well. The two terminologies of civilization and maturity were closely related in this worldview. Yet, although they were often interchangeable, each terminology also had its particular utility and significance. This interchangeability as well as these differences can perhaps best be glimpsed here by noting that popular child development theories of this time held that all boys started out with many of the supposed psychological characteristics of primitive man. Then, in the process of their growth and development they moved, through the acquisition of greater self-control, in the direction of more civilized personality structures. Puberty represented the most difficult challenge, and other boys were believed not to come through it as successfully as boys of old-stock background. These theories were in line with a tendency on the part of the leaders of American society to portray themselves as the mature, and therefore also responsible, members of humanity who needed to guide others deemed more childlike in nature. And they facilitated the adoption of a sometimes benevolent, but always essentially patronizing, condescending, and lecturing posture toward other people, especially those who were presumed to be humbly awaiting the help of a "big brother." However, the

interchangeability of these ideas also made available a quite different set
of images if such guidance was spurned. When they resisted U.S. power,
for instance, "childlike" Filipinos quickly turned into crazed, threatening
"hordes" in need of taming if not (as was the fate of many during the war
of 1899–1902) destruction.[30]

Social evolutionary thought offered the figures with whom we are concerned a satisfying and fundamentally self-serving view of the world (and
its disorders). Yet it was hardly an unproblematic view, and not only because
it could sometimes be a very dangerous guide to reality. This was also an
ideology capable of fueling profound tensions and anxieties on the part of
those who held it. In particular, for American policy makers much was seen
to be riding on the ability of "real Americans" to retain their self-mastery,
vitality, virility. The strong character they believed they possessed was also
something they believed they could lose—and with such loss would go the
fate of civilization, their nation, their race, and their family, everything for
which they saw themselves as having responsibility. Most of all, they stood
to lose their very identity and manhood.

As an example that supposedly proved the legitimacy of their concerns,
some American leaders pointed to China. It was impossible even for men
with their sense of cultural superiority to ignore the antiquity and complexity of such a civilization. And if they tended to scorn it in the present,
they could not deny that even on their own terms it had had past glories.
But China's present situation was defined as an object lesson of the consequences of failing to abide by the dictates of "self-mastery." Once proud and
mighty, it was held to be a civilization that had made great strides up the
"path of progress" in the distant past only finally to become "stationary" or
dormant because of a loss of virility in its men. Only now was it "awakening" because of the influence of the West. China had lost its momentum
because the fiber of its men had become "degenerate" and "soft." They
had lost the character of "self-mastery" through over-indulgence in the
material wealth their ancestors had created. As a result, they had become
"effeminate" and "effete." The supposed threat of the same kind of decay
eventually overtaking "real Americans" haunted the men of interest to us,
and none more so—perhaps not surprisingly—than Theodore Roosevelt,
whose own manly identity had been won at such a high cost against child-
hood infirmity. Avoiding this kind of "decadence," it was believed, could
only be ensured if "real Americans" continued to exercise and demonstrate
their own mastery. American men had to avoid over-refinement and over-
civilization, to keep in contact with nature, to rise to new challenges, and
to demonstrate courage in the face of adversity.[31]

One common tactic in domestic politics in the late nineteenth and early
twentieth centuries involved questioning a political opponent's virility.
This practice was engaged in by regular Republicans and others (like
Wilson) against what they saw as the too-pure Mugwump reformers and

the "anti-imperialists" (who opposed U.S. annexation of the Philippines). It was also a way by which some Republicans (and others) viewed and responded to the rhetoric and policies of President Wilson.[32]

But, as many of these men came to appreciate, charges that had more resonance with the country at this time were those that dealt with selfishness and greed.[33] Here, too, social evolutionary thought had something to offer, for it gave all the policy makers of this time the opportunity to identify their objectives with the good of the nation and the world, and to portray their actions as disinterested service, as the carrying out of their responsibilities to civilization. Simultaneously, it allowed to be cast as selfish those who opposed what was defined as the one proper way.

Throughout this era, and at no time more so than at the time of U.S. entry into World War I, American foreign policy was presented as being committed to the defense and advancement of liberty and democracy in the world. Although some historians have accepted this rhetoric at face value, at least for some presidencies, it has been hard for most to do so in the face of the rampant interventionism of these times. Nevertheless, no analysis of the ideology of these men would be complete without examining what they in fact meant by self-government. And the key to that can be had, it would appear, by noting how the term can in fact accommodate both the idea of the consent of the governed and the idea of "self-mastery."

American policy makers were strong believers in the *potential* advantages of political arrangements that placed checks on concentrated power and that provided for popular participation in government. And they believed that such a system belonged to people like themselves by right. But this was a far cry from believing that all men, not to mention all adults, had an inalienable right to self-government. For their "race," or peoples with a strength deemed close to their own, self-government was deemed to be a tonic. Indeed it was partly as a function of their nation's political arrangements that American leaders in this era frequently explained what they saw as America's greater dynamism by comparison with Europe. Germany and (much more) Russia they especially described as being held back by an old order of despotism and ignorance, of medieval survivals, that America had escaped.[34]

Self-government, however, was not deemed a right, or as good, for peoples who were not held to be "self-governed," anymore than it was deemed good for those members of a family not deemed mature. "Self-governing people must have the spirit which makes them self-controlled," wrote Elihu Root, head of the War Department under McKinley and of War and then State under TR (and, in terms of influence and importance, the most historically underrated figure of this era). According to William Howard Taft, it was "the question of self-imposed restraint that determines whether a people is fit to govern itself." Freedom, said Roosevelt, could "be used only by people capable of self-restraint." Democracy was "wrongly conceived when treated as merely a body of doctrine," wrote Woodrow Wilson. It was "not created by aspirations or by new faith." It came, instead, "like manhood, as the fruit of youth: immature peoples cannot have it, and the maturity to which it is vouchsafed is the maturity of freedom of self-control, and no other. It is conduct, and its only stable foundation is character." Robert Lansing wrote that, "The individual states in a federal state like the United States stand in the same relation to the federal sovereignty that the male citizens of legal age stand to the sovereignty in a single state ... the territories of the United States are similar to citizens of the male sex in a single state, who are minors, but who will in time attain to equality in sovereign rights; and colonies are like the females in a state, who owe it allegiance but lack the inherent qualities to become possessors of the sovereignty."[35]

Social evolutionary ideas had the unique quality of allowing policy makers to take direction over other people's lives while at the same time allowing them to claim that they were still being loyal to America's most sacred value of liberty. A perfect example is the Philippines, where U.S. leaders characterized what they were doing as freeing Filipinos both from the Spanish *and* from themselves. In their minds, essentially, the *right* of such countries to be free existed only when they would exercise that freedom as American leaders would have them.

Thus McKinley stated on July 12, 1900, on the occasion of his renomination for a second term, that

The Republican party was dedicated to freedom forty-four years ago. It has been the party of liberty and emancipation from that hour.... It broke the shackles of 4,000,000 slaves and made them free, and to the party of Lincoln has come another supreme opportunity which it has bravely met in the liberation of 10,000,000 of the human family from the yoke of imperialism."[36]

The Filipinos if left to themselves, he and others alleged, could only plunge into "anarchy" or, as John Hay put it, become "victims of misrule at the hands of their own agitators."[37]

The issue of forcible annexation as a betrayal of America's past was an important one, because it was a charge frequently made by critics of that course. In the process of replying to such charges, defenders were drawn into some of their most open disavowals of the political principles of the late eighteenth- and early nineteenth-century Age of Revolutions. Root replied by pointing to how often the principle of self-determination had in practice been violated before:

The Democrats declared that we had no right to succeed because our assertion of sovereignty was a violation of the Declaration of Independence, which declares that governments derive their just powers from the consent of the governed. That maxim, though general in its terms, was enunciated with reference to a highly civilized, self-governing people. Its unqualified application without regard to the rule and progress of humanity and ordered liberty among men, is contrary to the whole course of American history. Without the consent of the hundreds of thousands of Indians whom our fathers found in possession of this land, we have assumed and exercised sovereignty over them. Without the consent of the people of Louisiana, Jefferson ... purchased their territory and exercised sovereignty over them.[38]

"'The Consent of the Governed'," wrote Wilson, then a professor of politics at Princeton, to Allen Wickham Corwin on September 10, 1900,

is a part of constitutional theory which has, so far, been developed only or chiefly with regard to the adjustment or amendment of established systems of government. Its treatment with regard to the affairs of politically undeveloped races, which have not yet learned the rudiments of order and self-control, has, I believe, received next to no attention. The "consent" of the Filipinos and the "consent" of the American colonists to government, for example, are two radically different things.[39]

"The principles of the Declaration of Independence do not require the immediate surrender of a country to a people like this," argued Taft in 1907. "If they did, then it would be utterly impossible to defend rules which exclude women from the ballot, rules which exclude minors from the ballot, rules which exclude ignorant and irresponsible male adults from the ballot."[40]

This does not mean, of course, that U.S. policy makers wanted to exercise direct rule throughout those areas of the world deemed important to them. In fact, for a whole variety of reasons—including expense, domestic politics, and perhaps above all their fear of fueling the movement toward continued global political partition—this was quite undesirable. Instead, as numerous historians of this era have argued, they preferred informally to shape and structure the development of other countries so they would behave as desired.[41] And much of the impulse behind this effort was simply an extension of similar techniques in use at home.

Historians are by now well aware of the problems associated with use of the terms progressivism and progressive movement, one of the biggest of which is the unity they quite incorrectly suggest was characteristic of all new (non-socialist) approaches to social problems during the early years of the twentieth century.[42] Suffice it to say that with a couple of exceptions, John Hay, McKinley's secretary of state, and Robert Lansing (Wilson's) among key policy makers being the most significant, the men of interest to us here were all supporters to some degree of a more activist role for government in society than had been favored by their Gilded Age predecessors. Their motivations arose out of fears of social disorder, but also out of a desire to, as they saw it, fully realize the society that they led and see it operate at maximum efficiency. These people all worried that government involvement, especially if done in the wrong way, could actually fuel radicalism and labor militancy and, in other ways also, diminish the social efficiency they envisioned. But, at the same time, they also saw adamant adherence to laissez-faire not only as courting disaster, but as an admission of powerlessness before new challenges that they could not allow themselves. Characteristically, they charged that those Bourbons and other traditionalists with whom they disagreed were either selfish and narrow-minded or squeamish and unmanly before the problems of the age. When employed by these men, such charges of selfishness and lack of courage were, it should be noted, all themselves conceptualized within the framework of "self-mastery."[43]

To a greater or lesser degree, depending on the individual in question, this commitment involved being prepared to place some restraints on what were often referred to as the "mere money getters" in the business world when their behavior seemed to jeopardize either the overall performance of the economic system or its public reputation, or when their exploitation of workers or tenants seemed likely to undermine the social fabric. But socially responsible behavior, as most of them saw it, also meant positive efforts both to win loyalty and trust and to oversee and "uplift" the behavior of the masses.

Ultimately they sought to ensure the continued leadership of their kind in America by promoting conditions under which most Americans would accept and act in accordance with the ground rules of the existing social order. Albeit to different degrees, they supported a variety of social and political initiatives and approaches. These included institutional reforms at the state and local levels aimed at neutralizing the power of political bosses and radical labor leaders who would "mislead" the "weak" immigrant newcomers. In the case of urban political reform, the idea was to see this leadership replaced by what they considered to be the disinterested and responsible leadership of people like themselves. These initiatives also included selective support for social programs and improvements in social conditions, especially in the cities, which it was hoped would train and improve the character of the poor. Here the posture of the "state as parent" that historian David Rothman has written about very much characterized their approach. Finally, these men also generally supported new methods of conflict settlement—conferences, mediation, arbitration—which were designed to diminish potentially explosive confrontations, and promote the notion of commonly held interests.[44]

Just as a "search for order," to use historian Robert Wiebe's phrase, characterized much of American domestic politics in these years, so too did such a search characterize American diplomacy. And, at bottom, the same vision, the same values, and the same assumptions that informed the general domestic approaches these men endorsed also guided their foreign policy. It was not so much a matter of one field of concern acting as a model for the other, although comparisons were made, as it was of the same attitudes deriving from the same impulses and outlook.[45]

This can most clearly be seen in the case of diplomacy in Latin America and China in these years. In both regions, the urge to ensure stability and order was in a way overdetermined. The temperament of American policy makers, their values, as well as the development of concrete American interests all encouraged a desire to see these areas pacified. Yet the overarching concern of U.S. diplomatic activity in the two decades before World War I is best captured in the era's constant references to the Monroe Doctrine and the open door, policies by which American leaders sought principally to shore up and institutionalize the political boundaries and frameworks for trade that had been prevailing throughout those two regions. These were arrangements that Washington saw as being jeopardized by the twin threats, again, of greed and irresponsible behavior (each a reflection of "lower passions" out of control) in the late nineteenth and early twentieth centuries. But they were deemed important to American policy makers precisely because they were seen as offering the U.S., the world's great new political-economic force, broad opportunities throughout these arenas itself. As shall be seen below, American leaders believed that if these arrangements could be maintained, both East Asia and Latin America were likely in the coming century to fall in behind U.S. economic and political leadership. And that, in turn, was perceived as likely to ensure the men of strong "character" who led American society positions of influence and responsibility on the global stage that conformed with what they felt they deserved.

Leadership over Latin America and China was seen especially to depend on successfully responding both to the greed of other powers and to irresponsible behavior on the part of the peoples of the involved underdeveloped countries—behavior that might "invite" a political or military intervention by those other powers. As to the latter challenge, American policy makers throughout this period ideally sought governments that would on their own accept American leadership and the behavioral ground rules that it defined as appropriate. In practice, generally this did not mean governments based on wide popular participation. Elections might be promoted as a way of providing for orderly transfers of power, but what was not promoted was democracy.[46] Instead, policy makers generally opted for strong central governments based on propertied and/or military elements. Indeed there was in Washington throughout these years a considerable fascination with what American leaders saw as progressive strongmen and a belief that their kind of leadership was often appropriate for the level of development of the races in these countries.

Policy makers placed strong political figures in such countries in either of two categories, those who did and those who did not seem to be people with whom they might work. Those in the latter category were condemned as selfish and as misleaders of their people. Sometimes, as for instance in the case of Emilio Aguinaldo of the Philippines, they were compared to radical labor leaders at home.[47] Those placed in the former category, people for instance like Yuan Shikai of China, were meanwhile considered farsighted statesmen.

The narrowly controlled governments that had come into being in the late nineteenth century in the major exporting states of South America fit the model of what American policy makers in this era were after. These governments were deemed strong enough to ensure that their people behaved properly, but their actual policies often continued to constitute a challenge to American leaders. This happened because of differing views over such issues as the Calvo clause (pertaining to the rights that foreigners who wished to do business in their countries should have), and also because, with the partial exception of Brazil, these elites continued to be suspicious of the North American colossus and anxious to sustain their long-standing European economic and cultural ties.

To overcome such challenges, American leaders dealt with these governments much as they were inclined to deal at home with the more conservative representatives of strong labor unions. They tried to hold out inducements of greater recognition, participation, protection, and respect, in return for South American acceptance of the basic ground rules desired by the U.S. Through the Pan-American conference system, meanwhile, they sought to create a forum within which they might build trust, create a belief in common Western Hemispheric interests, and woo these governments away from Europe.

Much more serious challenges confronted American policy makers in the Caribbean and in China. In the former (desperately poor and socially inequitable) region the problem was defined as stemming from a habit of revolutions, whereas in the latter it was perceived as flowing from a governing elite that was too feeble to counteract the forces of "backwardness" at home and greed on the part of great powers such as Russia and Japan. In the case of many of the countries of the Caribbean, American policy makers ultimately came to endorse what they described as guardianships of their governments. Until conditions were deemed safe, much of the real, if not legal, sovereignty would actually be in the hands of outside financial advisors whose authority would ideally be protected through a compliant local president and military.

While the language of immaturity and incapacity dominated American discussions of such states' affairs, policy makers' approaches to them also corresponded to domestic approaches toward what was defined as misrule in America's cities. Indeed, America's great cities of this era clearly were associated in the minds of most American leaders with those places abroad that they found most foreign and different: especially the "exotic" land of China and the "tropical" lands of the Caribbean and the Philippines.[48] All were seen as exciting and tempting and, in part because of that, especially dangerous environs in need of taming. As was the case with much domestic urban political reform in this period, American policy makers saw themselves as taking away from corruption, or "out of politics," the infrastructure and key levers of power in the Caribbean states where they intervened. Supposedly disinterested hands would then provide the order and supervision demanded by the world and under which the political character of these countries might be "regenerated." Eventually, much the same kind of approach, although to be carried out multilaterally, was also proposed for China.

U.S. policy makers ideally hoped to get all the other great powers willingly to accept the frameworks that they wanted to see prevail in the Western Hemisphere and East Asia. In the Western Hemisphere, for instance, while they committed themselves to a policy of forcibly defending the Monroe Doctrine throughout all Latin America, they also pledged to respect the open door (the concept of equal terms of access for all commercial competitors) throughout the region (even if this was compromised in practice), and they assumed responsibility (if again not always lived up to) for policing the area on behalf of all the powers.[49]

Challenges to the open door in China were another matter. Here American policy makers were far from being in a political/military position of strength and certainly not in a position to declare themselves the sole superintendents of "civilization." Instead Washington sought to promote the idea that it was in the interest of all powers to accept the open door framework, and policy makers tried by various means to absorb the unilateral approaches of other powers into a collective supervision of the empire premised on that.

In connection with the most famous of such projects in China, Taft and Secretary of State Philander C. Knox claimed that they would "neutralize" the empire and take it "out of politics." Such an effort was in fact symptomatic of a broader drive during these decades to, as policy makers saw it, take world affairs in general "out of politics," this as a means of stabilizing an international order that advantaged states like the U.S. and Britain wished to see maintained. Arbitration was one means by which this was promoted, at the Hague conferences, at the Pan-American conferences, and on other occasions. A step beyond that was the simultaneous promotion of an effective world court and the codification of international law. Finally, against the backdrop of the Great War, Woodrow Wilson endorsed and promoted a League of Nations, the structure of which would eventually resemble a globalization (outside of the Western Hemisphere) of the above noted approach to China. At the top of its power structure would be the great powers, exercising an equal political weight, but operating in accordance with the guidelines desired by the U.S. Next would be the less powerful independent states, who could gain some measure of protection and recognition in return for acceptance of the system's ground rules. And finally there would be the trusteeships, or children, who would be internationally supervised until ready to behave.

Bidding for stability and consensus, American political leaders preferred to avoid confrontations and coercive methods in their conduct of foreign policy. But, as shall be seen, they did not rule out force when that was seen as the only way to secure behavior in accordance with the rules that they desired. Instead, what they frequently sought to do under such circumstances was to conceptualize such force as enforcement of the rules of civilization. "Good diplomacy," said Elihu Root in 1901, speaking quite directly to this point, "consists in getting in such a position that upon a conflicts flaming up between two nations the adversary will be the one who has violated the law."[50]

Chapter 2

The "Center of Gravity":
Caribbean Policy and the Canal

American policy makers saw control over the Caribbean as central to their hopes of realizing "wealth and greatness" for the U.S. in the coming twentieth-century world, and particularly to their ability to uphold and stabilize the kind of international order they wanted. American trade and investment in this region was growing, and was valued for political as well as economic reasons, but, with the one very significant exception of Cuba, nowhere near so much as to account for the amount of attention Washington directed here.[1] The region's exceptional importance is instead best explained by reference to the canal that Washington built during these years across the Panamanian isthmus. American officials saw the future economic and strategic role of the U.S. in the world as heavily dependent on its control of access to that waterway.

Policy makers saw the canal as pivotal to the ability of the United States to extend its trade and influence out into the Pacific in the twentieth century. But they also believed it would become the strategic hub, or pivot, of their ability simultaneously to deal with challenges in the Atlantic, particularly should Washington's interest in areas beyond North America bring it into conflict with one or more of the major European states.

To ensure that control, the United States increased its military posture in the Caribbean—particularly through the acquisition of bases in Cuba and Puerto Rico—while, through a revivified Monroe Doctrine (first loudly reasserted, as shall be seen in Chapter 3, within the context of all Latin America), it simultaneously warned other powers to keep out. Other major states were told that any effort to expand their political/military presence in the region would be viewed as an assault on the U.S.

Much more involvement soon seemed necessary, however, for by the early years of the century policy makers began to worry that other powers might in one way or another be "invited" by locals to play a greater role in the region. As a result, every administration from this time on pursued a policy of seeking to ensure the kind of "responsible" behavior it wanted in each of the Caribbean's independent states.

To comprehend why the Caribbean was seen to be so important, planning about the region needs to be placed against the backdrop of the "sea

Atlantic Ocean

Barbados (Br.)

Anguilla (Br.)
St. Martin (Fr. and Neth.)
St. Barthélemy (Fr.)
Antigua (Br.)
Guadeloupe (Fr.)
Montserrat (Br.)
Dominica (Br.)
Martinique (Fr.)
St. Lucia (Br.)
Tobago (Br.)
St. Vincent (Br.)
Grenada (Br.)
Port-of-Spain
Trinidad (Br.)

Virgin Islands
St. Croix (Den.)

Puerto Rico (U.S.)
San Juan

Mona Passage

Puerto Cabello
Caracas

VENEZUELA

Santiago
DOM. REP.
Santo Domingo

(Neth.)
Aruba
Curaçao

Puerto Plata
HAITI
Cap-Haïtien
Port-au-Prince

Windward Passage

Guantánamo Bay (U.S.)
Santiago de Cuba

Caicos Island

Mayaguana

Acklins Island
Great Inagua
Crooked Island

Caribbean Sea

COLOMBIA

Cartagena

Bahama Islands (Br.)

Grand Bahama
Freeport
Great Abaco
New Providence
Nassau
Eleuthera
Cat Island
San Salvador
Rum Cay
Long Island
Great Exuma

Andros Island

Camagüey
Holguín

Kingston
Jamaica (Br.)

CUBA
Santa Clara
Cienfuegos

FLORIDA

Straits of Florida

Key West, FL
Havana
Matanzas
Pinar del Río
Isle of Pines

Cayman Islands (U.K.)
George Town

Gulf of Mexico

Yucatán Channel

MEXICO

BRITISH HONDURAS
Belize

Isla de la Bahía

HONDURAS
Tegucigalpa
Matagalpa
León
Managua
Corinto

NICARAGUA
Mosquito Coast
Bluefields
San Juan River
Greytown
Liberia
Brito
San José

COSTA RICA

Pacific Ocean

Panama Canal Zone (U.S.)
Colón
Panama
Panama City
PANAMA

GUATEMALA
Guatemala
San Salvador
EL SALVADOR

The Caribbean, c. 1910.

power" doctrines through which leaders of the era had come to think about America's future relations with the rest of the world. These ideas had begun to be formulated by naval figures, in papers presented before the new U.S. Naval Institute at Annapolis, as early as the 1880s. They were then synthesized and given polished expression in lectures delivered by Captain Alfred Thayer Mahan at the new Naval War College, at Newport, Rhode Island, beginning in the late 1880s, and in Mahan's many books and articles published over the following years. He more than anyone else was responsible for the influence these ideas had come to command among policy makers by the turn of the century.[2]

Mahan's basic argument was that the key to the rise and fall of great world powers lay in their control of the sea. In America's case, such control would be a precondition for what had now become the world's greatest industrial state to develop, sustain, and protect a thriving commerce with other areas of the globe and thereby achieve for itself both "wealth and greatness." This was because there would also be other powers seeking the same objectives.

Challenges of this magnitude had generally not confronted the U.S. during its nineteenth-century rise to preeminence as the dominant power on the North American continent. But Mahan wanted America to "look outward" in the future, and sensed correctly that this idea was steadily gaining currency among the nation's most powerful political and economic leaders too.[3] If it did so, it was going to have to look to the sea. It was also going to have to compete in a world that, as the result of revolutions in the realms of transport and communications, was becoming progressively smaller and more crowded.[4]

Within such an environment, a rising maritime power would have to be prepared for the possibility of conflict with strong rivals over the political, military, and economic organization of other areas of the globe. This in turn would require it to be able to control the sea lanes of most economic and strategic importance to itself and to deny free use of the sea to its enemies. Such, Mahan argued, had been the key to Britain's success as the preeminent world power of modern times.

If America was going to emulate Britain it was going to have to adopt different naval strategies from those it had held to in the past. As befitted the U.S. continental position and orientation, American naval doctrine had traditionally emphasized commerce raiding and coastal defense. Cruisers and gunboats had sufficed to protect any interests in overseas, nonindustrial regions against the interference of locals. By contrast, Mahan emphasized the importance of an offensive battleship fleet, which could, by successfully engaging the capital ships of any potential great power opponent, ensure the U.S. "command of the sea."

Mahan's ideas not only found a receptive audience among American leaders seeking a broader world role for their nation. By the end of the 1890s his sea-power doctrines had also come to be celebrated abroad, among

the leaders of most other great powers. They are central to an understanding of the naval expansion the United States undertook from the 1890s
onward (the American navy ranked at most tenth in the world in 1890;
after 1906 the new battleship fleet never ranked less than third). At least
in their basic thrust, Mahan's ideas are likewise key to an understanding of
American strategic thinking once a more coherent and consistently activist foreign policy course began firmly to be embraced by Washington after
the mid-1890s.[5]

It was the Caribbean's geographic attributes that drew the attention of
Mahan and other naval strategists to that region in the late nineteenth century. Just as the opening of the Suez Canal in 1869 had had dramatic implications for British trade and strategy, so too was it recognized that a canal
built across Central America could have enormous implications for the
U.S. Mahan viewed a canal as a facility that would vastly enhance America's
ability to control the fate of the Western Hemisphere and bid for influence
in the Far East.

Like other American canal enthusiasts—the bulk of whom had been
looking at the issue principally from this perspective—Mahan saw that a
canal would give producers in the eastern, industrial half of the U.S. considerable advantages, in terms of distance and transportation costs, over
European rivals for the markets of the entire Pacific. He recognized—as
had Ferdinand de Lesseps of France, who had tried and failed to dig a
canal across Colombia's province of Panama in the 1880s—that such a
facility was also destined to have a still broader impact. An isthmian passageway would become a great international highway of commerce, redirecting much of the world's trade across the Western Hemisphere.[6]

But Mahan viewed the canal from a military standpoint as well. It would
enable the U.S. to project extensive sea power into the Pacific. It would also
make it possible for America quickly to concentrate virtually all its growing
naval strength in either ocean should its emergence as a world power
involve it in a war with another sea-power state. As one canal historian
has put it, for Mahan and his followers the project was the indispensable
"first step to American supremacy" on the two seas.[7] One such follower,
Theodore Roosevelt, proclaimed in 1899: "if we are to hold our own in the
struggle for naval and commercial supremacy, we must build up our power
without our borders. We must build the isthmian canal, and we must grasp
the points of vantage which will enable us to have our say in deciding the
destiny of the oceans of the East and the West."[8]

To ensure that such an important waterway would be used for these purposes, however, access to it would have to be controlled by Washington.
Otherwise, instead of enhancing the U.S. world posture the canal could
become a strategic liability. America would have to have strategic control
over the canal's approaches. It needed base facilities to bring its own naval
power to bear throughout the Caribbean region, and it needed to deny

any such facilities to potential great power enemies so they could not be employed to compromise American use of the canal—or to support naval operations against the U.S. coast (it was for precisely the same reasons—as well as to project American power out into the western Pacific—that the Hawaiian Islands were also deemed important to strategists). Indeed, without a Caribbean base it was believed that it would be impossible for any European great power to defeat the U.S. militarily.[9]

The U.S. acquired the most important of the Caribbean bases policy makers thought they would need as a result of the war with Spain. Issues directly related to the significant American stake in Cuba itself are sufficient to explain that conflict's origins. Yet worries about America's stature in the whole region were present as well, and the conflict erupted at a point when the navy was growing eager to obtain facilities in the Caribbean.[10] When it came, officials were anxious to take advantage of the opening the war provided to advance other concerns. Cuba also confronted Washington with the first of many challenges it would face in the Caribbean in taming what it defined as "irresponsible" behavior.

Had Spain been able to restore order to Cuba after the outbreak of revolution there in 1895, the U.S. would not have moved to eject it from the island in 1898 (although threats of force definitely would have greeted any effort by Madrid to sell Cuba to a more formidable European power). In fact, since the 1880s, as historian Louis Pérez has demonstrated, Spain had been providing political rule while the U.S. had increasingly been enjoying the economic benefits of that colony. Americans had invested between $30 and $50 million in sugar plantations, railroads, and other properties, and Cuba had emerged as one of America's largest trading partners.[11] Madrid's inability to restore order paved the way for Spain to be viewed as part of the problem, rather than the solution, however, as American leaders grew more and more appalled by the disorder and destruction taking place there. And Spanish resistance to American advice—especially given Cuba's self-evident strategic and economic value to the U.S.—posed a direct challenge to America's claim to be the preeminent power in this region.[12]

In late 1897 Madrid finally agreed to try to defuse the revolution through an offer of local self-government.[13] But after the apparent failure of this effort, the McKinley administration—despite its very great desire to show the world that it "had spared no effort to avert trouble"—decided to push Spain out of the way.[14] Preparations to employ force began in Washington. Madrid announced that it would seek an armistice, during which it would negotiate for peace with the revolutionists.[15] But it was not prepared to countenance the loss of Cuba as a solution, which had now become Washington's bottom line. As a result, McKinley requested authority from Congress on April 11 to remove Spain from the island.[16]

McKinley's objective, however, was to deal more effectively with the revolution, not to make Cuba literally independent. Indeed, his message to Congress defined America's posture as involving a "hostile constraint" on both parties to the contest, so that Washington could determine the island's future.[17] Assistant Secretary of State Alvey A. Adee had recently noted how this could be done. Washington, he asserted,

> would be free, if successful, to dictate the terms of peace and control the organization of an independent government in Cuba. We could hold the Cuban territory in trust until, with restored tranquility a government could be constitutionally organized which we could formally recognize and with which we could conclude a treaty regulating our future relations to and guarantee of the Republic.[18]

McKinley was determined to make American interests on the island secure and for that reason he adamantly opposed U.S. recognition of what he termed the "so-called Cuban Republic" that was being championed by the independence movement.[19]

He was confident that there were elements within Cuba that Washington could deal with and work through, including many leaders of the broad-based revolution. But McKinley and his advisors doubted that these "responsible" forces would come to dominate Cuban politics on their own. Cuba's social elite was composed of landed and middle-class light-skinned creoles, but the foot soldiers of the revolution were darker-skinned peasants and agricultural workers, people who in the eyes of American policy makers were by definition incapable, irresponsible, and dangerous. Moreover, pushed aside, dispossessed, and increasingly marginalized by enormous changes in Cuban land holding during the late nineteenth century—in no small part generated by the takeover and expansion of the sugar industry by American capital—these forces had been hoping for a government that would not only be independent, but that would also champion causes such as land reform. This social dimension to the revolution did not enhance its appeal in Washington. Rather, it spoke directly to the U.S. insistence since 1895 that Madrid stabilize the situation on the island. Grover Cleveland's secretary of state, Richard Olney, had pointed in horror at what he called "the heterogeneous combination of races" that threatened to inherit the governance of Cuba. Likewise, William J. Calhoun, an Illinois attorney who had gone to the island seeking information for McKinley, held up the specter of social upheaval and "black domination" should independence be achieved.[20]

None of this means that McKinley was not in fact affected by the draconian measures that Spain had resorted to in order to suppress the rebellion—most especially because of their impact on noncombatant women and children—even if his ideology would also make it possible for him shortly to sanction nearly identical tactics in the Philippines. But it does help us to understand how McKinley could see himself as going to the rescue of Cuba while he simultaneously pitted himself against the very cause for which most Cubans themselves had been fighting. The president instead asked Congress to empower him "to secure in the island the establishment of a stable government, capable of maintaining order and observing its international obligations, insuring peace and tranquillity and the security of its citizens as well as our own."[21]

The Cuban coast was put under blockade. Ground forces were assembled in Tampa for an invasion of the island near Havana, and American commanders offered supplies to the revolutionary army in order to ensure its assistance. Cuban military leaders, for their part, viewed such cooperation as perhaps the only hope they had of limiting the U.S. role.

But a great invasion ultimately proved unnecessary to the defeat of the Spanish. After Admiral Pascual Cervera y Topete's Spanish fleet evaded detection and slipped into Santiago Harbor, on Cuba's southeastern coast, Cuban fighters secured the beaches so that an American expeditionary force could land and drive it out into the hands of the waiting American navy. This set the stage for the only significant Spanish-American confrontations on land, including the battle for San Juan Hill on July 1.

Cervera bolted even before Santiago could be taken. His aged flotilla of ships was no match for the fleet under the command of the American Admiral William T. Sampson. Within a few hours all Spain's ships had been destroyed or run aground. The results seemed to vindicate Mahan's doctrines of sea power. Cut off from Cuba (as well as from the Philippines and Puerto Rico), and bereft of a navy, Madrid was soon ready to sue for peace.[22]

The pressure for cooperation with the Cuban forces ceased. Although anxious not to provoke a confrontation, U.S. authorities were now determined to move the Cuban army to the periphery, so—as Adee had put it—they could hold the island "in trust." The army was forbidden to enter Santiago with American forces after the city's formal surrender on July 17. In January 1899 (following the Spanish-American peace treaty signed the previous month), representatives of the Cuban army were excluded as well from the ceremonies in Havana that marked the end of Madrid's sovereignty over the island.[23] There were actually more U.S. troops on the island at the beginning of 1899 than there had been before the end of hostilities with Spain. And their first priority was to demobilize and disband the Cuban forces.[24]

Beyond this, the task of the U.S. occupation was to secure and guarantee for the future America's economic and strategic interests in the island. Cuba's strategic value to the defense of the U.S. itself had long been recognized, and officials were determined to ensure that no other power would ever be able to play a role there. But policy makers were now also looking at Cuba as a vital platform for the projection of American naval influence throughout the entire Caribbean. As early as August 1898, the Naval War Board formally recommended U.S. retention of naval bases in Cuba (especially in the vicinity of the vital Windward Passage) as well as in Puerto Rico.[25] To play all the roles envisioned for it, Cuba would have to be tied closely to the U.S.

Occupation officials were to be disappointed in their hope that the island's landed elite would constitute the leadership on which Cuba's government could be based. The upper class was reticent to become directly involved in politics, and, because so many of its members had opposed the revolution, they had become unacceptable to most of the populace. In their stead, however, American authorities were able to cultivate a relationship with some segments of the revolutionary leadership.[26]

During the three years of the occupation, economic ties between the U.S. and Cuba increased enormously. By 1902 the level of investment was twice what it had been in 1898, and this activity continued to promote development of the economy around big, increasingly American-owned plantations and the export of sugar and tobacco. For U.S. authorities no less than for private capital, rebuilding Cuba meant, by definition, reconstructing it along such lines. It also meant stimulating such activity through the promotion of numerous infrastructural projects, including new rail lines and the dredging of Havana Harbor.[27]

Overall policy was formulated in Washington by McKinley's new secretary of war, Elihu Root, while by late 1899 local responsibility for the occupation was vested in the hands of the well-connected General Leonard Wood, who had come to Cuba with TR's Rough Riders. Wood described his approach as one of "paternalism." As he saw it, those who had led the Cuban revolution were "transparent little rascals," out, unlike the U.S., for their own selfish ends. The people of Cuba meanwhile were by and large "a race that has steadily been going down for a hundred years." They constituted a threat to the kind of Cuba the U.S. wanted. To negate that threat and to promote a pro-American stability, Wood sought not merely to influence the island's political affairs and economy but also to shape its society.[28]

In his annual message for 1899, McKinley stated that Cuba was being fitted for what he called a "regenerated" existence by authorities who were "taking every rational step to aid the Cuban people to attain to that plane of self-conscious respect and self-reliant unity which fits an enlightened community for self-government within its own sphere, while enabling it to fulfill all outward obligations." Nevertheless, the "new Cuba" would also need to be "bound to us by ties of singular intimacy ... if its enduring welfare is to be assured."[29]

Over the following months, despite a purge of the civil administration employed by the occupation and an insistence on literacy and property qualifications for participation in both municipal elections and the election to select representatives to a constitutional convention, Root and Wood remained dissatisfied with the degree of independent-mindedness and radicalism existing in Cuban politics. This put an even greater emphasis on the kind of "ties" the president had referred to.[30]

General James H. Wilson had already suggested to Root how these might work. Washington could liquidate the occupation and still "practically bind Cuba, hand and foot, and put her destinies absolutely within our control," he pointed out. The key to this would be a treaty signed at the end of the occupation that would leave the U.S. government "as free to interpose for the prevention of rebellion and anarchy in the island of Cuba, as it is . . . to intervene in the affairs of any state of the Union."[31]

Root hoped to get the Cuban constitutional convention, which began meeting in November 1900, to propose such a relationship as if the idea was its own. When that was not forthcoming, however, the administration's demands were finally articulated by Congress in early 1901 in the form of the Platt Amendment, acceptance of which was made a condition of the occupation's termination. The Platt Amendment gave the U.S. the right to reintervene militarily in Cuba essentially at its own discretion. It accorded Washington the right to veto any foreign political or financial relationships Cuba might enter into. It compelled the new government to validate all the actions that had been taken by the military occupation. And it granted to the U.S. the right to establish naval bases on the island. These political-military connections were finally supplemented by commercial ties as well in 1903, when the new Roosevelt administration succeeded in getting Congress to ratify a reciprocal trade treaty with Cuba.[32]

By virtue of the Spanish-American War, American policy makers had come to control in Cuba what they saw as a vital, indeed perhaps *the* vital stronghold in the Caribbean region. By far the most populous and economically valuable of the states there, Cuba was also, as Root put it in 1904, "that island which guards the Caribbean and the highway to the Isthmus."[33] Meanwhile, the "lessons" of the war (when it took the battleship *Oregon* more than two months to travel from the coast of California to Key West to join the North Atlantic Squadron), simultaneous events in East Asia that presaged a new era of great power rivalry there (see Chapter 4), and the acquisition by the U.S. in 1898 of important territories in the Pacific, all gave additional impetus to the American desire to begin construction of a canal across that isthmus.

Before steps toward that end could be taken, however, Washington had first to address engagements that had been made to England. The Clayton-Bulwer Treaty of 1850 had stipulated that neither the U.S. nor Britain would construct a canal anywhere in Central America except in cooperation with one another. In the mid-nineteenth century, the agreement had worked to Washington's advantage in that it had blocked the prospect that Britain, then the dominant power in the region, might come to control a canal on the isthmus. However, Britain's rights had now become an obstacle to the construction of a canal that would be owned and operated by the rising new power in the region, the U.S.[34]

Although prepared to modify the treaty, Lord Salisbury's government in London was anxious for a quid pro quo (ideally in the form of a meaningful concession to Canada in the Alaska boundary dispute, discussed in Chapter 5). England would be yielding valuable rights. Moreover the War Office had pointed out that a canal would enhance American naval power, intensify the competition that Britain would face from U.S. trade, and create new burdens for the Royal Navy.[35] But neither the McKinley administration nor Congress were eager to bargain over what had by now come to be seen as the U.S. destiny in Central America, nor was Congress in particular willing, in any dealings with England, to tolerate delay.

Hard-pressed internationally (at the time particularly because of the Boer War in South Africa), and confronted with growing American power, which it was anxious to conciliate, London relented. Early in 1900, Hay and the British ambassador, Julian Pauncefote signed a new treaty relinquishing any direct role for England and paving the way for a canal to be built solely under American auspices.[36]

To Hay's surprise, however, this convention became the focus of domestic criticism, too. The Hay-Pauncefote Treaty followed the outline of the rules that had been laid down for the use of the Suez Canal. It banned fortifications in the immediate vicinity of the passageway, provided for its neutralization in time of war, and called on the rest of the world community to adhere to its terms. But, Roosevelt, now governor of New York, and other critics, including prominent members of the Senate, objected that these provisions would make it difficult for the U.S. to use the canal itself in wartime while denying its use to others. They also saw the issue of international adherence as potentially compromising the claims Washington was making under the Monroe Doctrine. Wrote TR to Hay, "If we invite foreign powers to a joint ownership, a joint guarantee, of what so vitally concerns us but a little way from our borders, how can we possibly object to similar joint action say in Southern Brazil or Argentina, where our interests are so much less evident?" The Senate eventually approved the treaty in December, but only after adding amendments that exempted Washington from the neutrality provision, allowed the U.S. to deploy military force at the site of the canal, and eliminated the call for international adherence.

Hay was fearful that the Senate had ruined any chance for a settlement with Britain. At the same time he believed there were advantages to an international guarantee of the canal's neutrality. He had by no means ignored the issue of control, but his discussions with naval authorities had led him to the conviction that this was not jeopardized by the treaty.[37]

Britain did balk at ratifying the agreement as amended. However, Lord Lansdowne, the foreign secretary, recognized that London ultimately had little alternative but to accede to America's wishes. And he understood as well that giving way on the fortification issue would only add to the naval preponderance in the region that the U.S. was destined in any event to enjoy. The Caribbean simply did not have the same importance in British policy. As a result, negotiations were resumed and a second Hay-Pauncefote Treaty was eventually concluded by the two powers in November 1901. Less offensively worded from the number one sea power's standpoint, it nevertheless explicitly superseded the Clayton-Bulwer pact and conceded all the points at issue.[38]

Washington was impatient with Britain, but it was even less willing to brook delay or opposition to its plans from within the Caribbean. Until the Spanish-American War, the general assumption had been that any waterway the U.S. built would follow a course across the southern border of Nicaragua, between the towns of Greytown and Brito. This route had been the favorite of American canal proponents since the 1870s, and a commission under Admiral John Grimes Walker again endorsed its feasibility in 1897. After 1898, however, as momentum for the project grew, McKinley and Congress agreed to have a more thorough examination made of the possible routes before reaching a final decision.[39]

When the second Walker Commission submitted its report in November 1901, the majority of its members felt compelled to reaffirm the choice of Nicaragua as "the most practicable and feasible route." However, they did so only because the price being asked for its rights by the New Panama Canal Company of France—which had inherited the rights of de Lessups's failed enterprise—made their route far more costly.[40] On engineering grounds, the commission actually came down strongly for that as the best site.[41]

In response to the report, the French company dramatically lowered its price. The Walker Commission changed its recommendation, and in mid-1902 Congress authorized the president to build the canal in Panama, provided a favorable treaty could be arranged with Colombia within a "reasonable" amount of time. Otherwise he was to turn back to Nicaragua.[42] Roosevelt had become convinced of the superiority of Panama, however, and after passage of the Spooner Act in June 1902 it seems unlikely that he would have settled for any other site. From this point on, Nicaragua's principal importance appears to have been the leverage it gave Washington in its bargaining with other parties involved in Panama.

And, at least at first, that leverage appeared to be quite substantial. Hay signed a canal treaty with Tomás Herrán, the Colombian chargé in Washington, in January 1903, which the latter described to his government as "not perfect" but "the best possible to make of a very difficult question." Under its provisions Washington was given the right, for the term of one hundred years, "renewable at the sole and absolute option of the United

States," to build, operate and collect tolls for the use of a canal and auxiliary facilities to be located in a zone six miles wide across the isthmus. Bogotá would retain nominal sovereignty over the area, but the U.S. was to be granted broad police and administrative powers, the right of military intervention, and substantial judicial authority. In return, Colombia was to receive a one-time cash payment of $10 million and an annual payment of $250,000 to begin nine years after the treaty's ratification.[43]

The Hay-Herrán Treaty easily secured ratification in the U.S. Senate in early 1903. But in Bogotá it ran into considerable opposition and then, in August, rejection. Attention focused both on the nature of the concession and on the amount of compensation Colombia was being offered for it. Unlike Herrán, Colombia's legislators were not intimidated by the presence of the Nicaragua alternative. They did not believe that the U.S. would easily abandon Panama. Nor did they believe that Washington would do other than seek to reopen negotiations. Their first assumption was right, but their second was profoundly mistaken.[44]

Roosevelt and Hay were furious about Bogotá's failure to ratify the convention. Indeed, its perfidy, as they saw it, placed Colombia on the lowest rungs of their civilization-backwardness scale. The Colombians were "contemptible little creatures," a "low," "inefficient," "pithecoid" community of "homicidal corruptionists." Its political "jack rabbits," they fumed, were consumed by a foolishness and greed that was jeopardizing the future of "civilization." They were nothing but "blackmailers," and as such it was hardly appropriate for the U.S. to continue to deal with them. Colombia had instead to be given "a lesson."[45]

That "lesson" wound up principally being one about power, particularly of the naval sort. The prospect that Bogotá's position might throw the Panama route into jeopardy had already sparked separatist discussions on the isthmus, as officials in Washington were aware. Roosevelt avoided open encouragement of such a revolt, while at the same leaving little doubt in discussions with involved parties, such as New Panama's Philippe Bunau-Varilla, as to how the U.S. would respond should one take place.[46]

Bunau-Varilla assured the separatists that, if an uprising occurred, the U.S. would act in such a way as to protect them from Colombian counteraction. Thus encouraged, they seized control of Panamá City and Colón on November 3–5, and U.S. naval power was deployed as had been expected. Washington quickly extended de facto recognition to the new government on the isthmus.[47]

Not only was the Roosevelt administration able to bypass Bogotá as a result of the Panamanian revolt, it was also able to acquire even more favorable rights on the isthmus than those that had been envisioned in the Hay-Herrán Treaty, a process that was abetted by the fact that Bunau-Varilla—whose principal loyalties lay with the Panama route rather than with Panama—had engineered his appointment as the new republic's diplomatic representative in the U.S.[48] Work on the canal, which would open in 1914, began the following year.

Mahan's ideas about American sea power placed an absolute premium on U.S. control of the new canal and its approaches, which in turn meant that potential great power enemies had to be prevented from establishing any military/political positions within the Caribbean. For that reason, policy makers like TR took every occasion to proclaim that the U.S. would not tolerate "territorial aggression by any non-American power at the expense of any American power on American soil," while the McKinley and Roosevelt administrations sought positions of strength in the vicinity of the canal zone themselves.[49]

Such preparations were designed to deter direct challenges by other great powers to this revived Monroe Doctrine. But, in part because of American strategic preparations, policy makers soon began to worry that their prohibition had a much greater likelihood of being compromised in an indirect, or as Root put it, "collateral" way.[50] This was the lesson that they felt was underscored by the Venezuela claims confrontation of 1902. And it was ultimately what led them to the conclusion that they would have to try to ensure the kind of order they wanted not just in "independent" Cuba, but throughout the Caribbean as a whole.

On the basis of a vigorous new expansionism of its own, Germany was seen as the power most likely to try to challenge the Monroe Doctrine (see Chapter 6). Consequently it was to Berlin that the most pointed warnings were made. At the turn of the century, Hay and Roosevelt (first as vice president and then as president) repeatedly reminded that state of American policy. Simultaneously, TR made assurances about the open door for trade in the region and insisted that, "If any South American State misbehaves towards any European country," that country could still "spank" it.[51]

Berlin was therefore doing no more than taking Roosevelt at his word when it began to consider administering such a "spanking" to Venezuela in fall 1901. It had been trying to get Caracas to pay for damages suffered by German nationals during Venezuela's civil wars of 1898–99, wars that had brought the new government of caudillo Cipriano Castro to power there. Faced with an empty treasury, scornful of the great powers, and soon confronted with renewed domestic warfare, Castro had, however, simply ignored the issue. Outraged German officials began in response to consider forcible collection, both to teach Castro a lesson and to set the tone they wanted for the treatment of German economic interests throughout Latin America.

At the end of 1901, Germany made it a point to inform the State Department of its plans and to render assurances that these did not include any permanent occupation of Venezuelan soil. Hay replied by reaffirming TR's recent statements (reiterated in his first annual message as president). Still uneasy about the possible impact of a naval expedition to Venezuela on German-American relations, however, Berlin kept its plans on hold throughout the first half of 1902. The project was then revived in July when Britain expressed interest in it.[52]

Planned for the late fall, the operation envisioned first a seizure of Venezuela's small fleet of gunboats and then the institution of a blockade at Puerto Cabello, the country's principal seaport. Washington was informed of the expedition by the British ambassador in November, and Hay replied as he had eleven months before. Once it began in early December, however, the action quickly assumed dimensions that none of the powers had counted on. Hostile fire erupted off the Venezuelan coast, and soon thereafter two of the country's gunboats were destroyed. Then the flotilla bombarded Venezuela's fortifications at Puerto Cabello. The prospect soon presented was of a protracted struggle rather than a quick Venezuelan capitulation.

As events drifted toward war, Roosevelt and Hay worried that there might be a more or less permanent seizure of territory by the expedition powers somewhere along the Venezuelan coast. Perhaps Germany was even anxious for that to happen. The president wrote editor Albert Shaw later in the month: "the chances of complication from a long and irritating little war between the European powers and Venezuela were sufficiently great to make me feel most earnestly that the situation should be brought to a peaceful end if possible." Castro, with the encouragement of the American minister, had expressed a willingness to accept an arbitral solution. Roosevelt and Hay now urged the intervening powers to agree to that as well. Elements of the U.S. fleet, which had been massed in the Caribbean for maneuvers, were despatched to the waters off Venezuela as a show of American strength.

The resolve of the intervening powers had in fact already been shaken, both by the failure of the operation to go off as planned and by the prospect of American displeasure. International opinion had deplored the fighting. The British government had come under severe domestic criticism for jeopardizing good relations with the U.S. And Berlin, for its part, was anxious not to occupy a more advanced position than its partner. On December 18, therefore, England and Germany jointly adopted a new position around which the confrontation might be contained and resolved. Once Venezuela paid the most important claims, and agreement could be reached on the terms of arbitration for the rest, the powers would end their blockade. Concerned all along not to "be put in the position of preventing the collection of an honest debt," TR quickly agreed.[53]

Roosevelt came away from the Venezuela crisis pleased with the deference that the European powers had felt compelled to show to American wishes in Latin America. However, the incident also raised serious concerns about the future, particularly since many of the impoverished countries of the Caribbean were beset by political instability and heavy public indebtedness to outsiders (still generally Europeans). Such issues might provide a favorable opening if a rival power was interested in securing a foothold in the area.

What would happen, the administration worried, if another such intervention were "invited" and the Caribbean state either refused to arbitrate or could or would not meet a European power's demands? Under prevailing international law, the intervening power would then have the right either to occupy a portion of the offending state's territory or to seize control of its customs houses. Either way, the result could pose a challenge to the Monroe Doctrine. The U.S. might be compelled to go to war to enforce its strategic hegemony in the Caribbean, and it would be placed in a more difficult military, and perhaps legal, position from which to do so. To prevent such a situation from arising, Roosevelt decided that the U.S. should subsequently itself address any conditions that might provide a "pretext" for such a challenge.[54]

The decision of the Permanent Court of Arbitration at The Hague in the Venezuela case, rendered in February 1904, encouraged Roosevelt to announce this as America's new policy. Most of the questions at issue between Caracas and the powers were in fact not sent to arbitration.[55] But the parties had not been able to agree on the contention of England, Germany, and Italy (which had joined the blockade on December 20) that they should be paid off before other countries that also had claims against Caracas. This one issue was referred to The Hague, and, to the surprise of many, the court found on behalf of the powers, seemingly encouraging more such interventions in the future.[56]

Hoping to show "those Dagos" that they had to behave as the great powers wished them to do, Roosevelt now articulated his new policy in the form of a warning. Before a dinner held in New York City in May to celebrate the second anniversary of Cuban "independence," Root read a letter from the president outlining his "corollary" to the Monroe Doctrine. "All that we desire," it said, "is to see all neighboring countries stable, orderly and prosperous.... If a nation shows that it knows how to act with decency in industrial and political matters, if it keeps order and pays its obligations, then it need fear no interference from the United States." But "Brutal wrongdoing, or an impotence which results in a general loosening of the ties of civilized society," Roosevelt continued, "may finally require intervention by some civilized nation, and in the Western Hemisphere the United States cannot ignore this duty."[57]

In the Caribbean, as in other regions of the world of special importance to them, American policy makers in the early twentieth century ideally wanted local governments that would accept U.S. leadership, that would behave according to the ground rules that Washington defined as appropriate, and that were strong enough to ensure that their populations were orderly.

But this region was instead, Roosevelt fretted, comprised of "weak," "irresponsible" governments and "disorderly" and "chaotic" peoples. Washington's initial concern had been confined primarily to Cuba and Panama, but in the aftermath of Venezuela, the Roosevelt administration became convinced of the need to ensure the kind of stability and order it favored throughout the entire Caribbean.

Roosevelt demonstrated his willingness to act on this policy within only a matter of months in the Dominican Republic. Here political turmoil had been almost perpetual since the overthrow (by assassination) in 1899 of the long dictatorship of Ulíses Heureaux. Now the country was nearly bankrupt, and it was far behind in paying back the large debts Heureaux had run up with foreign creditors.

Control of the capital, Santo Domingo, had been wrested back and forth among a handful of contending caudillos and factional leaders. In January 1904, one of them, Carlos Morales, whose forces had recently taken the city, initiated talks with Washington. Morales hoped to consolidate his position by forging a relationship with the U.S. that would enable him to deal both with his very sizable domestic opposition and with the republic's increasingly difficult debt situation. In return for assistance, which would involve military aid and American tariff reductions on Dominican exports of tobacco and sugar, he offered Washington leases to naval base sites at Samaná Bay and elsewhere on the country's coast. The money raised from such leases, Morales hoped, would help his government meet its foreign obligations.[58]

Roosevelt was especially perturbed that what he saw as inborn Dominican "incompetence" might present problems during a presidential election year, but felt that the situation had to be looked into. At the end of February, a mission led by Admiral George Dewey and Assistant Secretary of State Francis B. Loomis was sent to the island nation. It reported that American interests in the region would soon require intervention. Otherwise the republic's politics would continue to be unstable and there would eventually be trouble with European creditors. The president preferred to defer the problem, at least until after the elections were over, but to make sure that Morales was the still the person he would deal with, TR ordered the navy to block deliveries of arms to his opponents.[59]

American policy makers had already decided, however, that any arrangement would have to go beyond what Morales had suggested. It was at this point that the financial receivership idea first began to assume significance in American Caribbean policy. In 1903, the new German ambassador to the U.S., Roosevelt's friend Hermann Speck von Sternburg, had suggested that if there was more trouble with Venezuela the great powers ought to institute an international supervision of its finances. This would, he argued, not only ensure repayment of the country's obligations. It would also ensure domestic order by removing sources of revenue, such as the customs houses, as bones of contention within Venezuelan politics. As State Department planners began to appraise the situation in the Dominican Republic in 1904, they were attracted to this idea, although they were never willing to entertain the notion that Washington should share such an undertaking here with any other powers. As Loomis and others saw it, unless the U.S. gained some degree of direct supervision over the collection and disbursement of its revenues, Washington's concerns about the republic had no chance of being addressed in a lasting way.[60]

Right after the 1904 elections, Roosevelt acted. In October, pursuant to an arbitration that had been pushed for by Washington, an American creditor, the Santo Domingo Improvement Company, had been granted financial rights at the Puerto Plata customs house. Soon after, Italy, France, and Belgium began to agitate for their claims to be addressed. Morales simultaneously began to face new challenges from his rivals. At the end of December, Hay instructed Thomas Dawson, the new American minister to the Dominican Republic, to resume negotiations with the government.[61]

The resulting agreement departed in major ways from what Morales had proposed the previous January. Although the navy had looked on Samaná Bay with some interest prior to the Spanish-American War (and continued to be anxious that it not be occupied by another power), plans for bases in Cuba and Puerto Rico had, it was felt, obviated the need for another site here. Nor did Washington pursue the matter of trade concessions in the U.S. market, an issue that had proven very controversial with domestic interests in the case of Cuba. Instead, this arrangement provided principally for the American takeover of Dominican customs collections, which were the major source of revenue for the government. Of the monies collected, 45 percent were to be used for government expenditures and the rest to satisfy the republic's creditors. Washington would seek an adjustment of the country's debt, and, at Santo Domingo's request, it would also "grant such other assistance as may be in its power to restore the credit, preserve the order, and increase the efficiency of the civil administration and advance the material progress and the welfare of the Republic." The Dominican Republic undertook "to keep its administrative expenditures within the limits of the indispensable necessities of administration." According to Dawson, this clause, "not only gives us the power to insist on a reduction of expenditures whenever we may deem it advisable, but it opens the door to a real superintendence of all administrative matters, which in wise hands can be used to great advantage."[62]

Morales nevertheless declared himself willing to go along with the plan, "provided the American Government would stand by him." However, as the American minister acknowledged, in the country as a whole those who opposed the takeover were in the majority. To exercise a powerful "moral effect" on these "rash" and "ignorant" elements, U.S. naval vessels were put on display in Dominican waters during the negotiations.[63]

Eventually the State Department decided that the arrangement would have to be put in the form of a treaty and be submitted to the Senate. That there were not enough votes for ratification, however, became apparent almost immediately after that body was called into special session in early 1905. The treaty ran afoul of partisan politics, of senators from both parties who were anxious to reassert that institution's prerogatives in foreign (and domestic) affairs (recently challenged by the executive styles of both McKinley and TR), and of strong differences over foreign policy. Since 1898, some southern Democratic senators had consistently been critical of McKinley-Roosevelt diplomacy on the grounds that it represented a dangerous departure from the nation's tradition of "nonentanglement."[64]

Rather than risk defeat, the administration pressed for adjournment. Roosevelt then worked out a modus vivendi with the Dominican government whereby the protocol would in essence be implemented anyway even though it had not been ratified. Morales agreed to appoint American collectors to his customs service, and the president took steps to make sure that they were protected by the navy. Although it had been TR's hope that the treaty could be ratified when the Senate met again in regular session in December 1905, the *modus vivendi* was in fact left in place until, through political pressure and some changes in wording, enough votes could finally be mobilized behind a new convention in 1907.[65]

The Roosevelt administration had come away from the Venezuela claims crisis resolved that the U.S. should promote a pro-American order and stability throughout the entire Caribbean as a way of ensuring its strategic hegemony in the region. Stability would also enhance American control by accelerating the expansion of American business there. TR had warned the nations of Latin America that they could face U.S. intervention if they did not "behave." But what would happen if that warning was not sufficient? Roosevelt, as well as other policy makers, had long recognized how burdensome and problematic a protectorate over the entire area could in practice be.[66] In the period following the articulation of the corollary, finding the most effective means of promoting order throughout the Caribbean became a major concern of the administration, and especially of its new secretary of state, Elihu Root, the cool and methodical New York corporation lawyer to whom TR entrusted U.S. Latin American policy.

As secretary of war, Root had played a central role in formulating the Platt Amendment. He had also helped TR formulate the corollary. Just months before taking over at the Department of State in mid-1905, he wrote Henry M. Flagler, the Standard Oil Company cofounder who had become involved on a grand scale in the development of Florida, that, "The inevitable effect of our building the Canal must be to require us to police the surrounding premises. In the nature of things, trade and control, and the obligation to keep order which go with them, must come our way."[67]

Root, however, did not want such order to depend on a never-ending string of expensive, and potentially counterproductive, military interventions and occupations. If the states of the region could not, or would not, "behave," the U.S. ought to try to promote governments in them that could and would do so in the future. Local regimes, albeit with U.S. backing, could then carry the burden of maintaining stability and order. And, ideally, the mere threat of intervention would be sufficient to keep such governments from being overthrown.[68]

Intervention carried with it several other more immediate problems as well. First of all, after the administration's experience with the Senate over the Dominican treaty, it was by no means clear what level of activity Congress and the public were ready to support in the Caribbean, or what the political costs of administration interventionism there might be. In Cuba, the Dominican Republic, and Panama, meanwhile, Washington had obtained either a conventional right to intervene or an invitation to do so. But it as yet possessed no legal grounds to do so elsewhere, and Root worried about the international as well as domestic ramifications of acting without that.[69] Finally, it had become all too apparent by the time Root became secretary of state that all Latin America had taken offense at the corollary. This reaction seemed to jeopardize development of the kind of ties desired with local elites in the Caribbean. It also came at precisely the moment when the administration was concluding that U.S. relations with the continent of South America were at a vital crossroads (see Chapter 3).

Rather than emphasizing American coercive powers therefore, Root endeavored to keep these in the background and to concentrate instead on easing mistrust and fear of the U.S. among those figures in the Caribbean with whom Washington might work in the future. Toward this end he sought personally to cultivate such leaders and to treat more respectfully than had traditionally been the case the diplomatic representatives sent from the Caribbean states to Washington. To promote order in the region, Root drew on methods of conflict settlement, such as arbitration, that were also in vogue domestically within America in these years. He sought to tutor regional leaders in the behavior desired by the U.S., and through conferences and other mechanisms, he worked to bring them to a sense of commonly held interests with Washington. Root's hope was to promote the willing acceptance of American leadership among such elements in the region and eventually to enlist their support in the isolation of those who would not go along.[70]

His efforts to accomplish American objectives in the region without relying on force were exemplified by Root's policy toward Venezuela between 1905 and 1908. After the crisis of 1902–3, Castro had continued to "misbehave" toward foreign interests. The State Department unsuccessfully sought to have the claims of several American concessionaires settled either by negotiation or by international arbitration during 1904–5. Meanwhile, in

1905, France became involved in a dispute over Venezuela's interference with a French cable company. As early as 1904 TR had contemplated the prospect of forcefully intervening to have American claims addressed and to show Castro that he had to "behave." But by the following spring the president had concluded that there was for the moment "nothing to do but keep our temper." Castro had become for Roosevelt a "villainous little monkey," but an expedition against him would be inadvisable "alike from the standpoint of internal and of international politics." TR again considered intervention early in 1906 after Paris severed relations with Caracas, but Root opposed the idea, and the president accepted his lead. To the secretary, Castro was a "crazy brute." However, forceful action was not worth the detrimental effect it was likely to have on U.S. efforts to improve ties with the rest of Latin America. Force, moreover, he reasoned, would only help Castro if the objective was to remove him from power, whereas "if let alone," Root was ready to gamble, "Castro by following his methods would soon destroy himself."[71]

Root, however, was by no means averse to helping that process along. In June 1908 Washington broke diplomatic relations with Caracas. Then, when a crisis erupted between Venezuela and the Netherlands that fall, it gave its permission for the latter nation to conduct a naval demonstration off the Venezuelan coast. With Venezuela increasingly isolated and under the gun, Castro was overthrown in December by his vice president, Juan Vicente Gómez. Gómez promptly sought to repair relations with the U.S. and European states. He ruled Venezuela for the next twenty-seven years, largely on the basis of the same structures of dictatorship that had been fashioned by Castro. But, throughout that period there were no further confrontations with the great powers.[72]

Considerably greater challenges confronted Root in Central America, just to the north of the canal, where the most serious threats to stability in this era took the form of interstate conflict. American policy makers first became seriously concerned about events there when, in mid-1906, El Salvador supported exiled rebels from Guatemala in a war against the Guatemalan regime of Manuel Estrada Cabrera. After being invaded by Estrada Cabrera's forces, Honduras became involved as well. Seeking to mediate the conflict, the U.S. and Mexico were eventually able to bring all sides together for peace talks aboard the cruiser *Marblehead* on July 19–20. American authorities were anxious for Mexican participation both because that state had influence in Central America and because Root believed joint Mexican-American involvement would blunt Latin American concerns about U.S. overbearance.[73] Aboard the *Marblehead*, the belligerents agreed to an end to hostilities. Plans were also laid for a general peace conference to be held within two months. American diplomats hoped that they could eventually get the states of the region to agree to submit their disputes to joint Mexican and U.S. arbitration.[74]

At the subsequent conference, held in September in San José, Costa Rica, participants agreed to resolve future disputes between them through recourse to a Central American Tribunal of Arbitration. However, Nicaragua's leader, José Santos Zelaya, boycotted the conference, explicitly to protest what he saw as undue U.S. influence in Central America. As a consequence, the fiercely nationalistic Zelaya now became the most important focus of U.S. concern in the area. American diplomats would eventually justify much of their antagonism to him by citing the authoritarian nature of Zelaya's domestic rule. But that was not what set his government apart from the other regimes in Central America in this era. What differentiated Zelaya, was rather an ambitious agenda for Nicaragua and the region that appeared to constitute a direct challenge to Washington's objectives there. To the extreme irritation of American policy makers, Zelaya was unwilling to abandon the idea of a canal being built across Nicaragua, even after the U.S. had decided to build a passageway at Panama. After 1903 he repeatedly tried to interest Japanese and European investors in the project. Zelaya simultaneously tried to counterbalance America's growing influence in the region with political and, a bit more successfully, economic ties between Nicaragua and other industrial powers. Finally, he also refused to let the U.S. diplomatic offensive in the region prevent him from seeking to promote his influence and views beyond Nicaragua.[75]

It was this latter prospect that especially upset Washington in early 1907. Honduran exiles with aid from Zelaya attempted to unseat Honduran president and erstwhile Zelaya protégé Manuel Bonilla. Honduran forces chased the rebels back across the Nicaraguan border. Zelaya submitted the matter to the Central American tribunal, but he rejected its insistence that the states had to pull their forces back from the frontier before it could begin its deliberations. Instead, he invaded Honduras and overthrew Bonilla.[76]

The other Central American strongmen were all opposed to Zelaya dominating Honduras, and, in conversations with their representatives, Root made it clear that Washington was by no means against their using military force to stop him from doing so. El Salvador intervened, but the result was inconclusive and neither side was ultimately satisfied with the new Honduran government that emerged, led by Miguel Dávila. Hostilities between El Salvador and Nicaragua ended in late April, but it soon appeared as if these had merely been a preliminary to a general Central American war.[77]

Root had been optimistic about U.S. policy in the region at the close of the *Marblehead* conference the year before. But in May 1907, he told an audience at Yale that

The long period during which internal strife has prevailed in the Latin-American countries has been an illustration of the struggle between the capacity for self-control in a common national interest and the forces of selfish individualism and factionalism. The major part of those countries are now happily emerging from the stage of militarism and the condition of continual revolution into the stage of

industrialism and stable government; but in some of them on the borders of the
Caribbean the struggle is still waged and the result is in doubt.[78]

Moreover, as he saw it, broader policy concerns left him at the moment
without any options. As he opined to Second Assistant Secretary Alvey A.
Adee some weeks later, "nothing would be of real use except a long period
of armed intervention."[79]

A new opening did materialize in late August. Stepping back from the
uncertainties of war, all the Central American states including Nicaragua
agreed to attend another peace conference sponsored by Mexico and the
U.S. At this meeting, held in Washington at the end of the year, the Central
American governments agreed to an extensive list of provisions designed
to stabilize the region. The weak and pivotally located state of Honduras
was neutralized. Each government agreed not to harbor or provide support
to revolutionaries in neighboring states. What would eventually be known
as the Tobar Doctrine was adopted. It asserted that diplomatic recognition
would be withheld from any new government that did not come to power
through constitutional means. In addition, the delegates agreed to submit
future disputes between them to a Permanent Central American Court of
Justice, modeled after a plan for a new international court that the U.S.
had unsuccessfully promoted at the Second Hague Conference the previous summer (see Chapter 6).[80]

Conferences in and of themselves were seen as valuable by Root from
the standpoint of building up the kind of relations he wanted with leaders
in Central America. The Washington Conference provided him with the
opportunity to try to cultivate and tutor members of the various delegations with whom the U.S. might be able to work in the future.[81]

On this level at least, it is clear that, in its immediate aftermath, Root
saw the conference as a success. Two weeks after its conclusion, he wrote
Albert Shaw that he was "immensely interested in those poor people down
in Central America, and it is delightful to see how readily and gratefully
they respond to a little genuine interest combined with respectful consideration." "If we can maintain for a time the right sort of relations with
them, we can exercise an enormous influence over their conduct for their
own good and for ours." Eventually, concluded Root, "they will welcome
our advice and assistance, and gradually seek to conform their conduct to
our standards of what is praiseworthy ... and instead of wishing to hurt,
they will strive to help American enterprise."[82]

Conflict erupted again in the region in 1908, however. During the
summer, Guatemala and El Salvador instigated an unsuccessful rebellion
against the government of Honduras. With the very strong backing of Washington, the Central American Court asserted its jurisdiction in the dispute.
But the court's absolution of Guatemala and El Salvador in December just
as quickly raised questions about its ability to promote stability in the area.

As the new year began, and the Roosevelt administration left office, it seemed as if hostilities might recommence at any time.[83]

In a letter written in March 1909 to businessman and part-time diplomat William I. Buchanan, Root took note of this situation and expressed his frustration that the U.S. still did not possess a conventional right to intervene in the area. "The thing which I have always had in mind as the objective point towards which we were working," he wrote, "has been a joint guaranty of the neutrality of Honduras by Mexico and the United States, in such form that the President could use our naval force to prevent violations of that neutrality without himself over-stepping the constitutional limitations on his power." He argued: "The existence of the power would render its exercise unnecessary." However, Root still felt that such an arrangement "should be invited by Central America itself, and I have constantly had in mind the preservation of such an attitude on our part as to make such an invitation possible and probable." He felt "such a guaranty would be the pivot on which the whole political life of Central America would turn and that the Zelayas and Cabreras, unable to get at each other and confined to their own dominions, would be speedily disposed of by their own people."[84]

Philander Chase Knox, who succeeded Root as secretary of state in 1909 (after the brief interim appointment of Robert Bacon), was considerably less worried about deploying force in the Caribbean than his predecessor had been, but he did not want the order that the U.S. sought to promote in that region to have to rely on repeated interventions either. Where he and his influential assistant secretary, Francis M. Huntington Wilson, were prepared to break most sharply from the approach that Root had been pursuing was in their willingness to press much more heavy-handedly for the "invitations" that their predecessor had desired. Both were much more anxious about the drift of affairs in Central America. They were also more inclined by temperament to be impatient with such conditions. Like their president, Taft, they believed that the time had come for the U.S. "elder brother" to more actively "assert" a "guardianship" over the region.[85]

Early in 1909, Zelaya sponsored military activity designed to retaliate against El Salvador for its recent interference in Honduras. He also took steps that led U.S. diplomats to fear that he would openly violate Honduran neutrality and thus sweep away one of the key provisions of the accords of 1907. In its first meetings, the Taft cabinet discussed the situation, and the navy was directed to prevent expeditions from embarking across the Gulf of Fonseca.[86]

As had been the case with Root, Knox focused on Honduras in the hope that that state could be used as an instrument to contain and isolate Zelaya. He hoped that the current crisis could be used to gain for Washington a conventional right to intervene to ensure the country's neutrality. He also wanted to strengthen the government of Honduras (against its neighbors and domestic rebellion) by taking steps to reestablish its woeful credit. That could be done by getting Honduras to agree to the creation of a customs receivership.

The State Department asked if Mexico would assist Washington in responding to a possible Honduran request for an outside financial adviser. It also wanted Mexico to help the U.S. sponsor another regional conference. This time Zelaya would pointedly be excluded, and the aim would be for all the other Washington Conference signatories to join with Mexico and the U.S. in a collective guarantee of Honduras's neutrality. Mexico had been willing to help the U.S. keep the peace in the region. But it was not willing to single out Zelaya, whom it saw as a valuable counterweight to its neighbor immediately to the south, Estrada Cabrera. President Porfirio Díaz's regime was by this point also becoming more apprehensive about U.S. influence in both Mexico and Central America (see Chapter 5).[87]

Knox consequently decided to focus on the receivership idea and to deal with Honduras alone. The way was prepared for this by the fact that London had recently begun to press Tegucigalpa to agree to a plan for the repayment of its immense foreign debt. Knox moved to block these plans and also to look for U.S. bankers who would undertake a refunding operation for the country. Since the financial panic of late 1907, American bankers had become much more interested in undertaking such business, and the State Department had in fact become eager to have all the Caribbean states, if possible, eventually shift their indebtedness to American, as opposed to European, creditors. The secretary's objective was to secure a major loan for the government which would then be conditioned on its acceptance of U.S. control over its customs.[88]

By 1909, American policy makers had universally concluded that the Dominican receivership was highly successful and that it constituted a useful means for promoting stability and American influence in trouble spots around the Caribbean. In February, Roosevelt wrote Andrew Carnegie that the Dominican approach "may prove literally invaluable in pointing out the way for introducing peace and order in the Caribbean and around its borders."[89] Root and Bacon, meanwhile, had commented on what they saw as its particular relevance to the case of Honduras.[90]

In Honduras, the receivership's purpose would principally be to promote the kind of stability the U.S. wanted both within that country and among the states of Central America. Washington's formal relationship to the collection of customs would give it a right to intervene in Honduras, while the stability and strength the receivership would promote would presumably minimize the need for that. Zelaya would be thwarted, and a pro-U.S. Central American stability would be maintained.

Previously "there had never seemed to be much hope that American capital would flow into this channel," but by mid-1909 the State Department found that at least two New York investment houses, Speyer and Company and the House of Morgan, were interested in refunding Honduras's debt. J. P. Morgan and Company quickly arranged a settlement with the British Council of Foreign Bondholders and received the administration's support.[91]

Philip M. Brown, the American minister to Honduras, was convinced that the position of President Dávila was too weak and precarious for him to be able to commit his country to an intimate financial relationship with the U.S. But, taking the position that "the weakness of the present government" would actually be a "favorable factor" in facilitating the talks, the State Department and Morgan pressed forward. A tentative agreement, providing for a $10 million loan to be secured principally by customs revenues, was reached by the end of the year.[92]

Implementation of the contract was dependent on Honduras agreeing to a convention guaranteeing U.S. government control over the collection of these duties. This, however, proved much more difficult to obtain. By 1910, Dávila had become deeply worried about domestic opposition to the establishment of such a financial protectorate, and it was only through the application of enormous pressure that the State Department was eventually able, at the beginning of 1911, to get him to sign a treaty. That act, in turn, helped to bring about Dávila's overthrow just a few months later.[93]

In the meantime, the U.S. had become more directly involved with Nicaragua itself. Apparently on the advice of Mexico, Zelaya dampened his military preparations in the spring of 1909. But he continued to try to exert influence in neighboring states and to find counterweights to U.S. power. The Taft administration remained eager to see him driven from power.[94]

In the fall, Zelaya was confronted with a revolt centering around Bluefields, on the sparsely populated Mosquito Coast. Guatemala's Estrada Cabrera, dissatisfied foreign—including American—businessmen with interests in the area, and some members of Nicaragua's Conservative Party funded the rebellion, which was led by Juan Estrada, a former provincial governor. Estrada's initial hope was just to detach the east coast of the country from Managua's rule and to set up a separate republic.[95]

Although Knox did not want to appear to be contravening the Washington accords, he began immediately to look for ways of taking advantage of the situation. In mid-November, he unsuccessfully encouraged Costa Rica to make a major issue of a border incursion committed by Nicaraguan troops as they moved to engage the rebellion.[96] Then he seized on the opportunity provided by Zelaya's summary execution of two American soldiers of fortune, demolition experts who had been in Estrada's employ, to create a crisis between Washington and Managua.

Some within the State Department even considered using the executions as a pretext for U.S. seizure of the port of Corinto, but the response eventually decided on was a brusque severing of relations combined with the despatch of warships and marines to the waters off Nicaragua's coast. The note to the Nicaraguan chargé enumerated a long list of criticisms and complaints about Zelaya's foreign and domestic conduct. It then asserted that the current turmoil left no source of responsible authority to which Washington could look for reparations or for the future protection of American citizens and interests. The question of reparations, Knox indicated, would however be presented in a decidedly less punitive way if all vestiges of the current regime were replaced (the Estrada forces, he claimed, were more in tune with the majority wishes of Nicaraguans). Reserved for later consideration was the issue of "stipulating also that ... Nicaragua obligate itself by convention ... as a guaranty for its future loyal support of the Washington conventions and their peaceful and progressive aims."[97]

The confrontation had the effect of finally driving Zelaya into exile. Prompted by Mexico, which was anxious to see the Liberal Party remain in power, he resigned in favor of José Madriz, who had been a judge on the Central American court. The thinking was that Madriz's credentials might enable the government to repair its relations with the U.S. and bring the revolt to a close. But the Taft administration refused to recognize him. The State Department contended that the new government was still infected with "Zelayism" and therefore had to be removed. Its hope now was that Estrada or some other figure might be able to gain control and bring to power a far more pro-American regime.[98]

By the new year, Estrada's forces were emboldened to march west into the interior of the country and to seek to gain control of Managua. Anticipating their success, the State Department prepared two letters for Estrada to send back to the U.S. once he entered the capital. One requested recognition. The other made clear what that would be dependent on. It pledged that Estrada would secure justice for the execution of the two Americans, hold elections, and agree to the reorganization of Nicaraguan finances on the basis of a customs secured loan from American financiers.[99]

But the rebels suffered major reversals in late February and early March, and were compelled to retreat to Bluefields. Only the protection of the American navy, and the continued hostility of Washington to the regime in Managua kept them alive and, eventually, enabled them to regain the advantage. Madriz ultimately resigned and went into exile just before his opponent's forces entered Managua in late August.[100]

Estrada agreed, but to Washington's surprise only reluctantly, to the pledges and requests that had been demanded of him. Nicaragua was in fact not in desperate financial straits, but Estrada did want American recognition. In response, the State Department sent Thomas Dawson to Managua, where he quickly discovered that the ousted Liberals remained the most popular political party. It was also clear that the new government was divided, and that Estrada's position within it was weak.

The American emissary therefore abandoned plans for immediate national elections. Instead, he engineered Estrada's election to a two-year term as president by a constituent assembly. To appease the Conservatives, it was then agreed that Adolfo Díaz—a former employee of an American mining firm on the east coast who had funneled foreign contributions to Estrada's cause—would become vice president. A compromise figure, Díaz did not have a significant personal following within the party and was therefore not seen as a threat by Conservative chieftains like Emiliano Chamorro and Luís Mena. It was also agreed that Estrada would not succeed himself. Dawson's hope was that the Conservatives would be able to unite around one leader and to position themselves to control the outcome of presidential elections to be held in two years.[101]

Dissension continued to plague the government during the spring of 1911, however, ultimately leading Estrada to retire in favor of Díaz. The latter had an even weaker base of support, but for the moment what counted in Washington was that he could be depended on to complete the negotiations for the financial protectorate. The Knox-Castrillo Treaty, providing for the receivership, was signed by the two governments in June.[102]

American policy makers had become powerfully attached to the financial protectorate idea as the way by which they might bring the kind of pro-U.S. stability they wanted to Honduras, Nicaragua, and other potential trouble spots in the Caribbean.[103] Concerned that such countries would not act "responsibly" on their own, American officials saw receiverships as a cheap but effective means of taking charge of their affairs. Customs receiverships were seen to offer a systematic means of assuring the financial and social/political order desired and of avoiding the need for repeated military intervention. They would guarantee that each country's debts were paid and they would eliminate its revenues as a source of contention among disruptive or challenging forces. The authority of central governments tied to Washington could be strengthened, and more of their revenues could be directed towards the kinds of economic development projects deemed appropriate for these lands. The process, they believed, would then build on itself. Conditions would be enhanced for U.S. investment in plantation agriculture and extractive enterprises, and that in turn supposedly would generate general prosperity and still more harmony. Greater business ties would increase American control and make these states a source of profit to the U.S. Locals would, it was thought, benefit by economic as well as political training and tutelage.[104]

But the treaties still had to be approved by the Senate, where the climate was much less favorable now than it had been for the Dominican treaty. During its first year, especially because of its handling of tariff revision, the administration had come widely to be seen as dominated by large northeastern, particularly New York-based corporate and financial interests seeking to control the U.S. political economy. This had paved the way for significant Democratic gains in both houses of Congress in 1910, and for a split between the administration and many western "insurgent" Republicans who became a key bloc in the upper house.[105]

When the administration began working with a small number of the largest New York banks in connection with its policies in China and Latin America, its diplomacy was made vulnerable to the same criticism. Wisconsin senator Robert M. La Follette, a leading Republican insurgent, speculated in late 1909 that Taft was driven quickly to replace Charles R. Crane, the president's initial choice as minister to China, because the Chicago businessman was insufficiently "subservient to Wall St."[106] Soon thereafter, the influential Democratic newspaper the *New York World* began applying the term "dollar diplomacy" to the administration's foreign policies. It charged that the greed of bankers like J. P. Morgan was controlling U.S. diplomacy in Honduras and Nicaragua.[107]

Republican newspapers like the *New York Tribune* tried to make the issue one of manhood, maintaining that "There are certain timid souls on the Democratic side ... whose gentle, feminine temperaments are lashed almost into hysterics at the thought of 'entangling alliances'."[108] The State Department, however, took a different tack, launching a campaign during 1910 to bring out the "altruism and unselfishness" of the administration's diplomacy.[109] Opposition to the loan conventions was the really selfish course, it was implied, because that would prevent the U.S. from helping these weaker countries and from promoting peace. Rightly understood, Knox argued, this was "such a deviation from traditions as the American people will approve."[110] The administration maintained, moreover, that rather than entangling the country, the use of Wall Street "dollars" would reduce the need for the U.S. to use "bullets" to protect its interests in Central America.[111]

The administration got a favorable report on the Honduran convention from the foreign relations committee in spring 1911, but, because every Democratic member was opposed, further consideration of both pacts was delayed until the first regular session of the 62nd Congress. It was hoped that a good-will tour of the Caribbean by Knox during early 1912 could be used to promote the treaties. Instead, motions to report them favorably were defeated the following May by votes of 7 to 7. The solid opposition of the Democrats was now joined by the negative vote of the insurgent Republican junior senator from Idaho William E. Borah.[112]

The Nicaraguan government's financial situation had meanwhile deteriorated badly since the accession of Díaz.[113] In September 1911, two American investment houses, Brown Brothers and J. and W. Seligman, signed a $15 million loan contract with the government. However, the funds were dependent on U.S. supervision of the customs. To get new revenue immediately, Díaz began transferring key Nicaraguan assets to the bankers in return for short-term loans and small advances.[114] These developments horrified nationalist sentiment, especially among the Liberals. They also led Díaz's rivals within the Conservative Party to doubt whether Washington would ever willingly let anyone else contend for power. The result was an insurrection against the government, begun in late July 1912, led by Mena, the minister of war, and Liberal leader Benjamin Zeledón.

To the Taft administration, its entire policy, not only in Nicaragua but throughout the region, hung in the balance. Several hundred American bluejackets and marines were immediately landed to protect foreign lives and property. But once it became clear that Díaz's government was in jeopardy, the State Department began to call for an intervention that would defeat the forces in revolt and do so in demonstrative fashion. Failure to do this, Acting Secretary Huntington Wilson wrote the president, "would, we fear, be a blow to our prestige in all the neighboring republics."[115]

In the end, 2300 marines were landed to help Díaz put down the rebellion. The administration justified its involvement publicly by arguing both that the Nicaraguan government was asking for help and that the U.S. had a "moral mandate" to act stemming from the Washington conventions (even though all the other governments of Central America expressed their misgivings). Mena was condemned for his "selfish purposes," as were the revolutionary forces for their "uncivilized and savage" conduct. Their triumph, the administration asserted, would install a "regime of barbarity and corruption" just like that of Zelaya. The fighting ended in early October, after which most of the marines were quickly removed. However, a sizable legation guard—which would remain in the country until 1925—was left behind as a deterrent against future rebellions. In November, Díaz ran unopposed to succeed himself in the presidency, and, appropriately, his triumph was celebrated with a reception aboard the flagship of the U.S. Pacific fleet.[116]

American policy makers confronted instability elsewhere in the Caribbean during the last year of the Taft administration as well. In addition to the revolt in Nicaragua (and to the continued unfolding of the Mexican revolution, discussed in Chapter 5), a smaller rebellion broke out in eastern Cuba and factional conflict resurfaced in the Dominican Republic.[117]

Running for the presidency at this time, Woodrow Wilson pledged to end "dollar diplomacy" and also to repair U.S.-Latin American relations. Yet, referring to the recent unrest in the Caribbean, the candidate also told publisher Oswald Garrison Villard that "this was a period when the big nations of the earth were not going to put up with misbehavior by the small ones."

Following the election, concern arose within the State Department that Wilson's campaign rhetoric might actually have the effect of prompting "misbehavior," especially if it had encouraged the idea that the new president would take a hands-off attitude toward Latin American revolutions. As a result, within less than a week after taking office Wilson released a statement meant to make his opposition to such disorder clear. Positioning himself as the enemy of selfishness, he announced that "We can have no sympathy with those who seek to seize the power of government to advance their own personal ... ambitions." There could be no "stable peace in such circumstances." As friends, the U.S. would instead "prefer those who act in the interest of peace and honor, who protect private rights and respect the restraints of constitutional provision."[118]

Wilson believed, incorrectly, that "dollar diplomacy" had simply tied American policy to the narrow self-interest of the participating bankers. That was the policy that he was denouncing in 1912–13. But, while he asserted that his own diplomacy would instead be altruistic, the new president had no intention of dropping his predecessors' search for order and control (objectives that he feared "dollar diplomacy" threatened). To the contrary, Wilson's presidency would witness an unprecedented level of American armed intervention in the Caribbean on behalf of those goals.

Nor was Wilson's concern about disorder a product merely of temperamental or intellectual inclinations. The new president's determination to eliminate revolutions from the Caribbean (as well as his Mexican policy) cannot be understood without grasping the enormous significance that he, like his predecessors, attached to the construction of the Panama Canal. It was a topic to which Wilson returned again and again during the 1912 campaign as well as in the following months leading up to the project's completion. A historian and political scientist by training, Wilson believed that the waterway was going to alter the routes of world trade almost as much as "when the Turks captured Constantinople and blocked the course of the Mediterranean" in the fifteenth century, propelling European navigators out onto the Atlantic Ocean. "You know at that moment," he told gatherings of American businessmen in 1912, "England, which had been at the back of the nations trading with the East, suddenly swung around and found herself occupying a place at the front of the nations. ... Something not so great as that, but nevertheless as revolutionary in our trade, is going to happen as soon as the canal is opened."[119] Wilson believed that the canal was going to shift the "center of gravity of the world."[120] It had therefore become imperative for the Caribbean states and Mexico to have orderly and responsible governments. Otherwise friction would develop with other great powers and the U.S. would be confronted with more "such incidents as [the] Venezuela affair under Castro."[121]

This concern with stability and American influence in the region was shared by Wilson's secretary of state, William Jennings Bryan. The Nebraskan did not play as significant a role in overall policy formulation as his immediate predecessors in that office had. Wilson chose Bryan for his standing with key southern and western Democratic constituencies and aimed to superintend relations between the U.S. and all other major nations himself. But Bryan did figure importantly in the development of policy for the small countries of the Caribbean. Bryan—unlike Wilson—had long been a critic of Republican policy. But he too believed that he was rejecting a diplomacy that was selfish and destructive in favor of one that was not. This perception enabled him to successfully avoid the contradiction between his anti-imperialist rhetoric on the one hand and his actual determination to treat Latin Americans as if they were what he called "our political children" on the other.[122]

The administration confronted its first challenge in Nicaragua. The over-sized legation guard, a residue of the previous year's intervention, was left in place. But the Díaz government seemed in greater financial difficulties than ever before in 1913. If it could not meet basic expenses, the danger existed that unrest would swell again. Washington policy makers feared that there might yet be a return of "Zelayism." Knox had tried to strengthen pro-American regimes in Honduras and Nicaragua with his loan conven-tions, but Bryan had seen these as vehicles for the excessive enrichment of the involved bankers and as detrimental to stability. They had in any event failed to win Senate support.

He was, however, attracted to a project Knox had been working on dur-ing the last months of the Taft administration. After Díaz's election in the fall, the outgoing secretary had negotiated a treaty for the purchase by the U.S. of an exclusive option on the Nicaragua canal route, as well as naval base rights in the Gulf of Fonseca (on Nicaragua's Pacific coast) and on the Corn Islands (in the Caribbean). There had not been time for the treaty to be acted on by the Senate, but Bryan, like his predecessor, was drawn to the proposal for a variety of reasons. Washington would finally be able to rule out having to deal with the sale of the canal rights to European or Japanese interests. The $3 million purchase price would provide needed funds for the Díaz government. And the transaction might in its turn enhance that government's credit.

Bryan not only adopted the proposal. By the time he presented his own treaty to the Senate, it had also come to include language like that in the Platt Amendment that would have made Nicaragua into a formal American protectorate. "The proposed Nicaraguan treaty has my entire approval," Wilson wrote the secretary in mid-1913, "and I sincerely hope that the Senate may approve it, as well as our friends, the Nicaraguan government."[123]

Democratic senators were reluctant publicly to criticize the administra-tion's handiwork, but there was considerable dissatisfaction with the treaty among them, especially because of the protectorate feature. In August 1913 the majority of the Democratic senators on the foreign relations commit-tee voted with Borah, a more vocal opponent, in opposition. The treaty was then rewritten to exclude the Platt Amendment language. The foreign rela-tions committee reported on it favorably in December 1914, but the pact was then confronted with the threat of a filibuster. Only testimony from the General Board of the Navy, to the effect that the base rights included in the deal might be important if war were to come with Germany, finally made possible ratification of the Bryan-Chamorro pact early in 1916.[124]

As Bryan noted, Nicaragua under Díaz had "gone farther than any other Central American state in asking us to take part in her affairs."[125] Nevertheless, as the 1916 Nicaraguan presidential election approached, the State Department was anxious to secure a successor to Díaz who would work with the U.S. and yet have a broader base of political power in the country. This eventually led the Wilson administration into conflict with both Díaz and the Liberals, who despite being in the majority were still considered to be "Zelayist" and untrustworthy.[126]

Washington's candidate was Conservative strongman Chamorro, who had been working smoothly with the State Department since becoming Nicaragua's minister to the U.S. in 1912. The U.S. preference for him was made unmistakably clear when he was allowed to return to Nicaragua to begin his candidacy in May 1916 aboard an American naval vessel. Díaz had been planning to hand-pick his own successor, and he threatened to make common cause with the Liberals if Washington did not allow him to have his way. But the State Department warned that it might not recognize a government led by Díaz's choice, and that it might also hold up the money that had recently been pledged under the Bryan-Chamorro Treaty. Finally, in September, Admiral William B. Caperton, accompanied by a force of three cruisers and a regiment of marines, arrived to make it clear to the Nicaraguan president that he had no choice but to support Chamorro. The Liberals were informed that their candidate, Julian Irias, was considered unacceptable, and they, in response, withdrew from the campaign, leaving Chamorro to win unopposed in October.[127]

Another challenge to the administration's policy soon came in Haiti, where politics and public finance had become increasingly unstable after 1910. By early 1914, Bryan decided that Washington should seek to place that country under a Dominican-type financial protectorate ("Dear me, think of it," scoffed the deeply racist "Great Commoner" after a briefing about the country, "Niggers speaking French.")[128] Just as their predecessors had, Bryan and Wilson both looked to such receiverships as the means by which control and stability might best be ensured in the region. Bryan offered to protect then president Oreste Zamor in office if he agreed to such a plan, but Zamor balked at the amount of control the U.S. wanted. He changed his mind that fall when his position became less secure. Eight hundred marines were despatched to Port-au-Prince aboard the *Hancock*. But they arrived too late to save him.

The same offer was then tendered to the new president, Davilmar Théodore. When word that he was negotiating with the U.S. got out, however, demonstrations erupted both in the Haitian senate and on the streets of the capital. Theodore was himself overthrown in early 1915. This time the new president, Vilbrun Guillaume Sam, was informed that his government would not be recognized until and unless he agreed. However, he held back and was also able to obtain a loan from a French financier.

Outraged administration officials began to entertain fears that a plot was afoot by the French government, or even by the French and German governments (which were at war with one another), to obtain a naval base at Môle Saint Nicolas, strategically located on Haiti's northern coast. Lansing, now the secretary of state, fumed that "the African race are devoid of any capacity for political organization and [have no] genius for government."[129]

When Sam was assassinated that summer, the administration decided to move. At first American forces were landed only to restore order in the capital and to protect foreign lives and property. But Wilson quickly recognized the opportunity that this gave him to "amicably take charge" of "the dusky little republic."[130] An occupation force was landed. American marines seized the country's customshouses and began to censor its press. A pliant candidate, Philippe Dartiguenave, was chosen for the presidency and his election by the national assembly engineered. A treaty was then negotiated with Dartiguenave providing for American administration of the customs, for U.S. supervision of Haiti's finances, and for the creation of a new rural guard under American direction. All this was to be enforced for the foreseeable future by the continued presence of the marines (who would remain in Haiti for the next nineteen years).[131]

The Dominican Republic, Haiti's next-door neighbor, experienced a similar fate. Alfredo and Eladio Victoria, who had seized power in 1911, had been pushed aside by the Taft administration in late 1912 and replaced by a provisional president who was supposed to superintend national elections in 1914. Knox hoped that those elections would be accepted by all the contending factions in the country and that extra-constitutional, disorderly seizures of power could thenceforth be contained.

But tensions soon developed between the provisional president, Archbishop Adolfo Nouel, and most of the republic's major political leaders, culminating in Nouel's resignation early in 1913. José Bordas Valdés, who was elected by the Dominican congress to succeed Nouel, subsequently tried to pave the way for his own long-term rule. The Wilson administration warned that it would not recognize a government that came to power by overthrowing Bordas. It also promised to see to it that the elections would be held and that the provisional president would not control them.

But Bordas did rig the voting, and a full-scale revolt broke out. Under similar circumstances, the Victorias had been removed by Taft. Now the Wilson administration moved to restore stability by eliminating Bordas. New elections were held, and these brought one of the republic's major factional leaders, Juan Isidro Jiménez, to the presidency in December 1914. Washington pledged to protect him in office, but in return it insisted on still more extensive American control over the country's fiscal affairs. This undermined Jiménez's position within his country, and he was eventually confronted with a popular uprising in the spring of 1916.

A naval landing was undertaken to keep Jiménez in power. To the Wilson administration's astonishment, however, the latter decided that he would rather resign than cooperate further. Unlike the case in Haiti, American naval authorities could not now find even a single leader around whom to build a client relationship, and they refused to accept any of the replacements for Jiménez put forward by the Dominican congress. "I have never seen such hatred displayed by one people for another as I notice and feel here," reported Admiral Caperton when he arrived on the scene. We "positively have not a friend in the land." This was a telling comment on nearly a dozen years of American "guardianship" of the Dominican Republic, but it was not followed up by withdrawal. The country was instead now occupied and placed under direct military rule.[132]

Above all because the area—by virtue of its proximity to the canal—had come to seem critical to the American position in the coming twentieth-century world, U.S. involvement in the Caribbean expanded enormously during this period. Determined to control access to the isthmus, one administration after another dedicated itself, in particular, to the idea that it had to ensure a pro-U.S. stability on the part of all the region's independent states.

As policy makers saw it, their greatest challenge derived from the propensity of people in the Caribbean to "misbehave." Far from acting to protect self-determination in the region, as their rhetoric about the Monroe Doctrine claimed, officials kept themselves busy trying to make sure that locals, whom they saw as inherently "weak" and "irresponsible," governed themselves as the U.S. wanted. If that could be achieved, then "greedy" rival powers, it was thought, could be prevented from jeopardizing American hegemony in the region.

Drawing on methods in vogue at home, policy makers sought as best they could to bring to power and cultivate what they saw as elements with whom they might work in the region and to institute mechanisms which might serve to contain and settle conflicts among the Caribbean states. Where necessary, they also tried to assert real, albeit indirect, oversight over several nations in the area—both in the interest of order and control and so that a "disinterested" U.S. might try to instill the behavior it desired.

It was within this context that the financial receivership idea came to seem such a promising solution during the decade before the war. And yet policy makers were hardly willing to restrict themselves to financial methods. As the case of the Dominican Republic makes clear, in this region they placed such value on they were also prepared if necessary forcefully to impose their guidance on these "independent" states.

Chapter 3

Dominance Throughout the Hemisphere: South America

Caribbean policy, principally one supposes because of the high-profile interventions that it involved, is quite often treated as the sum total of U.S. policy toward Latin America at the turn of the twentieth century. But the entire continent of South America was given great importance by policy makers, and it was also a major focus of diplomatic activity. Along with East Asia, this was the extra-continental region of the underdeveloped world most highly prized for its economic potential by American leaders. Indeed, the canal was valued, at least in part, because it was felt that it would enhance the ability of the United States to expand its trade and influence into and over South America. Washington's aspirations were to dominate the development of this continent commercially, to shape the political future of the region, and, ideally, to organize South America as a bloc behind the U.S. in world affairs.

Fearing "selfishness" and "greed" on the part of other major powers, Washington took the position that it would enforce the Monroe Doctrine throughout this region as well as in the Caribbean. Meanwhile, it renounced any territorial acquisitions for itself in South America, pledged American respect for the commercial open door in the region ("save," said TR, "as the individual countries enter into individual treaties with one another"), and promised that the property, investments, and nationals of all the European countries doing business here would not be without protection.[1]

Other policies were a response to perceived conditions in the region itself. As the above noted pledge of protection suggests, policy makers were greatly worried about South American "irresponsibility." U.S. leaders were in many ways pleased with the upper-class, international trade-oriented regimes that had come into power in most of these states toward the end of the nineteenth century, particularly because they seemed a bulwark against "irresponsibility" on the part of the South American people.[2] By contrast with many of the governments of the Caribbean, the propertied, supposedly more "self-controlled," groups were in power here. Nevertheless, Washington was still fearful that the conduct of these states might open the way for other powers to intervene and play a greater political-military role. Policy makers were concerned about interstate, if not domestic, instability in South

Shipping Distances
(in approx. nautical miles)

New York – Buenos Aires	6000
New York – Rio	4800
New York – Panama	2000
Panama – Valparaiso	2650
Liverpool – Buenos Aires	6250
Liverpool – Rio	5200

South America, c. 1910.

America, especially because of the continent's numerous ongoing boundary disputes. They were also concerned because governments in the region frequently resisted the rules of behavior—particularly for the treatment of outside business interests—desired by the great powers, arguing that they constituted a challenge to their sovereignty or to their country's legal equality with other states.

Washington had other worries with regard to this region as well. Culturally and economically, all these nations had by tradition far closer ties to western Europe than to North America (a pattern seemingly reinforced yearly by the influx of new immigrants from across the Atlantic into the southern continent). And the Spanish-American states, in particular, were traditionally suspicious of the U.S. American leaders saw the U.S. as the "elder brother" of the Americas and sought to portray Washington as the champion of the sovereignty of all the nations of the hemisphere. This was not how things were viewed from South America. There there was generally much less concern about European threats to the region than there were fears of U.S. power and pretensions. At least since the Mexican-American War of the late 1840s, South Americans had been uneasy with the growth of the "Colossus of the North." The greatest consequence of the revival of the Monroe Doctrine at the turn of the century was that it had the effect of intensifying such fears of U.S. domination.[3]

Washington's principal response to these South American challenges came in the form of the Pan-American movement. Meant only to include the independent countries of the Americas, the movement's purpose was to provide the U.S. with a framework through which it might promote the kind of order and behavior that it wanted, overcome mistrust, undermine the influence of the European powers, and build up its own leadership of the hemisphere.

Other activities, both within and outside the Pan-American movement, were directed specifically toward the promotion of closer economic relations, and especially trade. South America was seen not only as a logical, but also as a very valuable market for American commercial expansion. As it always had in the past, Europe continued to take the greatest share of U.S. exports at the turn of the century. However, the consensus of opinion, in both Europe and America, was that the most important new opportunities for the industrial powers during the coming century would be found not in trade among themselves—which might in any event be jeopardized by protectionism—but rather in the development of markets in the non-industrial world. South America was viewed as one of the most valuable of these market areas, not only because of its size, but also because its buying power had been increasing steadily since the 1870s, when the economies of a number of countries there had begun to expand to meet the demand in industrial states for key food products and raw materials.[4]

While U.S. exports to South America had grown during the late nineteenth century, trade from the U.S. did not play anywhere near as important a role there as did imports from European sources, led above all by England. American policy makers fretted that these markets might not be available in the future if the commercial rivals of the U.S. became too firmly entrenched.

Although South American trade had long been a popular topic among American merchants and manufacturers, especially during times of slack home demand, consuls and trade experts complained that too few businessmen made a sustained effort to promote such commerce. For their part, manufacturers and merchants protested that they had to compete in South America without many of the advantages of their more established European rivals. Political leaders called on more businessmen to take the long view of their needs and opportunities. At the same time, and often in the face of significant domestic political resistance, they sought to provide exporters with greatly expanded forms of government assistance.

From the middle of the first decade of the new century onward, American exports to South America did begin to grow more rapidly. So too did programs of government help. Thus, when the U.S. was suddenly presented during the Great War with a golden chance to bid for outright economic leadership over the southern continent, it was well positioned, as well as eager, to make the effort.

Although nothing like a consistent forward policy toward the region was pursued until the late 1890s and after, South America had begun to attract the attention of some American political leaders as early as the 1880s. James G. Blaine was unquestionably the most important of these. Indeed it was he who first made Pan-Americanism a salient concept within American policy circles. Secretary of state during the brief James Garfield administration in 1881 and again under Benjamin Harrison in 1889–92, Blaine was also the Republican candidate for president in 1884. Early on he targeted South America as a "commercial empire that legitimately belongs to us."[5] But what worried him throughout these years was that other industrial powers were far more active on that continent than was the U.S. He asserted that "it would be demonstrated in the very near future that the United States will have to assume a much more decided tone in South America ... or else it will have to back out of it, and say it is a domain that does not belong to us, and we surrender it to Europe."[6]

Blaine was particularly concerned about Britain. He resented the central role that British financiers and merchants were playing in the commercial development of South America, and he was also fearful that Britain and British interests might seek by means of political intrigue to reinforce and expand the leading position that they had acquired on that continent. This was the explanation that Blaine later gave for the unsuccessful bid he made in 1881 to mediate the War of the Pacific and to see it settled without territorial transfers from the losers, Peru and Bolivia, to the victor, Chile. The conflict, he contended, was "an English war on Peru, with Chile as the instrument," the objective being control of the nitrate fields of southern Peru.[7]

Seeking to reduce possibilities for European political involvement in South America, Blaine invited all the Latin American states to a conference in the U.S. meant to address "means of preventing war among the nations of America." He hoped to promote an arbitral system that would head off flare-ups like the War of the Pacific in the future. Blaine was also anxious to establish a position for Washington as the ultimate, and only great power, peacemaker in the Western Hemisphere.[8]

Frederick T. Freylinghuysen, Blaine's immediate successor, backed away from the conference, principally out of a worry that Washington might not be able to control the results. But the Chester Arthur administration did launch a Latin American Trade Commission in 1884. And Freylinghuysen's sensitivity and opposition to European involvement in the hemisphere became no less intense than Blaine's. "The Department of State," he went so far as to state, "will not sanction an intervention of European states in South American differences *even with the consent of the parties* [emphasis added]. The decision of American questions pertains to America itself."[9]

A Pan-American conference once again received attention during the late 1880s. Now it was pushed by prominent figures in Congress (including William McKinley). In 1888, bipartisan majorities in both the House and the Senate called on President Cleveland to arrange for such a meeting to be held in Washington during the winter of 1889–90.[10]

Blaine's earlier proposal had focused on a conference to deal with peace-keeping. By 1888, however, the most enthusiastic Pan-Americanists envisioned a meeting that would address not only that topic, but also steps looking toward the rapid economic integration of the hemisphere. Their ultimate objective was a hemispheric customs union, under which the Latin American nations would discriminate in favor of American, as opposed to European, goods. Blaine shared this enthusiasm too once he was reappointed secretary of state and was slated to preside over the meeting.[11]

The South American states were indeed interested in expanding their commerce with the U.S. That was the principal reason why all sent delegates to the conference. They were, however, not willing to place their European economic connections in jeopardy for that purpose, and this put many delegates at odds with the U.S. agenda right from the start. In the end, the conference's only accomplishment with regard to trade was the establishment of the purely information-gathering institution, the Commercial Bureau of the American Republics.[12]

Nor were American hopes with regard to interstate order realized at the conference, in part because Chile, before agreeing to attend, insisted on a promise from Blaine that the meeting would seek only to provide for disputes that had yet to arise. In addition to annexing the territory of Tarapacá, Chile had extended its control over the more northerly Peruvian provinces of Tacna and Arica at the end of the War of the Pacific, and it worried that an arbitral treaty might place that possession in jeopardy.

At the conference, Argentina and Brazil nonetheless proposed a treaty of obligatory arbitration under which past issues could be addressed. The wording of their proposal would also have enabled questions to be raised about the vast U.S. territorial acquisitions stemming from the Mexican War forty-two years before. Blaine, as a result, finally settled for a very diluted treaty. It was signed by only a handful of the delegations and then went unratified even by the U.S.[13]

Finally, the U.S. found itself at cross purposes with other delegations at the conference over the extremely important question of the "rights" of outsiders doing business in South American countries. International law recognized a state's right to intervene diplomatically on behalf of its nationals to assure that they and their interests were treated in accordance with "internationally recognized" standards when operating in a foreign country. However, in Latin America this principle was viewed as affording special privileges to the great powers and their citizens and as detrimental to the sovereignty of small states. At Washington, many of the Latin American delegates were eager to see the conference endorse—as a cornerstone of what they saw as a more progressive "American international law"—a position that had first been articulated by the Argentine publicist Carlos Calvo in the 1860s. Essentially, this was that foreigners would have to conduct their business in Latin America on the same terms that citizens of those countries did.[14] But, the U.S. member on the International Law committee, William Henry Trescot resisted, insisting that any such changes required the consent of what he termed "the civilized world." He could "not concur in any opinions which diminish the right or reduce the power of a nation by diplomatic reclamation ... to protect the rights and interests of its citizens."[15] From Washington's perspective, this Latin American hesitancy to accept its "international obligations" constituted not only a challenge to the conditions desired for Americans interested in doing business in South America, it also "invited" confrontations with European states.

In an effort partially to compensate for the conference's failures, Blaine afterward hoped that he could forge new commercial, and ideally political, ties with the southern half of the hemisphere by means of bilateral reciprocal trade treaties. However, the politics of protectionism, especially within the Republican party, in combination with a continuing unwillingness on the part of most South American states to take steps that could jeopardize their European ties or substantially impact their own revenue systems, impeded progress in this direction too.[16]

Promoting American leadership in South America had clearly emerged as a more challenging task than any of its initial enthusiasts had expected. In part that may explain why the U.S. took the "decided tone" it did to assert its "rights" and protect its "honor" in the region during the early to mid-1890s. These first appeared to be under attack in Chile, where during the summer of 1891 a conflict that split the Chilean political establishment had culminated in the forcible overthrow of President José Manuel Balmaceda. Washington, like other foreign governments, had adopted a posture of "impartial forbearance" toward the struggle. But American diplomatic and naval personnel in Chile had made their preference for the president clear both by word and deed.

That guaranteed strained relations between the new government and the American minister, Patrick Egan, and it also contributed to the suspicion with which the triumphant forces viewed his determination to provide asylum to a large number of Balmaceda's supporters. During the fall, the Chilean government placed the U.S. legation under close surveillance, which in turn led to irritation in Washington. "The trouble with these people and their kindred seems to be that they do not know how to use victory with dignity and moderation," commented President Harrison: "someday, it may be necessary to instruct them."[17]

An occasion for such instruction was soon presented. On October 16, two American sailors, on shore leave from the cruiser *Baltimore*, were killed in a tavern brawl with Chileans in the port city of Valparaiso. From the start, the Harrison administration treated the affair as a major diplomatic incident, and ultimately it compelled Santiago, with a threat of war, to apologize, accept the American rendition of events, and pay reparations.[18]

Two years later, a U.S. naval squadron was used to thwart the efforts of rebellious Brazilian naval officers when they tried to establish a blockade of Rio harbor. The move was undertaken to keep the port open to American merchant shipping. But it also deprived the insurgents of their most important weapon and thus worked to the advantage of the side that Washington preferred to see win the struggle.[19]

The greatest confrontation of this period came in 1895, when the U.S. threatened Britain with war over a disputed boundary in northern South America. Blaine had asserted, that while the great powers of Europe would expand into Asia and Africa, it was "the especial province of this country to improve and expand its trade with the nations of America."[20] The scope and speed of European actions in the Eastern Hemisphere in the 1880s and 1890s, however, had stunned many U.S. leaders and made them fearful that the "scramble for Africa" might be repeated to their south. It was to warn against any such extension of European power into what it saw as the United States hemisphere that the Cleveland administration took the stand it did in this "Venezuela boundary dispute."

This was hardly a new controversy. Caracas and London had held conflicting positions as to the rightful boundary between Venezuela and British Guiana since the 1840s. Moreover, Venezuela had been trying to involve the U.S. in the matter for the better part of two decades. For all practical purposes, Washington had simply been indifferent. This changed, however, after Caracas in 1894 hired William L. Scruggs, a former American minister to Venezuela, as its lobbyist in the U.S. Quite familiar with the tenor of American anxieties about the region, Scruggs both publicized the case and artfully put a new construction on it, making its outcome appear to be crucial to the future of the U.S. role in the hemisphere.

Scruggs argued that Britain had never had a legitimate claim to any territory west of the line claimed by Venezuela (on the Essequibo River). It was simply trying to grab land that was not its own. And this territory was of enormous importance, because it would give London control over the main outlet of the Orinoco River—the key, so Scruggs claimed, to the control and commercial development of one-quarter of South America. Of even greater significance, Britain's effort constituted a direct challenge to the Monroe Doctrine, which would lie in tatters if London was not stopped. *British Aggressions in Venezuela—Or—The Monroe Doctrine on Trial* was the provocative title Scruggs gave to a long pamphlet he wrote and distributed about the controversy.[21]

Scruggs's campaign immediately elicited the concern of a broad cross-section of the nation's political establishment. Congress adopted without dissent a resolution calling for an unrestricted arbitration of the dispute. "If the United States are prepared to see South America pass gradually into the hands of Great Britain and other European powers and to be hemmed in by British naval posts and European dependencies," there was nothing more to be said, opined Republican senator Henry Cabot Lodge of Massachusetts in the *North American Review*. However, he hoped the American people were "not ready to abandon the Monroe doctrine, or give up their rightful supremacy in the Western Hemisphere." Prominent Democrat and Cleveland confidant Don M. Dickinson charged that Britain was quietly trying to close out and stifle the nation that had become its "leading competitor for the trade of the world."[22]

When diplomatic appeals to submit the dispute to arbitration did not meet with success in London, the Cleveland administration decided in mid-1895 to insist on that solution. A sharply worded note, penned by Olney, and later referred to by Cleveland as a "twenty-inch gun," was fired off to London in July. The note ranged well beyond the particular case at issue. Its concern having been aroused by the dangers identified by Scruggs, the administration was determined to set forth its views on the whole question of European political involvement in the Western Hemisphere.

Indeed, Olney went so far as to suggest that "distance and three thousand miles of intervening ocean" made "any permanent political union between an European and American state unnatural and inexpedient." Certainly, no extension of such influence beyond where it existed already would be tolerated. European powers should not think that the U.S. would shrink from enforcing the prohibitions included in the Monroe Doctrine.

"Today the United States is practically sovereign on this continent," he asserted,

and its fiat is law upon the subjects to which it confines its interposition. Why?... It is because, in addition to all other grounds, its infinite resources combined with its isolated position render it master of the situation and practically invulnerable as against any and all other powers.

All the advantages of this superiority are at once imperiled if the principle be admitted that European powers may convert American states into colonies or provinces of their own.

It was not inconceivable, argued Olney, "that the struggle now going on for the acquisition of Africa might be transferred to South America." One breach of territorial sovereignty by America's rivals would lead to others, and quickly to the necessity for the U.S. to arm on land as well as sea to preserve what he called the "predominance of the Great Republic in this hemisphere."[23]

In its reply, London insisted that Washington had "an erroneous view of many material facts" in the case, and it continued to reject any arbitration that might affect land already under British administration in the disputed territory. More importantly, it contested the grounds on which Olney was claiming a U.S. right to voice this demand. Monroe's doctrine had been addressed to quite a different situation and had, in any event, never been accepted by other powers, asserted Lord Salisbury. Now it was being expanded on by Olney. The secretary of state's assertion "that 'American questions are for American decision,'" he stated, "even if it receive any countenance from the language of President Monroe (which it does not), can not be sustained by any reasoning drawn from the law of nations." Like the U.S., Britain too opposed "any disturbance of the existing territorial distribution" in the Western Hemisphere. But that was ultimately why Salisbury—with his eye on Canada and the West Indies as well as Guiana—felt it important to challenge Olney's position. "He lays down," the reply concluded, "that the inexpedient and unnatural character of the union between a European and American State is so obvious that it 'will hardly be denied.'" Her Majesty's Government are prepared emphatically to deny it on behalf of both the British and American people who are subject to her Crown."[24]

Surprised and angered by Salisbury's response, doubly so because it took four months to be rendered, Cleveland and Olney moved toward a public challenge. The Monroe Doctrine, the president later explained, could not be left "a mere plaything with which we might amuse ourselves."[25] In a special message to Congress, delivered on December 17, Cleveland described the doctrine as of "vital concern" to the American people and insisted that this controversy came within its scope. He asked Congress to fund a U.S. commission which would determine the boundary for itself. Then, said Cleveland, it would "be the duty of the United States to resist by every means in its power as a willful aggression upon its rights" any extension of British power beyond that line.[26]

The president had taken the U.S. to the brink of hostilities with the world's greatest naval power—indeed, at this point, there was only one modern battleship in service in the American navy, compared with Britain's forty. But Cleveland had used the commission idea to buy time and had gambled, correctly as it turned out, that England would not want a war with the U.S. In the event, by early 1896 the two governments began to move toward a negotiated, and indeed amicable, settlement. So long as London recognized a U.S. right to involve itself in the controversy and agreed to submit more of the territory it was claiming to arbitration, Olney was willing to accord special status to those areas of long-time British occupation. In fact, no meaningful consultation took place with Venezuela, and in the final settlement the only parts of the disputed territory that were not assigned to British Guiana were those located immediately along the Orinoco. Anticipating Venezuelan protests, Olney commented revealingly that Caracas has "got to do exactly as we tell her."[27]

William McKinley had been one of the most avid proponents of the Pan-American conference held in Washington in 1889–90. Under Blaine's influence, he had also become a convert to the program of commercial reciprocity. He came to the presidency in 1897 eager to promote American interests not only in the Caribbean (and across the Pacific), but in South America as well.

Under section four of the new Dingley Tariff Act of 1897, the president was authorized to negotiate reciprocal trade agreements with other nations. Tariff reductions of up to 20 percent on any and all articles could be offered in return for concessions on American goods. McKinley hoped that this bargaining provision would finally provide the means for a considerable expansion of the U.S. commercial position throughout Latin America.[28] As soon as the measure was enacted, John A. Kasson, a former Republican congressman from Iowa, sometime special envoy, and longtime proponent of foreign trade expansion, was delegated to pursue such treaties as the head of a new Reciprocity Commission attached to the State Department.[29]

Numerous pacts were negotiated over the following three years. However, this activity was little more effective than Blaine's had been in eliciting South American interest. Indeed, in 1897, after a conference at the Brazilian legation in Washington, the Latin American ministers to the U.S. collectively voiced their opposition to reciprocity.[30] Kasson concluded treaties with France, with Britain (for five of its Caribbean possessions), with Denmark (for St. Croix), and with the Dominican Republic and Nicaragua. But as regards the southern continent, he was able by 1901 to negotiate agreements with only two states.[31]

The treaties also had to be ratified by the Senate, where they were greeted with much less favor than McKinley had hoped for. Section four had passed in part because of the depressed condition of the economy during the mid-1890s. With the return of more prosperous conditions, reciprocity encountered more resistance. The new trade agreements began to be submitted to the upper house at the end of 1899. But throughout 1900 and into 1901 the administration was unable to muster enough votes for the approval of any of them. A discouraged Kasson resigned his position.

Because of his mounting interest in foreign trade expansion, McKinley pressed on. Coming off his triumphant reelection, he hoped that he could capitalize on his popularity and build up public support for the pacts. Reciprocity was the central theme of a long cross-country speaking tour the president embarked on in the spring of 1901 (abbreviated because his wife became ill). It was also the subject of what would turn out to be his last public address, delivered at the Pan-American Exposition in Buffalo, New York the following September. The American system of all-embracing protection, with which McKinley's own political career had long been associated, now ought to be modified, the president maintained, so that the U.S. could "open up the widest markets in every part of the world for the products of American soil and American manufactures." "The period of exclusiveness," during which America had built up its industrial might, was past. "If perchance, some of our tariffs are no longer needed for revenue or to encourage and protect our industries at home," he asked, "why should they not be employed to extend and promote our markets abroad?"[32]

With McKinley's own sudden passing, however, there also disappeared any chance either for the existing agreements, or, at least in the immediate future, for the further pursuit of reciprocity. TR, except insofar as he sought to obtain special trade ties between the U.S. and its new colonies (and Cuba), deferred to Republican leaders' nervous opposition to the policy.[33]

McKinley had likewise come to office in 1897 eager to see Congress pass legislation which would promote an enlarged American merchant marine. Here too he ran into domestic political resistance. Protectionism, changing American patterns of investment and trade, plus a failure to keep up with an expanding and technologically innovative British industry had all contributed to the dramatic decline of American shipping on the high seas after the 1850s. McKinley was among those who believed that the resulting dependence on foreign carriers hampered the development of overseas trade, especially with areas outside of Europe, and most pressingly with South America. Congress had provided in 1891 for small mail subsidies to American carriers, but McKinley believed that much greater subventions were required. He hoped, in particular, that by such means new steamship routes could be opened up "between the eastern coast of the United States and South American ports." Legislation toward this end was introduced in Congress, where it was championed by the president's close friend Senator

Mark Hanna of Ohio. But southern and midwestern congressmen and senators from both parties opposed the proposal on the grounds that it constituted favoritism for a special interest. Although it passed the Senate immediately after McKinley's death, the measure could not get through the House. Virtually the same regional alignment, moreover, would continue to frustrate efforts in this direction during the administrations of Roosevelt and Taft.[34]

More success was registered when the McKinley administration set out after the Spanish-American War to revive Pan-Americanism, this time as an ongoing, institutional movement. In 1899, on the occasion of the tenth anniversary of the Bureau of American Republics, McKinley proposed that the states of the hemisphere convene a second inter-American conference. The results of the conference of 1889–90 hardly warranted such an effort. But, while they acknowledged their debt to Blaine, Hay and McKinley had no intention of simply trying again what had so demonstrably failed before. The U.S. had made sweeping proposals at the first conference, specifically about economic integration, which had not only failed to win support, but which had put much of Latin America on the defensive. Instead, this second conference was to be approached from an evolutionary perspective. The administration wanted to use the occasion to improve U.S.-Latin American relations (principally by cooperating with the other states to address noncontroversial commercial, legal, and health issues) and to try to get such meetings established on a regular basis. Its hope was that such a conference system might then increasingly develop into a useful vehicle for the promotion of hemispheric ties and American leadership.[35]

It was decided not to hold the meeting in Washington again. Hay was determined that the U.S. should have a lower profile than it had had in 1889. Instead, the trusted Díaz government of Mexico was asked to be the sponsor. Eager to see harmony reign at the conference, Hay also wanted to keep all potential sources of controversy off the agenda.

These concerns were reflected in the State Department's instructions to the American delegates. They were to try not to assume the leadership of the conference, but rather, by cooperating with the other states, to try to bring to fruition proposals of mutual interest around which a consensus existed. Every effort was to be made "to secure the greatest possible unity of action." Although the U.S. wanted to impress on Latin America the "deep interest" it had "in the peace and tranquility of all the American states," its delegates were also to avoid becoming enmeshed in current Latin American disputes. Nothing was of greater importance "than that the United States should be understood to be the friend of all the Latin-American republics and the enemy of none."[36]

What Hay was not prepared for was the degree to which the whole meeting might become enmeshed in such Latin American disputes. Disharmony among the South American states came close to torpedoing the second conference after it convened in October 1901 (with TR now in the White House). Especially because of the tense state of Chile's relations with its neighbors at this time, arbitration was an even more contentious issue at Mexico City than it had been in Washington. Several delegations, including those from Peru, Bolivia, and Argentina, arrived determined that the meeting not settle for anything less than a treaty that would provide for the obligatory arbitration of all disputes, pending or future. But that position was staunchly opposed by Chile, Ecuador, and Colombia.

Led by William I. Buchanan, the U.S. delegation was eventually able to defuse this controversy by invoking the assistance of the international arbitral system that had been set up at the Hague Peace Conference of 1899 (see Chapter 6). At that conference, which, among Western Hemisphere states, only the U.S. and Mexico had attended, a convention on the peaceful settlement of international disputes, providing for voluntary arbitration, had been signed. Now, in Mexico City, a settlement was reached whereby the participants as a whole would endorse and request adherence to this convention, while those states that chose to do so would sign a treaty providing for compulsory arbitration.[37]

Having prevented a break-up, and given some encouragement to arbitration, the U.S. delegates were subsequently able to achieve Washington's most important conference objective. Before they finally adjourned in January 1902, the participants accepted a proposal to hold future meetings on a regular five-year basis.

This bid for improved relations was, however, dramatically undercut in the period following the second Pan-American conference, partly as the result of American actions in Cuba and on the Isthmus of Panama, but above all because of Latin American concerns about the general U.S. policy on intervention. Hoping to gain acceptance for the Monroe Doctrine from all the European powers, Roosevelt, in his first annual message in December 1901, formally reiterated that it did not "guarantee any State against punishment if it misconducts itself, provided that punishment does not take the form of the acquisition of territory by any non-American power."[38] As has already been seen, the Roosevelt administration began to reappraise this policy in the wake of the Anglo-German expedition against Venezuela. But, its eventual response to that crisis—articulated in TR's 1904 "corollary"—did not stand it in any better favor in the southern half of the hemisphere (see Chapter 2).

Argentina also reacted to the Venezuela intervention, articulating at the end of 1902 what would come to be called the Drago Doctrine, so named for that country's foreign minister, Luis Maria Drago. Drago was particularly concerned that Caracas's tardiness in paying off its contracted public debt became an issue in the confrontation (it was not, however, its main cause), because Argentina, like most of the Latin American states, was also

heavily indebted to Europe. He proposed, in the spirit of his elderly coun-
tryman Calvo, that the nations of the hemisphere take a unified stance in
opposition to the use of force for the collection of such obligations. "Among
the fundamental principles of public international law ... one of the most
precious," wrote Drago, "is that which decrees that all states, whatever be
the force at their disposal, are entities in law, perfectly equal one to another,
and mutually entitled by virtue thereof to the same consideration and respect." "The loss of prestige and credit experienced by States which fail to
satisfy the rightful claims of their lawful creditors," he added, "brings with
it difficulties of such magnitude as to render it unnecessary for foreign
intervention to aggravate with its oppression the temporary misfortunes of
insolvency."[39]

Argentina's proposal was first broached to the U.S. in December 1902,
and then subsequently to other Western Hemisphere countries. In the hope
of winning Washington's favor, Drago suggested that it ought to be seen as
a logical extension of the Monroe Doctrine, the ostensible purpose of which
was to secure the sovereignty of the nations of the Americas. That argument, however, only further ensured an unenthusiastic reception from the
Roosevelt administration.

The fact is that for the U.S., as well as for other great powers, the use of
force for the collection of contracted debts was a practice that had increasingly come to seem problematic. Policy makers believed that it "generated
speculators who live on the people of the [debtor] country, who promote
revolutions by advancing money for arms and ammunition, and make at
times contracts with distressed governments which are seeking to avert political destruction." Rather than promoting, it undermined the development
in the underdeveloped world of governments that were stable and that
would "behave" on their own. It could draw bondholders' governments into
wasteful conflicts on behalf of dubious claims or unwise lending practices.
For the U.S., moreover, it seemed clear in the wake of the Venezuela confrontation that the practice of forcible collection posed a threat to the
Monroe Doctrine.[40]

Nevertheless, Washington strongly opposed the Drago Doctrine. William
Penfield, the State Department solicitor, worried that "If the United States
Government should definitely abandon all right of forcible intervention,
there are some communities ... in which Americans might ... be repeatedly ... despoiled."[41] Because of South America's indebtedness to creditors
on that continent, meanwhile, Drago's doctrine was seen as a major threat
to the U.S. objective of getting Europe to accept the Monroe Doctrine.

Lest Argentina get the wrong idea of Washington's position in the recent
confrontation, therefore, Hay replied to Drago in early 1903 that the administration continued to stand by the president's statement: the U.S. did "not
guarantee any State against punishment if it misconducts itself," provided
that this punishment did not involve "the acquisition of territory by any

non-American power." The way for Latin American states to avoid any chance of outside intervention was for them to "maintain order" and pay their "obligations." Disputes that arose over such matters had to be submitted to international arbitration.[42]

The Roosevelt administration instead wanted to see the admissibility of forcible intervention made contingent on the circumstances surrounding a failure to pay debts (or claims), hoping that this would encourage the kind of behavior it wanted to see in Latin America. In pursuance of this, Washington became a party to the Venezuela case at The Hague, where it argued that a differentiation should be made between countries that "misbehaved" and countries that would, but were simply unable to, pay.[43]

But the judges addressed only the issue of preference. As has been seen, the court's decision on that question quickly precipitated an announcement by TR of his "corollary." At odds with the position advocated by Drago, the U.S. here again warned the other nations of the Americas not to "misbehave" and now put itself forward as the policeman of the Western Hemisphere. South Americans generally recognized that the Caribbean was at the center of TR's attention. For the right of intervention that it asserted, and because of the condescending posture it appeared to take toward Latin America as a whole, however, Roosevelt's corollary inevitably bred unease and resentment on the southern continent.[44]

The problems created by the corollary for American policy in South America were apparent to TR and help to explain why he wanted the assistance of Root, its coauthor, in this arena.[45] They provide essential context for an understanding of the major offensive that Root launched toward those countries on assuming office as secretary of state in 1905.

The ideas of John Barrett, U.S. minister to Colombia, meanwhile, appear to have been helpful in shaping the contours of that offensive. An ex-journalist and commercial publicist, Barrett had been a delegate to the Mexico City conference and had also served as the U.S. diplomatic representative to Argentina and Panama.[46] His emergence as an important voice on Latin American policy began with what Root termed an "excellent memorandum" that he submitted in the fall of 1905, soon after the new secretary's appointment. In this and in subsequent communications, Barrett insisted that U.S. relations with Latin America were at a critical juncture. "The time is at hand that calls for what might be termed a widespread Latin American movement in the United States," he wrote. "To say that it may be 'now or never' with North American prestige and trade in Central and South America is not the statement of an alarmist or pessimist. It is a simple and logical conclusion drawn from a thorough study of the actual situation." Great opportunities existed. But, Barrett asserted, European nations and interests were competing much more effectively for them and were vigorously seeking to gain a hold in the region "of which they cannot be dispossessed." American prospects, meanwhile, were seriously hampered by the U.S. image in South America, and by a "holier than thou" attitude taken by too many U.S. statesmen, writers, and merchants.[47]

Given the traditionally large trade imbalance between the regions (because of American purchases of food and raw materials), argued Barrett, there was no reason why the U.S. could not sell much more than it did to South America. In addition to directing more energy in this direction, American businessmen had to learn more about the region's tastes and needs, employ agents who could speak the area's languages, and extend credit to reliable buyers. They would also benefit if American banks had branches in South America, and if North American capital participated in the development of the region's resources and infrastructure on a much larger scale. The government could help by sending more qualified representatives to South America and by trying, through careful diplomacy, to correct "the false impressions in regard to the intentions of the United States towards Latin America existing in the minds of some Latin American editors and publicists." Barrett did not place any emphasis on tariff policy, but he did push for better transportation facilities as a way of reaching these markets. Finally, he urged an expanded role for the Bureau of American Republics, viewing it as an agency that could promote broader cultural and educational exchanges between North and South America.[48] Few of Barrett's observations or ideas, especially about trade, were entirely new.[49] But his presentation had the special merit of speaking to the public relations problems that the U.S. faced in Latin America and of providing Root with the broadest possible plan of action.

"The South Americans now hate us," complained the new secretary to Senator Benjamin Tillman, "largely because they think we despise them and try to bully them."[50] He was determined to try to improve the situation. Efforts at what Root called his "rapprochement" began with the president's annual message. The year before, TR had announced his corollary to the Monroe Doctrine. Now Roosevelt, significantly, took care to inject that "There are certain republics to the south of us which have already reached such a point of stability, order, and prosperity that they themselves, though as yet hardly consciously, are among the guarantors of this doctrine."[51] Root was also convinced that better relations required the diplomatic representatives from South America to the U.S. to be courted and treated with greater consideration. The arrogance and anti-Hispanic prejudices that often permeated American dealings with South Americans, he felt, hurt U.S. diplomacy.[52] Root worked especially hard to have South American envoys brought more fully into the social life of official Washington.[53]

In one case at least, that of Brazil, a foundation for improved relations had already been laid. That country's foreign minister, the Baron do Rio Branco, had for several years been pursuing a strategy aimed at creating special ties between his country and the U.S. It was the number one market for Brazil's coffee and rubber. But even more important, Rio Branco grasped the fact that the U.S. was replacing Britain as the great power of most significance for South America. If Brazil greeted the expansion of American power with cooperation, rather than with the criticism emanating from the Spanish-American states, it was his hope that the U.S. might then tilt toward Rio and assist it to become the dominant regional power in South America. Toward this end, Rio Branco lobbied the Brazilian congress to grant tariff concessions to American products. He praised the Monroe Doctrine, refrained from criticizing TR's "corollary," and encouraged the Pan-American movement. In 1903–4 he took the lead in urging Latin American countries to recognize the independence of Panama. At his suggestion, the U.S. and Brazil in 1905 elevated each other's legations to embassy status.[54] And Rio Branco appointed the eminent diplomat, Joaquim Nabuco as Rio's first ambassador to the U.S. Root sought to take advantage of this opening when he became secretary. He immediately established a close working relationship with Nabuco, and by the end of 1905 it had been decided that Brazil would host the third Pan-American Conference.[55]

Root also decided that he would pay the conference the "compliment" of a personal appearance. Early in 1906, Lloyd Griscom was sent off to Rio as the new U.S. ambassador, his principal charge being to pave the way for the secretary's arrival the following summer. It was then decided that Root would also visit as many other South American states as he could. Plans were set in motion for a goodwill tour without precedent on the part of a secretary of state.[56]

"I hate banquets and receptions and ceremonial calls and drinking warm, sweet champagne in the middle of the day. All these are the fate of an honored guest in Spanish America," remarked Root when it was time for his departure.[57] He nevertheless expressed the hope that such a trip might help to diminish the feelings of resentment and mistrust that plagued American policy throughout much of the southern continent.[58]

In early July, Root and his family left New York for a trip that was to take the better part of the following three months. Traveling aboard the naval cruiser *Charleston*, they stopped at the new American territory of Puerto Rico and at several port cities along the Brazilian coast before arriving in Rio at the end of the month. There Root attended numerous receptions, met and exchanged pleasantries with key members of the Brazilian upper class, and on July 31 spoke before a special session of the Third Pan-American Conference. The secretary then reembarked for similar visits to the leading cities of Uruguay, Argentina, Chile, and Peru.

The themes for all Root's appearances in South America were set out in his address to the conference. Following Barrett's suggestion that "we should give Latin America more credit for . . . striving under difficult conditions to reach a higher standard of civilization," Root praised the South American nations for creating "strong and stable governments" and for replacing the

"forcible seizure of power" by "[p]eaceful succession." He lauded the decline of caudillism and hailed the fact that "Property is protected and the
fruits of enterprise are secure." Root also empathized with the leaders of
South America. As was also the case in the U.S., they had to cope with segments of their population that had not yet come fully to possess "character" and "self-control." Above all Root sought to disabuse his listeners of
any fears of U.S. domination. In the most widely noted passages of his
speech, he pledged:

We wish for no victories but those of peace; for no territory except our own; for
no sovereignty except sovereignty over ourselves. We deem the independence
and equal rights of the smallest and weakest member of the family of nations entitled to as much respect as those of the greatest empire; and we deem the obser-
vance of that respect the chief guarantee of the weak against the oppression of
the strong.[59]

As to the substance of the conference itself, Root had taken greater pains
even than had Hay in 1901 to ensure that the meeting would be harmonious and noncontroversial. Hay had failed to anticipate the struggle that
would break out among the South Americans over arbitration at Mexico
City. To avoid a repetition of that, Root worked throughout the spring of
1906 in Washington to make sure that the program for Rio would allow for
no surprises. He relied on the greater interest that the U.S. had in these
conferences, on his strategic position as the chair of the governing board
of the Bureau of American Republics, and on his cultivation of several of
the Latin American envoys to the U.S., to draft an agenda that would keep
the meeting under firm control.

Three things concerned him most. Root was determined to eliminate any
possibility for multilateral consideration of the Monroe Doctrine ("I lose
no convenient opportunity to impress upon them that it is a matter of our
own concern, not theirs," he wrote newspaper editor Henry Watterson) or
for criticism of Roosevelt's "corollary."[60] He was also intent on preventing
a repeat of the controversy over arbitration. To guarantee that, a compromise was agreed on whereby the Hague system would again be looked to
for assistance. Participants in the Rio meeting would deal with the question
by expressing their hope that the next conference at The Hague, scheduled
for 1907, would formulate an arbitral treaty that would find favor among
all the American states.

An even greater challenge, finally, was presented by the Drago Doctrine,
which had won broad support among the Latin American states over the
previous three years. Root could not keep it off the program, but he was
determined to prevent the doctrine from being endorsed, or even debated,
at Rio. Instead, he maneuvered to have the program simply include a resolution calling for forcible collection to be yet another issue taken up at
The Hague.[61]

Root warned the American delegation to the conference to stick to the program. It was to work to keep both the U.S. and the meeting from sailing into controversial waters. The conference, he argued, should not try to be "an agency for compulsion or a tribunal for adjudication." Nor should the delegates measure their success in terms of the meeting's accomplishment of "striking or spectacular final results." Rather, it was to be valued for the avenue it afforded for the promotion of closer relations between the U.S. and the Latin American republics, and for the opportunity it provided for the American delegates to bring the other states to Washington's views. In the end, it was this approach, Root thought, that held the strongest prospect for securing Washington's long-term goals.[62]

Judged in this light, the Rio conference was certainly more successful than either of its predecessors. Root's personal diplomacy made a particularly positive impression. Numerous relatively noncontroversial agreements, on such things as sanitation, patents, trademarks, and copyrights, all of which Root saw as working toward greater hemispheric integration, were made.[63] Still more important, the conference accepted a U.S. proposal for an expansion of the functions of the Bureau of American Republics. Root envisioned it now becoming the "permanent committee" of the conference. Dominated by Washington, it would have substantial power to guide and shape the development of the Pan-American movement. It could suggest topics for meetings. It would be given the resources to lobby governments so that they would adopt conference recommendations. The bureau would organize broad analyses of hemispheric economic opportunities, and it would promote cultural and educational exchanges.[64]

This success was in part, however, a function of what the conference avoided dealing with, above all the issue of forcible collection. In accordance with the secretary's plans, that was despatched to The Hague. Root had been eager to sidestep the challenge that the Drago Doctrine posed to American economic expansion, to the U.S. effort to shore up the Monroe Doctrine, and to more amicable U.S.-Latin American relations. Although his argument was that Latin America would hurt its case by acting on its own at Rio, and although he subsequently hailed Drago and spoke against forcible collection on his visit to Buenos Aires, the secretary had no intention of championing the Argentine diplomat's stance at The Hague.[65]

This was fundamentally, and significantly, because Root, like all U.S. policy makers in this era—and despite his comments on the subject at Rio—diverged sharply from Drago in his attitude toward sovereignty. That was in fact, as he saw it, something that was "held upon the condition" of a state performing what Root termed the "duties of sovereignty." In the parliament of man, he believed,

the rights of the weakest state are recognized; the right of the sovereign ruler or ... people to be protected against aggression is recognized.... But that right is held upon condition that the sovereign ruler or ... people performs the duties of sovereignty; that the citizens of other powers are protected within the territory; that the rules of international law are observed; that national obligations are faithfully kept.[66]

At The Hague, Root hoped to see the U.S. position on forcible collection endorsed instead. The use of force would be ruled out, but only if a country did not "misbehave" as that was defined under prevailing international norms. He also hoped that that outcome would be accepted by the Latin Americans as simply the best that could be obtained. At the very least, their disappointment would be focused on the powers in general, rather than on the U.S. alone.[67]

Washington had a strong interest in seeing the circumstances under which forcible collection could receive international sanction restricted, but it wanted great power standards to be upheld in Latin America and to counter the general attitude toward foreigners' rights that had come to be associated with Calvo. Root believed that the South American governments were "capable" of "behaving" and he wanted to ensure conditions that would pressure them to do so. The way to do that was for "mutual concessions" to be made. Force could be ruled out if, but only if, a debtor state did not refuse a request for a disagreement to be submitted to an outside tribunal (upholding, it was presumed, great power standards) for assessment and disposition. In that way, "wrongdoing," both on the part of debtors and on the part of "speculators," could, he thought, be addressed.[68]

"The position of this Government is thought by the European powers to be much more radical than it is," Root told the U.S. delegates before their departure for The Hague. However, he correctly anticipated that "when the subject is discussed in detail they will be pleased to learn that the views of the Government are really so moderate."[69] Indeed, Washington's proposal was supported by the European states, and, as a result, adopted at The Hague. In its final form, this Porter Resolution, so named for the American delegate Horace Porter, asserted that the "Contracting Powers agree not to have recourse to armed force for the recovery of contract debts claimed from the Government of one country by the Government of another country as being due to its nationals." This understanding was, however, "not applicable when the debtor State refuses ... an offer of arbitration."[70]

By contrast, there was considerable disappointment among many in the South American delegations. Instead of the principled opposition to the use of force that had been embodied in the Drago Doctrine, this convention specifically condoned intervention in certain instances. Drago, himself a delegate, futilely attempted to add an amendment that would have required any issue to be decided by the debtor nation's courts before the demand for arbitration could be invoked. This, and the express reservation that absolute nonintervention was a matter of national policy in cases involving such indebtedness, were attached as conditions to Argentina's approval. After the conference, not a single South American government ratified the Porter resolution.[71]

"In many parts of South America there has been much misunderstanding of the attitude and purpose of the United States," commented Roosevelt in his annual message for 1906.

> An idea had become prevalent that our assertion of the Monroe Doctrine implied, or carried with it, an assumption of superiority, and of a right to exercise some kind of protectorate over the countries to whose territory that doctrine applies. Nothing could be farther from the truth. Yet that impression continued to be a serious barrier to good understanding, to friendly intercourse, to the introduction of American capital and the extension of American trade. The impression was so wide-spread that apparently it could not be reached by ordinary means.
>
> It was part of Secretary Root's mission to dispel this unfounded impression, and there is just cause to believe that he has succeeded.[72]

TR was delighted with his secretary of state's "wonderful trip," and not only because of the improved tenor of U.S.-Latin American relations that he believed it had brought about. Like Root, it was his hope that the tour and the extensive publicity it generated at home would finally help to kick off that "widespread Latin American movement in the United States" that Barrett had spoken of.[73]

Root immediately moved to try to ensure such a result. In November 1906 he set off for the Midwest where he spoke before three different commercial gatherings. Then in January he addressed the National Convention for the Extension of the Foreign Commerce of the United States in Washington. His basic themes were the same on each occasion. Root emphasized the great trade prospects that he believed existed in South America, and he urged American businessmen to compete for them before the region came under the control of their rivals. Blaine had been in advance of his time, but now, Root contended, both North and South America had "grown up to Blaine's policy." The greater stability of South America, "our increase of capital, and the effects that must necessarily follow the opening of the great trade route of the Panama Canal all point to the development of American enterprise and American trade to the south." Repeating the suggestions that Barrett and others had long been making, Root argued that individual initiative would be necessary to conquer these markets. Yet he also sought to mobilize his listeners to lobby for more government assistance. Root noted two important steps that had already been taken by the Roosevelt administration. In 1903, it had overseen the establishment of a new Department of Commerce and Labor, and within it a Bureau of Manufactures, the chief purpose of which was to gather intelligence on foreign market conditions for American businessmen. Then, during 1906, the administration had finally brought to fruition reforms providing for the greater professionalization of the consular service. Root thought the

U.S. might benefit from a tariff with maximum and minimum rate schedules, but he did not think that reciprocity was "a question of first importance" with regard to relations with South America. On the other hand, he was very eager to see the government help underwrite better steamship facilities between the continents.[74]

To keep his campaign going, Root arranged to have Barrett appointed director of the Bureau of American Republics at the end of 1906. Drawing on his background as a publicist, Barrett undertook a vigorous schedule of writing and speaking to promote business interest in South America. He also expanded the functions of the Bureau so that it could provide greater information and assistance to manufacturers and investors. Root's friend Andrew Carnegie, meanwhile, agreed to pledge $750,000 towards the construction of a new Washington headquarters for the bureau. Two hundred thousand dollars more were appropriated by Congress.[75]

Others added their voices to the campaign. James Van Cleave, the president of the National Association of Manufacturers, told his members that "we are allowing our British and German rivals to beat us in trade" with South America.[76] Early in 1907, *Bankers' Magazine* mounted a concerted drive to promote more activity in the region on the part of American investors and financial institutions. "American enterprise and capital have already invaded Mexico, Canada and some of the South American countries," wrote its editor.

The South American countries, although more remote from our shores, offer opportunities for employing American energy and money quite as favorable as those which have been found in Mexico. While we have not been entirely indifferent to these inviting fields, our share of the rewards to be obtained there will be much smaller than it should be unless the attention of the moneyed men of the United States is persistently called to the opportunities awaiting them.[77]

In order to further this process, he began to feature regular contributions on South America by experts like Barrett and the financial writer Charles A. Conant.[78] By 1908, *Bankers' Magazine* was in the forefront of a campaign to promote legislation allowing for the federal chartering of American branch banks abroad.

The first decade of the twentieth century, no doubt at least in part because of this campaign, did witness an upsurge in export and investment activity directed toward the southern continent. Export levels moved upward, as did the U.S. share of the merchandise sold in South America's largest markets. Major American investment houses were also attracted to South America, as, in this period, they began to demonstrate a more serious interest in overseas prospects in general. Two significant pieces of business were obtained in 1906. Speyer and Company and the National City Bank secured a railway loan contract with the government of Bolivia. And the latter institution, in conjunction with Henry Schroder and Company of London, arranged to handle a loan for the state of São Paulo, Brazil.[79] These were a prelude to much greater banking activity in South America in the period following the Panic of 1907.

Dollar diplomacy came into its own during the Taft era less because of a change in administrations than because of this growing interest in foreign lending. Wall Street's curiosity about foreign business had risen noticeably in the wake of the successful sale of Japanese securities in the U.S. during the Russo-Japanese War. As noted above, significant new loan business began to be opened up in South America in 1906. Extremely high interest rates prevailed in the U.S. for fully a year in advance of the fall 1907 "Knickerbocker" panic. But by the end of the next year, American bankers were more eager to explore overseas possibilities than ever before.[80]

From early in 1908 there began a long period of extremely low money rates in New York, extending well beyond the general resumption of business activity. And for much of this time there existed a correspondingly strong market for bond sales. Some financial institutions were even driven to rely on their bond business to make up for small profits in other areas during this period.[81] These circumstances led American bankers to take a greater interest in the handling of foreign government loans, and when it was demonstrated how large and easy the profits brought in by such business could be, they were enthusiastic for more.

The São Paulo coffee loan of December 1908 provides an example. This was a $75 million loan, one-fifth of which was organized for sale on the American market by National City Bank. The president, Frank Vanderlip, reported to James Stillman, the board chairman, on December 11, "we have made a great success of the Brazilian loan. It will not be brought out until the first of next week, but it is already considered a little more than oversold." Referring to Morgan and Company, which participated in the underwriting, he commented: "The great success of the Brazilian loan, making them a very large profit without their having to turn a hand, has, I think, been most interesting to them."[82]

More business followed, including an important deal with Argentina. Late in 1908, the Argentine government entered the market for a $50 million dollar public works loan. American bankers were keenly interested. So too was the State Department. Root cabled the interim U.S. chargé in Buenos Aires, Charles F. Wilson, and instructed him to make representations on their behalf. Initially, Wilson was pessimistic. Traditional suspicions of Washington were still very much alive in Argentina, he replied. Wilson noted a "feeling among Argentines . . . that an American loan would not be a mere question of money, but would give the United States an influence in the country different from what would happen in the case of a loan raised in England, France, or other European countries." The history of the two countries' commercial relations, moreover, he felt, had "not been of a nature to give the Argentines a very high idea of either American business intelligence, methods, or honor." Nevertheless, the temporary, but unexpected, refusal of the French government to allow the loan to be listed on the Paris exchange enabled a group of American bankers, led by J. P. Morgan (with First National and National City), to obtain the right to a 20 percent participation in this flotation.[83] Early in 1909, National City sought to establish a financial relationship with Chile as well. Following the advice of W. R. Grace (the only American mercantile firm with lengthy experience on the west coast of South America), it solicited the assistance of the State Department in seeking to encourage Santiago to look to the U.S. for its future needs.[84]

To promote a government loan business more broadly, but also to pursue other banking and investment opportunities, financial institutions began to look toward the establishment of branch banks abroad, especially in South America. Here, too, Vanderlip took the leading role. Early in 1909, he investigated the organizational and legislative problems that needed to be overcome if such expansion was to take place. These proved formidable. Vanderlip quickly came to the conclusion that a revision of federal banking laws, to allow nationally chartered banks to establish overseas branches, would be the most effective means of carrying out such expansion. This began the process that, with the support of the Taft and Wilson administrations, would eventually see such legislation incorporated into the Federal Reserve Act of 1913.[85]

Symbolic of Wall Street's heightened interest in foreign business was the formation in mid-1909 of what came to be called the American Group. Initially this was brought into being at the instance of the federal government, which was seeking to promote American participation in Chinese financial matters. But the four institutions involved had already been cooperating in the foreign field. And a month after the creation of the syndicate for China, J. P. Morgan, National City Bank, Kuhn Loeb and Company, and the First National Bank all informed the State Department that they had also "agreed to cooperate as a 'North American Group' for the purpose of obtaining information and considering South American financial propositions and opportunities."[86] The expectation was that Morgan would take primary responsibility for the Group's affairs in East Asia, while National City would assume this role for South America.

With regard to South America, the Taft administration's chief interest was in seeing this new Wall Street activity lead to a dramatic increase in U.S. trade. "If we want foreign trade," asserted a State Department memorandum in 1909,

a share in foreign investments, a chance to exploit the riches of other lands, our share in the wealth of other nations, we must buy their bonds, help float their loans, build their railroads, establish banks in their chief cities. In South America the giving of good advice and the Monroe Doctrine should be made to yield a financial harvest by the establishment of banks in population centers. When their people want money they should come here for it. As a consequence, when railroads are to be built our mills will furnish the equipment; when mines are opened, bridges constructed, great enterprises started, the finished materials and machines will come from our plants. This is the way others do it and it is to be our way.[87]

The new president told Vanderlip, the latter reported to Stillman, that he was eager to "follow up the very good impression which Secretary Root made in South America." He was particularly anxious "to see some definite steps taken toward closer commercial relations."[88] Toward that end, Taft was "keenly interested and ready to do anything possible" to promote the establishment of branch banks on that continent.[89] The State Department, meanwhile, instructed U.S. diplomats in Latin America to make strong representations on behalf of American bankers.

But the department did not want to leave to chance the trade gains that it hoped would result from this new activity. At the suggestion of Charles Sherrill, the new U.S. minister to Argentina, Secretary of State Knox urged Milton Ailes, a representative of National City Bank, to arrange for future loans to carry a stipulation that funds borrowed through American institutions be spent on products manufactured in the U.S. The banker demurred, fearing that this might hurt his firm's chances of obtaining business. This might also create problems, he pointed out, when the banks involved were not just American. "It frequently happens that we are obliged to run such joint accounts in order to secure an international market for the loan," he added, expressing a persistent concern of Wall Street in this period. Knox nevertheless thought that "arrangements might be made for the purchase of American products ... to the extent of the American participation" in such business. The following day the Diplomatic Bureau was informed that this formula was to be kept in mind whenever government representatives extended their good offices to American bankers.[90]

Washington had in fact already inaugurated a campaign to get at least part of the recently concluded Argentine public works loan spent in the U.S., even though most of the money was to be spent on naval armaments. Although the State Department had attempted to ease the tensions that were rising at this time between Brazil, Bolivia, and Uruguay on the one hand, and Argentina on the other, it was also anxious to see the U.S. play a suppliers' role in the armaments race that those tensions had spawned.[91]

Buenos Aires's principal interest was in acquiring two modern battleships. Early in 1909 a purchasing commission was sent to London to review bids from shipbuilders. It was assumed that an English or German firm would do the work, but when the Fore River Shipbuilding Company of Quincy, Massachusetts expressed interest, Secretary of State Bacon instructed the U.S. ambassador to England to vouch for the firm's reliability and to secure it equality of treatment with the bidders of other nations.[92]

Three weeks later, the new Taft administration followed up with direct representations to the Argentine government. In April, it even offered confidential Navy and War Department designs to Argentina (a move that drew sharp criticism from insurgent Republicans and Democrats in Congress once knowledge of it surfaced in 1911).[93] Developments in London and Buenos Aires were carefully monitored in Washington, and, over the course of the next eight months, as many as eight telegrams per day left the State Department as it sought to coordinate this campaign.

From the outset, the Taft administration assumed that it would have to employ political means to obtain the contracts since the Argentine Naval Board and the Minister of Marine both had long-standing ties with Britain. In Buenos Aires, therefore, Sherrill directed considerable lobbying efforts toward the highest levels of government, arguing that Argentina should award the contracts to an American firm on grounds of national interest. Pressing his case in numerous personal interviews, the American minister presented the conciliation of the U.S. by way of warship orders as something useful, if not necessary, to Argentine diplomacy. Thus when the Argentine foreign minister "seemed desirous to know whether or not the United States really preferred the friendship of Brazil to that of Argentina," Sherrill responded "that our attitude was that of absolute impartiality, but ... he must realize that although it was general knowledge that Brazil had done everything possible and proper to cultivate our friendship, it could hardly be said that Argentina had made the same efforts." "I propounded the query," Sherrill reported, "that might not the people of our country believe that Argentina was really as desirous of our friendship as Brazil if they read in the newspapers that Argentina had taken so friendly a step as to place orders for her two battleships in our shipyards?"[94]

Finally, on January 21, 1910, the Argentine government awarded both battleship contracts to American firms. One ship was to be built by Fore River and the other by the New York Shipbuilding Company, under Fore River's guarantee. Bethlehem Steel was to provide the armor and artillery for both. In addition, Bethlehem was to supply the artillery for twelve torpedo boats which Argentina was having built in England, Germany, and France.[95]

The Taft administration mounted similar campaigns in both Chile and Brazil, as those countries sought to expand their navies in this period. But in none of these other instances did the outcome match the success registered in Argentina. In 1910, Chile, in an effort to keep up with its neighbor, went shopping for two new battleships. The State Department placed great faith in the ability of the new American minister, Henry P. Fletcher, to win this contract for the U.S. (the year before he had played an important role in securing American entry into the Hukuang loan project in China). However, it was immediately apparent both to Fletcher and to Commander A. P. Niblack, his Navy technical adviser, that long-standing suspicions and resentment of the U.S. (aggravated, as shall be seen, by Knox in 1909), plus the strength of Britain's position in Chile, would prevent American success.[96] Both battleship contracts were eventually awarded to English bidders.[97] In Brazil, as in Argentina, U.S. representatives sought to play on the importance of American friendship. Here, however, the tactic was, in the words of the Brazilian ambassador, "counterproductive," because officials in Rio came to see Washington as taking them too much for granted. Brazil continued to give such contracts to European firms in part as a way of asserting its independence.[98]

While the administration campaigned to win foreign government contracts for U.S. firms, it also tried to expand the number of American businesses interested in overseas activity, especially in South America. Secretary of Commerce and Labor Charles Nagel felt that it was crucial for the commercial intelligence gathered by his department to be distributed more widely within the business community. The key to expanding America's volume of trade, as he saw it, lay in getting medium and small-sized manufacturers, as well as large corporations, to take a greater interest in the foreign field. With this in mind, Nagel reorganized the Bureau of Manufactures. Then, in 1912, he oversaw its merger with the Bureau of Statistics, forming the new Bureau of Foreign and Domestic Commerce. With Taft's support, Nagel also helped to create the U.S. Chamber of Commerce.[99]

The administration simultaneously worked to coordinate its efforts with those of Barrett at the Bureau of American Republics. In February 1911, Barrett presided over the first Pan American Commercial Conference in Washington. Here representatives of American business groups were brought into contact with Latin American diplomats as well as U.S. government officials. Taft, Knox, Huntington Wilson, and ex-Secretary Root were among the many who addressed those in attendance.[100]

The Taft administration expanded on its predecessors' efforts in the area of trade promotion. But political relations with most of South America deteriorated badly over the course of its tenure in office. Part of the problem stemmed from Knox's inadequacies as secretary of state. After declining the job himself, Root had recommended the former attorney general (under McKinley and TR) and senator (from Pennsylvania) as his successor. However, he soon regretted doing so, principally because of Knox's handling of hemispheric affairs. Root later complained that for all his brilliance—the Pittsburgh native had been his rival as one of the nation's top corporate lawyers in the 1890s—Knox lacked diplomatic skills. "He got mad very easily," and was "absolutely antipathetic to all Spanish-American modes of thought and feeling and action."[101]

Anxious to increase the level of American trade with South America, the secretary employed an insistent and insensitive style of diplomacy that ultimately worked at cross purposes to all the long-term objectives of

Pan-Americanism, including trade expansion. Knox—and his equally impatient assistant secretary—not only lacked the ability to cultivate Latin American statesmen as Root had done. He also failed to appreciate just how essential such diplomacy was given the obstacles and competitive challenges confronting the U.S. in South America. Thus, in 1911, Knox sarcastically confessed to the president that he found it difficult to carry on "the delicate entente with the Latins" which, in the past, had largely been "nourished and maintained ... upon champagne and other alcoholic preservatives." It was mostly at Taft's behest that the secretary later undertook his good-will tour of the Caribbean, which was patterned on Root's South American voyage of 1906.[102]

The Taft administration's growing involvement in Central America, especially in Nicaragua, also contributed to this deterioration in relations. The reigning elites of South America looked down on the turbulent Caribbean states in this period much as their counterparts in the U.S. did, but they were increasingly unnerved by the expanding pattern of American intervention there. The Argentine leader Rogue Sáenz Peña felt that the "right of intervention is dangerous for all the states of South America." "The right that is adduced to avoid revolutions," he worried, "will it not be invoked tomorrow to foment them?"[103]

The first and most serious crisis in South American relations arose out of Knox's demand, shortly after taking office, that Chile submit to international arbitration the so-called Alsop Company Claims case that had long been pending between the two governments. For years the U.S. had sought to use arbitration as a way of ensuring greater security and regularity for its citizens, and others, doing business in Latin America. It had been pushing for a hemispheric agreement providing for the arbitration of pecuniary claims ever since the Pan-American conference in Mexico City. Arbitration offered the Latin American states protection against unilateral action on the part of the U.S. with regard to claims questions. But, it also required them to abandon the position that they had a sole right to dispose—through their own legal systems—of issues relating to business conducted within their countries. Claims cases would instead be referred to an outside body more likely to uphold the kind of guarantees and protections desired by the U.S.[104]

The problem, from Washington's standpoint, was that a policy of confrontation over such matters worked at cross purposes to the desire to improve relations with the South American states and to win them away from their European orientation. Such considerations clearly influenced Root in his efforts to settle the Alsop case on behalf of the company's U.S. stockholders.[105] But they were ignored by Knox, who, as part of his bid to expand the American business presence in Latin America, was determined to move claims matters onto what he saw as a more satisfactory plane.[106]

Chile finally agreed to submit the case to arbitration. But it stipulated that the protocol provide for Santiago's right to argue that the U.S. had no basis on which to interfere in the matter. And it also expressed a desire to have the president of Brazil named the arbitrator. In response, Knox, in November 1909, peremptorily insisted that Chile either agree to pay the amount determined by the U.S. or agree to an arbitration that would deal exclusively with that narrow monetary question. If Santiago did not accept at once, relations between the two countries would be suspended.

With the aid of Root and Nabuco, the Brazilian ambassador, this incident was quickly contained, and on terms largely favorable to Washington. Chile was allowed to include its stipulation in the protocol, but it had to accept reference of the dispute to the King of England, and this eventually led to a ruling that endorsed both the U.S. legal position and the American contention as to what was due the stockholders. In terms of its broader ramifications, however, the episode made an extremely unfavorable impression throughout South America and greatly antagonized Chile.[107]

Then, only two weeks after its ultimatum to Santiago, the Taft administration severed relations with Zelaya of Nicaragua and deployed marines off the coast of that country. These actions further upset opinion on the southern continent, and that in turn upset some long-time partisans of Pan-Americanism within the U.S. Before a Bureau of American Republics luncheon in his honor, attended by Knox and all the Latin American diplomats, Andrew Carnegie offered to give the State Department $20 million to be used to settle current difficulties between the U.S. and Latin America. Stunned and embarrassed, the secretary of state interrupted Carnegie to bitterly deny that any such problems existed.[108]

The acquisition by American firms of the Argentine battleship contracts early in 1910 was cited by the administration as confirmation "of the friendly relations which now exist between this country and all South America."[109] But such confidence clashed with the tone taken by Knox in his instructions to the U.S. delegation to the fourth Pan-American conference. Therein he voiced the hope that the "somewhat drastic action" taken against the "medieval despot" Zelaya "would not be misconstrued by the progressive American Republics."[110]

Knox's State Department employed just as much effort as Root's had four years before to ensure that the meeting in Buenos Aires during the summer of 1910 would be harmonious and noncontroversial. Nevertheless, this time there was a much stronger undercurrent of north-south tension. Brazil blundered badly when it proposed a motion in praise of the Monroe Doctrine. It had to be withdrawn before it reached the floor. And concerns were raised as well about U.S. dominance of the governing board of the Bureau of American Republics (here renamed the Pan-American Union).[111]

The situation worsened during the second half of Taft's presidency. Through no fault of Knox, the Justice Department threatened to bring suit against Brazil (or, more specifically, against its New York marketing agents), the one important friend the U.S. had in South America, over the coffee valorization program of the state of São Paulo. Aimed at stabilizing the price of coffee in the face of enormous overproduction, the program (which had been financed in part by National City Bank) was assailed by Attorney General George Wickersham as a violation of the Sherman Antitrust Act. Legal action was ultimately avoided. But Brazil had to abandon the scheme, and this left bruised feelings in Rio. "The United States position here," reported the British minister to Brazil near the end of the Taft era, "is at this moment weaker than it has ever been during my six years stay."[112]

Finally, in the last months of 1912 the U.S. intervened militarily in Nicaragua. This action ensured that Washington's South American policy would lay in tatters when the administration came to an end early the following year. "There is no Pan Americanism in South America," Argentina's ambassador to the U.S., Dr. Rómulo Naón, commented flatly in 1913, "it exists only in Washington."[113]

Woodrow Wilson criticized "dollar diplomacy." But he too was eager to see the government play an expanded role in the area of foreign trade promotion, and, like his predecessor, he placed a heavy emphasis on the markets of South America. Simultaneously, Wilson recognized the image problems that had been created for the U.S. in that region. He and his advisors felt that these had to be addressed if U.S. commercial and other objectives there were to be realized.

Wilson generally avoided discussion of foreign policy matters during the campaign of 1912, but he spoke quite frequently about foreign trade. The Democratic candidate derided what he described as the inadequate steps thus far taken by the government to expand the nation's overseas commerce. And he also criticized what he saw as the backwardness of much of American business in this regard. "We have been so rooted in our provincialism, so unaware of the very processes of our own industrial life," Wilson argued, "that we have cut ourselves off from the means of making ourselves supreme in the world from an economic point of view." Wilson proposed to lead the country toward such supremacy. He also argued that a vast expansion of American exports, particularly of manufactured goods, would soon be required by the nation. The time was approaching when American manufacturers would be producing more than the domestic market could consume. In addition, that domestic market was consuming more and more of the raw materials and foodstuffs that the U.S. traditionally had exported.[114]

Wilson wanted the U.S. to modernize its methods and to become socially and economically more efficient so that it could compete with greater effectiveness overseas. As soon as it was installed, his administration backed legislative steps aimed at promoting this "commercial conquest of the world."[115] One of the most significant involved revision of the tariff. Wilson had always been a low-tariff advocate, but the question had acquired a new significance for him as his interest in foreign trade grew. By the time he became president, a central concern was that protectionism was impeding the United States' development of a greater export trade in manufactures. During the campaign, Wilson complained that

The tariff question originally was a question of domestic development; and now the energies of the United States have been such, and her output in the field of manufacture has been such, that we need the markets of the world. If we continue to confine ourselves to domestic development, then we will be kept in a straitjacket. We will find it impossible to release our energies upon the great field upon which we are now ready to enter, and enter by way of conquest.[116]

Lower tariffs would open foreign markets, give manufacturers cheaper raw materials, and force U.S. business to be more efficient.

Protectionism had proven both ideologically and politically problematic for the Republicans. After a decade of mounting criticism from business constituents interested either in expanding their foreign markets or in obtaining cheaper raw materials (in many cases both), as well as from the public because of the rising cost of living, the Taft administration had twice tried to address the issue (once through a general revision and a second time via reciprocity with Canada, see Chapter 5), but without great success. It had sought to lower duties on raw materials and to obtain a bargaining mechanism with which Washington could protect its overseas trade. By contrast, the Wilson administration sought and, despite protectionist opposition, obtained a general lowering of duties.[117]

Legislation passed two months later was of even greater relevance for South America. The act providing for the establishment of the federal reserve system in December 1913 also contained provisions designed to help American bankers more effectively expand their international operations. Sections 13 and 14 opened the way for national banks to accept drafts drawn on foreign trade and to buy and sell foreign exchange, while Section 25 finally provided the legislative basis for nationally chartered banks to establish branches in foreign countries. Under the terms of the latter, National City Bank's Vanderlip immediately set up his institution's first overseas branch in Buenos Aires.[118]

The administration also sought to improve on the trade promotion machinery it had inherited from its predecessors. Here Wilson looked to the leadership of the man he appointed as secretary of commerce, William C. Redfield. A prominent New York manufacturer, former director of the Equitable Life Insurance Company, and congressional representative, Redfield had won national attention for his writings on the twentieth-century needs of American enterprise. The dominant theme of his book *The New Industrial Day*, published in 1912, was that American businesses had to become more efficient as organizations. In part this was so that they could compete more effectively in international markets (Redfield was himself a former president of the American Manufacturers' Export Association, founded in 1909). Wilson drew heavily on Redfield's views during the presidential campaign, and he hoped that at Commerce he would put his ideas into practice.

Immediately, the size and functions of the Bureau of Foreign and Domestic Commerce were expanded. With the backing of Wilson, Redfield succeeded in getting Congress to agree to a significant increase in its personnel. Overseas, a system was established whereby special commercial attachés were assigned to the most important U.S. trading partners. The number of roving commercial agents was increased. District offices of the bureau were established around the U.S. to bring it into closer contact with manufacturers. And, finally, a special fund was provided entirely to be targeted toward trade expansion with Latin America.

Like Nagel before him, Redfield was especially anxious to see the movement into foreign trade broadened to include as much of the business community as possible. Toward this end, the new secretary undertook an ambitious program of speaking tours around the country. And, in 1914, he played a prominent role in the founding of the National Foreign Trade Council, an organization that sought to unify all the most important export interests in the nation.[119]

Confronting a situation reminiscent of that facing Root in 1905, the Wilson administration simultaneously tried to improve U.S. political relations with South America. As a first step it sought to close out the Panama incident as an irritant in both U.S.-Colombian and, more broadly, U.S.-Latin American affairs. Hoping to restore good relations with Colombia and to regularize relations between that country and Panama, the Taft administration had already broached the possibility of compensating Bogotá financially for what it had lost in 1903. But Taft and Knox had been unwilling to meet Colombia's demand that Washington also apologize for its role at that time. Wilson, by contrast, felt far less need to uphold the Republican record, and he proceeded to negotiate an agreement that incorporated both provisions. Washington would express a general sense of regret for past difficulties and it would pay Bogotá $25 million. The treaty won considerable praise in Latin America. However, it also met bitter hostility from Republicans and from TR, who characterized it as an attack on American honor. As a result, Wilson was unable to get the pact ratified by the Senate.[120]

Elsewhere, the administration moved quickly to repair relations with Brazil, something desired no less intensely now in Rio. Efforts in this direction were capped off by a highly successful visit to the U.S. in mid-1913 by foreign minister Lauro Müller. Negotiations were also begun to elevate the status of Washington's ties with the two other powers of the southern continent. In 1914 it was agreed that the U.S. would begin to exchange representatives of ambassadorial rank with both Chile and Argentina, as it had been doing with Brazil for the previous decade.[121]

In the case of Argentina, however, it is worth noting that this effort to improve relations did not prevent the administration from taking a hard line when Buenos Aires tried to back out of its battleships deal with American firms. Given a world economic downturn in 1913–14 and a marked improvement in its relations with its neighbors, Argentina decided that it no longer wanted the ships. The Wilson administration, however, insisted that Buenos Aires honor the contract, which had of course been the Taft era's most noted instance of "dollar diplomacy" in South America.[122]

Another means by which mistrust could be reduced, it was thought, might be for the U.S. to try to solve hemispheric problems by enlisting the aid of adjutants or assistant policemen. This idea began to be discussed by individuals within and around the administration as early as 1913. But it was in fact similar to the approach that Root had tried to employ in Central America seven years before. He had sought Mexican cooperation in promoting stability there under the theory that this would make the U.S. seem less overbearing both to Latin America and to opinion back home.

Numerous experts were arguing that the Monroe Doctrine, especially since its association with TR's "corollary" and Taft's interventionism, had become a major problem for U.S. relations with South America. One of these was Yale professor Hiram Bingham, who went so far as to call the doctrine "an obsolete shibboleth" in a much discussed article published in the *Atlantic Monthly* in June 1913. On recent trips to the region, he had been profoundly impressed by the hostility that had developed toward the doctrine. South Americans resented its paternalism and implied superiority, and they suspected that the doctrine reflected a U.S. desire to monopolize and dominate the hemisphere. "The very words 'Monroe Doctrine'," Bingham reported, "are fraught with a disagreeable significance from our neighbors point of view." Such hostility could be defused, however, he suggested, if the unilateralism of the doctrine was replaced by a multilateral approach to hemispheric issues. This was the same idea that was beginning to be discussed within the administration. But for policy makers, at least, what was implicit was that other nations would be enlisted to help secure conditions and standards desired by the U.S. in the region.[123]

Actual recourse to such an approach was first seriously discussed in connection with Wilson's struggle to have Victoriano Huerta removed from power in Mexico (see chapter 5). As the president's campaign against the general intensified in 1913 and early 1914, John Barrett repeatedly implored him to avoid tactics that might offend and alienate Latin American opinion. Barrett urged Wilson to give a "Pan-American tone" to his policy.[124] Others specifically suggested that he seek to involve the three most important South American powers. Early in 1914, Wilson's close adviser and confidant Colonel Edward M. House told him that he felt Argentina, Brazil, and Chile were "strong enough to take their part in the policing of the Western Hemisphere."[125]

It was apparently at their own suggestion, however, that the A.B.C. powers finally became involved in the Mexican situation later that year. Their offer of mediation gave Wilson a way of extricating himself from a dangerous crisis that developed after the U.S. seized the port city of Veracruz in April. The possibility of war existed as Wilson, to his surprise, confronted nearly universal condemnation of this move by Mexicans. The intervention was also met with great criticism throughout Latin America and from within the U.S.

In accepting the offer of the A.B.C. powers to assist in a settlement of the crisis, the president was able both to escape more serious trouble and to turn much of the criticism into praise.[126] As shall be seen, however, it was not long before he was also trying to use the involvement of these states to advance his own agenda for the reorganization of Mexico's internal affairs (see Chapter 5).

The onset of World War I provided additional incentives as well as a new opportunity for the U.S. to improve its relations with South America and to diminish that region's ties to Europe. By late 1914, House was advising Wilson "to pay less attention to his domestic policy and greater attention to the welding together of the two Western Continents." Its past use of the "'big stick'" had lost the U.S. "the friendship and commerce of South and Central America and the European countries had profited by it." But now, by building on the policy inaugurated with the A.B.C. mediation, he argued, the Wilson administration could turn that situation around.[127]

House was concerned about what Germany might be able to do if the U.S. did not unify the hemisphere behind its leadership and end Latin America's disaffection. For he was convinced that Berlin "would never forgive us for the attitude we have taken in the war" and would challenge the Monroe Doctrine in South America if it was victorious.[128] To eliminate that prospect, House suggested that Washington offer to sign with the Latin Americans a pact whose central feature would consist of a guarantee by all the "Republics of the two Continents" of "each other's territorial integrity." He believed that such a treaty would alleviate the fears Latin Americans had about the ends of U.S. policy. House hoped that it would also pave the way for Latin American cooperation with Washington against both extra-hemispheric and hemispheric challenges to the kind of order in the Americas desired by the U.S. Finally, in addition to its impact on the Americas, House believed that this project might also help the U.S. to promote the kind of world order that it wanted after the war. As he recounted in his diary, House advised the president that he

might or might not have an opportunity to play a great and beneficent part in the European tragedy, but there was one thing he could do at once and that was to inaugurate a policy that would weld the Western Hemisphere together. It was my idea to formulate a plan ... which, in itself, would serve as a model for the European nations when peace is at last brought about.[129]

Wilson immediately warmed to House's proposal, and it was agreed that the latter would take responsibility for the preliminary negotiations on its behalf. It was felt that House should sound out the A.B.C. powers informally before any other states were approached. On December 17, he explained "this proposed League" to Bryan, after which the matter was laid, individually, before the ambassadors from Argentina, Brazil, and Chile.[130]

Taking the U.S. at its word, that it sought a new definition of the Monroe Doctrine and a more equitable relationship, Buenos Aires and Rio de Janeiro both responded positively.[131] However, Santiago was more cautious, because it feared that the pact, and especially the provisions it made for the expeditious settlement of outstanding territorial disputes, might jeopardize its hold over the territories of Tacna and Arica. At least in part because it did not oppose the treaty outright, House nevertheless doubted that Chile could not be satisfied and brought around.[132] Months of negotiations with Chile, and with the Argentine and Brazilian ambassadors followed, after which, in late 1915, a new draft was finally referred to Santiago.[133]

Optimistic that the project was about to be realized, Wilson discussed inter-American affairs at length in his annual message. Partnership was replacing guardianship as the hallmark of U.S. relations with Latin America, he maintained. The states of the hemisphere were becoming "cooperating friends." And "their growing sense of community of interest," the president believed, was even "likely to give them a new significance as factors in international affairs and in the political history of the world. It presents them as in a very deep and true sense a unit in world affairs."[134]

Wilson declared that "fears and suspicions" about the meaning of the Monroe Doctrine had heretofore prevented "intimacy and confidence and trust between the Americas," when, early in January, he at last made his plan public (in a speech before the Pan American Scientific Conference). But this mistrust could be put to rest by an agreement such as he had in mind. Great, cooperative strides could then, Wilson voiced hope, be made to promote not merely the "international" but also "the domestic peace of America." He asserted that it was "just as much to our interest to assist each other to the orderly processes within our own borders as it is to orderly processes in our controversies with one another."[135]

Pressed to decide, Chile, however, in early 1916 began more directly to oppose the pact by lobbying against it among the other A.B.C. powers. Lansing's first reaction was that "there may be some foreign power at work in the countries which seem to be lukewarm, or hostile to the proposed agreement."[136] He worried that Brazil might now also hold back. Infuriated, Wilson suggested that the A.B.C. nations ought perhaps to be made aware that the U.S. (their "cooperating friend") was "in a position to make their isolation very pronounced and unenviable" if any of them continued to oppose the treaty.[137] His inclination was to proceed with or without the prior agreement of all the big South American states. But Ambassador Fletcher pointed out that such a course was likely to be counterproductive from the standpoint of the purposes of the treaty.[138]

At the end of April, the submission of a new draft by Brazil, which was eager to maintain good relations with both the U.S. and Chile, revived hopes that Santiago and Rio might still go along. However, as historian Mark Gilderhus has detailed, the whole project then collapsed as a consequence of U.S. policy toward Mexico. Wilson's despatch of the Pershing expedition in March (see Chapter 5) brought the government of Venustiano Carranza and Washington to the brink of war by late June, whereupon the A.B.C. powers (just as they had done during the Veracruz crisis), as well as other Latin American states, proffered their good offices. Carranza welcomed outside involvement that might lead to the removal of U.S. forces from Mexican soil. But seeing his policy toward Mexico as hanging in the balance, Wilson was not ready to see that take place. He rejected mediation, gambling simultaneously that he could place responsibility for the crisis on Carranza and convince Latin America that U.S. actions did not constitute intervention. That was not, however, the effect that was achieved. Wilson's actions in Mexico and his rejection of a multilateral approach to the crisis, instead raised serious questions as to the sincerity of the professions that had accompanied the Pan-American pact. None of the key nations there were now prepared to move forward on the proposal.[139]

The Wilson administration was not able to bring its Pan-American pact to fruition. Yet, of much greater significance, and in the long run carrying vast political importance as well, the European war also created an opportunity for the U.S. to expand enormously its economic role throughout the Americas.

Latin America was highly vulnerable in 1914. The war began at a time when world economic activity was already sluggish. And, as was also the case for the U.S., the onset of hostilities had the impact of making conditions worse. Exports to Europe, particularly to the Allies, began to revive in 1915. However South America had long since become dependent on that area not just for markets, but also for finance, shipping, and many manufactured products. As these were diverted elsewhere by the conflict, the supply of such goods and services was dramatically disrupted. Even those Latin Americans who hoped that their country could take advantage of the war to pursue economic diversification recognized a need, at least in the short run, to look to the U.S. as Europe's replacement.[140]

Many Americans were immediately alert to the prospect that the war might enable them to encroach more significantly on the positions that had been occupied by the English, Germans, French and others. This was a prominent theme in consular reports from South America during late 1914, as it was also in the September issue of the *Bulletin* of the Pan-American Union. It was an "ill wind that blows no good," it announced, referring to the war. By winter, the new situation had become the focus of attention of manufacturers and merchant associations across the entire country.[141]

The administration had already taken steps to prepare the way for this new Latin American movement. Indeed, on August 7, only three days after Britain entered the war, the State and Commerce Departments established an Inter-Departmental Committee on Pan-American commerce. A Latin American Trade Conference was held in the capital in September. Presided over by Bryan and Redfield, it brought together government experts and representatives from major American export organizations. Credit and exchange facilities were among the deficiencies cited as standing in the way of the kind of commerce envisioned. Redfield and Secretary of the Treasury William Gibbs McAdoo subsequently sought to address these problems, while plans were also set in motion for a meeting with Latin American finance ministers to be held in the spring.[142]

That first Pan-American Financial Conference met in Washington in May 1915. Largely organized by McAdoo, its purpose was to promote cooperation in trade matters among all the republics of the hemisphere. Administration leaders also hoped to use the conference to improve the U.S. image and to encourage Latin America to view the new war-induced trade patterns as the desirable wave of the future.

Wilson, Bryan, Redfield, McAdoo, other members of the cabinet, and two members of the new Federal Reserve Board addressed the conference. Bryan, however, trod clumsily when he condescendingly likened the relationship he looked forward to to the growth of a "great Banyan tree." The U.S., he said, was the "parent stem." The "branches extending to the South have taken root in the soil and are now permanent supports, yes, important parts of that great tree."[143]

The principal accomplishment of the meeting was the establishment of an International High Commission, which was to pursue concrete solutions to hemispheric trade problems. McAdoo hoped to see it promote more uniform commercial and financial practices and standards throughout the region. In 1916, he personally led an American delegation to Buenos Aires for the first of the commission's meetings.[144]

From early 1915 on, exports to South America expanded at an unprecedented rate, gaining greatly at the expense of the European rivals of the United States.[145] Running parallel to this was a rapid growth of branch banking, led especially by National City. Once the war began, it quickly opened new branches in Rio, São Paulo, Santos, Montevideo, and then, by late 1916, Bahia and Valparaiso.[146]

Vanderlip also put together the American International Corporation in 1915. Going beyond the financial groups organized during the Taft years, this was a huge investment trust intended to promote the expansion abroad of major American financial and industrial interests. On its board of directors were leading executives not only from National City, but also from J.P. Morgan, Kuhn Loeb, Chase National Bank, and the Guarantee Trust Company, plus numerous corporate and shipping leaders such as Percy Rockefeller of Standard Oil, J. Ogden Armour of Armour and Company, and Charles Coffin of General Electric. Given its earlier antitrust and anti-"dollar diplomacy" rhetoric, Vanderlip at first worried that the administration might be hostile to this behemoth. But Wilson instead invited Vanderlip to the White House to assure him that he was "doing the things that the Administration wants done in respect to the expansion of our foreign trade."[147]

The A.I.C. also sought to develop maritime shipping facilities. In this area, its activities paralleled those of other steamship companies and of the federal government during this period. U.S. Steel had established the United States and Brazil Steamship Line in 1913. Two years later the Caribbean and Southern Steamship Company announced regular sailings to both Brazil and Argentina. Then, in 1916, the South American Steamship Company unveiled plans for regular sailings between Panama and Chile. The war, moreover, finally made possible an enhanced role for the federal government in the upbuilding of the merchant marine. Emphasizing the issue's importance from the standpoint of preparedness, Wilson was able to get Congress to create a United States Shipping Board in 1916. It was allotted $50 million to develop American shipping.[148]

American government and business figures were eager to take advantage of the opening that the war in Europe afforded them, for, as Wilson put it in his annual message for 1915, this was seen as "an opportunity which may never return again if we miss it now."[149]

By the turn of the twentieth century, American leaders had come to see the whole continent of South America as an area where the U.S. was destined to exercise commercial and political leadership. All the administrations in this period pursued policies aimed at promoting that relationship and at blocking any developments that might stand in its way.

The most dangerous of these appeared to be the possibility that one or more of the European powers would establish a political-military presence in the region and thus challenge the "predominance of the Great Republic in this hemisphere." To prevent that, Washington labored to get those powers, both by threats and assurances, to accept as permanent the existing political boundaries and framework for trade in South America.

This project, in turn, as policy makers saw it, required the U.S. to stifle conditions and trends in South America that might "invite" European involvement or impede such acceptance. Unlike the Caribbean, the states of this region seemed "capable" of "behaving" as the powers desired. The issue was getting them to do so. Washington worried particularly about instability arising from interstate rivalries in the region and about the region's proclivity to challenge the rules for the treatment of outside business desired by the U.S. and Europe. Drawing here again on approaches in fashion at home, policy makers sought to use settlement mechanisms like arbitration as a way both of limiting interstate conflict and of getting South Americans to accept those ground rules. They were offered inducements, principally in the form of greater protection from outside force, but were also pressured, principally by the continued legality of intervention, to behave as the U.S. desired.

Washington's efforts to ensure order and adherence to great power standards, however, had the capacity to work at cross purposes with its desire to increase its trade and influence in South America, particularly given the region's long-standing cultural and commercial ties with Europe and its fears of the U.S. Hoping to overcome such contradictions, officials had repeated recourse to multilateral institutions. They tried to use the Hague conference system as a way of integrating the South American states into the world system on the terms they wanted. Officials also sought through the ideological and institutional framework of Pan-Americanism to improve the U.S. image and to convince South Americans that Washington wanted not domination but partnership. The Pan-American conferences, in particular, bear comparison with similar such consensus building methods in vogue domestically within the U.S.

Pan-Americanism was only sporadically successful at achieving these objectives. But this era culminated, nevertheless, in a dramatic reorientation of trade and influence in the hemisphere. This was because of World War I, and because American business and political leaders—building on what was already more than a decade of accelerating efforts at trade promotion—were determined to take advantage of the opening that the war afforded.

Chapter 4

"Where the Far West Becomes the Far East": China

In China, the U.S. objective was to uphold and stabilize the "traditional" nineteenth-century open door framework for trade throughout that vast empire. Even if it did not compare in activity at this time with South America, observers in both Europe and North America were convinced, largely on the basis of its size and population, that China was destined in the coming century to become one of the world's most lucrative commercial frontiers.[1] American officials also believed that influence in and over China, especially by means of its commercial development, would, for much the same reasons, have a great impact on the relative international standing of the major powers. Their hope was that if the open door could be maintained, along ideally with the territorial integrity of the empire, that the U.S. would be well positioned eventually to take the leading role there economically and politically. The U.S. as they saw it had key advantages it could capitalize on in China, most notably the economic might that it was assembling and geography.[2] Especially with the construction of a canal across Central America, the U.S. would enjoy a great edge over the advanced industrial countries of western Europe in interacting with that region.[3]

By comparison with South America, however, far greater challenges appeared to confront the U.S. in East Asia. Worried that one or more other powers might act in such a way as politically to interfere with American access to part or all of the China market, policy makers doubted that they could as yet respond with force, or with the threat of force such as was embodied in the Monroe Doctrine. With its small army and distance from the scene, the U.S. seemed ill-prepared to match the might that an adjoining—albeit economically less advanced—land power, like Russia, could place in this theater. More disturbing still, officials came to doubt that American opinion would support even an aggressive naval posture—toward other powers—in East Asia. (In the Western Hemisphere, by contrast, the Monroe Doctrine was supported because it had come to be viewed as a traditional policy and as a measure of self-defense.)

China's behavior also appeared to constitute a greater challenge, principally because its government seemed weaker and less capable of acting "responsibly" than those in South America. Policy makers were particularly

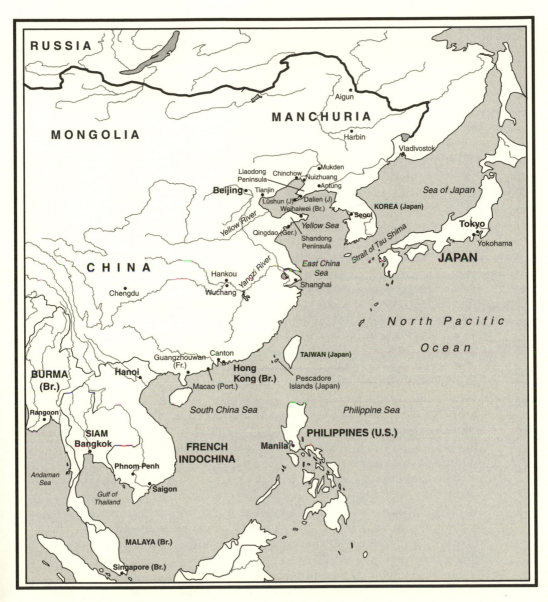

China and East Asia, c. 1910.

concerned about China's ability to protect foreigners and to promote and maintain the conditions that they wanted within the empire. Its deficiencies in that respect, as Washington saw it, threatened to "invite" more in the way of great power involvement that might be at odds with the open door.

U.S. policy toward this region therefore had to be different. Compelled to accept the presence of numerous other powers there, the basic trend was for Washington to try to encourage collective, rather than unilateral approaches, both to the supervision of China and to the protection of the open door, the hope being that this was a means of containing potentially "greedy" powers. With regard to the empire itself, policy makers meanwhile tried to promote the development of a government that could and would act as the U.S. desired. As was the case with a number of the Caribbean states, many officials were eventually drawn to the idea that some sort of "guardianship" had to be imposed on China before this could happen.

The "traditional" framework of foreign competition in China had been established in the 1840s and 1850s when Britain had taken the lead in opening the Qing (Manchu) empire up to outside trade.[4] Through the Canton system, the Manchus had tried to regulate and restrict foreign merchants, in part by confining them to that one port city in the south. But this system was brought crashing down by the British navy in the First Opium War of 1839–42. Afterward, China was compelled to cede Hong Kong, to allow British subjects to reside and do business in five cities along the coast, and to fix low tariff rates on its imports. At the same time, London obtained a "most favored nation" clause (whereby it would share in any privileges won by other powers), which set the tone for commercial treaties subsequently signed with China by numerous Western nations, including the U.S.

Eleven additional cities—both on the seacoast and up the Yangzi—were opened up to foreign trade in the aftermath of a Second Opium War (1856–60). Britain and other states secured the right to Western-style diplomatic representation at Beijing. Under a system of extraterritoriality, the foreign powers were also conceded legal jurisdiction over their subjects doing business in the empire.

Such claims compromised China's sovereignty at numerous points. However, once these "rights" were wrung from the Qing, Britain saw itself as having a stake in the dynasty's continued existence. England, along with other Western states, thus helped Beijing to put down the Taiping Rebellion in the 1860s. It also moderated the pace with which it had been pushing for its merchants and missionaries to have still greater access to the empire.

The Qing had confronted mounting problems since the second half of the eighteenth century. Rapid population growth, state neglect of public works, natural disasters, growing corruption within the bureaucracy and military, and poor leadership from the top all had combined to create conditions of internal crisis at the very time that the empire was confronted with unprecedented external challenges. But Qing officials now enjoyed something of a breathing spell, which they used to pursue a program referred to as "self-strengthening." Beginning in the reign of Tongzhi (1861–75), substantial public/private projects were undertaken especially to improve the empire's military might.

Beijing won new respect from the Western powers. But when Japan went to war with China in 1894, to challenge the latter's influence in Korea, Qing accomplishments were shown to be woefully overstated. Not only had "self-strengthening" been confined largely to the military sphere. The acquisition of new armaments had not been accompanied by institutional changes that would allow such strength to be coordinated and applied effectively. China found itself at the mercy of Japan, which since 1868 had been engaged in a much more thoroughgoing program of conservative modernization.

This Sino-Japanese War heralded Japan's emergence as a major power. It marked, as well, the beginning of a new era of great power pressure on, and rivalry over, the Qing state. Under the terms of the Treaty of Shimonoseki, Tokyo forced China to renounce its ties with Korea, but also to pay a large indemnity, and to give Japan Taiwan, the Pescadores, and the Liaodong Peninsula in southern Manchuria.[5]

Because St. Petersburg viewed this settlement as a preemptive attack on plans it had been developing to become a major East Asian power, it took issue with the treaty. In the hope of catching up with the industrial nations of Western Europe and of retaining its great power status, Russia had come to place much importance on its ability to develop its eastern provinces and to exploit the economic advantages it had relative to neighbors like China. To achieve these objectives it was building the Trans-Siberian Railway and looking for an ice-free Pacific port south of Vladivostok. Japan's treaty was seen as a threat to both projects.[6]

Russia enlisted the support of France and Germany to keep Japan from occupying territory on the Chinese mainland. Within a week of the signing of the treaty, all three powers protested the provision relating to the Liaodong. Tokyo felt compelled to retreat (subsequently demanding an even greater indemnity from Beijing). However, China's weakness had been underscored. It was not long before the interceding powers themselves began to pressure Beijing for favors to repay the "service" they had rendered.

At first these demands were confined to the empire's periphery. In 1896, Russia, for instance, won permission to build a stretch of its new transcontinental system (the Chinese Eastern Railway) across northern Manchuria to Vladivostok.[7] But after late 1897, changes were introduced much closer to the heart of the Qing state. In pursuit of a base of operations in East Asia, Berlin seized on the murder by bandits of two of its missionaries as a pretext to occupy the northerly harbor of Jiaozhou, on the Yellow Sea. It demanded port facilities there as well as a supportive sphere of influence in the surrounding Shandong province.

Germany's move, in turn, led Russia to occupy Lüshun, the most politically sensitive, strategically important harbor in the northern region. Located at the southern tip of the Liaodong, the site commanded the maritime approach to Tianjin, and thus to Beijing. St. Petersburg forced China to concede it a lease to the territory embracing both Lüshun (renamed Port Arthur) and the neighboring commercial port of Dalien. It also gained the right to build a rail line (the South Manchurian Railway) south to this leasehold from the town of Harbin on the C.E.R.[8]

These moves shattered the complacency of Great Britain. It feared that Russia might now challenge the open door in Manchuria, as it had done elsewhere in Asia. Still worse, the Salisbury government worried that Russia would soon have more influence over the rest of China by virtue of its growing political/military proximity to the Qing capital. The whole basis for England's traditional leadership in trade and influence seemed threatened.

To counter such prospects, London acquired rights to the port of Weihaiwei, one hundred miles to the south of Port Arthur. It pressured Beijing to confirm that a British citizen would continue to superintend the Qing maritime customs administration, a practice that dated back to the 1860s. England also began to look for allies who would help uphold the open door in the face of such a challenge.[9]

Eventually the topic would also be taken up with Germany and Japan, but the first power London turned to, in March 1898, was the U.S. Here it was confronted with a very cautious, though by no means unconcerned, McKinley administration. The president admitted to the British ambassador that the situation in China had "occupied his attention for some time." However, he was not ready to commit Washington to a policy in East Asia that might embroil it with another power. For a number of years the U.S. had been taking a more forceful tone with the Qing over the protection of Americans in the empire. Great power "entanglements" that might lead to conflict with another strong state in East Asia were considered a different story. Brewing trouble with Spain aside (and that by itself precluded action), neither the political nor the military preconditions were seen as existing as yet for that.

The McKinley administration took refuge instead in the hope that there was no "present reason" for Washington to depart from its traditional policy "respecting foreign alliances," because thus far no nation had in fact claimed "exclusive commercial privileges" in China. Immediately after conveying that negative reply to Great Britain, the State Department anxiously requested—and received—reassurances from St. Petersburg on this score.[10]

American policy makers were, however, interested in strengthening their position in the Far East so long as that could be done without incurring immediate risks. Indeed, on February 1, 1898, Secretary of the Navy John D. Long had already indicated to Commodore Dewey that the U.S. Navy might itself desire "the same concessions in some Chinese port, for the benefit of our ships, and the extension of our commerce, as are enjoyed by some other nations." Dewey, who had recently taken command of the Asiatic Squadron, was instructed to report on the best site remaining on the China coast.[11] The onset of the war with Spain interrupted this search. The subsequent U.S. decision to retain a major presence in the Philippines can, however, hardly be understood except against the background of this interest in a base in East Asia.

For the better part of two years, planning for a war with Spain had envisioned a naval attack—at the very outset of hostilities—on that nation's Pacific squadron, stationed in the Philippines. The objective was to neutralize those vessels and to make sure that they did not link up with the rest of Spain's forces. Early plans had also held that the U.S. could enhance its negotiating leverage with Madrid by obtaining a "controlling voice" in Manila Bay.[12]

But it took no time at all for the news of Dewey's victory on May 1, 1898 to suggest still broader possibilities. On May 9, only two days after firm word of the destruction of the Spanish fleet had reached Washington, Assistant Secretary of State John Bassett Moore completed a memorandum—prompted by British enquiries as to whether the evacuation of Cuba would still suffice—that asserted that a coaling station, either in the Philippine or Caroline Islands, should now be included among the conditions for ending the war.[13] Three and a half weeks later, the U.S. ambassador, John Hay, was told that the president would want two sites. The Philippines would "be allowed to remain with Spain," but minus "a port and necessary appurtenances, to be selected by the United States," while "an island . . . with harbor for a coaling station" would also be retained further to the east in the Marianas.[14] Policy makers were coming to envision a base system— or at least the sites for one—that would facilitate the projection of American power into East Asia.[15]

Concern for the strategic security of an American position in the Philippines soon led policy makers to consider an even more extensive role in those islands. As in Cuba, Spain had long confronted opposition to its rule. Madrid had suppressed an insurrection in 1896–97. But in the wake of the Battle of Manila Bay, armed struggle resumed. By mid-June, virtually all of Luzon outside of Manila was in insurgent hands. It was no longer clear to Washington what Philippine territory, if any, would "remain with Spain." And officials began to worry that if Madrid's authority was broken in the islands another great power, like Germany, might also be afforded the opportunity to establish a base there. By mid-July, McKinley had decided that the surrender of at least all Luzon by Spain would be necessary to protect the American hold on Manila.[16]

But would this be sufficient? And how would American interests in this territory be ensured? McKinley answered the second of these questions first. Initially he thought that a protectorate might suffice. On June 27, Dewey had cabled that he thought the Filipinos were "more capable" of "self-government" than the "natives of Cuba."[17] Building on this, the president voiced hope that "the insurgents will develop enough strength to solve the problem by setting up a government of their own under our protection—we to keep Manila."[18] On August 1, however, McKinley read an article entitled "Spain and the Philippine Islands" written by John Foreman, an Englishman, in the British periodical *Contemporary Review*. A Western "expert" on the islands, Foreman contradicted Dewey, arguing that the character of the Filipinos was such that they would only fall into conflict among themselves in the absence of an outside disciplining force. That in turn would open the way for constant complications between them and all outside powers with interests in the Philippines. For McKinley, such a prospect dictated that the U.S. start out with nothing less than direct and complete control over whatever territory was detached from Spain.[19]

The president was, however, still unprepared to stipulate how much that would be when the protocol ending hostilities was signed on August 12. McKinley did not want to place a limit on what the U.S. might take before he had heard from military figures, and others whose opinions he valued, who had been out to the islands. In mid-September, when he met with them before their departure for Paris, the president told his peace commissioners that the U.S. could not settle for less than the cession of Luzon. He also commented that, "for the safety of Luzon," it might ultimately be found necessary to demand other islands.[20]

The Naval War Board had already endorsed the idea that the Philippines should become the site for Washington's principal Far Eastern base, while the Office of Naval Intelligence had opined that all of the islands should "be the property of a single power." They were strategically "so intimately related that it is practically impossible to disassociate them in any scheme of offense or defense."[21] When, over the next several weeks, McKinley was presented with the same arguments from officers who had been out to the Philippines, he made up his mind. The commissioners were instructed to ask for all of the islands.[22]

With the annexation of the Philippines and Guam—as well as the formal acquisition of Hawaii, which had also been facilitated by the conflict with Madrid—the McKinley administration obtained valuable "stepping stones" across the Pacific in 1898.[23] It remained cautious, however, about taking new steps on the mainland of East Asia, and, indeed, saw itself as having its hands full dealing with the results of the just completed war.

Since the northern ports crisis at the beginning of the year, numerous observers, including especially textile exporters who had come together to form the American Asiatic Association, had been calling for the government boldly to assert its determination to defend American treaty rights in China. Some, like John R. Proctor of the U.S. Civil Service Commission, had gone so far as to call for Washington to join Great Britain in proclaiming "a new Monroe Doctrine applicable" to the Qing empire.[24]

In his annual message in December, McKinley assured such constituents that the government had been, and would continue to be, vigilant in looking out for the nation's interests in East Asia. But he insisted that commitments he had received from all of the powers with new leaseholds on the China coast for the time being "obviated the need of our country becoming an actor in the scene."[25]

As 1899 progressed, however, the McKinley administration grew more and more apprehensive about Russian policy and where it was leading. That, plus the nervousness of interested businessmen, led the secretary to approach St. Petersburg again for assurances in the spring.[26] It also made Hay receptive when, in the late summer of 1899, he was presented with a low-risk plan that he thought might boost American interests in East Asia onto firmer ground.

First-hand accounts of developments in East Asia clearly had an important impact on Hay in the months leading up to the despatch of his famous open door notes. Early in 1899 he met with Admiral Lord Charles Beresford who had just returned from an extensive tour of East Asia for the Associated Chambers of Commerce of England. He was prophesying "the break-up of China" under the pressure of Russian expansion.[27] Much the same specter was then raised by Jacob Gould Schurman, the president of Cornell University, who had been dispatched across the Pacific in January as the head of McKinley's first Philippine Commission. On his return to the U.S. in August, Schurman argued that the "great question" of the moment in "the Orient" was really China. "It is feared, now that Russia has taken Manchuria," he remarked, "it will try to encroach gradually on some or all of the other eighteen provinces ... and when it gets them it will ... put a duty on all foreign goods."[28]

Finally, and most importantly, there was Alfred E. Hippisley, who qualified as an exceptional authority on China by virtue of his service under Sir Robert Hart in the Imperial Maritime Customs Service.[29] Hippisley not only added to Hay's concern about Russia, he also proffered the key idea on which the first open door notes were based.

Hippisley came to the U.S. in the summer of 1899 to visit his wife's family in Baltimore before returning home for an extended leave to his native England. While in America he hoped that he might also help push the McKinley administration to take further steps on behalf of the open door for trade in China. Through an old friend, William W. Rockhill, an Orientalist currently serving as the director of the Bureau of American Republics, Hippisley was able to secure a personal meeting with Hay.[30] The

Englishman then began a regular correspondence with Rockhill, hoping that his suggestions might continue to be put before the secretary.

The actions of Germany and Russia with regard to Shandong and Manchuria in 1898 had ultimately led other powers already involved in China to take steps aimed at defining and defending specific regions of interest to them. These had included efforts to control railway building in particular areas. They had also involved demands that Beijing agree never to alienate certain territories. Even England had gotten into the act. Although it had opposed a policy of spheres in China, it had eventually felt compelled itself to pursue one in order to protect its position in the rich Yangtze region.[31]

Hay had thus far focused principally on the new coastal leaseholds. But Hippisley saw that these extensive, if thus far very imperfect, "spheres of interest" were of no less importance, especially since their proliferation seemed likely to encourage Russia to pursue further a policy of exclusivity in the north. Some agreement with regard to trade, he feared, had soon to be accomplished. Thus far, Hippisley wrote Rockhill, the "special rights and privileges" that several powers had tried to stake out in different parts of China had not been "extended to a claim to impose a differential tariff on merchandise consumed in or passing through" those areas. However, Russia might eventually take that step. The U.S. should therefore lose no time "in calling the attention of all of the Powers to the changes now taking place in China, and—while disclaiming any desire on her own part to annex territory—in expressing her determination not to sacrifice for her annually increasing trade any of the rights or privileges she has secured by treaty with China." It "should obtain an undertaking from each European Power that the Chinese treaty tariff shall without discrimination apply to all merchandise entering its spheres of influence; and that any treaty ports in them shall not be interfered with." Such a move, Hippisley argued, could simply be presented as a "logical completion" to previous enquiries that Washington had made about the intentions of the lease-holding powers. At the moment, he did not believe that "any Power would hesitate to agree." He warned, however, that "events move rapidly in China, and what is possible now might easily not be possible later on."[32]

Rockhill relayed these views to Hay, meanwhile replying that he agreed completely. Quite unrealistically, Rockhill even stated that he wanted to see the U.S. pledge itself publicly "to assist in maintaining the integrity of the Empire." But he doubted that, for the foreseeable future, the administration would take any new initiatives at all: "home politics and next year's elections" would, he thought, prevent this.[33] The secretary's initial response seemed to bear out the latter's fears.[34] But, less than two weeks later, on August 18, Rockhill reported that he was receiving indications Hay might in fact act along the lines that Hippisley had suggested.[35]

Thus encouraged, the Englishman sent on a memorandum summarizing his ideas. He had drawn this up after learning that the tsar had declared Dalien, the commercial port adjacent to Port Arthur, "an open port *for the whole period of the treaty*" with China, "i.e. for the next 23 years." "This is most satisfactory," he wrote Rockhill. "It gives a natural opportunity for opening negotiations to settle the conditions that are to hold in China for, at least, the immediate future, and it seems to promise co-operation on Russia's part in the direction we hope for."[36]

The decree clearly also struck Hay as affording a valuable opportunity for putting the open door in the region on a stronger footing. He told Rockhill that, although he had already received assurances, a "more formal engagement ... would be desirable."[37] Rockhill was asked to draw up draft instructions along the lines of the ideas that he had submitted, and the resultant "open door notes" were then sent out to the other powers.[38] Each was asked to give "formal assurances" and to "lend its cooperation in securing like assurances from the other interested powers," that they would not establish discriminatory barriers against the trade of other nations in the "spheres of interest" or leaseholds that they had claimed in China. The powers were also asked to affirm that the duties that were leviable on goods coming into these areas would continue to be collected by the Chinese government (the Customs Service).[39]

American officials were quite optimistic about the results they would get, for they found it hard to believe that Russia could reject a formula that seemed so in line with what the tsar himself had just declared. In a non-confrontational way, moreover, the U.S. had, by asking for a pledge before the world on the part of all of the powers, threatened St. Petersburg with potential isolation.

And, indeed, precisely because it feared, in Foreign Minister Count Muraviev's words, "the formation of a dangerous coalition of power against our interests in the Far East," Russia, like the other powers, announced itself as in agreement. It did so, however, only after much delay and with clear reluctance, in a reply hedged about with considerable qualification. This was not entirely what Hay had hoped for. Nevertheless, he decided that the appropriate strategy was to insist that it was.[40]

U.S. policy makers were pleased with the outcome of their initiative. But they continued to be uneasy about the division of China into spheres because of the commercial advantages that were likely to accompany them, because of the threat that such a trend might still pose to the open door, and because they wanted more opportunity for the expansion of American influence in China.

It was out of such concerns that Rockhill, in mid-August, had broached the idea of getting outside nations to commit themselves as well to maintenance of the integrity of the Qing empire.[41] There was little if any chance of that, Hippisley had replied, without steps first being taken to ensure the protection of foreigners and to reorganize the empire's systems of taxation and finance.[42]

Rockhill backed away from this "side of the China question," seeing it as too "big" for the moment. "All we can do," he wrote in mid-September, "is to instruct our Legation out there to adopt a general line of policy which may be favorable to the maintenance and the strengthening of the Peking Government."[43]

Nevertheless, in its note to Great Britain, the U.S. took the position that it would "in no way commit itself to a recognition of exclusive rights of any power within or control over any portion of the Chinese Empire under such agreements as have within the last year been made." It also voiced the hope that the open door notes might prepare the way for united great power action "in favor of the administrative reforms so urgently needed for strengthening the Imperial Government and maintaining the integrity of China," a goal justified on commercial grounds and as a way of ensuring peace and stability in East Asia.[44] Acting on its own, in March 1900 (two days after the replies of the powers were publicly described as "final and definitive" by Hay), Washington instructed its representative to Beijing to impress on the Chinese government the importance of upholding its international obligations.[45]

Events, however, were moving the other way. By early 1900, the agitations of the Boxers United in Righteousness, a loosely structured antiforeign movement, were already gaining ground among many poor in northern China. The official classes had been deeply affected by the empire's humiliation in the Sino-Japanese War and by the foreign inroads that had followed. Briefly, during 1898, a new and more thoroughgoing effort at "self-strengthening" had been launched. But reactionaries had rebelled against changes in the bureaucracy and educational system that might undermine their privileges. They mobilized behind Empress Dowager Cixi to push aside the young reformist emperor, Guangxu. Then, as popular sentiment against outside missionaries, businessmen, and diplomats and their privileges mushroomed into a mass movement over the following months, Cixi and other opponents of change were increasingly tempted by the thought that it by itself might deliver the empire from its problems. Attacks on missionaries and their converts and on foreign businessmen and railways mounted. Finally, by late June 1900, China was, at least technically, at war with all the powers, and the Boxers, along with some imperial forces, were laying siege to the diplomatic quarter in Beijing.[46]

Some 2500 American troops were dispatched from the Philippines to join an international great-power expedition to relieve the legations and subdue the Boxers. The overriding concern for Hay and Rockhill, however, was the prospect that this "misbehavior" might become the occasion for even greater Russian inroads in China. Indeed, they worried that a tightening of Russia's grip in the north might precipitate a process of general partition.[47]

There were great divisions within Chinese officialdom during the summer of 1900. Even in Beijing, the supreme commander of the government's forces forbade them to use fire power sufficient to take the foreign compound. At the provincial level, especially toward the south, many viceroys were convinced that the empress dowager was courting disaster. Such concerns prompted these officials to try to bargain independently with the powers. They maintained that what was really in progress in Beijing was a rebellion against the authority of the government and that the powers should therefore not consider themselves to be at war with China. In addition, they pledged to keep order in their provinces and to keep the military units in their regions out of the fray, so long as the powers refrained from intervening outside the vicinity of the capitol.[48]

Anxious to support such efforts to contain the scope of the intervention, Hay issued, in the form simply of a declaration of U.S. policy, a second open door note on July 3.[49] His circular announced that Washington regarded

the condition at Pekin as one of virtual anarchy, whereby power and responsibility are practically devolved upon the local provincial authorities. So long as they are not in overt collusion with rebellion and use their power to protect foreign life and property we regard them as representing the Chinese people, with whom we seek to remain in peace and friendship.

The U.S. purpose in intervening, it continued, was to rescue the besieged, protect American life, property, and interests, and prevent "a recurrence of such disasters." Moreover, in accomplishing that last result, Washington would seek "a solution which may preserve Chinese territorial and administrative entity, protect all rights guaranteed to friendly powers by treaty and international law, and safeguard for the world the principle of equal and impartial trade with all parts of the Chinese Empire."

In the end, all the powers refrained from declaring war against China. Hay's worries, however, persisted into the period following the bloody relief of the legations in mid-August. Once the rescue mission was over, McKinley, who was nervous about the upcoming presidential election, wanted to remove U.S. troops. But Hay persuaded him that they should be retained as the only way to keep pressure on the Chinese. More importantly, the presence of U.S. forces alongside units of other powers was critical if Washington was to make its voice heard in the post-Boxer settlement.[50]

Hay was convinced that the best way to prevent the detachment of any part of the empire was for the principle of collective action on the part of all of the powers to be maintained. But he worried that this might break down if the negotiations did not get started quickly. For this reason Hay became frustrated at Germany's behavior. Because Berlin's minister to Beijing had been slain during the rebellion, the kaiser had insisted that field Marshall Alfred von Waldersee be given overall command of the allied expedition. However, Waldersee and his forces did not get to China until after the capital had been occupied. Determined to see action, the German general then insisted on the right to conduct extensive punitive expeditions throughout the surrounding (Zhili) province, wherever the Boxers had been prominent. The U.S., as well as Russia, England, and Japan increasingly voiced opposition to such operations on the grounds that they were impeding a return to normalcy. But they did not come to an end until the fall.[51]

On September 18, Berlin also tried to make the surrender and punishment by the powers of pro-Boxer high officials a precondition for negotiations. As Hay saw it, this not only threatened further delay but contradicted U.S. efforts to uphold anti-Boxer officials and to promote a more "responsible" government in China. He wanted to see China given the task of carrying out these punishments.[52]

The post-Boxer scene presented both dangers and opportunities from Hay's perspective. He was above all anxious to obtain a settlement that would not see the empire's territorial integrity or its ability to keep order further undermined. But he also hoped the U.S. and other powers might now have an chance to initiate the kinds of changes in China for which he and Rockhill had been pushing.[53]

In October, the intervening powers finally began to formulate their demands. The starting point was a six-point French draft. Under it, China was to agree to the punishment of high officials who had supported the Boxers, the importation of advanced arms was to be forbidden, indemnities were to be paid, an enlarged foreign guard was to be stationed around the legations in Beijing, the coastal fortresses at Dagu (below Tianjin) were to be dismantled, and foreign forces were to be allowed to be posted at several points along the road leading from Tianjin to Beijing.[54]

Additional provisions were added over the next two months. At the suggestion of Britain the official exams were to be suspended for five years in cities where there had been Boxer disturbances, arrangements were to be made for the powers to negotiate another round of commercial treaties with the empire, and China was also to establish a new foreign office that was to have precedence over all the empire's external relations. Under a proposal pushed by the U.S., Beijing was to inform all local officials that they would henceforth be held strictly and personally accountable for order and for the treatment of foreigners in their districts.[55]

In December the completed note was finally presented to Li Hongzhang, the Chinese negotiator, who had little choice but to accept it as a basis for a settlement of the crisis. Many details yet remained to be worked out, however, particularly the level of indemnity that the empire would be asked to pay. The McKinley administration was concerned that Beijing have sufficient resources to keep internal order and pay its debts. Along with the British and the Japanese, it sought to have the overall bill for claims and damages held down. However, as part of his stratagem for accomplishing this, Hay presented an American estimate that he knew to be at least double what could really be justified. It was his hope that by pushing up the total he could secure an agreement on the part of all of the powers to a downward revision of claims. When this ploy failed, however, the secretary refused to reduce the U.S. share unilaterally.[56]

The Boxer negotiations were finally brought to a conclusion on September 7, 1901, when China and the powers signed a twelve-point protocol.[57] A month later, while trying to convey to his German friend von Sternberg American policy toward Latin America, the new president, Roosevelt, commented on what he hoped would be the policy adopted by the powers toward China. "I regard the Monroe Doctrine as being equivalent to the open door in South America," TR wrote. "That is, I do not want the United States or any European power to get territorial possessions in South America." He wished "that the same policy could be pursued in China. That is, if the Chinese could be forced to behave themselves—not permitted to do anything atrocious, but not partitioned, and with the ports kept open to all comers, as well as having the vexatious trade restrictions which prevent inter-Chinese trade in the interior, abolished."[58] It remained an open question whether this vision of a Chinese state that was both strong and cooperative had been advanced in the period since the rebellion, however. Indeed, Rockhill, who had served as the U.S. representative to the talks, was distinctly pessimistic. He could not fathom why the Chinese hesitated to accept American direction. To him the only answer was that the governing class was selfish and lacking in vitality.[59]

Russia meanwhile had been trying to strengthen its position in Manchuria. In August 1900, it had sent thousands of troops into the area, promising that its occupation would be only temporary. However, five months later news leaked of Russian plans to leave behind a far more thoroughgoing control over the region than had existed before the crisis. In both St. Petersburg and Beijing, Japan made representations against such a move. Hay felt compelled to tell Tokyo that the U.S. was "not at present prepared to attempt singly, or in concert with other Powers, to enforce ... [its] views in the east by any demonstration which could present a character of hostility to any other Power." Along with Britain, Germany, Austria-Hungary, and Italy, the U.S. did follow Japan in issuing warnings to Chinese authorities not to conclude any such arrangement "at least without the full knowledge and approval of all the powers now engaged in negotiations [in Beijing]."[60]

On February 16 such an agreement was in fact presented to China. Foreign Minister V. N. Lamsdorf proposed a treaty whereby St. Petersburg would end the occupation on the condition that Beijing grant it sweeping and exclusive economic (especially investment) privileges as well as informal military and political control. Hoping that the other

powers might oppose Russia, and also under great pressure from provincial officials, Beijing announced that it would refuse to sign. Tokyo dispatched a strongly worded note to St. Petersburg asserting that the accord
clashed both with China's sovereignty and with other power's rights in
Manchuria, and Russia decided to suspend temporarily its efforts to reach
a settlement.[61]

Renewed concern about Russian treatment of the trade and nationals of
other powers led the U.S., as well as Britain, to station a gunboat in Nuiz-
huang, the only existing Manchurian treaty port, for the winter of 1901–2.[62]
Then, in December, the U.S. minister to China, Edwin Conger, informed
the State Department that he believed St. Petersburg and Beijing were
again discussing an agreement that would be prejudicial to American interests. The political aspects of the new Russian proposal were actually a good
deal more moderate, at least for southern Manchuria, than what it had
pressed on the Chinese the previous spring. But St. Petersburg was also
demanding that China conclude a collateral agreement with the Russo-
Chinese Bank that would provide for a Russian monopoly of important
projects and concessions throughout the entire region.[63]

Hay protested against this envisioned arrangement, arguing that such
broad investment provisions constituted a violation of U.S. treaty rights in
China. Yet, in so far as Manchuria was concerned, it seems that the secretary had by now become reconciled to the idea that, for the foreseeable
future, Russia was going to occupy an exceptional position. It was his hope
that in exchange for informal recognition of that St. Petersburg would
agree at least not to interfere with American commerce.[64]

Japan, however, was unwilling to accept increased Russian control in
Manchuria, even if accompanied by equal treatment for trade. Korea could
not then be kept free of Russian predominance either, it believed. Since
the mid-1890s, the southern half of that peninsula had become a frontier
for the expansion of Japanese economic interests. Even more important,
Korea had been assigned a key role as part of a strategic "line of advantage"
around Japan that Tokyo was determined to hold.

It was to protect this perceived stake in the fate of northeastern Asia that
Japan concluded a military alliance with Great Britain in 1902. London had
come to accept the inevitability of a special position for Russia in Manchuria
by 1899, even though it had continued to hope that St. Petersburg would
respect the commercial open door in that region. It sought the alliance
because it did not want to see Russia become a more potent maritime, as
well as land, power in East Asia. England wanted Russia kept out of Korea
and blocked from any further expansion to the south.[65]

Announced to the world in mid-February, the Anglo-Japanese agreement
stiffened China in its resistance to Russia's demands. And it stunned Lamsdorf, who unsuccessfully tried during the following month to get France to
make a bold statement of its determination to stand by St. Petersburg in

the region. The two powers had been allies since the early 1890s, but their cooperation outside of Europe was by no means automatic. In what appeared to be a complete reversal, Russia on April 8 signed an agreement with China promising to evacuate its troops from Manchuria in three six-month stages during the next year and a half.[66]

Hay expressed hope that his minimum goals for the region would now be achieved. "What we have been working for two years to accomplish, and what we have at last accomplished, if assurances are to count for anything," he told Roosevelt in May, "is that, no matter what happens eventually in northern China and Manchuria, the United States shall not be placed in any worse position than while the country was under the unquestioned domination of China."[67]

Yet St. Petersburg's policy toward the region was still by no means settled. From within the tsar's inner circle, pressure was in fact growing for a stand to be made instead of a withdrawal. As historian Dietrich Geyer has put it, "superior competition had to be kept out and territories secured ... so that the state's financial investments would at least appear to have been justified from an economic point of view." The evacuation proceeded on schedule throughout the summer and early fall of 1902, but its completion was then delayed, and in April 1903 St. Petersburg presented China with yet another set of demands.[68]

Russian policy now began to clash with the Manchurian aspects of a broad program that Hay had been urging on Beijing since the conclusion of the Boxer protocol. He had been trying both to open up more of the empire to outside traders—in part as a way of reinforcing the open door—and to bring about a more forceful and "responsible" central Chinese governmental and administrative system. Hay sought a reform of the empire's finances and currency. He wanted to see China abolish the li-kin system, whereby significant duties were charged on the internal transit of goods, and he wanted to get the powers to agree on a restructuring of China's tariff schedules, this so as to address the empire's unfavorable trade balance and develop its potential as a market.[69]

In addition, Hay hoped to see more cities, including cities in Manchuria, converted into "treaty ports." When this topic was left out of Britain's new commercial treaty with Beijing, Washington included it in its negotiations with China, simultaneously informing St. Petersburg of its interest.[70]

Russia's demands of spring 1903 took on the appearance of a direct challenge to the U.S., because its new conditions for withdrawal included provisions that would bar additional treaty ports in Manchuria. Considering this a betrayal of a tacit understanding that had been reached between the two powers, Hay demanded an explanation, insisted on the U.S. request, and reserved the right to question any other aspects of the relationship that St. Petersburg was attempting to establish. "I am sure you will think it is out of the question," he wrote TR in frustration, that we should adopt any scheme of concerted action with England and Japan which would seem openly hostile to Russia. Public opinion in this country would not support such a course, nor do I think it would be to our permanent advantage. Russia is trying to impress us by the most fervent protestations that, whatever happens in Manchuria, our national interests shall not suffer. This is an object which I have been striving for for four years, and if worse comes to the worst I think we can gain it; but there is something due to self-respect also, and it is pretty hard to stand by and see an act of spoilation accomplished under our eyes.[71]

"Russia knows as well as we do," he complained three days later, "that we will not fight over Manchuria, for the simple reason that we cannot." The secretary could at this point only take comfort from his belief that the Russians were "really afraid of Japan."[72]

With U.S. prestige as well as its interests in Manchuria and China all on the line, Hay nevertheless was determined to do what he could to thwart St. Petersburg's challenge to the Washington-Beijing negotiations. He continued to press China to include provisions for the opening of additional ports in Manchuria in the new treaty. Meanwhile, he tried to take advantage of the fact that Russia was denying the existence of the April demands. Hay sought to "clinch" Russia's assurances by communicating them to the governments of England and Japan (Germany and France had already made clear their lack of interest), to the American press, and to Beijing.

"The bad feature of the situation," TR agreed, was "that as yet it seems that we cannot fight to keep Manchuria open, I hate being in the position of seeming to bluster without backing it up."[73] It was a position TR hated, but a tactic that the administration in any event employed. Throughout the late spring, St. Petersburg continued to deny the existence of the new demands while at the same time trying to prevent China from acceding to Washington's request for additional treaty ports. On June 18, Hay conducted a blunt interview with the Russian ambassador. He told him that he could not exaggerate the "gravity" of the situation that had been created between the two powers. Russia, Hay said, had pledged itself to the open door in principle but was doing everything it could to defeat it in practice. Soon he might have no alternative but to "lay the entire correspondence" between the two governments "before the President, [and] to confess my failure in coming to an amicable and honorable agreement with Russia." Hay also implied that the U.S. might explore a closer working relationship in East Asia with Britain and Japan.[74]

"All we ask is that our great and growing trade shall not be interrupted," the president told close friends in the press.[75] At the same time he took precautions to make sure that the navy was prepared for any contingencies that might arise in the region.[76] Finally, to demonstrate how endangered historically good American-Russian relations were, on July 1 Roosevelt publicly criticized recent actions by St. Petersburg toward Russian Jews.[77] Largely because of its fear of the U.S. actually joining the Anglo-Japanese alliance, these actions did lead to a tactical retreat on Russia's part. U.S. wishes were not granted in full. But in July St. Petersburg did agree to open additional cities in Manchuria to foreign trade.[78]

Russia's actual intentions remained unclear, and TR was still fuming. "I have not the slightest objection to the Russians knowing," he told Hay, "that I feel thoroughly aroused and irritated at their conduct in Manchuria; that I don't intend to give way and that I am year by year growing more confident that this country would back me in going to an extreme in the matter."[79] The secretary, however, was anxious simply to make what he could of the new situation. The way now seemed clear to get China to agree to open up the new Manchurian treaty ports and thus for there to be created a new legal situation that Russia would have to deal with.

During midsummer, great pressure was put on China to include the two new ports in the American commercial treaty. "We have done the Chinks a great service," Hay told Rockhill during the negotiations, "which they don't seem to recognize. It will never do to let them imagine they can treat us as they please, and that the only power they need fear is Russia."[80] At the end of August, Beijing relented. It agreed in writing that the cities would be included and that the new treaty would be signed on October 8, the original date for the conclusion of Russia's withdrawal. Hay conceded only that China could delay the actual opening of the cities until a time several months after the convention's ratification.[81]

When it was signed on schedule two months later, the treaty provided for both Antung (Dandong) and Mukden (Shenyang), in southern Manchuria, to become open cities. Beijing hoped that the U.S. might now be inclined in return to mediate an end to the occupation of Manchuria. Such, however, was not Washington's intention. Instead the administration restricted itself to monitoring Russia's treatment of American trade. During the winter of 1903–4 that seemed likely again to become an issue for discussion between the two powers. But it was rapidly overshadowed by the outbreak of the Russo-Japanese War.[82]

The concessions made by Russia to the U.S. in Manchuria in mid-1903 had never represented the basis for an acceptable settlement for Japan. For Tokyo, Russia's very presence in the region posed the crucial issue. Its leaders had been prepared to settle for St. Petersburg's dominance in China's northernmost provinces only in return for sweeping guarantees on Korea. Such were not forthcoming. As a result, Japan resolved to drive Russia away from Korea and southern Manchuria before St. Petersburg was able to complete the development of its East Asian railway and military systems. To maximize its prospect of victory, Tokyo began the conflict in February 1904 with a devastating surprise attack on the Russian fleet anchored at Port Arthur.[83]

No other leaders greeted this more enthusiastically than did those of the U.S. The Roosevelt administration was determined to observe a correct neutrality. Along with Britain and Germany it was also anxious to try to keep the war from engulfing other areas of China. But U.S. authorities were thrilled by the prospect that Tokyo might put Russia in its place. The administration had chafed at the limits on its abilities in the region, and Hay had been embarrassed to have to tell those "little people" (the Japanese) that the U.S. could not itself "take part in any use of force" in Manchuria. Now, according to TR, Japan seemed to be "playing our game."[84]

Confronted with a string of surprisingly easy Japanese victories in the early months of 1904, however, it was not long before Roosevelt began to wonder whether Japan might ultimately become a more formidable threat to American interests than Russia had been. He wrote his English friend Sir Cecil Spring Rice that

if the Japanese win out, not only the Slav, but all of us will have to reckon with a great new force in eastern Asia. The victory will make Japan by itself a formidable power in the Orient, because all the other powers having interests there will have divided interests.... If, moreover, Japan seriously starts in to reorganize China and makes any headway, there will result a real shifting of the center of equilibrium as far as the white races are concerned.[85]

Roosevelt did not change his sympathies. As he saw it, it was a question of balancing "the certainty of immediate damage" from Russia against "the possibility of future damage" from Japan.[86] Nevertheless, he began to hope that the war might be concluded without Russia's total elimination as a major power in the region.

Roosevelt wanted to see Japan established on the mainland.[87] However, he did not want to see the predominance of Japan substituted for that of Russia. The best solution, he came to think, was for Russia and Japan to exhaust themselves and then remain facing and worrying each other in northeast Asia. That would avoid "the creation of either a yellow peril or a Slav peril."[88]

His principal means of influencing the conflict's outcome was through the counsel that he gave to Japan.[89] TR wanted Washington's role to be that of a wise elder tutor to Tokyo. At the same time, he worried about the possibility that the "oriental," and therefore presumably mercurial, Japanese would spurn U.S. advice and—instead of becoming willing pupils—prove "insolent."

In a June 1904 meeting with Takahira Kogoro, the minister to the U.S., and Baron Kaneko Kentaro, a special emissary, Roosevelt promised that Washington would work to make sure Tokyo was not robbed of the fruits of its victories on the mainland as in 1895. But he also expressed his hope that Japanese troops would not try to advance beyond Mukden in southern Manchuria. After the war, he asserted, Japan should be granted a wide latitude in Korea and a "paramount interest in what surrounds the Yellow

Sea," but TR was anxious to see most of Manchuria returned to China. Perhaps, he suggested, a Chinese viceroy could be found who would be able to keep order there under the guarantee of the powers. The president admonished his guests at some length on the dangers that could come should Japan get a "big head."[90]

By the following winter, TR had grown even more concerned. On December 26 he wrote George Meyer, his new ambassador to St. Petersburg, that up until the present "Japan's diplomatic statements have been made good." "Yet Japan," he continued, "is an oriental nation, and the individual standard of truthfulness in Japan is low. No one can foretell her future attitude."[91] After the fall of Russia's base at Port Arthur Roosevelt was anxious to see the war ended. However, with the tsar and his advisers still convinced that they could turn the situation around, and Tokyo determined not to tip St. Petersburg off to its growing financial and military exhaustion by asking for talks itself, it was late spring 1905 before peace parlays could be arranged. By this time, Russia had lost a terrible land battle for Mukden and its Baltic fleet had been destroyed by the Japanese in the Straits of Tsu Shima. Social unrest and bankruptcy stalked the tsarist regime. TR fretted that St. Petersburg might be "driven out of East Asia." "Russia's triumph would have been a blow to civilization," he told Lodge in June, "but her destruction as an eastern Asiatic power would also be unfortunate. It is best that she should be left face to face with Japan so that each may have a moderative action on the other."[92]

TR played a pivotal role in bringing the two powers together for negotiations, in Portsmouth, New Hampshire, and—at least partly because of him—the treaty finally concluded there in September largely conformed to his desires. Russia recognized Tokyo's paramountcy in Korea and transferred its leasehold and railway rights in southern Manchuria to Japan. At the same time, the rest of Manchuria was restored to Chinese control, Russia remained a power in northeast Asia, and Japan failed to obtain a large indemnity.[93]

Other reassuring developments had meanwhile also taken place. Anxious to nail down U.S. acceptance of a free hand for Japan in postwar Korea, Prime Minister Katsura Taro had promised Secretary of War Taft in July that Tokyo had no interest in the Philippines and wished to continue to work in harmony with Britain and the U.S. in the region. Japan and Great Britain had then agreed, in August, to an extension of their alliance. U.S. officials accepted all of this as evidence that Tokyo would continue to be a good player—according to the rules Washington wanted—in East Asia.[94]

Juxtaposed against these hopes for the future of great power relations in East Asia, however, were developments in China in 1905 that Washington found alarming. Of most importance, the U.S. had since July been confronted with the organization of a popular boycott targeted specifically at the sale of its products in the empire. Initiated to protest American travel and immigration policies, the boycott was one of the first important manifestations of a new national spirit that had begun to take root in China since the end of the 1890s. Such an assertive and independent posture, however, did not fit the mold of the "regeneration," or "awakening," that the U.S. had been hoping for. Rather, as Washington saw it, the Chinese were demonstrating, again, their propensity to "misbehave." This threatened American trade, but also Washington's prestige in China and its standing among the other great powers.

The dispute had its origins in more than two decades of official American discrimination against immigrants and visitors from China.[95] During the late nineteenth century Chinese immigrants had become the target of intense European-American hostility on the west coast of the U.S. As those states gained population and political importance, the cause of prohibiting new immigration came to be championed by both of the nation's major political parties. Exclusion became federal policy in the 1880s, after which the Bureau of Immigration was given increasingly wide latitude to ensure that no Chinese took up residence in the U.S. under the guise of being visiting businessmen or students. By the turn of the century it had become a bastion of sinophobia. The policy of exclusion was extended to cover the Philippines and Hawaii (Cuba was also forced to incorporate exclusionist provisions into its constitution), and Chinese who came to American territory were regularly subjected to humiliating and intrusive physical examinations, interrogations, confinements, and delays.

Roosevelt had long supported exclusion. But in 1904 he suddenly began to worry that an overly zealous effort to enforce the policy might have a negative effect on U.S. objectives in China. What jolted him was Beijing's announcement that it did not want to extend the 1894 immigration treaty between the two countries.[96]

TR wanted the Bureau of Immigration to treat upper-class Chinese students and businessmen with greater consideration. That, he hoped, would stave off demands for treaty renegotiation, as well as prevent the development of attitudes that might undermine U.S. trade.[97] This initiative accomplished little, however, and Beijing persisted in seeking renegotiation. Washington was forwarded a draft treaty that provided firmer guarantees for travelers and for Chinese already in America. These suggestions were acceptable to Roosevelt and Hay. But, they were unwilling to go further unless they could line up support for such revisions from the politically influential exclusionists in the Bureau. To cross them, TR feared, would be to risk disaster for the Republican party.[98]

Throughout late 1904 and early 1905, Washington continued to hope that Beijing would simply give up and conclude that it had to settle for an extension of the old treaty. Policy makers failed to appreciate the degree to which immigration reform was becoming a popular cause in China. By spring, they were suddenly confronted with the prospect of a large-scale boycott of U.S. trade.[99]

Roosevelt lashed out at the bureau. It was "most wise and proper," he asserted, that Chinese immigrants generally be kept out of the U.S. But there was no reason for "insolence against Chinese gentlemen." By executive order, the president issued in June some modifications in the procedures that immigration officials were to use.[100] Consistent with its long-term policy in China, Washington meanwhile sought to get Beijing to clamp down on what the administration defined as unacceptable popular behavior. Rockhill, who was now the U.S. minister, was instructed to demand that Beijing suppress the activities of the boycott organizers.

The Chinese government was, however, both emboldened and intimidated by the agitation.[101] No significant steps were taken to stop the movement. Instead, in mid-summer, boycott activities began in a number of the major treaty ports from Canton (Guangzhou) north to Shanghai.[102] The boycott, Rockhill asserted, was "an unwarranted attempt of the ignorant people to assume the functions of government and to meddle with international relations."[103] Again he looked for redress from an authoritarian central government.

"Unless I misread them entirely," TR wrote Rockhill in late August, "they [the Chinese] despise weakness even more than they prize justice."[104] Rockhill now threatened to hold Beijing directly responsible for any losses suffered by American merchants as a result of the boycott. He also announced that there could be no further negotiations for a new treaty until the movement was ended. Rockhill applauded the northern viceroy Yuan Shikai for the way he suppressed the boycott in Tianjin by clamping down on freedom of assembly and freedom of the press, and he suggested that this approach be applied elsewhere in the empire.[105] Although he was anxious not to be perceived as acting under pressure, Roosevelt meanwhile began to explore the possibility of new legislation that might both reassure extreme exclusionists and secure better treatment for Chinese business travelers and students.[106]

Taken together, these steps gradually had some effect. Beijing began to apply pressure on the boycott organizers. Many Chinese merchants, hurt by their loss of business, now took the position that the campaign should be suspended until it became clear where Roosevelt's promises might lead. In most of the treaty ports, the boycott was over by October.

But it remained strong in Canton. And here the movement was also much more radical than it had been elsewhere. Its leaders insisted that Chinese people should be treated no differently than the immigrants of any other country who came to the U.S.[107] Pleased by the decline of the movement elsewhere, TR was furious that it continued to exist at all. He was also incensed at the rhetoric of the organizers. During the fall, he grew increasingly anxious to put the movement in (what he saw as) its place.[108]

In mid-November, Roosevelt inaugurated plans for a major concentration of U.S. naval forces off the China coast.[109] The idea at first was simply to employ on a much larger scale the kind of gunboat diplomacy that the navy had long practiced both in the Caribbean and along the rivers and coastways of China. A mere demonstration of power might, it was hoped, suffice both to ensure the protection of Americans and their interests and to bring an end to the boycott. But the president was less and less willing to take any chances with what he saw as a potentially vital threat to American prestige. Several weeks later, he instructed the War Department to plan for a military expedition to the Chinese coast. At least ten to fifteen thousand troops were to be assembled in the Philippines so that they could be ready to seize Canton.[110]

Not unintended was the possibility that such a military build-up would have an impact on the Chinese government. At the end of February, the U.S. again demanded that Beijing put an end to the boycott and take steps to ensure the safety of all Americans doing business in the empire. By this time, though, the government had already begun to do just that, and as news of this filtered back to Washington the prospect of a landing disappeared.[111]

Later the same year another immigration dispute broke out with Japan. This shattered the optimism with which the U.S. had looked at relations with Japan since late 1905. Now policy makers felt compelled to contemplate the possibility that the two powers might eventually go to war. And that, in turn, aroused more concern about what were seen to be the weaknesses of the U.S. military position in the Pacific. The controversy also led TR to conclude that Washington should modify its policy toward the northernmost regions of the Qing empire.

Japanese and Korean immigration to the U.S. was growing during the early years of the twentieth century. As a consequence, these people increasingly became the target of West Coast anti-Asian hostility. Faced with the possibility of a relaxation in federal policy toward Chinese travelers, the California legislature passed a resolution calling on Congress to extend exclusion to the new groups in March 1905. A Japanese and Korean Exclusion League was then launched in San Francisco two months later.[112]

Roosevelt was furious, especially since Japan had just registered some of its greatest successes in its war with Russia. "These Pacific Coast people," he told Lodge, "wish grossly to insult the Japanese and to keep out the Japanese immigrants ... and at the same time that they desire to do this ... they expect to be given advantages in Oriental markets; and with besotted folly are indifferent to building up the navy."[113]

But more such provocation was to come. By late 1906, the new campaign in California was gathering greater political strength. Playing to that, the San Francisco school board passed a ruling segregating all Japanese as well as Korean and Chinese pupils into a separate "oriental" public school.

This caused bruised feelings in Japan and led Tokyo immediately to protest. Washington, in response, lectured state and local authorities on the impact such discrimination might have on U.S. foreign relations. And when that proved unavailing it threatened to take legal action.[114]

Doubt soon arose, however, that the Japanese-American treaty of commerce of 1894 provided adequate grounds for a suit. The administration also grew more impressed with the depth of hostility toward the new immigrants. For reasons of both politics and policy, it decided that efforts to protect those Japanese already in America, as well as to block formal exclusion legislation, should be accompanied by a drive radically to reduce the number of future arrivals.[115]

Anxious to "smooth over" Japanese feelings, the president praised Japan and roundly condemned discrimination against Japanese immigrants.[116] But the administration now also worked to get Tokyo to restrict the number of Japanese coming to the U.S. in exchange for repeal of the offending San Francisco regulations. California authorities accepted this solution. Eager for both trade and policy reasons not to incite American animosity, Japan finally went along as well. It resisted having such a policy set down in the form of a treaty. But, in a "Gentlemen's Agreement" concluded early in 1907 Tokyo agreed to reduce voluntarily the number of Japanese henceforth allowed to go to the U.S.[117]

Roosevelt hoped that immigration would now be eliminated both as a point of friction between the two countries and as a political issue on the West coast. But it again required attention after Japanese-owned shops became the target of mob violence in San Francisco in May. Washington apologized to Japan and leaned heavily on San Francisco authorities to ensure adequate police protection to the city's Japanese population. Simultaneously, it pressed Tokyo to restrict immigration far more stringently.[118]

Many newspapers in Japan vented anti-American feelings in the weeks after the riots. And this heightened TR's fear that the two powers might someday clash. He had already identified Tokyo as a power that was "jealous, sensitive, and warlike." The possibility of a "mob outbreak" in Japan, TR now worried, increased the chances that that country would go to war over future incidents. Japan's rational interests did not lay in that direction. Its finances were not good. Such a war would destroy its alliance with Britain and leave Tokyo vulnerable in northeast Asia. But, as TR saw it, these considerations did not guarantee that a conflict would not occur.[119]

This concern, in turn, led Roosevelt to pay increased attention to questions of preparedness and deterrence. "We have a formidable navy, as compared with Japan, not only in material [a 3-to-1 edge in battleships at the time] but in personnel," he wrote in December 1906, "but in the event of war we should be operating far from our base."[120] If a war broke out, TR was fearful that Japan would be able quickly to seize the Philippines and perhaps Hawaii.

Profound changes had taken place in the military situation in the Far East over the previous several years. The Russo-Japanese War had eliminated Russia as a naval force in the region. But the Anglo-German naval rivalry and heightened tensions in Europe had led all the other European powers to diminish their forces off East Asia too. And the U.S. had also felt compelled to reduce its naval presence in the Far East dramatically.

For a time, U.S. battleships had been stationed in both the Atlantic and the Pacific. But war games in 1903 as well as the example of the Russo-Japanese War (where the division of Russia's forces had helped to make them more vulnerable) had since led to the belief that virtually all the battle fleet (at least until the navy was much bigger) had to stay together in one ocean. That ocean, moreover, it was felt, had to be the Atlantic (at least until the canal was opened), unless war with Japan was seen clearly to be imminent. America's most valuable assets were located along the Atlantic seaboard. Its position in the western hemisphere could, it was believed, only be challenged from this direction. And (in part for political reasons) base, building and repair facilities for the fleet had thus far all been located on that side of the continent.[121]

With a fleet that had meanwhile been expanding, Japan was thus left as the dominant naval power in East Asian waters. Possessed also of a formidable army, Tokyo, TR worried, was positioned to conquer and then occupy in force the Pacific outposts held since 1898 by the U.S.

Roosevelt was anxious to bolster the American strategic position, to "prevent Japan from feeling safe in attacking us," and to ensure victory in case such a challenge did come. He therefore pressed the service boards to generate a blueprint for the conduct of a war in the Pacific.[122] Although the resultant plans evinced confidence in such a conflict's eventual outcome, they began from the premise that the U.S. would have to assume the defensive and perhaps even sustain substantial losses during its opening phases. Only after the U.S. had successfully established its battle fleet in the western Pacific could offensive operations be begun. In true Mahanian fashion, what would eventually be called War Plan Orange then called on the navy to take command of those waters through decisive engagements with the enemy fleet.[123] The navy would, finally, take the war right to Japan itself. Through a complete blockade and unremitting attacks on enemy ports and shipping, it would seek the island empire's total capitulation.[124]

To facilitate such operations, TR sought to upgrade U.S. naval facilities in the Pacific. Work had barely begun on the development of bases there. Requests for significant expenditure on such projects had been resisted by Congress. But, repeated and exaggerated discussion of the possibility of war—even of the possibility of Japanese invasion—in the press and elsewhere during this period altered the political climate slightly. In 1908 Congress was willing to increase appropriations for installations in the Pacific, and, in particular, to meet TR's request for funds to build up Pearl Harbor.[125]

That site had come to seem especially important in the light of a dramatic reappraisal of plans for the Philippines that took place at this time. At the turn of the century the navy had selected Subig Bay, on the west coast of Luzon, as the optimal site from which it could operate in East Asian waters. Efforts to fortify the harbor were begun in 1904, and these were then stepped up in 1907. The navy ideally hoped that the Japanese could be prevented from taking the site so that it could provide a ready-made base of operations once the entire fleet had been assembled in the region. However, critics in the army maintained that Subig Bay could not easily be made defensible against a major attack from the rear, against the kind of amphibious assault, in other words, that Japan, in particular, was capable of launching. Generals J. Franklin Bell, the army's chief of staff, and Leonard Wood, the Philippine commander, argued that defensive preparations within the islands should instead be centered on Manila. Strategic security for the islands ought to be provided for by a battle fleet operating out of an invulnerable base located to the east in Hawaii. These ideas finally prevailed before both the Joint Army and Navy Board and the president in 1908, all but guaranteeing that Pearl Harbor would henceforth have to be looked at as the most important fortified base of operations in the Pacific.[126]

Unready for a major war in that ocean, TR was eager to defer conflict with Japan, at least until more of these preparations had been made and, ideally, until after the canal, which would diminish travel distance between the Atlantic and East Asia by 8,000 miles, was open. This was, in part, why he decided in 1907 to dispatch the huge "Great White Fleet" on its unprecedented around-the-world journey. Roosevelt hoped that such a dramatic step would silence any thoughts of war in Tokyo. The president also thought that it was time the navy practiced carrying out a transfer of the battle fleet from one ocean to the other.

After careful preparation, sixteen battleships and their auxiliaries departed from Hampton Roads in December. In February 1909, to great fanfare, the flotilla—even larger than when it left because four new battleships had joined it en route—returned home. Both because of the speed with which the ships had covered the various legs of their voyage and because few serious breakdowns were recorded, TR and his advisers were pleased with the fleet's performance. Nevertheless, the cruise underscored again the navy's deficiencies in terms of support facilities for keeping its warships fueled and supplied in far distant waters.[127]

Talks between the American secretary of war and officials in Tokyo in the fall of 1907 clearly demonstrated the desire of *both* governments to avoid a confrontation over immigration. But Tokyo still resisted a treaty that would single out Japanese immigrants. Taft telegraphed TR that he was sure "we can obtain practically the same exclusion" by new administrative measures. Nevertheless, because of the domestic political furor that the issue had raised, it soon became apparent that the Japanese government was not eager to move on these points either.[128]

The State Department finally warned Japan that unless there was "a very speedy change in the course of immigration" the executive branch would no longer oppose exclusion legislation by Congress. Unwilling to chance that, Tokyo moved to put in place a much more restrictive version of the Gentleman's Agreement during the early weeks of the new year.[129]

The crisis at an end, both powers henceforth strove to repair and stabilize their frayed relations. Pursuant to a request by Root, Japan signed an arbitration treaty with the U.S. in May. It also invited the U.S. fleet to stop in Yokohama during its round-the-world tour. The two states pledged reciprocally to protect their trademarks, copyrights and patents in China and Korea. Then, in the fall, a new government led by Katsura Taro offered to exchange with Washington sweeping guarantees about the objectives of Tokyo's policies in the Pacific and the Far East.[130]

On his side, TR now proved more and more willing to concede Tokyo an essentially free hand in southern Manchuria. As a consequence of the Portsmouth settlement, the U.S. had already accepted the transfer to Japan of Russia's leasehold and railway rights in that region. But TR had initially wanted to see the rest of Manchuria restored to Chinese control. And both Britain and the U.S. had voiced displeasure when the Japanese army of occupation sought to secure broad economic and political influence throughout the area immediately following the war.[131]

Restrictions were placed on the activity of the military after mid-1906, and few complaints were subsequently heard about discrimination toward other powers' trade. The occupation came to an end in early 1907. For both strategic and economic reasons, Tokyo nevertheless continued, in other ways, to try to control the region, particularly by trying to monopolize its railway development. Fearful of losing Manchuria, some Chinese officials began to hope that they could use American capital and political power to create a counterweight to this influence.[132] In 1907–8 they held out the prospect of railway contracts and of a central role for Americans in the creation of a development bank for the region. They also proposed a Sino-American alliance that would be premised on the preservation both of China's integrity and of the open door.[133]

Some American officials were eager to take advantage of these opportunities. But not Roosevelt. After the immigration crisis, he opposed the adoption of any policy that might bring the U.S. into conflict with Japan in that region. As he saw it, Tokyo would fight to protect what it saw as a vital sphere of influence. Back in 1900, some, like Mahan, had argued that the open door powers should concede Manchuria to Russia and concentrate on China proper. TR felt that the U.S. had even less chance of challenging Japan there now. To try to do so, moreover, would be counterproductive, for Manchuria gave a vent to Japanese energies that otherwise might crash up against more important U.S. interests.[134]

Having achieved a settlement of the immigration issue largely on his terms and eager for an agreement with Japan applicable generally to East Asia and the Pacific region, TR was prepared to make informal assurances with regard to China's northeastern provinces. In September he told Taka-hira that with regard to China's sovereignty he was willing tacitly to treat Manchuria as in a separate category from the rest of the empire. Two months later, Root and the Japanese ambassador signed a joint declaration in which both nations professed their dedication to the "free and peaceful development of their commerce on the Pacific," their respect for each other's territorial possessions, and their support for the open door and the "independence and integrity" of China.[135]

The diplomacy of the Taft administration in China was influenced tremen-dously by the renewed interest that Wall Street was, by 1909, beginning to take in foreign activities.[136] Since the turn of the century, such investment had come to seem increasingly important if the U.S. was going to be a major factor in that empire's commercial development. But Taft era policy makers, in addition, welcomed investment capital as an instrumentality that could help the U.S. to reshape China and shore up the open door.

The first major opportunity, and test, for dollar diplomacy in the empire came right after Taft's inauguration, and it involved a concession, for a railway from Hankou to Canton, that Americans had for a time held (and managed poorly) but then surrendered during the nationalist upsurge in China three and a half years before. After the contract was revoked, provin-cial elites had unsuccessfully tried to come up with sufficient funding. Bei-jing had then reasserted control and begun to look again for foreign capital to build the railroad.[137]

The Hankou-Canton project was eventually merged with a still larger piece of business, namely, a major segment of China's planned imperial trunk line, running for hundreds of miles from Hankou west into Sichuan Province. Then the three traditional competitors for investments in China proper, France, England, and Germany, came together to cooperate on this now much bigger undertaking. They concluded a deal for its construction with Beijing in May 1909.[138]

State Department officials were stunned.[139] As they saw it, the U.S. was being shut out of what had become a vast and potentially pivotal enter-prise. Moreover, since Chinese governmental revenues were to constitute the loan's security, the settlement also seemed to carry with it the possibil-ity that the involved powers would come to exercise a great deal of power over China's fiscal and administrative affairs. Knox refused to accept this outcome. He decided to insist on American inclusion in what was now termed the "Hukuang (Hu-guang)" loan. The secretary was not only eager to see Americans involved in such an important enterprise. He also wanted to guarantee Washington a role in any political decisions that might grow out of it. At the same time, Knox was clearly also attracted to this scheme precisely because of the political objectives that it might further.

Knox hoped that American participation might mark a precedent whereby all China's infrastructural projects would henceforth be approached cooperatively by the major creditor states. Not only would such cooperation provide for regular American involvement in important Chinese business. By removing that infrastructure from competition and interlocking the interests of the various states, it would, in addition, help to secure the open door and give the powers greater leverage over China's reform. For all of China, Knox was already moving toward the neutralization proposal that he would later be known for, and he was doing so on the premise that America's new financial resources might be the means by which Hay's collective approach toward the empire could be revitalized.

Third Assistant Secretary William Phillips suggested an avenue by which Washington might gain entry into the project. The U.S., he offered, could argue that it had not relinquished its right to be given, along with Britain, first chance at the Hankou-Chengdu concession, a claim based on assurances given the American minister to China in 1903 and 1904. A protest was lodged in Beijing in these terms, and the matter was raised with the British Foreign Office in the same way.[140] These claims were met with evasive replies.[141] Not to be put off, Knox sent off a circular instruction outlining the grounds on which the U.S. case was to be argued in the interested capitals. This pointed to a "menace to foreign trade likely to ensue from the lack of proper sympathy between the Powers vitally interested in the preservation of the principle of equality of commercial opportunity." Cooperation, defined as including American participation, was "best calculated to maintain the open door and the integrity of China." Still claiming priority on the westward route, it said that Washington was prepared to share the business to further the creation of a "highly desirable community of interests" in China.[142]

The British, French, and German interests, and their respective governments, still resisted, but the State Department applied great pressure on China.[143] After Taft, on July 15, took the unusual step of addressing a personal appeal to Prince Chun (who had assumed the role of regent on the death of Cixi the previous November), the loan agreement was finally opened up for renegotiation.[144]

Elated by his success, Knox moved during the next six months to extend this approach to China's three northeastern provinces. Far from accepting the idea that conceding Manchuria was either inevitable or in America's best interests, Taft era policy makers wanted to see if Washington's now dollar-fortified diplomacy could not dissolve the Japanese sphere that had been developing there. The president was, for his part, far less worried about Japanese antipathy than either TR or Root had been. Indeed, he was not convinced that Japan could not be won over to American plans.[145]

Attitudes in the State Department, meanwhile, were heavily influenced by the views of people like Huntington Wilson and Willard Straight (who resigned from the Far Eastern Division in 1909 to represent the interests of the American Group in London and Beijing). They had both been in the Far East during the war and had hoped that Russia's defeat would open the way to a new era of U.S. economic expansion in Manchuria. Both had become hostile to Japan for what they saw as its interference with that destiny and they were eager to see Washington challenge its policy.[146]

Three specific developments prompted Knox to take the initiative in Manchuria in late 1909. The first had to do with agreements between China and Japan covering the latter's railway rights there. Since the beginning of the year, Tokyo had been pressing Beijing to acquiesce in new plans that it had not only for the S.M.R. but also for a line that Tokyo had built during the war from Antung (on the Korean border) to Mukden. During August and early September, Beijing finally granted Tokyo broad new mining privileges along the routes of both railways.[147] Officials in the State Department saw this as a bold new step by Japan to secure dominance in Manchuria.[148]

A second development, meanwhile, seemed to offer Washington new leverage in the area. This was the signing by Straight, on October 2, of a preliminary agreement by which the American Group would finance, and a British construction firm would build, a Chinese railway running the entire length of Manchuria from Chinchow (Jinzhou) in the south to Aigun (Aihui) in the north. Straight had gone to the Far East to represent the Group in the Hukuang loan negotiations. But he had been drawn irresistibly into a discussion of Manchurian affairs as well. Knox looked at the scheme much as he had the American claim to the Hankou-Chengdu route in the spring. The line might be promoted by itself, he thought, and used to pierce into and challenge the Japanese and Russian spheres. Or, more fruitfully, it might be used to promote collective great power development of all the region's railways. The secretary hoped that the British connection would ensure London's diplomatic support for U.S. plans in the region.[149]

Finally, Knox also received some indication that Russia might now be leaning toward policies that would dovetail with Washington's. Just before his death in September, the American railway magnate E. H. Harriman had negotiated with parties in Russia who suggested that St. Petersburg might be willing to sell the C.E.R. And some weeks later Straight announced that he thought it was interested in cooperating in the Hukuang loan. To Knox, these reports implied that Russia might be used to further isolate Japan.

No request specifically aimed at the Hukuang loan was forthcoming, but during the first week in October the chargé of the Russian embassy did ask for U.S. support for equal Russian participation in future Chinese opportunities.[150] This had the effect of encouraging Knox to formulate more concretely the approach that he was seeking to promote in the Qing empire. "The development of China," he wrote State Department counselor Henry Hoyt, "had not progressed to such an extent, at the time the doctrine of the 'open door' was promulgated, as to make it much more than a theory for harmonious action. This theory has not been really tested in a concrete way and in its application to matters of great importance as it seems likely now to be."

Knox referred to the "limited application" of the open door policy in practice and cast the Russian proposal as a request for U.S. support for the extension of that policy to the investment realm. He had formulated three propositions, as "a starting point to reach what I desire, namely, that we set down in some concrete and simple form the rules by which we are willing to be guided and to which we would desire the other Powers to adhere." They were

(1) In all cases where the Imperial credit . . . is pledged for railway construction, the Powers which have pledged themselves to the principle of equal trade opportunities . . . and the preservation of China's political integrity have such a direct interest as to entitle them to participation in the loans and equitable consideration for their nations and materials.

(2) In no case where a railroad is constructed upon Imperial credit . . . should exclusive rights be granted to the nationals of any country to do business of any kind within the territory served by the railroad. . . .

(3) The United States Government not only does not crave territory in China but disavows any desire or intention to secure for its nationals or its products any monopoly or preferences that will interfere with the right of the nationals of the other Powers to engage in business with China.[151]

Knox saw these rules as providing, in effect, for the institutionalization of the open door in China. But in the three eastern provinces of the empire the secretary faced an especially formidable task.

Knox thought that he could use the Chinchow to Aigun, or "Chin-Ai," contract to create a working model of the kind of arrangements that he wanted in Manchuria. But he decided first to play for bigger stakes, namely, the "neutralization" of all the railways in the region. He first broached the idea to Britain in the hope that he could enlist its support with Japan. In a lengthy memorandum transmitted to the Foreign Office on November 6, he announced that the U.S. was prepared to cooperate with London in diplomatic support of the Chin-Ai project. Tokyo, he suggested, could be compensated for losses inflicted on the, at some points nearly parallel, S.M.R. by admission into the scheme. But Knox first wished to propose a broader arrangement as the "most effective way" of guaranteeing equal opportunity and protecting Chinese territorial integrity. This was that the Chin-Ai should become part of a completely "neutralized" Manchurian railway network. All present and future lines in the area should be brought under "an economic, scientific, and impartial administration by some plan vesting in China the ownership of the railroads through funds furnished for that purpose by the interested powers willing to participate." During the term of the loan, the system should be supervised by representatives of the participating powers, and these powers would enjoy "the usual preferences for their nationals and materials upon an equitable basis *inter se.*"[152]

Such was the essence of Knox's most daring dollar diplomacy venture. In one fell swoop, "dollars," many of which would be supplied by other powers, would extricate Manchuria from "politics," as he saw it. The Hukuang model would be brought north where it would absorb the exclusive approach of Japan and make the region into one large commercial "neutral" zone. In the absence, as yet, of a strong China, the empire would be held together and much of its economy overseen by the cooperating powers, including the U.S.[153]

But the proposal was not accepted. However brilliant in the abstract, Knox's plan reflected a poor grasp of the contemporary drift of international affairs. In particular, Knox grossly misestimated the Foreign Office's likely attitude toward his project, and this for the simple reason that neither he nor his advisors sufficiently appreciated the changes that had been taking place in British policy. The secretary hoped that London might be guided by the commercial and investment opportunities offered by the scheme. But Britain had little appetite for antagonizing its Far Eastern ally. Issues in Europe, and its rivalry with Germany, had become too pressing. Sir Edward Grey, the foreign secretary, delayed providing a direct answer, and focused instead on ways by which Japan's participation in the Chin-Ai might be facilitated.[154]

Knox had misread Russia as well. When it learned of the plan its reaction was shaped principally by its concerns about the Chin-Ai line. St. Petersburg perceived that project as a strategic threat both to its own territory and to its position in northern Manchuria. As a result, it turned against the whole idea of the U.S. mixing in the region's affairs. Japan, for its part, was left with no reason not simply to demand participation in the Chin-Ai line on its terms.[155] Washington appealed to Russia and Japan on the grounds that neutralization of their lines "would afford an opportunity for both . . . to shift their onerous duties . . . to the shoulders of the combined Powers, including themselves." It also argued that neutralization would promote peace and security for both nations precisely because it would bring the interests of other states into the area. Finally, the administration sought to make participation a test of fidelity to the open door, and thereby embarrass both powers into compliance. St. Petersburg and Tokyo remained unmoved, however. Indeed, in January 1910 they coordinated their rejections of Knox's scheme.[156]

Knox thought that the Chin-Ai route still offered an opportunity for him to push the cooperative approach, to challenge the Japanese and Russian spheres, and to promote an American presence in Manchuria. But this plan was rather quickly cast in doubt too. Britain warned China against completing arrangements for construction without conferring with its entente partner, Russia, and its ally, Japan. Since Tokyo was by no means strongly committed to the railway, this meant that Washington was left to deal with the misgivings of Russia alone. Although the U.S. refused to recognize any Russian right to hold up the project, little could be accomplished so long as China feared reprisals from that quarter.[157]

Straight now urged a middle course. He suggested that Washington push for construction at first of just part of the line. But such an approach, the State Department realized, risked a full revelation of the limits of U.S. power in the region and, potentially, the loss of any influence at all with Beijing. Retreat was also too humiliating a course to accept immediately. To cover itself, therefore, the department, in July, decided simply to temporize and hope that some element of the situation might change.[158]

Pursuit of such a nonpolicy required coordination with the Group as well as with Beijing. Both were by this time growing restive. J. P. Morgan's Henry P. Davison commented, "that while it was all right to be making history, their business was to make money, and he expressed some doubt as to the wisdom of groups continuing operations in China."[159] Taft worried about a "severe blow to our prestige," and the State Department spent much of the rest of the summer trying to keep the bankers in line.[160]

Meanwhile, the attitude of the Chinese government also required attention because the American offensive had unintentionally had the effect of contributing to a rapprochement between Tokyo and St. Petersburg. After Russia and Japan formally agreed to defend the status quo in Manchuria by whatever means necessary, Beijing demanded to know Washington's intentions.[161]

The reply could only have been disappointing. The State Department announced that the American position on the Chin-Ai project would be formulated in "due time." In the meantime, it hoped to "stiffen" Beijing and counseled a program of "prompt and strenuous" currency and tariff reform. "I should think her role," commented Huntington Wilson, "was to strengthen herself as fast as possible and make all possible reservations on paper."[162]

China hoped that it might be able to enlist one or both of the major powers not affiliated with the entente, namely Germany or the U.S., in an alliance. Prince Chun had already tried to pave the way for this by initiating a new program of army and navy expansion. The U.S. was eager to compete for any contracts that this might entail, and it also aspired to guide China's naval development. However, Knox cautioned Taft that the administration was hardly in a position to pledge the U.S. to a "policy in opposition to the aims and acts of other powers."[163]

Other ideas attracted greater American interest. By the end of the summer, Beijing embarked once more on a search for a large loan for Manchurian development. This was followed by an attempt to finance the reform of the empire's currency. These actions opened up new opportunities to the hard-pressed American bankers and policy makers. It quickly became apparent that the members of the American Group, although frustrated with the Chin-Ai project, remained interested in China. Although the British Hong Kong and Shanghai Bank held the inside track, the American Group, with Washington's backing, worked vigorously to land the Manchurian loan.[164]

It achieved a quick triumph in the matter of the currency reform business. Anxious to maintain freedom of action in the face of the cooperation that had been developing among the European banks, Beijing made the loan prospect known to the U.S. on September 22. Four days later, Huntington Wilson personally laid the matter before representatives of the Group. Their acceptance was subsequently cabled to the new U.S. minister, along with Knox's stipulation that Beijing engage an American financial advisor, preferably Professor Jeremiah W. Jenks of Cornell, to oversee the reform and the use of the loan.[165]

Acceptance of this proposal unexpectedly proved to be the key to the other as well, for China almost immediately decided to merge the two pieces of business together (because it did not want a loan for the northeastern provinces to be treated separately from business for the rest of the empire). A preliminary agreement for a loan of $50 million was concluded on October 27.[166]

Quite contrary to Beijing's desires, however, the Group had no intention of pursuing an independent course. The European bankers had already invited the Americans to combine with them for future Chinese financing. J. P. Morgan and the other members wanted to join the consortium. They wished, however, to bargain for optimal terms of entry. In particular, the Americans wanted an agreement that would allow the internationalization of all bond issues, which would lessen their dependence on their own home capital market.[167] To this end, control of the currency reform loan business was now to be applied as leverage.[168]

The State Department was also encouraged by the new turn of events. The Manchurian aspects of the loan seemed to provide one more chance for what had become a stalemated policy in that region. The financial aspects provided for what was considered a much needed reform as well as a new opportunity for Knox to promote the kind of arrangement that he wanted for the empire as a whole. Like the Group, he too was looking toward international participation.[169]

The European members of the new consortium, organized in November, insisted that their participation be accompanied by their signature of the final loan agreement. Although Washington was willing to press Beijing to accept this, it was nevertheless anxious to continue to control the

negotiations and to secure a financial adviser who was an American. The
U.S. wanted to influence the direction of reform in China as much as possible and to protect the Manchurian portions of the loan.[170]

Much to the discomfort of the Group, however, Knox's maneuvering on
these matters threatened to upset the entire deal. The Europeans objected
to his efforts with regard to the advisor, and in the end he was forced to
abandon his claim. Beijing signed a final agreement with all four groups in
April 1911, at which time it also agreed to accept a neutral advisor chosen
by the bankers.[171]

Despite its failure to reap the desired advantages, the State Department
still felt justified in claiming a major triumph for its China policy. This was
doubly the case after Beijing finally bowed to consortium terms and signed
the concluding agreement for the Hukuang loan just one month later. "By
the successful completion of the two loans," one key memorandum boasted,
the U.S. "has now for the first time such a substantial interest in the material development of China ... as to give it more than a moral right to have
a voice in all questions affecting China's welfare." Furthermore,

Those interests have been so associated with the interests of other leading Powers
by common financial ties that it is to the interest of all alike to join in maintaining
the political integrity of China and to unite in sympathetic and practical cooperation for the peaceful development of the Chinese Empire.... The first step only
has been taken on the road to the essential monetary and fiscal reforms of the
Chinese Empire, but it has been a long and practical step and the interests of the
Powers have been so clinched as not only to secure an open door for all the world
but virtually to neutralize the whole broad field of China's commercial, industrial,
and fiscal enterprises.[172]

It quickly became apparent, however, that these arrangements could not
guarantee the kind of framework that the administration wanted in Manchuria.[173] Knox had hoped that British and French participation in the
Manchurian part of the loan would lead them to discourage interference
by their allies, Japan and Russia. But Tokyo and St. Petersburg were determined to keep the consortium out of the three eastern provinces. And,
instead of eliminating this threat, the British and French were ultimately
prepared to bow to their allies' concerns.

In response to the continued opposition, Knox, as early as spring 1911,
endorsed the entrance of capital-poor Russia and Japan into the financial
syndicate. His idea was that it still might be possible to absorb the two powers into a pattern of "harmonious action."[174] At the advice of the French,
both the Russians and the Japanese did seek entry at the end of the year.
But they did so in order to combine their votes with those of Britain and
France, and thereby block any challenges to their Manchurian positions.[175]

By the end of 1911 there was another reason why Knox wanted Russia and
Japan to be part of the consortium, even if that did further compromise

U.S. objectives in the north. As a revolt against imperial authority unfolded in central China that fall, he became convinced that the framework of cooperative action among all the great powers was more important to sustain than ever before (in fact, in 1912 the secretary would finally be ready to write off Manchuria in order to try to hold onto the threads of American policy south of the Great Wall).

Over the summer, Beijing's plan to take over the Hankou-Chengdu route and to fund its construction through foreign capitalists had come up against growing opposition from within Sichuan. Then, in October, elements of the New Hubei Army mutinied and took control of Wuchang. These events crystallized what had for several years been a mounting anti-Qing sentiment, and they set off a collapse of imperial power throughout most of the country.

The dynasty had embarked on a program of more dramatic change in the years since the Boxer catastrophe, but it had nevertheless been unable to retain the confidence of local elites and of many students, merchants, and members of the army. Its efforts at railway development and at military, educational and constitutional reform had in fact served to swell the ranks of those who saw Qing rule as inadequate to the tasks that confronted China. Acting largely through the empire's new provincial assemblies, one province after another declared its independence of the government in Beijing.[176]

In the face of this instability, "harmonious action" seemed crucial to Knox, both as a means by which the powers could coordinate the protection of their interests in China and as a mechanism that would inhibit forms of unilateralism dangerous to U.S. policy. From the very beginning of the disturbances, he took a leading role in efforts to ensure such a common front. The powers quickly agreed to coordinate their efforts and to act in unison if and when the situation warranted. Unlike the case with the Boxer Rebellion, however, their inclination was to be cautious. This reflected a sense that events were for the time being beyond the ability of outsiders either to predict or control. Western powers were also afraid that Japan might take advantage of any intervention to extend its influence in China as Russia had done in 1900.[177]

The powers were at the same time concerned as to where the revolution might lead. On the one hand, despite activists' promises to protect foreign residents and property, they worried about the revolutionaries' attitude toward outside interests. On the other hand, the powers were fearful that a new government would be unable to ensure the conditions that they wanted in China. There was particular unease about the objective, proclaimed by many of the revolution's leaders, of creating a republic. Nearby, monarchical Japan may have felt most threatened, but it was not a course favored by the republican U.S. either. The preference of all the powers was to see the imperial system upheld and modified, rather than overthrown.

Yet they were afraid that their interests might suffer if they tried to assist the Qing even just financially.[178]

During late 1911 the court launched a military counteroffensive against the main centers of revolutionary influence. But to accomplish this, it felt compelled to turn over inordinate political and military power to Yuan Shikai, the official who had overseen much of the military modernization program and built up a strong personal following within the pivotal New Northern Army. Yuan, however, had no intention of going down with the dynasty. Ambitious and opportunistic, by December he was negotiating with the revolutionary leaders and offering to facilitate the Manchus' abdication in return for a position of prominence in the new China. The revolutionaries respected Yuan's military power, they also hoped that his leadership might lend stability to their government and gain it acceptance by the powers. In February, therefore, after the abdication, he succeeded Sun Yat-sen as provisional president of a newly declared Chinese republic.[179]

Most of the great powers, perhaps Britain and the U.S. above all, were pleased about Yuan's rise, for he had long been viewed as the kind of strongman they could deal with and potentially cultivate. The powers, and their banking groups, nevertheless remained uneasy about the regime of which Yuan was a part. As a result they decided to withhold their recognition of the new government. This created political problems for Taft, because many in the U.S. saw in the republic a reaffirmation of their own country's political heritage. Many Protestants, in particular, celebrated what they took to be a triumph for the American missionary movement in China. The administration was, however, determined not break ranks with the other interested states.[180]

The powers and bankers also took a stern attitude when approached by the new government about a loan. The bankers were convinced that much greater controls could and ought now to be insisted on. Their governments, meanwhile, saw in such a course an opportunity to promote a financial protectorate over the country.

Knox was anxious to obtain such controls because to him this was the path by which China might finally be supervised and forced to accept Western-desired reforms. Four years later he was to describe what he was trying to foster here as a "league of nations" for China. Its objectives were completely in keeping with what had already been the secretary's objectives in the country. As he saw it, this "common policy of cooperation" would protect the open door (at least throughout China proper), secure the U.S. a front row seat in that country's economic future, and enable the powers, as Knox might have put it, to take China "in hand." China's renewal had to be "aided and guided" by more "responsible" states and this task could best be accomplished by all the powers working together.[181]

To ensure that there should be no interruption in China's payment of its by now immense foreign obligations, the bankers and powers, led by

Britain, had already increased their control over the country's customs collection. Foreign administrators had overseen the system for decades. But when provinces in revolt against the central government tried to gain access to these revenues, such control was extended to include the actual collection of duties. The proceeds were then deposited in foreign banks as well.[182]

Now, in connection with this so-called "Reorganization Loan," the powers and bankers began to demand much more sweeping supervision over the policies of the new republic. With their governments' support, the members of the consortium insisted on a financial advisor who would oversee all China's finances as well as supervise the reorganization of the country's taxes and public administration (including the post-revolution demobilization of the army). They sought a veto over expenditures. In addition, the consortium members wanted to see the accounting and railroad departments of the Chinese government staffed by foreigners.[183]

So far as many Chinese were concerned, however, such outside "guardianship" was one of the things that they had been hoping to diminish. Those handling the negotiations were exhorted to resist the controls and supervision that the consortium was demanding and also to find other sources of funding.[184]

This resistance had some effect. By 1913 most of the banking groups were ready to modify their demands in the hope of wrapping up the business. Such a posture was also endorsed by the majority of the participating governments, including the U.S. However the American bankers held back. They had long been concerned about having a sufficient market for their foreign loan flotations. And now, because of mounting tensions in Europe, they were beginning to worry that France and England might take steps that would bar internationalization of the sale of the bonds for the loan.

The American Group was growing increasingly nervous about its China business, and it felt that it was no longer receiving the degree of understanding and support that it deserved from the Taft administration. It doubted, moreover, that the situation would improve under Wilson. Picking up on the "dollar diplomacy" theme, the president-elect had made implied criticisms of the consortium during the campaign. The bankers therefore sought an audience with the new administration as soon as it took office. They announced that they would consider continuing in the negotiations, but they wanted specifically to be requested to do so by the government. To the disappointment, at least of outgoing Taft administration officials, however, Wilson refused to make that appeal.[185]

Since he was at the same time pledging to have the government play a greater role in the promotion of American trade, why did Wilson take this stance? Part of the answer needs to be sought, again, in his interpretation of "dollar diplomacy." Throughout the campaign, Wilson had been critical of what he saw as a small minority of the banking and business community in America that sought to profit through what he described as "concerted arrangements" and political favoritism. Such practices, he argued, artificially restricted entrepreneurial opportunity in the U.S. They had a debilitating effect on overall economic development. And they undermined public support for the business system.[186]

Similar consequences, he feared, were the logical end product of dollar diplomacy, for that constituted, in Wilson's view, an extension overseas of such practices.[187] As the incoming president saw it, China policy had under Taft simply become subordinated to the narrow self-interest of those banks that had formed the Group and then become part of the international consortium. The bankers' objective had been to fasten a financial monopoly and high interest rates on China and then have that relationship guaranteed by Washington.[188] Such a policy could be costly and dangerous. It was likely to beggar China, to slow down its development as a market, and to promote instability in the region, none of which was in the long-term best economic or political interest of the U.S.

At the same time, Wilson believed that breaking with the consortium offered the U.S. an opportunity to guide events in China and to benefit economically and politically from Chinese friendship. The U.S. could win a position of special favor and influence, he felt, if it broke with the policy of the other powers. And by so doing it could ensure that revolutionary China did not develop in ways that were likely to be disruptive to the international order Washington desired. Wilson wrote in January 1913 that "probably nothing more nearly touches the future development of the world than what will happen in the East and it ought to happen, so far as our influence extends, under the best possible guidance."[189]

Moreover, the way had already been prepared. In company with the bulk of the American press and a number of prominent missionaries, Wilson was eager to believe that the revolution since 1911 was principally a product of Western, and especially American, educational and missionary initiatives. To him this suggested the possibility that a new China was emerging that would be both strong and eager to take guidance from the U.S.[190]

Wilson's response to the bankers came in a policy statement released to the public on March 18. The administration, it said, did not want even by implication to be a party to the conditions that the bankers were demanding, conditions that might conceivably require its "forcible interference in the financial, and even the political, affairs of that great oriental state." Nevertheless, the new president wanted to make it clear that

The government of the United States is not only willing, but earnestly desirous, of aiding the great Chinese people in every way that is consistent with their untrammeled development and its own immemorial principles. The awakening of the people of China to a consciousness of their possibilities under free government is the most significant, if not the most momentous, event of our generation. With this movement and aspiration the American people are in profound sympathy. They certainly wish to participate, and participate very generously, in opening to the Chinese and to the use of the world the almost untouched and perhaps unrivalled resources of China.[191]

Wilson saw himself as returning American policy to the posture that had been adopted by Hay in the open door notes. And he told his cabinet that he thought the U.S. position in China would be stronger because of this. Its members agreed. Bryan felt that Wilson had put the U.S. in line to win the "lasting gratitude" of the Chinese by breaking with the consortium. And Secretary Redfield cited trade evidence that, he thought, showed America to be ready to assume a position of economic leadership in that country.[192]

On April 1 Wilson informed the cabinet that he intended to have Washington take the lead in recognizing the republic once its newly elected National Assembly was formally organized. The next week Bryan reported a "fatherly talk" with the Chinese minister, his purpose being to convey Washington's hope that China's government would comport itself in such a way as to encourage the other great powers to follow the U.S. lead. Finally, on May 2, U.S. recognition was extended. In his announcement, Wilson welcomed the new republic into the "family of nations." He also made a special point of admonishing it to be faithful to its "international obligations."[193]

Wilson's concern about guiding China through its revolution meanwhile led him to conduct a search for someone with educational or missionary experience as the next U.S. minister to that country. After Charles W. Eliot, former president of Harvard, and John R. Mott, organizer of the Student Volunteer Movement for Foreign Missions, were approached, the position finally went, in July, to Paul S. Reinsch, a noted political scientist from the University of Wisconsin. Reinsch had written extensively on the Far East. He also served under TR and Taft as a delegate to the Pan-American conferences in Rio (1906) and Buenos Aires (1910).[194]

The Wilson administration's approach toward China in 1913 rested on five key assumptions: (1) that the U.S. "position would be stronger" than it had been "not to be in partnership" with the other powers; (2) that breaking with the other powers would yield the U.S. (as some of its diplomats in East Asia had suggested as early as December 1911) an inside track with the new government; (3) that the end of Washington "favoritism" for any specific interests would not diminish, and would most likely increase, American business and investor involvement in China; (4) that a Chinese government that could and would conduct itself more consistently as the outside powers wanted now had a good prospect of coming into being; and (5) that this government would be strong enough to contend not only with "irresponsible behavior" within China, but also—and with only limited American political/military assistance—with "greedy" behavior on the part of Washington's rivals.[195] The second of these assumptions was certainly true. There was even a chance of the fourth proving accurate as well. However, neither

China nor the U.S. possessed the strengths hoped for by the administration, and as a consequence Washington's position in East Asia became weaker rather than stronger over the next several years. That, in turn, would eventually lead the administration to revise its methods for shoring up the open door.

Chinese politics were in fact heading toward another period of instability by the spring of 1913, arising principally out of Yuan's ambition to consolidate power in his own hands. Elections had been held in 1912–13 for a new National Assembly, and Sun's followers, organized in the Guomindang Party, had won the largest share of seats. Even before the assembly convened, however, Yuan responded by placing restrictions on the political activities of his opponents. Many of these held Yuan responsible as well for the assassination of the Guomindang's principal strategist, Song Zhiaoren. The backlash that this aroused led the remaining members of the consortium to conclude the Reorganization Loan on somewhat more generous terms in the hope that they could reinforce Yuan's power. He then signed that agreement without referring it first to the Assembly.

A portion of the Guomindang leadership finally resorted to armed opposition in July. This Revolution of 1913 was, however, crushed in less than two months. And once it was over, Yuan resumed his efforts to consolidate rule. He now had himself elected as the (no longer provisional) president. He ordered the complete dissolution of the Guomindang. He dissolved the National Assembly and all the provincial assemblies and then promulgated a new constitution that essentially turned the post of president into that of dictator.[196]

As this split developed, the Wilson administration not only accommodated itself to Yuan's consolidation of power. It tilted in his direction. Yuan was viewed, as he had been by many Western governments for a decade or more, as the kind of strongman who might rule China as the outside powers desired. Fearful of losing him, Washington came to blame Sun and his nationalist followers for the instability there. The administration also eventually concluded that China was simply unready to be governed as a republic.[197]

Yuan's government was recognized by all the major Western states by the middle of October 1913. Nevertheless, because of its break with the other powers, Washington was positioned to reap his special attention. Yuan's so-called "cabinet of talents" of late 1913–14 was eager to obtain more foreign lending, and it hoped it could do so on terms that were easier than those being demanded by the consortium. This led the government to look hopefully toward the U.S. as well as toward nonconsortium financial sources in Britain. It also hoped that the U.S. (as well as Germany and England) might be drawn into a political relationship such as would balance off the potential growth of Japanese influence in northern China.

The Chinese government suggested that it would look to the U.S. for advice and be receptive to American enterprise undertaking major projects in the country. Rockhill became an advisor to Yuan, and the constitution of 1914 owed much to a draft prepared by the prominent American political scientist (and expert on municipal reform) Frank Goodnow. Several large concessions were offered to U.S. corporations, the hope being that substantial amounts of money might be raised quickly by the government and that such involvement would pave the way to more extensive American investment.

While the U.S. quickly gained influence, it did not, however, witness a similar boost in its economic role. The assumption had been that the end of "favoritism" for any specific parties would not affect the overall level of American investment that might flow toward China. Particularly given the uncertainty as to political conditions there, however, this proved not to be the case. Even the proffered concessions were in 1914 only pushed forward slowly.[198]

The outbreak of the Great War opened up a new chapter in Far Eastern affairs as it created conditions under which Japan made a bid dramatically to improve its position in that region. Tokyo quickly plunged into the conflict on the side of its British ally, hoping that by so doing it could eliminate Germany permanently as a force in China and in the western Pacific. It also hoped to secure Germany's possessions for itself. By November 1914, Japan's forces had taken control over Qingdao and the principal fortress guarding Berlin's leasehold in Shandong. They also seized all Germany's western Pacific island possessions north of the equator.[199]

While its other rivals, including the U.S., remained distracted by events in Europe, Tokyo then moved to try to enhance its position in China. In January 1915, it presented Beijing with a sweeping set of proposals, which came to be known as the Twenty-One Demands. Their principal purpose was to consolidate Japan's preexisting dominance in Manchuria and its new role in Shandong. But they pointed in the direction of a new role for Tokyo in the rest of China as well. Economic concessions in other parts of the country were discussed. Beijing was asked to agree that it would not permit any other power to establish naval bases on the coast. And, in a final, fifth, cluster of desiderata, China was asked to appoint Japanese advisors throughout its administration and military, to give Japan a dominant role in the supply of China's arms, and to agree to joint policing in areas of special Japanese interest.[200]

These developments powerfully brought home to Washington the fact that it could not rely just on its own strength or on that of China. In December Reinsch wrote Bryan that he was fearful that the U.S. might lose the confidence of the Yuan government. When he learned of the existence of the Twenty-One Demands, he counseled Chinese officials to drag out discussion of them and, despite Tokyo's insistence on secrecy, to leak their contents to all the powers. But even this degree of activism was seen as dangerous back home. Fearful of antagonizing Japan and of encouraging it to act more boldly, officials in Washington preferred at first to believe that the demands were not as serious as Reinsch thought. In a discussion with Wilson and Lansing, Colonel House urged "great caution" as well. The U.S., he warned, was "not at present in a position to war with Japan over the 'open door' in China."[201]

Lansing suggested that Washington try to strike a deal with Tokyo. As a result of the exhaustion of the Europeans and the continued growth of American economic power, he believed that the U.S. was destined to emerge as the leading power in East Asia after the war. The crucial thing was to prevent Japan from establishing itself throughout all China in the meantime. Its principal influence had to be contained to the north and to Shandong. Japan was extremely anxious to have its rivals recognize a special position for itself there. The U.S., he felt, should make explicit assurances with respect to those areas in return for Japanese guarantees regarding the rest of the country.[202]

In the end, on March 13, the administration only cautioned Tokyo mildly about some of its demands. It voiced concern about the fifth group in particular, and about the issue of preferential claims to concessions. But the note also stated that Washington was disposed to "raise no question, at this time," about the demands relating to Shantung, Manchuria, and eastern Inner Mongolia. In a phrase that Japan was later to seize on, it even asserted that the U.S. "frankly recognizes that territorial contiguity creates special relations between Japan and these districts."[203]

Other language was also included that was intended to reassure Tokyo and to show that Washington could be flexible. However from Reinsch's standpoint in Beijing, this approach seemed likely only to encourage Japan and to lose the U.S. leverage with China. Tokyo could not be appeased or co-opted, in his opinion. Nor did Washington understand the scope of what Japan intended.

After several vigorously worded telegrams from Reinsch—and after it also became clear that Japan still intended to press the fifth group of demands—the administration began to modify its stance. In mid-April, Wilson instructed Bryan to be "as active as the circumstances permit" in preventing the Japanese domination of China.[204] Frank discussions were held with the Japanese ambassador, and an unsuccessful effort was made to arrange for a joint British, French, Russian, and American intercession with Japan. Farther than this the administration still did not believe it could go. It would only reserve the right not to recognize any changes that, in its opinion, contravened American rights.

In fact, the negative international publicity, the protracted nature of the talks, plus the evident displeasure of Britain and the U.S. finally did lead Japan to defer the demands in its fifth group. It then presented Beijing with an ultimatum on the rest. After this was met, Washington informed

Tokyo that it could not "recognize any agreement or undertaking" that impaired its treaty rights , the "territorial integrity of the Republic of China, or the international policy relative to China commonly known as the open door policy."[205]

Although Japan retreated on the fifth group of demands, that did not signify an intention to abandon its efforts to become more influential throughout all of China. Like the U.S., it sought to cultivate close relations with political factions in that country. Tokyo also strove to expand its role in the Chinese economy. Japan now began aggressively to use political pressure, as well as financial leverage, to secure concessions from Beijing and to block contracts from being offered to Americans or others.[206]

On a trip home during the summer of 1915, Reinsch told Wilson that "the only promise of safety for the future lies in attempting ... to develop every individual American interest in China quickly and with energy while there is yet time; to oppose at every point all attempts to establish an exclusive policy; and to have if possible a clear understanding with Great Britain and Russia as to means for averting the common danger."[207] A much greater urgency on the part of the administration with regard to economic matters ensued. U.S. bankers and businessmen were exhorted to become involved in China and to loan money to the government. And Taft era practices, that previously had been criticized, began again to be employed. Businessmen were offered help in the negotiation of contracts and the use of government cables for their communications.[208]

A significant increase in the U.S. economic role in China at first seemed likely. Vanderlip's new investment trust, the American International Corporation, was prompted to explore opportunities in East Asia. At the end of 1915, it agreed to take over an important conservancy project on the Huai River. And in spring 1916, in coordination with the Siems-Carey Railway and Canal Corporation, it obtained preliminary contracts for railway projects in three widely scattered regions of the country. Later that year, at the behest of the State Department, the Chicago Continental Trust and Savings Bank agreed to advance $5 million to the Chinese government and to consider a further loan of $25 million.

All these projects were soon in trouble, however. Lansing had hoped that the Europeans would drop their long-standing claims to investment spheres in the face of Tokyo's challenge. But France and Russia lodged strong objections to two of the railway schemes. Meanwhile, Japan objected to the Huai River conservancy. Despite the administration's efforts, these complications made the involved American businessmen increasingly uneasy.

The situation was then made worse by the collapse of political peace again in China during 1916. This came as a direct result of Yuan's efforts to restore the monarchy and imperial institutions. Reinsch had actually come to favor a return to constitutional monarchy as early as 1914. However, he wanted some of the political reforms of the late Qing era retained in the hope that these would cement the loyalties of provincial elites to Yuan's regime. He worried that a bid for absolute power would be destabilizing, and this proved to be the case. Yuan precipitated a wholesale rebellion against his rule, even among many of his own generals. And China was plunged into turmoil that persisted even after the would-be emperor's death by illness in the middle of the year. Confronted with a rise in disorder, as well as a likely decline in U.S. influence, and finding much more favorable prospects elsewhere at this time as well, American investors turned away from China.[209]

Frustrated by these setbacks, and angry at Japanese successes, Reinsch took increasingly bold steps on his own. After hearing of Tokyo's suggestion that it participate in the Huai River project, he proposed, in early 1917, that the two countries also cooperate in development schemes in southern Manchuria.[210] Opposed to any such invasion of its sphere, Japan turned Reinsch's idea aside. But the minister then looked to Washington for support. He wanted Japan to be forced to pay a price in terms of its policy toward the rest of China if it wished American acceptance of its claims in the north.

Reinsch also began, in February, to push for a Sino-American alliance. The occasion was the severing of relations between the U.S. and Germany. The Wilson administration called on other neutral nations to support its response to German submarine warfare. Reinsch used this as an opportunity to propose that China likewise break relations. He hoped in this way to get the government in Beijing to align itself firmly with Washington. He offered, in return, guarantees of U.S. political and economic support. Indeed, it was Reinsch's hope that this scheme would make it easier for Washington to involve itself politically and militarily in East Asia.[211]

The State Department, however, refused to support these initiatives, and Reinsch was, in the latter case, reprimanded for acting on his own. Both Lansing and Wilson worried that he would prompt countermoves that Washington might not be able to meet. And, indeed, Japan now stepped up its efforts to induce Chinese politicians to follow Tokyo's lead in international affairs.[212]

At the same time, coming as they did on the heels of two years of worsening Japanese-U.S. relations, Reinsch's initiatives also led Tokyo to hope that it could come to an understanding with Washington. Although it shared the goals of its predecessors, the Terauchi ministry that came to power in October 1916 was much more nervous about potential American opposition. This may, in part, have had to do with the recent passage by Congress of legislation providing for a great expansion in American capital ship construction, designed eventually to give the U.S. the capacity to fight major enemies in both the Atlantic and Pacific at the same time (see chapter 6). The new ministry also worried about American economic power—which was expanding so much more rapidly now as a byproduct of the war—and about Japan's dependence on U.S. trade. The use of economic leverage could, it was feared, seriously impede Japan's own development and its expansion onto the continent. If the differences between the two powers could be settled, on the other hand, it was thought Japanese entrepreneurs might be able to enlist the cooperation of American capital after the war. Japan wanted U.S. assurances about Shandong and about Manchuria. It also wanted Washington to concede to Japan political and strategic dominance in East Asia. In return, Tokyo was prepared to promise that it would not pursue an exclusive economic approach to China proper.[213]

In May 1917 Japan asked if it could send a special emissary to the U.S. for talks. Now at war, the administration saw its bargaining posture as anything but ideal. However, policy makers wanted if possible to restrain Japan, and they were also concerned about rumors that Tokyo might defect to the Central Powers. The way was thus cleared for parleys between Lansing and envoy Ishii Kikujiro.

A detailed discussion of those talks is beyond the purview of this study, but their outcome should be noted, for they produced a joint declaration in which the U.S. recognized "special interests" that Japan had in East Asia, while both powers reaffirmed a commitment to the open door and to China's independence and territorial integrity. Each side could read this "agreement" as it wished. However, from Washington's perspective, it deferred a confrontation while it also provided language that could constitute the basis for a challenge of Tokyo's policy at a later date.[214]

At the same time, the administration continued its shift back toward dollar diplomacy and the cooperative approach. Discussions were undertaken in 1917 to assemble another American Group and to make this part of a reconstituted international consortium.[215]

Along with South America, East Asia was a region where American leaders hoped to see the U.S. play a role of political and economic leadership in the twentieth century. The value they placed on China was reflected in the interest they displayed, from the 1890s on, in trying to uphold and stabilize the "traditional" economic and political framework that had been established there under England's influence roughly fifty years before. Only in Manchuria were policy makers at times tempted to abandon, or compromise, on that goal. If the open door, better yet the territorial integrity of China, could be maintained, their assumption was that the U.S.—because of geography and economic power—would eventually replace Britain as the most important outside power in that part of the world.

The open door appeared to be under considerable pressure, throughout this era, both because of the "greed" of some other powers and because of Chinese "irresponsibility," which, policy makers worried, constituted a standing invitation to great power intervention in, and conflict over, the vast country. The U.S. was not in a position to put itself forward as the

only power to play a role in the region (or as yet to use force against vio-
lators of the framework it wanted even in combination with other powers).
Instead, what policy makers sought to do was to encourage a unified great
power approach. They argued that all powers shared an interest in avoiding
conflict and in doing business in China on the basis of the existing framework. Once American resources became available, American leaders also
tried to employ financial arguments and incentives as a means of solidify-
ing such a "community of interests" and of taking that framework "out of
politics." The hope was that enough powers would be attracted to this
approach to at least isolate and intimidate those who were not.

Simultaneously, U.S. policy was aimed at trying to promote a strong
and cooperative Chinese government, a government that could and would
"behave." For most of this period, Washington sought to enlist the other
powers in this effort, and accomplishment of this goal was held up as one
potential benefit of "harmonious action." The Wilson administration initially thought that the revolution of 1911–12 had brought into being a much
stronger, more stable and "responsible" China. And that indeed was one
reason why it decided to break with the cooperative approach. Continued
instability and weakness likewise was one of the reasons the administration
decided to return to that approach in 1917.

Chapter 5

The Home Continent: Canada and Mexico

As the United States sought to position itself for "wealth and greatness" in more distant areas, it also exhibited greater interest in its North American neighbors, Canada and Mexico. This era witnessed unprecedented efforts by Washington both to influence the behavior of those states and to try to ensure that their economies continued to develop as part of what might best be described as an extension of the U.S. home base in the world.

Canada and the U.S. had quarreled repeatedly over land and resources throughout the nineteenth century, and such disputes continued to dominate the two countries' relations at the very beginning of this period. The most important was a controversy that had erupted in the 1890s over the boundary of Alaska. Convinced that Ottawa only dared challenge the U.S. over such questions because of its connection to London, American leaders were determined to give both governments a lesson. They wanted not merely to defend what they saw as a rightful claim, but also to use the dispute to establish guidelines for the future conduct of Britain and Canada in North America. Responding vigorously, Washington sought to show London that a drastic curtailment of its role would be the price of the international rapprochement with the U.S. that it was trying to achieve. It also sought to force Ottawa to accept a more subordinate position.

After the issue had been settled on their terms, policy makers adopted a new attitude toward Canada. Drawing on methods of conflict adjustment in use at home, they worked to bring greater regularity to the settlement of Canadian-U.S. issues, and, employing many of the techniques of Pan-Americanism, they tried to get this British dominion now to line up behind U.S. global policy. The goal was to stabilize relations between the countries and to integrate Canada into a framework of American continental leadership.

Eventually Washington also sought a comprehensive new trade agreement with Canada. Alongside their determination to ensure strategic predominance in North America and their aspiration to rally, if possible, both their neighbors behind American diplomacy, policy makers came during the first decade of the century to place a high value on the economic relations that had been growing up between the U.S., Canada, and Mexico. Over the course of the late nineteenth and early twentieth centuries, Canada and (to a still greater extent) Mexico had come to occupy roles relative to the urban-industrial U.S. not unlike that of the trans-Mississippi American West.[1] Their economies had to a great degree been developing as extensions of the U.S. resource base for food and raw materials. In 1910–11, the Taft administration sought through a reciprocity pact to secure the continuation of this pattern with Canada—one that it saw as of utility to the position of the U.S. in the larger twentieth-century world.

By contrast with Canadian relations, U.S.-Mexican relations had never been more harmonious than they were at the outset of this period. In foreign areas of interest to them, American leaders wanted local governments that would accept U.S. leadership, that would behave according to the ground rules Washington deemed appropriate, and that would be strong enough to ensure that their populations behaved in an orderly way. The Canadian government had failed this test by virtue of the fact that, as Washington saw it, it had repeatedly acted in an insolent fashion. Canadians were viewed as unsophisticated upstarts who did not understand their proper place. Again and again Ottawa had tried to claim a role on the continent beyond that to which it was entitled (the dominion's alleged backwardness and immaturity being explained, it appears, by recourse to the idea that it was a ward of the mighty British Empire and had never had to rise to the challenges that had strengthened the American character). Mexico, meanwhile, worked with the U.S. in international, and especially hemispheric, affairs. While Ottawa had pursued close economic, as well as political, ties with Britain, Mexico City had thrown its doors open to U.S. trade as well as investment. And Porfirio Díaz, the country's dictator, had ensured order amidst a population deemed by Washington to be composed of people overwhelmingly weak and unstable. He was proclaimed "the greatest statesman now living" by TR in 1908.[2]

Precisely because of these relations, and because of the enormous emphasis placed on Díaz, American policy makers wanted to give him their support when unrest developed in Mexico during the first decade of the twentieth century. And they became increasingly apprehensive as the strongman began to show signs of age. When revolution finally swept Díaz from power, Washington's overriding objective came to be to promote the order it wanted in Mexico under new auspices. At the same time, policy makers quickly grasped that there were significant limits on what they could do. Given the size of Mexico, and the nature of the explosion that had been set off there, interventions of the sort that had taken place elsewhere in upper Latin America seemed out of the question.

The Taft administration worked to uphold Díaz's successor, Francisco Madero, simultaneously pressuring him to create the conditions that the U.S. wanted. However, its ambassador to Mexico eventually facilitated a seizure of power by General Victoriano Huerta. Out of the mistaken belief that Huerta held the key to a restoration of stability, European governments moved to recognize him. But the incoming U.S. president, Wilson, held back.

His principal fear was that recognition of the general would undermine U.S. efforts to ensure order throughout the Caribbean. Wilson urged authorities in Mexico City to take steps that would enable him to declare that Mexico had returned to orderly, constitutional processes. The president, however, overestimated the ease with which he could bring this about. Resistance on Huerta's part led to a personalized test of strength between the two leaders. It sent Wilson in search of European powers on whom he could blame the defiance and it led him to interfere further in Mexican affairs.

But Huerta's eventual removal in late 1914 by no means spelled an end to U.S. concern. Only involvement in the European war, two and one-half years later, brought about a pause in its campaign to secure the conditions that it wanted.

In Canada and Mexico, the challenges that worried the U.S. in this period came mostly from within those countries themselves. U.S. leaders pitted themselves against the recent thrust of Canadian political and economic nationalism (albeit a nationalism compelled to draw strength from Canada's connection to England). To the south, they faced social and political unrest (caused at least partly by the new economic relationship that had begun to form between the U.S. and Mexico since the late nineteenth century).

Policy makers were looking at both countries in a new way in this era, however, to a great extent because of the importance it was felt they bore to the U.S. role in the world. They were seen as having special political and strategic value to the U.S. as it set out to compete economically and politically with other great powers. They were seen as valuable from the standpoint of the effect they, and developments in them, might have on events elsewhere (Latin America in Mexico's case, the British Empire in Canada's). And their nearby economies offered bountiful supplies of the resources for which many rival powers were combing the globe.

Although the Venezuela boundary confrontation arose over issues in Latin America, it also had an impact on Canada and, of even more importance, on the general posture of Britain toward the U.S. Not lost on the dominion in 1895–96 was the fact that it would be an obvious target if war did come. Twice before, in 1775 and 1812, invasions of Canada had arisen out of British-American disputes. Public statements by U.S. military figures in late 1895 confirmed that the conquest of Canada would again be an American priority. Moreover, General Nelson A. Miles offered that this time, if war did come, there was no doubt but that the U.S. would succeed. Ottawa, in response, engaged in a flurry of military preparation.[3]

Undoubtedly more long lasting was the impression left by the tone of Olney's note. His statement that the U.S. was "practically sovereign on this

Canada, c. 1912.

continent" was guaranteed to revive traditional Canadian fears of the economic and political power of the republic to the south. The dominion's development in the nineteenth century, especially in the realm of economic policy, was in many ways patterned after that of the more populous and industrially advanced U.S. Yet fear and rejection of American domination had helped define Canadian nationalism from its very inception. Olney's suggestion that "any permanent political union between an European and American state" was both "unnatural and inexpedient" actually reinforced the belief in Ottawa that the development of Canadian nationhood still had to be accompanied by close ties with England.[4]

In Ottawa the crisis reignited attitudes of alarm but also of defiance. It had a somewhat different impact in London. Policy makers there were eager to improve relations with Washington and to reduce the possibility of conflict. They recoiled at the thought of war with the U.S., both because of the difficulties that would present and because such a conflict would jeopardize Britain's ability to keep in check its rivals in Europe. The global foreign policy posture of the U.S. also seemed less at odds with that of Britain than did that of continental powers like Russia and France.[5]

Not only did London become more conciliatory over British Guiana, Ambassador Pauncefote was instructed to work on an arbitration treaty between the two powers. When a limited pact was concluded at the end of 1896, Pauncefote exclaimed that it would "take the wind out of the sails of the [American] Jingoes ... the Eagle will have to screech at other Powers, and let the British Lion nurse his tail." He spoke too soon, however, because in spite of the support it received from both Cleveland and McKinley, the treaty failed of ratification in the Senate the next spring.[6]

During the Far Eastern crisis of the following year, London suggested that the two powers might work together to uphold their common interest in the open door. Joseph Chamberlain, the colonial secretary, went so far as to suggest that Britain and the U.S. could enforce the peace all over the world. London maintained a neutrality that tilted noticeably in Washington's direction during the Spanish-American War. And this finally led to an agreement on the part of London and Washington to try to remove the sources of controversy outstanding between them. A Joint High Commission, which convened in August 1898, was organized for this purpose.[7]

Virtually all these issues had actually arisen out of disputes between the U.S. and Canada, however, and their resolution had to be accomplished in the face of the tensions that continued to plague those relations. These transcended the specific questions at stake, and were rooted in the emotions that had been reawakened by Olney's note and in Washington's long-standing resentment of what it saw as Ottawa's impudent behavior. Three questions, in particular, awaited attention. They had to do with pelagic (or ocean) sealing by British Columbians in the Bering Sea, with rights for American fishermen in the Canadian Maritimes, and with the boundary between Canada and Alaska. Of these, the third issue was by far the most difficult and dangerous.[8]

What should be the line demarcating Canadian from U.S. sovereignty along the landward side of the Alaska panhandle? That was the question confronting the commission.[9] Washington took the position that in 1867 it had acquired the entire coastline in this region. On the basis of an 1825 treaty between England and Russia (from whom Alaska had been purchased), however, Canadian officials argued that some of the longer fjords in the area extended into territory that belonged to British Columbia.

The issue had suddenly assumed pressing importance for Ottawa when in 1896–97 gold was discovered in the Canadian Yukon. Although prospectors and others flooded into the region, it had quickly become clear that most of the commerce they generated was going to be controlled by the U.S. Such would not be the case if Canada had the coastal access that it claimed.

In particular, Ottawa asserted that the headwaters of the Lynn Canal, which was the best gateway to the lower Yukon, were really in Canada. Two settlements at its northern end, Dyea and Skagway, had been occupied by Americans for some time. Canada was prepared to concede these as long as it was allowed to develop a port of its own. It hoped that the U.S. would grant control over a corridor connecting British Columbia to the Lynn Canal at Pyramid Harbor.

The U.S. commissioners refused to consider the question of sovereignty. In what they saw as a conciliatory move, they did offer Canada transshipment rights and a port facility in the Pyramid Harbor region. This concession was subsequently withdrawn, however, after news of it leaked to the press and protests from West Coast statehouses and Pacific Northwest shipping companies bombarded Washington.

Diplomacy then appeared at an impasse. For British and Canadian commissioners there seemed no alternative but arbitration. But American negotiators would agree only to submission of the dispute to another panel composed of three members from each side. They took this position less because they lacked confidence in the American legal case, which they in fact felt was strong, than because the McKinley administration did not want to take any steps that might risk a loss of valuable territory. The State Department worried, in particular, that an arbitral tribunal might resolve the matter through compromise.

The problem with this stance was that it appeared a direct contradiction of the position that the U.S. had taken just three years earlier over the boundary between British Guiana and Venezuela. Hay fully recognized this. As he later told Whitelaw Reid, "After we had put forth our entire force and compelled—there is no other word for it—England to accept arbitration in the Venezuela matter, we cannot feel entirely easy in refusing an arbitration in this.... And yet if we went into arbitration on the matter, although our claim is as clear as the sun in Heaven, we know enough of arbitrations to foresee the fatal tendency of all arbitrators to compromise."[10]

Greatly disappointed, the British delegate, Lord Herschell, wrote Salisbury that it would be useless to try to find agreement on the other issues before the commission "if we leave unsettled the question which is most likely to give rise to conflict and which, moreover, is capable of adjustment by methods well recognized among friendly Powers."[11] The Canadians reacted even more angrily. By 1899, this issue had come to occupy not only great real but also great symbolic importance for Canadian political leaders. As they saw it, the Dominion had made most of the concessions over the years with regard to issues like sealing and the fisheries. Washington meanwhile had maintained an unneighborly attitude with regard to trade between the two countries. And with regard to territory, particularly on the Pacific coast, it had repeatedly tried to box Canada in.[12] Canada's national dignity and long-term interests—especially in view of Washington's new international assertiveness—as well as its interests in the Yukon, seemed to compel a stand.

"There is a question of dignity involved," asserted Prime Minister Wilfrid Laurier, himself one of the delegates. The Americans were "certainly in the wrong" in the position they were adopting and he was not going to be "bulldozed" by them. It was, moreover, "incumbent upon us to refuse to negotiate on anything else."[13] Announcing that what they would do on the other questions would be affected by the outcome of this dispute, the Canadian delegates finally insisted on a suspension of all the Joint High Commission's negotiations. Ottawa also elicited from Britain a promise that it would not go forward with revision of the Clayton-Bulwer Treaty relating to a Central American canal until the Alaska boundary had been settled.

Canada's leaders now thought that the U.S. was going to have to come to them. But the British government was eager not to see its chances of improved relations destroyed. It continued to work throughout 1899 for a solution to the boundary problem. And when Ottawa refused to endorse its proposals London became annoyed.[14]

Increasingly frustrated, London also began to entertain doubts about the strength of Canada's case. An argument could be made "based on letter of Treaty of 1825," but the Colonial Office worried that this was likely to be undercut by the subsequent history of events.[15] Canada could not be assured of a victory, it asserted, even if an arbitration was achieved, most importantly because it had for too long tacitly acquiesced in the U.S. claims.

In the fall, London agreed to a modus vivendi on the boundary that yielded no significant points to Canada. Then, early in 1900, as has been seen it signed with the U.S. the first Hay-Pauncefote Treaty. Ottawa lost whatever leverage it had had. Not least because of the political fervor that the controversy had stirred up, however, it was still reluctant to alter its stance.[16] Only in 1902 did the Canadian government's attitude change. During meetings with Lansdowne that summer in England, Laurier finally gave his assent to an even-numbered tribunal (and to assurances being given over Dyea and Skagway).[17]

U.S. leaders meanwhile had become increasingly more irritated with Ottawa since the demise of the commission. To Hay, Canada was a "'spoiled child' ... unsetting the American apple cart."[18] Roosevelt had never taken the dominion seriously. "The American ... regards the Canadian with the good-natured condescension always felt by the free man for the man who is not free," he commented in 1896.[19] For him, as for many late nineteenth century U.S. leaders, the great rub was the relationship with England.[20] Like both Hay and Root, TR had lent his name in 1892 to the short-lived Continental Union League, an annexationist organization that had called on the "Canadian people to cast in their lot with their continent."[21] As TR and others saw it, it was this English relationship that had both enabled and encouraged the dominion to challenge the U.S. "I entirely agree with you," he wrote James Harrison Wilson in mid-1899, "that it would be the greatest possible good fortune if we could hand the Philippines over to England, if she would leave this continent. The relations between Canada and England always tend to bring on friction between us and both of them."[22]

And now things had been allowed to go too far. For, as Roosevelt saw it, the Alaska boundary matter actually constituted a conscious bid on Ottawa's part to steal from the U.S. a part of its territory. The nation's integrity was at stake, as was its international credibility as a great power. This view led the new president at first to reject even the idea of an even-numbered tribunal as a means of resolving the controversy. He finally relented after Hay persuaded him that the U.S. could be assured against losing under such a formula and when it became clear that his stance could undermine Washington's efforts to have the European powers arbitrate their differences with Venezuela's Castro. Thus the way was cleared for signature of the Hay-Herbert Treaty in January 1903.[23] Under its provisions, Washington agreed to submit the boundary to a tribunal composed of "six impartial jurists of repute," three to be selected by each side.[24]

Partly for domestic political reasons, specifically to get the treaty through the Senate, Roosevelt decided to be much less subtle than Hay had intended in his selection of the American judges. For the three "impartial jurists of repute" he named two U.S. senators, Henry Cabot Lodge, of Massachusetts, and George Turner, of Washington, both of whom had already publicly criticized Canada's claims, and Elihu Root, a member of his own administration. These appointments elicited astonishment and outrage in Ottawa. They also caused disappointment in London. Nevertheless the Foreign Office pleaded that Britain could not risk the great ill will likely to be aroused if it made a fuss, and it moved to exchange ratifications with Washington even before hearing back from Canada.[25]

Nor was TR content to ensure that the U.S. could not lose. Convinced that Ottawa's claims were fabricated, and that the tribunal ought to be viewed merely as a mechanism to allow the British and Canadian governments to save face, he intended to get "ugly" if the tribunal did anything other than return an award favoring Washington. Specifically, Hay, Root, U.S. ambassador to England Joseph Hodges Choate, and Roosevelt all agreed at a White House meeting in mid-1903 that the U.S. should send troops to the region and simply enforce its own position in such an eventuality.[26]

TR subsequently made sure that his attitude became known in England. Through intermediaries he informed British leaders that an award by the tribunal in basic accord with U.S. claims constituted the "last chance" for an amicable settlement of the boundary matter. If such were not forthcoming, Washington would "run the line" as it saw it. That would be "unpleasant for us," Roosevelt commented, but "it will be a thousandfold more unpleasant for them."[27]

TR and other officials justified this politicking on the grounds that it was necessary to prevent London from being intimidated by the Canadians ("[t]hat collection of bumptious provincials," Lodge called them).[28] In fact, Washington brought far more pressure to bear on London than the Canadians were in a position to do. Alarmed at the prospect of a break with the U.S., and of embarrassment at its hands, Prime Minister Arthur Balfour and Lansdowne both interceded—as TR intended they should—with Lord Alverstone, the one English judge on the panel. He had, it appears, already decided for Washington on the central issue of control over the headwaters of the Lynn Canal. Eventually, however, Alverstone also changed his position as to how far south American territory extended. Outvoted four to two on these issues, the Canadian judges refused even to sign the award. The U.S. was able to claim a major victory, while north of the border, popular and political upset at the dominion's defeat wound up being focused to a great extent on England.[29]

As historian Norman Penlington has written, TR was able to "make Britain the instrument of Canada's humiliation."[30] Roosevelt nevertheless was also pursuing a broader objective, namely to confront London with the implications of what any future such impertinence—as Washington defined it—on Ottawa's part would be.

London took his point. Moreover, during the next three years it also relinquished any significant strategic presence in the Americas. This was motivated by a number of considerations. British leaders believed that they had to prioritize their commitments and concentrate the empire's strength at its center (see Chapter 6). They also hoped that U.S. policy would be consonant with their basic interests in the Western Hemisphere. But they were impelled as well by a growing appreciation of U.S. power. By the late 1800s, Britain had already come to view a successful war against America as problematic. Given the rise of the U.S. Navy, it now saw such a war as all but impossible. A policy of friendship appeared imperative, which in turn added weight to the idea of a reduction in London's posture.[31]

Beginning in 1904, London undertook a withdrawal of its troops from Barbados, Trinidad, Jamaica, St. Lucia, and Bermuda, and a dramatic reduction of its naval presence in that part of the world. A similar withdrawal took place from Canada. Ottawa was encouraged to assume responsibility for the garrisoning of Halifax and Esquimalt; however, neither facility continued to be an important base for the British navy.[32] There was less point to such bases given Britain's loss of regional naval superiority, but a lower profile also seemed more likely to ensure peace with Canada's neighbor.

These ideas were spelled out in great detail in an Admiralty memorandum of February 1905 (at a time when this perspective had already become the reigning one within the British cabinet).[33] Asked to comment on possible measures to bolster the defenses of Canada, the Admiralty stressed its belief that a war with the U.S. was "the greatest evil which could befall the British Empire in its foreign relations." America, it held, could

employ every ship she possesses in the Western Atlantic, but the conditions under which England could employ her whole naval force in such a distant locality are hardly conceivable. And, as though disparity were not enough, the time is now approaching when, by the completion of the Isthmian Canal, the United States will possess the enormous advantage of moving her war-ships at will from her Pacific to her Atlantic coasts in war by a route some 10,000 miles shorter than that which would be open to the vessels of our own country.

The implications for Canada, the document held, were that it ought to be compelled to rely principally on its own resources in preparing "for defence against invasions by the United States." This was because "any action on the part of the Mother Country is conditional upon British sea supremacy in the Western Atlantic, which cannot, even now, under all circumstances, be guaranteed in such a war." But it was also because it was in Britain's interest to avoid any strategic role there which might upset the Americans and because forcing Canada to rely only "upon her own resources" would "tend to inculcate in her statesmen a wholesome caution." Britain would concede the kind of supremacy after which Roosevelt had quested.

With the boundary matter decided, the way in theory lay open for Canada, Britain, and the U.S. to take up the other questions that had been before the Joint High Commission. In practice, however, a resumption of such talks had to wait until Ottawa had digested and adjusted to its defeat. Laurier finally signaled a willingness to proceed in 1906, and over the next several years negotiators sought to address not merely all pending issues, but "all the questions that are likely to arise between the United States and Canada."[34] London was anxious to promote this process, and crucial roles in it were played by James Bryce, its ambassador to the U.S., and the British governor general in Canada, the fourth Earl Grey.[35] But Washington was also eager to see progress, not least because it believed that its relations with Canada might now be put on a different basis. Having helped to create more distance between London and its dominion, policy makers were eager to promote a diplomatic and economic leadership over Canada much along the lines of what they were trying to promote throughout the rest of the Western Hemisphere. Root's Canadian diplomacy, for this reason, warrants comparison to his contemporaneous pursuit of Pan-Americanism.

Especially noteworthy are the secretary's efforts in this period to cultivate Canadian leaders and opinion. The highlight was a trip north early in 1907 that, at least in the rhetoric employed, greatly resembled Root's just finished visit to South America.[36] He delivered his most important address at a banquet of the Canadian Club of Ottawa on January 22. Here, as he had in Latin America, Root focused on themes emphasizing shared heritage, experience, and values. Before an audience composed of many of Canada's most prominent business and political leaders, he expressed admiration for the dominion's accomplishments, something that U.S. leaders had generally been loath to do in the past. Root also pledged American respect for its neighbor.[37]

Root was even looking forward to Canada's eventual participation in the Pan-American system. Construction began on the building to house the Bureau of American Republics in Washington in the spring of 1908. At Root's initiative, Canada's coat of arms was included with those of the other American states in the patio of the building. As his biographer notes, he likewise gave orders that a bronze frieze in the meeting room of the Governing Board "include a panel depicting Champlain's negotiations with the Indians." A Board Room chair with Canada's name and coat of arms carved on it was contracted for as well.[38]

Laurier, however, recognized that both Washington and London wanted to repair relations with Ottawa, and he was determined to drive as hard a bargain as he could. For this reason, Bryce urged Canada and the U.S. to try to avoid getting bogged down over the aged issues of sealing and the Atlantic fisheries. He was successful in getting less difficult matters that had been on the commission's agenda, as well as new problems that had arisen since 1898, taken up first.[39]

At the same time, precisely because Canadian-U.S. relations had traditionally been affected so much by domestic political considerations, Root and Laurier sought solutions that would take those relations "out of politics." "What was significant about the twentieth-century Canadian-American approach to the outstanding points of contention," write historians John Herd Thompson and Stephen J. Randall, "was the effort to institutionalize and depoliticize the mechanisms of conflict resolution.... This preference to avoid diplomatic disputes that might become hotly debated public issues paralleled the emergence of a more bureaucratic and 'scientific' approach to conflict management during the years of progressive reform." It was thus not surprising, they argue, that Washington and Ottawa created in this period a number of commissions, of "bilateral bureaucratic institutions," to deal with what were likely in many cases to be ongoing common problems.[40]

Treaties to establish two such institutions were signed in April 1908. An inland fisheries agreement provided for the creation of a mixed Canadian-American commission that was to regulate the fisheries in fourteen bodies of water divided by the boundary between the two countries.[41] Simultaneously, an International Boundary Commission was established to address continuing questions about the precise location of the Canadian-American border.[42] The following January, the Boundary Waters Treaty was concluded. It provided for the creation of an International Joint Commission, whose broad charge was to render advice about all questions affecting the usage and management of the rivers and lakes shared by the two countries. Issues having to do with power generation, dams, irrigation, water levels, and pollution were all supposed to be within its purview.[43]

The Atlantic fisheries controversy, meanwhile, had to be settled by arbitration. A special agreement referring that issue to The Hague was finally concluded at the beginning of the Taft administration in 1909, and hearings took place the following summer, with Root, now a U.S. senator, representing the U.S. Outmaneuvering a disunited legal team from Canada, Newfoundland, and England, he secured a ruling that won key points for American fisherman even as it appeared to preserve British North American amour propre.[44] The pelagic sealing issue was then settled in 1911, when terms were worked out to compensate Canadians for abandoning that practice. Ottawa subsequently agreed to participate, along with the U.S., in a conference with Russia and Japan aimed at arresting the depletion of the Bearing Sea herds.[45]

By the end of his term in office, Root had still not achieved the kind of cordiality in relations that he hoped for. Indeed the degree to which this had not taken place seems to have engendered in him considerable frustration. In mid-1908, for instance, the normally unflappable secretary blew up at a Canadian envoy in terms reminiscent of American complaints during the Alaska boundary dispute. As the emissary reported to Laurier,

He broke out and talked for fifteen minutes about the unfriendly attitude that had been displayed by Canadians generally towards the United States for many years. . . . He said that one party seemed to vie with the other in saying nasty things and all seemed to imply that the American people had always overreached them heretofore and were lying in wait to do so again.

He spoke about the freedom with which people, who had not resumed [sic] "responsibilities" of a nation, were able to talk. He said that it was unbearable; denied that we had been put to any unfair advantage by the Alaska award.[46]

Along with Bryce and numerous officials from Ottawa, Root had nonetheless largely accomplished a "cleaning of the slate" of the outstanding issues between the two countries, and this, as he saw it, was a vital precondition for achievement of long-term U.S. objectives with regard to both Britain and Canada.

One of those goals was to enlist Canada behind American foreign policy. Roosevelt and Root were in fact already trying to exercise such influence in 1907 and 1908 in connection with the crisis over Japanese immigration.[47] Indeed, the administration suggested in this period that British dominions bordering the Pacific ought in the future look to the U.S. as their proper protector should their own immigration policies lead to conflict with Japan. Washington also sought to use the Canadians as a means of pushing Britain into an anti-Japanese coalition.

Root had raised the issue of immigration with Ottawa officials as early as his trip to Canada in January 1907.[48] Then, later that year, Vancouver was the scene of violent anti-Japanese rioting, and Canada began to pursue an immigration restriction agreement of its own with Tokyo. The administration saw in these developments an opening whereby it might successfully influence British foreign policy. Eager to get Japan to agree to much tighter restrictions than had yet been introduced, TR and Root hoped that a common Anglo-American front could be created around the immigration issue and that London would bring pressure on its Far Eastern ally.

Rather than approach England on his own, Roosevelt calculated that his objective stood a better chance of success if he could work through Canada. In January 1908, the president arranged for William Lyon Mackenzie King, then Ottawa's deputy minister of labor and immigration, to visit him in Washington. TR surprised his guest by suggesting that King convey Washington's concerns and hopes to officials in London. King also met with Root who told him that the U.S. had gone "too far in the number of foreigners" it had permitted to enter. Such a "silent invasion" he asserted, was "as effective as that of the Huns and Goths in the days of the Roman Empire."[49]

King subsequently apprised both Laurier and Bryce of the nature of his meetings, and on his next visit the British ambassador joined in the talks. Apparently in an effort to create doubt in London, however, TR wrote a well-connected English friend that the discussions had been begun at the initiative of Canada. He wrote to the Canadian prime minister in a similar vein. Dubbing this "a smart Yankee trick," Laurier nevertheless dispatched King to England.[50] TR simultaneously told a visiting delegation of Canadian legislators that the Great White Fleet's trip to the Pacific was in the interest not only of the U.S., but of western Canada and even Australia. The Monroe Doctrine, he suggested, applied to these areas as well.[51]

In London, the foreign secretary turned aside Roosevelt's proposals. He did not want to jeopardize the Anglo-Japanese alliance. His advisors in the Foreign Office also opined that the president was "playing a very dangerous game," and that it was fortunate he had "such cool-headed people as the Japanese to deal with." These were judgments quite at odds with those then prevailing in Washington. Grey promised King that Canada could count on London should there ever be a lack of cooperation on Tokyo's part with regard to immigration.[52]

The Taft administration, as has been seen, presided over many of the latter phases of the slate-cleaning process undertaken by Root. It also retained Root's emphasis on trying to improve the U.S. image north of the border. This conditioned Washington's response when in 1909 a major political storm erupted in Canada over the U.S. naval posture on the Great Lakes.

This portion of the Canadian-American frontier had witnessed significant fighting between British and American forces during the War of 1812. It had then, for all practical purposes, been demilitarized under the Rush-Bagot Agreement of 1817. By this understanding, both sides were to maintain no more than four small armed vessels throughout the Lake Ontario, Upper Lakes, and Lake Champlain region. During the opening years of the twentieth century, however, the increasingly sea power-conscious U.S. began regularly to exceed that limit. A growing number of vessels, larger and larger in size, were assigned as training ships to state naval militias throughout the region. Washington asked permission and temporarily disarmed its ships each time one traveled between the Atlantic and the Great Lakes by means of the St. Lawrence River and the Canadian canal system. But, as historian Alvin Gluek notes, in the force levels it now began to maintain on the lakes, the U.S. was carrying out an "invisible revision" of the Rush-Bagot Agreement.

Officials in London advised Ottawa that there was nothing to be gained by raising questions about this, since, if offended, the U.S. might simply renounce the accord—which it had the right to do on six months notice— and then do as it wished. After the formidable gunboat *Nashville* was transferred to duty on the lakes in 1909, however, the Laurier government no longer could avoid the issue. Wide notice was taken of the ship's passage, after which it became the subject of a considerable furor in the Canadian press and of hostile questioning by the Conservative opposition. Recognizing that any other course would only inflame the debate, the Taft administration finally informed Bryce that the U.S. would henceforth be more careful to adhere to the accord.[53]

By far the boldest effort of Washington to draw Canada closer came with its pursuit of commercial reciprocity with that country in 1910–11. Historically, reciprocity between the two countries had mostly been a Canadian idea, one first broached in the era before the American Civil War. A reform coalition of agrarians and expectant capitalists had begun to clamor for a reduction of trade barriers in the 1840s. The governor-general at the time, Lord Elgin, then took up the proposal, because he was convinced that reciprocity with the U.S. would stimulate the Canadian economy, satisfy those interested in what seemed to be a growing American market for lumber, grain, fish, and coal, and isolate those interests that, in reaction to the end of British mercantilism, had called for annexation to the U.S.[54]

Elgin initially met with success.[55] An agreement (the Elgin-Marcy Treaty), which removed tariffs on a wide range of natural products, was concluded in 1854. It soon came under growing attack from within the U.S., however. Critics charged that its advantages were all on the Canadian side. In 1865, with protectionism rapidly becoming a hallmark of the new American order and resentment of all things British running high (a result of Civil War related friction), Washington gave notice of its intention to terminate the experiment.[56] Canadian governments continued to pursue reciprocity, at least in natural products, throughout the rest of the century. But such proposals evoked little enthusiasm to the south. American tariff walls were instead only raised and extended.[57]

Meanwhile, the new confederation adopted a policy of industrial protectionism itself. This trend became pronounced from the late 1870s onward, as high tariffs on industrial products became a central feature of the "National Policy." Under this, vigorous government activity was aimed at the creation of an economy that would operate on a west-east geographic axis. Industrial protection and state-subsidized railway and immigration programs were designed to harness expanding western agricultural, resource, and market opportunities to central Canadian industrialization.

Though this enormously expensive program was pushed relentlessly by the governments of Conservative John A. MacDonald, it seemed destined for years to bring forth little more than national bankruptcy as well as permanent antagonism toward the central government on the part of western agrarians, Maritimers, and some segments of the French community. With the end of the long depression in the late 1890s, however, and the subsequent boom in world demand for wheat and other natural products, the program's promises finally seemed borne out. Laurier's Liberals presided over this era of growth, dubbed the dawn of "Canada's Century." But they retained the essentials of the "National Policy." Amid this prosperity, and for political and nationalistic reasons as well, Ottawa refrained from any active pursuit of reciprocity, even restricted to natural products, with the U.S.[58]

When the issue was raised diplomatically again, it was as an American initiative. Taft thought that reciprocity might help his administration to recover politically from its failure to achieve a meaningful downward revision of tariff rates in 1909. However, there were broader policy objectives as well. In particular, he and Knox hoped that reciprocity would help to solidify the creation of an integrated economic order throughout North America, organized around the needs of the American industrial system.[59]

The first decade of the twentieth century witnessed dramatic developments in U.S. economic ties with its immediate neighbors. Exports of finished manufactured goods to immediately adjacent nations climbed impressively.[60] Still more important, these neighbors came to be highly prized as handy, secure, and plentiful sources of food and raw materials. Widely commented on by the end of the Roosevelt era was the fact that the economy was devouring an ever greater quantity of natural resources and agricultural products.[61] Indeed, one reason frequently cited for encouraging industrial exports was that the U.S. would have to pay for greatly enlarged imports of natural products (including food) in the future. The rising cost of many such commodities, it was alleged, was threatening to price American industry out of competition in the world market.[62]

To trade analysts in the U.S., these trends put the booming growth of agriculture in western Canada and the discovery of major new mineral deposits in the Laurentian Plateau during this period in a new light. In fact, the dramatic growth of U.S. export trade with adjacent countries after the turn of the century to a large extent followed a growth in investment in their natural products possibilities. During the Roosevelt years, investment in Canada nearly quadrupled, to a great extent oriented toward its mining and timber opportunities.[63] American imports of natural products from Canada, Mexico, Cuba, and Newfoundland were also growing rapidly.[64] The central purpose of achieving "commercial union"—as Taft termed it—with Canada was to try to solidify these trends with that country.[65]

By implication this objective pitted Taft against the "National Policy." Reciprocity also constituted a quite conscious effort to undermine forces in Canada and England that had been trying to turn the British Empire toward a policy of imperial preference and "Tariff Reform." In 1897 the Canadian government had begun to discriminate in favor of imports from Britain, the greatest purchaser of Canada's raw materials and alimentary products, and the dominion's primary creditor. This policy had by no means halted the growth of U.S. exports to Canada. It had, however, as Bureau of Trade Relations experts noted in 1908, limited the growth of the U.S. share of Canada's import market.[66]

Simultaneously, a movement had developed in Britain since 1903 in opposition to that nation's historic policy of free trade. Led initially by Joseph Chamberlain and lavishly funded by segments of heavy industry, these Tariff Reformers demanded protective duties on all but colonial imports into the United Kingdom. They wanted protection against competition from German, American and other imports in their home market, and they wanted to reward and encourage the kind of preferential treatment that British trade had recently been accorded by Canada and other self-governing colonies.[67] The cause was dealt a major setback when the Liberal party came to power in 1906. Nevertheless, members of the Taft administration still feared that Tariff Reform would eventually be victorious and lead to a substantial disruption of American trade with Canada and with the British Empire as a whole.[68]

Following his trip there in 1907, Root had remarked that Canada "has definitely entered upon a career of protection and of building up her own infant industries, in order to secure a market for her own food products. She is going to travel the same road that we have traveled."[69] During the Taft administration, however, State Department trade analysts were no longer so sure. They believed that changes in the U.S. tariff could create pressures that would both undermine the "National Policy" and thwart the program for imperial preference.

These ideas were first outlined for Taft in the summer of 1909. As the House and Senate, or Payne and Aldrich, tariff bills headed to conference committee, Charles M. Pepper, of the Bureau of Trade Relations, sought to draw the president's attention to the impact that each would have on America's economic relations with Canada. "The revision of the tariff in the United States," noted Pepper in a long memorandum, "reopens the whole question of commercial relations with the Dominion. Broadly stated, the House bill opens the door to Canada. The Senate bill does not." The House had placed hides, coal, iron ore, and wood pulp, among other products on the free list, and it had slashed existing rates on, among other products, lumber and newsprint. Pepper argued that the reductions of natural products rates contained in the House measure would not materially damage any substantial U.S. interests. On the other hand, they would definitely benefit those American businesses and individuals who consumed such products and encourage changes in Canadian commercial policy beneficial to the sale of American manufactures north of the border. Furthermore, some provisions (a duty drawback on Manitoba hard wheat, for instance) would put America in "a stronger position to compete in the European markets." "If the House provisions prevail," he continued,

important results are sure to follow. In the first place the British Imperial preferential system will prove non-workable. With the United States offering fair treatment to Canada, the Dominion will be unable to fix rates for England far enough above the reciprocal or intermediate tariff rates to hold more than a shred of its market for Great Britain. The program of the British protectionists when they come into power will be found impracticable.... Holding the trade of Canada is a very important feature in their program.... While in the end the system would break down this would not happen for several years and in the meantime there would be a serious dislocation of exports ... to England and to Canada and an inevitable loss to producers and exporters in the United States.

Finally, the Payne bill would not only result in the blocking of imperial preference and the dangers that it posed for American interaction with Canada and the rest of the empire. It would also go a long way toward destroying what had been "the positive policy of the Dominion government," namely, its encouragement of commercial channels running "from west to east and from east to west." In their place would be substituted a "natural movement of trade," running from "north to south and south to north."

Pepper understood that Laurier professed no desire for closer commercial relations with the U.S., a position clearly supported by Canadian

industry. There were, however, many reasons for believing that in the face
of U.S. concessions, "this position could not be maintained." Laurier was
anxious to stay in power and concessions might make it difficult for him
not to make a gesture that would please western farmers and Maritime
interests.

If the House provisions did not prevail, Pepper warned, "the Canadians
who want to keep as far away from the United States as possible are given
fresh encouragement." "The McKinley and the Dingley bills [of 1890 and
1897] put Canada fifty years away" from the U.S. The Senate bill, which did
not significantly alter traditional protectionism, "would put it another fifty
years away."[70]

Generally speaking, of course, the House provisions did not prevail.
Moreover, a maximum/minimum feature of the final Payne-Aldrich Act
soon threatened to bring on a trade war between Canada and the U.S.
Embodied in section two of the law, this provision established two rate
levels. The maximum (supposedly general) level constituted the already
high, legislatively designated, minimum rates, plus a full 25 percent of the
value of the articles imported. After March 31, 1910 it was to apply to the
trade of any nation that, as of that date, had not been specifically granted
the minimum level as a result of the president's determination that it did
not "unduly" discriminate against American trade.[71]

Drawn up with several European powers in mind, the provision actually
had its greatest impact on Canadian-American relations. Canada had established a triple schedule tariff system in 1907. This was composed of a high
general schedule, a British preferential schedule, and, between them, an
intermediate schedule that could be bargained for by other (non-Empire)
countries. The fact that France had bargained for and received these intermediate rates placed Canada, according to the provisions of the Payne-
Aldrich Act, on the list of those nations subject to the maximum U.S. tariff
level.[72]

Laurier and his finance minister, W. S. Fielding, argued that France had
bought the intermediate schedule of the Canadian tariff with concessions.
They adamantly insisted that granting this benefit for free to the U.S. would
amount to surrender of Canadian commercial policy autonomy.[73] But a
trade war was the last thing Taft wanted. Indeed, by early 1910 he had committed himself to a bid for reciprocity, and he desperately looked for a way
out. In March, as the deadline approached, he said that he "was very anxious not to have a war with Canada.... If they will only give me something
upon which I can hang a decision, I will be glad to seize an excuse and
make the announcement required."[74]

Laurier finally gave Taft his "excuse" in the form of a brief list of Canadian intermediate rates. He too wished not only to avoid commercial war
but also now to explore U.S. hints about reciprocity. Laurier apparently
believed that a limited agreement could reverse the Liberals' recent decline

in support and rally the sympathies of western agriculturalists who were eager for tariff revision.[75]

In May, Pepper and Mack Davis, also of the Bureau of Trade Relations, submitted a planning document to Knox that once again made the case for continental economic integration and discussed how this could be promoted via reciprocity. They argued that

Trade treaties of a reciprocal nature with a view to cheaper food products for consumers in the United States might be negotiated with Canada, Newfoundland and Mexico on the basis of geography, that is the special relations resulting from contiguous territory. The Dominion of Canada is by far the most important, but the other countries also come within the sphere of a North American commercial policy. Newfoundland in the commercial sense is a prolongation of the New England coast, while Mexico, as relates to trade and industry, is an extension of the southwest.

Canadian reciprocity was the dominant concern of the memorandum. It suggested that a pact revolve around free entry of wheat, livestock, and fish, reduced rates on other farm products as well as nonagricultural natural products, and an approach toward Canada's intermediate rates for manufactured goods and semi-raw materials. Important gains could be expected. Reciprocity along these lines would attain a guaranteed long-term source of natural products that would hold down prices in the U.S. market. It would block closer British-Canadian trade relations. It would set a precedent for still further reductions of duties in the future. Important industries, such as flour, would be helped to maintain their competitiveness on the world market. And an expanding volume of commerce along a north-south axis would be assured.

Pepper and Davis counted on American reduction of duties on natural products to ensure dominance of the Canadian market for U.S. manufacturers. Such reductions, not Canadian reductions on American goods, were seen as the key to the process that would guarantee the realization of continental integration. It was deemed necessary to push for substantial Canadian concessions on manufactured rates primarily to obtain sufficient political support for the agreement within the U.S.[76]

During the talks that took place the following fall and winter, Knox and other negotiators (of whom the most important was Pepper) vigorously pushed for Canadian extension of the French treaty rates to U.S. manufactures.[77] To obtain an agreement, however, they had to settle for much less. Laurier and Fielding always had been intent on limiting the agreement primarily to natural products, and they became much more rigid at the appearance of a powerful Canadian antireciprocity coalition backed by industrialists and by those interested in closer British ties.[78]

Nevertheless, the essential concerns of the administration were met in the agreement reached in January 1911. Its principal features were embodied in four separate schedule classifications. Schedule A contained a very long list of natural products that were to enter each country free of duty. Schedule B consisted primarily of a long list of processed food products and a number of manufactures on which identical rates would be levied by both countries. Finally, Schedules C and D included a brief number of American and Canadian rate classifications that were lower than the existing levels but not equal to those of the other nation.[79]

The agreement seemed destined to ensure the broad structural goals outlined earlier by the Bureau of Trade Relations, goals now those of the entire administration. In his message accompanying presentation of the accord to Congress, Taft spoke about reciprocity from the standpoint of one concerned about the competition among industrial states for assured sources of food and raw materials.[80]

The policy also had clear implications for costs of production in the U.S., for America's export trade, and, as the president made clear in a letter to TR, for Canadian development and American sales opportunities north of the border. Reciprocity, he wrote,

> might at first have a tendency to reduce the cost of food products somewhat; it would certainly make the reservoir much greater and prevent fluctuations. Meantime, the amount of Canadian products we would take would produce a current of business between western Canada and the United States that would make Canada only an adjunct of the United States. It would transfer all their important business to Chicago and New York, with their bank credits and everything else, and it would increase greatly the demand of Canada for our manufactures. I see this as an argument against reciprocity made in Canada, and I think it is a good one.[81]

Reciprocity also seemed destined to block imperial preference. Taft spoke of Canada and the U.S. as being at a "parting of the ways."[82] "The forces which are at work in England and in Canada to separate her by a Chinese wall from the United States and to make her part of an imperial commercial band, reaching from England around the world to England again, by a system of preferential tariffs, will derive an impetus from the rejection of this treaty," he told one audience.[83] Such statements enabled Canadian opponents of the treaty to do much damage. As Fielding later told Knox,

> the appeal of Mr. Taft to the American people to prevent the accomplishment of the policy of British preference throughout the Empire was a most unfortunate one. The Opposition leader, Mr. Borden, was quick to seize this point, and throughout the whole campaign he held up Mr. Taft's words and asked the people to accept them as proof that reciprocity was an anti-British movement and that the President aimed at the annexation of Canada. In this he received powerful help from the English Conservative press and the English leaders of what is called the "Tariff Reform" movement.[84]

Reciprocity faced opposition in the U.S. from staunch protectionists and from farm interests, especially along the border. Nevertheless, with substantial majorities in each chamber, Taft was able to get congressional endorsement for the agreement by mid-summer.[85] To his and Laurier's surprise, however, the policy had meanwhile engendered a huge controversy in Canada. Opposition was led by the Conservative Party and by central Canadian business interests fearful for the fate of the "National Policy."

Unable to curtail debate in parliament, Laurier finally called for a new election. This poll, held in September, was decided by a number of factors.[86] But trade relations with the U.S. was the dominant topic of discussion. And it seems clear that popular Canadian fears of the U.S., skillfully appealed to by the opposition, were critical in bringing about a Liberal defeat.[87] Reciprocity was consequently rejected.[88] Taft's effort to ensure through legislation the continued development of continental integration, and to bail himself out politically, had failed.

Signs of Canada's growing dependence on and deference to the U.S. nevertheless continued to proliferate after the defeat. The new prime minister, Robert Borden, was eager to explain that there was "no spirit of unfriendliness or hostility" to the U.S. meant by his campaign.[89] His finance minister hastened off south to reassure Wall Street about Canada's receptivity to American investment. Laurier had been holding back, but, anxious to patch things up, Borden moved to give final approval to the fisheries settlement.[90]

Taking cognizance of the Anglo-American rapprochement, but also of the growing influence of the U.S., Borden strove in subsequent years to carve out a "mediating role" for Ottawa between London and Washington. But neither power responded to the idea.[91] Passage of the Underwood Tariff, meanwhile, meant that during the Wilson era wheat and many other food products, as well as lumber, coal, and additional raw materials, were admitted to the U.S. duty free.[92] Before the World War more than four hundred American enterprises were already doing business in Canada. As historians J. L. Granatstein and Norman Hillmer have noted, the goal of developing "an interlocking North American economic system" advanced "even without reciprocity."[93]

Participation in the war, from August 1914, prompted an upsurge of imperial sentiment throughout much of Canadian society, as well as a degree of resentment of the U.S. for, until 1917, its nonbelligerency.[94] At the same time, however, the war, by the deep blow that it registered to the British economy, also helped to ensure the long-term economic and political reorientation of the dominion.

In the early twentieth century, Mexico meanwhile was, as Pepper and Mack put it, increasingly coming to be viewed by American political and business leaders as an economic "extension of the [U.S.] southwest."[95] Boasted banker James Speyer to the German minister to Mexico in 1904: "In the United States there is a pervasive feeling that Mexico is no longer anything but a dependency of the American economy, in the same way

Mexico, c. 1910.

Legend:
- National Capital
- City or town
- International Boundary
- State (estado) Boundary
- Railways

Labels on map:
CALIFORNIA
ARIZONA
NEW MEXICO
TEXAS
UNITED STATES
Columbus
El Paso
Ciudad Juárez
Carrizal
Parral
Rellano
San Pedro
Torreón
Aguascalientes
León
Celaya
Mexico City
Tampico
Veracruz
Gulf of Mexico
Bahía de Campeche
Yucatán Peninsula
BRITISH HONDURAS
GUATEMALA
HONDURAS
EL SALVADOR
Golfo de Tehuantepec
Sierra Madre Occidental
Golfo de California
Baja California
North Pacific Ocean

that the entire area from the Mexican border to the Panama Canal is seen as part of North America."[96]

From the late nineteenth century onward, and with an accelerating momentum from the late 1890s, American business interests had poured across the border. And here, too, natural products were the most important draw. Investment was concentrated in extractive enterprises and in railways designed to transport materials north. The overall stake in the country was approximately a billion dollars by 1910. Three quarters of Mexico's pivotal mining and smelting industry and half of its new, but rapidly growing oil industry was American owned. American investment outstripped that of all other foreign countries, and the overwhelming bulk of Mexico's trade had also come to be with its northern neighbor.[97]

Porfirio Díaz had facilitated these developments. After consolidating power in the late 1870s and 1880s, he had gone to great lengths to create a climate conducive to foreign investment. New tariff, rail, mining, and labor policies had been implemented. Order and stability became hallmarks of his reign. On the basis of these achievements the former general built up a formidable reputation among business and political leaders in the U.S.[98]

Washington also found Díaz a useful foreign policy adjutant in the early twentieth century. He agreed to sponsor the crucial second inter-American conference in 1901. In 1906 he collaborated with the U.S. to bring an end to fighting in upper Central America. Mexico was a cosponsor of the Washington conference on Central America the following year. In 1907 Root traveled to Mexico City on another of his good will tours. There he lauded Díaz and congratulated him on advancing his people "steadily along the pathway of progress."[99]

As the first decade of the century progressed, Díaz actually began to manifest concern about the degree of influence Americans were coming to exercise over Mexico's economy and about the practices of some U.S. firms. His government took steps to increase its control over the railways. Efforts were made to attract more European investment, and favoritism was shown to British oil interests.[100] As seen in Chapter 2, differences also began to emerge over policy toward Central America, especially with regard to Nicaragua.

Continued movement in this direction would at some point have begun to tarnish Díaz's luster in the eyes of U.S. policy makers (as had already begun to happen in the case of some oil executives). But such a transformation clearly did not take place in the years he had remaining. On the contrary, as Díaz aged and Mexico began to display more and more signs of social and political unrest, American leaders worried principally about what would happen when he was gone.

Such concerns were expressed with growing frequency after Díaz suggested in 1908 that he might not stand again for office in 1910.[101] Despite growing evidence of dissatisfaction with his dictatorial rule, the president then announced, in March 1909, that he would be a candidate after all. In October, on a long trip through the West, Taft met Díaz at El Paso. With great fanfare, he crossed back over the border with him. This was the first such venture ever by an incumbent U.S. president onto foreign soil, Taft's purpose being to demonstrate his support for the aging leader. "There is a great fear, and I am afraid a well-founded fear," he wrote his wife the next day,

that should [President Díaz] die, there will be a revolution growing out of the selection of his successor. As Americans have about $2,000,000 [sic] of capital invested in the country, it is inevitable that . . . we should interfere, and I sincerely hope that the old man's official life will extend beyond mine, for that trouble would present a problem of the utmost difficulty. . . . He thinks, and I believe rightly, that the knowledge throughout his country of the friendship of the United States for him . . . will strengthen him with his own people, and tend to discourage revolutionists' efforts.[102]

But a major revolt did come, and well before Díaz was ready to leave the scene.[103] Indeed, the dictator's vacillation clearly had the effect of stimulating political activity. In April 1910 Francisco Madero agreed to run as the presidential candidate of a new Anti-Reelectionist Party. This movement was principally an expression of growing restiveness on the part of Mexico's "urban middle class," a stratum of the society that had expanded significantly as the result of the economic changes of the Díaz era. Eager to participate more fully in the running of the country, the Anti-Reelectionists wanted an opening up of Mexico's political process.

Alarmed at the support that the wealthy young Coahuilan was able to garner, Díaz soon resorted to repression. Madero and many of his campaign organizers were jailed. The government manipulated the outcome of the mid-summer polling, and the Mexican congress, in September, confirmed Díaz's victory. In October, Madero escaped. He fled to Texas, denounced the elections, and called on Mexicans to mount an insurrection beginning on November 20.

Some of Madero's core supporters did stage uprisings, but these were generally weaker than hoped for and easily suppressed by the regime. The merchants, shopkeepers, clerks, civil servants, and professionals who had filled the ranks of the Anti-Reelectionists hesitated to take up arms, and those who did so found the towns and cities unfavorable terrain on which to do battle. Madero himself quickly crossed back over the border into the U.S.

It soon became clear, however, that the call for revolt had elicited a much greater response throughout large sectors of rural Mexico. The overwhelming majority of Mexicans still resided in the countryside, and here a deep sense of grievance against the Díaz regime had been mounting since the late nineteenth century. The new railways of the Porfiriato had opened the way to a much closer integration between interior regions of the country and foreign markets, especially in the U.S. This in turn had prompted large agricultural estate owners, eager to take advantage of new export possibilities, to try to increase their holdings. Their efforts were encouraged and facilitated by the government—particularly through legislation designed to take advantage of the lack of legal documentation for much traditional peasant land—with the result that this era witnessed a vast encroachment by the haciendas on communal village properties and small holdings. The process created an ever larger army of landless laborers, who subsequently were faced with falling wages and rising food prices. Meanwhile, in the drier and less heavily populated north, Díaz's policies had led to the opening up of much new territory, to the displacement of many in old occupations, and to the emergence of powerful new land barons who were given sweeping preferential rights to much of the region's pasturage, timberland, and water. These developments likewise stimulated enmity toward the regime.

Although insurrectionary activity in the towns quickly died down, it spread throughout the countryside, with the "pioneer" regions of the north leading the way. By late 1910, armed bands composed of rancheros, small farmers, muleteers, herders, and cattle rustlers were operating out of the foothills of the western Sierra Madre. Only lightly armed, they were nevertheless quickly able to contest the authority of the federal army everywhere beyond the region's railways and towns. Their success, in turn, sparked uprisings in central and southern Mexico in early 1911. Heartened by the developments, and eager to assert leadership over them, Madero crossed back into Mexico again.

In March the U.S. ambassador to Mexico, Henry Lane Wilson, met with Taft in Washington. He told the president that "Díaz was on a volcano," that his popularity seemed spent, that a "general explosion" was imminent, and that this would inevitably have an impact on American citizens and property in Mexico.[104] Taft immediately ordered a force of 20,000 troops to be assembled in south Texas. His hope was that such a demonstration of power would discourage any interference with Americans or their interests by the Mexican populace and that it would also pressure the Díaz government to protect such interests. He likewise assumed that his action would serve to reassure—and warn off—other major powers.

The troops would also be ready to intervene if deemed necessary. But Taft hoped that his rapid deployment would reduce the likelihood that that would be required. If the U.S. intervened, an administration-inspired article in the *New York Tribune* suggested, its goal would be to restore order and then to push for elections as a way of containing further unrest. The president, however, did not want to intervene. He worried that that would be expensive and burdensome. It might also inflame Mexican opinion and actually promote attacks on Americans and their property. It would have a negative impact on U.S. relations with Latin America. In addition, Taft was concerned about the political impact that intervention in Mexico might have at home.[105] Knox, who had been vacationing in Florida, shared the president's perspective. On his return, he told Wilbur J. Carr of the consular service that he was fearful that if troops were sent into Mexico they might "never come out."[106]

Taft hoped that ideally the mobilization would also "hold up the hands of the existing government."[107] This it clearly did not do. Indeed, one historian suggests that the opposite was the case. To some in Mexico, the American troop movements were taken as confirmation of how weak Díaz had become. Others suspected that the dictator was working to bring about foreign intervention. In fact, Díaz and his advisors were enraged at the action. Finance Minister José Limantour, who was in New York at the time, warned that any crossing of the frontier would mean war.[108]

Far from feeling that the U.S. was behind him, Díaz came to believe that it wanted him out of the way. The dictator was convinced that Washington had not done all it could to hamper the activities of the Maderistas in Texas, and to him this confirmed a suspicion that Taft had decided to punish him for his independence. Nothing that happened subsequently dissuaded Díaz from this view. Indeed, his capitulation may have come about sooner than otherwise as a result.[109]

The end, in any event, came quickly. Although the major cities and towns were still under the control of the federal army, it was clear by April that the regime had lost control of rural Mexico. Even more apparent was its loss of public support. On May 10 Juárez fell to the revolutionary forces. Díaz now consented to resign and go into exile, and Madero agreed that Foreign Minister Francisco Léon de la Barra, who until recently had been Díaz's ambassador to Washington, should head an interim government pending elections in the fall.[110] The fighting over, Knox and Henry L. Stimson, the new secretary of war, decided to demobilize U.S. forces.[111]

Washington was pleased, as it had expected to be, by de la Barra's interregnum. Madero meanwhile gave explicit guarantees of his intention to respect and protect foreign interests doing business in the country. Elected president in October, he was inaugurated early the following month.[112]

The Taft administration was anxious to see Madero consolidate his rule and hopeful that his accession to power would signal an end to Mexico's period of instability. It was not to be. Many who had rallied to his banner the previous winter and spring were deeply disappointed by the deference Madero gave to groups and institutions—including the army—central to the old regime, by the favoritism he displayed toward the "urban middle class"—and even former officials of the Porfiriato—in his political appointments, and by his limited commitment to social reform. As historian Alan Knight has put it, a "viable regime" in Mexico at this time had "to put down roots into the soil whence popular rebellion sprang." This Madero failed to do, and as a result he soon had to deal with renewed revolutionary activity on the part of many of his former rural allies.

Madero also confronted armed uprisings on the part of figures ambitious to reestablish the old order with themselves in the role of Porfirio Díaz. To Díaz's traditional supporters they held out the promise of a restoration of the privileges and power that they had enjoyed under the old regime. These challengers also argued that Madero was too weak and that only a dictatorship could deal with the country's unrest. Such plots did not appear a significant threat to the government in its early stages. The first, launched by General Bernardo Reyes, collapsed immediately for lack of support in December 1911. But support for action of this sort mounted with the persistence of agrarian movements in the countryside.

In the regions surrounding Mexico City, many agrarian leaders had grown distrustful of the new Maderista politicians by late 1911. Rather than demobilize as the new regime demanded, Emiliano Zapata, the most well known, announced his determination to continue fighting for the return of peasants' land in Morelos. Morelos, Guerrero, Tlaxcala, and parts of two other states were placed under martial law early in 1912. They then became the focus of a brutal counterinsurgency campaign lasting into the spring.

Perceived as a much greater threat to the survival of the regime was the revival of insurrectionary activity in the north early in 1912. This was led by Pascual Orozco, one of the most important of the military leaders in 1911. His forces won control of Chihuahua. Federal troops were sent to disperse them. But, on March 23, Orozco's army won a stunning victory (at Rellano).[113]

Against the backdrop of these events, the attention of the Taft administration shifted again toward Mexico. Military precautions began to be discussed in February. Contingency plans were readied, and U.S. troops once more went on alert, albeit in a less obtrusive manner than the year before. When fighting took place in and around Juárez, both sides were warned not to let it spill across the border.

Such actions were coupled with other steps designed to alleviate friction between the two governments and to help Madero. On March 2 a presidential proclamation warned American citizens living in Mexico that it was illegal for them to seek to undermine a government with which their country was at peace. Americans were advised to withdraw from dangerous areas of the country. Then, at Taft's behest, Congress passed a resolution making it illegal for arms to be exported to any American republic experiencing a rebellion unless such sales were expressly approved by the president. Madero's government was subsequently allowed to purchase arms, while they were denied to his opponents.[114]

Orozco's army was eventually broken up by federal forces under the leadership of General Victoriano Huerta. Guerrilla activity nevertheless continued in the north as well as in the center of the country.[115] In response, the Taft administration decided during the summer that U.S. naval vessels should begin making regular visits to Mexican ports. These were to be "friendly and casual," according to Knox, but he also hoped that they would have a "desirable moral effect upon the minds of the local population."[116] Washington stepped up its diplomatic pressure on Mexico City too, insisting that it do more to protect Americans and their interests.[117]

At the same time, the administration continued to believe that it should go no further unless conditions grew far worse. When unrest continued even after the defeat of Orozco, criticism of Taft's policy was expressed by some members of Congress, chief among them Senator Albert B. Fall, a Republican from New Mexico. The State Department insisted, however, that forcible intervention would be counterproductive, that it would generate an antagonism that would immediately be vented toward Americans and their interests in Mexico, and that this would happen on a scale that would vastly eclipse any damage that had already occurred.[118]

Another figure prominently associated with the old order made a bid for power in October. General Felix Díaz, a nephew of the former president, seized control of Veracruz. Within ten days his forces were however surrounded and compelled to surrender by loyal troops. Like Reyes, Díaz was sent off to jail in the capital.[119]

But the regime drew the wrong conclusions from this victory. Madero and many of those around him felt that they had rounded a corner with Díaz's defeat (and this appears to have been the belief in Washington as well).[120] In fact, more serious military plots against the president were yet to come. Another revolt, by officers who freed and then rallied to the support of Reyes and Díaz was launched in February 1913, this time in the capital city. Huerta, the hero of the previous year's campaign against Orozco, was called on to put the rebellion down. But after ten days of furious and destructive fighting, he finally betrayed Madero, formed an alliance with Díaz, and put the president under arrest.

Although American forces once more went on alert during these disturbances, Taft, his term soon due to expire, remained eager to avoid intervention. Long of the opinion that Madero was too weak, and that Washington failed to understand the situation, the American ambassador, on the other hand, worked to undermine the regime. Wilson likewise played a major role in composing the issues that remained between Díaz and Huerta after Madero's arrest. With his mediation, it was agreed that Huerta would become the provisional president, that Díaz would select the cabinet, and that Huerta would throw his support to Díaz at the time of the next presidential election. In exchange for a pledge of safe conduct out of the country, and a promise of immunity for his followers, Madero agreed to resign. He was, however, shot and killed three days later.

As soon as Huerta was confirmed in office, the ambassador urged Washington to recognize the new government. But Taft held back, maintaining that Huerta ought first to render assurances about a number of outstanding disputes and claims. Settlement of these matters had yet to be reached when the administration's term ran out eleven days later.[121]

The Wilson administration's policy toward Huerta's government, which came eventually to focus on a new presidential election as the price of U.S. recognition, needs principally to be understood as an expression of its resolve to put an end to revolutionary disorders in Latin America.[122] This issue greatly influenced its view of events in Mexico when it came to power in 1913. Against the background of the turmoil in the Caribbean throughout 1912, and of warnings that new revolts might be in the offing there, Wilson, as has been seen, announced on March 12 that he had "no sympathy" with those in Latin America who would "seize the power of government." The U.S. would instead "prefer those who act in the interest of peace and honor, who protect private rights and respect the restraints of constitutional provision." Wilson entered office fearful that continued political instability would jeopardize American control in the Caribbean. And he saw such control as especially important now given the imminent completion of the Panama Canal, an event in his eyes of epochal importance. Particularly after taking this position, Wilson believed that how the U.S. reacted to events in Mexico could not but have a profound impact on developments throughout the region.

An instructive comparison can be found in U.S. policies toward China and Mexico in 1913–14. The Wilson administration embraced Yuan Shikai, even after he worked to undermine the new Chinese republic and consolidate dictatorial powers. Meanwhile, it accepted the idea that Huerta was a "brute" for doing much the same thing (both were even suspected of assassinating key opponents). The unifying thread between these policies was the theme of order and American leadership. Support of Yuan was seen as functional to the promotion of those objectives in China, while Huerta was seen as a threat to the realization of those goals in upper Latin America. Rather than coming to be viewed as a progressive strongman, Huerta came instead to be seen as the first of several "selfish" adversaries against which the administration campaigned in these years (the other most important being Great Britain and Venustiano Carranza). Meanwhile, Washington also saw Mexico as threatened by "irresponsible" forces, principally in the form of that country's revolutionary rank and file, which it likewise sought to contain.

Initially the Wilson administration simply withheld recognition from the new government.[123] But its hope appears to have been that Huerta would, on his own, soon announce concrete plans for an election, in conformity with what was taken to be his agreement with Díaz. In spring 1913 this step would almost certainly have won recognition for Huerta.

During this period, meanwhile, it became clear that Huerta's authority had by no means been universally accepted in Mexico. Unrest was in fact on the rise, especially in the north. His seizure of power had actually helped to recreate there, if in uneasy collaboration, something like the revolutionary coalition of 1911. Several Maderista governors, in command of local military forces, spurned Huerta's claims of legitimacy and announced their intention of driving him from power, while popular forces, generally of a more social revolutionary complexion, took the field as well.[124]

Wilson was also coming to appreciate what the consequences of U.S. military intervention were likely to be. Members of his cabinet expressed concern that action of that sort here would be extremely costly.[125] Then, when the president asked Colonel House whether he thought "intervention and war would be as bad as his Cabinet thought," House replied that he did.[126] Several prominent Americans with substantial property interests in Mexico simultaneously voiced concern about the damage that would be done to their operations if that were to come to pass.[127]

Elections came to be valued both for the long-term effect they might have on the region as a whole and as a means of addressing the immediate situation in Mexico.[128] The administration grew impatient with, and increasingly antagonistic toward, Huerta personally. By June, it was no longer willing to recognize him on a conditional basis. It worried that that might help him to consolidate power and then defy the U.S. from a position of greater strength.[129]

In May, Wilson had sent the journalist William Bayard Hale to Mexico as a special executive agent. Reports began to come back from him in early June. These confirmed American newspaper speculation about Henry Lane Wilson's role in the February coup (the ambassador was subsequently recalled and discharged from the foreign service). Hale also claimed that Huerta was losing control of the country. He suggested that the "psychological moment" had arrived for a "positive policy." Indeed, he felt that if matters were allowed to drift too much further there would be little hope of avoiding U.S. military occupation. The country was being ravaged. America was, after all, Hale argued, the natural guardian of "order and justice and decency on this Continent." For good measure, he opined that Huerta was "an ape-like old man" and that the average Mexican was either hopelessly passive or "a savage."[130]

In mid-July, a number of European diplomatic representatives in Mexico City "expressed a great desire that the United States should recognize General Huerta provisionally in the interests of stability."[131] After meeting together they agreed to ask their home governments to raise this issue with Washington. Cecil Spring Rice reported back to London, however, that recognition was out of the question. This, he said, was "on the ground of insecurity of the present régime and bad effect on South American peoples of recognizing a Government which attained power by unconstitutional and murderous methods."[132] Wilson was nevertheless by now feeling pressure from a number of directions to clarify his course.

A more active policy finally began to take shape in August. Another agent, John Lind, was sent to Mexico, significantly, on board a U.S. battleship. His instructions were to make it clear to the Huerta government that Washington no longer felt at liberty "to stand inactively by while it becomes daily more and more evident that no real progress is being made towards the establishment of a government at the City of Mexico which the country will obey and respect." "The present situation," was "incompatible with the fulfilment of international obligations on the part of Mexico, with the civilized development of Mexico herself, and with the maintenance of tolerable political and economic conditions in Central America." Wilson proposed that Mexico bring about an immediate cessation of fighting and arrange for an early and free election in which all parties would agree to participate. Huerta should agree not to be a candidate.[133]

When Huerta's foreign minister, Federico Gamboa, spurned these proposals, as uninvited interference in Mexico's affairs, Lind threatened him. He told Gamboa that the U.S. might tilt toward the rebels or intervene itself if his government did not change its mind.[134] Wilson, however, was not really prepared to pursue either of those options.[135] Instead, on August 27 he went before Congress to announce that he intended to isolate the Huerta government, to shut off sales of arms to it from the U.S., and to await a change in attitude in Mexico City. For that, "only a little while will be necessary," he asserted. In an effort to explain his policy, Wilson argued that not just the U.S., but the whole world desired that country's "peace and progress." "Mexico lies at last," he said,

where all the world looks on. Central America is about to be touched by the great routes of the world's trade and intercourse running free from ocean to ocean at the Isthmus.... America north and south and upon both continents—waits upon the development of Mexico; and that development can be sound and lasting only if it be the product of a genuine freedom, a just and ordered government founded upon law.[136]

Meanwhile, in Gamboa's formal reply to Lind he pointed out that under the Mexican constitution, Huerta could not in any event be a candidate in October.[137] This statement was seized on by the administration and led it to decide that its essential demands had finally been met. Remarks by Huerta in mid-September, pledging that he would not run and promising neutrality in the election, reinforced this optimism. As things were developing, Gamboa seemed likely to become the next president. But that outcome was satisfactory to the Wilson administration. "I feel that we have nearly reached the end of our trouble," Bryan wrote the president.[138]

The administration appears principally to have been looking for the creation of a "constitutional" government to which it could lend its support. But Hale questioned whether this would be sufficient from the standpoint of restoring order to Mexico. The northern revolutionaries had still not agreed to participate in the elections. "The Mexico City people may come to some sort of a settlement among themselves, may even set up a government which we may recognize," he wrote, "but it may be set down as certainty that the North will remain in revolt; we shall have months more of disturbances along the frontier, destruction of the property of Americans and occasional murders to provide material for intervention agitators." The "one chance for peace," he thought, was to induce the "Constitutionalists," now loosely organized behind the leadership of Venustiano Carranza, the Maderist governor of Coahuila, to participate.[139]

In response, Wilson instructed Lind to encourage officials in Mexico City to strive "to secure the participation and cooperation of the leaders in the north."[140] Hale meanwhile directly approached the Constitutionalists. He warned them that the U.S. would "support Gamboa or any other man who won . . . on October 26" whether the Constitutionalists participated or not. It would also not "recognize a government which was produced by a revolution." In a preview of disputes yet to come, the Constitutionalists nevertheless insisted that they could have no faith whatsoever in these elections.[141]

Suddenly, another political upheaval took place in the capital. The Mexican Congress, including most Maderist members, had been relatively quiescent during the first six months of Huerta's rule, but by the end of the summer this changed. At the very same time that Constitutionalist forces were beginning to win major victories, congressmen began to challenge Huerta's heavy-handed dictatorial rule. Huerta, on October 10, responded by dissolving the lower house and arresting 110 deputies. The Senate immediately adjourned. Huerta assumed the full powers of government and announced that a new Congress would be chosen during the upcoming election.[142]

The general appeared intent on retaining supreme control in Mexico City. "Huerta has his back to the wall and may now be considered an absolute military dictator," reported the U.S. chargé, Nelson O'Shaughnessy.[143] Enraged at what he saw as this second coup, and direct challenge to American wishes, Wilson now decided that Huerta would have to leave the scene before the kind of order he wanted could be established.[144]

Wilson was eager above all to force the European powers, and especially Britain, to dissociate themselves from the general. He was convinced that London was behind Huerta's boldness and that it was attempting to prop him up in spite of U.S. wishes. To Wilson, this constituted a challenge not merely to his Mexican policy, but also to Washington's claim of preeminence in the hemisphere.

The ensuing U.S.-British confrontation took shape against the background of a struggle that American and British oil interests in Mexico had been engaged in since Madero's overthrow, a struggle heavily influenced by the belief that Mexico was soon destined to become the richest oil-producing region in the world (it was already number three). Because of the role Henry Lane Wilson had played in his coming to power, the major U.S. firms, all allies of Standard Oil, had hoped that Huerta would give preference to them over their main rival, the powerful English business-man S. Weetman Pearson (Lord Cowdray). The opposite turned out to be the case. For much the same motives that had governed Díaz in his latter years, Huerta was determined to favor British and European interests over those of his northern neighbor. This orientation preceded, although it was clearly later reinforced by, President Wilson's critical stance.

During the summer of 1913, Lionel Carden was appointed as London's minister to Mexico. Because he was outspoken in his belief that Huerta should be supported and, even more, because he presented his credentials on October 11, the day immediately following the general's move against the Chamber of Deputies, Wilson and Bryan decided that the British gov-ernment bore significant responsibility for the failure of their policy. Since Carden had connections to Cowdray, moreover, they concluded that the latter had come to control this area of British diplomacy.[145]

Walter Hines Page, the American ambassador to England, was subse-quently instructed to urge British authorities to pursue a "wider view" toward Mexican affairs than one dictated simply by the desire to promote Cowdray's interests.[146] Wilson and Bryan also discussed sending a sternly worded note to all the powers with representatives in Mexico City. After they worked on a draft, however, the president simply outlined his desires and turned the task over to State Department counselor John Bassett Moore. Wilson asked that six points be set forth. These were (1) that the U.S. was the govern-ment that was "most interested" in the situation in Mexico ("This govern-ment ... is and must continue to be of paramount influence in the Western Hemisphere," the draft read); (2) that the development of all Central Amer-ica was involved; (3) that Huerta's government would already have broken down "but for the encouragement and financial aid derived from its recog-nition by other nations, without regard to the wishes or purposes" of the U.S.; (4) that Huerta's continuation in the face of American opposition was impossible; (5) that the other powers could either be cooperative or they could antagonize Washington and make its "task one of domination and force"; and (6) that the U.S. would not accept joint intervention in the country. Bryan handed the outline to Moore with the added suggestion that the Monroe Doctrine be invoked over the issue of European powers recognizing Huerta's government before consulting with Washington.[147]

Taken aback, Moore pointed out the resentment and antagonism that such a position on recognition would breed among Latin American as well as European countries. Indeed, he argued, the whole tone of the commu-nication, as prefigured in the outline, threatened unnecessarily to damage U.S. international relations.[148]

In the end, the note was not sent. Instead, through a speech delivered in Mobile, Alabama on October 27, Wilson made an only slightly more veiled attack on Britain. Declaring that the completion of the canal would open up a fresh chapter in the history of the world that would have "unimaginable significance," the president asserted that the U.S. would oppose European efforts to use financial means to take over Latin American countries and deprive them of their new opportunities. Wilson cast the U.S. in the role of defender of Latin America against such selfish schemes and as the opponent of the corrupt local influences through which they might be effected.[149] A week and a half later, in a circular note, Washington formally notified the powers of its intention to compel Huerta's removal from power.[150]

As historian Friedrich Katz has made clear, there were those in the British government who had been hoping to see Huerta remain in power. He had enjoyed support in London because of the influence of Cowdray, but for broader reasons as well. The general had been seen as critical to Mexican stability and thus to the protection of numerous British investments. Moreover, Cowdray's oil concessions were seen as having strategic consequence. The Royal Navy was in the process of shifting from coal to oil fuel, Cowdray held a key suppliers contract, and, in the event of a war in Europe, this was seen as a region where Britain could be assured of access.[151]

In fact, London had for several years been doubtful that following the U.S. lead was the best way of protecting its interests in upper Latin America. Early in the century, Britain accepted the idea that the entire area would be a sphere of influence for the U.S. But it had not meant to abandon British economic interests, and London had taken seriously U.S. pledges of support for the open door. It subsequently grew disenchanted with the U.S. record in these areas. British creditors alleged discrimination in the final settlement of the accounts of the Dominican Republic. The Taft administration worked to gather solely into American hands the finances of countries such as Honduras and Nicaragua. And during the campaign of 1912, Wilson, Taft, and TR all endorsed the Panama Canal Act, by which U.S. vessels were to be charged lower tolls than those of other nations when they used that waterway (despite the fact that the Hay-Pauncefote Treaty had pledged that the canal would be open on an equal basis to the ships of all nations). These developments encouraged London to act more independently in the Caribbean. And they help explain why it was not initially disposed to defer to Washington in Mexico City. "Our interests in Mexico are so big that I think we should take our own line, without making it dependent upon that of other governments," Grey had commented when Britain recognized Huerta.

London was not, however, about to support the general at the risk of serious damage to the Anglo-American rapprochement. And once it became clear that that would be the price, it changed course. Grey told Carden on October 17, that "His Majesty's Government cannot with any prospect of success embark upon an active counter-policy to that of the United States, or constitute themselves the champions of Mexico or any of these republics against the United States." Huerta was explicitly told that this was British policy on November 10.[152]

Several days later, the president was visited at the White House by Grey's private secretary, Sir William Tyrrell, for a meeting intended to iron out the differences between the two nations. Wilson laid out and sought to defend his policy in Mexico, and the gist of his remarks was communicated to Grey the following day. "With the opening of the Panama Canal," Tyrrell wrote,

it is becoming increasingly important that the Governments of the Central American Republics should improve, as they will become more and more a field for European and American enterprise: bad government may lead to friction and to such incidents as Venezuela affair under Castro. The President is very anxious to provide against such contingencies by insisting that those Republics should have fairly decent rulers and that men like Castro and Huerta should be barred. With this object in view, the President made up his mind to teach these countries a lesson by insisting on the removal of Huerta. The mode of procedure which he proposes is that Huerta should convoke the Congress of last May, which he considers the only legal one in Mexico, and that he should proclaim a general amnesty so as to enable the contingents of the North to share in the election of a new President. If the latter refused to come in, they would be treated as rebels by the United States Government. The President assured me that, should Huerta agree to this, he would go to almost any length to enable him to save his face. After that, he does not propose to examine with a microscope what happens in Mexico, but he is under no illusion with regard to the capacity of Mexicans for maladministration. Huerta, however, exceeded the limit of what is permissible. The President is confident that the Mexican Congress would and could elect a President capable of maintaining law and order.

"It seems to me," commented Tyrrell to Grey,

that we [Great Britain] have neither the intention nor the power to oppose this policy.... The Administration has, by its own mistake, got itself into a difficult position, as it wishes to avoid intervention if possible. If we can do anything to help the President, he will be most appreciative.

Wilson was a strong partisan of a "sympathetic alliance" with England, he concluded, and this was the proper "psychological moment" for cementing such a relationship.[153]

In exchange for going along with his policy toward Huerta, London wanted the president to push for revision of the Panama Canal Act, and it wanted assurances about the protection of British investments and property in Mexico. Wilson had already come to the conclusion that London's interpretation of the Hay-Pauncefote Treaty was right. He had dragged his feet on the matter, both because revision was politically unpopular and because he wanted to use the issue as leverage with England. He now took up revision and pushed it to a successful conclusion the following spring.[154]

As for British investments in Mexico, the president wrote Tyrrell on November 22 urging him to assure Grey that the U.S. "intends not merely to force Huerta from power, but also to exert every influence it can exert to secure Mexico a better government under which all contracts and business concessions will be safer than they have been." Grey was to feel free to convey the contents of this letter to British and Canadian investors.[155]

Having succeeded in getting Britain to accept his lead, Wilson turned his attention to the elimination of Huerta. Washington wanted his retirement and then for new elections to be held. If Huerta agreed to turn over power to an acceptable *ad interim* government, Washington would try to ensure his personal safety.[156] The general refused these demands. For Wilson, the question then became one of forcing the "desperate brute's" removal.[157] Still anxious to avoid the direct involvement of American troops, his thoughts increasingly turned to the armies of the Constitutionalists. Lind had been arguing that "if order and pacification can be accomplished by Mexican means it will be necessary to utilize the rebel organization."[158] By the end of October, Wilson's mind was moving in this same direction. On the thirtieth, he discussed with House "the feasibility of recognizing the Constitutionalists as belligerents in order that they might obtain arms and ammunition upon the same terms as the Federalists."[159]

Wilson had serious misgivings about the Constitutionalists, however, and disagreements continued with them. Some of these were highlighted in talks that the president, through Hale, conducted with Carranza near the Sonora-Arizona border in mid-November. The president wanted assurances that Carranza could and would ensure the behavior of all those who fought under him. He wanted to make sure that everything would be done to protect foreign lives and property and to minimize destruction. Carranza willingly complied. But Wilson could not understand why the Constitutionalist leader objected to the stationing of U.S. troops in his country for such duty. Nor could he comprehend the Constitutionalists' unwillingness to trust to American supervised elections, if they could still be arranged, as a way of settling Mexico's unrest. For his part, Carranza was coming to suspect that the president aspired to control the revolution. He therefore broke off the talks on the eighteenth.[160] Wilson sympathized with the Constitutionalists, Bryan later wrote Lind, "but their attitude makes it impossible at present to give any open manifestation of that sympathy."[161]

What soon put these issues in the background for the president were the successes that the Constitutionalists began to enjoy in the field. By the end of 1913, virtually all northern Mexico was in their hands. The administration had formed a strong antipathy to Carranza, indeed some officials were already looking for some other revolutionary with whom they might work. But what now mattered most was that the Constitutionalists seemed on the verge of putting an end to the president's protracted confrontation with

Huerta. When their momentum seemed to slow at the end of January 1914, Wilson finally decided to lift the embargo that had blocked the legal sale of American arms to them.[162]

The fighting nevertheless seemed to settle back into stalemate. Wilson became increasingly impatient, as did foreign powers and their nationals. Lind suggested that if Huerta was not on the run by mid-March the U.S. itself should intervene.[163] His reports became increasingly pessimistic. Lind warned that with his oil revenues and the extraordinary levies and taxes he was applying, Huerta might be able to hang on for months. A relatively minor deployment of U.S. force, on the other hand, he assured Washington, would now tilt the balance and send him on his way.[164]

It was against this backdrop that the administration responded to news of a confrontation between a U.S. naval commander and Mexican authorities at Tampico. On April 9, bluejackets from a U.S. squadron patrolling off the coast had been arrested when, on an errand to purchase gasoline, they had docked their small boat in a restricted part of that city's harbor.[165] When the Federal commander learned of the arrests, he apologized and ordered the release of the sailors, who were returned to their ship within an hour. However, Rear Admiral Henry T. Mayo, the commanding officer of the squadron, deemed the incident an "inexcusable" insult, and on his own authority issued an ultimatum. He demanded not only a formal apology and punishment of the responsible officers, but also that the U.S. flag be hoisted above the harbor and given a twenty-one-gun salute.[166]

The president understandably considered the incident itself "of no great importance" (House remarked that the goings on reminded him of the dueling codes of an earlier age), but he nevertheless seized on the incident as an opportunity to try to hasten Huerta's departure. O'Shaughnessy was told to insist on the demands in Mexico City and to threaten serious repercussions if they were not complied with. From Wilson's standpoint, Huerta would be humiliated if he went along. If, on the other hand, he refused, Washington could use the incident as a pretext to take action against the general that would hopefully decide his fate. A blockade was the first idea entertained. In preparation for that, much of the Atlantic fleet was directed to assemble off Mexico's gulf coast.

Huerta agreed to simultaneous and reciprocal salutes. But this was rejected, as was the idea that the dispute be submitted to arbitration. The general then sought a guarantee that the Mexican salute would be returned. This was spurned as well. On April 20, a Monday, Wilson went to Congress seeking a resolution that would allow him to compel recognition of the "rights and dignity" of the U.S., though this barely hinted at his objective.[167]

The navy began to move even before the Senate had finished its deliberations. But the focus of its attention had shifted from Tampico to Veracruz. Over the weekend, news had arrived that a German steamer, the *Ypiranga*, was about to land there with a large shipment of arms and ammunition for the Huerta government. Wilson, in response, had decided to seize the customs house.

Washington assumed that there would be little or no resistance. Indeed, policy makers believed American forces might even be welcomed by the people of the city. Quite the opposite! Bluejackets and marines were confronted by Federal troops, citizen volunteers, and cadets from Mexico's Naval Academy. And, as a result, a struggle ensued for control of all of Veracruz. Before it was over, 126 Mexicans and 19 Americans had been killed.[168]

Demonstrations against the intervention broke out throughout Mexico, again to the president's surprise, and it was also condemned by Carranza. "The invasion of our territory, the stationing of American troops in the port of Veracruz, the violation of our rights as a sovereign, free, and independent state could provoke us to an unequal but just war, which we wish to avoid," he proclaimed. In response, Wilson reimposed the arms embargo.[169]

As has been seen, the seizure of Veracruz elicited condemnation throughout the rest of Latin America as well. Wilson was determined to cripple Huerta by holding onto the port, but he was also anxious to keep the situation that had developed from getting out of hand. He therefore eagerly welcomed the offer of mediation made by the governments of Argentina, Brazil, and Chile.[170]

Mediation offered Wilson not only an escape from the danger of broader military complications. The president also came quickly to see it as an avenue through which the termination of Huerta's government might finally be arranged. As he accurately perceived, Huerta was all but finished. The occupation of Veracruz, plus U.S. naval control of the coast meant that Huerta would now be starved both of needed revenues and of many supplies. Moreover, in April, the Constitutionalists, had dealt the Federal army stunning new defeats (at Torreón and San Pedro).

Wilson likewise hoped that the U.S., cloaked in Pan-American multilateralism, could use the mediation to determine the political conditions that would follow the departure of the general. He had characterized his antagonism toward Huerta as being driven by a desire to assure free self-development for the Mexican people. Yet the president fully intended to continue to try to shape the course of that country's affairs even if such involvement was not wanted. Wilson saw no inconsistency between this posture and his professions. As he saw it, he was the one competent and "disinterested" force on the scene. All he was trying to do was to guide a neighboring state back onto the correct path, which it could not find alone. As the president phrased it for an interview in the *Saturday Evening Post*, the situation required "the strong guiding hand of the great nation on this continent."[171]

Wilson thus informed the A.B.C. powers that he would not participate in the mediation unless its members were willing to involve themselves in the promotion of a settlement of the entire Mexican conflict. It was out of conditions related to that conflict, he argued, that the differences leading up to the seizure of Veracruz had arisen. Specifically, the president insisted that no settlement would be acceptable which did not provide for Huerta's retirement and for the immediate establishment of a provisional government that would pave the way toward a return of constitutional orderliness.[172] Wilson's hope was that this provisional government would be beholden to the U.S. and look to it for guidance.

In late April Wilson suggested that "the essence of any hopeful settlement would ... be a concert of the contending elements" in Mexico. However, over the ensuing weeks the Constitutionalists continued to make great gains against the Federal forces. By the time of the mediation conference, which convened a month later at Niagara Falls, Canada, the president had decided that the Constitutionalists would have to be offered the dominant role in any such arrangement.[173]

Immediate peace and predominance in the provisional government, plus arms that Washington was now willing to let get through to them, were the favors and inducements that Wilson hoped would lead the Constitutionalists to accept his plan. But Carranza was not willing to countenance a government set up under U.S. auspices (under a plan, moreover, that stipulated that he himself could not be the provisional president), nor the precedent that this would set of Washington acting as the arbiter of Mexico's internal affairs. He therefore rejected Wilson's proposal. The conference finally broke up on June 24 without achieving any of these broader objectives.[174]

Furious, Wilson resorted to threats. As Huerta turned over power to his foreign minister in mid-July and then fled, and the revolutionaries pressed on toward the capital, the president warned that the Constitutionalist government might itself not be recognized unless it behaved properly. It was "evident," moreover, he wrote, that the U.S. was the "only first-class power that can be expected to take the initiative in recognizing the new government."[175] He later added that if the U.S. did not recognize the government, "it could obtain no loans and must speedily break down."[176]

Carranza's forces entered Mexico City in triumph on August 22, 1914. Just as the revolutionary coalition of 1911 had broken apart after the victories of that spring, however, so too were serious divisions now beginning to develop within the ranks of the Constitutionalists. A great rivalry, in particular, had emerged between Carranza and the most successful of the Constitutionalist generals, Francisco (Pancho) Villa. A former sharecropper turned bandit, Villa had taken the field alongside Orozco in Chihuahua in 1911 and then fought for Madero against Orozco the following year. He had acknowledged Carranza as leader of the revolt against Huerta in 1913, but relations between the two had then become strained. Carranza worried that Villa's unrivaled military success and popularity would make him difficult to control, while Villa resented what he saw as Carranza's unwillingness to accord him his due.

Carranza also saw Villa, like Zapata and other agrarian leaders in the south, as a threat to his goals for the revolution. Determined to avoid the mistakes of Madero, Carranza saw some steps in the direction of land reform as necessary. But a *hacendado* himself, the Constitutionalist's first chief, as he was called, was not prepared to push this very far. Villa was often not consistent on the question of agrarian reform. By contrast with someone like Zapata, he better fit the mold of *caudillo* than social revolutionary. Villa was nevertheless prepared to endorse much more redistribution than was Carranza. Simultaneously, Carranza embraced a vision of Mexico's future that was more urban and commercial than Villa's. And the first chief was also eager to promote a powerful and centralized Mexican state, quite the opposite of what many of the popular leaders throughout the countryside had been contending for.

During the late spring, Carranza had become concerned that Villa's army might reach Mexico City first. His efforts to prevent that almost precipitated a confrontation between the two men then. A break was avoided only when Carranza appeared to agree to a convention to discuss the course of the revolution.[177]

The Wilson administration was hostile to Carranza for reasons of its own, mostly because of his resistance to U.S. direction, but also because it doubted that Carranza was a man of sufficient strength to impose order on his fighters. It thus withheld recognition from the interim government that was established in Mexico City. Through two new agents, Paul Fuller and George C. Carothers, the administration then worked to have the first chief shunted aside. Fuller and Carothers pressed on prominent Constitutionalist generals the idea that the upcoming convention should lay the groundwork for elections to be held in the near future. Carranza might serve as provisional president, but he should be declared ineligible to succeed himself in that office.

As leverage on Carranza, Fuller tried to use the continued American occupation of Veracruz. But this only further antagonized the first chief. In his subsequent report to Wilson, Fuller asserted that more strife in Mexico was preferable if that was the only way to "purge away unworthy ambitions." Carranza was a man without "sufficient force to dominate his petty surroundings."[178]

Washington's hopes for the convention, which met in October at Aguascalientes, were to some extent realized. It declared itself a sovereign body, demoted Carranza, and elected a new provisional president. But Carranza rejected its authority, with the result that by mid-November, he and the "Conventionists," increasingly dominated by Villa, were moving toward a test of arms.[179]

Most observers assumed that Villa would easily triumph, and this was clearly the outcome that the Wilson administration preferred. Not only would Villa dispense with the uncooperative Carranza. Washington, at this time, also saw him as a strongman who might ensure the success of its policy. Officials were hopeful that the charismatic Villa was someone capable of guaranteeing order in Mexico. In addition, and again in contrast to Carranza, they viewed him as someone who would cooperate with the U.S.

This was because of the deference that Villa had shown Washington and American interests up to this point. The Chihuahuan general had early on become convinced of the critical importance of American good favor, especially to his ability to get arms and to conduct the trade that would allow him to finance his army. He had therefore been eager to address American concerns about the conduct of the revolution whenever they had been raised.[180]

American special agents had sung Villa's praises since late 1913. Carothers was one of his most important boosters. General Hugh L. Scott also met on several occasions with Villa. At a meeting along the border in February 1914, he lectured the Mexican general on the proper provisions to be made for foreigners within Mexico's war zones. Afterward, American officials voiced their conviction that Villa was a "savage" who could be tutored. The general also won points in Washington by distancing himself from the criticisms most Constitutionalist leaders made of Wilson's occupation of Veracruz. Villa had by this time come to believe that he had allies in Washington, and he did not want to lose them.[181]

In August 1914, House and Wilson "went into the Mexican situation carefully and agreed that Villa is the only man of force now in sight."[182] The same view was expressed by another special agent, Leon Canova, in November. As Mexico headed toward conflict again, the president told the French military attaché that Villa had "gradually succeeded in instilling sufficient discipline into his troops to convert them into an army. Perhaps, he added this man today represents the only instrument of civilization in Mexico. His firm authority allows him to create order and to educate the turbulent mass of peons so prone to pillage."[183]

Serious dissent from this view only seems to have arisen in 1915. After several months of indecisive military engagements and much political maneuvering, Wilson felt that he was losing "the threads" of the Mexican situation. He thus commissioned another agent, Duval West, to inquire into the prospects and likely policies of the contending sides. West reported that Villa still seemed the likely victor. But, when he met with the general, West was startled to hear Villa say that he felt foreigners exercised far too much influence over the Mexican economy.[184]

Meanwhile, relations between the Wilson administration and Carranza remained unfriendly. Carranza continued to insist on the evacuation of Veracruz. Anxious—especially with the onset of war in Europe and the possibility of renewed fighting in Mexico—to extricate American forces, the administration nevertheless demanded guarantees for Hueristas who had taken refuge there and for Mexicans who had served the occupation. For his part, the first chief maintained that the U.S. had no right to set pre-conditions. Faced with the possibility that his army might be cut off from the coast, however, Carranza finally proclaimed an amnesty at the beginning of November. Leaders of the convention having already adopted the same position, Veracruz was evacuated later that month and subsequently seized by the Constitutionalists.[185]

More friction occurred during the new year. At the beginning of March 1915, Washington strongly protested the conditions that confronted the foreign community in Mexico City (where Carranza was temporarily back in control). At the same time, a confrontation developed over the Constitutionalists' (generally unsuccessful) efforts to blockade the ports of the Yucatán Peninsula, a region from which the U.S. imported large supplies of sisal hemp, a material of great importance to its agriculture. These controversies led to an expansion of the U.S. naval presence off Mexico's east coast.[186]

During the winter, Carranza moved to shore up his popularity by pledging support for more land reform and by appealing to elements of the Mexican labor movement. Villa's concentration on the north (plus the relative ineffectiveness of Zapata's forces outside their home region), allowed the Constitutionalists crucial time and space within which to regroup.

In late March, the first chief's leading general, Alvaro Obregón, began slowly and systematically to move north. As Obregón hoped, Villa immediately raced south to confront him. Villa's high-spirited cavalrymen threw themselves at the Constitutionalists. However, they paid dearly for their daring and for their leader's relative lack of familiarity with conventional military tactics. By its second day, the first major battle between these two armies, at Celaya, had come to resemble what was then transpiring in Europe. Using machine guns, from behind well-prepared defensive positions, Obregón's forces took a devastating toll of Villa's army. Later in the spring, Villa suffered another major defeat, outside León.[187]

Beginning to despair of a (from its standpoint) satisfactory resolution of the Mexican situation anytime soon, the Wilson administration, at the end of May, seized on an idea for a new American initiative suggested by newspaperman David Lawrence. He argued that beneath the level of Villa and Carranza there were many important figures within and among the contending factions who wanted the fighting to come to an end. By appealing to this sentiment, Wilson might be able to bring about a peace conference which in turn could construct a new provisional government. The U.S. might then lend its support to that government as against any elements that remained aloof from the conference.[188]

On June 2, Wilson called for the leaders of the contending sides to try to conciliate their differences. He warned that "if they cannot ... unite ... this Government will be constrained to decide what means should be employed by the United States in order to help Mexico save herself and serve her people."[189] Carranza, however, was feeling stronger than ever, and the president was unable to pry away from him any of the lesser Constitutionalist leaders.[190]

The administration then tried once more to use the vehicle of Pan-Americanism as a means of influencing Mexican events. In late June, it approached the A.B.C. powers about a conference on Mexican affairs. Mexico, in this view, might be a potential testing-ground for the Pan-American peace-keeping system that House had been pushing for. House wrote in his diary that the plan should involve a multilateral insistence "upon the different factions in Mexico getting together." He advised that, "if they once get a government in Mexico started, [Wilson] should throw all the moral and financial weight of the United States back of it, and insist upon there being no change until peace and order reigned."[191]

Lansing was given responsibility for pursuing this approach. At first he considered the possibility of finding secondary figures in the Constitutionalist camp who might constitute the core of such a government. Then he pondered backing a single individual around whom a new government might somehow be created. Early in August, when the Pan-American conference convened, Lansing still hoped that the U.S. could block Carranza's triumph. Toward that end, in fact, Washington worked to keep the conflict in Mexico going. Its hopes for Villa's victory had long vanished. So too had the administration's favorable opinion of the northern general. But, in the wake of still more defeats, like that at Aguascalientes in July, it was eager to see Villa remain in the field as a way of pressuring and/or forestalling the first chief.

Wilson, however, eventually began to voice doubts. Given the Constitutionalists' momentum, it seemed increasingly clear that—in the absence of massive American intervention—Carranza was going to win. Carranza rejected Pan-American mediation. But Lansing and Wilson ultimately decided that dealing with him was the only course they had left. In October, the administration recognized Carranza as the de facto head of the Mexican government.[192]

By continuing to withhold de jure recognition, Washington indicated that it would yet seek to monitor Carranza's course. However, for the time being, the goal was to try to smooth over relations and defer any direct confrontations between the two governments. The war in Europe was coming to influence all the administration's thinking. Lansing wrote in his diary: "Germany will undoubtedly seek to cause a quarrel between that government and ours; therefore, we must avoid a quarrel regardless of criticism and complaint in Congress and the press."[193]

The administration's policy as spelled out by Lansing, however, failed to reckon with what an increasingly desperate Villa's reaction might be to the American change of course. Once Washington had been trying to find ways to keep Villa's army in the field. In October, all aid to him was cut off. Villa was enraged at what he took to be this betrayal. He was also convinced that Carranza had secured recognition by agreeing to U.S. demands that would compromise Mexican sovereignty. In response, he set out deliberately to try to embroil the two governments in conflict.

Carrying out attacks on Americans in northern Mexico and then raiding the border town of Columbus, New Mexico on March 9, 1916, Villa hoped both to get revenge and to draw American forces into Mexico. He expected that this would make it clear to Mexicans that Carranza had sold out. If, on the other hand, Carranza decided to resist, the first chief would forfeit Washington's support and his regime would in that way be weakened. Either way, Villa would be able to assert himself as the defender of Mexican sovereignty.[194]

In Washington the decision was made to despatch forces across the border to destroy what remained of Villa's army. Lansing told Carranza's representative in Washington that he understood it was Villa's intent to embroil the two governments in conflict, but he said that it was up to Carranza to prevent that from happening. Mexico should not consider the American action an invasion of its territory, but rather a case of "hot pursuit" after raiders.[195] Mexican authorities rejoined that they would condone genuine "hot pursuits" that were limited in terms of distance, the number of troops that could be involved, and how long they could stay, so long as this would be a reciprocal privilege. The open-ended mission that the U.S. was contemplating, involving the deployment of a sizable contingent of soldiers, however, had to be considered an invasion. Carranza nevertheless decided not to challenge the five thousand troops led by General John J. Pershing when they finally crossed the border into Mexico on March 15.[196]

Villa enjoyed a six-day head start. Moreover, he was familiar with the vast expanses of northern Mexico into which he had retreated. Weeks passed. American forces wandered deeper into and around the state of Chihuahua. At the end of March, Pershing warned his superiors not to be optimistic about Villa's apprehension. His mission nevertheless continued. The longer Pershing stayed in Chihuahua, the more territory he covered, the more inevitable it was that friction would arise between his forces and the increasingly wary local population. Finally, on April 12, fighting broke out between units of the 13th Cavalry, who were in search of supplies, and inhabitants of the town of Parral.[197]

At this, the Carranza government finally lodged a formal protest. And, in response, Wilson despatched General Scott to the border to negotiate with Obregón. Although willing to concentrate Pershing's forces, Washington still wanted to keep them in northern Mexico. It asserted that the troops would go home only when the U.S. had satisfactory assurances about the future. The Mexican government, meanwhile, refused to discuss any other matters until a date for withdrawal had been set. Carranza also asserted that the expeditionary force would be allowed to move only north.

Relations became increasingly tense during late May and early June. Then, on June 20, Mexican and American troops clashed when a detachment of the latter insisted on passing through the town of Carrizal. Fourteen Americans died and seventeen were taken prisoner. Viewing this as a sign of hostile intent on Carranza's part, Wilson prepared to go to Congress to request authority to occupy northern Mexico. He was still anxious for war not to come, however, and his mail also ran ten to one against that. When Carranza released the American prisoners, therefore, Wilson decided to hold his message back. Lansing suggested that Mexico might propose that a joint commission take up the issues between the two countries, and the Carranza government took that step on July 12.[198]

The president told his secretary that he did not want to intervene in Mexico because that was what Germany wanted, and if war came with Germany, he wanted the U.S. to be able to turn all its attention in that direction.[199] The establishment of a commission defused the crisis. Nevertheless, in combination with the continued presence of U.S. troops in northern Mexico, the commission also came to be seen as yet another opportunity to try to influence the broader direction of Carranza's government. The administration wanted the commission to address a whole range of topics that touched directly on Mexican internal affairs, including especially the conditions and guarantees that would be provided for foreigners doing business in that country.

In fact, when the commission began its deliberations in the fall, Washington urged Mexican acceptance of a relationship that resembled that of Cuba under the Platt Amendment. Mexico's delegates were asked to consider a proposal that would give the U.S. formal and sweeping rights to intervene in their country. It read:

the Government of Mexico solemnly agrees to afford full and adequate protection to the lives and property of citizens of the United States or other foreigners, and this protection shall be adequate to enable such citizens ... [to operate] industries in which they might be interested. The United States reserves the right to re-enter Mexico and to afford such protection by its military forces, in the event of the Mexican Government failing to do so.[200]

But in session after session Mexican negotiators refused to discuss any other issues until the questions of troop withdrawal and future border security were settled.

After the fall elections were over, the administration adopted a sterner tone. Secretary of the Interior Franklin K. Lane, who led the U.S. delegation, informed his counterparts that "the President's patience is at an end, and that he regards present conditions in Mexico as intolerable."[201] The Carranza government stood its ground, however, and in fact began to explore prospects for German economic and military assistance in case Washington was not bluffing.[202] Faced with this resistance, it in the end became necessary for the administration again either to court war with Carranza or to change course. Once German-American tensions rose sharply early in 1917, there was really no decision to be made. In late January, Pershing's forces began a withdrawal that was completed early the following month.[203]

The Wilson administration remained deeply dissatisfied with Carranza's government. Indeed, the list of its concerns was growing as the U.S. moved toward entry in the European war. On the very day that the Pershing expedition completed its withdrawal, Mexico promulgated a new constitution. Among other things, the document laid the basis for much more national control over the Mexican economy, especially with regard to the exploitation of subsoil minerals and resources. Expropriation, if necessary for national development, was affirmed, as was the Calvo principle. The Wilson administration was willing to countenance, indeed favored, land reform in Mexico as an outcome of the revolution. Creating a greater body of actual property holders and destroying "medievalism" were seen as valuable from the standpoint of long-term stability. But Washington was greatly alarmed by proposals that seemed to touch more directly on the question of the country's foreign "obligations." In subsequent years, these questions would come to dominate, and bring further crises, to U.S.-Mexican relations.[204]

Additional concerns lay in the area of foreign policy. On February 11, Carranza addressed a note to other neutral countries, including the U.S., suggesting that they collectively urge a mediated settlement on the European powers. If this failed, neutral countries should then suspend trade with those powers to try to bring about an end to the conflict. Carranza was apparently anxious to try to keep the U.S. out of the conflict, fearing that its entry might either revive the danger of American intervention in Mexico or drag Mexico itself in. However, his initiative was not viewed kindly in Washington. It challenged its leadership of the Western Hemisphere nations in world affairs, and came precisely at the point when the U.S. was moving toward a confrontation with Germany.[205]

Less than two weeks later, British intelligence turned over to the State Department the text of the Zimmermann telegram, which it had intercepted and deciphered. Germany's foreign minister, Arthur Zimmermann, hoped that Carranza might still be interested in a military arrangement if the U-boat campaign Berlin was about to inaugurate led to a U.S. declaration of war. Ideally, he wanted to induce Mexico to attack the U.S. and thus tie down a portion of its forces. His telegram to the German minister in Mexico City spelled out the terms of this proposal.

Carranza saw nothing to be gained in provoking military conflict with the U.S. The incident nevertheless greatly added to the Wilson administration's mistrust of his government. In April, after Washington entered the war, the State Department demanded, and received, a guarantee of strict neutrality from Mexico City.[206]

At about this time, an unfounded rumor reached Washington that Carranza would carry out the course of action he had proposed for neutral countries in February, namely, that they should refrain from commercial intercourse with either side. The story drew concern especially because of the desire of the Allies and the U.S. to have uninterrupted access to Mexican oil. "Unfortunately," responded Wilson when apprised of the rumor by Lansing, "the Mexican government has, no doubt, a legal right to prohibit exports; and I feel quite clear that we could not make such an action on its part a justification for invasion and (virtual) war." A week later, the president added another reason why he thought Washington should be cautious about seizing the Tampico oil fields, and this was that the U.S. could not "afford to be too 'practical.' She is the leading champion of the right of self-government and of political independence everywhere." The ideological posture that the U.S. had assumed on entering the war was at stake. None of this meant, however, that the problem would have to be ignored. Instead, Wilson proposed to have the British seize the fields if that was necessary. They could be told, he informed Lansing, that in this case such action would not be considered as prohibited under the Monroe Doctrine.[207]

As they set out to compete on the world stage, American leaders gave new importance to U.S. relations with the other countries of North America. Ideally they hoped to marshal the entire continent behind their effort to establish the U.S. as one of the globe's leading powers in the coming century.

Washington wanted to occupy a position of unquestioned strategic predominance in North America, an entire continent that it saw as, in essence, its home base in the world. It was determined that its leadership of the continent be recognized and accepted by its neighbors. The U.S. aspired to rally these countries behind its broader foreign policy objectives and to influence events in other parts of the world through them. Not least, it also hoped to see the Canadian and Mexican economies continue to develop as an extended resource base, as well as market, for U.S. industry.

Policy makers saw this vision challenged principally by what they took to be forms of irresponsibility and greed emanating from within Canada and Mexico. To the north, the Alaska boundary dispute presented them with the specter of "spoiled" upstarts refusing to accept their place because they thought that they could draw on the power of Great Britain. Later, Canada's "National Policy" came to be perceived as interference with the "natural movement of trade" on the continent. To the south, turbulent masses and diverse "selfish" figures appeared after 1910 to pose a threat to the behavior that the U.S. wanted.

Washington responded to the Alaska dispute in such a way as profoundly to demonstrate to Canada its true strategic position. Employing Pan-American style rhetoric, as well as methods for conflict settlement currently popular at home, it subsequently sought to promote the idea that Canada's interests were the same as its own, to put the U.S. forward as Ottawa's natural protector, and to inject more order and regularity into the adjustment of Canadian-American affairs. The bid to secure a reciprocity agreement can be seen as running parallel to these other efforts to draw the two nations closer.s

Washington interfered repeatedly in Mexico's affairs. Here its objective was to promote the creation of a new regime that would defer to U.S. leadership internationally and that could and would ensure the conditions within Mexico that it desired. What was different about the Wilson administration, especially during 1913–14, was its conviction that how this was done would also have a profound impact on the U.S. "search for order" throughout the rest of upper Latin America. And yet Wilson's emphasis on constitutional forms was also consistent with the means by which his predecessors had often sought to neutralize "selfish" forces, contain disorder, and promote "peaceful succession" elsewhere in the region. As noted earlier, the nature of his commitment to Pan-Americanism—and, it might be suggested, to internationalism—was also made evident here, as the president sought to involve other American states only when, and in ways, that would serve Washington's purposes.

Diplomatic and military means were employed, and various factions in Mexico were played off against one another. The U.S. was able to isolate its southern neighbor and greatly influence the course of its politics. But, in 1917, when Washington felt compelled to turn elsewhere, it had yet fully to achieve its objectives.[208]

Chapter 6

World Order (to 1914)

As they directed their gaze toward regions of the less developed world of particular interest to them, American policy makers also felt compelled to pay more attention than they had to broader questions of world politics, above all to rivalries within the European state system from which the United States had historically sought to remain aloof. In the wake of the Venezuela boundary dispute and of the rise of German Weltpolitik, successive administrations accepted the proposition that it was not in the U.S. interest to see Britain's position in the Eastern Hemisphere, and, especially, on the high seas undermined. Policy makers still did not want to become enmeshed in European power politics (in part because they did not wish to undercut the sweeping claims that they were making in regard to the Western Hemisphere under the Monroe Doctrine). They also faced extremely strong domestic political sentiment against such "entanglement." Stopping far short of an alliance, Washington nevertheless adopted a more friendly and supportive posture toward Britain in this period, one that was intended to help uphold that empire's power relative to its continental rivals.

This still constituted a "pro-American" rather than a "pro-British" policy. As has already been seen, during the early twentieth century British and American diplomacy frequently diverged with regard to the Far East and Japan as well as the Western Hemisphere,. The two powers' particular interests consistently governed their attitudes toward European questions as well. As evidence of this, in 1916 Washington and London clashed at a quite fundamental and telling level, right at the height of the Great War.

Anxious to avoid embroilment in European power politics, American leaders, albeit to varying degrees, meanwhile tried to reduce the need for that by encouraging reforms in the conduct of international affairs. In particular, from the turn of the century on, policy makers promoted arbitration and other mechanisms by which they hoped to diminish the chances of upheaval and to institutionalize the existing Anglo-American-oriented international order. Such activities carried fewer political or policy risks than did participation in Old World power politics. They were also popular with a growing number of Americans and were pointed to as evidence of Washington's disinterested foreign policy objectives.

Policy makers hoped that reforms of this sort offered a way of overcoming at least some of the threats and uncertainties hanging over the kind of

global environment that they wanted. As has already been seen in the case
of Latin America, arbitration was seen as a means of encouraging order in
certain regions of the underdeveloped world. It was also seen as a means
of fostering "responsible" behavior on the part of small states and, as a
byproduct, of limiting the need for direct great power involvement in their
affairs. In both cases, arbitration was valued as a mechanism that might
reduce the likelihood of conflict among the great powers as their economic interests expanded around the globe.

For the disruption it entailed and the territorial redivisions it could bring
in its wake, such conflict was seen as the most serious problem confronting
the kind of world the U.S. wanted. Policy makers were somewhat hopeful
on this score, at least up to 1914. Their general belief was that war between,
or among, great powers was likely to be less and less common in the future.[1]
As U.S. leaders in this era saw it, the growth of "self-control," and therefore
of rationality, was the most important force working in this direction. The
great powers were by definition composed of growing numbers of more
"responsible" people. And these people, it was believed, were less willing
than people had been in the past to take war lightly as an instrument of
national policy. They were coming to see modern warfare (at least between
great powers) as extremely costly and as bringing with it the danger of
domestic upheaval. And they were coming to see the annexation of new
territories—as a way of expanding trade—as no longer necessary. The people of the great powers were also, it was felt, becoming more cosmopolitan
in their outlook, less prejudiced toward—and more anxious to stand well
in the opinion of—those who lived in the other industrial states.

Policy makers nevertheless continued to believe that wars between great
powers remained a threat, and not just because of the instability that prevailed in areas of the underdeveloped world. As they saw it, all the industrial societies contained large masses of people who were still ignorant and
irresponsible with regard to foreign affairs (these were often the same people who were viewed as a threat to the internal order of such states). These
constituted a ready-made audience for those "agitators" who for selfish reasons might play to popular emotions and thereby bring on war.

There was also no guarantee that the views of "responsible" people would
prevail even where such conditions did not apply. This was especially the
case with states like Germany and Russia, where foreign policy decision making remained extremely autocratic. Here "greedy" and/or irrational leaders or cliques, it was feared, could fairly easily lead their countries into war.[2]

It was hoped that arbitration could help diminish the likelihood of great
power war arising from these causes as well. Arbitration treaties could assist
in the resolution of politically controversial and highly emotional issues
between states, partly by just providing the time within which tempers might
cool. Meanwhile, the failure to agree to an arbitration or to an arbitral finding might carry with it the penalty of diplomatic isolation and international

opprobrium for an offending state. In their promotion of such schemes, American policy makers were here again striving toward what they saw as the depoliticization of world affairs. The ultimate objective was to contain actions on the part of other great powers (as well as on the part of public opinion within the U.S.) and actions by small states that were seen as threatening to the stability of the existing international order. As has been seen, there were a number of disputes that Washington was itself unwilling to arbitrate. Nor was it unwilling when necessary itself to use force. However, this behavior merely underscores the fact that U.S. policy makers were by no means after just any peace.

In the aftermath of the Venezuela boundary dispute, London succeeded in convincing Washington that it had no intention of pursuing a forward policy in the Western Hemisphere, and that indeed its hope was to see upheld the existing territorial boundaries and open door commercial framework throughout Latin America. Even before Britain set about liquidating its own strategic presence in the region, in 1904 and after, this position led American policy makers to radically reevaluate their attitude toward that power.

Suspicion and hostility toward Britain was a long-standing tradition in the U.S.[3] Indeed, it was one that continued to be honored by large segments of the American public until well into the twentieth century. American national identity and culture had to a great extent been formulated, and over time reformulated, in opposition to that power and to things English. The two countries had clashed not only during the American war for independence, but repeatedly during the late eighteenth and early nineteenth centuries, both in North America and on the Atlantic. Throughout the nineteenth century, England had been seen as the biggest opponent of U.S. efforts to realize its "manifest destiny" in North America. It had also antagonized much American sentiment by real and perceived instances of unneutrality during the Civil War. Other developments helped give Anglophobia political weight during the second half of the century. Large numbers of immigrants from Ireland brought with them to America their hostility to the power that controlled their home country. And, as the center of world finance, England also came to be seen by many hard-hit southern and western farmers in the 1880s and 1890s as the source of hurtful international economic policies.

In the wake of the Venezuela boundary dispute, however, and then real and perceived British favors during the Spanish-American War, Washington policy makers downgraded Britain as a potential threat to American policies and instead came to see its power, at least on the high seas and in the Eastern Hemisphere, as something that worked to the advantage of the U.S.

This alteration in the official U.S. attitude was undoubtedly facilitated by the racialist Anglo-Saxonism then in favor among so many prominent old stock Americans, an Anglo-Saxonism that was also avidly played to by British politicians such as Arthur Balfour. The same is true for the Anglophile sentiments that during the late nineteenth century became prominent among important sectors of propertied and "cultured" eastern American society.[4] It was more than anything else, however, the product of a more hardheaded reappraisal on the part of policy makers as to how British power related to their vision of America's proper place in the coming twentieth-century world. TR, for instance, felt that there were distinct branches of the "English-speaking race," and he never had any trouble identifying which of them he thought was the greatest.[5]

In the aftermath of Cleveland's confrontation with London in late 1895, the Anglophile Woodrow Wilson expressed the belief that, if united, the two countries would hold "the future destinies of the world" in their hands.[6] This attitude did not prevent Wilson as president two decades later from forcefully confronting British policy himself on several occasions (beginning with Mexico in 1913). The same is true of Hay, who though equally enamored of British institutions and culture, was not unwilling to press London hard over such issues as Alaska.[7] TR's traditionally greater suspicion of British policy, and his pronounced criticism of Americans he thought were in awe of England, meanwhile, did not prevent him from advocating a new U.S. attitude toward London by the late 1890s.[8]

On the one hand, U.S. policy makers became convinced that Britain did not have the stature it once had, that it was at the very least a power in relative decline. And this encouraged them to play on Britain's predicament, on what in later twentieth-century parlance would be called its "imperial overstretch." Anxious for stable relations with the U.S. and intimidated by America's growing power, London was subsequently, as has been seen, compelled to pay for the rapprochement with a series of one-sided concessions, at least in the Western Hemisphere.[9]

On the other hand, Britain's power on the Atlantic, even in Africa and around the periphery of Eurasia, came to be seen as beneficial to U.S. policy. Above all, British naval power was seen as a formidable factor working to uphold the existing political and economic organization of Latin America. For policy makers continued to worry that other European naval powers might try to challenge the Monroe Doctrine.

Indeed, at almost the precise moment that they began to dismiss British opposition to the doctrine, U.S. leaders began to focus on Germany as such a threat. Historians may never agree as to Berlin's aims with regard to the Western Hemisphere in these years. It is clear that Germany's leaders saw the Monroe Doctrine as an arrogant conceit, equally that its naval commanders would ideally have liked to have had a presence of their own in the Caribbean. It seems no less evident, however, that this was not seen as a goal that could be realized anytime soon. In practice Berlin was cautious in its dealings with the U.S., and after the turn of the century it appears to have subordinated all else to the hope that it might woo Washington away from its developing relationship with Britain.[10]

American policy makers certainly seem to have exaggerated the immediacy of any such German challenge. Yet there can be no doubt that their concern was real. They based it in part on their recognition of the resentment and envy held by many German leaders of the U.S., but above all, it would seem, on what they took to be that state's needs and what they saw as the recklessness of its—in the realm of foreign policy at least—essentially unchecked leaders. It must be said that Germany, to some degree, seems also simply to have fit the bill as a potential challenger to American policy.

Germany was seen as the one major power that had yet to acquire territory on which to settle its surplus population. This, even more than its quest for markets and raw materials, was held as likely to be the motor force behind Berlin's foreign policy. And U.S. policy makers convinced themselves that such a need would almost inevitably drive Germany to look not just to expansion in the Caribbean, but to the creation of German colonies in South America (thus their fixation on the German immigrant community in Brazil). The kaiser had already shown in the case of the Kruger telegram that he had no qualms about intruding on the spheres other powers claimed, in that case Britain's in South Africa. And unless the U.S. continued to build up its own strength, it was argued, it would find this rapidly growing industrial and military state trying to do the same thing in the Americas.[11]

Britain's position in the Old World and on the high seas came to be valued for additional reasons as well. By contrast with that of Russia and France, British power came to be appreciated as a force working not only for stability but also for a high degree of American commercial access to much of Africa and Asia. At the same time, Britain came to be seen as an essentially "satiated" power working against a territorial expansionism on the part of other states that Washington feared might lead not only to its exclusion from many regions, but also to disruptive war and/or the creation of more powerful great power combinations in the Old World.

This new appreciation of Britain and its role began to be articulated by leading policy figures soon after the Venezuelan clash of 1895–96. In spring 1897, right after his arbitration treaty with Britain failed of ratification, ex-Secretary Olney—the author in 1895 of the "twenty-inch gun"—wrote Henry White that Americans were "part of one great English-speaking family whose proud destiny it is to lead and control the world."[12] He told an audience at Harvard's Sanders Theatre the following winter that there was no question but that the two powers would soon start to cooperate more in international affairs. "[O]ur material interests alone," said Olney, dictate this: "through what agency are we so likely to gain new outlets for our products as through that of a Power whose possessions girdle the earth and in whose ports equal privileges and facilities of trade are accorded to the flags of all nations?"[13]

Roosevelt's reassessment began at the same time. Convinced that Britain had to be stood up to in 1895–96, he expressed a much more sanguine view as assistant secretary of the navy in spring 1897. He had already also come to focus on Germany as England's replacement. In a letter to Mahan, TR opined that

We should acquire the Danish [Virgin] Islands, and by turning Spain out [of Cuba] should serve notice that no strong European power, and especially not Germany, should be allowed to gain a foothold by supplanting some weak European power. I do not fear England; Canada is a hostage for her good behavior; but I do fear some of the other powers.[14]

The next year he told another correspondent that "of all the nations of Europe, it seems to me Germany is by far the most hostile to us ... with Germany, under the Kaiser, we may at any time have trouble if she seeks to acquire territory in South America."[15]

The Spanish-American War accelerated this shift in attitude toward Britain. American leaders were struck by the extent of British power on the high seas. British neutrality, as already mentioned, also tilted in Washington's direction. The Spanish fleet, for example, was not allowed to take on coal in Egypt, but Dewey was afforded use of cable facilities at Hong Kong and British authorities also delayed officially proclaiming their lease of Mirs Bay from China so that U.S. naval vessels would not have to be ordered away when the war broke out.[16]

Friction developed between Dewey and the commander of a German flotilla sent to Manila Bay soon after the destruction of Spanish maritime power there. And a legend soon took shape that only the interposition of British vessels, also on the scene, prevented the commander from interfering.[17] In late 1898 TR, now governor-elect of New York, wrote his British friend Arthur Lee that, "I shall not forget, and I don't think our people will, England's attitude during the Spanish War." "[T]he English-speaking peoples are now closer together than for a century and a quarter, and ... every effort should be made to keep them close ... for their interests are really fundamentally the same." He only hoped that "the Kaiser does not make it necessary for one or the other of us to take a fall out of Germany, for the Germans are a good people, and there is really no need to have their interests clash with ours. But at least we must stand together!"[18]

The U.S. and Britain had convened their Joint High Commission during the summer of 1898, and in September John Hay became secretary of state. In his capacity as ambassador to Britain, Hay had already called publicly for closer relations between the two powers, and his desire to bring about such a new relationship quickly became a central objective of his diplomacy. "As long as I stay here," he wrote in 1899, "no action shall be taken contrary to my conviction that the one indispensable feature of our foreign policy should be a friendly understanding with England."[19]

This new attitude toward British power was clearly in evidence during the Boer War of 1899–1902.[20] The conflict arose out of London's determination to solidify its control over the interior of South Africa, and especially, in this case, over the Transvaal state that had been set up by Boers (or Afrikaners)—colonial settlers of Dutch descent—after their "great trek" out of the Cape Colony a half century before. Britain had a loose form of overlordship over the territory dating to the early 1880s, but it grew increasingly anxious to consolidate its hold after a gold rush began in the Rand later that decade. Tensions rose steadily following an unsuccessful Cape Colony effort (the Jameson Raid) in early 1896 to overthrow the Boer government of Paul Kruger. London was nevertheless inadequately prepared for the opposition it would face when full-scale war finally erupted three-and-a-half years later. British forces suffered a string of calamitous defeats during the fall and winter of 1899–1900, and a much more serious effort had to be mounted before the tide finally began to turn in 1900.

Popular and official sentiment on the continent of Europe was overwhelmingly critical of Britain, and this criticism mounted when the kinds of tactics that had already become commonplace in colonial wars against non-European peoples began at the end of 1900 to be employed against the Boers. London worried that its rivals might take advantage of the crisis to test its power elsewhere.

The attitude of other powers toward Britain's predicament, however, was not shared by policy makers in the U.S. Although American public opinion was generally (if not excitedly) pro-Boer, there was never any question as to which side Washington preferred. U.S. officials expressed concern and dismay over England's early setbacks, and they adopted a diplomatic posture toward the conflict that leaned heavily in London's direction.[21] Hay rejected a request from the president of the Orange Free State to mediate the controversy. And a later Boer appeal, made during the war, was handled in such a way as to give London a chance to make clear to all powers how hostile its attitude toward such intervention would be. The U.S. became a key source of supplies for the British war effort. A one-sided relationship was able to develop without any technical compromise of U.S. neutrality because of Britain's control of the sea. But Washington also refused to hold London strictly accountable when that power challenged American neutral rights. When the British navy began to treat Delagoa Bay, in the nearby Portuguese colony of Mozambique, as though it were an enemy port, for instance, Hay simply worked out an agreement whereby London would compensate American exporters for any ship seizures it made.[22]

There are several explanations for the posture assumed by Washington. As historian Thomas Noer points out, many U.S. leaders had come to view the government of the Transvaal as too provincial and as economically

backward. American trade with southern Africa had grown since the opening up of the Rand, but the consolidation of British power was seen as something that would greatly accelerate the development of mining in the region
and thus promote far more rapid expansion. Hay, for example, absorbed
this perspective through discussions with his friend John Hays Hammond,
an associate of Cecil Rhodes and one of many American mining engineers
who had spent time in South Africa.[23]

U.S. policy makers were grateful for the position that Britain had adopted
during the Spanish-American War. They were also in much the same boat
as Britain at this time, fighting a war of their own to subdue the Philippines.
Above all, however, Washington adopted the course that it did during the
Boer War because it was convinced that Britain's strength and credibility
as a great power were at stake and that that, in turn, was of consequence
to American interests. "If the existence of the British Empire should be
called in question," Hay commented, during the period when one after
another serious setback for England was being registered, "there is no knowing what constellation might then make its appearance among the powers."[24] "The fight of England," he wrote some weeks later to Henry White,
"is the fight of civilization and progress and all of our interests are bound
up in her success."[25]

The same concern dominates TR's correspondence on South Africa
throughout this period. As early as 1896 he wrote, "though I greatly admire
the Boers" (he was himself of Dutch ancestry), "I feel it is to the interest of
civilization that the English-speaking race, should be dominant in South
Africa, exactly as it is for the interest of civilization that the United States
themselves, the greatest branch of the English-speaking race, should be
dominant in the Western Hemisphere."[26] In the aftermath of Black Week,
a period in December 1899 when the British army suffered record losses,
Roosevelt told his sister that "The downfall of the British Empire I should
regard as a calamity to the race and especially to this country."[27] Should
that power suffer a serious disaster, he subsequently predicted, "in five
years it will mean a war between us and some one of the great continental
European nations, unless we are content to abandon the Monroe Doctrine
for South America."[28]

During these same turn-of-the-century years the U.S. began to assume an
important role in the promotion of international arbitration. Historically,
the U.S. and Britain had often had recourse to arbitration as a method
of resolving differences. Since Blaine, the U.S. had also pushed for its expanded use in the Americas. In its quest to stabilize the existing international order, Washington now began to promote the global relevance of this
method of conflict settlement.

The starting point for such activity was the Hague Conference of 1899.
It, in turn, had its origins in a Tsarist rescript of August 1898. Financially

hard-pressed and eager to avoid the expenditures that would be necessary if it were to keep up with the weapons modernizations being carried out by its European neighbors, St. Petersburg proposed that an international conference be held to discuss arms limitation. The other major powers, including the U.S., responded positively. But their lack of enthusiasm was apparent, and they assented principally out of deference to world opinion. Most were suspicious of Russia's intentions and all were ill-disposed toward discussion of either limitation or disarmament.[29]

After Tsar Nicholas suggested a broader agenda for the conference, however, it elicited more support. In January 1899, Count Michael Muraviev, the foreign minister, offered that it ought also to address outstanding questions as to the rules for the conduct of war, as well as methods by which disputes might be settled short of armed conflict.[30] The McKinley administration now saw the meeting as an opportunity to exert influence on behalf of international stability.[31]

Delegates from twenty-six countries assembled at The Hague for the start of the conference in May. Representing the U.S. were Andrew Dickson White, Washington's ambassador to Germany and former president of Cornell University; Seth Low, president of Columbia University; Stanford Newel, U.S. minister to the Netherlands; William R. Crozier, an army ordnance expert; Alfred Thayer Mahan; and Frederick W. Holls, an international law expert who served as the delegation's secretary.[32]

Russia had hoped that such a conference might lead to a freeze both on spending and on the size of all the powers' military establishments. But such ideas received little support at The Hague. Confronted with a military challenge in the Philippines and immersed in a major program of naval expansion, the U.S. explicitly instructed its delegates to stay clear of such questions.[33]

More agreement was forthcoming with regard to Russia's proposals for action on the rules and conduct of war. Meeting in Brussels in 1874, representatives from fourteen states had undertaken to produce a draft code of law on land warfare (building in part on regulations written during the Civil War by Francis Lieber for the U.S. army). The conference revised these rules and made them the basis of an international convention. It also adapted and extended to warfare at sea the Geneva Convention of 1864, which had established the Red Cross and set down rules for the protection of sick and wounded on land battlefields.[34] The U.S., however, continued to see itself as likely to be neutral in any European war. It was more interested in seeing the conference endorse the idea that all private property, exclusive of contraband, be granted immunity from capture at sea. White pressed hard to have this topic taken up at The Hague. But he had to settle for an expression of support that the issue be addressed at some future meeting.[35]

Muraviev had also proposed that the conference consider "Acceptance,

in principle, of the use of good offices, mediation, and voluntary arbitration ... with the purpose of preventing armed conflicts between nations."[36]
The State Department saw these topics as "likely to open the most fruitful
field for discussion" at the meeting, and they did indeed draw the most
attention.[37] It culminated in the signing of a Convention on the Peaceful
Settlement of International Disputes.

There already existed means—beyond bilateral negotiations—whereby
disputes between countries might be settled short of war. The thrust of the
conference was to publicize these, to make recourse to them easier, and to
get all the powers on record as supporting them, the belief being that such
conflict management might thereby become more regular. Before an appeal
to arms, the signatory states agreed ("as far as circumstances allow") to
employ "the good offices or mediation of one or more friendly Powers." And
"strangers to the dispute" were encouraged, and seen as having the right
under the convention, to "offer their good offices or mediation" to the
"States at variance." Countries could accept such mediation without having
to interrupt their military preparations. Where disagreements arose "from
a difference of opinion on points of fact," the treaty endorsed the creation
by the involved parties of impartial international commissions of inquiry
or elucidation.[38]

Such approaches sought essentially to widen the scope of diplomacy, but
the conference also sought to make easier recourse to arbitration, hoping
that it might more frequently be employed for the settlement of disputes
that eluded such methods.[39] Indeed, most of the articles of the convention
were on this topic.

The U.S. position was that this could best be done through the creation
of an international court, and to promote that its instructions included a
detailed plan for such a body.[40] Britain's principal representative, Sir Julian
Pauncefote, seized the initiative on this question, however, and the U.S.
delegates soon found themselves falling in behind his leadership. "Many
arbitration codes and rules of procedure have been made," he told the conference, "but the procedure has up to the present time been regulated by
the arbitrators or by general or special treaties. . . . If we want to make a step
forward, I believe that it is absolutely necessary to organize a permanent
international tribunal which may be able to assemble at once on the request
of the disputing nations."[41]

Most of the delegations then began to gravitate toward arbitral provisions based on the Russian proposals and on Pauncefote's plan for a court.
Inexperienced with arbitration, and fearful of how it might compromise
its pursuit of its interests, or interfere with its need to mobilize rapidly in
time of war, Germany, however, balked at the entire thrust of this part of
the meeting.[42]

White played a leading role among those who worked to overcome
this opposition. In conversations with Count Herbert von Münster, one of

Germany's delegates, and in a long letter to Foreign Minister Bernhard von Bülow, he argued that Germany was courting international public censure by its opposition and that the defeat of the conference would also work to "promote the designs of the socialistic forces which are so powerful in all parts of the Continent."[43] White sought to disabuse the Germans of any fear that the convention constituted a threat to their sovereignty. He pointed out to Münster "that the plan thus far adopted contemplated entirely voluntary arbitration, with the exception that an obligatory system was agreed upon as regards sundry petty matters."[44] "No rational man here," he told Bülow, "expects all wars to be ended by anything done here; no one proposes to submit to any such tribunal questions involving the honor of any nation or the inviolability of its territory, or any of those things which nations feel instinctively must be reserved for their own decision."[45] But White held out practical benefits that might be advanced by the scheme. "Take ... matters as they now stand between Germany and the U.S.," he told Münster.

There is a vast mass of petty questions which constantly trouble the relations between the two countries.... What a blessing it would be if all these questions ... which make the more important questions constantly arising between the two countries so difficult to settle, could be sent at once to a tribunal and decided one way or the other! ... [T]he sovereign and his government would thus be relieved from parliamentary chicanery based, not upon knowledge, but upon party tactics or personal grudges or inherited prejudices.[46]

Germany ultimately relented, albeit on the condition that the court's bureaucracy be scaled back and all references to obligatory arbitration in the project be removed (the U.S. had itself already insisted on some categories being excluded, for fear, in particular, that they might obligate it to arbitrate over Alaska).[47]

The final convention recognized arbitration, in "questions of a legal nature" and "especially" in the interpretation of treaties, "as the most effective, and at the same time the most equitable, means of settling disputes which diplomacy has failed to settle." It also established a Permanent Court of Arbitration, to meet at The Hague, and set down rules of procedure that, "unless otherwise stipulated by the parties," were to be employed in connection with its use. Each power was entitled to appoint as many as four people to serve as "Members of the Court." These names were to be placed on a list from which arbitrators could whenever necessary be chosen. The convention envisioned "arbitration tribunals" composed of five judges, two selected by each side, with a fifth, an umpire, then designated by those four.[48] McKinley endorsed the treaty in his annual message for 1899—Cleveland, and former secretaries of state Evarts, Foster, Olney, and Day, also announced their support—and it was ratified by the Senate the following February.[49]

The Hague conference of 1899 gave a great boost to the "peace movement" in the U.S. Activism around issues of war and peace had a long history in America, going back to the days of pre-Civil War reform. But in this era of dramatically increasing American economic and political involvement and interest in the globe, it grew as never before. Old organizations, like the American Peace Society, expanded, and many new ones were founded. At the same time, as many studies have detailed, peace activism during these years tried to shed whatever associations it earlier had had with pacifism or nonresistance. Instead it focused on how mechanisms like arbitration or regular international conferences might serve to promote world order and stability. As historian Charles DeBenedetti puts it, the ranks of the peace movement came to be composed in this period of "people of status," of businessmen, educators, philanthropists, journalists, clergymen, and lawyers, whose principal desire it was "to regularize order in the industrial age."[50] Heartened by the arbitral convention, these reformers subsequently campaigned for more achievement in this same direction.

Early twentieth-century U.S. policy makers wanted to stand well in the eyes of the peace movement and to enlist its support. The movement shared policy makers' emphasis on order and stability. It also shared their belief in Anglo-American superiority and leadership as well as their fear that "the masses" at home and abroad could by their behavior destabilize international affairs. Policy makers were at the same time concerned, however, that many peace leaders were not as practical in their attitudes as they made themselves out to be. And they fretted that some activists—Andrew Dickson White referred to them as "cranks"—entertained and, worse, preached unrealistic ideas about what arbitration and other peaceful settlement schemes could be relied on to achieve. This was especially the case with TR, who always harbored the suspicion that many men of his social background—including many political leaders—lacked what it took to embrace "the strenuous life."

Roosevelt worried that the rise of the peace movement might bring about the triumph of what he called "peace at any price" men.[51] At a minimum he felt that the movement's outlook was dangerously short-sighted. Arbitration could not be resorted to as a means of settling all disputes. At least, that is, not if the U.S. was going to have the kind of world order, the kind of peace "of righteousness," that he wanted and that he believed many in the peace movement wanted too. For that, the U.S. would need force that it was able to deploy (indeed TR argued that Washington would have less need to resort to force to keep such a peace if it maintained a powerful navy and if foreign countries were convinced that it was willing to use it). "To be rich, aggressive, and yet helpless in war," Roosevelt lectured Theodore Burton, an Ohio Republican who was also a peace reformer and skeptical of naval expansion, "is to invite destruction."[52] Americans, he admonished on another occasion, "would dearly purchase a hundred arbitration treaties if they lulled us into trusting to them alone to preserve the peace."[53]

The new president did not oppose what had been done at The Hague though. However cautious he could sometimes be about arbitration for the U.S., Roosevelt at the same time saw merit in "the Hague idea" for what he thought it might do to help promote the kind of world order he desired. Although careful to emphasize that he felt the U.S. had been able to play a worthwhile role in 1899 only because it was a strong and well-armed power, TR had in its aftermath spoken in praise of the conference. He commented that

a very marked feature in the world-history of the present century has been the growing infrequency of wars between great civilized nations. The Peace Conference at The Hague is but one of the signs of this growth. I am among those who believe that much was accomplished ... and I am proud of the leading position taken in the conference by our delegates.[54]

Right after he took office, his administration, as noted, tried to use the Hague system as a means of promoting order in Latin America.

The following February, TR received a visit at the White House from the Baron d'Estournelles de Constant, a prominent member of the French Chamber of Deputies and one of his country's delegates at The Hague. D'Estournelles was concerned that as yet no cases had been sent to the court, and he was in Washington as part of a personal crusade he was conducting to drum up such business. He worried that the institution might die of neglect otherwise. Roosevelt took an immediate liking to his visitor and praised him for being the kind of peace advocate that he respected. He then arranged for a long-standing dispute between the Catholic church of California and Mexico (the Pious Fund case) to be referred to the court.[55] TR drew attention to the Hague system again in his next annual message. "The last century has seen a marked diminution of wars between civilized powers," he commented (while wars with "uncivilized" powers were largely "mere matters" of what he called "international police duty"). "Wherever possible, arbitration or some similar method should be employed ... to settle difficulties between civilized nations, although as yet the world has not progressed sufficiently to render it possible, or necessarily desirable, to invoke arbitration in every case."[56] Several weeks later, the administration found a much more important use for the court in connection with the Venezuela claims confrontation.[57]

The referral of that case to The Hague helped simultaneously to cinch a campaign that the outgoing ambassador to Germany had been conducting to get Andrew Carnegie to build a headquarters for the court. White had taken the matter up with the retired steel magnate—and aspiring peace leader—on visits to his estate in Scotland. And these were then followed up by a meeting between Carnegie and the assistant secretary of state, David

Jayne Hill, in New York at the end of January 1903. The following April, Carnegie announced that he would donate $1.5 million to construct a home at The Hague for the court and its library.[58]

By the end of 1904, Washington had come to be even more closely identified with the Hague system. Although the Olney-Pauncefote treaty's fate before the senate was still fresh in their minds, Hay and Roosevelt decided in the spring to pursue treaties of arbitration between the U.S. and each of the other powers that were signatories to the Hague convention. Article 19 of that document, drafted after Berlin blocked any provisions for obligatory arbitration, stated that the signatories still reserved the right to conclude "general or private" agreements among themselves "with a view to extending obligatory arbitration to all cases which they may consider it possible to submit to it."[59] Reflecting at least in part their broader effort to improve relations in this period, London and Paris signed such a pact late in 1903. This then stimulated a campaign to have Washington pursue, and by implication promote, such bilateral treaties as well.

The Anglo-French treaty provided that differences between those two powers "of a legal nature, or relating to the interpretation of treaties" that could not be settled by diplomacy, would be referred to the Hague court, so long, that is, as such differences did not affect the "vital interests, the independence, or the honor" of either state and "did not concern the interests of third parties." In each instance, the two governments were to conclude a special *compromis* defining clearly the matter in dispute, the scope of the powers of the arbitrators, and other specific details.[60]

The treaty was quickly followed by the negotiation of many others along the same lines on the continent, more than a dozen just by the end of 1904, including one between London and Berlin in July. It also gave rise to efforts to have the U.S. follow suit. Thomas Barclay, who was president of the Paris branch of the British Chamber of Commerce and had played a key role in promoting the Anglo-French treaty, crossed the Atlantic at the end of 1903 hoping to revive interest in a new Anglo-American treaty.[61]

Hay, at first, was hesitant. Replying to the U.S. ambassador to France, who had urged him to consider a treaty with that country as well, he commented in December that it "would never do to send another arbitration treaty with England to the Senate unless the President were absolutely sure in advance that it would not be rejected, and it is impossible at this moment to see that this is the case." It would meanwhile "be awkward," he asserted, "for us to make an arbitration treaty with any other European power." Nor was Hay convinced that there was "the same necessity" for such treaties "that there was before the organization of the Hague Tribunal." "We are in as good a position to carry matters to The Hague as we would be if we signed with France and England arbitration treaties on the line of the recent one, a copy of which you enclose," he commented. "As a matter of fact, the United States is, so far, the only country which has done anything to make use of The Hague court and to build up its authority and prestige. We have brought before it the only two cases it has ever considered, and we hope to make use of it hereafter in the same way."[62]

Hay's reservations were eventually left behind, however, both as it became clear that the treaty had set off a trend and as enthusiasm for such a pact, especially with England, gained influential support within the U.S. Prominent Anglophiles and peace activists held a meeting in Washington early in 1904 to lobby on behalf of this goal. Ultimately the administration decided that it should sign such treaties and that the wisest course would be for it simultaneously to offer pacts on the Anglo-French model to all the powers that had expressed support for arbitration at The Hague. By January 1905, conventions along these lines were concluded with Britain, France, Germany, Italy, Austria-Hungary, the Kingdom of Norway and Sweden, Switzerland, Spain, Portugal, and Mexico.[63]

Uncertain as to what the fate of the treaties would be, the president meanwhile took another, more dramatic, step to reaffirm U.S. support for The Hague. Responding to an appeal from the Interparliamentary Union, an organization of European and American legislators interested in promoting arbitration, TR announced in September that he would call for another international conference.[64]

Just a few days later, Hay was the opening speaker before the International Congress of Peace, meeting in Boston. Seeking, in this election year, to win support for the president from the American peace movement, Hay trumpeted the McKinley-Roosevelt record with regard to the Hague system. "No Presidents in our history," he said, "have been so faithful and so efficient as the last two in the cause of arbitration and of every peaceful settlement of differences." Hay did not mention Alaska, or the U.S. refusal to respond to a demand from Colombia for an arbitration over Panama. At the same time, he characterized the government's use of troops in the Caribbean and in the Far East since 1898 as also being in the interests of peace.[65]

Although they did not go as far as many of its members would have liked, there was no question but that the administration's arbitration treaties would receive the overwhelming support of the peace movement. Like the Olney-Pauncefote Treaty before them, however, the conventions came under careful scrutiny when submitted to the Senate. A large majority in that body took the position that it was wrong for its "advice and consent" not to be required for the "special agreements," or *compromis*, that would set the terms, scope, and details of each arbitration entered into. To redress this, the senate voted 50 to 9 in February 1905 to substitute the term "treaty" for "agreement" in the appropriate clause.[66]

Roosevelt was furious. He wrote prominent Republicans that the amendment, promoted most actively by his friend Lodge, turned the whole business of the treaties "into a sham." "The point of having the arbitration treaties at all," he told John Coit Spooner, "is to make it easier to arbitrate in the future." The pacts, TR said, were a short but real step toward increasing the chances for the peaceful settlement of differences between the U.S. and other nations. "[T]his point is entirely destroyed when ... we go through the solemn farce of ratifying an arbitration treaty that says nothing but that under certain conditions we shall again go through the matter of considering whether or not we will have another arbitration treaty." Rather than accept the conventions in their amended form, he chose to have them withdrawn.[67]

Although the U.S. pressed Britain vigorously over the canal treaty and Alaska in the period during and after the Boer War, its position on British power in the Eastern Hemisphere was once again demonstrated during the first great European diplomatic crisis of the new century. This was the controversy that developed between Germany and France in 1905 over the latter's plans for Morocco.

TR's preference was to avoid involvement. Asked to play a role, the president initially did so because he was afraid that there might otherwise be a European war. But once a conference to address the issues in dispute had been agreed on, the administration became more explicitly concerned to work for an outcome that would uphold the recently concluded entente between London and Paris. TR preserved good relations with Berlin. However, his participation in the conference marked a departure for the U.S. (and one that his domestic critics took careful note of).

The previous several years had seen a major reorientation in the foreign policies of all the European great powers who were parties to this dispute. French policy throughout the 1890s had been based on the alliance concluded with Russia at the beginning of that decade. This had been sealed with Germany—France's enemy in the Franco-Prussian War of 1870–71—in mind. But French leaders also came to hope that the new relationship could strengthen them in their rivalry with Britain for influence and positions of advantage in Africa and Southeast Asia.[68]

France's greatest immediate ambition in the underdeveloped world in this period was to unseat Britain from the position of control it had achieved at Suez by virtue of its occupation of Egypt in 1882. After the tripartite intervention in the Far East over the Treaty of Shimonoseki in 1895 there were hopes that Germany and Russia might also exert leverage on behalf of a multi-power "neutralization" of Egypt. But these were misplaced, and in succeeding years French policy toward northeastern Africa continued to be stymied by British opposition.[69]

Foreign Minister Théophile Delcassé meanwhile became interested in extending French influence over Morocco.[70] His goal was eventually to make it, together with Algeria and Tunisia, part of what historian Christopher Andrew has called "a Greater France built round the shores of the Mediterranean, with an African hinterland stretching southward to the Congo."[71]

Convinced finally that he had no chance of overturning London's occupation of Egypt, Delcassé in 1903 began to hope that Paris might be able to exchange acceptance of the situation there for the removal by Britain of any objections to French ambitions in the Maghrib.

Important changes had meanwhile also been underway in British policy.[72] By the turn of the century, the leaders of Britain had become greatly concerned about that power's future position in the world. England's preeminence had throughout the previous century been based to a great extent on its economic lead over all other nations. From mid-century on, however, it had lost its position as the only major industrial state. It retained a position of supremacy in finance, and in shipping and many other services, but in manufacturing it was being overtaken by the U.S. and Germany. Its goods no longer dominated the markets of continental Europe and North America. Since the 1870s, Britain had also come to face more competition in the tropical world and in the Eurasian periphery—regions that now seemed more vital to the Empire's future than ever before. To ensure the framework and influence it wanted in those places, and to address the instability often caused by Western penetration there, London assumed much greater political/military burdens in Asia and Africa during the 1880s and 1890s. During such events as Queen Victoria's Diamond Jubilee in 1897, the British upper classes gloried in the extent of their nation's role around the world, but their leaders were beginning to wonder how many more commitments their state could undertake.

The Boer War proved extremely expensive. It revealed glaring inefficiencies in preparedness and coordination, and, still more important, underscored what seemed to be a position of diplomatic isolation and global over-extension. It became, for these reasons, a catalyst for change. As the new century opened, the Salisbury and then, from July 1902, Balfour governments undertook a number of initiatives to try to address these problems.[73] One involved the hope that the self-governing colonies might contribute more resources toward the Empire's defense. Although many foreign leaders were awed by the scale of the British Empire, its leaders were often more impressed by what they saw as the greater cohesiveness of such giant countries as Russia and the U.S., states that had grown principally by colonizing neighboring territories. They believed that Britain would be able to compete with those powers over the long run only if it could more effectively draw on and coordinate the resources of the dominions. An appeal to this effect was made at the Colonial Conference in 1902, but in the face of the independent identities and interests that had grown up throughout the Empire it achieved only mixed results. Joseph Chamberlain pressed subsequently for his program of Tariff Reform and imperial preference as a way of drawing the Empire together, saving British industry (by creating a larger, protected "home" market), and raising revenue for social programs to address what he saw as the deteriorating fibre and flagging loyalty of England's lower classes. However, the leaders of both the major parties resisted this course on policy as well as electoral grounds.[74]

Other initiatives involved diplomacy and the reposturing of the navy. For the security of its empire London had traditionally been able to rely on its naval supremacy. But that too had come under pressure, in part because of budgetary concerns and in part because of the rise of other powers' fleets. Throughout most of the nineteenth century, dominance in the waters around Europe had secured England control over the sea lanes between its home ports and the rest of the globe as well as security against any direct attack on Britain. "By blockading enemy fleets in their home ports and by attacking them as they attempted to pass through the confined waters of the English Channel, the North Sea, the Suez Canal, and the mouth of the Mediterranean," political scientist Aaron Friedberg notes, British warships were able to "control access to the world's oceans."[75] Indeed, as naval historians Harold and Margaret Sprout put it, "Great Britain could virtually dictate the terms of Europe's access to the 'outer world.'" "As long as no important center of naval power existed outside Europe, England's grip on the ocean portals of that Continent constituted in effect a global command of the seas."[76]

These conditions had, however, changed by the turn of the century. For one thing, extra-European powers like Japan and the U.S. started to build oceangoing navies. It became clear that Britain could not maintain supremacy in the Far East and in the Western Hemisphere and still hope to control the waters off Europe (including the sea lanes between Europe and India). Nor could England unaided contain Russian expansion in the Far East. To address these problems, London, as already noted, entered into understandings with Japan and the U.S. by which it hoped its essential interests in those regions would be protected even as it lost that supremacy.

Yet keeping ahead of the combined might of the French and Russian navies—whose growth and potential cooperation seemed especially to pose a challenge to British control in the Mediterranean—had already proven to be expensive. As a result, London grew eager to explore possibilities for an improvement in relations with one or both of those powers. This disposition intensified in the face of Germany's efforts to build its own large navy, a program that began to register concern, at least within the admiralty, by 1902. For these reasons, Britain responded positively to French feelers about a deal, and in April 1904 the two powers reached a general settlement of their colonial differences, centering on support for each other's ambitions in Morocco and Egypt.[77]

Berlin had meanwhile also adopted a new course. After unification in the early 1870s, Germany had quickly established itself as the leading military and industrial power in Europe. But, by the late 1890s, its leaders were convinced that their state's future power, prestige, and wealth would be dependent on the position it occupied relative to the globe as a whole.

They therefore embarked on a long-term strategy that they hoped would make Germany at least the equal of any other power during the coming century.[78]

The centerpiece of their plan was the construction of a great battleship fleet. In true Mahanian fashion, Germany was seen to require a navy that could not only protect trade, but also give Berlin the ability to influence the political/economic organization of distant regions of the globe. The future strength of the economy and state was seen to depend on the continued growth of exports and on Germany's ability to import raw materials and food from around the world. The kaiser and his advisors also believed that Germany needed a greater number of colonies so that it could hold its own in competition with rivals on the scale of the British Empire, Russia, and the U.S. Since the most appropriate places for such expansion seemed already to have been parceled out, they felt that these would come only if Berlin was strong enough to insist on its share of the spoils when decline overtook older, less dynamic European colonial powers. Berlin had failed to benefit substantially by the collapse of the Spanish Empire, but it was, for instance, hopeful that it would fare better once similar weaknesses overtook Portugal.

Above all, a large fleet was looked on as an instrument that would give Berlin more leverage in its relations with London. Britain still had the most say about the disposition of the extra-European world. It also controlled the sea lanes running to and from the continent. As things stood, Germany's leaders were convinced that England would never willingly allow them the role they wanted. And in a dispute, Britain could, without fear of serious repercussion, cut Germany off from its overseas trade and possessions. If Germany could amass a sufficiently powerful fleet just across the North Sea, however, a process expected to take fifteen to twenty years, its leaders thought that London would then be compelled to grant them their wishes, to cede them, as the kaiser's most influential admiral, Alfred von Tirpitz, put it, "sufficient naval presence . . . for the conduct of a grand policy overseas."[79]

Germany's leaders assumed that European great power relations would continue to be dominated by the rivalry between Britain and the Dual Alliance. Indeed that was seen as functional to, if not a prerequisite of, the realization of Berlin's objectives. They were surprised and chagrined therefore to learn of the signing of the entente. Berlin worried that it was now in fact in danger of being isolated and encircled by those three other powers. London and Paris, working together, could block any initiatives in the extra-European world that they did not favor. And should an Anglo-Russian agreement also be concluded, that would alter the position of strength on the continent that Berlin had taken for granted.[80]

Principally in the hope of foreclosing an Anglo-Russian accord, Berlin tried unsuccessfully during the fall of 1904 to forge an alliance with St.

Petersburg. Anglo-Russian relations remained strained, however. Moreover, Russia's power promised for some time to be at a low ebb as the result of the beating it was taking in the Far Eastern war. As France moved at the beginning of 1905 to begin to assert its influence in Morocco, these circumstances suggested to Germany another means by which it might respond to the entente.[81]

Delcassé had tried to lay the groundwork for his initiative through negotiations not only with Britain, but also with Italy and Spain (which was to be given a small sphere of influence in northern Morocco). He had decided, however, not to consult or offer compensation to Germany.[82] In response, Berlin decided to challenge French policy forcefully. It hoped to show France that it could not be disregarded. Paris would also see that it could not count on Britain in a crisis, and a wedge would be driven into the entente before it could develop into a closer relationship.[83]

While on his yearly Mediterranean cruise, the kaiser stopped at Tangiers at the end of March, and dramatically proclaimed his government's support for the independence and integrity of Morocco, as well as for the preservation of the open door there. Many European states and the U.S. had pledged themselves to uphold those principles in the Treaty of Madrid in 1880, and, fully expecting majority support, Germany insisted that the convention's signatories meet again collectively to consider Morocco's fate. Hoping that a deal could be done, the French prime minister forced Delcassé from the cabinet. But Berlin continued to insist on a conference, and some observers feared that the two countries might go to war.[84]

Largely because of the emphasis the U.S. placed on the open door in China, Germany counted on Washington to support its demand. It also hoped that such support would encourage Britain to go along. Protesting that the U.S. had but limited interests in Morocco, Roosevelt at first begged off. But, fearful of a war in Europe, and anxious for German help in ending the war in the Far East (that a year before both powers had been happy to see break out), TR eventually weighed in on the side of those calling on Paris to agree to a meeting. The kaiser was delighted. And his ambassador went so far as to exceed his instructions and pledge that Berlin would accept Roosevelt's decision as to what was most fair and practical if differences arose between Germany and France at such a conference.[85] In July, partly due to the U.S., France finally agreed to a meeting, to be held at Algeciras, Spain, early the following year.

Of crucial importance, however, TR simultaneously promised the French ambassador, Jules Jusserand, that Washington would not act in such a way as to undermine Paris. I wanted "to keep on good terms with Germany, and if possible to prevent a rupture between Germany and France," he subsequently confided to Henry White, then the U.S. ambassador to Italy. "But my sympathies have at bottom been with France and I suppose will continue so."[86]

These concerns continued to shape American policy throughout the following year. U.S.-German relations had in fact improved since the turn of the century. Disappointed by the developing rapprochement, and ideally hoping for an American counterbalance to England, Berlin had worked hard to bring such improvement about. The kaiser's brother, Prince Heinrich, was sent on a good-will tour of America in 1902. Roosevelt's friend Speck von Sternburg was appointed as German ambassador, in the wake of the Venezuelan crisis of the following winter, and he brought reassurances about the Monroe Doctrine. Cultural and intellectual exchanges and a public relations campaign were initiated. Wilhelm sought to establish a personal relationship with TR. The two corresponded directly. The emperor asked the president's daughter Alice to christen a yacht that he had had built in America. And the kaiser donated works of art to TR's alma mater, Harvard University.[87]

TR testified to this change in relations in a letter to Spring Rice in late 1905. "When I first came into the Presidency," he wrote,

I was inclined to think that the Germans had serious designs upon South America. But I think I succeeded in impressing on the Kaiser ... that the violation of the Monroe Doctrine by territorial aggrandizement ... around the Caribbean meant war ... immediately, and without delay. He has always been as nice as possible to me since and has helped me in every way, and ... the relations of the two countries have been, I am happy to say, growing more close and more friendly.[88]

But this fact in no way altered the president's conviction that Washington's interests were best served by a continuance of British predominance along the eastern shores of the Atlantic. For, as Roosevelt saw it, Germany would desist from challenging the Monroe Doctrine only so long as it faced formidable obstacles to doing so.[89]

Just four weeks later, Root outlined American policy to Henry White, who was going to lead the U.S. delegation at Algeciras. His instructions echoed the considerations TR had raised the summer before. Washington certainly wanted to look out for any commercial interests it had in the region, and it wanted to maintain good relations with Berlin. However, the secretary also felt that Paris might have special interests in Morocco that needed to be safeguarded. The U.S. was willing "to acquiesce in whatever special protection the legitimate interests of France appear justly to require, without becoming the advocate of those interests in such a way as to appear to be opposing any other country." He concluded, "bear in mind that, while we are friendly to Germany, and wish to remain so, we regard as a favorable condition for the peace of the world, and therefore, for the best interests of the United States, the continued entente cordiale between France and England, and we do not wish to contribute towards any estrangement between those two countries."[90] The entente "is useful to us as well as agreeable," he added in another letter.[91] Root might have added that the

U.S. also did not want to see a deal struck whereby Berlin might obtain a Moroccan port on the Atlantic. That possibility had been a worry in London from the start of the crisis, and, as historian Peter Larsen has shown, it became a concern of Washington in 1906.[92]

Germany got its conference, but it was a hollow victory. Almost as soon as the meeting of thirteen states convened it became clear that, on the key issues, Berlin stood virtually alone. The most important debate revolved about the command and control of Morocco's police, with all agreeing that they should be organized from the outside. Berlin wanted this job to be undertaken by one or more small European states or by the great powers on a collective basis, while Paris insisted that the task be shared simply between Madrid and itself. The conference came close to breaking down before Germany finally accepted a face-saving gesture and substantive defeat. TR helped to secure this outcome by invoking Sternberg's promise and by making it clear that German-American relations would be affected if that were disowned.[93]

In the meantime, questions were raised in Congress as to the nature of America's participation in the conference. The administration deemed it politic to defend its involvement on the grounds that issues of importance to American trade were being discussed there. But figures like Augustus Bacon, of Georgia, in the Senate asked whether political topics were not also being discussed. Was America entangling itself in European affairs? When the meeting finally concluded in early April, the U.S. accompanied its adherence to the Act of Algeciras with a declaration that its interest in the proceedings had been nonpolitical in nature. While Washington would be guided by the "regulations and declarations" agreed to at the conference, White also stipulated that it would not assume responsibility for their enforcement. Nevertheless, back home, the administration still had to struggle before it was able to get the Senate to ratify the convention at the end of the year.[94]

Roosevelt also felt compelled to explain his policy to the new Liberal government in Britain, which had strongly supported France. Grey and others had misperceived TR's exchanges with the kaiser and the role that the U.S. played throughout the crisis, a fact that the president blamed on the inadequacies of Mortimer Durand, London's representative in Washington. With Jusserand, of France, he had been in effective communication throughout the entire year. Through Whitelaw Reid, the U.S. envoy in London, and a correspondence that then developed with the British foreign minister, TR explained that while he wished to "keep on good terms with" the Germans, he felt "it even more important that we should keep on good terms or better terms with the English."[95] And "your good relations with France," he told Grey, "are an excellent thing from every standpoint."[96]

Those "good relations" became in fact much closer as a result of this pivotal early twentieth-century crisis. Grey had worried that in the absence of

British support Germany might come to dominate France, and thus achieve a position from which it could more easily and effectively challenge Britain at sea. As a result, secret military talks began between the two governments even before the Algeciras conference got under way.[97]

The crisis also added stimulus to England's efforts to achieve an understanding with Russia (something the kaiser had in 1905 again tried to head off via discussions with the tsar). After its defeat in the Far East, many British leaders had worried that St. Petersburg would shift its attention back to Central Asia, where it had been developing new railways. For this reason, the Anglo-Japanese alliance was extended to include the subcontinent when it was renewed in 1905. British colonial officials in India called for a land military buildup and for a forward policy in the north to secure a large buffer zone between the two empires. Grey, however, in 1906, decided to pursue an entente, hoping that he could avoid that and that an Anglo-Russian agreement in Asia would lead Russia to focus its attention on Europe. An agreement between the two powers was finally concluded in late 1907.[98] Subsequent efforts by Germany to dissolve it (most notably in the second Moroccan crisis of 1911), only led to a tightening up of the Triple Entente that was thus created, which in turn led Berlin to be ever more solicitous of the standing of Vienna, its one remaining great power ally.

Planning had meanwhile begun for the second Hague conference. Pursuant to TR's meeting with the Interparliamentary Union delegates in 1904, Hay had raised the question of another meeting with the other powers who participated in the first conference. He avoided outlining an agenda, but noted that numerous topics had been deferred at that time, including that of immunity. Hay also broached the subject of broader participation by Latin America in the Hague system.[99] Although all the powers responded favorably, Russia opposed having the conference meet while it was still at war in East Asia. Further planning was therefore put off until after Portsmouth. Then, when the tsar indicated a desire to be the meeting's sponsor, as he had been in 1899, Roosevelt conceded him that role.[100]

TR articulated his hopes for the conference in his annual message of 1905.[101] He prefaced his comments by again insisting that, particularly in the face of armed "barbarism" and "despotism," the U.S. had to be ready to use force to uphold "righteousness." It was, however, he argued, worthwhile to "try to minimize the number of cases" in which the sword would have to be the arbiter of disputes, "and to offer, at least to all civilized powers, some substitute for war which will be available in at least a considerable number of instances." In this spirit, Roosevelt voiced the hope that a "general arbitration treaty" would be negotiated at the conference. TR praised the "Hague tribunal" as "a symptom" of the "growing closeness" among "civilized nations," and also as "a means by which" that "growth can be furthered." "Our aim," he said, "should be from time to time to take such steps as may be possible toward creating something like an organization of the civilized nations."

The president wanted to see the conference protect "[n]eutral rights and property" at sea. He also hoped that it might "be possible to exercise some check upon the tendency to swell indefinitely the budgets for military expenditure." In 1899 Washington had opposed any agreements on arms limitation. But now, with a powerful navy (he had written recently to Carl Schurz that he didn't "think it necessary to increase the number of our ships—at any rate as things look now"), Roosevelt wanted the U.S. to maintain its relative naval strength at as little cost as possible. He hoped that an agreement might be concluded at The Hague that would let the U.S. "rest."[102]

Most of the U.S. delegation was named in January. Joseph Hodge Choate, former ambassador to England and prominent New York lawyer, was chosen to head the group. He was joined by Horace Porter, former ambassador to France and president of the Navy League; Uriah M. Rose, a prominent Democrat and former judge from Arkansas; and David Jayne Hill, who was now minister to the Netherlands. Admiral Charles S. Sperry and General George B. Davis were named as specialists from the navy and army. Later additions included James Brown Scott, solicitor of the state department and a prominent expert on international law, and William Buchanan, who had experience in Latin American affairs.[103]

Russian planning began in earnest in spring 1906. The hope initially was that the conference could be held that July, but it was soon put off until the following summer.[104] St. Petersburg, in the meantime, drew up and circulated a program. This called for discussion of the pacific settlement of international disputes and of the laws and customs of land and maritime warfare, but it explicitly declined to endorse consideration of arms limits. Root, in response, reserved for the U.S. the liberty of raising that issue (as well as forcible collection) at the meeting.[105]

Britain also was hopeful that the second Hague conference might address this question. Its efforts to control naval spending, while still retaining sea primacy, had gone into high gear with the elevation of the forceful Sir John Fisher to the post of first sea lord in 1904. He sought to achieve "increased efficiency" while holding down overall spending. Fisher set out to do that by rearranging priorities and by incorporating new designs and technologies into Britain's construction of capital ships. He slashed what he saw as wasteful or nonessential expenditures, retiring or selling, for instance, small or obsolete craft. The number of overseas docking facilities was also reduced, and, for both strategic and financial considerations, naval strength continued to be redistributed back toward the waters off Europe. Such savings were then redirected toward the construction of capital ships of unprecedented speed and firepower, like the battleship *Dreadnought,* which was laid down in October 1905 and launched the following February, and the armored cruisers of the *Invincible* type that began to be built that spring (and that, according to historian Jon Sumida, were more in tune with Fisher's own thinking). Although more expensive than earlier battleships, the turbine-driven, all-big-gun *Dreadnought* was held to be more economical because it was so much more potent than any ship then afloat. Britain's budgetary problems were likely only to get worse, however, if the powers henceforth began a vigorous competition in the construction of such vessels.

The new Liberal ministry, meanwhile, had committed itself in the recent general election to the enactment of social reforms (particularly an old-age pension system) without a significant increase in taxation. This created yet another incentive for London to press for arms limitation in 1906–7. Calling for a "league of peace," Sir Henry Campbell-Bannerman, the prime minister, offered that the funding of such programs could be accomplished through a limitation in military spending. In the wake of Tsu Shima the battleship strength of the Royal Navy was superior to that of Russia, France, and Germany combined. But the British government was still concerned, particularly about the building program of Germany. Determined not to yield its naval advantage, Britain hoped that it might be frozen in place by means of an international agreement.[106]

Yet London was reluctant to raise the topic itself for fear of antagonizing Berlin and because it did not want to appear to be displaying weakness. It preferred to see TR, who seemed to enjoy good relations with the kaiser, broach the issue. Such a course was urged on Reid by Grey and on Henry White by Richard B. Haldane, the war secretary, in conversations held in England in July.[107]

Roosevelt was determined to impress on the new government his vision of arms control. He wrote Reid that he wanted "to see the British navy kept at its present size, but only on condition that the Continental and Japanese navies are not built up."[108] That, he hoped, was what London too had in mind. The president subsequently told Carnegie that he thought a possible approach might be to pursue an agreement limiting in the future the size of battleships. Surely, he thought, all the powers "must be a little appalled by going into an era of competition in [the] size of ships."[109]

Over the next several months, Washington and London both sought to promote serious arms limitation at The Hague. They found little interest, however. St. Petersburg did not want any barriers placed on its efforts to rebuild its navy, while Paris was afraid of the debate that might be opened up in France by any talk at all of arms limits. Berlin was only the most indignant of the opponents. It insisted that armaments were an issue for each nation to decide. By early 1907, U.S. policy makers had adopted the position that an effort still ought to be made to have the issue discussed, but only to the extent that it did not jeopardize progress on the rest of the program.

"Personally I think that the strengthening of The Hague Court is of more consequence," TR wrote Grey. By May, the British government had assumed this posture as well.[110]

In mid-April, the peace movement held a large meeting in New York to rally support for what it hoped would be achieved at The Hague. The impetus for the gathering had originally come from Benjamin Trueblood and Edwin Mead, two long-time leaders, but its scale was largely due to their success in enlisting the involvement of Carnegie, with his connections and money. Organizations from all over the country sent some twelve hundred delegates to this four-day National Arbitration and Peace Congress. Thousands more people attended its sessions, held at Carnegie Hall, the Hotel Astor, and Cooper Union. A number of cabinet officers, justices of the Supreme Court, senators, representatives, and other national, state, and local politicians were also in attendance.[111]

Carnegie (the meeting's president) had asked Roosevelt to send a message of greeting. However, as historian Calvin Davis puts it, the resultant letter had an unintentionally "dampening effect" since TR was determined to use this opportunity to again push his theme that "righteousness" needed to be put before peace. For months the president had been predicting that his "chief trouble" in connection with The Hague was likely to come from those he described as "crazy to do the impossible." He therefore seems to have been greatly agitated when the meeting went on to pass a resolution calling for all disputes to be settled by arbitration.[112]

Concrete planning for The Hague, meanwhile, had been left up to Root. He invited the American delegates to his Washington home in 1906 and met with most of them again at the State Department shortly before their departure for Europe in late spring 1907.[113] His instructions called on the delegates to push for consideration of the topic of forcible collection, and to support, if others raised it, discussion of arms limitation. In the area of arbitration, "two lines of advance" were "indicated." Root wanted the delegates to work for a general treaty on the model of the bilateral pacts many countries had recently signed. To ensure ratification, American signature would have to be accompanied by an "explanation" embodying the claim put forward by the Senate in connection with the Hay treaties, namely, that any specific *compromis* negotiated by the U.S. would have to be ratified by that body. The delegates were also directed to push for a new world court. The administration had concluded that weaknesses in the structure of the existing institution were in part responsible for it not receiving more cases.

In addition, Root instructed the delegation to support "the traditional policy of the U.S. regarding the immunity of private property of belligerents at sea," and to discuss with the other powers agreements relative to the conduct of war on land and sea and the rights and duties of neutrals. The success of the conference was, however, according to the secretary, not to be measured simply in terms of its "immediate results." In terms redolent of his instructions to the delegates to Rio the year before, Root wrote that the crucial thing was to try to keep in motion a process whereby over time a willing agreement on U.S. goals might be achieved. Toward this end, he encouraged them to "favor the adoption of a resolution by the Conference providing for the holding of further Conferences within fixed periods" on a regular basis.[114]

The second Hague conference met from June 15 to October 18, 1907. Because of the opposition of the continental European powers, little time was spent on the issue of arms limitation. After a very brief discussion, the participants simply agreed to endorse a nonbinding resolution—similar to one passed in 1899—recommending this as a topic worthy of each government's study.[115]

A very considerable proportion of the time and energy of the conference was dedicated to issues having to do with the rules and conduct of war at sea. This was a topic that had been slighted in favor of discussions of land warfare at the first conference. Two of the conference's four principal subcommittees, or "commissions," were organized around maritime questions, and another related proposal formed part of the agenda of the first commission, which was dedicated to the subject of the peaceful settlement of disputes.

This last dealt with the creation of an international court of prize. Britain signaled its willingness to depart from past practice by arriving at The Hague with a detailed blueprint for such an institution. Historically it had insisted on its own admiralty courts having the final say as to the disposition of neutral prizes captured by the British navy during war. Now England was ready to join Germany—which also arrived with a plan—and other traditional critics of that policy in seeking to establish an international court to which appeals from all national admiralty courts could be taken. The initiative reflected British irritation with the rulings of Russia's prize courts during the recent Far Eastern war. It also corresponded with London's overall strategy on maritime questions at the conference. In essence, Britain sought to restrict measures that could interfere with its trade, whether it was a neutral or a belligerent, while ensuring its ability when at war to use its naval power, particularly through blockade, to cripple the trade of its enemy (ideally without unduly antagonizing powerful neutrals).[116]

The U.S. eagerly endorsed the idea, and Choate played a major role in helping to compromise the British and German plans. Eventually, England, Germany, the U.S., and France got behind the same proposal. And it was accepted, albeit not without criticism from smaller nations who objected to a formula that guaranteed that the majority of the judges would always be selected by the major powers.[117]

Far more complex was the question of what kind of rules would govern such a court. This and more general matters having to do with maritime warfare were dealt with in commissions three and four. One principle that historically had been contended for by the U.S. was that of the "immunity of private property at sea, that is, of private and unoffending property, not contraband, even in enemies' ships ... in time of war."[118] Largely because this doctrine enjoyed enormous domestic political support, as evidenced by a resolution that in 1904 received unanimous approval in Congress, the American delegates were instructed to push for it at The Hague.[119] As a result of discussions leading up to the conference, however, TR and Root had come to have "grave doubts" about immunity. They were much less upset than figures like Choate, therefore, when the idea failed to gain acceptance.[120]

These doubts reflected the advice administration leaders were getting in this period from American naval experts, who were arguing that the U.S. had to rethink some of the positions on maritime policy that it had promoted in the past in order to bring them into line with its growing global interests. Immunity, the now-retired Mahan, Dewey, and others argued, might work against the maintenance of international stability, undercut Britain's power, and hamper the U.S. in any struggles it might get in over the Monroe Doctrine.[121] Mahan wrote Roosevelt that the question was one "of expediency; and what was expedient to our weakness of a century ago is not expedient to our strength today." He no longer even thought that the doctrine of "free ships, free goods," accepted by all the European powers in the Declaration of Paris in 1856, fit U.S. interests. "We need," Mahan wrote, "to fasten our grip on the sea."[122] "Great Britain, and the British Navy," he told the president, "lie right across Germany's carrying trade with the whole world. Exempt it and you remove the strongest hook in the jaw of Germany that the English-speaking people have."[123] These ideas anticipated attitudes that Washington would adopt during the Great War, particularly after the U.S. itself became a belligerent in 1917.

The "English-speaking" powers did in fact take the same side on many issues related to maritime war raised at The Hague. Both, for instance, worked, unsuccessfully, to have the conference endorse the "doctrine of release," the principle that belligerent warships should have to let neutral vessels they captured go if they could not be conducted into a port for prize court adjudication (this as an alternative to cargoes being destroyed and their seizure being adjudicated later). Each power thereby sought to provide not only for the safety of its commerce (whether it was a belligerent or not), but also to maximize advantages (particularly of a geographic nature) it expected to have over its most likely enemies.[124]

Likewise, both powers pushed for severe restrictions on the use by belligerent warships of neutral ports. Along with Tokyo, Washington and London sought thereby to deprive the continental European navies of adequate facilities for the projection of their power into distant waters.[125] Britain and the U.S. found themselves essentially on the same side as well in arguing for the conference to endorse the idea of distant blockades.[126]

These were both areas, again, where no agreement could be reached at the conference.

The U.S. was not willing to go as far as the number one sea power, however, in fighting for restrictions on the use of torpedoes and contact mines.[127] And it also responded negatively to London's proposal, broached early in the meeting, to simply put an end to seizures of neutral ships for contraband.[128] After learning the details of the proposal, U.S. policy makers worried that it might afford England dangerously broad rights to throttle neutral trade.[129]

Japan abstained, while all the other powers voted against London's suggestion. But when the fourth commission subsequently failed to agree on definitions with regard to contraband, or blockade, the prize court project was left in an untenable position. For that reason, British delegates began to sound out representatives of the other major maritime powers about the possibility of a future meeting on naval law where such work might be completed.[130]

From the standpoint of the U.S., the most important issues taken up at The Hague were those having to do with arbitration. TR had earlier written Grey that, "Every effort should be made to extend the number of ... disputes which are to be subjected to arbitration, and above all to make it easier to secure effective arbitration."[131] In consequence, American delegates lobbied for the adoption of a general arbitration treaty that would resemble in scope the bilateral pacts that had recently been signed (explaining at the same time that Washington's signature would have to be accompanied by a proviso allowing *compromis* to be put before the Senate). Adherents would pledge to refer to The Hague differences with another signatory that were of a legal nature, or that related to the meaning of treaties, unless such differences were held to affect "vital interests," independence, or "honor."

This approach competed from the start with a more ambitious alternative championed by Portugal. Its idea was for there to be a list of stipulated topics to which such reservations could never apply. Germany and its allies, however, strongly opposed both models. Baron Marschall von Bieberstein, Berlin's chief delegate, criticized a general treaty as likely to promote rather than alleviate friction. He also announced that his government would continue to consider only bilateral conventions with what seemed appropriate partners. The conferees decided ultimately to abandon the general treaty idea in the face of this opposition.[132]

Although disappointed at this defeat, Washington was far more anxious to see the conference endorse the creation of a new court, a course that Germany, as well as other powers, announced it favored. The court established in 1899 had by 1907 handled only four cases, a minority in fact of the arbitrations carried out in those years. U.S. policy makers were convinced that fundamental deficiencies in the Permanent Court were largely responsible for this and that the creation of a new, more truly judicial institution, would contribute more than anything else could to the growth of arbitration.[133]

American policy makers felt that the existing court, while useful, failed to inspire confidence. This was to a large extent due to the fact that parties to disputes before it each selected two of the judges. It also reflected the fact that many of the people on the list from which "judges" were to be chosen were in fact diplomats and statesmen rather than people whose training was in the law. The arbitral bodies that resulted thus inevitably tended to resemble mixed commissions more than courts of law. And their decisions, rather than being judicial, were more likely to be the product of negotiation and compromise. Root asserted that for many nations the "objection to obligatory arbitration was not to the principle of the thing," but rather to a submission of their interests to this kind of process. Most countries, he felt, would be much more ready to submit their controversies to a different institution.[134]

Although its title suggested otherwise, the Permanent Court of Arbitration created in 1899 actually comprised just a permanent list. The court itself was constituted afresh from among the names on the list whenever a case was to be heard. This was a process fraught with dangerous delays. American diplomats also felt that a lack of real continuity in the court deprived it of prestige and of the ability effectively to contribute to the development of the kind of international legal order that they wanted.

The new court they desired was not intended to replace the Permanent Court, but rather to stand (and be housed) alongside it as an institution specifically designed to deal with justiciable questions. It was intended to be a continuous body in fact, consisting of a specific number of designated judges who would be called on to render decisions based on legal criteria. Also, its expenses were to be borne not by the litigants, as was the case with the Permanent Court, but by all the nations who participated in the new institution's creation. On August 1, Choate asked the members of the first commission of the Hague Conference to seek to develop out of this proposal a truly permanent court "which shall hold regular and continuous sessions ... consist of the same judges ... pay due heed to its own decisions ... speak with the authority of the united voice of the nations, and gradually build up a system of international law, definite and precise, which shall command the approval and regulate the conduct of nations."[135]

At this level the U.S. proposal found widespread support at the conference. All the participants realized, however, that the kind of order provided by such a court would be dependent on more specific aspects of its construction. As they moved on to these, the project foundered. In the end, a scheme outlining the nature and jurisdiction of such a court was approved, but that could only be accompanied by a *voeu* expressing the hope that at some later date the institution would be established.[136]

The critical question was that of membership on the bench. During the conference, each major power made clear its desire for constant representation, as well as its preference for a bench dominated by the great powers collectively. Individually, the major powers wished to protect their interests against each other and against smaller, "less responsible," nations. Collectively, they appreciated the development of international law that would naturally result from the continuity provided by the new court, and they were anxious to see their common standards predominate. The most prominent attempt to implement these considerations was a British-German-American plan that was also supported by France. "It provided," Choate noted, "for a Court of seventeen judges to be organized for a period of twelve years and that of the seventeen, eight nations, *who will be generally recognized as having the greatest interests at stake in the exercise by the Court of its powers* [emphasis added], should each have a judge sitting during the whole period of the organization."[137] The eight were Germany, the U.S., Austria-Hungary, France, Great Britain, Italy, Japan, and Russia. Spain, the Netherlands, and Turkey were each to have a judge seated for ten years, while all other nations were allotted one for four years or less.[138]

Any such weighted representation was unacceptable to most other states (indeed it had been controversial in connection with the more narrowly focused prize court). And, much to the embarrassment of Root's boasted entente with that country, Brazil led the underdeveloped nations in demanding a system that would recognize juridical equality in the actual make-up of the bench.[139]

Against the backdrop of failure in the areas of maritime law and, especially, arbitration, American diplomats took comfort in the passage of the Porter Resolution and in the progress they felt had been made at The Hague with regard to the creation of the Prize Court and the new Court of Arbitral Justice. Indeed, they remained optimistic as the conference came to an end that both of those institutions would soon be functioning. They took solace as well in the fact that the delegates, in late September, passed a resolution looking ahead to the convocation of a third conference at The Hague in another seven or eight years.[140]

In the aftermath of the Second Hague Conference, Root continued to try to promote arbitration as well as a new world court that would be more capable of rendering judicial decisions. The secretary of state believed that, over time, the existence of such an institution could help to transform more and more (though never all) international conflicts into cases. The decisions of such a court would also generate increasingly precise definitions of nations' rights and obligations. Law, Root thought, could thus become a much more important means of containing upheaval and of stabilizing the existing international order. Just as law was, in the eyes of this leading corporate attorney, the handmaiden of order at home, so too could it serve as a means of securing order internationally.

Root believed the prospect existed for law increasingly to play this role, particularly because growing numbers of people in the major industrial states were coming to see themselves as having a stake in international stability. Such people constituted a natural constituency for arbitration as well as a potential counterweight to "greedy" governments and "irresponsible" elements. Governments did not make war "nowadays," he asserted, unless they had "support among their people" or were "driven into" it by "popular feeling."[141]

This constituency for arbitration itself needed to be guided and educated, however. That was a major reason why Root welcomed, and participated in, the creation of several organizations for the promotion of international law in this period, the most important being the American Society of International Law (1906). Its membership came to include such figures in the worlds of law and diplomacy as Choate, Andrew D. White, John Bassett Moore, Professor George W. Kirchwey of Columbia University, Supreme Court Justice David J. Brewer, James Brown Scott, Robert Lansing, John W. Foster, Chandler P. Anderson, Philander C. Knox, and Taft. Root served as the organization's first president.

It was also why Root sought to boost such people and organizations, and what he saw as their more sensible approaches and outlook, to a position of foreign policy leadership in and over such forums as the American peace movement. The secretary's considerable success in this regard was due, at least in part, to his close relations with Carnegie. Root played an increasingly important role in guiding the former industrialist's thinking and benefactions in the period after 1907. Then, when Carnegie decided to set up a lavishly funded "peace trust" in 1910, he turned to the former secretary of state for advice. Root went on to become the first president of the decidedly safe and nonoppositional Carnegie Endowment for International Peace.[142]

Root's efforts to promote arbitration in the wake of the second Hague conference began with the influence he exerted to have the peace conference on Central America, which met in Washington in November 1907, establish a court for that region. He hoped, of course, that such an institution would help to contribute to order in Central America. But Root also looked at the court, as his biographer puts it, as a kind of "laboratory experiment" and as a way of sustaining the momentum for a new global tribunal.[143]

In view of The Hague's failure to produce a general treaty, Root also persuaded Roosevelt that the U.S. should pursue bilateral arbitration treaties on the Anglo-French model, again conceding the Senate's demands with regard to its role, with as many countries as possible. The first of these was concluded with France in early 1908, and more than twenty more were signed over the following year. Britain, Italy, Japan, and Austria-Hungary were other major powers among the signatories. Russia and, despite a great deal of personal lobbying by TR, Germany remained aloof. Russia wanted tariff and trade issues to be explicitly exempted from obligatory arbitration. Germany balked at the treaty on the grounds that, with Root's concession to the Senate, the two powers would be committed in an unequal way (unlike the treaty signed with the U.S. in 1904).[144]

None of this activity, it should be emphasized, set Root at odds with TR's conviction that the nation needed to be able to subordinate peace to "righteousness." Indeed, the ex-secretary of war repeatedly made the same argument (while much more successfully eluding peace movement criticism). "The world is growing more pacific," he asserted at the dedication of the Army War College, in 1908. "Nevertheless, selfishness, greed, jealousy, a willingness to become great through injustice, have not disappeared, and only by slow steps is man making progress. So long as greed and jealousy exist among men, so long the nation must be prepared to defend its rights. It must be possessed of virile manhood and a capacity to prevent wrongdoing."[145] The army and navy needed to be strong so that they could, in the face of "injustice" and misbehavior, act as "the policeman."[146]

In 1908 Britain announced that it would not ratify the prize court convention adopted at The Hague until further agreement had been achieved as to the rules by which that institution was to be guided. The other major naval powers were invited to send delegates to a conference in London for that purpose.[147]

Root took an interest in this meeting not only for the questions of law to be addressed. Here American delegates were basically instructed to protect the interests that had been the U.S. concern at The Hague. He also viewed the conference, composed just of major powers, as another, and potentially more favorable opportunity, to bring into being a new world court.[148]

Meeting at the Foreign Office from December 1908 through February 1909, the London Naval Conference revisited many of the issues that had been discussed at The Hague, with the negotiations this time culminating in an agreement, the so-called Declaration of London. A definition of blockade was accepted that opened the way to something less than a close maritime siege. A narrow list of trade was defined as absolute contraband. This included arms and ammunition. Food, fuel, clothing, and a few other categories were defined as conditional contraband. Such goods could be seized only if they were for an enemy's armed forces. Many other commodities were explicitly declared as beyond the reach of such treatment. The "doctrine of release" was accepted, but in modified form. A prize ship could be destroyed (after all on board were removed), if taking it to port placed the capturing vessel in danger.[149]

Root (and then Robert Bacon) wanted the conference to make it possible for the judges of the prize court to take on the functions of the Court of Arbitral Justice, for those nations willing to accord them that role. This procedure would circumvent the controversy that had arisen in 1907 over the composition of the bench for the arbitral body, and it would create an institution that might then come to be accepted by the rest of the world. Despite considerable effort on the part of the U.S. delegation, and sympathetic responses on the part of some other powers, the conferees, however, refused to consider the matter, taking the position that it was outside the purposes for which the meeting had been called.[150]

The U.S. continued its role in the promotion of such schemes under Taft. In particular, his administration conducted a vigorous drive for the court and it sponsored the idea of new, "unlimited" treaties of arbitration.

In fall 1909, the State Department issued an identic circular to the nine other London Conference participants.[151] It proposed that they include as part of their instrument of ratification of the prize court a specific agreement stipulating

that the International Court of Prize ... and the judges thereof, shall be competent to ... decide any case of arbitration presented to it by a signatory of the international court of prize, and that when sitting as a court of arbitral justice the said international court of prize shall conduct its proceedings in accordance with the Draft Convention for the establishment of a court of arbitral justice.[152]

In response, several great powers reaffirmed their interest in establishing the new court. However concern continued to be voiced about procedure, and Grey, in particular, expressed misgivings about the reaction that the plan would arouse among those "[small] powers which refused every plan of proportional representation at The Hague." Hoping for ratification of the prize court treaty by "as many powers as possible," he worried that that would be jeopardized by the U.S. proposal. Grey appeared ready to wait until the entire subject could be discussed again at the next Hague conference.[153]

But the Taft administration did not want to wait. It raised the topic of the new arbitral court again at an informal meeting, held to discuss prize court procedure, in Paris in March 1910. James Brown Scott, the State Department solicitor, was the U.S. representative. Paris, London, and Berlin, he later reported, "approached the establishment of the court of arbitral justice with very considerable diffidence and misgiving. They proposed to consider the Prize Court and then to take up the court of arbitral justice when the Prize Court Convention had been disposed of, thus separating the two propositions." But, "[p]ursuant to my oral instructions," Scott "refused to consider the two projects as separate" and made agreement on the one court the price of American adherence to the other.[154] This insistence resulted in the four nations pledging to cooperate in the establishment of an arbitral court modeled on the prize court. It was to come into existence as soon as eighteen nations had agreed to it. However, no effort was to be made to create the institution (and the plan to do so was to be kept confidential) until the prize court was fully established.[155]

So long as progress on the prize court continued (it was ratified by the U.S. in February 1911), Scott was optimistic. By March 1911 nine powers had "formally or informally accepted" the arbitral court project. These included Austria-Hungary, Japan, Italy, Belgium, and the Netherlands, as well as the four powers that had participated in the March 1910 meeting. Scott told Knox he did not think it was "too much to expect that another group of nine Powers may be found" once the issue began to be taken up more openly.[156]

This, however, was before formal debate on the Prize Bill had gained momentum in England.[157] The British government had been eager to see the creation of the prize court. At The Hague and after it had also promoted a system of maritime law that it felt would protect both the instrument of a blockade and, whether it was a neutral or a belligerent, British trade and shipping. On balance, the government felt that its objectives had been achieved. But by 1911 it was faced with critics who argued that the Declaration of London embodied unacceptable trade-offs. Some of the controversy that subsequently developed was due to the intense partisan political scene in Britain at this time. But genuine opposition was reflected as well, particularly on the part of journalists, MPs, and others who shared a different conception of the kind of war(s) London needed to be prepared to fight and who took a more dismissive attitude toward neutrals (for their part, many senior naval figures who were uncertain about the Declaration simply took the view that it should be adhered to so long as it served Britain's interests—particularly when it was a neutral—and abandoned as soon as it did not). The harsh debate clearly also reflected the anxieties that had arisen in connection with what since 1907 had become a stepped up naval construction rivalry between Germany and Britain.[158]

Critics argued that the Declaration and Prize Court involved too great a surrender of British power, of the belligerent rights London had claimed and exercised in the past. They focused in particular on the Declaration's provisions on contraband, which were seen as impeding the Royal Navy's ability to destroy an enemy's trade. Cabinet ministers rejoined that Britain stood to gain, especially as a neutral, from the prize court. And Grey insisted that the Declaration did "not diminish the belligerent rights which this country is in a position to enforce in a war under present conditions."[159] Parliament nevertheless did not ratify the bill, and as a consequence creation of the prize court had again to be delayed.[160]

This setback for the prize court constituted, in turn, a major reverse for Washington's plans with regard to establishment of the new arbitral court. In its waning days, Taft's State Department considered, but drew back from, an effort to convince the other great powers to move ahead on the Court of Arbitral Justice without waiting for the creation of the other institution.[161]

The Taft administration also pursued bilateral arbitration pacts that would dispense with the articulated exceptions (covering "vital interests," independence, and "honor") characteristic of the Anglo-French model (and Root) treaties. Taft first broached this as an idea in a talk before the American Peace and Arbitration League in March 1910.[162] He then publicly invited other powers to negotiate such conventions with the U.S. at the end of that year.[163]

A number of considerations lay behind this move. As the president later admitted, one was the hope that the promotion of such treaties would offset opposition to his plan to build more battleships.[164] Developments in Europe and concern about Japan had led TR, from 1907, and then Taft to press for increases in the size of the fleet.[165] The topic was also broached at a time when Taft's political fortunes were plummeting and when his foreign policy had begun to be described as "bullying" and "dollar" diplomacy. Taft hoped that his pacts, making "peace," as one official put it, "a purely American proposition," would "draw the sting" of such criticism and, if possible, enhance his administration's public standing.[166]

At the same time, the administration saw these treaties as having policy value. They came to be paired in policy makers minds with the court and prized as another means of promoting stability and discouraging international conflict.[167] In spring 1911, Grey let it be known that England was interested in signing a treaty with the U.S. along the lines suggested by Taft. "The example would spread," he asserted, with the consequent likelihood of a real effect on "the 'morale' of international politics."[168]

The president apparently wanted to sign such a treaty first with England, before negotiating with any other government, seeing this as an occasion safely to reaffirm the close relations between, and similarity of outlook of, the U.S. and Britain. Ambassador Bryce was eager to oblige. But the French ambassador, Jusserand, immediately asked to be included, so Taft thought, to either isolate Germany or compel it to follow along. In the end, Berlin held back, objecting both to the role that Washington insisted on for the Senate and to the fact that bondholders in Germany would under this treaty still be unable to press longstanding claims they had against the state of Georgia. Knox and Bryce agreed on the text of a British-American treaty by mid-summer and the French government accepted their handiwork, thus making it possible for both of those powers to sign the new conventions with the U.S. on August 3.[169]

It is evident from the draft proposals that Knox had things largely his own way in the construction of these pacts. The finished documents clearly also reflect his conception of what needed to be done with an initiative that Taft had at first set rolling in a fairly offhand way. Knox recognized that both the public relations and policy goals of the treaties required them to be free of the standard statements of exempted topics, which they were.[170]

With these treaties, Knox also sought to institutionalize procedures he thought would facilitate the settlement of disputes. His, and the administration's, commitment has generally been misunderstood as representing a radical emphasis on the utility of arbitration. In reality, Knox did not want to make arbitrations "too cheap and easy," partly because, in the absence of the kind of world court the administration sought, they tended to result in "diplomatic compromises" rather than decisions. His emphasis instead, reflected in Articles 2 and 3 of the pacts, was on provisions that would allow for "cooling off" time and for an "exhaustion of diplomatic effort, plus a commission's recommendations before resort to arbitration." Knox envisioned two stages of settlement effort before the issue of arbitration would become relevant. The first consisted of a year of diplomatic negotiation. The second, of fact finding and nonbinding recommendation by a Joint High Commission composed of three nationals from each side.[171]

Knox hoped these treaties would encourage the peaceful settlement of international disputes. He was, however, not about to bind the U.S. to arbitrate all questions not settled by diplomacy or advisory investigation, despite the "unrestricted" language that surrounded the pacts. In Article 1, the pacts bound the signatories to submit to impartial arbitration differences "relating to international matters in which the High Contracting Parties are concerned by virtue of a claim of right made by one against the other under treaty or otherwise, and which are justiciable in their nature by reason of being susceptible of decision by the application of the principles of law or equity."[172] Knox chose his words carefully. By employing the concept of "justiciability," he believed he was excluding "the idea that governmental policies or vital interests or national honor will be subjects of arbitration unless in respect thereto we have, by treaty or otherwise, given another country a rightful claim that may involve these subjects."[173]

Of greater significance was the fact that the mechanism the treaty provided for the determination of "justiciability" allowed for substantial maneuvering. If the U.S. refused another party's claim that an issue was "justiciable," the Joint High Commission was to make a ruling on that claim. A loss before that body, however, could only result from the defection of two of the three commissioners appointed by the president. This mechanism gave the executive some independence from domestic politics as well. Although the Senate had to consent to every *compromis*, recourse to the commission provided the executive branch a means of applying considerable "moral" pressure when it wished to cross that body and encourage the arbitration of a dispute.[174]

As the administration hoped, signing these treaties proved a popular move. Hundreds of chambers of commerce submitted resolutions in favor of the pacts. The peace movement, in cooperation with many church groups, organized a campaign on behalf of their ratification. And editorial opinion throughout the country was overwhelmingly enthusiastic. Many Democratic newspapers, like the *World*, were positive, as were usually critical journals, like the *Nation*. In the opinion of the *New York Times*, the treaties were the "crowning achievement" of the Taft presidency.[175]

Criticism from some Republican and Democratic politicians was, however, forthcoming too. One opponent was TR. His early disapproval, well before he possessed any specifics concerning the treaties' contents, plus the fact that his attacks shifted focus as he became aware of his misconceptions, supports the notion that TR's opposition was politically motivated. Roosevelt had already begun to move down the road toward another presidential candidacy. Yet there was also some consistency in his criticism. TR recognized that the pacts seemed to promise more than they did. Arbitration should not and, he was convinced, would not be resorted to as a means of settling all disputes. It was therefore, so far as he was concerned, wrong and destructive to suggest—as the administration seemed to be doing—that it would.[176]

Meanwhile, Lodge, who penned the Senate Committee on Foreign Relations' report on them in mid-August, took issue with the treaties on the grounds that they compromised the role of the Senate in a way that was unwise if not unconstitutional. He held that the term "justiciable" was not as restrictive as Knox claimed. But he had no quarrel with the pacts' definition of arbitral issues so long as the third clause of Article 3—which allowed the Joint High Commission to rule on the "justiciability" of an issue if the parties disagreed—was eliminated. Recognizing that the conventions allowed the president to control the formation of the commission, Lodge's proposed amendment reflected a desire, shared by the majority of the committee, to give the Senate the chance to block arbitrations to which the executive branch was prepared to accede.[177]

In a critique that partly overlapped with that of TR, Root, now a senator from New York, worried that U.S. conduct under the pacts might sharply conflict with the promises surrounding them. This could ultimately discourage the very tendencies that the treaties were designed to promote. For this reason, he reintroduced the concept of exemptions in a report written to express the views of a Republican minority on the Foreign Relations Committee.[178] Root was prepared to back ratification without amendments. But, to neutralize senatorial objections and to limit the possibility of foreign accusations of bad faith, he suggested a resolution of ratification "clarifying" the term "justiciable." This would express the understanding that the treaties exempted from arbitration "any question which depends upon or involves the maintenance of the traditional attitude of the United States concerning American questions, or other purely governmental policy."[179]

The administration found both suggestions distasteful. Aside from diluting the executive's leverage, it feared that elimination of the third clause of Article 3, especially at this stage, was destined to compromise the "moral influence" on international affairs which it was hoped ratification of the treaties would exert. With regard to Root's proposal, the conventions were seen as both distinctive and popular precisely because they lacked any list of exemptions.

The administration, meanwhile, had also hoped that the popularity of the treaties would force the Democratic party to follow, as Carnegie put it, in "Taft's wake." But Taft's obvious, almost desperate, effort to use the pacts to revive his standing ultimately worked against that. Some southern and western Democrats, moreover, like Senator Bacon, were concerned that the conventions (or subsequent replicas of them with other nations) might become vehicles by which positions they wished to see maintained were overridden by Washington. To block this, the Georgian proposed a resolution of ratification specifically denying that the rulings of the commission were in any way binding on the Senate. It also suggested that Root's resolution be amended to stipulate as exempted issues "the admission of aliens," "the admission of aliens to the educational institutions of the several States," state boundaries, or the "alleged indebtedness" of any state. And where Root had been content to refer to "American questions," Bacon wanted a frank exemption of the Monroe Doctrine.[180]

In the hope of saving the pacts as signed, the president asked that their consideration be postponed until the next session of Congress.[181] Taft hoped that he might meanwhile "set a fire under the senators which may change their views."[182] In the tradition of McKinley's campaigns for the Treaty of Paris and reciprocity, he took his case directly to the country, promoting the conventions during a fall cross-country speaking tour.[183] Taft also wrote a widely distributed article entitled "The Dawn of World Peace."[184]

The gap between the White House and the Senate Republican foreign policy leadership finally closed in January. Lodge and Knox agreed to promote the treaties with the third clause of Article 3 and without a statement of exemptions, but prefaced by a resolution of ratification that both secured the Senate's right to approve nominees to the Joint High Commission and stipulated that only the executive, not the Senate, was bound by its findings. Root reluctantly fell in line behind this agreement, but it remained to be seen whether it would attract sufficient votes from the Democrats and the as yet quiet Republican insurgents.[185]

The full Senate took up the treaties in late February 1912. Bacon and Hoke Smith, also a Democrat and from Georgia, argued that the treaties were sloppily written and unclear in meaning (for which they could cite previous Republican differences in interpretation). Administration assurances that the issues of concern to Democrats could not be arbitrated and that the commission's rulings were not binding on the Senate also gave these and other critics an opening to ask what harm could be done by removing the third clause of Article 3 and by attaching an explicit list of exemptions.[186] On March 7, these positions prevailed. By a 42–40 vote the controversial section of Article 3 was stricken. Joining most Democrats in backing this move were six Republicans, of whom four were insurgents.[187]

Then Bacon's resolution of ratification, containing the exemptions he desired, passed by an even greater margin, picking up the votes of seven Republicans, including Borah and four other insurgents.[188]

Thus altered, the treaties easily won the assent of two-thirds of the senate.[189] However, in their final form they did not serve the administration's purposes, and Taft refused to press them further.

This emphasis on international stability continued into the Wilson era. Many of the Root arbitration pacts terminated in 1913. In the months before the Great War broke out in Europe, the U.S. negotiated the renewal of two dozen of these. In early 1914, it also issued a call for a third Hague conference, to be held in 1915. James Brown Scott was named to the international committee vested with the responsibility of preparing for that ill-fated meeting.[190]

However, the new administration did not display the same enthusiasm for the particular mechanisms of arbitration and the Hague system as its predecessors had. It in fact had to be prodded by peace groups and by Root and the Carnegie Endowment before it acted with regard to the conference. Given the Taft administration's record, there appeared to be little chance that broader arbitration treaties would be accepted. At the same time, as historian David Patterson has noted, Wilson himself was someone who harbored a fairly strong "anti[international]court attitude," and who agreed with those who saw "the problem of world order as the province of political leaders rather than jurists removed from the practical exigencies of everyday diplomacy."[191] In this period, a greater emphasis was therefore placed on initiatives other than these.

One involved William Jennings Bryan's so-called "cooling-off" treaties.[192] These were based on an idea that the secretary of state had been promoting since 1905. Eager to get beyond arbitration treaties laden with exemptions, and Senate insistence on the ratification of individual *compromis*, Bryan wanted to see the U.S. negotiate treaties with other countries under which both parties would simply bind themselves to turn over any disputes between them that could not be settled otherwise to what were essentially mixed commissions of inquiry (with a neutral umpire). Neither side would be compelled to accept the findings of this commission. However, Bryan hoped that the light shed on a dispute, plus the delay involved, would be sufficient to eliminate the prospect of war.

Although Bryan's enthusiasm for them was unmatched, these conventions won support from figures like Wilson and Colonel House because they were seen—as the Taft treaties of 1911 had been—as a means of exerting "moral influence" on the international scene and of isolating those powers that would not go along. If another power did not wish to sign such a treaty, said the president in April 1913, "let them say so, it will put them to their trumps to give a reason for not talking over the matter."[193] As a consequence, twenty such pacts were concluded over the following sixteen months.

These pacts received the overwhelming assent of the Senate when they were submitted as a group for ratification in mid-August 1914. They did not raise the same issues that the arbitration treaties had. But this support undoubtedly also reflected the strong desire many senators had to see the U.S. isolated from the European war (a sentiment shared by Bryan). Germany refused to negotiate such a treaty on the grounds that the "cooling off" idea, if it became the pattern of other treaties, might jeopardize Berlin's mobilization timetables and continental defense. But the other major European powers were unenthusiastic as well. Britain, France, and Russia signed such treaties with the U.S. only after the onset of the war.

Far more indicative of the long-term thrust of the Wilson administration's foreign policy was the diplomacy conducted by House in this period.[194] Having observed the recent development of the alliance systems in Europe and an increase in international tension, House supported peaceful settlement mechanisms (including both the world court idea and arbitration) and proposals for arms limits. But he also wanted to see more in the way of inducements and reassurances extended to Germany (mostly by Britain), which had shown itself resistant to those ideas. House hoped that this could head off war in Europe. As important, he also believed that such an approach offered a way to create a more effective association of great powers, on behalf of international stability, than was possible just through such institutions as the proposed great power-dominated court. House thought that Germany could be transformed into an upholder of, rather than threat to, the existing international order. The leading industrial powers would then not only settle peacefully conflicts among themselves, they would also cooperate in supervising the underdeveloped countries (though not in the Western Hemisphere) and protect this international order against any great power challengers (by far the most likely, as House saw it, being Russia).

This constituted a new approach toward Germany, and it also implied somewhat more international political "entanglement" for the U.S. (although the premise was that there would be less likelihood of the peace being disrupted), but House's policy was not without its precedents in the diplomacy of Wilson's predecessors.

His project, for instance, bears similarity to the efforts of the Taft administration to promote the notion of commonly held interests among the great powers in China and to substitute cooperation and "harmonious action" for competition among them there.[195] Nor was House the first U.S. policy figure of prominence to think about the creation of a great power political association as a way of securing order on the global level. In his speech accepting the Nobel Peace Prize in 1910 (for his role in ending the Russo-Japanese War), for instance, ex-President Roosevelt had opined that it "would be a master stroke if those great powers honestly bent on peace would form a League of Peace, not only to keep the peace among them-selves, but to prevent, by force if necessary, its being broken by others." And TR's successor, Taft, had similarly told newspaper publisher Harrison Gray Otis that he thought the way "to bring about peace" was "to enforce it" if an arrangement to do that could be effected "between England, Germany and the United States, and possibly two or three more Powers."[196]

House's approach drew on methods in vogue within the U.S. in this era, by which inducements and appeals to a "community of interest" were used to promote social order and efficiency. It also ran parallel to the scheme he put forward in 1914 to promote collaboration, in line with U.S. goals, among the nations of the Western Hemisphere (predicated on arms lim-its, mutual guarantees of territorial integrity, and arbitration). What House was at work on was, in its genesis, what the administration would later refer to as the League of Nations, a project that, despite its advocates' charac-terizations, was aimed not at world peace per se, but rather at upholding and stabilizing a particular international order.

In 1913 House set out to ensure such stability by returning to the issue of arms limitation, in particular by getting Germany to scale back its ambi-tious naval building program. But he hoped to do this not merely by having Britain and the U.S. offer cutbacks in their programs, but also by convinc-ing Berlin that its interests would be much better served if it abandoned the course that London had come to define as a challenge to its naval supremacy.

House felt that to date England had been too "intolerant of Germany's aspirations for expansion." He hoped that the problem of Berlin's emer-gence as a world power might be favorably resolved if it was reassured that the door for German emigration and trade would remain open in South America and if London conceded to Berlin a "zone of influence" through-out a large section of the Near East (particularly, and significantly, in areas bordering on Russia). By this means, the Anglo-American understanding might be extended to include Germany. Moreover, a powerful, if informal, "pact" could even be created whereby those powers (probably France, and maybe Japan as well) would collectively guarantee the peace, maintain the open door, and see to the "proper development" of the underdeveloped world.[197]

House was laying plans for this effort to "depoliticize" the Anglo-German rivalry from the very beginning of the administration. In early May 1913, he casually suggested to the German ambassador, Count Johann von Bernstorff, "that it would be a great thing if there was a sympathetic understanding between England, Germany, Japan, and the United States." Together, "They could ensure peace and the proper development of the waste places, besides maintaining an open door and equal opportunity to every one everywhere." He was encouraged by the fact that Bernstorff seemed to agree with him.[198]

House thought that the U.S. might have to nudge Britain to get it to go along with his plans. At the same time, he was convinced of the importance of the two powers maintaining good relations with one another. This topic first came up in discussion with Wilson in spring 1913 in connection with the Panama tolls controversy. House urged "the necessity of keeping on good terms with England." Both men then "deplored the short sightedness and ignorance of our public men. They talk and bluster and then are unwilling to maintain an army or navy in any way adequate to meet their pretensions."[199]

Traveling in England that summer, Wilson's close friend and advisor talked over his plan with Walter Hines Page, the new U.S. ambassador to that country. He also met with Grey and recounted Bernstorff's conviction that "good feeling would soon come between England and Germany." House's purpose was "to plant the seeds of peace" between the two powers.[200]

Page later wrote House deploring the arms buildup and the "withdrawals of men from industry—an enormous waste" that had taken place in Europe. "They'd like to find a way to escape," he said. But Page was skeptical both of the Hague system and of arms limitation. ("The Hague programmes, for the most part," as he saw it, "just lead them around a circle in the dark back to the place where they started.") The answer was to find something for the powers to do together, such as "cleaning up the tropics." The leadership for such a redirection of energies had to come from the U.S., since it, he claimed, was the only one with the capacity to think unselfishly.[201]

In late 1913, Sir William Tyrrell, Grey's private secretary, visited the U.S. He discussed Mexico and the Panama tolls question with Wilson and then, as already noted, conveyed to the foreign secretary the president's desire for a "sympathetic alliance." Subsequently, House informed Tyrrell of his interest in bringing "about an understanding between France, Germany, England and the United States regarding a reduction of armaments, both military and naval." Tyrrell, House wrote in his diary, advised that House should travel to Germany and tell the kaiser "that England and America had 'buried the hatchet' and there was a strong feeling that Germany should come into this good feeling and evidence their good intention by agreeing to stop building an extravagant navy." "Sir William assured me," House continued, that England would henceforth "cooperate with Germany cordially." "With England, United States, France and Germany we both thought the balance of the world would follow in line and great change would come about."[202] House received Wilson's approval to go on such a mission during the coming spring. The president also offered to "try and get Congress to put in a clause authorizing him to eliminate the building of the two battleships which are now being considered," provided a "naval holiday" of the sort that First Lord of the Admiralty Winston Churchill recently had proposed was "approved by other nations."[203]

As part of the preparation for his trip, House, in April, met with Irwin

Laughlin, who had served for three years as first secretary at the American embassy in Berlin. Laughlin doubted that Germany would accept the idea of a naval holiday. But House convinced him that the effort was worth making by explaining that his approach would be to try to prove to Berlin that such a step would be to its "material advantage." "I went into some detail," he wrote, "as to giving Germany a zone of influence in Asia Minor and Persia, and also lending a hope that they might be given a freer hand commercially" in areas of Latin America.[204]

House departed for Europe in mid-May (just three and a half weeks after the U.S. occupation of Veracruz). On his arrival, he wrote Wilson that the situation was extraordinary.

It is jingoism run stark mad. Unless some one acting for you can bring about an understanding, there is some day to be an awful cataclysm. No one in Europe can do it. There is too much hatred. . . . Whenever England consents, France and Russia will close in on Germany and Austria. England does not want Germany wholly crushed, for she would then have to reckon alone with her ancient enemy, Russia, but if Germany insists upon an ever increasing navy—then England will have no choice. The best chance for peace is an understanding between England and Germany in regard to naval armaments, and yet there is some disadvantage to us by these two getting too close. It is an absorbing problem and one of tremendous consequence.[205]

In addition to his efforts to entice Germany into an understanding, House also employed this vision of the dangers that power faced when three days later he sought to get the kaiser to consider his proposals. "I told him," he later wrote,

that the English were very much concerned over his ever-growing navy, which taken together with his enormous army constituted a menace; and there might come a time when they would have to decide whether they ran more danger from him . . . than they did from Russia. . . . I thought when that point was reached, the decision would be against Germany.

House spoke of the "community of interests" between England, Germany, and the U.S., and said that "if they stood together the peace of the world could be maintained."[206] He "made it plain" that it was the policy of the U.S. "to have no alliances . . . but we were more than willing to do our share towards promoting international peace."[207]

House felt sufficiently encouraged by the kaiser's response to his offer to try to compose European "difficulties" to continue to promote his project in Britain. There he likewise held up a vision of what might happen if he did not succeed. He told of "the militant war spirit in Germany and of the high tension of the people." He "feared some spark might be fanned into a blaze. . . . [T]he Kaiser himself and most of his immediate advisers did not want war, because they wished Germany to expand commercially . . . but the army was militaristic and aggressive."[208]

On July 3, Tyrrell informed House that the government wanted him to convey to the kaiser its interest in pursuing further the prospects of a "better understanding."[209] The American envoy concluded his trip by writing a letter to the German emperor to that effect.[210] House was genuinely, if cautiously, optimistic. Even had events not overtaken him in the summer of 1914, however, his plan probably carried little prospect of success. Britain had in fact already made some overtures to Germany in the direction suggested by House. But there were limits beyond which it was unwilling to go, and, perhaps even more important, it was anxious not to take any steps that might unsettle the relations that had been established with Russia and France. Meanwhile, even though the navy had taken a back seat to the army by this time in Germany, that power was still unwilling formally to renounce its aspirations at sea.[211] House's mission is crucial, however, for the light it sheds on what would continue to be the central foreign policy concerns of the Wilson administration.

Chapter 7

World Order (1914–17)

The search for order (of a particular sort) remained a central theme of American diplomacy throughout the period from August 1914 to April 1917. When war broke out in Europe, key policy makers like Wilson and House saw the incidents that precipitated it as having little to do with them and were relieved to be detached from the conflict (the president announced that he wanted "to have the pride of feeling that America, if nobody else," had her "self-possession").[1] At the same time, administration leaders considered important American interests to be at stake and were anxious to see the war brought to a conclusion—so long as it was an acceptable conclusion—as soon as possible. Although it clearly presented opportunities (especially in the Western Hemisphere), they worried that the conflict, particularly if extended, would be profoundly disruptive, not just to American trade (especially with Europe) but to the whole economic and institutional fabric of the world system that the "white" powers had, in the nineteenth century, created. Key leaders were also anxious that the war not lead to new assemblages of power in the Old World that could present greater challenges to the political and commercial frameworks that Washington wished maintained, especially in the Western Hemisphere and in East Asia. They did not want to see Germany's ability to dispute U.S. ascendancy in Latin America enhanced. Nor—and here lay the source of what would develop into a major difference with Britain—did they want what they saw as a tragic war among the western European powers to open the way for Russia and Japan, both of whom were viewed as threats to the existing order in East Asia, to become stronger.

U.S. leaders were anxious for the war to end without such destruction to, or changes in, the existing (and, from Washington's standpoint, advantageously organized) world order taking place. They were also eager that the settlement of the conflict be structured so as to guard against such an upheaval ever occurring again. For Wilson and House, this concern carried implications as to what kind of victory (assumed as all but inevitable in 1914) the Entente (or Allies) should seek over Germany. But it also dictated renewed efforts to achieve something along the lines of the great power "pact" that House had pursued in 1913–14. Toward these ends, Washington sought to insert itself as a (indeed as *the only possible*) mediator of the war, beginning within weeks of its onset.

Anglo-American relations at the outset of the war followed directly from the "sympathetic alliance" idea that Tyrrell and Wilson had discussed in 1913 and that had generally characterized American policy toward British power (in the Eastern Hemisphere) during the previous decade and a half. The administration saw British power as a force working in favor of the framework that Washington wanted in Latin America. Britain and British-dominated colonies and facilities represented a vast and important part of the international market within which the U.S. economy operated. And London was also seen as a power interested in working for the preservation of, and stability in, the existing international order (by contrast, House told Wilson that a German victory would mean the triumph of "militarism"— the U.S. would have to "build up a military machine of vast proportions" to guard its interests).[2]

This appraisal of British power and of London's posture is key to explaining the "benevolent neutrality" or, more accurately, "unneutrality" engaged in by the administration (and more or less acknowledged by House).[3] The essential form this took was forged early in the conflict when it became clear that Britain was determined to assert belligerent maritime rights comparable in scope to those that had brought on war between itself and the U.S. during the Napoleonic era a century before.[4] The administration very much wanted to sustain publicly the claim that it was behaving in a neutral fashion, both for domestic political reasons and so as to keep out of war with— and be seen as a potential intermediary by—Berlin. Nor did it want formally to surrender to London any rights it claimed. But it also did not want to clash with Britain.

As the blockade (never formally declared as such) developed, Washington found what it hoped would be a way around this dilemma in a response that was in fact suggested by Grey when he made it clear that England would not abide by the Declaration of London. In October 1914 the foreign secretary suggested that the U.S. neither accept nor protest against the measures that Britain was about to proclaim, but rather "be content to declare that we reserve all rights under international law ... if ... any harm be done to our commerce and that we will take up cases of damage if any occur as they arise."[5] From this point on, for at least the next year and a half, Anglo-American dealings over the blockade were diverted away from confrontation. They were channeled instead toward informal discussion of particular cases, toward the postwar settlement of claims, or toward protests intended principally for public consumption (which is not to say that U.S. officials were always pleased by the workings of the blockade). For its part, Britain sought to mitigate the impact of its measures on the American economy and to reward the U.S. for its informal collaboration. The U.S., as historian John W. Coogan forcefully argues, not only failed to fulfill the legal obligations it had as a neutral to Germany, it also, in essence, became a partner in the blockade.[6]

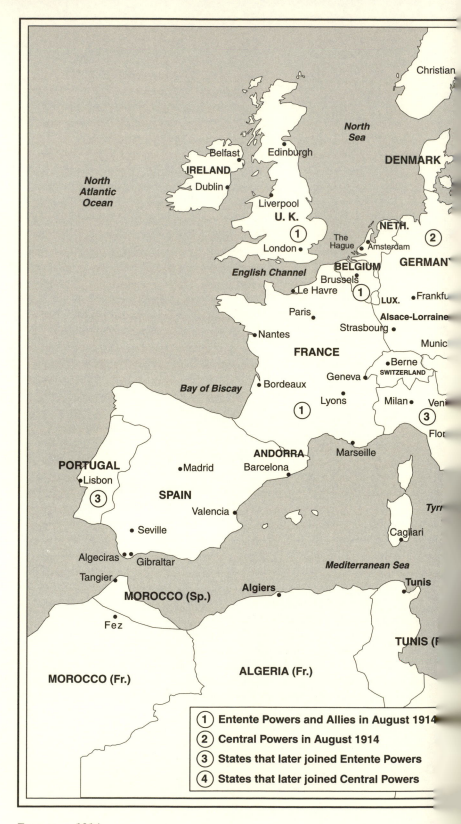

Europe, c. 1914.

St. Petersburg

Stockholm

Revel

Moscow

teborg

Riga

Baltic Sea

penhagen

Vilna

Minsk

R U S S I A

Warsaw

①

Kiev

Prague

AUSTRIA–HUNGARY

Vienna

②

Budapest

③

Belgrade

ROMANIA

Black Sea

BOSNIA
Sarajevo

SERBIA

Bucharest

①

MONTENEGRO

BULGARIA

①

Sofia

④

Constantinople

Adriatic ALBANIA

Naples

③

Dardanelles

④

GREECE

Aegean Sea

OTTOMAN EMPIRE

Ionian Sea

Smyrna

Athens

CYPRUS

CRETE

Beirut

Damascus

Alexandria

Jerusalem

Cairo

Suez
Canal

LIBYA (It.)

EGYPT (Br.)

A major reason why Washington wanted to avoid a confrontation with Britain over maritime policy was that it looked to London as the most likely and important partner it had in settling the war as it desired. Its effort to enlist London in such a partnership was, however, fraught with difficulty, because, early on, the two powers developed different ideas as to what would constitute an acceptable peace. In particular, Britain was bent on a greater destruction of Germany (at least as a power capable of conducting world policy) than the U.S. was. London took the attitude that a decisive defeat of Berlin was the only way that its interests would be secure. The Wilson administration worried that such a result would work against long-term international stability (because it would breed a spirit of revenge) and open the way for Russia to become a more formidable challenger of U.S. (and, it insisted, British) interests. It wanted German efforts to alter the prewar status quo checked, for Berlin to be taught a lesson, and for the influence of Germany's "irresponsible" military to be reduced, but it also wanted Berlin to remain strong and to be able to participate in a postwar international "pact."

The U.S. tried to bargain for British acceptance of its position with promises that Washington would be a full participant in a postwar great power league to enforce the peace. It even suggested that it might intervene militarily to put an end to the current disorder. But London was skeptical, particularly of the administration's ability to overcome domestic American opposition to military involvement in the war. It continued to believe that its best interests would be served by a decisive defeat of Germany, by acquisition of the strategic assets that would be available after the destruction of the Central Powers (including the Ottoman Empire), and by close adherence to its French and Russian allies.

Once it seemed clear that London would not cooperate, the tenor of U.S. policy changed. Washington became more suspicious and confrontational. In part because the Allies had become dependent on American trade and money, Wilson decided in mid-1916 that he would try to compel them to adopt the U.S. position.

By contrast with its response to British measures, the U.S. assumed a much sterner attitude toward German infringements of international law. Its announced objective was to secure to Americans the "full enjoyment" of their rights on the high seas. Washington simultaneously warned Berlin, after the latter proclaimed the waters around Britain a submarine war zone early in 1915, that a "critical situation" would be created if any of those rights were violated.[7] This posture can be explained again, at least in considerable measure, by reference to the administration's desire to influence Britain and the peace. Policy makers wanted to bolster the standing of the U.S. as a global power and in particular to convince London that Washington would not shrink from challenges in the Eastern Hemisphere.

Wilson was extremely anxious to see the U.S. itself stay out of military involvement with Germany. This was his attitude at the outset of the war, and, except for some occasional musings, it remained his attitude even after key advisers came to feel that U.S. interests might require intervention. There were many reasons for this. Wilson was especially conscious of, and sensitive to, the great domestic American opposition to participation. He was fearful that involvement would lead to disarray in his party and would open the way to the resurgence of what he saw as "greedy" and unenlightened elements associated with the Republicans. From an international policy perspective, he worried that U.S. participation would diminish the chances of the war ending as he wanted and of Washington shaping the peace. None of these reasons, however, prevented the president, on several occasions in 1915–16, from taking harsh stands toward Berlin—stands that could have led to war—principally on the belief that that was necessary to maintain U.S. prestige.

For a time, in late 1916 and early 1917, Wilson felt that he might finally be within reach of bringing the war to an end under American auspices and along the lines he wanted. The president believed he could control the Allies. He also believed that Germany was ready, or felt the need, to end the war on those terms. But he turned out to be profoundly mistaken. Rather than accept Wilson's settlement, German leaders announced a campaign of unrestricted submarine warfare. They accepted the likelihood of U.S. military intervention, but that was no longer a deterrent. Their gamble was that they could carry out a "blockade" of their own, of Britain, and that that would be sufficient to achieve a pro-German settlement before U.S. intervention could become effective.

Wilson broke relations, eased his pressure on London, and took other steps that he thought might encourage Berlin to forgo its campaign and move back toward his plan. He continued to maintain that nonintervention was the preferable course for the U.S. from the standpoint of the reconstruction of the kind of world it wanted after the war. But attacks on American merchant vessels eventually made it impossible for that course to be sustained short of what Wilson saw as an unacceptable diminishment of U.S. credibility.

Anxious to mediate, House thought the first real chance to do so had come when Germany failed to achieve a rapid defeat of France.[8] For him, the principal problem remained Berlin's military leaders and their influence. But House hoped that the German army's setback at the Marne in September 1914 meant that the kaiser and his civilian advisors, along with what he took to be their more cautious attitude, might be strengthened. Berlin, he also believed, was fearful that a longer war would make Germany vulnerable to starvation in the face of what already appeared to be a British intention of preventing food from reaching the Central Powers. House hoped that London would be willing to settle for a return to prewar boundaries, an "indemnity for Belgium," and "an agreement for general disarmament." And he hoped to get talks going while England still "dominates her allies," under the theory that France and Russia held objectives that might make an accord more difficult.

At Wilson's encouragement, his confidant held discussions with the German and British ambassadors, Bernstorff and Spring Rice. Confronted with an unwarranted optimism on the part of Bernstorff, however, he at first concluded that it was just the Entente powers who were not ready to talk. House urged the importance of ending the war before Russia came to dominate the continent and that Britain could not afford to be seen as the one that was standing in the way of a return to normalcy. But Britain appeared to be moving toward the position that a thorough defeat of Germany was necessary. Former ambassador Bryce summed up that attitude when he wrote Wilson that anything short would lead "to a sort of truce rather than peace" between the two powers. Worried that continued pressure would merely antagonize London, House decided to ease up and wait for a more propitious time.[9]

House refrained from making any further effort to mediate the war for over two months. It was in this period that he turned his attention to the Pan American pact idea. The U.S. ought to use this time to solidify its position relative to Latin America, he told the president, especially if there was any chance at all of Germany winning. Such a "League" as he had in mind, pivoting around a collective guarantee by the signatories of each other's territorial integrity, and premised in turn on arms control and the arbitral treaties that had already been agreed to, would promote Latin American cooperation with Washington on both hemispheric and extra-hemispheric issues. No less important, it might also provide a "model" for the stabilization of Europe after the war.[10]

House told Wilson at the beginning of December that he still doubted that the time had come to revive the issue of mediation. "[T]he Allies would consider it an unfriendly act, and further it was not good for the United States to have peace brought about until Germany was sufficiently beaten to cause her to consent to a fundamental change in her military policy."[11] Within two weeks, however, his attitude had changed. In mid-month House received a letter from Zimmermann, then the undersecretary at the Foreign Office, suggesting that it was "worth while trying to see where the land lies in the other camp."[12] This suggested to House that perhaps Germany was ready. He told Bernstorff that "there was no use taking it up with the Allies excepting upon a basis of evacuation and indemnity of Belgium and drastic disarmament," but the latter responded that he thought this would be "no obstacle."[13] "Germany was asserting her willingness to listen to peace proposals," House told Spring Rice the next day, and he "thought the Allies would be placed in a bad light if they refused to consider peace upon these terms" (essentially those he had been pushing for in September).[14]

In fact neither coalition was interested in settling the war at this time, either on the terms Washington was suggesting or on any basis that the other camp was likely to accept. The confusion stemmed principally from each side's desire to throw responsibility for continuance of the conflict onto their opponents. By no means ready to accept House's estimate that it had lost the war because of the failure of the Schlieffen Plan, Berlin remained intent on breaking up the Triple Entente and on bringing about a significant alteration in the prewar status quo, at the very least with regard to France and the smaller countries along its northern and northwestern border. It hoped for territorial adjustments in those areas (it already occupied substantial territory) and for a pro-German economic realignment of the countries of northwestern Europe.[15] London was less interested in acquiring new territory, at least at this time, than in seeing Berlin denied the gains it sought and dealt a decisive defeat. And to achieve those ends it was extremely anxious to keep together, and if possible enlarge, the coalition that it led. That strategy, in turn, required Britain to countenance territorial adjustments at the expense of the Central Powers on the part of its allies.[16]

Spring Rice asked why Berlin would "consent to peace parlays now when they seemingly were so successful." House conceded that the "German military party" and the expectations that had been built up among the German people would constitute formidable obstacles. On the other hand, he "thought the Kaiser, the Chancellor, the Foreign Secretary, and their entourage knew that the war was already a failure and did not dare take the risk involved, provided they could get out of it whole now."[17]

Anxious to see Germany checked, but not destroyed, to secure guarantees with regard to stability in the future, and to see "normal conditions" return as soon as those goals were possible, House decided to set off for England and the continent early in 1915.[18] By the time of his departure at the end of January, he may already have given up on the idea that either side was ready to talk peace. Hoping to put House off, Grey had in fact informed Wilson that he thought the time for parlays had not yet come. Not wanting London to appear as the obstacle, the foreign secretary noted that Paris wanted an indemnity from Germany as well as the territory of Alsace-Lorraine, which it had lost to Berlin at the end of the Franco-Prussian War fifty years before. St. Petersburg wanted to acquire Constantinople and the Dardanelles from the Ottoman Empire (which had recently entered the conflict on the side of the Central Powers).[19] For Germany's part, Zimmermann, meanwhile, had not provided Washington with confirmation of Bernstorff's assurances.

House nevertheless still saw the trip as worthwhile. He thought it might pave the way for him eventually to become the mediator of the conflict, hopefully in a few months, after the belligerents had made the next military moves for which they were preparing. He reckoned that by that time, in mid-1915, both sides would be forced to rethink the price (and in Berlin's

case, he thought, the very possibility) of an unequivocal victory. They would
then perhaps be ready to settle the war along the lines desired by the U.S.

Their willingness to do so would also depend on the alternatives they
had, and here House hoped through his trip to pick up where he had left
off on his last journey to Europe, before the war, the previous year. As he
saw it, the "permanent guarantees" of security and peace that both sides
asserted they wanted could only be accomplished if a framework for peace
was outlined that both saw as in their interest. The trip provided a means
of promoting his conception of such a framework in the hope that it might
eventually win the support of the two sides.

House had already told Spring Rice before leaving that it was his "purpose not to discuss terms with Germany so much as to discuss a plan which
would ensure permanent peace."[20] After hearing of the situation at the
front, he told Grey, when he met with him in London at the beginning of
February,

> that I had no intention of pushing the question of peace, for in my opinion, it could
> not be brought about, in any event, before the middle of May or the first of June.
> I could see the necessity for the Allies to try out their new armies in the Spring, and
> I could also see the necessity for Germany not to be in such an advantageous posi-
> tion as now, for the reason she would be less likely to make terms that would insure
> permanent peace.[21]

In the meantime, House wanted to talk about postwar stability. He raised
with Grey the idea of a "general guarantee of territorial integrity," as well as
a proposal for a ten-year moratorium on the manufacture of munitions and
the building of warships as a way of addressing the issue of arms limitation.[22]

Grey threw his visitor off balance by urging that the U.S. become a formal party to the peace made in Europe. House thought the tradition of
nonentanglement made that impossible. Having already stated that all of
the territory between Germany and France—including Alsace-Lorraine—
ought to be neutralized after the war, he suggested, however, that Washington could join in a more general covenant aimed at preventing the violation of neutral territory and at enforcing limits on the conduct of war—
including, he ventured, conduct that involved gross interference with merchant shipping.[23]

House pointedly avoided making "an immature suggestion of peace"
when he met with Delcassé (who had returned as foreign minister) in the
French capital in mid-March. Instead, he tried to pave the way for France
eventually to accept him as mediator.[24] House asked Willard Straight, who
was then in Paris and who knew men prominent in the French government,
to reinforce his effort. He later recorded in his diary:

> Straight is to convey the thought that it will be of advantage to the Allies to have
> the good will of the President, and that the best way to get it is through me.
> Another idea I wished conveyed was that the really essential thing ... was to strive

for a permanent settlement and not for any small territorial advantage, which in itself would leave wounds which in time would lead to further trouble.[25]

Comments made to him in Britain, especially by Tyrrell, had led House to believe that London might be prepared to support, as part of a postwar covenant, some sort of broad immunity for merchantmen—regardless of nationality—during wartime. Wilson's envoy termed this "the freedom of the seas."[26] London would come around to this idea, he thought, because it would see it as in its interest to do so. Otherwise, it would be difficult in the future to protect its trade given the emergence of the submarine.

This gave House the idea that he might use "the freedom of the seas" both to get Germany to accept U.S. mediation and to try to sell Berlin on the kind of settlement he desired.[27] Particularly if London was depicted as a staunch enemy of the idea, a pledge of U.S. support for "the freedom of the seas" might convince Berlin to accept an American role. House also hoped that Germany would come to see that realization of "the freedom of the seas" made the retention of Belgium unnecessary. Berlin's interests would be better served by an evacuation of the territory it had occupied and by entering into a great-power agreement for the limitation of arms. House hammered away at these themes in talks with Zimmermann, Foreign Minister Gottlieb von Jagow, Chancellor Theobald von Bethmann Hollweg, and other officials when in Germany in late March.

He reported to the president from Berlin that it seemed clear that peace talks would have to await some major new battlefield development, particularly given the degree to which public sentiment had been led to expect a great victory. In the meantime, House looked "to put us on a good footing." "If nothing arises to disturb the relations we are establishing in these several belligerent countries," he wrote, "I feel hopeful that your influence will dominate to a larger degree than it ever seemed possible."[28]

House sought to show the Germans "the different points where our interests and theirs touched," and he "expressed a desire that we work together to accomplish our purpose." In the spirit of his trip before the war, he "endeavored to make it clear to the German government that their best interests could be served by working along harmoniously with us." He drew "particularly upon our desire for the freedom of the seas," and promised Berlin that Washington was committed to bringing this about. If London's consent for that could be obtained, House suggested to Bethmann Hollweg, then Berlin could say to its people that "Belgium was no longer needed as a base for German naval activity, since England was being brought to terms." In conversations with Wilhelm Solf, of the Colonial Office, House urged that outlets for German overseas expansion could be found without a repartition of the underdeveloped world. He argued that "colonies in themselves were not sources of strength to a country, but were oftentimes a weakness." "I also pointed out that in the future there would be far less segregation of interests throughout the world than there had been in the past, that intercommunication had become so general that a new and better outlet for expansion would probably take place."[29]

House left Berlin at the end of March. He spent several weeks in France, conferring with the U.S. ambassadors to Spain and Italy and briefing French officials, before finally returning to London—there to take up again with British leaders his ideas about freedom of the seas.[30] Generally overestimating the impression he had made in the capitals he visited, and still fairly sure that parlays were at most a matter of a few months away, House felt there was little more he could do but wait. He felt compelled to alter his expectations, however, after the torpedoing of the *Lusitania.*

Seeking to interrupt British trade, but unable to challenge the Royal Navy on the surface of the sea, Berlin had announced in early February that it was declaring the waters around the British Isles a war zone. Germany proclaimed that it would "endeavour to destroy every enemy merchant ship that is found in this area ... without its always being possible to avert the peril that thus threatens persons and cargoes." On the grounds that accidents could happen, and that Allied vessels often illegally flew the flags of nonbelligerents, the government also warned that it would be dangerous for neutrals' ships to travel in the area.[31]

Washington replied that it would "take any steps it might be necessary to take to safeguard American lives and property and to secure to American citizens the full enjoyment of their acknowledged rights." It would also hold Germany to a "strict accountability" if any American ships or lives were lost.[32] Some such incidents were nevertheless recorded that spring. One American died when the British liner *Falaba* was torpedoed. Several weeks later, two American ships were hit. The *Cushing* was slightly damaged by a bomb from a German airplane. Then, two days later, three Americans died when a submarine torpedoed the *Gulflight.* Because of these events, administration officials had already begun to discuss possible responses when the British liner *Lusitania* was torpedoed on May 7. Among those killed on the Cunard flagship vessel were 128 Americans.[33]

The sinking of the *Lusitania* intensified the discussion in Washington.[34] Berlin gave assurances that it would make every effort to avoid attacks on the vessels of neutrals, and it expressed regret at the loss of American life in all of these incidents, but the question of the status of Americans who took passage on Allied merchant and passenger ships remained. The predominant view within the administration (including most of the cabinet, Wilson, House, and Lansing) was that the U.S. should threaten Germany with serious consequences unless it agreed to conduct that would make it safe for Americans to travel on board such vessels.[35]

Bryan was the principal holdout from this view.[36] He was upset by, and willing to support a protest of, Germany's act. But the secretary wanted the U.S. also to make a serious protest to London over its interference with American trade and shipping. The U.S. had to defend its "rights from aggression from both sides."[37] This was critical if the U.S. was going to retain the trust of both powers, necessary, as he saw it, to Washington's hope of being able to mediate the conflict. It was also necessary if the U.S. was going to stay out of the war itself, particularly since Berlin—on the basis of a swelling trade in munitions between America and Britain—was already quite angry with Washington. Bryan did not see that commerce as unneutral, but Germany did. For much the same reason, the secretary worried about a condemnation of submarine warfare on the grounds that it was inhuman if that was unaccompanied by a condemnation of Britain's starvation policy on the same grounds.

In the spirit of his "cooling-off" treaties, Bryan insisted that Washington ought not to demand an immediate settlement of the *Lusitania* case. Rather it should be receptive to the idea that all of the facts should first be determined. Finally, the secretary wanted Americans to be warned about the dangers of traveling aboard belligerent vessels in the war zone. Had this been done when he originally called for it in April, Bryan argued in May, the crisis created by the sinking of the *Lusitania* would not have occurred. The secretary expressed outrage that the British, as he saw it, had been using the presence of American passengers as a way of trying to protect the shipment of ammunition that the liner had been carrying. It was, Bryan argued, "like putting women and children in front of an army."[38] Meanwhile, Americans who deliberately took passage on belligerent vessels, knowing the risks involved, were guilty of "contributory negligence."[39] They put their own private business interests over the interests of the rest of their countrymen. They should not to be allowed to embroil their nation in international complications. He maintained that Americans had no more business being on belligerent vessels traveling through such a war zone than they did walking through the conflict's land battlefields.

Wilson, however, was determined to keep British and German relations separate. He also did not want the U.S. to be seen as backing away from the positions it had taken when the submarine campaign was first announced, namely, that Berlin would be held to strict accountability and that "any steps" would be taken to secure American citizens in the "full enjoyment" of their rights. This was in line with a cable House sent the president from England on May 9. "Our action in this crisis will determine the part we will play when peace is made," it said. "We are being weighed in the balance."[40] Page claimed that in Britain, the feeling was "that the United States must declare war or forfeit European respect."[41] "It is a very serious thing to have such things thought," Wilson subsequently commented to Bryan, "because everything that affects the opinion of the world regarding us affects our influence for good."[42]

On May 13 a note was despatched to Berlin stating that a "grave situation" had been created as the result of the recent acts and expressing disbelief that they had the sanction of a government traditionally committed to "freedom of the seas." Germany, the note insisted, was obliged to conduct its naval operations in such a way as to provide for the safety of noncombatants, just as it also had to "take the usual precaution of visit and search to ascertain whether a suspected merchantman is in fact of belligerent nationality or is in fact carrying contraband of war under a neutral flag." It expressed skepticism that submarines could actually be used against merchantmen without an "inevitable violation" of these rules. Washington expected Berlin to disavow the recent acts, to make reparation for them, and to ensure against their recurrence.[43]

In its response two weeks later, Berlin side-stepped most of these demands. It reiterated that its policy was not to attack neutral vessels, it blamed those attacks that had occurred on the misuse of neutral flags, and it avowed that it would pay compensation if, on investigation, Germany proved responsible. The reply insisted that the *Falaba*'s commander was responsible for what had happened to that ship. He had disregarded an order to lay to and then sent up flares to summon help. As for the *Lusitania*, it belonged in a different category. It was armed, and London encouraged such ships to take aggressive action toward submarines. Germany also alleged that the vessel was carrying high explosives. Berlin wanted to delay a final response to Washington's demands pending an American consideration of these questions.[44]

Determined to press the broader issue of what it had insisted were Germany's obligations, Washington dispatched a second note on June 9, essentially restating its demands. It reiterated that the U.S. "cannot admit that the proclamation of a war zone from which neutral ships have been warned to keep away may be made to operate as in any degree an abbreviaton of the rights either of American shipmasters or of American citizens bound on lawful errands as passengers on merchant ships of belligerent nationality," and it again asked for assurances that such would not be the case.[45]

Bryan was fearful that the president was steering the nation toward war (and was hurt at the degree to which he had been forced to play the role, as his wife bitterly described it, of a mere figurehead secretary). He now submitted his resignation.[46]

In disagreement with Bryan, the president had, as one historian has put it, clearly opted for a course that put "more stress on American rights," at least with regard to Germany, "and less on maintaining noninvolvement."[47] Nevertheless, Wilson was still eager to avoid war if possible and he hoped that the outcome of his diplomacy would be to get Berlin to change its behavior.

Anxious to accomplish both objectives, the president slightly altered his stance. Although Berlin's reply to the second note continued to defend its practices, on the grounds of self-defense and by pointing to Britain's actions,

Germany also professed an interest in working out practical ways by which traveling Americans might be protected.[48] Neither Wilson nor House was prepared "to bargain with the German Government for less than our inalienable rights." However, House also noted that, "Since your first note the German Government has not commited any act against either the letter or the spirit of it." He continued, "it may be [that] even though they protest that they are unable to meet your demands, they may continue to observe them."[49] That continued observation, plus an apology and reparations for the *Lusitania*, rather than a renunciation of the submarine campaign, now came to constitute Wilson's irreducible minimum. He told House, "Apparently the Germans are modifying their methods: they must be made to feel that they must continue in their new way unless they deliberately wish to prove to us that they are unfriendly and wish war."[50] That sentiment was incorporated into a third note, which was dispatched on July 21 and meant to put an end to the correspondence.[51]

For a time it appeared as if this would indeed put an end to the crisis, for, wanting to avoid war with the U.S., Berlin had in fact modified its conduct of submarine warfare. Bethmann Hollweg and the army had successfully struggled for a policy shift in the face of navy opposition and despite a German public opinion that seemed to want the government to use to the maximum whatever weapons it had. In June, submarine commanders received secret orders not to take aggressive action against any large liners.[52]

Relations were again thrown into turmoil, however, after the British liner *Arabic* was sunk off Ireland. Two Americans died. Wilson told Edith Galt, his future wife, of his disappointment. He had hoped that the "undersea craft" had been reined in. The act was one of "brutal defiance of the opinion and power" of the U.S. The next step would be to break off relations, which could lead to war.

The president recognized that "the people of the country"—even though obviously upset at such incidents—"were still demanding of me that I take no risk of war." He also worried that Washington would lose the ability to play a mediatory role—the ability to bring an end to the conflict in line with the kind of settlement that it wanted—if it itself became involved.[53]

There were other concerns as well. Two weeks earlier, Wilson and Galt had discussed an article, sent to the former by House, that explained how continuance of the war was likely to prove suicidal for Europe from the standpoint of its role in the world. It argued that the U.S. stood as the "likely heir to the influence and power hitherto possessed and exercised by England and her continental neighbors and rivals." Wilson thought that this was a "pretty safe prediction." However, it was "always supposing we succeed in keeping out of," what he called, "the deadly maelstrom ourselves."[54]

But the U.S. had to do something, House and Lansing insisted. Its correspondence with Germany over the *Lusitania* had put America's prestige and credibility as a great power on the line over the submarine issue. In

House's opinion, "Unless Germany disavows the act and promises not to repeat it, some decisive action upon our part is inevitable, otherwise, we will have no influence when peace is made or afterwards."[55]

The president was finally saved from a need to take such action when the U.S. ambassador, James W. Gerard, was told that Berlin had in fact, in June, altered its commanders' instructions. Germany now formally pledged that no liners would be sunk "without warning and without safety of the lives of non-combatants, provided that the liners do not try to escape or offer resistance."[56]

Disagreement flared again in September and early October, when Germany at first refused to disavow the sinking of the *Arabic* (on the grounds that it had tried to ram the submarine). Fearing that Berlin was prepared to say one thing and then do another, Wilson became much more belligerent. Convinced that the alternative was war, Bernstorff finally capitulated and offered to negotiate an indemnity, compelling Berlin to go along.[57] Issues still remained, particularly with regard to a settlement over the *Lusitania*. However, by mid-October the issue of how submarine warfare would be conducted appeared, from Washington's standpoint, to have been favorably, if perhaps not permanently, resolved.

Grey had continued to exchange letters with House (after the latter returned home) throughout the summer of 1915. Again and again he came back to his hope, first raised months before, that the U.S. would help enforce the peace once the war was over.[58] Indeed, the foreign secretary suggested, it was only in that context that London could consider the proposal for freedom of the seas. In the wake of the *Arabic* settlement, and in the face of ongoing Allied frustration on the battlefield, House seized on these appeals, hoping that they constituted an opening through which the U.S. could once again push for a settlement along the lines that it wanted.[59]

House wanted to see Germany checked in its efforts to alter the prewar status quo and he wanted to see its "militarism" ended. In the interest of long-term stability and of ensuring that Russia did not achieve a stronger position, however, he did not want Germany destroyed. The preservation and stability of the existing world order would be better served, as he saw it, if a strong Berlin could instead be turned into a collaborator of the U.S. and England on the international stage.

The great-power pact idea as it had been developed by House to this point had focused on a "general guarantee of territorial integrity," on arms limits, on schemes for the peaceful settlement of international disputes, on rules regulating the conduct of war, and on cooperative major-power oversight of the underdeveloped world. House hoped that such a scheme would promote greater order in the international system (at least beyond the Western Hemisphere, there he and Wilson were looking to the U.S.-led Pan-American pact) as well as the containment of unwanted unilateral activites on the part of all of the other big powers (either through their absorption into this collective framework or through their isolation).

Wilson's emissary had suggested to Grey in early 1915 that while Washington could not guarantee a European peace in specific terms, he thought it could accomplish much the same thing by participating in a more general covenant. He now hoped that a firm understanding with regard to such a pact, plus an intimation that the U.S. would even go to war with Germany if that power refused to give up its ambitions, might succeed in getting Britain to agree to the kind of settlement that Washington desired.

House acted against a backdrop of growing criticism from within the U.S. of the British blockade and of growing personal frustration on Wilson's part with the continuation of the war. At the height of his confrontation with Berlin over the *Arabic* in September, the president also told his advisor that "he had never been sure that we ought not to take part in the conflict and if it seemed evident that Germany and her militaristic ideas were to win, the obligation upon us was greater than ever."[60]

This all emboldened House to present to Wilson in early October a new initiative for bringing the war to an end. He suggested that the Allies be asked unofficially to let House know "whether or not it would be agreeable to them to have us demand that hostilities cease." Such a demand could be put "upon the high ground that the neutral world was suffering along with the belligerents and that we had rights as well as they, and that peace parlays should begin upon the broad basis of both military and naval disarmament." In terms redolent of the way he had tried to use "freedom of the seas" earlier in the year, House suggested that it should "be understood that the word 'militarism' referred to the Continental Powers and the word 'navalism' referred to Great Britain." "If the Allies understood our purpose," he continued,

we could be as severe in our language concerning them as we were with the Central Powers, the Allies, after some hesitation, could accept our offer or demand, and if the Central Powers accepted, we would then have accomplished a master stroke in diplomacy. If the Central Powers refused to acquiesce, we could then push our insistence to a point where diplomatic relations would first be broken off, and later the whole force of our Government, and perhaps the force of every neutral, might be brought against them.[61]

A week later, House received another letter from Grey referring to the postwar peace.[62] The president thought it gave "ground for hope," and both men decided that House should pose to Grey his plan by way of reply.[63] House thus wrote the foreign secretary, on October 17, that "the time may soon come when this Government should intervene between the belligerents and demand that peace parlays begin upon the broad basis of the elimination of militarism and navalism." House said that he did not want to suggest this to Wilson until he had confidentially been informed that it would meet with the approval of the Allies. On that score, however, he told Grey that "it would be a world-wide calamity if the war should continue to a point where the Allies could not with the aid of the United States bring about a peace along the lines you and I have so often discussed." "It is in my mind," House continued,

> that after conferring with your Government, I should proceed to Berlin and tell them that it was the President's purpose to intervene and stop this destructive war, provided the weight of the United States thrown on the side that accepted our proposal could do it.
>
> I would not let Berlin know of course of any understanding had with the Allies, but would rather lead them to think that our proposal would be rejected by the Allies. This might induce Berlin to accept the proposal, but if they did not do so it would nevertheless be the purpose to intervene. If the Central Powers were still obdurate, it would probably be necessary for us to join the Allies and force the issue.

(Wilson had inserted the word "probably" here, telling his friend: "I do not want to make it inevitable . . . because the exact circumstances of such a crisis are impossible to determine.")

In conclusion, House warned Grey of the "danger of postponing action too long" on his proposal. "If the Allies should be unsuccessful and become unable to do their full share," he wrote, "it would be increasingly difficult, if not impossible, for us to intervene."[64]

Grey cabled back asking whether what House meant by eliminating militarism and navalism entailed a U.S. commitment to a "League of Nations" that would enforce the peace.[65] With Wilson's endorsement, his adviser replied immediately back, in code, "yes."[66]

House was looking for the British to show interest in the scheme, with the idea that Washington could then give the Allies leeway to suggest when it was opportune for it to be activated.[67] But the first letter he received back from Grey expressed mostly skepticism. The foreign secretary did not see how the Allies "could commit themselves in advance to any proposition, without knowing exactly what it was," and without knowing that the U.S. was definitely prepared to intervene if they accepted.[68] "Sir Edward is evidently taking a pessimistic view of the situation," wrote House in his diary on November 25. "He had not received my cablegram when he wrote, but, even so, the offer which I made in my letter—which was practically to ensure victory to the Allies—should have met a warmer reception."[69] A short time later he received a letter from Bryce "to say that there is not the slightest change in British sentiment regarding the duty and necessity of prosecuting the war with the utmost vigor, and listening to no suggestions for negotiations with the German Government."[70] The conclusion House drew was that he had to make a greater effort to convince London that the plan was in its interest.

The new year found House back in England trying to sell that government on his scheme. For two weeks in mid-January he met with key figures, particularly Grey, Balfour, and David Lloyd George. The battlefield disappointments of the previous six months notwithstanding, he reported back to Wilson that "Their confidence seems greater now than it did when I was here before."[71] One of the things that House tried to do was to shake that. He also raised the prospect that Russia might at any time pursue a separate peace.[72]

The U.S. would be the one making sacrifices under his plan, House asserted. "We were willing to consider some means by which we could serve civilization," he told Balfour, "but if we did it, we felt it would be at a sacrifice of our traditional policy and entailed some danger which does not now confront us."[73] As to freedom of the seas, House argued that it would "accomplish for Great Britain what her predominant naval power does for her now, but it would be less costly, more effective, and would not irritate neutrals."[74] With Lloyd George he spoke of using Asia Minor to compensate Germany for the territories it would relinquish in Europe.[75]

Without pushing these discussions to a conclusion, House, on January 20, departed for the continent. He spent the last days of the month in Berlin, trying to determine what the attitude of the German government was toward a settlement.

His most important interviews were with Bethmann, Jagow, and Zimmermann. Wilson's emissary felt that the chancellor was at least for the moment more powerful than his rivals in the army and navy. Yet House did not find the civilian officials with whom he spoke willing to entertain terms that fell short of a major victory. At most, Bethmann hinted that he might be willing to see Germany give up the territory it had come to control in Belgium and France in return for a large indemnity. House sought to plant doubt that Berlin would ever be able to realize its objectives. He also told the chancellor that "western civilization had broken down, and there was not a market-place or a mosque in the East where the West of to-day was not derided."[76]

When reporting his findings to Wilson, House commented that he also felt there was rising pressure, and a growing temptation, in Germany to resort to use of the submarine in ways that would be at variance with the pledges it had made. "They think," he wrote, "war with us would be not so disastrous as Great Britain's blockade."[77]

On his way back to England, House stopped in Paris, where he decided to broach the topic of American intervention with leading officials of the French government. In his discussions, in particular with Aristide Briand and Jules Cambon, he stressed, as he had in London, "the gamble that a continuance of the war involves."[78] House pointed to the failures that the Allies had thus far had, emphasized Germany's strengths, and spoke of the danger of Russia and/or Italy agreeing to a separate peace with the Central Powers.[79] It was not probable, he told Cambon, that "the Allies would be able to have a decisive victory on any of the fronts during the coming spring and summer."[80]

Then, before crossing the Channel, House met with King Albert, of Belgium, at La Panne. He suggested that Belgium should be paid an indemnity by all the belligerents after the war. He also raised the idea of that country possibly selling Germany the Congo.[81]

On February 10, another round of discussions began with British officials, and this finally culminated in a memorandum of understanding, signed by Grey, but drawn up by both men, and dated the twenty-second:

Colonel House told me that President Wilson was ready, on hearing from France and England that the moment was opportune, to propose that a Conference should be summoned to put an end to the war. Should the Allies accept this proposal, and should Germany refuse it, the United States would probably enter the war against Germany.

Colonel House expressed the opinion that, if such a Conference met, it would secure peace on terms not unfavorable to the Allies; and, if it failed to secure peace, the United States would leave the Conference as a belligerent on the side of the Allies, if Germany was unreasonable. Colonel House expressed an opinion decidedly favourable to the restoration of Belgium, the transfer of Alsace and Lorraine to France, and the acquisition by Russia of an outlet to the sea, though he thought that the loss of territory incurred by Germany in one place would have to be compensated to her by concessions to her in other places outside Europe. If the Allies delayed accepting the offer of President Wilson, and if, later on, the course of the war was so unfavorable to them that the intervention of the United States would not be effective, the United States would probably disinterest themselves in Europe and look to their own protection in their own way.[82]

House subsequently returned to America and in early March obtained the president's approval of the document "so far as he can speak for the future action of the United States."[83] It was the hope, and at this point strong belief, of the two men that the House-Grey memorandum had secured "an active working arrangement between Great Britain and the United States in the settlement of the world's affairs," and that this would enable those powers to, in the not distant future, bring the conflict to an end roughly on the basis of the terms Washington had been wanting.[84] House and Wilson had worried that an Allied commitment to the destruction of Germany would lead either to an indefinite prolongation of the war or to a peace that would break down quickly or involve Russia becoming a far more formidable rival. Now, not only would Washington's basic conception of appropriate peace terms prevail. Once "normal" conditions were restored, the stability of Europe and of the existing international order might rest on unprecedently firm foundations, principally as a result of the kind of pact that they had in mind.

Britain was in the process of fielding much larger ground forces at this time, and the Allies were preparing for a massive offensive on the Western Front. House doubted that the British and French would achieve a breakthrough, but he hoped they would soon turn the tide sufficiently to get Germany to acquiesce in the kind of peace that he wanted. There was also the chance that the U.S. would have to get involved militarily itself to bring that about. Although Wilson had recently felt compelled to pledge to congressional Democrats from the South and West that the U.S. would only go to war if its honor or interests were directly attacked, House clearly had great faith in Wilson's ability to steer the country in any direction he wanted. He also believed that the president's ability to do that would be enhanced if the end could be characterized as a struggle for permanent peace.[85]

The president meanwhile appears to have been quite confident that he could still avoid military intervention, which he, much more than House, was eager to do. He seems to have been convinced that the receptivity of the Allies to talks would confront Germany with an irrestible amount of pressure.[86]

House's plan soon seemed in jeopardy of being thrown off track by Germany, however. On March 24 a French steamer, the *Sussex*, was torpedoed by a U-boat in the English Channel. Four American passengers were injured. The incident touched directly the issue that had been the subject of the *Arabic* pledge and thus threatened the prospect of a break with Berlin before the plan discussed with Grey had been activated.[87]

Wilson voiced concern that if the U.S. broke relations it would lose the ability to "lead the way out."[88] He was receptive therefore when House suggested that they contact Grey immediately to ask whether it "would not be wise to intervene now."[89] Their subsequent message to Grey (composed by both but signed by House) read:

Since it now seems probable that this country must break with Germany on the submarine question unless the unexpected happens and since if this country should once become a belligerent the war would undoubtedly be prolonged I beg to suggest that if you had any thought of acting at an early date on the plan we agreed upon you might wish now to consult with your allies with a view to acting immediately.[90]

"We have another reason for this," read a follow-up letter sent by House, "and that is we are not so sure of the support of the American people upon the submarine issue, while we are confident that they would respond to the higher and nobler issue of stopping the war."[91] Neither man seems to have been particularly surprised, however, when the foreign secretary responded that the time was not right.

But House was convinced that Washington had to take a firm line with Berlin regardless. Otherwise its credibility and influence would be lost. The U.S. "[w]ould lose the respect of the world unless he [Wilson] lived up to the demands he has made of Germany."[92] Attempting to press that course on the president, he insisted that,

Our becoming a belligerent would not be without its advantages in as much as it would strengthen your position at home and with the Allies. It would eliminate the necessity for calling in the conference any neutral because the only purpose in calling them in was to include ourselves.

Your influence at the peace congress would be ... enhanced....We could still be the force to stop the war when the proper time came.[93]

Finally accepting House's counsel, Wilson on April 18 despatched a note that was virtually an ultimatum and that could certainly have meant war. It did not sever relations (as Lansing had urged), but it threatened to do so unless Germany immediately declared that it would avoid sinking "passenger and freight-carrying vessels" without warning.[94]

American leaders held their breath. But, Bethmann, who continued to fear military conflict with the U.S., was once again successful in selling his policy to the kaiser. In early May, Germany pledged that it would use submarines only in accordance with traditional rules. It reserved the right to alter that if Washington did not effect changes in London's conduct of the blockade, but Wilson pointedly refused to accept such a condition.[95]

House had been urging the president "not to allow the war to continue beyond the Autumn." Indeed, he told Wilson on May 3 that he now thought he could end it "whether the belligerents desire it or not." He could "so word a demand for a conference that the people of each nation will compel their governments to consent."[96]

But with the conclusion of the *Sussex* crisis, the president began to think that he could and should set the ball rolling right away. Not only did Berlin's reply—in phrases that drew much comment in the U.S.—claim that Germany was open to peace discussions. The outcome of that affair, plus the seeming failure of Berlin's ongoing offensive at Verdun, suggested that the time might be appropriate. If Wilson waited, on the other hand, the war would go on, he was bound to face growing pressure for Britain to be confronted over the blockade, and there was no guarantee that a new crisis might not erupt over the use of Germany's submarines.

Wilson might also be able to use the league again now as leverage to get Britain to move on the House-Grey memorandum. For, come what may, the president seems to have been intent on publicly announcing his support for that idea within a matter of weeks, seemingly so as to preempt a possible Republican endorsement of a postwar league at that party's upcoming national convention. "I thought the republicans were holding their convention a week before ours [in early June] because they intended to put something in their platform concerning the war, its settlement and its aftermath in order to forestall the democrats," House wrote in his diary.

I felt so certain of this that I advised him [Wilson] to make a speech prior to the Republican Convention outlining our policy in such a manner that they could not appropriate it. The President was keen about this.... In outlining this policy we agreed that I should ... cable Sir Edward Grey and get his approval of the policy and when the President announced it as his own, the approval of Great Britain would follow.[97]

On May 7 House sent Wilson a draft of such a cable. It stated that the president wanted to "intimate that in the near future he contemplated calling a conference looking to peace." At the same time, he would "suggest to our people that the United States ought to be willing to do her share towards maintaining peace when it comes."[98] House told Wilson that Grey "may not wish a statement made concerning calling of a peace conference believing that it will stimulate Germany to a maximum effort during the summer." Nevertheless, it was "better for you to have both proposals come together because of the effect upon our people." "In order to force Sir Edward to accept the one with the other," he concluded, "I have intimated that he might lose the second if he does not take the first and I have also tried to alarm him as to public feeling in America."[99]

The day after his cable to this effect went off (on May 10), House also wrote Grey a letter arguing that

The wearing down process, as far as Germany is concerned, has gone far enough to make her sensible of the power we can wield.... A year ago we could not have made her come to the terms to which she has just agreed [the Sussex pledge], and it seems certain that at a peace conference she would yield again and again rather than appeal to the sword.[100]

But London was not receptive. British leaders were anxious to maintain good relations with the U.S. Nonetheless, they viewed the House-Grey memorandum only as an insurance policy that might be of use if their upcoming military efforts were unsuccessful. They doubted that Germany was as worn down as House suggested, and they were unconvinced of Wilson's ability to bring the U.S. into the war in accordance with his advisor's plan. Some thought that Wilson was merely trying to position himself as the champion of peace for the upcoming presidential campaign. British officials feared that talk of peace in Europe would break apart the Allied coalition and diminish the popular support they needed to continue on. Misgivings existed as well about the role that Washington seemed to want to play in the peace settlement. Above all, Allied leaders still wanted to win a decisive victory, and they were at this point more confident than they had been for some time that they could achieve that.[101]

Grey cabled House back on May 12 saying that he thought his colleagues and Britain's allies were most unlikely to favor a discussion of peace talks at this time.[102] "I see evidences of the Allies regaining their self-assurance and not being as yielding to our desires as they were when they were in so much trouble," wrote House to Wilson. "We have given them everything and they ever demand more."[103] With the president's encouragement, he composed and despatched yet another appeal to the foreign secretary.[104]

Simultaneously, Wilson went to work on a speech endorsing a league along the lines of what House and Grey had been discussing. The president had been invited to speak before a meeting of an organization, formed in mid-1915 and headed by Taft, dedicated to the creation of a postwar League to Enforce Peace.[105] House had been critical of what he saw as the impracticality of some of that group's ideas for ensuring international stability after the war, at least as they stood, but he encouraged Wilson in the thought that its banquet would provide "the occasion" for him to make the announcement that they had been planning.[106]

Having not heard back from Grey, Wilson avoided calling outright for a peace conference and concentrated instead on the league idea in his speech, delivered in Washington on May 27. The president endorsed the creation—with American participation—at the end of the war of a "universal association of the nations to maintain the inviolate security of the highway of the seas for the common and unhindered use of all the nations of the world, and to prevent any war begun either contrary to treaty covenants or without warning and full submission of the causes to the opinion of the world—a virtual guarantee of territorial integrity and political independence."[107] Shortly after the speech, however, House received a cable from Grey that again rejected as premature an American call for peace.[108] The ungrateful "Allied Governments and press overlook the weight the President has thrown on their side at almost every turn," wrote back the disappointed presidential advisor.[109]

Wilson now began to plan for a showdown with the Allies. He was determined to try to position himself so as to coerce them to agree to peace, along the lines desired by the U.S., as soon as an opportunity was provided. He told House angrily, "it will be up to us to judge for ourselves when the time has arrived for us to make an imperative suggestion."[110] House had already offered that Wilson might be able to end the war in the autumn—whether the belligerents desired it or not—by making a public demand for a conference that the war-weary people of both sides would by then be ready to compel their governments to attend. He and the president reverted back to this idea in the weeks after Grey's response.[111] Their attention was also beginning to focus on the enormous power that Washington was developing by virtue of the economic changes that were being stimulated and accelerated by the war—which included in particular the mounting Allied dependence on, and indebtedness to, the U.S. As early as the spring of 1915, the president had noted that "we are more and more becoming, by the force of circumstances, the mediating nation of the world in respect to its finance."[112] "We are growing stronger as they grow weaker," House had written back from London in January, "consequently our power is increasing in double ratio."[113] Wilson referred again to this leverage in an article, "America's Opportunity," that he wrote but did not publish in mid-summer 1916.[114]

Rejection of mediation confirmed the existence of sharp policy differences between Washington and London. And that in turn colored the Wilson administration's attitude toward British (and Allied) policies on trade and the blockade. Neither power had been free of suspicions and resentments over these questions prior to this. Since the start of the war, British leaders, for instance, had seen themselves as fighting on behalf of a world order from which the Americans stood to benefit, and they had thus been disposed to see the U.S. as getting a free ride from their efforts. This had led London to resent the (far from vigorous) protests that the State Department had occasionally felt compelled to make over the operation of the blockade. British leaders were also displeased by the alacrity with which the U.S. moved to benefit from the economic opportunities opened up by the war.[115] The Americans, meanwhile, had been on the lookout since the beginning of the conflict for signs that London might use the blockade as a means of holding onto its primacy and of stifling the surging commercial development of the U.S.[116] In fact, from their own vantage points, both powers had felt entitled to take advantage of opportunities that the war (in the U.S. case) or the blockade (in Britain's) offered.[117]

But once broader questions of policy were raised, it was inevitable that the two powers would be both more critical and more suspicious of one another. London's reluctance to act on the House-Grey memorandum increased apprehension in the U.S. as to how American interests might fare if the Allies in fact won a decisive victory. House had already described that as a "danger" back in December.[118] In May he wrote that "A situation may arise, if the Allies defeat Germany, where they may attempt to be dictatorial in Europe and elsewhere."[119] This consideration added to Washington's desire to see the war halted short of Germany's destruction.

Concern that the Allies were not going to be cooperative, in American terms, was also heightened by what officials heard about the Allied Economic Conference, held in Paris in mid-June 1916. The meeting's principal objective was to promote greater coordination among the participants in financial and commercial matters so that the war could be prosecuted more effectively. But it also envisioned carrying such collaboration over into the postwar period. As historian Gerd Hardach notes, no firm commitments were made about the future. Even the mention of such plans, however, alarmed the U.S. Lansing reported that the results of the meeting might make the negotiation of peace more difficult. Moreover, while the envisioned combination would be aimed in the first instance at revitalizing the Allies and hampering the economic recovery of Germany, it would also pose problems for the countries that had been neutral.[120]

U.S. officials were upset as well at Britain's further tightening up of the blockade (which reached a point where, in July, London dispensed with any pretense of continuing to adhere to the Declaration of London subject to "modifications and additions").[121] The State Department was particularly concerned about two new steps that were taken. Measures were instituted to inspect not merely cargo but also correspondence on board ships sailing into European neutral ports.[122] Then, the names of eighty-five U.S. firms were added to Britain's blacklist—a list designed to punish companies held to be doing business with the Central Powers.[123]

Throughout the previous two years, House had argued for the importance of keeping British-American relations on an even keel, even though demands for a firmer line had been growing in the U.S. He had insisted that disputes with England over neutral rights and maritime issues were not worth jeopardizing mediation for.[124] Now that British policy was being viewed in a more sinister light, however, now that the Allies were proving uncooperative, and now that the administration was under more pressure—from both at home and abroad—to demonstrate neutrality, Washington began to adopt a more assertive posture. Vigorous protests of the Royal Navy's interception of American mail and of the inclusion of U.S. firms on the blacklist were despatched.[125] More significant, retaliatory measures began to be considered. Wilson wrote House on July 23 that he was "about at the end of my patience" with Britain, the "black list business" being the "last straw." "I am seriously considering," he continued, "asking Congress to authorize me to prohibit loans and restrict exportations to the Allies. It is becoming clear to me that there lies latent in this policy the wish to prevent our merchants getting a foothold in markets which Great Britain has hitherto controlled and all but dominated."[126]

London's rhetoric about what it was contending for House and Wilson now derided as hypocritical and as simply a cloak for self-interest. When Page came home on leave in late summer, they sought to jolt him out of an Anglophilia that they felt limited his utility as a representative of the administration. House told Page he "resented some of the cant and hypocrisy indulged in by the British," such as the claim that they were fighting to free Belgium.[127] "I spoke," continued House in his diary, "of the traditional friendship between Germany and Great Britain, which existed until Germany began to cut into British trade and to plan a navy large enough to become formidable." He wondered whether London did not now "see us as a similar menace both as to their trade and supremacy of the seas" as Germany.[128] Wilson meanwhile told Page that the war was the result of "England's having the earth and of Germany wanting it."[129]

In September, at the administration's request, Congress empowered the president to retaliate against British trade with the U.S. and against British shipping in order to challenge not only the black list but the whole tenor of the blockade.[130] Wilson was reluctant to use this power, but he did hope that it would strengthen his hand in bargaining with London over policy.

A similar attitude was now also adopted with regard to the upbuilding of the navy. At the beginning of the war, Wilson had rejected advice that he should push for an accelerated program of naval expansion and for the creation of a larger army. The president knew how unpopular such measures would be among southern Democrats and among westerners of both parties. He also felt, as historian Kendrick Clements puts it "that a military buildup was more likely to create than to avert trouble."[131] Wilson resented criticism of his posture, which he saw as constituting a threat to his management of foreign relations, and he was inclined to retort that northeastern Republicans who called for such measures had lost their "self-possession."[132]

This attitude changed, however, in the aftermath of the *Lusitania* sinking, and by the winter of 1915–16, the president was ready to undertake a major political effort on behalf of "preparedness."[133] Initially this was conducted with Germany principally in mind. But by mid-1916, the naval aspects in particular were being thought about more broadly. House insisted that the U.S. should have a navy "commensurate with our position in the world."[134] "We have the money," he told Wilson, and a program even bigger than what the administration had originally envisaged would "give us the influence desired in the settlement of European affairs, make easy your South American policy, and eliminate the Japanese question."[135] House's concern was with Britain as well as Germany and Japan, and it was from the same perspective that Wilson subsequently lent his support to an even more ambitious bill. At the end of the summer, Congress passed the landmark Naval Act of 1916, which appropriated funds to make the American navy, within three years, a very close second in size to that of Britain.[136]

In September, House repeated to Wilson his argument that "the real difference with Great Britain now was that the United States had undertaken to build a great navy; that our commerce was expanding beyond all belief, and we were rapidly taking the position Germany occupied before the war," to which the president replied: "Let us build a navy bigger than her's [sic] and do what we please!"[137]

The president did not believe that he could make another move to end the disorder in Europe before the conclusion of the fall election campaign, which now claimed all of his attention. He was not in a position to commit the country to a long-term course of diplomatic action, and he realized that that would also affect how foreign leaders viewed him.[138]

Wilson had won only 42 percent of the popular vote in 1912, running against Taft, TR (who had tried to use the Progressive party as vehicle to return to the presidency), and the Socialist candidate, Eugene V. Debs. With the Republican party reunited, victory in 1916 seemed to rest heavily on which of the two major-party domestic agendas appeared more attractive to those who had voted for the Progressives four years before. Democratic party leaders were stunned, however, by the scale of the demonstrations for peace at their national convention in June, and they concluded that success would hinge as well on how each candidate addressed the continuing anxiety in the country about the possibility of involvement in the war. Wilson was thus put forward in 1916 as the man who "kept us out of war." Simultaneously, the Democrats sought to brand his opponent as someone destined to get the U.S. into the conflict.[139]

These intimations hurt Charles Evans Hughes, the Republican candidate—despite his insistence that he was for a strict neutrality—perhaps especially because of the loud campaigning that was done on his behalf by Roosevelt. The former president had for some time been critical of Wilson's foreign policy, charging that it was timid and selfish, in particular that it was not assertive enough toward Germany. This was a familiar role for TR, who had in the past made comparable critiques of the policies of Cleveland, McKinley, and Taft, but it proved to be of little help to the Republicans in 1916.[140]

Once the election was over, Wilson again began to think about steps that might be taken to bring about an end to the war along the lines that he desired. During the fall, he had become increasingly optimistic that Germany was ready for the kind of peace that he wanted after James W. Gerard, the U.S. ambassador, reported in September that Berlin would be receptive to a proposal for talks of the sort that TR had made to Russia and Japan in 1905.[141] It had subsequently appeared, however, that Germany was impatient for that to be done as soon as possible. In mid-October, Bernstorff sent House a memorandum stating that Berlin foresaw "the time at which it will be forced to regain the freedom of action," in regards to the use of its submarines, that it had "reserved to itself" in the *Sussex* pledge in May. House forwarded this to the president with the thought that Germany's intent was to force Wilson's hand.[142]

After the armed British steamer *Marina* was sunk without warning on October 28, with six Americans among the crew, Wilson worried that Berlin was carrying through on its threat. It might only be a short while before German-American differences over submarine warfare once again became serious. "[I]n order to maintain our position, we must break off diplomatic relations," he told House just a week after the election, and this would cut short any hope of making a bid for peace.[143] In the coming days, however, Bernstorff insisted that it was still German policy to adhere to the restrictions agreed to in the *Sussex* pledge, that the sinking of the *Marina* was a mistake, and that Berlin would be issuing an apology and making reparations.[144] This reassured Wilson and led him to look back toward the Allies as the principal obstacle he had to face.

The president had mentioned to House (as the latter reported in his diary) that he wanted to write a note "demanding that the war cease." Wilson hoped that he could use public diplomacy to make the Allied governments go along. But House worried that the way had not yet been prepared for that. Instead, the danger existed that such a move might promote an estrangement in Allied-U.S. relations. He argued that the Allies would consider Wilson's effort unfriendly coming as it did when they were "beginning to be successful." It also might seem as if Wilson was giving in to Berlin. House contended that any peace proposal made at that moment would be accepted by Germany and rejected by the Allies. The president "wondered whether we could not have a separate understanding with the Allies by which we would agree to throw our weight in their favor in any peace settlement brought about by their consent to mediation." But his advisor was convinced that this would get the U.S. into a "hopeless tangle" of territorial discussions.[145]

Wilson nevertheless remained determined to try. He set about drafting a note to the powers. He asked House if he would in the meantime write to Grey and impress on him that America's feeling was now "as hot against Great Britain as it was at first against Germany and likely to grow hotter still against an indefinite continuation of the war."[146]

Wilson was suddenly also presented with an opportunity to demonstrate to the Allies the degree of economic leverage that the U.S. was coming to have over them, this materializing in connection with frantic efforts on the part of Morgan and Co. (the purchasing and financial agent for London in America) to find new means of raising funds for the Allied war effort.

At the beginning of the war—to protect the American financial system against potential shock, to avoid political controversy, and to guard against embroilment in the conflict—the Wilson administration had taken the position that "loans by American bankers to any foreign nation which is at war are inconsistent with the true spirit of neutrality."[147] The administration rapidly began to retreat from this policy, however, after it became clear how dramatically it would interfere with American trade. Within months it announced a willingness to accept a distinction between loans and the arrangement of short-term commercial credits between the Allies and American bankers. Then, in 1915, it reversed its policy completely. In September of that year, Lansing approached Wilson about "the necessity of floating government loans for the belligerent nations, which are purchasing such great quantities of goods in this country, in order to avoid a serious financial situation which will not only affect them but this country as well."[148] The banking community was afterward informed that Washington would not object to such transactions, and over the next year, nearly $2 billion were borrowed by Britain in the U.S.

London found that it had not only to pay high interest rates but also to put up substantial collateral to attract these funds, however. Its effort to float an unsecured loan to the American public in the fall of 1915 fared poorly and would have ended in failure had not DuPont, Westinghouse, Bethlehem Steel, and a few other companies with large British contracts come forward to purchase one fifth of the bonds (the syndicate that underwrote the loan was still left holding nearly twice that amount). England henceforth looked to private loans from American banks. But, by the end of 1916 it was running short of the kind of high-grade collateral required by those institutions. Hope over the long term now rested on the possibility of another unsecured loan being floated to the public if the ground for that could be prepared for adequately.

Until such could be attempted, J. P. Morgan wanted to see if it could not meet England's needs by selling short-term, unsecured British Treasury bills to American bankers. The scale of the operation it envisioned, however, raised serious concern on the part of the Federal Reserve Board as to its impact on the liquidity of the American banking system. The board suggested to Morgan partner Henry P. Davison that a recession might be preferable to banks loading up on too great a quantity of securities which would almost certainly have to be refunded into long-term bonds.

After Davison's visit to Washington, the board drafted a statement cautioning member banks against investing too heavily in these notes. But that statement was then, at the president's behest, strengthened. Banks and private investors were to be informed that it was not considered "in the interest of the country ... that they invest in foreign Treasury bills of this character." The public release of this warning, on November 27, made pointless any effort to issue the Treasury bills at this time.[149]

Although the White House did not wish publicly to reveal or to explain its role, it did not take long for British officials to get Wilson's message. "President Wilson believed that the War could be wound up now on reasonable terms," noted Grey, "but those terms we should regard as unsatisfactory and inconclusive." It was the president's intention, he believed, "to bring pressure to bear."[150] Spring Rice cabled the Foreign Office on December 3 that the board governor, William Procter Gould Harding, had acknowledged to him privately that the statement had been altered by the "highest authority." "The object of course," the ambassador reported, "is to force us to accept President's mediation."[151]

Wilson's idea for his note was to cast it in the form not of a demand for peace, but of a request for each side to state the terms under which it would consider ending the war. On the grounds that the interests of neutrals were also affected, the president took the position that he had a right to ask the combatants, "What sort of ending, what sort of settlement, what kind of guarantees will ... constitute a satisfactory outcome ...?" The simplest way for such terms to be defined, he suggested in a draft finished about November 25, would be by means of a conference held for that purpose, which would also include "the governments not now engaged in the war whose interests may be thought to be most directly involved."[152]

At the behest of House, and to enhance the chances of success, Wilson dropped this suggestion from his second draft, completed on December 9.[153] He nevertheless continued to hope that the adversaries would feel pressured to respond in such a way as to make it possible for a conference, under his auspices, to be organized. Both sides, he asserted, had said that they were not fighting for territorial conquest and that their object was to obtain permanent guarantees of security and peace. The U.S. agreed with this and would join a league for that purpose. It wanted to be able to assess its position, however, if the war's end was not in sight.

Before Wilson could go any further, however, Germany, on December 12, issued a call for the Allies to meet with delegates from the Central Powers to discuss an end to hostilities.[154] From London, Page reported that Berlin's proposal would not even get "serious consideration" by Britain "unless definite and favorable terms" were put forward, and "Nobody believes that such terms will be authoritatively put forth."[155] The president fretted that his own initiative would now be seen as connected to Germany's by the Allies. Yet, if he postponed, he took the risk that the Allies would reply in such strong language as totally to foreclose a positive response to his own note. Before the situation became "even more hopeless," Wilson therefore sent off his proposal on December 18.[156] The final note, differing little in its essentials from the draft of December 9, included a request that it be considered on its own merits and not be seen as having been prompted by Germany.[157]

Germany responded first, on December 26. Picking up on Wilson's assertion, in his final draft, that he was "indifferent" as to the means by which the warring powers articulated their terms, Berlin simply stated, in the spirit of its own December 12 note, that it felt that a "direct exchange of views" between the two sides was "the most suitable way of arriving at the desired result." The question of "the prevention of future wars" could most appropriately be taken up "after the ending of the present conflict" in a conference that would include other powers.[158]

This fell well short of the response that Wilson wanted. Nevertheless, it did not extinguish his hope that Germany would accept the kind of settlement he desired. No doubt fueling this optimism was the fact that for the past month he had been receiving reports that Berlin was eager for peace, that it was ready to evacuate France and Belgium, and that it would join a postwar league (even while Wilson was also hearing that the food situation and the fear of defeat were prompting the German military to clamor more and more loudly for greater latitude in the conduct of submarine warfare).[159] Bernstorff moreover suggested to House that his government might be willing to state its terms if that could be done in strict confidence.[160]

So long as this hope remained alive, Wilson continued to focus on the Allies. They took longer to formulate an official response. But Wilson doubted that it would be favorable, and his advisors may possibly have ensured that it would not. House, still worried about antagonizing them, went so far as to reassure Jusserand of U.S. sympathy for the Allies. The secretary of state, meanwhile, took the Allied position. He believed that international stability would in the future best be served by the decisive

defeat of Germany and by the destruction of its autocratic system of decision making. He felt that the U.S. should enter the war to help the Allies
to bring such results about. Intending perhaps to advance that entry, Lansing
at first intentionally mischaracterized the December 18 note in comments
he made to the press, asserting that it was not really "a peace Note." He then
suggested privately to both Jusserand and Spring Rice that the Allies should
include in their reply a demand for such German "democratization."[161]

Whatever the effect of these actions, London had already decided to
resist, albeit as diplomatically as possible, should it be confronted with an
American peace effort. Both in anticipation of such a move and as a byproduct of their battlefield hopes and expectations, British policy makers
had begun discussing the question of war aims several months before. Some,
like Lansdowne—the former foreign secretary who was a minister without
portfolio in Herbert Asquith's (post-May 1915) coalition—had ventured
the opinion that England should cut its losses and settle for something less
than a total victory.[162] But the bulk of his colleagues, as well as the leaders
of the military, responded that the fight should go on. While differences
were voiced as to how weak or strong postwar Germany should be, there
was a general desire to see its military dealt a convincing defeat and to see
its decision making processes changed. However weak or strong it might
be on the continent, there was also a desire to see Berlin eliminated as a
significant naval and colonial power.[163]

Such resolution was, if anything, even more characteristic of the Lloyd
George ministry that came to power in early December. In September, Lloyd
George had himself tried to warn off any Wilson peace bid by declaring to
a United Press correspondent that he was intent on a fight "to the finish—
to a knock-out" over Berlin.[164] He moreover brought with him into posi-
tions of prominence in the government individuals such as Lords (George)
Curzon and (Alfred) Milner and Leo Amery who were convinced that
Britain's future needs required it to fight on to obtain control over some
territory in the "colonial world" that currently belonged to the Central
Powers. As historian Paul Guinn puts it, a number of these people felt that
"Only the failure of 'Britons' to make the Empire strong and cohesive
enough to ignore the balance of power in Europe had required war against
German domination of the Continent." Such cohesion would henceforth
be necessary to meet American as much as German, French, or Russian
rivalry. And to achieve that, influential members of Lloyd George's new
War Cabinet did not want to see Britain end the war without having assured
itself of dominance over at least German East Africa, Palestine, and Meso-
potamia so as to perfect the security of what they described as the "Southern British World" around the rim of the Indian Ocean (and so as to control
the oil of that region).[165]

London's concerns (no less than those of St. Petersburg and Paris) thus
continued to put it in direct conflict with Wilson. Yet it was one thing to

turn the German proposal down flat, quite another to take a defiant tone with Washington. That was particularly important to avoid in the wake of the Federal Reserve Board announcement of late November. At least since October, British leaders had been acutely conscious of how economically dependent they were on America. The passage of retaliatory legislation by Congress in September had triggered an examination of the issue, and subsequently the critical state especially of Britain's finances had become clear. Reginald McKenna, the chancellor of the exchequer, reported on October 24 that "If things go on as present, I venture to say with certainty that by next June or earlier the President of the American Republic will be in a position, if he wishes, to dictate his own terms to us."[166]

London hoped to disguise the desperateness of its predicament and simultaneously to respond in such a way as might prevent a confrontation. The Treasury had already begun quietly but dramatically to reduce purchases in the U.S. On December 29, the Allies collectively dismissed Germany's call for a conference. But, on the same day, Lloyd George told Page that he felt there was a special relationship between Britain and the U.S. London could not talk now because of the advantageous position that Germany still occupied on the map, and it would fight on even if Washington imposed an economic embargo. However, Wilson was the only one who could bring an end to the war once the proper time came.[167]

On January 10, the Allies finally made a formal reply, with France—as opposed to Britain—expressly delegated to speak on their behalf. The note praised the league idea and asserted that the Allies had a strong desire to see the war ended. Present circumstances, however, did not favor the establishment of a satisfactory peace. Addressing Wilson's deprecation of territorial conquest as a basis for that, the note asserted that the Allies were not fighting for "selfish interests," but to "safeguard the independence of peoples, of right and of humanity." Allied war aims were articulated in a general way, so as to comply with the president's request, and these were mostly cast in terms of the liberation of "Europe from the brutal covetousness of Prussian militarism."[168] Balfour, the new foreign minister, then followed up with an explanatory note of his own, meant to make the case, as he told his colleagues, that "A reversion to the *status quo ante bellum* would not be in the interests of the world at large."[169]

From the president's standpoint these aims, taken in their entirety, were not such as might enable peace discussions to take place. The Allied response irritated but did not unnerve Wilson, however, because he believed that he could also employ public diplomacy on behalf of his objectives. The president and House had several times in 1916 discussed the possibility of phrasing a call for peace that might mobilize the war-weary people of Europe against their governments. Then, on January 3, Wilson had announced that he was thinking of making such an effort just as soon as the formal Allied response was in. House approved of this step, and the two "thought if he made his speech before the Senate, the occasion could be arranged in answer to a request from" that body "for information as to what America would demand if she consents to join a league to enforce peace."[170]

Wilson immediately set to work on what was described as this "more important move." By January 5 he had produced an outline, entitled, significantly, "Americanism for the World." He completed a draft over the following week, which he then discussed with House when the latter was back in Washington on January 11–12.[171] The president delivered his address before the Senate ten days later.[172]

Wilson was seeking to get European opinion to rally behind his bid for the war to be concluded now on the lines that he desired. Peace could not only be had at this time, he meant to suggest, it was only by taking up his proposals that it could be made permanent. Such arguments ran directly counter to the Allies' insistence that a durable peace required a decisive defeat of Germany.

The speech opened with a reference to the president's note requesting that the belligerents' define their terms, with Wilson stating that that initiative had brought "nearer a definite discussion of the peace." As a consequence, it had also brought nearer, he insisted, discussion of the "international concert" which "must thereafter hold the world at peace." According to Wilson, it was "inconceivable" that the U.S. would not participate in that enterprise. Obviously anticipating that there were those of his fellow citizens for whom that would be conceivable, however, the president maintained that to do otherwise would be inconsistent with America's principles and traditions—the U.S. could not "in honor" withold such a "service" to mankind.

Yet, he continued, Americans owed it "to themselves and to the other nations of the world to state the conditions" under which they would feel free to render such a service. The present war had first to be ended. And it also made "a great deal of difference in what way and on what terms" that was done. The U.S. would have nothing to do with a settlement that merely served the "immediate aims of the nations engaged." It had instead to be a settlement that contained within it what the president maintained were the ingredients of permanent peace. That meant a settlement that constituted, above all, a "peace without victory," rather than a peace of conquest.

The president then enumerated what he felt were the other ingredients of the long-term peace he sought. These included arms limitation, access to and freedom of the sea, and (crucial elements of the guarantees for territorial integrity that he wanted) recognition of the legal equality of states and of the right of people henceforth not forcibly to be handed about "from sovereignty to sovereignty." Wilson had told House that he wanted this to be a "main principle" of his speech. But it, of course, begged the question of real self-determination, especially given that American forces were, for instance, still in Mexico and in occupation of several smaller Latin American countries. In a revealing summation, the president announced that what he really was proposing was "that the nations should with one accord adopt the doctrine of President Monroe as the doctrine of the world."[173]

It was Wilson's hope that the reaction to his speech would enable him to end the war and bring about the sort of peace that he desired (namely, one in which Germany would not be destroyed but rather integrated into the kind of great power pact for which the administration had long been eager, premised on arms control, peaceful settlement schemes, freedom of the seas, and territorial integrity). He and House immediately began to consider what their next step might be to bring this result about.

Optimistic as to the affect of the address on Allied public opinion, House, on January 23, passed on a suggestion from Herbert Hoover (then serving as chair of the Commission for the Relief of Belgium). This was to the effect that the president should solicit reactions from each of the belligerent governments about the principles he had outlined in his address, hopefully as a way of opening up a dialogue that might lead to a peace conference.[174] But Wilson felt that he should first find out for sure "what Germany is thinking," for he was certain that "if Germany really wants peace" he would be able to "bring things about."[175] This House, in confidential communications with Bernstorff, now set out to do.[176]

It soon became clear, however, that Wilson had overestimated how close Berlin's position had been to his own, and that Germany's peace drive was already in the process of being abandoned in favor of a new, unrestricted campaign of submarine warfare.

Berlin had indeed been serious in its quest for peace in the fall (at the same time, Bethmann Hollweg had hoped that if that was unattainable he might at least create a better reception within the U.S. for a German resort to unrestricted submarine warfare). But the terms that Germany's leaders had in mind diverged considerably from what Wilson was after. They still wanted a settlement that would either break up the Entente or, at least, strengthen Berlin's strategic position relative to it.

As the war turned into a struggle of attrition, Bethmann had during 1916 become more and more concerned about Germany's prospects. He and other German leaders came to worry that the greater resources of the Entente, combined with the effectiveness of the blockade, would lead, by mid-1917, to their defeat. German naval officers (and now army leaders as well) began to press for the adoption of unrestricted submarine warfare on the grounds that this, even if it brought the U.S. and other nonbelligerents who traded with Britain into the conflict, would turn the tables on their enemy and starve London quickly into submission. But Bethmann, as well as officials in the foreign ministry and treasury, worried that the result might instead be a more perilous situation.

Until the beginning of 1917, these political figures were able to hold off the advocates of unrestricted submarine warfare, in part with the argument that less risky paths to an "acceptable" peace had yet to be exhausted. Unable to achieve a separate peace with either Russia or France, the chancellor finally came to hope that he might be able to engage the Entente as a whole in negotiations where Germany would be able to cash in on the favorable position that it still occupied on the ground. An "acceptable" peace achieved by these means consisted of one in which there would be, if not extensive annexations, a considerable expansion of German influence, at the very least in next-door Belgium and Poland.

Bethmann's hope had been that Wilson could bring such a conference about, but he did not want the American president to participate in it. He did not trust Washington and believed that that would diminish Germany's leverage (although Berlin was ready to pledge itself to a subsequent, all-inclusive conference dealing with means of guaranteeing the peace). Worried that Wilson would not act, and anxious to take advantage of recent successes in the field—in particular the fall of Bucharest—Germany dispatched its own call for negotiations on December 12. (Some members of the military hoped that it would not be accepted. If it was, Germany, as they saw it, would either lose valuable time—to have the intended effect on British food supplies it was felt that the move to unrestricted submarine warfare had to start by February—or wind up with what they considered an inadequate peace.)

But the call was rejected, and the Allies' negative response precipitated the ascendance of those who were in favor of unleashing the U-boats.[177] On January 31, Bernstorff presented to Lansing memoranda complaining of the blockade, invoking the "freedom of action" that Berlin had reserved to itself in its reply to the *Sussex* note the previous year, and announcing that Germany would henceforth try to sink all ships, of whatever nationality, it found sailing into or out of Allied ports.[178]

Lansing urged an immediate break in relations, if not a declaration of war. Berlin was an untrustworthy power, he argued, in the midst of a "reversion to barbarism." In the face of its challenge, a break in relations was the only possible action in keeping with U.S. "[h]onor, dignity and prestige."[179] Wilson, though—as the secretary put it—"deeply incensed" at the "insolent notice," was taken off guard given the hope that he had placed on his initiative.[180] He told House that "he could not get his balance." Germany was a "madman" who ought to be "curbed." Yet the president was determined to be deliberative and not lose self-control.[181]

Wilson reiterated some of the reasons why he felt it would be a mistake to become a belligerent if that could be avoided. He told House "that it would be a crime for this Government to involve itself in the war to such an extent as to make it impossible to save Europe afterward."[182] Connected to this, Wilson told Lansing "that he was not yet sure what course we must pursue and must think it over; that he had been more and more impressed with the idea that 'white civilization' and its domination in the world rested largely on our ability to keep this country intact, as we would have to build up the nations ravaged by the war."[183] The president also floated past his cabinet the thought that it might even be wise to do nothing if it seemed necessary "to keep the white race or part of it strong to meet the yellow race —Japan, for instance, in alliance with Russia, from dominating China."[184]

But House and Lansing responded, as they had in previous submarine crises, that if the U.S. did not act, and do so immediately, it risked a profound diminution of its international influence. And Wilson, as he had before, accepted this thinking. A prompt break was also made more palatable for him by the thought that it might just save, rather than foreclose, the possibility of Washington remaining above the fray, and continuing to occupy a mediatory position. Lansing argued that it was unlikely that such a move would bring a declaration of war by Berlin, while House and Wilson spoke of Germany as a power that had lost its self-possession, but might yet, by a decisive U.S. act, still be brought back to its "senses."[185]

Once it had become clear that southern and western Democratic senators would support him, the president went before Congress to announce a severance in relations.[186] At the same time, he asserted that only "overt acts" on Germany's part could make him believe that it actually intended to adopt its recently proclaimed course. Further action would depend on Germany.[187]

Wilson would meanwhile continue try to intimidate, or in some other way influence, Berlin to abandon its course and to move back toward the settlement desired by the U.S. One thought was that most of the European neutrals might also be induced immediately to break with Berlin and that that might in turn get Germany to rethink its policy. An appeal toward that end was included in his address to Congress. However, it elicited little response, partly because the administration—intent on charting its own course and on cornering by itself the role of mediator—had so often rebuffed the initiatives of other nonbelligerents looking to collective action in the past.[188]

Wilson also decided to retain relations with Austria-Hungary—despite the fact that it too adopted unrestricted submarine warfare—as a way potentially of keeping alive his drive to end the war. The administration was already aware that Vienna might be looking for some way out of the conflict, and the possibility appeared to exist that Berlin would be compelled to negotiate if that took place. Early in February, Austria-Hungary's new foreign minister, Count Ottokar Czernin, informed Washington that it in fact looked favorably on the president's "peace without victory" formula, but that Vienna could never talk of peace so long as the Entente maintained its commitment, contained in the war aims it announced in January, and justified on the "principle of nationality," to a dismemberment of the multiethnic empire.[189]

Hopeful that something less threatening might lead to negotiations, Wilson instructed Page to ask for reassurances on this score.[190] Lloyd George denied that the Allies were intent on "sheer dismemberment," but he at first also asserted that they preferred to see Vienna remain in the conflict as what he called a "burden" on Germany (instead, the prime minister called for the U.S. to enter the war).[191] Ten days later, London reversed itself and announced that it would be receptive to a peace offer.[192] Although Washington explored the possibility, it soon became clear that Austria-Hungary was not ready to act independently of Berlin.[193]

The Wilson administration meanwhile eased up on Britain, determined now, in the wake of Germany's announcement, to do nothing that might lessen the war's pressures on the Central Powers. Government authorities ceased raising any objections to the use of American ports by armed Allied merchant vessels. At the end of February, Washington avoided comment when London announced, in a new Order in Council, still more stringent measures of blockade.[194] Then, on March 8, after consultation with the administration, the Federal Reserve Board issued a statement meant to retract the warning that it had issued to investors at the end of November. Claiming that it had been misunderstood, the board now pronounced foreign loans "a very important, natural and proper means of settling the balances created in our favor by our large export trade."[195]

The president also took up the subject of arming American merchant ships.[196] He ultimately endorsed such a policy both as a signal to Berlin, and to give confidence to American shippers, who otherwise, it became apparent, were not eager to send their vessels through the war zone.[197] The administration ideally wanted formal congressional endorsement of this course and hoped to receive it on the grounds that the U.S. needed to defend its rights. Congressional sentiment had become more militant in the wake of Germany's announcement, and party considerations were leading most Democrats to line up behind the president. After an armed ship bill was met with a filibuster by several Republican insurgent hold-outs in the senate, however, Wilson (insisting that older statutes gave him the authority to do so) simply acted on his own on March 9.[198]

The hope that Germany might still turn around reflected Wilson's long-held misgivings about the ramifications of American belligerency. If that took place, he felt there would inevitably be a price to the country in lives and treasure. In addition, under wartime conditions, Wilson believed that the forces of what he saw as narrow and irresponsible greed (the Republicans and their allies) might triumph at home.[199] Of perhaps greatest concern, the president also remarked in this period that if the U.S. went in, "we should lose our heads along with the rest." The U.S. then could not stop the Allies. "Germany would be beaten and so badly" that there might be no chance to achieve the settlement and postwar order that Wilson and House had been seeking.[200]

But how he would act if "overt acts" occurred and American vessels were destroyed had already been foreshadowed in the president's behavior during earlier submarine crises. When Germany finally extended its new campaign to nonbelligerent vessels in March, and several American merchantmen in quick succession were sunk en route to Britain, Wilson moved toward war.[201]

A greater interest in the rivalries of the European state system developed side by side with the expansion of the U.S. into new regions of the underdeveloped world at the turn of the twentieth century. This emerged as policy makers became convinced that events in the Old World could have a profound impact on their ability to prevent interference with the arrangements they wanted throughout the rest of the Western Hemisphere and in East Asia. It reflected as well their belief that access to, and order in, broad areas of the Eastern Hemisphere was also in their interest.

In the eyes of American leaders—throughout *most* of this era—continued British preeminence in the Eastern Hemisphere was seen as important to the stabilization of what they viewed as an advantageously organized international order. For that reason they sought, at several key junctures, to support London's position relative to its continental rivals.

At the same time, policy makers worked—often in conjunction with what they saw as that other most "responsible" power, Britain—to shore up and stabilize the existing international order by pushing for reforms in the conduct of world politics (many of which paralleled strategies for domestic stabilization employed in the U.S. in these years). Hoping to diminish the chances of upheaval, and worried about the territorial redivisions that could come from great power wars, administrations from McKinley's day onward took a leading role internationally in promoting mechanisms like arbitration. To encourage not just arbitration but the adjustment of disputes and the reduction of upheaval in general, Washington also pushed for the establishment of two different world courts. The first of these, founded in 1899, provided, in essence, for the creation of mixed arbitral commissions with a neutral umpire to deal with disputes. The second, which failed of establishment in this period, was premised on the idea that a truly judicial court would garner more confidence and use. Policy makers expected this second court over time also to generate a more complete system of international law that would regulate not just competition among the great powers, but in addition, and in accordance with collective great-power standards, the behavior of countries in the underdeveloped world.

Arms limitation, of a sort that would freeze in place the relative naval standing of the Old World powers was promoted, starting in late 1905. And some policy makers were talking by the end of the first decade of the new century about a "league" of some or all of the "civilized powers" that might collectively secure or "enforce" the kind of peace that the U.S. wanted.

No less eager than its predecessors to stabilize world affairs, but less hopeful about the Hague system (at least by itself), the Wilson administration gravitated early toward the idea of such a great power understanding ("the surest guaranty of peace," House told Wilson, "was for the principles [sic] to get together frequently and discuss matters with frankness ... as Great Britain and the United States were doing").[202] It was attracted particularly to the idea that Berlin, through inducements and reassurances, might be brought into such a pact. The administration hoped to defuse Anglo-German tensions and instead turn Berlin into an upholder of the existing international order (in its essentials). With pivotal Germany joined to a "sympathetic alliance" of (at least) Britain and the U.S., the balance of the world would "follow in line." The leading powers would then be inclined to settle peacefully disagreements among themselves. They would cooperate in supervising, and policing, the "backward" peoples (of the Eastern Hemisphere) without further struggles over territory and on the basis of the open door, and they would work collectively to protect this order against any "selfish" great-power challengers.

These hopes were blasted by the outbreak of war in Europe in 1914. Glad to be detached from the fighting, American leaders nevertheless continued to view affairs in Europe as of importance to them. They wanted to see the war end without the positions of Germany or Russia (as possible challengers of the existing order) enhanced. There was an added urgency to their desire to have the international order they wanted bolstered by new security arrangements. And they wanted the disruptive conflict to come to an end just as soon as these other objectives were within reach.

Such concerns fundamentally shaped the kind of "neutrality" adopted by the U.S. They were central to repeated efforts by Wilson and House to mediate, and preside over, the settlement. They influenced America's relations with Britain. They greatly impacted the attitude Washington assumed toward Berlin with regard to maritime rights. And they dominated the war aims of the U.S. when it finally became a belligerent in that conflict itself.

Conclusion

When viewed as a whole, it can be seen that there was a dominant thrust, or trajectory, to U.S. diplomacy during this turn-of-the-century "age of emergence." Throughout the era policy makers worked to shore up and stabilize an international order that they believed would guarantee the U.S. (or, implicitly, its society's leading elements) a position of commercial "wealth" and political "greatness" in the coming twentieth century.

A position of world leadership not only appealed to those who made U.S. policy. To them it was simply axiomatic that such leadership coincided with what was in the interest of the entire globe. This was principally by virtue of the fact that "real Americans" like themselves were the most mature people in creation. They were, by definition in this view, the disinterested agents of civilization, as well as civilization's guardians against "selfish" and "irresponsible" people who did not have their strong character.

In the Western Hemisphere and East Asia, policy makers labored to secure prevailing and, they believed, advantageous political boundaries and frameworks for trade against interference by other major powers. This was largely because these seemed logical places for the extension of American trade and influence as well as regions on which a position of much broader international leadership for the U.S. could be developed. At the same time, Washington sought elsewhere (at least during most of this period) to help uphold British power and to promote mechanisms that would diminish the prospects of major power war and upheaval.

The U.S. was a rising power on the world stage at the turn of the twentieth century, as for instance was Germany, but it was also in key respects a status quo power. It saw itself as having a vested interest in the current political-economic organization of broad areas of the underdeveloped world and in the existing distribution of power and territory among the globe's major states. And for these reasons it also saw itself as having a strong general interest in the stability of the existing international system. Its thrusts, on both the regional and general level, to reform that system were in fact aimed principally at enhancing that stability.

By contrast with some of the other powers, American leaders did not see the U.S. as requiring more territory or population (indeed they were struggling to assimilate, to "Americanize," as they saw it, those people it already had). They saw the U.S. as already occupying an extremely strong and competitive position relative to the other powers of the globe, both economically and politically.

The U.S. did want to diminish Britain's political-military role in the Western Hemisphere, but it was precisely the attachment of both powers to broader features of the existing international order (as well, admittedly, as the fact that the U.S. could not be denied) that encouraged Washington and London to avoid conflict and often collaborate in this period. Although they differed as to what they meant by it, each government was hoping thereby to ensure (in TR's words) that "the twentieth century" would "still be the century" of "men who speak English."[1]

There was also a broad similarity to the methods policy makers employed in this search for international order. And, in an age when order was a great concern on that front as well, these methods tended to echo or parallel approaches being developed for the promotion of stability domestically. Throughout the era, policy makers worked to promote consensus and (more selectively) collaboration on the part of other powers with regard to the organization and supervision of regions of the underdeveloped world, generally by trying to convince other major states that such frameworks would be in their best interest. They sought to rein in real or perceived behavior by major states or private parties that could undermine the promotion of the kind of long-term stability they wanted in underdeveloped countries (examples here would include Hay's efforts to restrain Germany during the Boxer Rebellion, the posture adopted by Root toward the rights of foreign bondholders in Latin America, and Wilson's objection to what he took to be the thrust of dollar diplomacy). All of the administrations in this period simultaneously sought to promote new and more effective mechanisms for the settlement of conflicts between and among the major states. Through the promotion of consultation, conferences and leagues, or through devices such as arbitration and mediation, they hoped, as they saw it, to depoliticize great-power international relations. They were of course prepared as well—where the circumstances were propitious—to endorse more forceful methods of reshaping the behavior of other powers when such efforts to stabilize the arrangements they desired failed.

Similarities are evident as well in policy makers' efforts to promote the kind of order they wanted in the underdeveloped regions of interest to them—a necessary "corollary," as American leaders saw it, of their campaign to shore up the political boundaries and economic frameworks prevailing across Latin America and China. Here the idea was to create inducements and pressures (codified where possible into law) that would encourage the governments in those areas to behave as Washington desired. Since such behavior hinged in turn on the existence of regimes that were capable of it, one administration after another labored to build up, or bring to power in

Latin America and China, what were defined as "strong" and "responsible" rulers (and to neutralize those held to be dangerously "weak" or "irresponsible"). And this included, where necessary, placing countries into "receivership" (or "guardianship" or "trusteeship") status—still, technically, without any breach of sovereignty—until that sort of regime could be created.

Throughout the period, albeit with growing vigor over time, policy makers sought to justify this stepped up overseas activity, including the use of force, by arguing that their intent was to protect, or promote, self-determination (or democracy, or freedom) and peace. These arguments were a predictable response on the part of policy makers to the challenges they faced, perhaps above all from within American society (where skepticism about such activity remained strong). But they by no means constitute an accurate description of Washington's commitment. As this study has shown, U.S. policy makers did not equate formal independence and territorial integrity with self-determination, which they in fact saw as contingent on a nation's "behaving." Nor was it peace per se, but rather the stabilization of particular kinds of regimes and of a particular international order, that they set out to uphold, or police.

This diplomacy, it should be noted finally, plotted out much of what would continue to be characteristic of the U.S. approach toward twentieth-century world affairs.[2] In their efforts to stabilize international affairs before World War I, American policy makers developed a basic vision of the kind of international arrangements they wanted and of how these might be achieved (how, in particular, they might contain the unilateralism of rivals and get underdeveloped countries to "behave") that would be drawn on again and again by their successors—both in their efforts to organize the Western Hemisphere and East Asia, and in their efforts to secure similar conditions for the United States elsewhere around the globe.

Abbreviations

CR	U.S. Department of Commerce and Labor, *Commercial Relations of the United States* (Washington, D.C.)
ERP	Elihu Root Papers (Library of Congress, Washington, D.C.)
EMHP	Edward M. House Papers (Yale University Library, New Haven, Conn.)
FR	U.S. Department of State, *Papers Relating to the Foreign Relations of the United States* (Washington, D.C.)
FVP	Frank Vanderlip Papers (Rare Book and Manuscript Library, Columbia University, New York)
GCP	Grover Cleveland Papers (Library of Congress, Washington, D.C.)
HWP	Francis M. Huntington-Wilson Papers (Myrin Library, Ursinus College, Collegeville, Pa.)
JHP	John Hay Papers (Library of Congress, Washington, D.C.)
LTR	Elting E. Morison, ed., *The Letters of Theodore Roosevelt*, 8 vols. (Cambridge, Mass., 1951–54)
PCKP	Philander C. Knox Papers (Library of Congress, Washington, D.C.)
PCJP	Philip C. Jessup Papers (Library of Congress, Washington, D.C.)
PWW	Arthur S. Link et al., eds., *The Papers of Woodrow Wilson*, 69 vols. (Princeton, N.J., 1966–94)
RLP	Robert Lansing Papers (Library of Congress, Washington, D.C.)
SDDF	Department of State, Decimal File, General Records of the Department of State, Record Group 59 (National Archives, Washington, D.C.)
SDNF	Department of State, Numerical File, General Records of the Department of State, Record Group 59 (National Archives, Washington, D.C.)
TRP	Theodore Roosevelt Papers (Library of Congress, Washington, D.C.)

WEBP   William E. Borah Papers (Library of Congress, Washington, D.C.)

WHTP   William Howard Taft Papers (Library of Congress, Washington, D.C.)

WJCP   Wilbur J. Carr Papers (Library of Congress, Washington, D.C.)

WMP   William McKinley Papers (Library of Congress, Washington, D.C.)

WTR   Hermann Hagedorn, ed., *The Works of Theodore Roosevelt*, 20 vols. (N.Y., 1926)

WWRP   William W. Rockhill Papers (Houghton Library, Harvard University, Cambridge, Mass.)

Notes

Preface

1. Reservations about that label have occasionally been voiced. See, for instance, Thomas A. Bailey, "America's Emergence as a World Power: The Myth and the Verity," *Pacific Historical Review* 29 (1961): 1–16; Richard W. Leopold, "The Emergence of America as a World Power: Some Second Thoughts," in *Change and Continuity in Twentieth-Century America*, ed. John Braeman Robert H. Bremner, and Everett Walters (Columbus, Ohio, 1964), 3–34; and Paul A. Varg, "The United States a World Power, 1900–1917: Myth or Reality?" in *Twentieth-Century American Foreign Policy*, ed. John Braeman, Robert H. Bremner, and David Brody (Columbus, Ohio, 1971), 207–40.

2. Two of the best are Lloyd C. Gardner, "American Foreign Policy, 1900–1921: A Second Look at the Realist Critique of American Diplomacy," in *Towards a New Past: Dissenting Essays in American History*, ed. Barton J. Bernstein (New York, 1969) and Joseph A. Fry, "In Search of an Orderly World: U.S. Imperialism, 1898–1912," in *Modern American Diplomacy*, ed. John M. Carroll and George C. Herring (Wilmington, Del., 1986).

3. Narrative surveys focusing on the same period as this study include Julius W. Pratt, *America and World Leadership, 1900–1921* (New York, 1967); Samuel F. Wells, Jr., *The Challenges of Power: American Diplomacy, 1900–1921* (Lanham, Md., 1990); and John Dobson, *America's Ascent: The United States Becomes a Great Power, 1880–1914* (De Kalb, Ill., 1978). In *From Wealth to Power: The Unusual Origins of America's World Role* (Princeton, N.J., 1998), Fareed Zakaria is ultimately more interested in why an already wealthy country did not expand before the 1890s (it did, of course, in North America)—the reason being, he argues, that it had an inadequate state structure—than in why and how the U.S. did expand during and after that decade.

4. This continues to be a problem with much Wilson scholarship, as witness, for instance, Thomas J. Knock's recent study of the postwar settlement and the 1919 treaty fight, *To End All Wars: Woodrow Wilson and the Quest for a New World Order* (Princeton, N.J., 1992). Although full of useful information, the value of Knock's book is undermined by his failure to get inside, to try critically to analyze Wilson's rhetoric and terminology. In the author's view, Wilson was motivated in 1919 by a genuine internationalism and by a desire to spread democracy and self-determination around the globe (his approach to the League, according to Knock, being prefigured by how he supposedly sought to promote these goals in Mexico, during its revolution, and in Latin America generally, through the Pan-American Pact). It is what Wilson meant (as demonstrated above all in his practice) by self-determination, however, that remains the crucial question.

5. Such as "big stick diplomacy," for instance. Where involvement in the promotion of peaceful settlement schemes has been noted, meanwhile, the tendency has been to see it as inconsistent with the thrust of the rest of diplomacy in these

years. See, for instance, George Mowry, *The Era of Theodore Roosevelt and the Birth of Modern America, 1900–1912* (New York, 1962), 278–79 and Robert E. Osgood, *Ideals and Self-Interest in America's Foreign Relations* (Chicago, 1953), 95–97, 102–3. To the extent that such activity has been addressed in detail it has principally been within the framework of studies of the American peace movement, and there official activity has usually been explained as a result of that movement's pressure. For example, see Merle Curti, *Peace or War, The American Struggle, 1636–1936* (New York, 1936) and Warren F. Kuehl, *Seeking World Order: The United States and International Organizations, to 1920* (Nashville, Tenn. 1969). Francis Anthony Boyle's *Foundations of World Order: The Legalist Approach to International Relations, 1898–1922* (Durham, N.C., 1999) marks something of a departure from this. Because his principal interest lies elsewhere—in arguing for the merits of international law over realpolitik—Boyle, however, does not say much about the social outlook of his legalists. Nor does he adequately explore the kind of world order they sought or how their efforts were related to other phases of policy.

6. One partial exception is N. Gordon Levin's study *Woodrow Wilson and World Politics: America's Response to War and Revolution* (New York, 1968), which, however, focuses mostly on 1917–19.

Chapter 1. Ideology and Interest

1. I have focused in this chapter on Presidents McKinley, Roosevelt, Taft, and Wilson, on Secretaries of State John Hay (1898–1905), Elihu Root (1905–9), Philander C. Knox (1909–13), and Robert Lansing (1915–20),on Assistant Secretary of State Francis M. Huntington-Wilson (1909–13), an exceptionally influential figure during the Taft years, and on Edward M. House, a key advisor to President Wilson. The ideas and attitudes outlined below, however, were clearly shared, for the most part, by most less influential officials and advisors as well. Virtually all these people were part of what T. J. Jackson Lears has usefully called the "metropolitan bourgeoisie" of turn-of-the-century America. William Jennings Bryan, who was Wilson's secretary of state from 1913 to 1915, does not fit that description, yet his differences with the general spirit dominant among other policy makers in this era have often been exaggerated. More important, Bryan's significance as a major shaper of foreign policy directions is open to question. Principally for that reason, I have for the purposes of this chapter left him aside.

2. Julius W. Pratt, *Expansionists of 1898: The Acquisition of Hawaii and the Spanish Islands* (Baltimore, 1936). Also see. Pratt, "The Ideology of American Expansion," in *Essays in Honor of William E. Dodd*, ed. Avery O. Craven (Chicago, 1935).

3. It has figured prominently mostly in discussions of Roosevelt, although even here historians have had much less success in relating it to his diplomacy while president than they have to his ideas about policy prior to 1901. See especially Howard K. Beale, *Theodore Roosevelt and the Rise of America to World Power* (Baltimore, 1984) and Thomas G. Dyer, *Theodore Roosevelt and the Idea of Race* (Baton Rouge, La., 1980). Also see David H. Burton, "Theodore Roosevelt's Social Darwinism and Views on Imperialism," *Journal of the History of Ideas* 26 (1965): 103–18; Frank Ninkovich,"Theodore Roosevelt: Civilization as Ideology," *Diplomatic History* 10 (Summer 1986): 221–45; (dealing with other policy makers as well as TR) Stuart Anderson, *Race and Rapprochement: Anglo-Saxonism and Anglo-American Relations, 1895–1904* (Rutherford, N.J., 1981).

4. Here see especially J. D. Y. Peel, *Herbert Spencer: The Evolution of a Sociologist* (New York, 1971), 192–223. Indeed, social evolutionary and Social Darwinian premises were employed, as historian Christopher Lasch among others long ago pointed

out, by critics as well as advocates of America's acquisitions in the aftermath of 1898. See Lasch, "The Anti-Imperialists, the Philippines, and the Inequality of Man," *Journal of Southern History* 14 (August 1958): 319–31.

5. David W. Noble, *The Progressive Mind, 1890–1917* (Minneapolis, 1981), 187–88; Paul F. Boller, Jr., *American Thought in Transition: The Impact of Evolutionary Naturalism, 1865–1900* (Chicago, 1969), 12, 48–56; John S. Haller, Jr., *Outcasts from Evolution: Scientific Attitudes of Racial Inferiority, 1859–1900* (New York, 1975), 97–98; Carl N. Degler, *In Search of Human Nature: The Decline and Revival of Darwinism in American Social Thought* (Oxford, 1991), 13.

6. For background, see Irvin G. Wyllie, *The Self-Made Man in America: The Myth of Rags to Riches* (New York, 1954), and John Cawelti, *Apostles of the Self-Made Man: Changing Concepts of Success in America* (Chicago, 1965).

7. Eric Foner, *Free Soil, Free Labor, Free Men: The Ideology of the Republican Party before the Civil War* (New York, 1971), 23–31; Daniel T. Rodgers, *The Work Ethic in Industrial America, 1850–1920* (Chicago, 1979), 30–36.

8. See, for instance, the discussion in Alan Trachtenberg, *The Incorporation of America: Culture and Society in the Gilded Age* (New York, 1982), 70–100.

9. These changes are discussed at greater length below. Also see Daniel T. Rodgers and Sean Wilentz, "Languages of Power in the United States," in *Language, History and Class*, ed. Penelope J. Corfield (Oxford, 1991), 240–59.

10. Stephen Jay Gould, *The Mismeasure of Man* (New York, 1981), 19–145.

11. As a real force, racism had of course long been present and important in American society, and that importance had grown throughout the nineteenth century as Europeans and European-Americans extended their influence over non-European peoples. The literature here is immense. With regard to racism and expansion, important studies include Reginald Horsman, *Race and Manifest Destiny: The Origins of American Racial Anglo-Saxonism* (Cambridge, Mass., 1981); Richard Drinnon, *Facing West: The Metaphysics of Indian-Hating and Empire-Building* (Minneapolis, 1980); and Ronald T. Takaki, *Iron Cages: Race and Culture in Nineteenth-Century America* (New York, 1979). The broader Western context is surveyed in V. G. Kiernan, *The Lords of Human Kind: Black Man, Yellow Man, and White Man in an Age of Empire* (New York, 1986). Also see Edward W. Said, *Orientalism* (New York, 1978).

At the same time, racism assumes different specific shapes within different contexts, sometimes, as historian George Frederickson points out, within different groups in the same society at the same time. See his *The Black Image in the White Mind: The Debate on Afro-American Character and Destiny, 1817–1914* (New York, 1972).

12. An important starting point for the study of gender and history is Joan W. Scott, *Gender and the Politics of History* (New York, 1988). On gender and the study of American foreign policy, see Emily S. Rosenberg's contribution to the round table "Explaining the History of American Foreign Relations," *Journal of American History* 77 (June 1990): 116–24. Relevant also is the symposium on "Culture, Gender, and Foreign Policy," *Diplomatic History* 18 (Winter 1994): 47–124. A new work that perceptively relates social evolutionary ideas to a culture of "manliness" in this era, specifically in connection with international financial advisers and advising, is Rosenberg's *Financial Missionaries to the World: The Politics and Culture of Dollar Diplomacy, 1900–1930* (Cambridge, Mass., 1999). See especially pp. 33–39.

13. Although clearly offering something to all old-stock Americans, this ideology offered particular succor to the men who held it. Much has been written, both by cultural historians like T. Jackson Lears and by students of gender such as Carroll Smith-Rosenberg, about feelings of uncertainty and fears of disorder experienced by late Victorians, especially by that age's privileged men. They felt threatened by the emergence of the New Woman of this time, whose aspirations and activities they saw as tied to and symptomatic of still other threats to order. And

they worried as well about what they saw as a feminization of their culture, their living circumstances, and the kind of work they did. In the face of all these developments and people before whom they felt threatened, this ideology—with its emphasis on the supreme challenge of "self-mastery"—offered upper-middle- and upper-class men a way of buttressing their masculinity.

That it was the males of different backgrounds who were principally being compared in this worldview is apparent from its very emphasis on the mastery theme. As E. Anthony Rotundo and other students of manhood in America have pointed out, mastery had been claimed as a specifically male trait throughout the previous century. By the men we are interested in at least, women meanwhile continued to be looked at as neither strong nor self-controlled, but rather as children. See, for instance, Roosevelt's address "The Woman and the Home," March 13, 1905, *WTR*, 16: 164–71; Taft, "Remarks Before the Forty-Second Annual Convention of the National American Woman Suffrage Association," April 14, 1910, WHTP; "From the Diary of Nancy Saunders Toy," January 6, 1915, *PWW*, 32: 21–22. Within the home, women did have a role of course in promoting the character formation of young boys. "There is not a man anywhere in our country," asserted McKinley, "who, remembering the affectionate counsels of his mother, has not been helped in resisting wrong and adhering to right." *Speeches and Addresses of William McKinley* (New York, 1900), 275. Also see T. J. Jackson Lears, *No Place of Grace: Antimodernism and the Transformation of American Culture, 1880–1920* (New York, 1981), 4–139; Carroll Smith-Rosenberg, *Disorderly Conduct: Visions of Gender in Victorian America* (New York, 1985), 176, 245–96; E. Anthony Rotundo, "Boy Culture: Middle-Class Boyhood in Nineteenth-Century America," in *Meanings for Manhood: Constructions of Masculinity in Victorian America*, ed. Mark C. Carnes and Clyde Griffen (Chicago, 1990), 19–22.

14. Degler, *Human Nature*, 54–55.

15. Noble, *Progressive Mind*, 53; Robert B. Westbrook, *John Dewey and American Democracy* (Ithaca, N.Y., 1991), 80–81, 166.

16. Degler, *Human Nature*, 20–24; Haller, *Outcasts*, 153–54; George W. Stocking, *Race, Culture, and Evolution: Essays in the History of Anthropology* (New York, 1968), 234–69. Also see Stocking's *Victorian Anthropology* (New York, 1987). Stocking's discussion of social evolutionary ideas in these volumes and in a talk he gave in Boston sparked in me a new interest in the language and terminology that I had been reading in documents on early twentieth-century American foreign policy. Such a reexamination has been central to my efforts to understand the ideology of this period. I have also found useful in this regard the editor's excellent opening essay in Corfield, ed., *Language, History and Class*, 1–29; Daniel T. Rodgers, *Contested Truths: Keywords in American Politics Since Independence* (New York, 1987); and Raymond Williams, *Keywords: A Vocabulary of Culture and Society* (New York, 1976).

17. For early arguments among intellectuals that joined social evolutionism to state intervention, see Morton Keller, *Affairs of State: Public Life in Late Nineteenth Century America* (Cambridge, Mass., 1977), 295–96.

18. William Appleman Williams, *The Tragedy of American Diplomacy* (Cleveland, 1959).

19. Michael H. Hunt, *Ideology and U.S. Foreign Policy* (New Haven, Conn., 1987).

20. Ibid., 18.

21. He seemed to be voicing reservations himself when he later wrote that "a system of culture can seem sprawling and amorphous and far too static to suit the needs of historians." See Hunt's contribution to the round table, "Explaining the History of American Foreign Relations," *Journal of American History* 77 (June 1990), 110.

22. This is now a large as well as diverse body of work. See, for example, the citations in Robert E. Shalhope, "Republicanism and Early American History," *William and*

Mary Quarterly 39 (April 1982): 334–56. For outstanding examples dealing with later periods, see for instance Sean Wilentz, *Chants Democratic: New York City and the Rise of the American Working Class, 1788–1850* (New York, 1984), and Foner, *Free Soil.*

23. Mary P. Ryan, *Cradle of the Middle Class: The Family in Oneida County, New York, 1790–1865* (Cambridge, 1983), 147, 160–61; Wyllie, *Self-Made Man,* 34.

24. Speech at the Mechanics' Pavilion, San Francisco, May 22, 1901, WMP.

25. Rotundo, "Boy Culture," 19, 27–29.

26. "Bodily vigor is good, and vigor of intellect is even better, but far above both is character," wrote Roosevelt in *The Strenuous Life: Essays and Addresses* (New York, 1905). Also see Roosevelt's reviews of Charles Pearson's *National Life and Character* and Benjamin Kidd's *Social Evolution* in his *American Ideals and Other Essays* (New York, 1897), 271–328; Taft's address at Norwich, Connecticut, July 5, 1909, in William H. Taft, *Presidential Addresses and State Papers* (New York, 1910), 173; and Wilson's address "The Nature of Democracy in the United States," May 1889, in *PWW,* 6: 221–39.

27. Roosevelt, *Strenuous Life,* 329. On these characteristics, also see, for example, the language and terminology employed by McKinley in his Home Market Club speech in Boston, February 16, 1899, in *Speeches and Addresses of William McKinley,* 193; by Hay in his speech "The Platform of Anarchy," October 6, 1896, JHP; by Root in his Nobel Peace Prize address of 1912, printed in *Addresses on International Subjects by Elihu Root,* ed. Robert Bacon and James Brown Scott (Cambridge, Mass., 1916), 155–56; by Knox in his address "The Spirit and Purpose of American Diplomacy," June 15, 1910, PCKP; by Taft in his collection of speeches *Political Issues and Outlooks* (New York, 1909), 71; by Wilson in "The Modern Democratic State," December 1885, *PWW,* 5: 61–92; and by Wilson and House in their discussion of the onset of World War I, "From the Diary of Colonel House," August 30, 1914, *PWW,* 30: 461–67.

28. Here see, for instance, Dyer, *Roosevelt,* 45–68; William Howard Taft, *Four Aspects of Civic Duty* (New York, 1907), 13–20; and Wilson, "Democracy and Efficiency," October 1900, *PWW,* 12: 10–13.

29. See, for instance, McKinley, "Letter Accepting the Nomination," September 8, 1900, WMP; Hay, "Fifty Years of the Republican Party," July 6, 1904, in *Addresses of John Hay* (New York, 1906), 287–88, and Hay's novel, *The Breadwinners* (New York, 1883), especially 74–87; Root, "The United States and the Philippines," October 24, 1900, in *The Military and Colonial Policy of the United States: Addresses and Reports by Elihu Root,* ed. Robert Bacon and James Brown Scott (Cambridge, Mass., 1924), 42–43; Dyer, *Roosevelt,* 69–142; Taft, "Administration of Criminal Law," June 26, 1905, in William Howard Taft, *Present Day Problems* (New York, 1908), 341–42; Wilson, "The Ideals of America," December 26, 1901, *PWW,* 12: 223–24; "Remarks by Wilson and a Dialogue" (with William Monroe Trotter), November 12, 1914, *PWW,* 31: 301–8.

30. Gould, *Mismeasure,* 113–19; Haller *Outcasts,* 114, 136–40; Stuart Creighton Miller, *"Benevolent Assimilation": The American Conquest of the Philippines, 1899–1903* (New Haven, Conn., 1982).

31. For references that include such allusions to China, see especially Root, "The Character and Office of the American Army," January 27, 1903, in *Military and Colonial Policy,* 16; and Roosevelt, *Strenuous Life,* 6. Trying to prepare Americans for the annexation of the Philippines, McKinley asserted that "The progress of the nation can alone prevent degeneration." See his speech in Chicago, October 19, 1898, in *Speeches and Addresses,* 135. In his Memorial Day address of May 30, 1908, Taft felt that "This day ... should for a time take us out of the atmosphere of self-seeking, of money-making, of pleasure-hunting, and of peaceful sloth, that we may value again the many instances it revives of mental and physical courage, self-denial, self-restraint, and self-sacrifice" of the Civil War era. *Present Day Problems,* 62. The conquest of the Philippines, commented Wilson in a speech on December 14, 1899, "means that

this country has young men who prefer dying in the ditches of the Philippines to spending their lives behind the counters of a dry goods store in our eastern cities. I think I should prefer that myself." *PWW*, 11: 299. Also see the chapter on Roosevelt in Tom Lutz, *American Nervousness, 1903: An Anecdotal History* (Ithaca, N.Y., 1991), 63–98. Many policy makers spoke about the "Latin nations" of Europe in terms similar to this discussion about China.

32. The Democrats had "lost the virility of the founders" of their party, charged McKinley on September 8, 1900, in his letter accepting the Republican nomination, WMP. Roosevelt denounced as "shrill eunuchs" those who criticized his actions in connection with Panama in fall 1903. See Roosevelt to Otto Gresham, November 30, 1903, *LTR*, 3: 663. Wilson described the anti-imperialists in similar terms. They were also impractical and lacking in true Americanism. "Because of our Americanism," he said in an address of January 28, 1904, "we had no patience with the anti-imperialist weepings and wailings that came out of Boston, not because we didn't think them entitled to their fair opinion, but because we knew that the crying time was over and that the time had come for men to look out of dry eyes and see the world as it is." *PWW*, 15: 143. Also see Geoffrey Blodgett, "The Mugwump Reputation, 1870 to the Present," *Journal of American History* 66 (March 1980): 883–84; William C. Widener, *Henry Cabot Lodge and the Search for an American Foreign Policy* (Berkeley, Calif., 1983), 215; John Milton Cooper, Jr., *The Warrior and the Priest: Woodrow Wilson and Theodore Roosevelt* (Cambridge, Mass., 1983), 208, 282–83, 315. After their final rift in 1920, Robert Lansing also attacked Wilson for having a "feminist" mind. See "The Mentality of Woodrow Wilson," November 20, 1921, RLP.

33. For an excellent example of Wilsonian rhetoric on this topic, see "A Draft of the National Democratic Platform of 1916," c. June 10, 1916, *PWW*, 37: 191.

34. "Popular government is organized self-control—organized capacity for the development of the race," pronounced Root in his lectures at Yale in May 1907. See *Addresses on Government and Citizenship by Elihu Root*, ed. Robert Bacon and James Brown Scott (Cambridge, Mass., 1916), 6. "Why has democracy been a cordial and a tonic to little Switzerland and big America, while it has been as yet only a quick intoxicant or a slow poison to France and Spain, a mere maddening draught to the South American states?" asked Wilson in "The Modern Democratic State," December 1885, *PWW*, 5: 63. Also see his "Constitutional Government in the United States," March 24, 1908, *PWW*, 18: 87–88. "I like the Russian people and believe in them," wrote Roosevelt to Cecil Arthur Spring Rice on June 13, 1904, but, "I see nothing of permanent good that can come to Russia, either for herself or for the rest of the world until her people begin to tread the path of orderly freedom, of civil liberty, and of a measure of self-government. Whatever may be the theoretical advantages of a despotism, they are incompatible with the growth of intelligence and individuality in a civilized people. Either there must be stagnation in the Russian people, or there must be what I should hope would be a gradual, but a very real, growth of governmental institutions to meet the growth in, and the capacity and need for, liberty." *LTR*, 4: 829.

35. Root, "The Spirit of Self-Government," November 21, 1912, in *Addresses on Government and Citizenship*, 381; Taft, "Address Before the New York State Bar Association," January 20, 1912, WHTP; Roosevelt to Charles William Eliot, April 4, 1904, *LTR*, 4: 769; Wilson, "The Modern Democratic State," December 1885, *PWW*, 5: 63; Lansing, *Notes on Sovereignty from the Standpoint of the State and of the World* (Washington, D.C., 1921), 26. "They are children and we are men in these deep matters of government and justice," said Wilson of the Filipinos. See "The Ideals of America," December 1901, *PWW*, 12: 223.

36. Address of July 12, 1900, WMP. What is striking, in fact, is the degree to which colonialism and domestic rule over disfranchised African-Americans were

justified and thought about in the same terms by some American leaders in this period. And this extended to the belief that what the Filipinos most needed was training in the habits of industry. For example, see Taft, *Four Aspects of Civic Duty*, 85. Also see Taft's speech "The Future of the Negro," September 15, 1908, in his *Political Issues and Outlooks*, 68–69.

37. See McKinley to Lodge, September 8, 1900, WMP and Hay, "Speech at Carnegie Hall," October 26, 1904, JHP. Also see Roosevelt, "The Treaty with Spain," February 3, 1899, *WTR*, 14: 312–13.

38. See Root, "American Policies in the Philippines in 1902," September 24, 1902, in *Military and Colonial Policy*, 87–88. Along these same lines, also see Roosevelt, "The Issues of 1900," September 15, 1900, *WTR*, 14: 365.

39. *PWW*, 11: 573.

40. See Taft, "Southern Democracy and Republican Principles," in *Present Day Problems*, 233.

41. This was a line of argument first delineated in Walter LaFeber, *The New Empire: An Interpretation of American Expansion, 1860–1898* (Ithaca, N.Y., 1963); Thomas McCormick, "Insular Imperialism and the Open Door: The China Market and the Spanish-American War," *Pacific Historical Review* 32 (May 1963): 155–69; David Healy, *The United States in Cuba, 1898–1902: Generals, Politicians, and the Search for Policy* (Madison, Wis.,1963), among other works.

42. See, for instance, Peter G. Filene,"An Obituary for 'The Progressive Movement,'" *American Quarterly* 22 (1970): 20–34.

43. "The greatest impediment to progress in this country is the squeamishness of refined men in respect to politics," said Wilson. See "A Newspaper Report of an Address in Philadelphia," January 3, 1900, *PWW*, 11: 356. Also see "The Democratic Opportunity," November 1909, *PWW*, 19: 465–66 and Wilson's speeches, for instance, in Boston on January 27 (*PWW*, 24: 83–84) and in Albany, Georgia on April 18 (*PWW*, 24: 346), during the 1912 campaign. "The friends of property, of order, of law, must never show weakness in the face of violence or wrong or injustice," wrote Roosevelt to Knox on November 10, 1904, "but on the other hand they must also realize that the surest way to provoke an explosion of wrong and injustice is to be shortsighted, narrow-minded, greedy and arrogant." *LTR*, 4: 1023. Also see the speeches of Root and of Knox, who had handled the Northern Securities case as Roosevelt's Attorney General, before the Union League Club in 1904. Root's, dated February 3, is reprinted in *Miscellaneous Addresses of Elihu Root*, ed. Robert Bacon and James Brown Scott (Cambridge, Mass., 1917). Knox's, dated October 20, is available in PCKP. Taft outlined his attitude toward laissez-faire at some length in a speech at Syracuse, New York on September 16, 1911, available in WHTP. Both Taft and Root were major officers in the National Civic Federation.

44. There is a vast literature on the domestic views and policies of Roosevelt and Wilson. One useful point of entry for both is Cooper, *Warrior and the Priest*. For those of Root, Philip C. Jessup, *Elihu Root*, 2 vols. (New York, 1938) remains the key source. For Taft, see Paolo E. Coletta, *The Presidency of William Howard Taft* (Lawrence, Kan., 1973). For McKinley, who had staked out a more sophisticated approach toward labor as early as the mid-1890s when he was governor of Ohio, the place to begin is Lewis L. Gould, *The Presidency of William McKinley* (Lawrence, Kan., 1980). A number of works have shaped my understanding of the social policy approaches discussed here. These include Robert H. Wiebe, *The Search for Order, 1877–1920* (New York, 1967); James Weinstein, *The Corporate Ideal in the Liberal State, 1900–1918* (Boston, 1968); and Paul Boyer, *Urban Masses and Moral Order in America, 1820–1920* (Cambridge, Mass., 1978). An important synthesis of much of this literature is Alan Dawley, *Struggles for Justice: Social Responsibility and the Liberal State* (Cambridge, Mass., 1991), especially 98–171. On economic regulation, see Martin J. Sklar, *The Corporate*

Reconstruction of American Capitalism, 1890–1916 (Cambridge, 1988). Rothman develops the "state as parent" idea in Willard Gaylin, David J. Rothman, S. Marcus, and I. Glasser, *Doing Good: The Limits of Benevolence* (New York, 1978).

45. This is not to deny—and here I would certainly agree with Walter LaFeber's observation, made in his *The American Search for Opportunity, 1865–1913* (New York, 1993)—that disorder was frequently the result of American policy. Policy makers were also willing consciously to act in ways that were counter to order at times, particularly so as to end a regime that worked against perceived American interests (they then, however, generally sought to establish a new order that might conform to those interests). These points granted, they do not to my mind diminish the utility of the "search for order" idea, as I use it below, as a way of thinking about the overarching goal of American world policy at this time.

46. On this topic, see also the discussion in David Healy, *Drive to Hegemony: The United States in the Caribbean, 1898–1917* (Madison, Wis., 1988), 219–37.

47. See Kenton J. Clymer, *John Hay: The Gentleman as Diplomat* (Ann Arbor, Mich., 1975), 134. "We are fighting against the selfish ambition of a military dictator," argued Root on October 7, 1899. See "The American Soldier," in *Military and Colonial Policy*, 10.

48. Taft commented that "we owe to our less fortunate [international] neighbors that come under our guardianship the same degree of neighborly feeling and aid that a successful man in a community owes to his less fortunate fellow citizens," in an address at Marquette, Michigan on September 20, 1911, WHTP. Because of his tenure as governor-general in the Philippines, Taft considered himself an expert on the tropics. He saw them as holding opportunities both for gain and for the demonstration of American leadership abilities. See his lecture "The Duties of Citizenship Viewed from the Standpoint of Colonial Administration," in *Four Aspects of Civic Duty*. Yet they also were a place where the character of American men could be dangerously undermined. See his address at Augusta, Georgia, January 17, 1909, on the national (urban) and international ("the tropics and the Orient") work of the YMCA in *Political Issues and Outlooks*, 245–55.

To Wilson, the "primeval" Philippines offered a replacement for the disappearing frontier of the American West. The islands were valuable in part because it was "always well to have a frontier on which to turn loose the colts of the race." See "Address in Montclair, New Jersey," January 28, 1904, *PWW*, 15: 143. While voyaging through the Caribbean en route to inspect the work at Panama in November 1906, Roosevelt wrote letters to his son Kermit that spoke powerfully of what the region meant to him. The "fourth day out," he related,"was in some respects the most interesting," when the U.S.S. Louisiana passed between Cuba and Haiti, "in each case green, jungly shores and bold mountains—two great, beautiful venomous tropic islands." They inspired TR to recount what he saw as the region's history of "turbulence," "splendor," and "wickedness," and to contrast that with "the effort we are now making to bring Cuba and Porto Rico forward." See *LTR*, 5: 495.

49. Warren G. Kneer, *Great Britain and the Caribbean, 1901–1913: A Study in Anglo-American Relations* (East Lansing, Mich., 1975) is especially good on how these pledges were compromised.

50. Quoted in David Healy, *U.S. Expansionism: The Imperialist Urge in the 1890s* (Madison, Wis., 1970), 153–54.

Chapter 2. The "Center of Gravity": Caribbean Policy and the Canal

1. For a classic statement of the argument that Washington's involvement in the region stemmed from its desire to protect these economic interests, see Scott Nearing

and Joseph Freeman, *Dollar Diplomacy: A Study in American Imperialism* (New York, 1925). In his *Intervention and Dollar Diplomacy in the Caribbean, 1900–1921* (Princeton, N.J., 1964), Dana G. Munro explained Washington's diplomacy as an essentially defensive effort to protect American national security, especially by preventing the establishment near the Panama Canal of hostile foreign lodgments. The trend in recent studies, however, has been to put more emphasis on the canal's importance as a conduit of American trade with, and military power to, other regions of the world. Especially important studies are David F. Healy, *Drive to Hegemony: The United States in the Caribbean, 1898–1917* (Madison, Wis., 1988), and Lester Langley, *The Banana Wars: United States Intervention in the Caribbean, 1898–1934* (Lexington, Ky., 1985). Quite a different tack is taken, however, in Richard H. Collin, *Theodore Roosevelt's Caribbean: The Panama Canal, the Monroe Doctrine, and the Latin American Context* (Baton Rouge, La., 1990), where the author contends that TR was not an expansionist.

2. The two books most directly relevant here are Alfred Thayer Mahan, *The Influence of Sea Power upon History, 1660–1783* (Boston, 1890) and Mahan, *The Interest of America in Sea Power, Present and Future* (Boston, 1898), a collection of articles published during the 1890s.

3. See here, especially, Walter LaFeber's classic *The New Empire: An Interpretation of American Expansion, 1860–1898* (Ithaca, N.Y., 1963), 85–101. Also see Milton Plesur, *America's Outward Thrust: Approaches to Foreign Affairs, 1865–1890* (DeKalb, Ill., 1971) and Robert L. Beisner, *From the Old Diplomacy to the New, 1865–1900* (New York, 1975).

4. All countries "touch one another more closely than of old" was the way Mahan put it in *The Problem of Asia and Its Effect upon International Policies* (Boston, 1900), 18.

5. On the navy, and on Mahan, his ideas and impact, see Mahan's works cited above and the following: Kenneth J. Hagan, *This People's Navy: The Making of American Sea Power* (New York, 1991), 161–258; Philip A. Crowl, "Alfred Thayer Mahan: The Naval Historian," in *Makers of Modern Strategy: From Machiavelli to the Nuclear Age*, ed. Peter Paret (Princeton, N.J.,1986), 444–77; William E. Livezey, *Mahan on Seapower* (Norman, Okla., 1947); Clark Reynolds, *Command of the Sea: The History and Strategy of Maritime Empires* (New York, 1974), 402–18; Richard D. Challener, *Admirals, Generals, and American Foreign Policy, 1898–1914* (Princeton, N.J., 1973), 12–23; and John Tetsuro Sumida, *Inventing Grand Strategy and Teaching Command: The Classic Works of Alfred Thayer Mahan Reconsidered* (Washington, D.C., 1997).

6. On Mahan, the navy, the canal, and the Caribbean, see especially Mahan, *Interest* and Charles H. Stockton, "The American Interoceanic Canal: A Study of the Commercial, Naval, and Political Conditions," *Proceedings of the United States Naval Institute* 26 (December 1899): 753–97.

7. David McCullough, *The Path Between the Seas: The Creation of the Panama Canal, 1870–1914* (New York, 1977), 250.

8. Roosevelt, *The Strenuous Life: Essays and Addresses* (New York, 1905), 9.

9. Mahan, *Interest*, 26, 102, 265; Challener, *Admirals*, 35.

10. See Challener, *Admirals*, 12–110.

11. Louis A. Pérez, *Cuba Between Empires, 1878–1902* (Pittsburgh, 1983). Also see Jules Robert Benjamin, *The United States and Cuba: Hegemony and Dependent Development, 1880–1934* (Pittsburgh, 1977), 1–10.

12. Until well into the twentieth century, it was not atypical for historians to describe President McKinley as simply being swept into this war by public opinion and Congress. Those really responsible for the conflict, some suggested, were William Randolph Hearst and Joseph Pulitzer, whose newspapers had been carrying sensationalized accounts of Spanish brutality on the island in order to build up circulation. This historical literature is discussed in Joseph A. Fry's "William McKinley and

the Coming of the Spanish-American War: A Study of the Besmirching and Redemption of an Historical Image," *Diplomatic History* 3 (Winter 1979): 77–97. Also see Thomas G. Paterson, "United States Intervention in Cuba, 1898: Interpretations of the Spanish-American-Cuban-Filipino War," *History Teacher* 29 (May 1996): 341–61 and Louis A. Pérez, Jr., *The War of 1898: The United States and Cuba in History and Historiography* (Chapel Hill, N.C., 1998).

A few memorable contemporary depictions of McKinley lent support to this interpretation. Political cartoonist Homer Davenport's biting caricature (in the *New York Journal*) of a president being overwhelmed by public sentiment and Roosevelt's alleged comparison of McKinley to a cream-filled pastry are among the most famous. See the discussion in Fry, "William McKinley," 77. Both of these, it is worth noting, questioned the president's manhood. Davenport drew McKinley in a bonnet and dress and with a broom, as an "old woman" fussily and futilely seeking to brush back waves of public sentiment that were flooding in, while TR is said to have exploded in April 1898 that the president had "no more backbone than a chocolate éclair." Also see Edmund Morris, *The Rise of Theodore Roosevelt* (New York, 1980), 610 and Kristin L. Hoganson, *Fighting for American Manhood: How Gender Politics Provoked the Spanish-American and Philippine-American Wars* (New Haven, Conn., 1998), 88–106.

While the public and Congress were certainly prepared for war in spring 1898 (especially after the sinking of the *Maine*), and while that mood is important, this traditional explanation of the war's origins—as well as the image of McKinley as a weak president without a foreign policy of his own—has largely been cast aside by modern scholarship. McKinley did not want war if his objective could be accomplished by other means. But he came to office intent on ending the disorders in the nearby island and was willing to risk a conflict if other methods did not fairly quickly lead to success. For other recent treatments, see Robert C. Hilderbrand, *Power and the People: Executive Management of Public Opinion in Foreign Affairs, 1897–1921* (Chapel Hill, N.C., 1981), 4–28; Lewis L. Gould, *The Presidency of William McKinley* (Lawrence, Kan., 1980), 59–90; and Richard J. Barnet, *The Rockets' Red Glare: War, Politics, and the American Presidency* (New York, 1990), 125–35. John Offner, in his *An Unwanted War: The Diplomacy of the United States and Spain over Cuba, 1895–1898* (Chapel Hill, N.C., 1992), argues that domestic political considerations did finally, in April 1898, become central to McKinley's concerns. But he does not really contend that this did anything more than hasten a conflict which was "inevitable" given the two governments' objectives. Nor does he challenge the idea that it was McKinley who defined what the goals of the war would be.

13. American pressure to try this had begun under Grover Cleveland and his secretary of state, Richard Olney. The McKinley administration came to power early in 1897 hopeful that Cleveland's proposals were "all that is necessary" to restore calm to the island. In late spring, the new president sent his friend William J. Calhoun to determine how things stood in Cuba. He reported that the Spanish army was still not succeeding in its effort to suppress the rebellion. Moreover, the measures it was employing were tending toward the outright ruination of the island. After this, Washington told Madrid that it would be given until November 1 to embark on a course such "as would satisfy the United States that early and certain peace can promptly be secured." The crisis precipitated a change in government, and in late October the new ministry announced that it would institute a policy of autonomy. Washington's response was that it would "maintain an attitude of benevolent expectancy," but only long enough "to prove the asserted efficacy of the new order of things" due to be inaugurated at the beginning of the coming year. See Olney to Dupuy de Lôme, April 4, 1896, *FR 1897*, 540–44; Message of the President, December 7, 1896, *FR 1896*, xxix–xxxvi; Gerald G. Eggert, *Richard Olney:*

Evolution of a Statesman (University Park, Pa.,1974), 265–69; Philip S. Foner, *The Spanish-Cuban-American War and the Birth of American Imperialism, 1895–1902,* 2 vols. (New York, 1972), 1: 209–14; Gould, *McKinley,* 68; Offner, *An Unwanted War,* 42, 46–47; H. Wayne Morgan, *America's Road to Empire: The War with Spain and Overseas Expansion* (New York, 1965), 29; Message of the President, December 6, 1897, *FR 1897,* x–xxi. Also see the exchanges between Woodford and the State Department in *FR 1898,* 558–613. On the Spanish side of the coming of the war, see Thomas Hart Baker, Jr., "Imperial Finale: Crisis, Decolonization, and War in Spain, 1890–1898" (PhD dissertation, Princeton University, 1977).

14. McKinley concluded that autonomy was not the solution he had been hoping for early in 1898. Not only did it fail to win over any significant proportion of the forces in opposition to Spain, it also sparked protests and riots in Havana among angry *peninsulares* and Spanish army officers. The morale and effectiveness of the army as a fighting force appeared to be deteriorating rapidly, while the revolutionaries were growing in influence and self-confidence. On March 1 McKinley informed Stewart L. Woodford, U.S. minister to Madrid, that he was "as yet unable to discern the favorable advances which were gladly anticipated from the changed order of things." See Pérez, *Cuba Between Empires,* 144–69; LaFeber, *New Empire,* 342–44; David F. Trask, *The War with Spain in 1898* (New York, 1981), 22–26; Sherman to Woodford, March 1, 1898, *FR 1898,* 666–69. The sinking of the *Maine* simply underscored for McKinley the feeling that things were getting out of control.

15. On March 9, Congress granted a presidential request for a huge $50 million supplemental defense appropriation. See Gould, *McKinley,* 76; Woodford to Sherman, March 25, 1898, *FR 1898,* 698–701; and Woodford to McKinley, March 26, 1898, *FR 1898,* 703–4.

16. For statements of the McKinley administration's final position, see Day to Woodford, March 26, 27, 28, and April 3, 4, 1898, *FR 1898,* 704, 711–13, 732–33. For Madrid's, see Woodford to Day, April 9, 1898, *FR 1898,* 746; Polo de Bernabé to Sherman, April 10, 1898, *FR 1898,* 747–49; and Ernest R. May, *Imperial Democracy: The Emergence of America as a Great Power* (New York,1961), 157. McKinley's message to Congress is in *FR 1898,* 750–60.

While long considered an inferior nation, Spain had until 1897 been considered a force acting in the interest of American policy in Cuba, and therefore supposedly in the cause of civilization. No more. By 1898, Spain had come instead to be labeled as an incurably backward and inefficient enemy of progress that had to be removed from Cuba by force. It was depicted as a country inhabited by a "medieval" and "decadent" race. Earlier eras of rivalry with Madrid, extending back to colonial times, were drawn on for images to confirm this verdict. See, for instance, *Speeches and Addresses of William McKinley* (New York, 1900), 3; Roosevelt to Robert Bacon, April 8, 1898, *LTR,* 2: 814; and Gerald F. Linderman, *The Mirror of War: American Society and the Spanish-American War* (Ann Arbor, Mich., 1974), 119–27.

17. *FR 1898,* 757.

18. Quoted in Pérez, *Cuba Between Empires,* 182.

19. *FR 1898,* 757. The president might have been compelled to start from that point had Madrid granted the island its freedom, but he was not going to do so now.

20. Pérez, *Cuba and the United States* (Athens, Ga., 1990), 55–96; Olney to Dupuy de Lôme, April 4, 1896, *FR 1897,* 540–44; Foner, *Spanish-Cuban-American War,* 1: 213–14.

21. *FR 1898,* 759. His opposition to the recognition of Cuba's independence caused consternation among a number of members mainly because it had been around that issue that American public opinion had crystallized. As a result, the Senate, like the House, supported intervention, but it also passed resolutions recognizing independence (the so-called "Turpie Amendment") and disclaiming any American intention to exercise sovereignty over Cuba "except for the pacification

thereof" (the "Teller Amendment"). The first of these constituted the serious challenge, since it would be up to the executive to define "pacification." But once talks on a joint resolution were taken up in a conference committee, McKinley was able to have the Turpie Amendment removed. See David F. Healy, *The United States in Cuba, 1898–1902: Generals, Politicians, and the Search for Policy* (Madison, Wis., 1963), 22–28.

22. As naval historian Kenneth Hagan has put it, "The Americans could not lose. Their three battleships—the *Indiana, Iowa,* and *Oregon*—were themselves sufficient to demolish a few obsolete cruisers scurrying along the coast." See Hagan, *This People's Navy,* 211–27. Also see Trask, *War with Spain,* 73–434 and John Offner, "The United States and France: Ending the Spanish-American War," *Diplomatic History* 7 (Winter 1983): 1–21.

23. Healy, *The United States in Cuba,* 30–50; Pérez, *Cuba Between Empires,* 199–204, 215–27; Langley, *Banana Wars,* 11–15.

24. Healy, *United States in Cuba,* 51–55, 62–64, 67–80; Pérez, *Cuba Between Empires,* 227–65.

25. See the discussion in John A. S. Grenville and George Berkeley Young, *Politics, Strategy, and American Diplomacy: Studies in Foreign Policy, 1873–1917* (New Haven, Conn., 1966), 295.

26. Especially from among its urban middle class, but also including some former military leaders. See Pérez, *Cuba and the United States,* 100–117.

27. Pérez, *Cuba and the United States,* 117–48; Benjamin, *United States and Cuba,* 7–10.

28. Wood is cited in Hermann Hagedorn, *Leonard Wood: A Biography,* 2 vols. (New York, 1931), 1: 250–53; and in James H. Hitchman, *Leonard Wood and Cuban Independence, 1898–1902* (The Hague, 1971), 78. Also see Howard Gillette, Jr., "The Military Occupation of Cuba, 1899–1902: Workshop for American Progressivism," *American Quarterly* 25 (1973): 410–25.

29. Message of the President, December 5, 1899, *FR 1899,* xxviii–xxix.

30. Healy, *United States in Cuba,* 126–32, 143–49; Pérez, *Cuba and the United States,* 102–9.

31. See Healy, *United States in Cuba,* 94–96, 110–11, 113–15.

32. Within two decades, roughly three-quarters of the island's trade would be with its giant neighbor. Washington insisted that the Platt Amendment's provisions be accepted as part of Cuba's new constitution. The amendment was then also secured by treaty. See Root to Wood, Jan. 9, 1901, ERP; Root to Hay, Jan. 11, 1901, ERP; Philip C. Jessup, *Elihu Root,* 2 vols. (New York, 1938), 1: 311; Healy, *United States in Cuba,* 150–78, 194–206; Pérez, *Cuba Between Empires,* 315–24; Louis A Pérez, *Cuba Under the Platt Amendment, 1902–1934* (Pittsburgh, 1986), 72–76; Healy, *Hegemony,* 203–18.

33. Root, *The Military and Colonial Policy of the United States: Addresses and Reports by Elihu Root,* ed. Robert Bacon and James Brown Scott (Cambridge, Mass., 1924), 100.

34. Walter LaFeber, *The Panama Canal: The Crisis in Historical Perspective* (New York, 1979), 11–12.

35. J. A. S. Grenville, *Lord Salisbury and Foreign Policy: The Close of the Nineteenth Century* (London, 1964), 371–73.

36. Charles S. Campbell, Jr., *Anglo-American Understanding, 1898–1903* (Baltimore, 1957), 186–92; Grenville, *Salisbury,* 374–81; A. E. Campbell, *Great Britain and the United States, 1895–1903* (London, 1960), 49–53; U.S. Congress, Senate, *Diplomatic History of the Panama Canal,* S. Doc. 474, 63d Cong., 2d sess., 1914, 289–91.

37. See Roosevelt to Hay, Feb.18, 1900, *LTR,* 2: 1192; Campbell, *Anglo-American Understanding,* 193–212; Challener, *Admirals,* 86–89, 91, 176. The issue of fortification

was in fact not held to be of as great importance by the navy as it was by the treaty's critics. Control of the canal was seen to depend instead on the size of the naval units that any power would be able to deploy in the region and on the base facilities the administration was working to obtain elsewhere in the Caribbean.

38. Grenville, *Salisbury*, 382–88; Campbell, *Great Britain and the United States*, 53–72; Kenneth Bourne, *Britain and the Balance of Power in North America, 1815–1908* (Berkeley, Calif., 1967), 347–51; U.S. Congress, Senate, *Diplomatic History of the Panama Canal*, 292–94.

39. The launching now of a second Walker Commission was above all the product of intense and skillful lobbying on the part of representatives of the New Panama Canal Company of France (the successor to de Lesseps's failed enterprise, which had gone bankrupt in 1889), especially its American counsel, William Nelson Cromwell. See Dwight Carroll Miner, *The Fight for the Panama Route: The Story of the Spooner Act and the Hay-Herrán Treaty* (New York, 1940), 75–91; Charles D. Ameringer, "The Panama Canal Lobby of Philippe Bunau-Varilla and William Nelson Cromwell," *American Historical Review* 68 (January 1963): 347–48; McCullough, *Path*, 259–63, 273–74.

40. The company estimated the value of its assets at $109 million, while the commission appraised them at $40 million.

41. A canal across Panama, it noted, would be shorter and would require fewer locks and curves. Harbors were already in existence at each end of the route, at Panama City and Colón, and a railway, the Panama Railroad that American entrepreneurs had built during the California gold rush, connected them. The technical and other problems that had plagued de Lessups in the 1880s were no longer seen to be as relevant. And costs of operation, as well as construction, seemed likely to be cheaper. See Miner, *Fight*, 91–92, 99, 101–4, 113–20; McCullough, *Path*, 274–91.

42. Miner, *Fight*, 120–55, and, for the text of the Spooner Act, 408–12; McCullough, *Path*, 260–67; 274–94.

43. Lewis L. Gould, *The Presidency of Theodore Roosevelt* (Lawrence, Kan., 1991), 93; Miner, *Fight*, 47–74, 109–13, 128–42, 157–240, and, for the text of the treaty, 413–26; Collin, *Roosevelt's Caribbean*, 172–222.

44. Colombia's traditional plans had envisioned a canal being built by a private company. The hope had also been that the concession would eventually revert back to national control. Such terms had governed the agreement with de Lesseps and his successors. However something far more extensive and permanent was now being proposed, and within Colombia's senate the position was taken that Bogotá ought to receive greater compensation for what it would part with. See Miner, *Fight*, 200–334; McCullough, *Path*, 332–38; Collin, *Roosevelt's Caribbean*, 219–35.

45. Roosevelt to Hay, August 19, 1903, *LTR*, 3: 566–67; Roosevelt to Hay, September 15, 1903, *LTR*, 3: 599; Roosevelt to Hanna, October 5, 1903, *LTR*, 3: 625; Miner, *Fight*, 350–51; Collin, *Roosevelt's Caribbean*, 243; LaFeber, *Panama Canal*, 22–23.

46. The region had in fact witnessed many earlier rebellions, but Washington had historically been strong in its support of Bogotá's control. Indeed, under a treaty signed in 1846 in response to British moves in the region, the U.S. had secured a guarantee from Colombia of free passage across the isthmus in return for a pledge to uphold its sovereignty. During periods of unrest in the late nineteenth century, American marines and naval forces had often been deployed not merely to enforce those transit rights along the Panama Railroad, but also to hamper the operations of insurgents until Colombian reinforcements could arrive. Given the mountains and jungles of eastern Panama, such reinforcements had to come by sea from Cartegena, and given American naval control of the Caribbean, U.S. power could just as easily be used, during another revolt, to prevent their landing. That appeared to be the easiest way for the administration to move ahead in Panama, but if such a rebellion misfired or was deferred beyond November, Roosevelt planned to

"recommend to Congress that we should at once occupy the Isthmus anyhow, and proceed to dig the canal." See *Theodore Roosevelt: An Autobiography* (New York, 1913), 563.

47. Philippe Bunau-Varilla, *Panama: The Creation, Destruction, and Resurrection* (New York, 1914), 304–19; Roosevelt, *Autobiography*, 563, 572–73; Miner, *Fight*, 335–70; McCullough, *Path*, 339–80; LaFeber, *Panama Canal*, 23–34; Collin, *Roosevelt's Caribbean*, 237–68.

48. Under the Hay-Bunau-Varilla convention, the U.S. was granted rights in perpetuity to a zone ten rather than six miles wide, within which it would exercise power as "if it were the sovereign." Any objection to these terms, or any delay, the Panamanians were warned, might still lead Washington to turn to Nicaragua or even back to Colombia. See Healy, *Hegemony*, 86–88.

49. First Annual Message, December 3, 1901, *WTR*, 15: 116.

50. Minutes of the American Commission to the Second Hague Conference, April 20, 1907, PCJP.

51. Howard K. Beale, *Theodore Roosevelt and the Rise of America to World Power* (Baltimore, 1984), 403–4; Roosevelt, *Strenuous Life*, 234–35; Roosevelt to Lodge, June 19, 1901, *LTR*, 3: 97–98; Roosevelt to Hermann Speck von Sternberg, July 12, 1901, *LTR*, 3: 116; Roosevelt to Sternberg, October 11, 1901, *LTR.*, 3: 172.

52. Theodor von Holleben to Hay, December 11, 1901, *FR 1901*, 192–94; Hay to von Holleben, December 16, 1901, *FR 1901*, 195; D. C. M. Platt, "The Allied Coercion of Venezuela, 1902–3—A Reassessment," *Inter-American Economic Affairs* 15 (Spring 1962): 6; Holger H. Herwig, *Germany's Vision of Empire in Venezuela, 1871–1914* (Princeton, N.J., 1986), 80–109; Collin, *Roosevelt's Caribbean*, 75–91; John V. Lombardi, *Venezuela: The Search for Order, the Dream of Progress* (New York, 1982), 160–62. England had even larger unsettled claims stemming from the civil wars. More important, during the spring Castro had confiscated, and in one case summarily destroyed, British-owned vessels that he held had been ferrying supplies from Trinidad to his domestic opponents. London took the attitude that it had to make an example of the general too.

53. Roosevelt to Shaw, December 26, 1902, *LTR*, 3: 397; Roosevelt to George W. Hinman, December 29, 1902, *LTR*, 3: 400; Warren G. Kneer, *Great Britain and the Caribbean, 1901–1913: A Study in Anglo-American Relations* (East Lansing, Mich., 1975), 11–56; Healy, *Hegemony*, 101–6; Collin, *Theodore Roosevelt's Caribbean*, 89–123.

54. Roosevelt to Cleveland, December 26, 1902, *LTR*, 3: 398; Roosevelt to Taft, December 26, 1902, *LTR*, 3: 398–99; Roosevelt to Hinman, December 29, 1902, *LTR*, 3: 399–400; Roosevelt to Hay, March 13, 1903, *LTR*, 3: 446; Dexter Perkins, *A History of the Monroe Doctrine* (Boston, 1963), 235.

55. To save time and expense, all parties had agreed in early 1903 to have those claims that were not to be paid immediately referred to mixed commissions with neutral umpires instead. Arrangements to pay these claims, and to have Venezuela resume payment of its bonded debt, had also been made.

56. Kneer, *Great Britain*, 40–56; Calvin DeArmond Davis, *The United States and the Second Hague Peace Conference: American Diplomacy and International Organization, 1899–1914* (Durham, N.C., 1975), 82–85, 89; Collin, *Roosevelt's Caribbean*, 107–23; Munro, *Intervention*, 74–75.

57. Roosevelt to Hay, September 2, 1904, *LTR*, 4: 917; Roosevelt to Root, May 20, 1904, *LTR*, 4: 801.

58. Healy, *Hegemony*, 113; Munro, *Intervention*, 89–90; Collin, *Roosevelt's Caribbean*, 390.

59. Roosevelt to T. Roosevelt, Jr., February 10, 1904, *LTR*, 4: 723–24; Roosevelt to Dewey, February 20, 1904, *LTR*, 4: 734; Healy, *Hegemony*, 117; Munro, *Intervention*, 92; Challener, *Admirals*, 127–31; Collin, *Roosevelt's Caribbean*, 392–97.

60. Roosevelt to Hay, March 13, 1903, *LTR*, 3: 446; Healy, *Hegemony*, 112, 117; Munro, *Intervention*, 90.

61. Hay to Dawson, December 30, 1904, *FR 1905*, 298; Healy, *Hegemony*, 119; Munro, *Intervention*, 80–87, 94–98. For the history of the Santo Domingo Improvement Company and its role in the republic, see especially Cyrus R. Veeser, "Remapping the Caribbean: Private Investment and United States Intervention in the Dominican Republic, 1890–1898" (PhD dissertation, Columbia University, 1997).

62. See *FR 1905*, 311; Dawson to Hay, January 23, 1905, *FR 1905*, 301–9; Munro, *Intervention*, 101.

63. "There is always the dread," Dawson quipped, "that the men I have been at so much pains to negotiate with may suddenly be standing up against a wall instead of sitting in the Minister's arm chair." See Dawson to Hay, January 2, 1905, *FR 1905*, 298–300; Dawson to Hay, January 23, 1905, *FR 1905*, 301–9; Challener, *Admirals*, 133; Healy, *Hegemony*, 120.

64. See Gould, *Roosevelt*, 177; Healy, *Hegemony*, 122; Collin, *Roosevelt's Caribbean*, 424–29; Shelby M. Cullom, *Fifty Years of Public Service* (Chicago, 1911), 387–93; Dorothy G. Fowler, *John Coit Spooner* (New York, 1961), 353–58; Lala Carr Steelman, "The Public Career of Augustus Octavius Bacon" (PhD dissertation, University of North Carolina, 1950), 213–29; W. Stull Holt, *Treaties Defeated by the Senate* (Baltimore, 1933), 212–28.

65. Healy, *Hegemony*, 122; Munro, *Intervention*, 104–6, 116–21; Challener, *Admirals*, 135–41; Holt, *Treaties*, 225–27; Collin, *Roosevelt's Caribbean*, 441–47. On Roosevelt's role in expanding the use of such executive agreements, see Walter LaFeber, "The Constitution and U.S. Foreign Policy: An Interpretation," in *A Less Than Perfect Union: Alternative Perspectives on the U.S. Constitution*, ed. Jules Lobel (New York, 1988), 234–35. One thing still not in place at that time, however, was the Morales government. The administration had finally decided not to "stand by him" when at the end of 1905 he was outmaneuvered by another, much stronger, political faction under the leadership of Vice President Róman Cáceres.

Meanwhile, conditions in Cuba had come again to claim Washington's attention. Invoking the Platt Amendment, the U.S. reoccupied the newly "independent" state in 1906. Its objective was to contain popular forces that had risen up in rebellion there, but also to try to implement a yet greater reorganization of that island's politics and military forces, so that it might "behave" in the future as Washington wanted. On this intervention, see Roosevelt to Quesada, September 14, 1906, *LTR*, 5: 411–13; Pérez, *Platt Amendment*, 91–94, 97–98, 100–107; Pérez, *Cuba and the United States*, 153–58; Langley, *Banana Wars*, 36, 39–41, 43–48; Lester Langley, *The United States and the Caribbean in the Twentieth Century* (Athens, Ga.,1982), 41–43; Healy, *Hegemony*, 128–33; and Collin, *Roosevelt's Caribbean*, 535–39.

66. See, for instance, Theodore Roosevelt, *American Ideals and Other Essays* (New York, 1897), 230–31.

67. Root to Flagler, January 3, 1905, ERP.

68. "We have to deal with all the countries surrounding the Caribbean," wrote Root to editor Lyman Abbott. "In that region the United States must exercise a predominant influence.... We must control the route to the Panama Canal. How are we to do it? I should state the answer in three propositions. The first is furnished by the Monroe Doctrine. We cannot permit any un-American power to obtain possession of any of these countries. The second ... is that we do not ourselves wish to take possession of any of these countries. We do not wish ... to dilute our electorate ... by the inclusion of all or any part of these peoples who in race and traditions and customs and laws and systems of government are so unlike our own. The third proposition is that to prevent the possibility of the one and the necessity of the other we wish to help all these peoples to build up and maintain peaceable, orderly

and free governments of their own." Root to Abbott, December 24, 1908; Root to Watterson, March 5, 1908, ERP.

69. See, for instance, Root to Buchanan, March 20, 1909, cited in Jessup, *Root*, 1: 510–11. Also see Collin, *Roosevelt's Caribbean*, 516.

70. See also the valuable discussions of Root's approach in Healy, *Hegemony*, 135–44; Langley, *United States and the Caribbean*, 44–49; and Munro, *Intervention*, 112–16.

71. Roosevelt to Hay, September 2, 1904, *LTR*, 4: 917; Roosevelt to Hay, April 2, 1905, *ibid.*, 1156; Jessup, *Root*, 1: 497–99; Embert J. Hendrickson, "Roosevelt's Second Venezuelan Controversy," *Hispanic American Historical Review* 50 (August 1970): 482–95; Healy, *Hegemony*, 133–34.

72. At his behest, U.S. warships quickly appeared off the Venezuelan coast to bolster his government in 1908, and negotiations aimed at settling American claims were begun. See Hendrickson, "Roosevelt's Second Venezuelan Controversy," 495–98 and Healy, *Hegemony*, 134.

73. With its emphasis on stability and its desire to meet the needs of foreign business, the regime of strongman Porfirio Díaz was, moreover, viewed as an exemplary model for the U.S. to endorse throughout the region (see Chapter 5).

74. Healy, *Hegemony*, 139–41; Langley, *United States and the Caribbean*, 44–46; Munro, *Intervention*, 141–46; Collin, *Roosevelt's Caribbean*, 465–87; Ralph Lee Woodward, Jr., *Central America: A Nation Divided* (New York, 1985), 192; Jessup, *Root*, 1: 501.

75. Here see especially Thomas D. Schoonover, *The United States in Central America, 1860–1911: Episodes of Social Imperialism and Imperial Rivalry in the World System* (Durham, N.C., 1991), 130–42.

76. Healy, *Hegemony*, 141; Woodward, *Central America*, 166, 192; Langley, *United States and the Caribbean*, 46–49.

77. Schoonover, *United States in Central America*, 142–43.

78. Root, *Addresses on Government and Citizenship by Elihu Root*, ed. Robert Bacon and James Brown Scott (Cambridge, Mass., 1917), 13–14. Also see Jessup, *Root*, 1: 502.

79. "That we cannot undertake," wrote Root, although Costa Rica, which had a government of which he approved, was an exception. "She is so near Panama that we must not let her be overturned." Quoted in Jessup, *Root*, 1: 505.

80. James Brown Scott, "The Central American Peace Conference of 1907," *American Journal of International Law* 2 (1908): 121–43; Healy, *Hegemony*, 141–42; Langley, *United States and the Caribbean*, 48; Munro, *Intervention*, 151–55; Walter LaFeber, *Inevitable Revolutions: The United States in Central America* (New York, 1983), 40–41.

81. In his opening speech he told the delegates that, "It can be nothing but the ambition of individuals who care more for their selfish purposes than for the good of their country that can prevent the people of the Central American states from living together in peace and unity." Quoted in Scott, "Central American Peace Conference," 129–30.

82. Root to Shaw, January 3, 1908, ERP.

83. Healy, *Hegemony*, 142; Langley, *United States and the Caribbean*, 48–49; Munro, *Intervention*, 156–58.

84. Quoted in Jessup, *Root*, 1: 510–11.

85. See Taft's address at Marion, Indiana, July 3, 1911, WHTP.

86. The American chargé in Managua, John H. Gregory, fueled these concerns, reporting that the Nicaraguan leader was an admirer of the recently overthrown Castro of Venezuela, that Zelaya was hoping the transition between administrations would mean a slackening in American attention to the region, and that the Nicaraguan president was determined to destroy the Washington conventions. See Gregory

to Department, December 11, 1908 and February 6, 1909, SDNF 6369; Gregory to Department, February 23, 25, 1909, SDNF 18432; Walter V. Scholes and Marie V. Scholes, The *Foreign Policies of the Taft Administration* (Columbia, Mo., 1970), 45–46; Challener, *Admirals*, 293–94; Munro, *Intervention*, 164.

87. Knox to de la Barra, March 26, 1909, PCKP; Scholes and Scholes, *Foreign Policies*, 46, 69. Also see "Mexico, Honduras, and Central American Affairs," July 26, 1909, PCKP, and Knox to Taft, September 28, 1909, PCKP.

88. See, for instance, Root to Hay, January 7, 1905, ERP. Also see Healy, *Hegemony*, 149–50; Scholes and Scholes, *Foreign Policies*, 68–70; and Munro, *Intervention*, 217–20. For a discussion of the growth of banking interest in such foreign business, see Chapter 3.

89. Roosevelt to Carnegie, February 26, 1909, *LTR*, 6: 1538–39.

90. Munro, *Intervention*, 218. Also see Healy, *Hegemony*, 150.

91. See *FR 1912*, 549–54.

92. Most of the funds were to be applied to outstanding debts and claims, while the rest were to be used for improvement and extension of the national railroad, which the bankers would operate during the life of the loan, and any other infrastructural projects that the bankers decided on. See Scholes and Scholes, *Foreign Policies*, 70–71; Munro, *Intervention*, 220–22.

93. Scholes and Scholes, *Foreign Policies*, 71–72; Munro, *Intervention*, 222–25.

94. His government's official newspaper editorialized that the country should seek the aid of another strong nation. See Healy, *Hegemony*, 152–53 and Langley, *United States and the Caribbean*, 50.

95. Scholes and Scholes, *Foreign Policies*, 50–52; Healy, *Hegemony*, 153; Langley, *United States and the Caribbean*, 50–51.

96. Schoonover, *United States in Central America*, 144.

97. *FR 1909*, 455–57; Challener, *Admirals*, 295. Equally fascinating is the twenty-six-page "Indictment of Zelaya" drawn up within the department at this time. It contained a catalog of Zelayan crimes that portrayed the strongman as a total threat to order and appropriate behavior. Among these, prominent place and pertinence were now suddenly assigned to allegations about Zelaya's sexual conduct. The confrontation with Zelaya was described, at least in part, as motivated by a desire to protect the people of Nicaragua. "It may be safely asserted," the document stated, "that without exception Zelaya is the most reprehensible ruler that ever oppressed an aspiring people." PCKP.

98. Scholes and Scholes, *Foreign Policies*, 53–57; Healy, *Hegemony*, 154; Challener, *Admirals*, 300; Schoonover, *United States in Central America*, 145.

99. Munro, *Intervention*, 180.

100. Challener, *Admirals*, 300–301; Healy, *Hegemony*, 155; Munro, *Intervention*, 183–86.

101. Scholes and Scholes, *Foreign Policies*, 59–60; Healy, *Hegemony*, 155–56; Munro, *Intervention*, 187–89.

102. *FR 1912*, 1074–75; Healy, *Hegemony*, 156–57; Scholes and Scholes, *Foreign Policies*, 60–62; Munro, *Intervention* 189–93.

103. Huntington-Wilson wrote that the Honduran treaty was "a test case of the utmost importance, because failure here will be the doom in advance of our Nicaraguan projects, and because the principle we seek to act upon in Honduras is one we are bound to have to resort to in still other cases." Huntington-Wilson to Adee, January 13, 1911, SDDF 815.51.

104. See, for example, Knox to Taft, January 23, 1911, PCKP; Knox to Sutherland, May 3, 1911, PCKP; Taft address at Marquette, Michigan, September 20, 1911; Taft address in New York, December 30, 1911, WHTP.

105. Coletta, *Taft*, 45–120.

106. *La Follette's Weekly* 1 (October 23, 1909): 3. In spring 1911, Knox appealed to University of Wisconsin academic, reformer, and international affairs expert Paul Reinsch for assistance in dealing with La Follette. See Knox to Reinsch, May 3, 1911 and Reinsch to Knox, May 7, 1911, SDDF 815.51. For the details of the "Crane incident," see Jerome Israel, *Progressivism and the Open Door: America and China, 1905–1921* (Pittsburgh, 1971), 60–82.

107. *New York World,* January 30, 1910.

108. *New York Tribune,* June 7, 1911.

109. Knox to Huntington-Wilson, May 20, 1910, PCKP.

110. Knox address, "The Spirit and Purpose of American Diplomacy," University of Pennsylvania commencement, June 15, 1910, PCKP (also in *Congressional Record,* 61st Cong., 2d sess., Appendix, 470–74).

111. See, for instance, "Rough Notes on Honduras Loan," February 1911, PCKP.

112. Cullom to Knox, May 17, 1911, SDDF 815.51; "Statement of the Secretary of State Before the Senate Committee on Foreign Relations," May 24, 1911, *FR 1912,* 583–95; Cullom to Knox, June 12, 1911, SDDF 815.51; Knox to Senators, January 22, 1912, *FR 1912,* 1082–92; Taft to Knox, February 10, 1912, PCKP; Taft to Senators, March 14, 1912, WHTP; Munro, *Intervention,* 203. Also see Williams to Knox, January 27, 1912, SDDF 817.51 and Borah to Clark, April 27, 1914, WEBP. For Borah, the Nicaragua treaty was "simply a scheme to locate a protectorate there for a time and then to take over the country." See here also Robert David Johnson, *The Peace Progressives and American Foreign Relations* (Cambridge, Mass., 1995), 34–41.

113. In no small part this was because prominent Conservative families and political figures, including Díaz himself, had eagerly rushed to compensate themselves for real and alleged damages suffered under Zelaya.

114. Along with these went control over the national bank and other important concessions. The bankers instituted their own customs collectorship in December. During the spring, they assumed operational control over the nation's railway network, located on the Pacific coast, having already laid plans to build new lines linking this railway and the coffee growing region around Matagalpa to Caribbean port facilities.

115. "We think," he continued, "that if the United States did its duty promptly, thoroughly and impressively in Nicaragua, it would strengthen our hand and lighten our task, not only in Nicaragua itself in the future, but throughout Central America and the Caribbean and would even have some moral effect in Mexico." See Scholes and Scholes, *Foreign Policies,* 65–66.

116. Scholes and Scholes, *Foreign Policies,* 63–67; Healy, *Hegemony,* 157–60; Munro, *Intervention,* 194–216; Challener, *Admirals,* 302–9; Langley, *Banana Wars,* 65–76; Langley, *United States and the Caribbean,* 58.

117. For Cuba, see Pérez, *Platt Amendment,* 148–52; Challener, *Admirals,* 341–44; Langley, *Banana Wars,* 49–50. For the Dominican Republic, see Healy, *Hegemony,* 160–62; Scholes and Scholes, *Foreign Policies,* 40–44; Munro, *Intervention,* 259–65.

118. Mark T. Gilderhus, *Pan American Visions: Woodrow Wilson in the Western Hemisphere, 1913–1921* (Tucson, Ariz., 1986), 8; Healy, *Hegemony,* 164–65; E. David Cronon, *The Cabinet Diaries of Josephus Daniels, 1913–1921* (Lincoln, Neb., 1963), 6–7; "From the Diary of Oswald Garrison Villard," August 14, 1912, *PWW,* 25: 24–25; "A Statement on Relations with Latin America," March 12, 1913, *PWW,* 27: 172–73. Also see the undated memorandum on this topic by Huntington-Wilson in HWP.

119. "An Address in New York to the National League of Commission Merchants," January 11, 1912, *PWW,* 24: 33.

120. "An Address on Latin American Policy in Mobile, Ala.," October 27, 1913, *PWW.,* 28: 449.

121. "An Address on Mexican Affairs to a Joint Session of Congress," August 27, 1913, *PWW.*, 28: 228; "The British Embassy to Sir Edward Grey, November 14, 1913; *PWW.*, 28: 543.

122. See Arthur S. Link, *Wilson: The New Freedom* (Princeton, N.J., 1956), 335.

123. Díaz proposed the Platt Amendment feature himself, out of a desire to do whatever he could to pave the way for Washington to keep him in power. But Bryan saw it as an additional means of stabilizing the country, and, as he later put it to Wilson, "it will give us the right to do that which we might be called on to do anyhow." Bryan is quoted in Healy, *Hegemony*, 183–84. The Wilson quote is in Link, *New Freedom*, 334. Also see Munro, *Intervention*, 388–91; George W. Baker, Jr., "The Wilson Administration and Nicaragua, 1913–1921," *Americas* 22 (1966): 342–44; Langley, *United States and the Caribbean*, 85–86.

124. "From William Jennings Bryan," c. July 20, 1913, *PWW*, 28: 47–48; Bryan to Wilson, August 16, 1913, *PWW*, 28: 175–77; Link, *New Freedom*, 337–40; Healy, *Hegemony*, 184–86; Munro, *Intervention*, 391–97; Baker, "Wilson Administration and Nicaragua," 344–62.

From the outset, meanwhile, neighboring Central American states had reacted to the pact with concern. They worried that a now compliant and dependent Nicaragua might open the door to far greater American involvement in the region. All the other states opposed the Platt Amendment provision, fearing that similar rights of intervention might subsequently be asked of them. But opposition to the treaty continued even after that provision was withdrawn. Costa Rica insisted that it had a right to be consulted before Managua entered into any arrangement over the canal route, since the San Juan River, which the route would incorporate, ran along its border with Nicaragua for almost fifty miles. And El Salvador maintained that it had to be consulted, along with Honduras, before Nicaragua could sell naval base rights to an outside power in the Gulf of Fonseca. Once the treaty was ratified, both states took Managua before the Central American Court of Justice. It upheld the plaintiffs, but, supported by Washington, Nicaragua defied this institution that the U.S. had itself, a decade before, done so much to found. Not only was the treaty protected, but the court was destroyed. It never heard another case and was formally dissolved in March 1918 (with Secretary of State Lansing commenting that it had outlived its usefulness). See Healy, *Hegemony*, 186–87; Munro, *Intervention*, 397–404; Baker, "Wilson Administration and Nicaragua," 370; LaFeber, *Inevitable Revolutions*, 40–41.

125. Quoted in Munro, *Intervention*, 398.

126. The Liberal Party was composed, a State Department memorandum of December 1915 complained, "in great part of the ignorant masses of people who either do not appreciate the intentions or policies of this [the United States] government or who are readily acceptable to political oratory." Quoted in Baker, "Wilson Administration and Nicaragua," 358.

127. Healy, *Hegemony*, 234–36; Munro, *Intervention*, 406–13.

128. Quoted in Langley, *Banana Wars*, 123. For background on Haiti's crisis, see Brenda Gayle Plummer, *Haiti and the Great Powers, 1902–1915* (Baton Rouge, La., 1988).

129. Cited in Langley, *Banana Wars*, 125. Also see Healy, *Hegemony*, 187–90; Langley, *United States and the Caribbean*, 69–72; David Healy, *Gunboat Diplomacy in the Wilson Era: The U.S. Navy in Haiti, 1915–1916* (Madison, Wis., 1976), 3–61.

130. Wilson to Edith Bolling Galt, August 15, 1915, *PWW*, 34: 208–9.

131. Healy, *Hegemony*, 190–92; Langley, *United States and the Caribbean*, 72–77; Healy, *Gunboat Diplomacy*, 62–231; Langley, *Banana Wars*, 126–41, 155–65.

132. Healy, *Hegemony*, 192–97 (Caperton quotation from 197); Langley, *Banana Wars*, 121–22, 141–54.

Chapter 3. Dominance Throughout the Hemisphere: South America

1. Roosevelt to Sternberg, October 11, 1901, *LTR*, 3: 172.
2. A superb introduction to this era of South American history is provided in E. Bradford Burns, *Latin America: A Concise Interpretive History* (Englewood Cliffs, N.J., 1990). See especially pp. 130–87. Racism played a role here. See, for instance, the story about TR cited in Wilfrid Hardy Callcott, *The Western Hemisphere: Its Influence on United States Policies to the End of World War II* (Austin, Tex., 1968), 100.
3. For insightful background on U.S.-South American relations, see Lester D. Langley, *America and the Americas: The United States in the Western Hemisphere* (Athens, Ga., 1989), 1–132; and Gordon Connell-Smith, *The United States and Latin America: An Historical Analysis of Inter-American Relations* (London, 1974), 1–145.
4. Bill Albert, *South America and the World Economy from Independence to 1930* (London, 1983), 17–36; D. C. M. Platt, *Latin America and British Trade 1806–1914* (New York, 1973).
5. James G. Blaine, *Political Discussions: Legislative, Diplomatic, and Popular, 1856–1886* (Norwich, Conn., 1887), 419; Joseph Smith, *Illusions of Conflict: Anglo-American Diplomacy Toward Latin America, 1865–1896* (Pittsburgh, 1979), 38–43.
6. Quoted in Connell-Smith, *United States and Latin America*, 96.
7. This "Peru-Chilean war," Blaine stated, "destroys American influence on the South Pacific coast and literally wipes out American commercial interests in that vast region.... Chile's victory throws the whole Peruvian business into English hands." See Smith, *Illusions*, 59–80 (quotation 65); Frederick B. Pike, *Chile and the United States, 1880–1962: The Emergence of Chile's Social Crisis and the Challenge of United States Diplomacy* (Notre Dame, Ind., 1963), 47–59.
8. Arthur P. Whitaker, *The Western Hemisphere Idea: Its Rise and Decline* (Ithaca, N.Y., 1954), 74–76.
9. Quoted in Callcott, *Western Hemisphere*, 44–45. Also see Smith, *Illusions*, 118–30; and David M. Pletcher, *The Diplomacy of Trade and Investment: American Economic Expansion in the Hemisphere, 1865–1900* (Columbia, Mo., 1998), 212–14.
10. Whitaker, *Western Hemisphere Idea*, 76–85.
11. Smith, *Illusions*, 130–34, 135–36; Joseph S. Tulchin, *Argentina and the United States: A Conflicted Relationship* (Boston, 1990), 22.
12. Smith, *Illusions*, 134–43; Gordon Connell-Smith, *The Inter-American System* (London, 1966), 39–42; J. Lloyd Mecham, *The United States and Inter-American Security, 1889–1960* (Austin, Texas, 1961), 52–58; Tulchin, *Argentina*, 19–23; Thomas F. McGann, *Argentina, the United States, and the Inter-American System, 1880–1914* (Cambridge, Mass., 1957), 121–64.
13. Pike, *Chile*, 62–65.
14. "The foreigner, with all the rights of the native, with no right less, yet with no right more," was how the Latin American majority on the Committee of International Law put it.
15. Donald R. Shea, *The Calvo Clause: A Problem of Inter-American and International Law and Diplomacy* (Minneapolis, 1955), 3–77; Connell-Smith, *Inter-American System*, 42–43.
16. In formulating the high McKinley Tariff of 1890, protectionists in Congress were determined to keep rates on some key items of South American trade, such as wool, virtually prohibitive. Meanwhile, to placate American consumers, other items produced on that continent, such as hides, coffee, and sugar were put on the free list. Given these constraints, Blaine was left with little with which he could deal. Instead he was compelled to accept from Congress a "bargaining" mechanism that provided for what historian Joseph Smith has described as "forced rather than

voluntary reciprocity." All the administration could do to try to influence another country's treatment of American trade was to threaten it with a reimposition of duties on one or more of the exempted products. Among the South American countries, only Brazil, because of the importance of the American market to its coffee and sugar exports, felt a sufficient need to respond to such pressure. But, even here, as Smith has shown, the preferences obtained in the resulting agreement did not lead to significant results. The agreement was in force from 1891 to 1894, when it was abrogated under the terms of the Wilson-Gorman Tariff. See Smith, *Illusions*, 143–54; Joseph Smith, *Unequal Giants: Diplomatic Relations Between the United States and Brazil, 1889–1930* (Pittsburgh, 1991), 14–19; Steven C. Topik, *Trade and Gunboats: The United States and Brazil in the Age of Empire* (Stanford, Calif., 1996), 73–78; F. W. Taussig, *The Tariff History of the United States* (New York, 1964), 278–83; and Pletcher, *Diplomacy of Trade and Investment*, 256–79. In his *Power, Protection, and Free Trade: International Sources of U.S. Commercial Strategy, 1887–1939* (Ithaca, N.Y., 1988), economic historian David Lake has argued that the free wool provision of the Cleveland era tariff was also aimed at redirecting Latin American trade from Europe to the United States.

17. Quoted in Smith, *Illusions*, 197.

18. Smith, *Illusions*, 192–201; Pike, *Chile*, 44–46, 66–85; Kenneth J. Hagan, *This People's Navy: The Making of American Sea Power* (New York, 1991), 198–200; Joyce S. Goldberg, *The Baltimore Affair* (Lincoln, Neb., 1986), 1–19, 86, 124.

19. Smith, *Unequal Giants*, 19–25; Topik, *Trade and Gunboats*, 138, 144–47, 151–54.

20. Quoted in Connell-Smith, *United States and Latin America*, 95.

21. William L. Scruggs, *British Aggressions in Venezuela—Or—The Monroe Doctrine on Trial* (Atlanta, 1895); John A. S. Grenville and George Berkeley Young, *Politics, Strategy, and American Diplomacy: Studies in Foreign Policy, 1873–1917* (New Haven, Conn., 1966), 127–54; Charles S. Campbell, *The Transformation of American Foreign Relations, 1865–1900* (New York, 1976), 194–221; Smith, *Illusions*, 205–9.

22. Grenville and Young, *Politics, Strategy, and American Diplomacy*, 139–48; Nelson M. Blake, "Background of Cleveland's Venezuela Policy," *American Historical Review* 17 (January 1942): 259–77; Walter LaFeber, *The New Empire: An Interpretation of American Expansion, 1860–1898* (Ithaca, N.Y., 1963), 250–51, 254; Alan Nevins, *Grover Cleveland: A Study in Courage* (New York, 1932), 630–31; Gerald G. Eggert, *Richard Olney: Evolution of a Statesman* (University Park, Pa., 1974), 199–208; Henry Cabot Lodge, "England, Venezuela, and the Monroe Doctrine," *North American Review* 160 (June 1895): 651–58; Dickinson to Cleveland, May 10, 1895, GCP.

23. Olney to Bayard, July 20, 1895, *FR 1895*, 545–62.

24. There are in fact two notes, each Salisbury to Pauncefote, November 26, 1895, *FR 1895*, 563–76.

25. Cleveland to Bayard, December 29, 1895, *Letters of Grover Cleveland, 1850–1908*, ed. Alan Nevins (Boston, 1933), 418.

26. *FR 1895*, 543–45.

27. See Grenville and Young, *Politics*, 170–77; Eggert, *Olney*, 225–43; Campbell, *Transformation*, 209–21.

28. He also hoped that it would enable him to stabilize American trade relations with France, where there was considerable dissatisfaction with many features of the new American law. Lewis L. Gould, *The Presidency of William McKinley* (Lawrence, Kan., 1980), 244–45.

29. Taussig, *Tariff History*, 352–55; Percy Ashley, *Modern Tariff History* (London, 1920), 229–30; T. E. Terrill, *The Tariff, Politics, and American Foreign Policy, 1874–1901* (Westport, Conn., 1973), 159–219; Paul Wolman, *Most Favored Nation: The Republican Revisionists and U.S. Tariff Policy, 1897–1912* (Chapel Hill, N.C., 1992), 19–37; Gould, *McKinley*, 6–7, 40–44, 244–51.

30. Smith, *Unequal Giants*, 31.

31. These were Ecuador and Argentina, the latter in particular having been hit hard by the Dingley Tariff's reimposition of duties on wool (which had been placed on the free list in 1894) and on hides (which had been free since 1872). See McGann, *Argentina*, 176–78.

32. Tyler Dennett, *John Hay: From Poetry to Politics* (New York, 1934), 416–17; "Address of President McKinley at the Pan-American Exposition," Buffalo, N.Y., September 5, 1901, WMP.

33. Lewis L. Gould, *The Presidency of Theodore Roosevelt* (Lawrence, Kan., 1991), 24–25.

34. "Address of President McKinley at the Pan-American Exposition," Buffalo, N.Y., September 5, 1901, WMP; Gould, *McKinley*, 34, 232; Merle Fainsod, Lincoln Gordon, and Joseph C. Palamountain, Jr., *Government and the American Economy* (New York, 1959), 105–8; Edward P. Crapol and Howard Schonberger, "The Shift to Global Expansion, 1865–1900," in *From Colony to Empire: Essays in the History of American Foreign Relations*, ed. William Appleman Williams (New York, 1972), 157–68; Milton Plesur, *America's Outward Thrust: Approaches to Foreign Affairs, 1865–1890* (DeKalb, Ill., 1971), 93.

35. On the calling of the conference, see Calvin DeArmond Davis, *The United States and the Second Hague Peace Conference: American Diplomacy and International Organization, 1899–1914* (Durham, N.C., 1975), 41–44.

36. The main purpose of the conference was to sow "the seed of friendly relations, of business confidence, and of permanent feelings of good will." See Roosevelt to Hay, October 8, 1901, *LTR*, 3: 164–70.

37. Robert Burr, *By Reason or Force: Chile and the Balance of Power in South America, 1830–1905* (Berkeley, Calif., 1974), 241–44; William I. Buchanan, "Latin America and the Mexican Conference," *Annals of the American Academy of Political and Social Science* 22 (July 1903): 53–55; John Bassett Moore, "Application of the Principle of International Arbitration on the American Continents," *Annals of the American Academy of Political and Social Science* 22 (July 1903): 40–41; A. Curtin Wilgus, "The Second International American Conference at Mexico City," *Hispanic American Historical Review* 11 (1931): 59–61; Pike, *Chile*, 126–31; McGann, *Argentina*, 198–209; Mecham, *Inter-American Security*, 59–61; Davis, *Second Hague*, 46–49. Brazil had also been invited to The Hague, but declined to attend.

38. December 3, 1901, *WTR*, 15: 116.

39. Drago to García Merou, December 29, 1902, *FR 1903*, 1–5.

40. See, for instance, Elihu Root's discussion of this question in "Meeting of the American Commission to the Second Hague Conference," April 20, 1907, PCJP. Also see Smith, *Illusions*, 18–20; Charles Lipson, *Standing Guard: Protecting Foreign Capital in the Nineteenth and Twentieth Centuries* (Berkeley, Calif., 1985), 45–50; Edwin M. Borchard, "Calvo and Drago Doctrines," *Encyclopedia of the Social Sciences*, 15 vols. (New York, 1930–35), 2: 153–56.

41. Quoted in Harold F. Peterson, *Argentina and the United States, 1810–1960* (New York, 1964), 260.

42. Hay to García Merou, February 17, 1903, *FR 1903*, 5–6.

43. Hay to MacVeagh, June 27, 1903, JHP; Davis, *Second Hague*, 85–88.

44. Mecham, *Inter-American Security*, 67.

45. On Root and the corollary, see chapter 2 and also Philip C. Jessup, *Elihu Root*, 2 vols. (New York, 1938), 1: 469–71.

46. For background on Barrett, see Salvador Prisco, *John Barrett, Progressive Era Diplomat: A Study of a Commercial Expansionist, 1887–1920* (Birmingham, Ala., 1973), 1–58.

47. Prisco, *Barrett*, 56–57; Barrett to Bacon, August 1, 1906, SDNF 550.

48. Barrett to Bacon, August 1, 1906, SDNF 550.

49. Indeed, on trade matters his views simply reinforced those being expressed by people like Frederic Emory, recently retired as chief of the State Department's Bureau of Trade Relations, or of Lincoln Hutchinson, who toured South America in 1905 as a special agent for the Department of Commerce and Labor. See Frederic Emory, "Causes of Our Failure to Develop South-American Trade," *Annals of the American Academy of Political and Social Science* 22 (July 1903): 153–56; Richard Hume Werking, *The Master Architects: Building the United States Foreign Service, 1890–1913* (Lexington, Ky., 1977), 139; U.S. Congress, Senate, *Report on Trade Conditions in Brazil* by Lincoln Hutchinson, S. Doc. 164, 59th Cong., 1st sess., 1906.

50. Root to Tillman, December 13, 1905, ERP.

51. December 5, 1905, *WTR*, 15: 301.

52. "We have been treating those gentlemen like yellow dogs," he asserted, "and they resent it." Root to Watterson, May 16, 1906, ERP.

53. See Root to Dewey, January 6, 1906, ERP; Jessup, *Root*, 1: 471–74.

54. The latter thereby joined Mexico as the only other Latin American state with that ranking in Washington at the time.

55. E. Bradford Burns, *The Unwritten Alliance: Rio Branco and Brazilian-American Relations* (New York, 1966), 74–108; Burns, *A History of Brazil* (New York, 1980), 320–30; Smith, *Unequal Giants*, 33–53.

56. Smith, *Unequal Giants*, 36–37; Jessup, *Root*, 1: 474–75, 489.

57. Quoted in Jessup, *Root*, 1: 475.

58. Diplomatic representatives in South America were instructed to make preparations for the secretary to exchange hospitalities with his hosts. And Root, at his own expense, took along a large supply of Havana cigars and expensive European wines for that purpose. See Jessup, *Root*, 1: 476–77.

59. Root's address is in *Latin America and the United States: Addresses by Elihu Root*, ed. Robert Bacon and James Brown Scott (Cambridge, Mass., 1917), 6–11. Also see Jessup, *Root*, 1: 478–79; Burns, *Unwritten Alliance*, 111.

60. Root to Watterson, May 16, 1906, ERP.

61. McGann, *Argentina*, 239–41; Connell-Smith, *Inter-American System*, 49; Mecham, *Inter-American Security*, 63, 67; Pike, *Chile*, 131–32; Callcott, *Western Hemisphere*, 92; Petersen, *Argentina*, 262–63.

62. June 18, 1906, *FR 1906*, 2: 1567. The delegation was led by Buchanan and by political scientists Leo S. Rowe and Paul Reinsch.

63. For the report of the U.S. delegation, see *FR 1906*, 2: 1576–94. Also see Paul S. Reinsch, "The Third International Conference of American States," *American Political Science Review* 1 (February 1907): 187–99; and McGann, *Argentina*, 244–49.

64. *FR 1906*, 2: 1578–80; Reinsch, Third International Conference," 190–92; Clifford B. Casey, "The Creation and Development of the Pan American Union," *Hispanic American Historical Review* 13 (November, 1933): 437–47.

65. McGann, *Argentina*, 248; Jessup, *Root*, 1: 485–86.

66. Root, "The Monroe Doctrine," December 22, 1904, in *Miscellaneous Addresses of Elihu Root*, ed. Robert Bacon and James Brown Scott (Cambridge, Mass., 1917), 270. In subsequent years, Root repeatedly sought to counter the arguments of Calvo and Drago. See "The Relations Between International Tribunals of Arbitration and the Jurisdiction of National Courts," April 23, 1909; "The Basis of Protection to Citizens Residing Abroad," April 28, 1910; and "The Real Monroe Doctrine," April 22, 1914, in *Addresses on International Subjects by Elihu Root* , ed. Robert Bacon and James Brown Scott (Cambridge, Mass., 1916), 33–50, 107–23. He also used a variant of this argument to defend Roosevelt's actions in Panama in 1903. See "The Ethics of the Panama Question," February 22, 1904, *Addresses on International Subjects*, 180–206.

67. Root also wanted Latin American participation at The Hague in order to further confirm European acceptance of the political status quo in the Western Hemisphere. See *Addresses on Latin America*, 10.

68. "Meeting of the American Commission to the Second Hague Conference," April 20, 1907, ERP; Joseph H. Choate, *The Two Hague Conferences* (Princeton, N.J., 1913), 61.

69. Choate, *Two Hague Conferences*, 61.

70. U.S. Congress, Senate, *The Second International Peace Conference*, S. Doc. 444, 60th Cong., 1st sess., 1908, 89.

71. Peterson, *Argentina*, 263–64; Samuel Flagg Bemis, *The Latin American Policy of the United States: An Historical Interpretation* (New York, 1967), 228–29; Whitaker, *Western Hemisphere Idea*, 102–3. Root maintained in a private letter to the editor of the *Outlook* that this attitude was due to "a peculiarity of the Latin races." They pursued "every line of thought to a strict, logical conclusion" instead of stopping to "achieve a practical benefit as the Anglo-Saxons do." Quoted in Jessup, *Root*, 2: 74

72. December 3, 1906, *WTR*, 15: 392–93.

73. Jessup, *Root*, 1: 483, 488–89.

74. Root, *Addresses on Latin America*, 245–81; Jessup, *Root*, 1: 489–91; Werking, *Master Architects*, 44–142; Burton Kaufman, "The Organizational Dimension of United States Economic Foreign Policy, 1900–1920," *Business History Review* 46 (Spring 1972): 29–31.

75. Prisco, *Barrett*, 59–61. Carnegie had himself been a delegate to the first Pan-American conference.

76. James Van Cleave, "What Americans Must Do to Make an Export Business," *Annals of the American Academy of Political and Social Science* 29 (May 1907): 470–71.

77. *Banker's Magazine* 74 (June 1907): 868.

78. See, for instance, John Barrett, "Latin America as a Field for United States Capital and Enterprise," *Banker's Magazine* 74 (June 1907): 920–26; Charles A. Conant, "The Economic Benefits of Investments Abroad," *Banker's Magazine* 74 (May 1907): 699–705.

79. For the changing U.S. market share, see the table provided in *CR 1912*, 12–13. For U.S. exports to the continent as a whole, which soared upward in the decade before the war, see U.S. Department of Commerce, *Statistical Abstract of the United States, 1914* (Washington, D.C., 1915), 340. The total in 1913 was $146,147,993 (versus $41,137,872 in 1903). The U.S. was the source of 12.7 percent of Argentina's imports in 1903 and 15.4 percent in 1912. For Chile, the increase over the same period is from 8.6 to 13.8 percent, and for Brazil, from 11.3 to 15.6 percent. With regard to investment, see Cleona Lewis, *America's Stake in International Investments* (Washington, D.C., 1938), 340–41, 343; Margaret A. Marsh, *The Bankers in Bolivia* (New York, 1928), 74–79; Benjamin H. Williams, *Economic Foreign Policy of the United States* (New York, 1929), 400. Direct investments also increased. Swift and Co. and National Packing Co. acquired meat-packing facilities in Argentina and the Guggenheims were beginning to become involved in Chilean copper mining. See McGann, *Argentina*, 262; Pike, *Chile*, 161. Also see Mira Wilkins, *The Emergence of Multinational Enterprise: American Business Abroad from the Colonial Era to 1914* (Cambridge, Mass., 1970), 215.

80. Maurice Flamant and Jeanne Singer-Kérel, *Modern Economic Crises and Recessions* (New York, 1970), 45–47; Herbert Feis, *Europe the World's Banker, 1870–1914* (New York, 1965), 424–25; Lewis, *America's Stake*, 340–41.

81. William C. Schluter, *The Pre-War Business Cycle* (New York, 1923), 13–55.

82. By the end of 1908, Morgan had closed a deal to handle a small Bolivian loan for the construction of school buildings. The business was divided between the Morgan houses in London and New York, First National Bank, National City Bank, and W. R. Grace and Company. We "expect to sell them at a clear ten points

profit," wrote Vanderlip to Stillman. See Vanderlip to Stillman, December 11, 1908, and January 1, 1909, FVP.

83. Root to American Legation, Buenos Aires, January 14, 1909, SDNF 8503; Wilson to Department, January 29 and February 22, 1909, SDNF 8503; Feis, *Europe*, 126. Also see Vanderlip to Stillman, February 22 and 26, 1909, FVP. An interesting exchange, illustrating the value attached to such transactions, transpired during the week the loan was first advertised. At a National City board meeting, some members expressed the desire to have more of them consulted before the bank decided on such participations. Vanderlip replied by "pointing out ... the absolute impossibility of operating a bond department in that way." Immediate decisions on such matters were necessary. "So far as the Argentine business was concerned," Vanderlip recounted, "I explained that it was engaged in by perhaps the strongest international group of bankers that had ever united in bringing out a loan; that, as a matter of fact, the subscription had opened three hours before ... and had been so large that it had been closed at twelve o'clock; that the bank had already made a profit of some $60,000 or $70,000 and the bonds were already quoted at a premium. I called attention to the fact that the Bond Department had, the day before, turned over to the General Department, $500,000 as its profits for February, and the month before had transferred $300,000, making $800,000 for the two months of the calendar year, and that in the present low interest market, assistance of that sort was absolutely necessary to a satisfactory result in general earnings." See Vanderlip to Stillman, March 5, 1909, FVP.

84. Nor was South America the only focus of Wall Street's attention. National City Bank, James Speyer and Company, and J. P. Morgan all began to canvass the Caribbean region for business in these months. See Vanderlip to Don Anibal Cruz, February 16, 1909, FVP; Ailes to Knox, April 7, 1909, SDNF 9484; Vanderlip to Stillman, February 22 and April 8, 1909, FVP. And prospects in China likewise began to receive fresh interest (see Chapter 4).

85. Meanwhile, National City sought to work through subsidiaries. For a time Vanderlip explored the prospect of purchasing the International Banking Corporation, a bank that had been chartered under Connecticut state law to meet American banking needs in the Philippines. Then, feeling that he could not acquire that institution on satisfactory terms (National City would eventually absorb I.B.C. in 1915), he looked to his institution's National City Company (which had been organized outside of the banking laws) to lay the foundations for such expansion. See Vanderlip to Stillman, February 4, 12, 26, March 5, October 22, 29, 1909, September 23, 1910, September 8, 22, 1911, March 2, 16, 29, April 22, September 6, November 8, 1912, FVP; Vanderlip to Sielken, January 30, 1911, FVP. British banking interests became so concerned at one point that they approached Vanderlip about an alliance. They offered a share of their business to the Americans in return for abandonment of "our South American banking project and working out what we wish to do through them." Vanderlip to Stillman, October 29, 1909, FVP. The International Banking Corporation had been established in 1909. In 1909 it had sixteen foreign offices, mostly in the Far East. Lewis, *America's Stake*, 194.

86. Morgan et al. to Knox, July 15, 1909, SDNF 20606. Also see Vincent P. Carosso, *The Morgans: Private International Bankers, 1854–1913* (Cambridge, Mass., 1987), 591–93.

87. "Latin America, The Bureau of Latin American Affairs, The Pan-American Bank, A Ship Subsidy," October 6, 1909, PCKP.

88. Vanderlip to Stillman, May 1, 1909, FVP.

89. Vanderlip to Stillman, May 7, 1909, FVP.

90. Sherrill to Knox, May 27, 1909, SDNF 8503; Knox to Ailes, April, 7, 1909, SDNF 9484; Huntington Wilson to American Legation, Santiago, April 9, 1909, SDNF

9484; Ailes to Knox, April 7, 1909, SDNF 9484; Huntington Wilson to Diplomatic Bureau, April 8, 1909, SDNF 9484.

91. Seward W. Livermore, "Battleship Diplomacy in South America: 1905–1925," *Journal of Modern History* 16 (March 1944): 31–48; Tulchin, *Argentina*, 26; Smith, *Unequal Giants*, 62–66.

92. Bacon to Reid, February 11, 1909, SDNF 1070.

93. Huntington Wilson, Memorandum dated March 7, 1909; Knox to American Legation, Buenos Aires, March 8, 1909; Portela to Knox, April 12, 1909; Huntington Wilson to Meyer, April 13, 1909; Meyer to Knox, April 27, 1909; Huntington Wilson to Portela, April 28, 1909; Huntington Wilson to Dickinson, April 29, 1909; Huntington Wilson to Portela, May 7, 1909; all SDNF 1070 Also see Richard D. Challener, *Admirals, Generals, and American Foreign Policy, 1898–1914* (Princeton, N.J., 1973), 316–18. For criticism, see *Congressional Record*, 61st Cong., 3d sess., 3113, 3519–20; *La Follette's Weekly* 3 (March 4, 1911): 1, 8–9.

94. Sherrill to Department, July 29, 1909, SDNF 1070. Also see Sherrill to Department, July 8, August 21, September 4, October 8, 1909, SDNF 1070.

95. Sherrill to Department, January 22, 1910, SDDF 835.34; Dawson to Knox, January 22, 1910, SDNF 1070.

96. As Niblack reported to the Navy Department in October, "I do not believe that the Chilean Government wants, intends, or can order its ships elsewhere than in England, except by a political upheaval of which there are now no signs; and I believe further that the national financial condition of Chile dictates the same policy." Quoted in Livermore, "Battleship Diplomacy," 41.

97. A small consolation was the award of a $2 million coastal defense contract to Bethlehem Steel. See Livermore, "Battleship Diplomacy," 43.

98. The State Department conducted a lengthy campaign on behalf of Niles-Bement-Pond Company of New York, which wanted to build a large naval arsenal near Rio. During late 1911, it also tried to land a submarine building contract for the Electric Boat Company of Connecticut. But these projects went to French and Italian companies. See Smith, *Unequal Giants*, 72–74.

99. Werking, *Master Architects*, 190–215; Kaufman, "Organizational Dimension," 32–33.

100. Robert Neal Seidel, "Progressive Pan Americanism: Development and United States Policy Toward South America, 1906–1931," *Cornell University Latin American Studies Program Dissertation Series* 45 (January 1973): 43–46.

101. Quoted in Jessup, *Root*, 2: 250–51. Also see Walter V. Scholes and Marie V. Scholes, *The Foreign Policies of the Taft Administration* (Columbia, Mo., 1970), 6–7.

102. Quoted in Scholes and Scholes, *Foreign Policies*, 12–13. Also see Taft to Knox, February 10, 1912, PCKP.

103. Quoted in McGann, *Argentina*, 267.

104. Shea, *Calvo Clause*, 20; Mecham, *Inter-American Security*, 61–62. Also see Francis M. Huntington-Wilson, *Memoirs of an Ex-Diplomat* (Boston, 1945), 211–12.

105. Pike, *Chile*, 139–40.

106. A departmental memorandum later asserted that the alternative was either "to abandon a just case and recede from the position of protecting large American interests, or else to take the next and logical step, i.e., to press for impartial arbitration or an equitable cash settlement." "Current Business of the Department of State," n.d., PCKP.

107. Pike, *Chile*, 140–42; Jessup, *Root*, 2: 250–51; Burns, *Unwritten Alliance*, 135–39; Peterson, *Argentina*, 296.

108. *New York Times*, December 21, 1909; Carnegie to Knox, December 21, 1909, PCKP; Carnegie to *New York Times*, December 21, 1909, PCKP; Knox to MacVeagh, December 30, 1909, PCKP.

109. Taft address before the Americus Club of Pittsburgh, May 2, 1910, *Congressional Record*, 61st Cong., 2d sess., Appendix, 469–70.

110. Quoted in McGann, *Argentina*, 277. The delegation included the diplomat Henry White, international law expert John Bassett Moore, Paul Reinsch, General Enoch Crowder, and the shipbuilder Lewis Nixon.

111. McGann, *Argentina*, 276–77, 282–84; Mecham, *Inter-American Security*, 71–72; Connell-Smith, *Inter-American System*, 52–53.

112. See Smith, *Unequal Giants*, 82–92.

113. Quoted in Mecham, *Inter-American Security*, 72.

114. "A Political Address in Nashville," February 24, 1912, *PWW*, 24: 194. Also see "An Address in New York to the National League of Commission Merchants," January 11, 1912, *PWW*, 24: 32–37; "An Address in Philadelphia to the Periodical Publishers' Association of America," February 2, 1912, 122–31.

115. "An Address to the General Assembly of Virginia and the City Council of Richmond," February 1, 1912, *PWW*, 24: 111.

116. "A Nonpartisan Talk to the Commercial Club of Omaha," October 5, 1912, *PWW*, 25: 341.

117. Taussig, *Tariff History*, 361–446; Robert H. Wiebe, *Businessmen and Reform: A Study of the Progressive Movement* (Chicago, 1968), 56–61; David W. Detzer, "The Politics of the Payne-Aldrich Tariff of 1909" (PhD dissertation, University of Connecticut, 1970); Paolo E. Coletta, *The Presidency of William Howard Taft* (Lawrence, Kan., 1973), 45–75; Wolman, *Most Favored Nation*; Burton I. Kaufman, *Efficiency and Expansion: Foreign Trade Organization in the Wilson Administration, 1913–1921* (Westport, Conn., 1974), 68, 73, 84; Kendrick A. Clements, *The Presidency of Woodrow Wilson* (Lawrence, Kan., 1992), 36–40.

118. Kaufman, *Efficiency and Expansion*, 74–76, 104–5; Robert Mayer, "The Origins of the American Banking Empire in Latin America," *Journal of Interamerican Studies and World Affairs*, 15 (February 1973): 66–67; Barbara Stallings, *Banker to the Third World: U.S. Portfolio Investment in Latin America, 1900–1986* (Berkeley, Calif., 1987), 64–66.

119. Kaufman, *Efficiency and Expansion*, 68–70, 76–82.

120. David Healy, *Drive to Hegemony: The United States in the Caribbean, 1898–1917* (Madison, Wis., 1988), 180–81; Arthur S. Link, *Wilson: The New Freedom* (Princeton, N.J., 1956), 321–24.

121. Smith, *Unequal Giants*, 93–96; Mark T. Gilderhus, *Pan American Visions: Woodrow Wilson in the Western Hemisphere, 1913–1921* (Tucson, Ariz., 1986), 27–30.

122. Gilderhus, *Pan American Visions*, 26–27.

123. Thomas L. Karnes, "Hiram Bingham and his Obsolete Shibboleth," *Diplomatic History*, 3 (Winter 1979): 42–46; Gilderhus, *Pan American Visions*, 15–16. Bingham had gained fame in 1911 for discovering the ruins of Machu Picchu. For Root's efforts to work with Mexico, see Chapter 2.

124. Gilderhus, *Pan American Visions*, 16–17.

125. "From the Diary of Colonel House," January 16, 1914, *PWW*, 29: 135.

126. Gilderhus, *Pan American Visions*, 31–33.

127. "From the Diary of Colonel House," November 25, 1914, *PWW*, 31: 354–55.

128. "From the Diary of Colonel House," *PWW*, 31: 355.

129. "From the Diary of Colonel House," December 16, 1914, *PWW*, 31: 469–70.

130. "From the Diary of Colonel House," December 17, 1914, *PWW*, 31: 481; December 19, 1914, *PWW*, 31: 497–98.

131. In fact, American policy makers saw the pact not as superseding or replacing the Monroe Doctrine, but as a possible way of reinforcing it. See Bryan to Wilson, April 27, 1915, *PWW*, 33: 77–80; House to Lansing, October 12, 1915, *PWW*, 35: 54–55. In a lengthy memorandum on the Monroe Doctrine dated November

24, 1915, Secretary of State Lansing was quite explicit and detailed as to what he saw as the doctrine's relationship to Pan-Americanism. He noted that "it may be invoked against an American government as well as against a European government." The Monroe Doctrine "is not a Pan-American policy," asserted Lansing. "In its advocacy of the Monroe Doctrine the United States considers its own interests. *The integrity of other American nations is an incident, not an end* [emphasis added]." See *PWW*, 35: 248–49. "The argument of this paper seems to me unanswerable," the president commented. See Wilson to Lansing, November 29 1915, *PWW*, 35: 263.

132. "From the Diary of Colonel House," January 13, 1915, *PWW*, 32: 64; House to Wilson, January 21, 1915, *PWW*, 32: 98–99; Pike, *Chile*, 150–51; Gilderhus, *Pan American Visions*, 52.

133. See "Diary of Colonel House," June 24, 1915, *PWW*, 33: 449; House to Wilson, July 25, 1915, *PWW*, 34: 24–25; Lansing to Wilson, September 10, 1915, *PWW*, 34: 444; Wilson to Lansing, September 11, 1915, *PWW*, 34; 448; Gilderhus, *Pan American Visions*, 64–67.

134. "Annual Message on the State of the Union," December 7, 1915, *PWW*, 35: 296.

135. "An Address to the Pan American Scientific Congress," January 6, 1916, *PWW*, 35: 444–45.

136. Lansing to Wilson, February 16, 1916, *PWW*, 36: 197.

137. Quoted in Gilderhus, *Pan American Visions*, 69.

138. "From the Diary of Colonel House," March 29, 1916, *PWW*, 36: 380; House to Wilson, with enclosure, April 13, 1916, *PWW*, 36: 478–79.

139. Gilderhus, *Pan American Visions*, 74–77.

140. Albert, *South America and the World Economy*, 36–37; Tulchin, *Argentina*, 30–36; Smith, *Unequal Giants*, 103–5; Flamant and Singer-Kérel, *Modern Economic Crises*, 49–51; Schluter, *Pre-War Business Cycle*, 127–73; Kaufman, *Efficiency and Expansion*, 91–93; Gilderhus, *Pan-American Visions*, 37–42.

141. Gilderhus, *Pan-American Visions*, 39–45; Kaufman, *Efficiency and Expansion*, 93–95, 103.

142. Kaufman, *Efficiency and Expansion*, 100–103; Gilderhus, *Pan American Visions*, 43–45; Seidel, "Progressive Pan Americanism," 70–74; Joseph S. Tulchin, *The Aftermath of War: World War I and U.S. Policy Toward Latin America* (New York, 1971), 3–10.

143. Quoted in Gilderhus, *Pan American Visions*, 60.

144. Gilderhus, *Pan American Visions*, 61–62; Kaufman, *Efficiency and Expansion*, 113–16; Seidel, "Progressive Pan Americanism," 74–103; Emily S. Rosenberg, *World War I and the Growth of United States Predominance in Latin America* (New York, 1987), 34–38.

145. Indeed the pace only slackened slightly once the United States itself entered the war. Joseph Tulchin has provided the most careful analysis of these trends. See *Aftermath of War*, 39–41. The most telling figures are those for the relative shares of the (overall) Latin American import market held by Britain and the United States. In 1912 these were 29 and 18 respectively. By 1920 they were 20 and 42 (39–42).

146. Seidel, "Progressive Pan Americanism," 68–69; Mayer, "American Banking Empire," 69–70; Gilderhus, *Pan American Visions*, 71–72; Kaufman, *Efficiency and Expansion*, 104–6, 117–18.

147. Kaufman, *Efficiency and Expansion*, 145–47.

148. Kaufman, *Efficiency and Expansion*, 96–100, 146–47, 124–29; Seidel, "Progressive Pan Americanism," 49–50; Gilderhus, *Pan American Visions*, 72.

149. December 7, 1915, *PWW*, 35: 302.

Chapter 4. "Where the Far West Becomes the Far East": China

1. For a time in the 1890s there had been great expectations about the trade that could be done right away. These had been aroused by the considerable growth in exports to China in that decade, particularly of plain cotton goods and lamp oil. But American trade, never large in absolute terms, expanded much more slowly after 1900. Consuls complained about insufficient interest and attention on the part of U.S. businessmen. Interference by foreign powers was sometimes blamed. However, policy makers were also increasingly of the belief that, for reasons having to do with conditions in China itself, trade possibilities were for the time being limited. Impediments were seen to include a serious balance of payments problem, extensive duties on internal trade, and the lack of adequate transportation throughout the empire's interior. Confidence remained, however, that China would offer great opportunities in the future. After touring the empire in 1906 as special agents for the Department of Commerce and Labor, for instance, Harry R. Burrill and Raymond F. Crist frankly acknowledged the existing limits to trade expansion there. But they nevertheless thought that a new era of immense growth might only be a short time away. In their report they noted the "growing sentiment among the Chinese in favor of railway construction." This, they felt, indicated the beginning of a "radical departure from the narrow, commerce-paralyzing prejudices of centuries and the dawn of an era of trade expansion difficult to comprehend by those unfamiliar with the vast resources of the Empire." On this topic, see Francis E. Hyde, *Far Eastern Trade, 1860–1914* (London, 1973); Barry Lee Knight, "American Trade and Investment in China, 1890–1910" (PhD dissertation, Michigan State University, 1968); Paul Varg, *The Making of a Myth: The United States and China, 1897–1912* (East Lansing, Mich., 1968); Eileen P. Scully, "Taking the Low Road to Sino-American Relations: 'Open Door' Expansionists and the Two China Markets," *Journal of American History* 82 (June 1995): 62–83. The quotes above are from U.S. Congress, Senate, *Trade Conditions in China* by Harry R. Burrill and Raymond F. Crist, S. Doc. 484, 59th Cong., 1st sess., 1906, 38. Also instructive is a "Memorandum Relative to American Trade Possibilities in the Far East," September 15, 1909, written by J. B. Osborne of the Bureau of Trade Relations, Department of State, PCKP.

2. The geographic reference in this chapter's title suggests how China was an extension of the American frontier. The phrase is from a speech by John Hay. See "Fifty Years of the Republican Party," July 6, 1904, in *Addresses of John Hay* (New York, 1906), 283–84.

3. See here Chapter 2 above; also Alfred Thayer Mahan, *The Problem of Asia and Its Effect upon International Policies* (Boston, 1900), 124–38.

4. These paragraphs draw heavily on Jonathan D. Spence, *The Search for Modern China* (New York, 1990), 143–224; Jean Chesneaux, Marianne Bastid, and Marie-Claire Bergère, *China from the Opium Wars to the 1911 Revolution*, trans. Ann Destenay (New York, 1976), 3–292; Ranbir Vohra, *China's Path to Modernization: A Historical Review from 1800 to the Present* (Englewood Cliffs, N.J., 1992) 22–78; and Peter Lowe, *Britain in the Far East: A Survey from 1819 to the Present* (New York, 1981).

5. Ian Nish, *Japanese Foreign Policy, 1869–1942: Kasumigaseki to Miyakezaka* (London, 1977), 34–44; W. G. Beasley, *Japanese Imperialism, 1894–1945* (Oxford, 1987), 14–68.

6. The tsar's powerful finance minister, Sergei Witte, maintained that a Japanese presence in Manchuria would greatly complicate security for the railway. It would also isolate Korea and pave the way for increased Japanese influence there. No appropriate site would remain for a base. Russia's position in the Far East would be weaker than before, and Tokyo rather than St. Petersburg would gain predominant influence in northern China. See Dietrich Geyer, *Russian Imperialism: The Interaction of Domestic and Foreign Policy, 1860–1914* (New York, 1987), 18–193 and David

Gillard, *The Struggle for Asia, 1828–1914: A Study in British and Russian Imperialism* (London, 1977), 147–61.

7. France meanwhile secured a favorable adjustment of China's border with its territories in Southeast Asia and the right to construct railway lines from Indochina into the adjoining provinces of Yunnan and Guangxi.

8. Geyer, *Russian Imperialism*, 193–98.

9. L. K. Young, *British Policy in China, 1895–1902* (Oxford, 1970), 51–67; Lowe, *Britain in the Far East*, 64–67.

10. Marilyn B. Young, *The Rhetoric of Empire: American China Policy, 1895–1901* (Cambridge, Mass., 1968), 93–95. Also see R. G. Neale, *Great Britain and United States Expansion: 1898–1900* (East Lansing, Mich.,1966), 117–18; A. L. P. Dennis, *Adventures in American Diplomacy, 1896–1906* (New York, 1928), 170–71, 181–82.

11. See William R. Braisted, *The United States Navy in the Pacific, 1897–1909* (Austin, Tex., 1958), 19–20.

12. Braisted, *Pacific, 1897–1909*, 21–22; John A. S. Grenville, "American Naval Preparations for War with Spain, 1896–1898," *Journal of American Studies* 2 (1968); David F. Trask, *The War with Spain in 1898* (New York, 1981), 72–81.

13. John Offner, "The United States and France: Ending the Spanish-American War," *Diplomatic History* 7 (Winter 1983): 4.

14. See Tyler Dennett, *John Hay: From Poetry to Politics* (New York, 1934), 190.

15. A seminal work on the topic of insular expansion is Thomas McCormick, *China Market: America's Quest for Informal Empire, 1893–1901* (Chicago, 1967).

16. Braisted, *Pacific, 1897–1909*, 34; Trask, *War with Spain*, 379; McCormick, *China Market*, 110; Lewis L. Gould, *The Presidency of William McKinley* (Lawrence, Kan., 1980), 101; John A. S. Grenville and George Berkeley Young, *Politics, Strategy, and American Diplomacy: Studies in Foreign Policy, 1873–1917* (New Haven, Conn. 1966), 285–86.

17. Quoted in Trask, *War with Spain*, 409.

18. Quoted in Gould, *McKinley*, 101.

19. See Margaret Leech, *In the Days of McKinley* (New York, 1959), 325, 328, 644.

20. For the protocol, see *FR 1898*, 823–25. For the negotiations leading up to it, see Trask, *War with Spain*, 431; and Offner, "United States and France." McKinley's instructions can be found in *FR 1898*, 904–8. Also see H. Wayne Morgan, ed., *Making Peace with Spain: The Diary of Whitelaw Reid, September-December 1898* (Austin, Tex., 1965), 31.

21. Braisted, *Pacific, 1897–1909*, 52–53; Grenville and Young, *Politics*, 294–95; U.S. Congress, Senate, *Message from the President transmitting a treaty of Peace between the United States and Spain*, S. Doc. 62, 55th Cong., 3d sess., 1899, Part 2, 520–21.

22. Day to Hay, October 6, 1898, *FR 1898*, 918–22; Day to Hay, October 9, 1898, *FR 1898.*, 925–27; U.S. Congress, Senate, *United States and Spain*, 362–70, 374–78, 386–89, 441–71; Morgan, ed., *Whitelaw Reid*, 42, 54–56, 64, 88–113; Peace Commissioners to Hay, October 25, 1898, *FR 1898*, 932–35; Hay to Day, October 26, 1898, *FR 1898*; Hay to Day, October 28, 1898, *FR 1898*, 937–38; Paolo E. Coletta, "The Peace Negotiations and the Treaty of Paris," in *Threshold to American Internationalism: Essays on the Foreign Policies of William McKinley*, ed. Coletta (Jericho, N.Y., 1970), 121–75. Also see Ephraim K. Smith, "'A Question from Which We Could Not Escape': William McKinley and the Decision to Acquire the Philippine Islands," *Diplomatic History* 9 (Fall 1985): 363–75.

There remained the issues of both domestic and Filipino acceptance of this step. Despite the criticisms of an "anti-imperialist" movement and of some prominent Democrats, the administration was successful in getting the Treaty of Paris ratified during a lame-duck session of the Fifty-fifth Congress on February 6, 1899. A war of resistance had meanwhile broken out in the islands on February 4. By the time most though by no means all of this had been suppressed, two years later, some 200,000 Filipinos and 5,000 American soldiers had lost their lives. On the battle over ratification, see Lala C. Steelman, "The Public Career of Augustus Octavius Bacon," (PhD dissertation, University of North Carolina, 1950), 131–96, 213–38; Francis B. Simkins, *Pitchfork Ben Tillman, South Carolinian* (Baton Rouge, La., 1944), 353–54, 386; J. Rogers Hollingsworth, *The Whirligig of Politics: The Democracy of Cleveland and Bryan* (Chicago, 1964), 125–241; Richard E. Welch, *Response to Imperialism: The United States and the Philippine-American War, 1899–1902* (Chapel Hill, N.C., 1979), 61–63; William J. Pomeroy, *American Neo-Colonialism: Its Emergence in the Philippines and Asia* (New York, 1970), 106–8, 118–32; Stuart Creighton Miller, *"Benevolent Assimilation": The American Conquest of the Philippines, 1899–1903* (New Haven, Conn., 1982), 23–30; Christopher Lasch, "The Anti-Imperialists, the Philippines and the Inequality of Man," *Journal of Southern History* 14 (August 1958), 319–31; Paolo E. Coletta, "Bryan, McKinley, and the Treaty of Paris," *Pacific Historical Review* 26 (May 1957): 131–46; Gould, *McKinley*, 143–50; and Robert C. Hilderbrand, *Power and the People: Executive Management of Public Opinion in Foreign Affairs, 1897–1921* (Chapel Hill, N.C., 1981), 28–42. On the "anti-imperialist" movement of 1898–1900, outside Congress, see in particular Robert L. Beisner, *Twelve Against Empire: The Anti-Imperialists, 1898–1900* (New York, 1968); David Healy, *U.S. Expansionism: The Imperialist Urge in the 1890s* (Madison, Wis., 1970), 213–47; Welch, *Response*, 43–57; Geoffrey Blodgett, "The Mugwump Reputation, 1870 to the Present," *Journal of American History* 66 (March 1980): 867–87; Miller, *"Benevolent Assimilation"*, 104–28; E. Berkeley Tompkins, *Anti-Imperialism in the United States: The Great Debate* (Philadelphia, 1970); and Daniel B. Schirmer, *Republic or Empire: American Resistance to the Philippine War* (Cambridge, Mass., 1972). On the war, see especially Miller, *"Benevolent Assimilation"* and two articles by Glenn A. May: "Filipino Resistance to American Occupation: Batangas, 1899–1902," *Pacific Historical Review* 48 (November 1979): 531–56 and "Why the United States Won the Philippine War," *Pacific Historical Review* 52 (November 1983): 353–77. Also see David Haward Bain, *Sitting in Darkness: Americans in the Philippines* (Boston, 1984), 79–101, 185–220, 244–55, 275–94, 319–27, 344–50, 361–74 (focusing on the capture of Emilio Aguinaldo) and Brian McAllister Linn, *The U.S. Army and Counterinsurgency in the Philippine War, 1899–1902* (Chapel Hill, N.C., 1989).

23. On Hawaii, where the United States had already come to exercise great influence, see Merze Tate, *Hawaii: Reciprocity or Annexation* (East Lansing, Mich., 1968); Thomas J. Osborne, *"Empire Can Wait": American Opposition to Hawaiian Annexation, 1893–1898* (Kent, Ohio, 1981); Charles S. Campbell, *The Transformation of American Foreign Relations, 1865–1900* (New York, 1976), 230–38; Michael J. Devine, "John W. Foster and the Struggle for the Annexation of Hawaii," *Pacific Historical Review* 46 (February 1977): 29–50; Allen Lee Hamilton, "Military Strategists and the Annexation of Hawaii," *Journal of the West* 15 (April 1976): 81–91; and William Michael Morgan, "The Anti-Japanese Origins of the Hawaiian Annexation Treaty of 1897," *Diplomatic History* 6 (Winter 1982): 25–44.

24. Charles S. Campbell, Jr., *Special Business Interests and the Open Door Policy* (New Haven, Conn., 1951), 25–36; Young, *Rhetoric*, 96.

25. *FR 1898*, lxxii. Basically the same position was articulated by the new secretary of state in a letter he wrote to Paul Dana, the editor of the *New York Sun*, at the beginning of 1899. "It is not very easy to formulate with any exactness the view of the Government in regard to the present condition of things in China," Hay commented. The U.S. was "of course, opposed to the dismemberment of that Empire," and "keenly alive to the importance of safeguarding our great commercial interests." To protect the latter, its representatives had orders "to watch closely everything that may seem calculated to injure us, and to prevent it by energetic and timely representations."

By way of illustration, Hay noted that the administration had not been willing to support Italy's unsuccessful recent effort to obtain a port for itself. Yet at the same time it had not been prepared "to assure China that we would join her in repelling that demand by armed force." "We do not consider our hands tied for future eventualities," Hay concluded, "but for the present we think our best policy is one of vigilant protection of our commercial interests without formal alliance with other powers interested." Hay to Dana, March 16, 1899, JHP.

26. Edward Zabriskie, *American Russian Rivalry in the Far East, 1895–1914* (Philadelphia, 1946), 52–53.

27. He was calling for a British-German-Japanese-American guarantee of China's integrity as a way of upholding the open door. While still ambassador to England the year before, Hay himself had urged formal cooperation between Britain and the U.S. in East Asia. But he had since come to believe that such an alliance would be more difficult than any other for the administration to advocate, given the strength of popular American Anglophobia. On Beresford and Hay, see Dennett, *Hay*, 286–88; Young, *Rhetoric*, 118–19; Michael H. Hunt, *The Making of a Special Relationship: The United States and China to 1914* (New York, 1983), 181–82.

28. Hunt, *Special Relationship*, 125.

29. For background on Hippisley, see Neale, *Great Britain*, 168–69, 197–200 and A. Whitney Griswold, *The Far Eastern Policy of the United States* (New Haven, Conn., 1938), 63–65.

30. For background on Rockhill, see Peter W. Stanley, "The Making of an American Sinologist: William W. Rockhill and the Open Door," *Perspectives in American History* 11 (1978): 419–60.

31. Young, *British Policy*, 77–86.

32. Hippisley to Rockhill, July 25, 1899, WWRP. Other detailed discussions of this correspondence include Griswold, *Far Eastern Policy*, 62–75; Harvey Pressman, "Hay, Rockhill, and China's Integrity: A Reappraisal," *Harvard University Papers on China* 13 (Cambridge, Mass., 1959): 61–79; Young, *Rhetoric*, 123–30.

33. Rockhill to Hippisley, August 3, 1899, WWRP. The Englishman replied that prompt action by Washington along the lines of the note that he had suggested would forestall any damaging charges that the administration "was following the lead of ... England." Moreover, he argued, the Russification of the northern provinces of China was proceeding so rapidly that "it would be suicidal for America to drift and do nothing for another year." See Hippisley to Rockhill, August 16, 1899, WWRP.

34. "I am fully awake to the great importance of what you say, and am more than ready to act," wrote the secretary in early August from his summer estate in New Hampshire. "But the senseless prejudices in certain sections of the 'Senate and people' compel us to move with great caution." Hay to Rockhill, August 7, 1899, WWRP.

35. Rockhill to Hippisley, August 18, 1899, WWRP.

36. Hippisley to Rockhill, August 21, 1899, WWRP. The memorandum, which bears the date August 17, 1899, has been reprinted in Griswold, *Far Eastern Policy*, 475–91.

37. Hay to Rockhill, August 24, 1899, WWRP.

38. Initially England, Germany, and Russia. Although it claimed a sphere in southernmost China, France was not at first included among the powers addressed by Hay, in part because it was not one of the governments with which Washington had already had exchanges, but also because there were doubts initially that the Quai d'Orsay would assent. In subsequent weeks, however, France as well as Italy and Japan were invited to adhere.

39. Hay to Vignaud, September 6, 1899, WWRP; Hippisley to Rockhill, August 21, 1899, WWRP; *FR 1899*, 129–36, 140–42.

40. "We got all that could be screwed out of the [Russian] Bear," he later told his friend Henry Adams, "and our cue is to insist we got everything." See Young, *Rhetoric*, 131–35. For the correspondence over the notes, see *FR 1899*, 128–29, 130–32, 138–39, 141–43.

41. Rockhill to Hippisley, August 18, 1899, WWRP.

42. Hippisley to Rockhill, August 26, 1899, WWRP.

43. Rockhill to Hippisley, September, 14, 1899, WWRP. Of course the open door notes did include a gesture on behalf of China's integrity in their request for respect for the official Chinese customs system.

44. Hay to Choate, September 6, 1899, *FR 1899*, 132.

45. See Young, *Rhetoric*, 138–42. For Hay's characterization of the powers' replies on March 20, 1899, see *FR 1899*, 142–43.

46. Spence, *Search*, 224–35; Chesneaux et al., *1911 Revolution*, 307–39; Meribeth E. Cameron, *The Reform Movement in China, 1898–1912* (Palo Alto, Calif.,1931), 9–57; Chester C. Tan, *The Boxer Catastrophe* (New York, 1955); Vincent Purcell, *The Boxer Uprising: A Background Study* (Cambridge, 1963).

47. For a very good discussion of the administration's concerns, see Young, *Rhetoric*, 143–71. On the military response, see Braisted, *Pacific, 1897–1909*, 104–7.

48. Purcell, *Boxer Uprising*, 255–56; Tan, *Boxer Catastrophe*, 76–92.

49. *FR 1901, Appendix: Affairs in China*, 12.

50. Young, *Rhetoric*, 180–87. On the American occupation of its zone in Beijing, see Michael H. Hunt, "The Forgotten Occupation: Peking, 1900–1901," *Pacific Historical Review* 48 (November 1979): 501–27. On U.S. reaction to the Chinese-Russian suggestion that the talks be moved to Tianjin, see Adee circular, August 29, 1900, *FR 1901, Appendix: Affairs in China*, 9–10; Conger to Hay, September 13, 1900, *FR 1901, Appendix: Affairs in China*, 33–34; Conger to Hay, September 12, 1900, *FR 1901, Appendix: Affairs in China*, 340–41; Hay to Adee, September 14, 1900, JHP; Hay to McKinley, September 17, 1900, JHP; Tan, *Boxer Catastrophe*, 100–128.

51. Hunt, "Forgotten Occupation," 527; Young, *British Policy*, 208–13; Hosea B. Morse, *The International Relations of the Chinese Empire*, 3 vols. (London, 1918), 3: 314–18.

52. *FR 1901, Appendix: Affairs in China*, 23–25; Dennis, *Adventures*, 234; Tan, *Boxer Catastrophe*, 127–28, 144–45, 149; Young, *British Policy*, 208; Young, *Rhetoric*, 200–201.

53. See *FR 1901, Appendix: Affairs in China*, 3–7, 24–25, 27–28, 356, 368; Hay to McKinley, October 25, 1900, JHP; Hay to Hippisley, January 5, 1901, JHP; Hay to Cambon, April 20, 1901, JHP; Hay to Cassini, April 20, 1901, JHP; Young, *Rhetoric*, 139–42, 181–83, 200–202; Hunt, *Special Relationship*, 196–200; Warren I. Cohen, *America's Response to China: An Interpretative History of Sino-American Relations* (New York, 1971), 58–59.

54. *FR 1901, Appendix: Affairs in China*, 26–28, 345–46; Hay to McKinley, October 4, 1900, JHP; Young, *Rhetoric*, 202; Tan, *Boxer Catastrophe*, 149–50.

55. *FR 1901, Appendix: Affairs in China*, 43–45, 58–60; Morse, *Chinese Empire*, 3: 339–43; Young, *British Policy*, 214–32; Tan, *Boxer Catastrophe*, 15–56; Young, *Rhetoric*, 203.

56. Tan, *Boxer Catastrophe*, 223–26; Young, *British Policy*, 255–58; Morse, *Chinese Empire*, 3: 346–47, 350–54, 366–67; Michael H. Hunt, "The American Remission of the Boxer Indemnity: A Reappraisal," *Journal of Asian Studies* 31 (May 1972): 539–59.

57. For the text, see *FR 1901, Appendix: Affairs in China*, 312–18.

58. Roosevelt to Sternberg, October 11, 1901, *LTR*, 3: 172–73.

59. It had "no life, energy or patriotism," was how he put it. See Hunt, *Special Relationship*, 267.

60. *FR 1901, Appendix: Affairs in China*, 363–64; Dennis, *Adventures*, 242; Tan, *Boxer Catastrophe*, 164–67, 175–77, 181–82; Geyer, *Russian Imperialism*, 207.

61. Tan, *Boxer Catastrophe*, 172–201; Masataka Kosaka, "Ch'ing Policy over Manchuria," *Harvard University Papers on China* 16 (1962): 126–53, Young, *British Policy*, 283. Hay now informed the Russian minister that he "would be gratified to be assured ... that in any arrangements which may hereafter be entered into ... the citizens of the United States shall suffer no diminution of their rights and privileges," and Lamsdorf provided such assurances on June 9. See Hay to Cassini, April 20, 1901, JHP; and Tan, *Boxer Catastrophe*, 201–13.

62. Zabriskie, *American-Russian Rivalry*, 74–77; Varg, *Myth*, 59–62; Hunt, *Special Relationship*, 60; Braisted, *Pacific, 1897–1909*, 137–38.

63. For their part, many Qing officials now believed that some such settlement with St. Petersburg was going to be the only way that they could retain even a semblance of control in the north. See *FR 1902*, 271–73; Kosaka, "Ch'ing Policy," 137–41; Zabriskie, *American-Russian Rivalry*, 77–79; Michael H. Hunt, *Frontier Defense and the Open Door: Manchuria in Chinese-American Relations, 1895–1911* (New Haven, Conn., 1973), 61–62.

64. *FR 1902*, 275–76. Rockhill had suggested to Hay in March 1901 that the Manchurian provinces were "irretrievably lost" to China. See Hunt, *Frontier Defense*, 59. Also see the language of Hay to Cassini, April 20, 1901 quoted above.

65. Ian Nish, *The Anglo-Japanese Alliance: The Diplomacy of Two Island Empires, 1894–1907* (London, 1966). See pp. 216–18 for the text of the treaty. Also see Young, *British Policy*, 295–318; Beasley, *Japanese Imperialism*, 46, 74–77.

66. Kosaka, "Ch'ing Policy," 141; Hunt, *Frontier Defense*, 63; Zabriskie, *American-Russian Rivalry*, 79–83; Andrew Malozemoff, *Russian Far Eastern Policy, 1881–1904* (Berkeley, Calif., 1958), 173–75; Nish, *Anglo-Japanese Alliance*, 238.

67. Hay to Roosevelt, May 1, 1902, JHP.

68. Geyer, *Russian Imperialism*, 208–14; *FR 1903*, 53–54; Zabriskie, *American-Russian Rivalry*, 82–87; Malozemoff, *Russian Far Eastern Policy*, 175–76, 200–201; Ian Nish, *The Origins of the Russo-Japanese War* (London, 1985), 142–47.

69. Hay to Cambon, April 20, 1901, JHP; Hay to Hippisley, January 5, 1901, JHP, Hay to Rockhill, April 11, 1901, *FR 1901, Appendix: Affairs in China*, 368; Hunt, *Special Relationship*, 267–71, 390; Varg, *Myth*, 40, 81; Stanley F. Wright, *Hart and the Chinese Customs* (Belfast, 1950), 755–58, 761–62.

70. Wright, *Hart*, 755, 758–62; Dennis, *Adventures*, 377–80.

71. Hay to Roosevelt, April 25, 1903, JHP; *FR 1903*, 54, 708–9.

72. Hay to Roosevelt, April 28, 1903, JHP; Hay to Roosevelt, April 28, 1903, JHP.

73. Roosevelt to Hay, May 22, 1903, *LTR*, 3: 478; *FR 1903*, 54–58; Hay to Roosevelt, May 4, 1903, JHP; Hay to Roosevelt, May 12, 1903, JHP; Zabriskie, *American-Russian Rivalry*, 89–90; Raymond A. Esthus, *Theodore Roosevelt and Japan* (Seattle, 1966), 9–10.

74. See Dennis, *Adventures*, 377–80. Also see Hay to Conger, June 13, 1903, JHP; *FR 1903*, 60, 63, 65.

75. Roosevelt to Shaw, June 22, 1903, *LTR*, 3: 497–98; Roosevelt to Abbott, June 22, 1903, *LTR*, 3: 500–502.

76. Braisted, *Pacific, 1897–1909*, 144–46.

77. Roosevelt to Hay, July 29, 1903, *LTR*, 3: 532–33; Esthus, *Japan*, 10.

78. The railway junction of Harbin was excepted, and severe restrictions on foreign settlements were also insisted on. See Zabriskie, *American-Russian Rivalry*, 93; *FR 1903*, 67.

79. Roosevelt to Hay, July 18, 1903, *LTR*, 3: 520.

80. See Hunt, *Frontier Defense*, 72.

81. *FR 1903*, 66–71; Hunt, *Frontier Defense*, 73; Kosaka, "Ch'ing Policy," 144.

82. For the text, see *FR 1903*, 91–101. Also see Wright, *Hart*, 758–62; Hunt, *Frontier Defense*, 80–84.

83. Nish, *Origins of the Russo-Japanese War*, 83–220, 238–57; Shumpei Okamoto, *The Japanese Oligarchy and the Russo-Japanese War* (New York, 1970), 57–102; Beasley, *Japanese Imperialism*, 78–81.

84. See Esthus, *Japan*, 12; Roosevelt to T. Roosevelt, Jr., February 19, 1904, *LTR*, 4: 724; Hunt, *Frontier Defense*, 84–87. There was also great admiration in the U.S. for Tokyo's preparation. Elihu Root, who had just stepped down as secretary of war, wrote the president in mid-February: "Was not the way the Japs began the fight bully? Some people in the United States might well learn the lesson that mere bigness does not take the place of perfect preparation and readiness for instant action." "Oh," rejoined TR, " if only our people would learn the need of preparedness, and of shaping things so that decision and action can alike be instantaneous. Mere bigness, if it is also mere flabbiness, means nothing but disgrace." See Root to Roosevelt, February 15, 1904, ERP; Roosevelt to Root, February 16, 1904, *LTR*, 4: 731.

85. Roosevelt to Spring Rice, March 19, 1904, *LTR*, 4: 759–61.

86. Roosevelt to Spring Rice, June 13, 1904, *LTR*, 4: 832. For the broad background of Japanese-American relations to this point, see Walter LaFeber, *The Clash: U.S.-Japanese Relations Throughout History* (New York, 1997), 3–80.

87. As early as 1900 he had commented that he would "like to see Japan have Korea" because "She will be a check upon Russia." Roosevelt to Sternberg, August 28, 1900, *LTR*, 4: 832.

88. Roosevelt to Spring Rice, March 19, 1904, *LTR*, 4: 760; Dennis, *Adventures*, 364–65.

89. The two countries had grown closer through their opposition to Russian policies. And Japan was now more anxious than ever to maintain good relations with Washington, especially because Tokyo was eager to obtain loans, to pay for its war, on American and British financial markets.

90. Roosevelt to Spring Rice, June 13, 1904, *LTR*, 4: 829–33; Esthus, *Japan*, 41–43.

91. Roosevelt to Meyer, December 26, 1904, *LTR*, 4: 1079–80. Also see Roosevelt to Spring Rice, December 27, 1904, *LTR*, 4: 1085–88; Roosevelt to Meyer, February 6, 1905, *LTR*, 4: 1115–16; Roosevelt to Hay, April 2, 1905, *LTR*, 4: 1157.

92. Roosevelt to Lodge, June 16, 1905, *LTR*, 4: 1230; Esthus, *Japan*, 56–80; Okamoto, *Japanese Oligarchy*, 105–50; John Albert White, *The Diplomacy of the Russo-Japanese War* (Princeton, 1964), 201–12; Eugene P. Trani, *The Treaty of Portsmouth: An Adventure in American Diplomacy* (Lexington, Ky., 1969), 50–112; Zabriskie, *American-Russian Rivalry*, 101–21; Nish, *Anglo-Japanese Alliance*, 295–96, 340.

93. Esthus, *Japan*, 80–96; White, *Russo-Japanese War*, 238–309; Trani, *Portsmouth*, 112–55; Raymond A. Esthus, *Double Eagle and Rising Sun: The Russians and Japanese at Portsmouth in 1905* (Durham, N.C., 1988), 47–57, 80, 116–17, 131–53; Okamoto, *Japanese Oligarchy*, 153–55; Zabriskie, *American-Russian Rivalry*, 121–30.

94. They also hoped that the alliance would diminish any need for Japan dramatically to expand its navy. On September 27, 1905, Elihu Root (who had recently succeeded Hay as secretary of state) wrote to James Bryce that he was "much gratified by the change which has taken place in Eastern affairs during the last few months." Root to Bryce, September 27, 1905, ERP. On reception of the treaty in Japan, see Esthus, *Double Eagle*, 167–69, 184–87. Also see Roosevelt to O'Laughlin, August 31, 1905, *LTR*, 4: 1328–29; Roosevelt to Lodge, September 6, 1905, *LTR*, 5: 12–13; Braisted, *Pacific, 1897–1909*, 184–85; Esthus, *Japan*, 95–96, 102–4; Nish, *Anglo-Japanese Alliance*, 298–340; Walter LaFeber, "Betrayal in Tokyo," *Constitution* 6 (Fall 1994): 4–11; John E. Wiltz, "Did the United States Betray Korea in 1905?" *Pacific Historical Review* 54 (August 1985): 243–70. In an 1882 treaty, the U.S. had indicated that it would help to protect Korean independence.

95. For background, see Delber L. McKee, *Chinese Exclusion Versus the Open Door Policy, 1900–1906: Clashes over China Policy in the Roosevelt Era* (Detroit, 1977), 21–82;

Hunt, *Special Relationship*, 85–108, 227–32, 241–42; Alexander Saxton, *The Indispensable Enemy: Labor and the Anti-Chinese Movement in California* (Berkeley, Calif., 1971). Also see Robert McClellan, *The Heathen Chinee: A Study of American Attitudes Toward China, 1890–1905* (Columbus, Ohio, 1971); A. Gregory Moore, "The Dilemma of Stereotypes: Theodore Roosevelt and China, 1901–1909" (PhD dissertation, Kent State University, 1978).

96. Ten years before, the Chinese government had accepted exclusion, believing that it might thereby secure better treatment and protection for visitors and for Chinese already resident in America. Beijing did not, however, feel that those hopes had been realized. See McKee, *Chinese Exclusion*, 59–60, 82–84.

97. "We wish to enlarge our trade with China," he told the secretary of commerce and labor (within whose department the bureau was housed). "We wish to make even firmer our intellectual hold upon China. It is for our interests that Chinese merchants should come here and that Chinese students should come here." See Roosevelt to Cortelyou, January 25, 1904, *LTR*, 3: 709–10.

98. McKee, *Chinese Exclusion*, 84–102; Hunt, *Special Relationship*, 234.

99. On the origins of the boycott, see Margaret Field, "The Chinese Boycott of 1905," *Harvard University Papers on China* 11 (1957): 63–75; McKee, *Chinese Exclusion*, 104–8; Hunt, *Special Relationship*, 234–36.

100. Roosevelt to Metcalf, June 16, 1905, *LTR*, 4: 1235–36; McKee, *Chinese Exclusion*, 116; Hunt, *Special Relationship*, 243.

101. Some senior officials were even beginning to think in terms of a treaty that would be characterized by full reciprocity between the two countries.

102. McKee, *Chinese Exclusion*, 109–23, 148–64; Hunt, *Special Relationship*, 235–38; Field, "Chinese Boycott," 78, 84, 87; Shih-shan H. Ts'ai, "Reaction to Exclusion: The Boycott of 1905 and Chinese National Awakening," *Historian* 39 (November 1976): 98–102.

103. See Howard K. Beale, *Theodore Roosevelt and the Rise of America to World Power* (Baltimore, 1984), 232–33.

104. Roosevelt to Rockhill, August 22, 1905, *LTR*, 4: 1310.

105. McKee, *Chinese Exclusion*, 120, 124; Ts'ai, "Reaction to Exclusion," 104–5.

106. After Taft, who was already in East Asia, met with boycott representatives in Canton in September, the president was able to line up most of his cabinet behind such legislation. See Roosevelt to Perkins, August 31, 1905, *LTR*, 4: 1327–28; McKee, *Chinese Exclusion*, 138–41, 172, 178–79; Beale, *Theodore Roosevelt*, 219–20, 234–38.

107. Canton was in the heart of the region from which most Chinese who were resident in America had come. It was also the home of the movement's most nationalistic student organizers. See McKee, *Chinese Exclusion*, 149, 161; Field, "Chinese Boycott," 75–80; Hunt, *Special Relationship*, 239–40.

108. Simultaneously, although only on the basis of a few incidents, Roosevelt also began to worry that if that were not done there would be a replay of the Boxer Rebellion in southern China with Americans and their interests as the primary targets. See McKee, *Chinese Exclusion*, 147, 163–66; Beale, *Theodore Roosevelt*, 238.

109. Roosevelt to Bonaparte, November 15, 1905, *LTR*, 5: 77.

110. Roosevelt to Taft, January 11, 1906, *LTR*, 5: 132–33; Richard D. Challener, *Admirals, Generals, and American Foreign Policy, 1898–1914* (Princeton, 1973), 215–18.

111. McKee, *Chinese Exclusion*, 168–69; Beale, *Theodore Roosevelt*, 240–45. Once it became clear that the boycott was unlikely to be revived, the Roosevelt administration relaxed its efforts to modify American immigration policy. With Chinese money, however, it did continue to pursue an initiative aimed at improving the U.S. image among that country's students. The role of foreign-educated Chinese youth in the immigration dispute underscored the importance of this educational trend as well as the extent to which the U.S. was losing out to Japan and even Europe as a

destination for overseas study. Rockhill had been arguing that this challenge might be met if the large surplus left over from the Boxer indemnity was used to fund a special program for the education of Chinese students in America. Although Beijing insisted that this money was rightfully its own and ought to be spent as it thought best, Washington was determined that the return of the indemnity should be tied to projects that would advance American interests. After the boycott began, TR decided to support Rockhill's plan. The idea ran parallel to a proposal put forward by Root during this same period looking toward the creation of Rhodes-type scholarships to bring Latin American students to the U.S. See McKee, *Chinese Exclusion*, 140–45, 178–85, 192–97, 204–9; Hunt, *Special Relationship*, 245–47; Hunt, "American Remission."

112. Esthus, *Japan*, 128–30; Roger Daniels, *The Politics of Prejudice: The Anti-Japanese Movement in California and the Struggle for Japanese Exclusion* (Berkeley, Calif., 1962), 1–45; Akira Iriye, *Pacific Estrangement: Japanese and American Expansion, 1897–1911* (Cambridge, Mass., 1972), 86–90.

113. Roosevelt to Lodge, June 5, 1905, *LTR*, 4: 1205. Also see Charles E. Neu, *An Uncertain Friendship: Theodore Roosevelt and Japan, 1906–1909* (Cambridge, Mass., 1967), 23–24; Iriye, *Pacific Estrangement*, 151–52.

114. Neu, *Uncertain Friendship*, 27–36; Esthus, *Japan*, 128–45.

115. Neu, *Uncertain Friendship*, 40–44.

116. See Sixth Annual Message, December 3, 1906, *WTR*, 15: 387.

117. Neu, *Uncertain Friendship*, 46–72; Esthus, *Japan*, 146–66.

118. Neu, *Uncertain Friendship*, 75–80, 84–85.

119. Neu, *Uncertain Friendship*, 103–4; Braisted, *Pacific, 1897–1909*, 184–85. Also see Roosevelt to Knox, February, 8, 1909, *LTR*, 6: 1510–14.

120. Roosevelt to Grey, December 18, 1906, *LTR*, 5: 529. Also see Braisted, *Pacific, 1897–1909*, 193.

121. Braisted, *Pacific, 1897–1909*, 73, 117–18, 148–51, 169–75, 184, 188, 226; Braisted, *The United States Navy in the Pacific, 1909–1922* (Austin, Tex., 1971), 7; Challener, *Admirals*, 34, 215, 227–32; Hagan, *This People's Navy*, 233.

122. The first in what would be a long succession of these had in fact already begun to take shape (in response to the changed conditions brought about by the Russo-Japanese War). But now study of the problem, particularly by the General Board of the Navy and the Naval War College, intensified.

123. Orange was the code designation for Japan.

124. Edward S. Miller, *War Plan Orange: The U.S. Strategy to Defeat Japan, 1897–1945* (Annapolis, Md., 1991), 13–29, 33, 162; Braisted, *Pacific, 1897–1909*, 193, 195, 199, 212; Challener, *Admirals*, 30–31, 232, 235–36; Hagan, *This People's Navy*, 238–39.

125. Harold Sprout and Margaret Sprout, *The Rise of American Naval Power, 1776–1918* (Princeton, N.J., 1967), 281; Neu, *Uncertain Friendship*, 100–103, 224, 242–43.

126. Braisted, *Pacific, 1897–1909*, 175, 216–223, 238; Miller, *War Plan Orange*, 66–67.

127. Challener, *Admirals*, 248, 253, 260, 263; Braisted, *Pacific, 1897–1909*, 205–6, 224–28; Hagan, *This People's Navy*, 240–41; Sprout and Sprout, *Rise*, 265, 284; Ronald Spector, *Admiral of the New Empire: The Life and Career of George Dewey* (Baton Rouge, La., 1974), 163; Neu, *Uncertain Friendship*, 104–44, 201–36, 258–73, 307–9. For the cruise itself, see James R. Reckner, *Teddy Roosevelt's Great White Fleet* (Annapolis, Md., 1988).

Roosevelt also hoped that the cruise would "arouse popular interest in and enthusiasm for the navy" and thereby facilitate his efforts to get Congress to support an expanded building program. During the first years of his presidency, TR had presided over a steady expansion of the fleet. Ten new battleships were authorized by

Congress within the space of four years. In 1905, the president conceded that the nation could "afford to rest." Roosevelt announced that he would ask henceforth for the construction of only one new battleship per year to prevent the fleet from aging. Developments in Europe (see Chapter 6) and concern about Japan soon led TR to abandon this policy, however. See Sprout and Sprout, *Rise*, 259–69; Neu, *Uncertain Friendship*, 110–12, 129, 211, 237–53; Braisted, *Pacific, 1897–1909*, 180; Spector, *Dewey*, 171–75; Roosevelt to Taft, *LTR*, 5: 762.

128. See Neu, *Uncertain Friendship*, 150–62.

129. Neu, *Uncertain Friendship*, 163–79. Also see Esthus, *Japan*, 170–228, 246–65; Lewis L. Gould, *The Presidency of Theodore Roosevelt* (Lawrence, Kan., 1991), 262.

130. Neu, *Uncertain Friendship*, 180, 207, 254, 272–75.

131. Beasley, *Japanese Imperialism*, 94–99.

132. Yuan Shikai, a former protégé of Li Hongzhang and favorite of the empress dowager who came to head the foreign ministry in this period, and Tang Shaoyi, who was the governor of the southernmost Manchurian province, were especially central.

133. Iriye, *Pacific Estrangement*, 174; Nish, *Japanese Foreign Policy*, 65, 78–81; Hunt, *Special Relationship*, 202–5.

134. Mahan, *Problem of Asia*, 64–74; Knox to Taft, December 19, 1910, PCKP; Neu, *Uncertain Friendship*, 283; Iriye, *Pacific Estrangement*, 169.

135. Raymond A. Esthus, *Theodore Roosevelt and the International Rivalries* (Claremont, Calif., 1970), 139; Neu, *Uncertain Friendship*, 275–82; Esthus, *Japan*, 119–21, 240–42, 265–82.

136. On the occasion of his ill-fated nomination of Charles R. Crane as minister, the new president told his wife that he was "especially anxious to secure ... the investment of American capital" in China. It was "looking in that direction," and was "much more likely to go into investments with a Minister of the standing of Crane, than with one who does not understand anything about it." See Taft to Helen Taft, July 14, 1909, WHTP.

137. Spence, *Search*, 252–53. For the story of the American China Development Company and its concession, see William R. Braisted, "The United States and the American China Development Company," *Far Eastern Quarterly* 11 (February 1952): 147–65; En-han Lee, *China's Quest for Railway Autonomy, 1904–1911: A Study of the Chinese Railway Rights Recovery Movement* (Singapore, 1977), 51–78; Hunt, *Special Relationship*, 149–51, 277–78; Daniel H. Bays, *China Enters the Twentieth Century: Chang Chih-tung and the Issues of a New Age, 1895–1909* (Ann Arbor, Mich., 1978), 167–74. Also see Roosevelt to Morgan, July 18, 1905, *LTR*, 4: 1278–79.

138. Rockhill to Department, March 10, 1909, SDNF 5315; Rockhill to Department, March 13, 1909, SDNF 5315; Knox to American Legation, Peking, March 19, 1909, SDNF 5315; Knox to American Legation, Peking, May 3, 1909, SDNF, 5315; Walter V. Scholes and Marie V. Scholes, *The Foreign Policies of the Taft Administration* (Columbia, Mo., 1970), 127–29; Charles Vevier, *The United States and China, 1906–1913* (New Brunswick, N.J., 1955), 96–98.

139. "The failure of the United States to execute its part in the Hankow-Canton railway concession becomes more and more important as we see the European powers seizing the opportunity which was once entirely and exclusively in the hands of American capitalists," reported Third Assistant Secretary William Phillips. See Phillips to Knox, May 13, 1909, SDNF 5315.

140. Phillips to Knox, May 21, 1909, SDNF 5315; Knox to American Legation, Peking, May 24, 1909, SDNF 5315; Knox to American Embassy, London, June 2, 1909, SDNF 5315. "American capital," the ambassador to England was told, "is interested in this western line to such an extent that it would be glad to cooperate with the British interests in accordance with the understanding of 1904."

141. The interested parties gave their most telling response by quickly concluding their preliminary agreement. See Rockhill to Department, June 1, 1909, SDNF 5315; Reid to Department, June 8, 1909, SDNF 5315; Fletcher to Department, June 7, 1909, SDNF 5315.

142. Knox to American Embassies in London, Paris, and Berlin, June 9, 1909, SDNF 5315

143. Included was the threat that the rest of the Boxer indemnity might not be returned in any form.

144. *FR 1909*, 178; Scholes and Scholes, *Foreign Policies*, 136–46; Hunt, *Special Relationship*, 213.

145. On his two diplomatic visits to Tokyo since the Russo-Japanese War, in 1905 and 1907, Taft had been greatly impressed by that country's financial inadequacies. At the same time, during the latter trip, he had been tantalized by Beijing's seeming enthusiasm to get the U.S. involved in Manchuria. See Braisted, *Pacific, 1909–1922*, 13, 20; Challener, *Admirals*, 246; Iriye, *Pacific Estrangement*, 198.

146. Neu, *Uncertain Friendship*, 260–62; Esthus, *Japan*, 230–40; Scholes and Scholes, *Foreign Policies*, 14–17, 116–20.

147. Japan had already obtained the right to rebuild and operate the Antung-to-Mukden line, but now it was also formally given a status similar to that of the S.M.R.

148. Scholes and Scholes, *Foreign Policies*, 148–49; E. Carleton Baker, "Regarding Recent Chinese-Japanese Agreements Respecting Manchuria," memorandum dated October 7, 1909, PCKP.

149. Scholes and Scholes, *Foreign Policies*, 151–55; Vevier, *United States and China*, 117–31; Herbert Croly, *Willard Straight* (New York, 1925), 295–300.

150. Knox to Phillips, October 6, 1909, PCKP; Alvey Adee, "Memorandum of Interview," October 7, 1909, PCKP.

151. Knox to Hoyt, October 8, 1909, PCKP.

152. *FR 1910*, 234–35.

153. Some weeks later, Huntington Wilson made the connection with the Hukuang project explicit in a letter sent to Elbert Baldwin, the editor of the *Outlook.* "It is impossible not to see," he wrote, "that arrangements like the Hukuang loan, where Great Britain, France, Germany and the United States join in acquiring an interest in a great railway system in China, such interests including the possible hypothecation of Chinese revenues, is an arrangement in direct opposition to the dangerous principle of 'spheres of influence.' Its commercial advantages in the supplying of railway materials, etc., and its general political advantages in increasing prestige are too obvious to touch upon. The Manchurian neutralization plan is an application of the same principle in a case of more urgent need and upon a vast scale. If accepted in its entirety it will substitute real for nominal Chinese sovereignty in those provinces, and if accepted in part only will ensure the neutrality of the regime concerned." Huntington Wilson to Baldwin, January 19, 1910, HWP.

154. Grey to Reid, November 25, 1909, *FR 1910*, 235–36.

155. Scholes and Scholes, *Foreign Policies*, 159 164–68.

156. Division of Information, "Commercial Neutralization of the Railways of Manchuria," January 6, 1910, PCKP; *FR 1910*, 234–35, 248–52.

157. Frustrated in Beijing, Straight proceeded to St. Petersburg in late spring only to find Foreign Secretary Alexander Izvolsky immovable. See *FR 1910*, 255–57; Division of Far Eastern Affairs, "Memorandum on the Chinchow-Aigun Railway Project," February 10, 1910, PCKP; Division of Far Eastern Affairs, memorandum dated March 31, 1910, PCKP; Croly, *Straight*, 326–28.

158. Huntington Wilson to Knox, July 15, 1910, HWP; Huntington Wilson to Knox, July 27, 1910, PCKP; Ransford Miller, memorandum dated July 22, 1910, PCKP.

159. Ransford Miller, memorandum dated July 14, 1910, PCKP.

160. Taft to Knox, September 1, 1910, WHTP; Huntington Wilson, undated memorandum, HWP; Huntington Wilson to Knox, August 12, 1910, HWP; Knox to Huntington Wilson, August 16, 1910, HWP.

161. Scholes and Scholes, *Foreign Policies*, 180–83.

162. Huntington Wilson to Knox, July 15, 1910, HWP. On American efforts to bring about currency reform in China in the early twentieth century, see Emily S. Rosenberg, "Foundations of United States International Financial Power: Gold Standard Diplomacy, 1900–1905," *Business History Review* 59 (Summer 1985): 184, 189–92; Carl P. Parrini and Martin J. Sklar, "New Thinking About the Market, 1896–1904: Some American Economists on Investment and the Theory of Surplus Capital," *Journal of Economic History* 43 (September 1983): 573–77.

163. Braisted, *Pacific, 1909–1922*, 77–93; Challener, *Admirals*, 271.

164. Vevier, *United States and China*, 173–75; Scholes and Scholes, *Foreign Policies*, 192–93.

165. Calhoun to Knox, September 22, 1910, SDDF 893.51; Huntington Wilson to Knox, September 26, 1910 (with accompanying memorandum of September 24, 1910), SDDF 893.51; Group to Knox, September 27, 1910, SDDF 893.51; Knox to Calhoun, September 29, 1910, SDDF 893.51. For background on Jenks, including efforts to bring about currency reform in China, see Parrini and Sklar, "New Thinking," 562, 571–77; Rosenberg, "Foundations," 190–92; Hunt, *Special Relationship*, 390n17.

166. Calhoun to Knox, October 2, 1910, SDDF 893.51; Calhoun to Knox, October 27, 1910, SDDF 893.51. Members of the Group were now optimistic that their relationship to affairs in China was returning to a profitable track. See Vanderlip to Stillman, September 28, 1910, FVP; Vanderlip to Stillman, October 7, 1910, FVP.

167. Morgan and Company to Morgan, Grenfell, and Company, October 3, 1910, SDDF 893.51.

168. Vanderlip reveled in the position that he felt the American Group had attained. See Vanderlip to Stillman, October 7, 1910, FVP.

169. Such involvement, a department memorandum noted, "in loans where Chinese national or provincial revenues are pledged as security is in harmony with the policy of the Department and moreover such participation would tend to insure the cooperation of the other Powers so essential to the success of the plans of the Chinese Government for currency reform." Knox to Calhoun, October 6, 1910, SDDF 893.51.

170. Knox to American Embassy, Paris, November 30, 1910, SDDF 893.51; Knox to American Legation, Peking, November 25, 1910, SDDF 893.51.

171. *FR 1912*, 95–96; Scholes and Scholes, *Foreign Policies*, 201–10.

172. "Chinese Railway and Currency Loans," undated memorandum, PCKP. Also see Miller to Knox, June 19, 1911, PCKP; Vevier, *United States and China*, 187–88.

173. At the end of 1910, Roosevelt had finally broken his silence over the determination of his successor's administration to include those provinces in its China campaign. Since TR's return from Africa the previous spring, many issues of personality, method, and policy had come to upset his once close relations with Taft. On this topic, Roosevelt wrote the president that the vital interest of the U.S. was to "keep the Japanese out of our country" and at the same time preserve Tokyo's goodwill. It was therefore wise not to make Japan in any way feel challenged in an area that it felt was so important. The Taft administration was nevertheless intent on continuing its efforts. It rejected the idea that Washington was threatening any legitimate Japanese interests. At worst, the U.S. might fail in the short run to achieve its objectives. But in the future, argued Knox, it might be prepared to take a more forceful approach in the region, and it should not prejudice its case beforehand by

abandoning its position. See Roosevelt to Taft, December 8, 1910, *LTR*, 7: 180–81; Roosevelt to Taft, December 22, 1910, *LTR.*, 7: 189–91; Knox to Taft, December 19, 1910, PCKP.

174. Division of Far Eastern Affairs, memorandum dated May 16, 1911, PCKP; *FR 1912*, 96; Scholes and Scholes, *Foreign Policies*, 212–13, 218–20, 227–38.

175. Early in 1912, William J. Calhoun, the U.S. minister, commented on what had happened. "The tendency," he wrote, "seems to be for the English and Japanese to work together, and the intimacy between the French and Russians is marked. These combinations are, for many reasons, to be expected, but they leave the Germans and the Americans very much to themselves." It was likely, he concluded, that "for some time to come," American influence would be obstructed "in every way possible." *FR 1912*, 64–65.

176. Spence, *Search*, 253–65; Chesneaux et al., *1911 Revolution*, 369–77.

177. Scholes and Scholes, *Foreign Policies*, 221–26; Vevier, *United States and China*, 200; Hunt, *Special Relationship*, 216; Lowe, *Britain in the Far East*, 86–87; Braisted, *Pacific, 1909–1922*, 103, 109. On Japan, see Beasley, *Japanese Imperialism*, 105.

178. Daniel M. Crane and Thomas A. Breslin, *An Ordinary Relationship: American Opposition to Republican Revolution in China* (Miami, 1986), 37–41, 47–51; Hunt, *Special Relationship*, 271; Braisted, *Pacific, 1909–1922*, 107, 111; Lowe, *Britain in the Far East*, 88.

179. Spence, *Search*, 266–68, 277. Yuan had betrayed the reformers of 1898 in order to solidify his position with Cixi. Since her death he had been out of favor.

180. Crane and Breslin, *Ordinary Relationship*, 110–22; Scholes and Scholes, *Foreign Policies*, 226, 239–40; Lowe, *Britain in the Far East*, 91; Braisted, *Pacific, 1909–1922*, 117; James Reed, *The Missionary Mind and American East Asia Policy, 1911–1915* (Cambridge, Mass., 1983), 115–40.

181. The Chinese were "like children" in financial matters, opined the American minister. See Knox address in Cincinnati, Ohio, October 1916, PCKP; Vevier, *United States and China*, 202–11; Herbert Feis, *Europe the World's Banker, 1870–1914: An Account of European Foreign Investment and the Connection of World Finance with Diplomacy Before World War I* (New York, 1965), 442–49; Hunt, *Special Relationship*, 216; Scholes and Scholes, *Foreign Policies*, 239–46, Crane and Breslin, *Ordinary Relationship*, 71–73, 78.

182. Crane and Breslin, *Ordinary Relationship*, 64–65.

183. Crane and Breslin, *Ordinary Relationship*, 71–82.

184. Efforts to do the latter are detailed in Scholes and Scholes, *Foreign Policies*, 232–46.

185. Crane and Breslin, *Ordinary Relationship*, 86–107; Warren I. Cohen, *The Chinese Connection: Roger S. Greene, Thomas W. Lamont, George E. Sokolsky, and American-East Asian Relations* (New York, 1978), 46–47; "Message to Democratic Rallies," November 2, 1912, *PWW*, 25: 502–3.

186. See, for example, "A Speech Accepting the Democratic Nomination in Sea Girt, N.J.," August 7, 1912, *PWW*, 25: 3–18.

187. "A News Report of an Address in Philadelphia to the Universal Peace Union," February 19, 1912, *PWW*, 24: 181–83; "A Message to Democratic Rallies," November 2, 1912, *PWW*, 25: 502–3.

188. See, for instance, Josephus Daniels, *The Cabinet Diaries of Josephus Daniels, 1913–1921*, ed. E. David Cronon (Lincoln, Neb., 1963), 7–8.

189. Wilson to Charles William Eliot, January 20, 1913, *PWW*, 27: 65.

190. While he was the president of Princeton, that institution had supported the work of the Y.M.C.A. in China and the policy of bringing students to the United States with the surplus from the Boxer indemnity. See Roy W. Curry, *Woodrow Wilson and Far Eastern Policy, 1913–1921* (New York, 1957), 15; Crane and Breslin, *Ordinary Relationship*, 43–45, 57–61, 110–21; Reed, *Missionary Mind*, 140–43.

191. "A Statement on the Pending Chinese Loan," March 18, 1913, *PWW*, 27: 192–94.

192. Daniels, *Cabinet Diaries*, 17–18. There were also critics, such as Straight and Huntington Wilson. See Curry, *Far Eastern Policy*, 24–25; Crane and Breslin, *Ordinary Relationship*, 108; Cohen, *Chinese Connection*, 47; Huntington Wilson to Wilson, March 19, 1913, *PWW*, 27: 195–97.

193. Daniels, *Cabinet Diaries*, 19–21, 23, 25–26; Curry, *Far Eastern Policy*, 29–30.

194. Curry, *Far Eastern Policy*, 36–38; Noel H. Pugach, *Paul S. Reinsch: Open Door Diplomat in Action* (New York, 1979), 3–63; In 1900, he had published *World Politics at the End of the Nineteenth Century as Influenced by the Oriental Situation* (New York), in which he had chronicled the intensification of great power international competition in the late-nineteenth century and emphasized what he saw as the global significance of China's fate. This was followed in 1911 by a survey of contemporary *Intellectual and Political Currents in the Far East* (Boston).

195. Daniels, *Cabinet Diaries*, 17, 23; Curry, *Far Eastern Policy*, 26; Key Ray Chong, *Americans and Chinese Reform and Revolution, 1898–1922: The Role of Private Citizens in Diplomacy* (Lanham, Md., 1984), 156.

196. Spence, *Search*, 279–84; Curry, *Far Eastern Policy*, 32–34; Crane and Breslin, *Ordinary Relationship*, 106, 128–34.

197. Crane and Breslin, *Ordinary Relationship*, 127–28, 130–34. Also see Chong, *Reform and Revolution*, 172.

198. Crane and Breslin, *Ordinary Relationship* 136–55; Hunt, *Special Relationship*, 219–20; Pugach, *Reinsch*, 89–107, 125–27.

199. These included the Mariana, Caroline, and Marshall Islands. See Nish, *Japanese Foreign Policy*, 93–96; Beasley, *Japanese Imperialism*, 109–10, 116; Lowe, *Britain in the Far East*, 100–102. Tokyo declared war on August 23, 1914.

200. Nish, *Japanese Foreign Policy*, 96–99; Beasley, *Japanese Imperialism*, 112–14.

201. Pugach, *Reinsch*, 143–52; Burton F. Beers, *Vain Endeavor: Robert Lansing's Attempts to End the American-Japanese Rivalry* (Durham, N.C., 1962), 37; "From the Diary of Colonel House," January 25, 1915, *PWW*, 32: 120.

202. Lansing also hoped that Tokyo might agree to refrain from protesting legislation in California that was designed to prohibit landholding there by Japanese immigrants. Immigration had again begun to smolder as a problem in Japanese-American relations, and this in fact was another reason why the State Department counselor was attracted to something along the lines of a Rooseveltian approach toward northeast China. Between the British dominions, where such sentiment had also spread, and the U.S., much of the Pacific rim had now been closed off to East Asian immigration. Lansing's belief was that stable relations required there to be somewhere for Japan to expand demographically. See Beers, *Vain Endeavor*, 39–41. On Britain's Pacific dominions and East Asian immigration, see Avner Offer, *The First World War: An Agrarian Interpretation* (Oxford, 1991), 164–214.

203. For the text, see *FR 1915*, 105–11.

204. Pugach, *Reinsch*, 152–55; Beers, *Vain Endeavor*, 45; Hunt, *Special Relationship*, 223; Lloyd C. Gardner, *Safe for Democracy: The Anglo-American Response to Revolution, 1913–1923* (New York, 1984), 83.

205. Bryan to Guthrie, May 11, 1915, *FR 1915*, 146; Wilson to Bryan, May 10, 1915, *PWW*, 33: 140–41; Nish, *Japanese Foreign Policy*, 99–103; Beasley, *Japanese Imperialism*, 114–15; Curry, *Far Eastern Policy*, 122–27; Beers, *Vain Endeavor*, 45–47; Pugach, *Reinsch*, 156.

206. Nish, *Japanese Foreign Policy*, 92; Lowe, *Britain in the Far East*, 92–97; Curry, *Far Eastern Policy*, 154.

207. Reinsch to Wilson, July 25, 1915, *PWW*, 34: 25–26.

208. Pugach, *Reinsch*, 165–75; Beers, *Vain Endeavor*, 72–74.

209. The Chicago bankers backed away from their commitment; the A.I.C. lost interest in its railways. It accepted a Japanese offer to cooperate in the Huai River scheme. In the end, the whole operation was abandoned. Pugach, *Reinsch*, 175–214; Beers, *Vain Endeavor*, 74–92; Crane and Breslin, *Ordinary Relationship*, 146–57. Also see Reinsch's comments on Chinese political reform in his 1911 book *Intellectual and Political Currents*, 269–71.

210. In particular, he suggested a revival of the Chin-Ai project.

211. At the time, the government was led by Li Yuanhong, Yuan's vice-president, and Premier Duan Qirui, who had served under Yuan in the army. See Reinsch to Wilson, January 10, 1917, *PWW*, 40: 436–38; Pugach, *Reinsch*, 214–28; Beers, *Vain Endeavor*, 93–94.

212. Wilson to Lansing, February 9, 1917, *PWW*, 41: 175–79; Pugach, *Reinsch*, 229–35; Beers, *Vain Endeavor*, 97–99.

213. Nish, *Japanese Foreign Policy*, 106–15; Beasley, *Japanese Imperialism*, 117, 163; Beers, *Vain Endeavor*, 79–80, 108, 111–12; Braisted, *Pacific, 1909–1922*, 188–208.

214. For the text, see *FR 1917*, 264–65; Nish, *Japanese Foreign Policy*, 115–18; Beasley, *Japanese Imperialism*, 163–64; Beers, *Vain Endeavor*, 100–116.

215. Beers, *Vain Endeavor*, 86–89, 134–42.

Chapter 5. The Home Continent: Canada and Mexico

1. For background here a good starting point is William G. Robbins, *Colony and Empire: The Capitalist Transformation of the American West* (Lawrence, Kan., 1994).

2. Roosevelt to James Creelman, March 7, 1908, *LTR*, 6: 963–64.

3. Miles, however, was not advocating war. See C. P. Stacey, *Canada and the Age of Conflict: A History of Canadian External Policies*, 2 vols. (Toronto, 1977), 1: 49–51.

4. Here see Robert Craig Brown, *Canada's National Policy, 1883–1900: A Study in Canadian-American Relations* (Princeton, N.J., 1964). Also see J. L. Granatstein and Norman Hillmer, *For Better or Worse: Canada and the United States to the 1990s* (Toronto, 1991), 1–34; John Herd Thompson and Stephen J. Randall, *Canada and the United States: Ambivalent Allies* (Athens, Ga., 1994), 1–65.

5. Aaron L. Friedberg, *The Weary Titan: Britain and the Experience of Relative Decline, 1895–1905* (Princeton, N.J.,1988), 163–64; Paul Kennedy, *The Realities Behind Diplomacy: Background Influences on British External Policy, 1865–1980* (Glasgow, 1981), 107–9.

6. Bradford Perkins, *The Great Rapprochement: England and the United States, 1895–1914* (New York, 1968), 26–29. Pauncefote is quoted on p. 28.

7. Perkins, *Great Rapprochement*, 59, 33–47; Charles S. Campbell, Jr., *Anglo-American Understanding, 1898–1903* (Baltimore, 1957), 56–57; Brown, *Canada's National Policy*, 323–51.

8. For the sealing controversy, up to 1898, see Brown, *Canada's National Policy*, 42–54, 92–124, 328–35, 373–78; for the fisheries controversy, to 1898, see 3–6, 13–41, 54–90, 361–66, 404.

9. This topic is treated extensively in Stacey, *Age of Conflict*, 86–97; Campbell, *Anglo-American Understanding*, 65–76, 102–19, 134–50, 188–92, 225–28, 240–44, 256–59, 263–64, 301–45; Norman Penlington, *The Alaska Boundary Dispute: A Critical Reappraisal* (Toronto, 1972); Brown, *Canada's National Policy*, 281–322, 378–401, 408–9.

10. Quoted in Calvin DeArmond Davis, *The United States and the Second Hague Peace Conference: American Diplomacy and International Organization, 1899–1914* (Durham, N.C., 1975), 64–65.

11. See Brown, *Canada's National Policy*, 385.

12. Seward had in fact quite frankly stated this as one of his objectives in pushing

for the acquisition of Alaska. See Gordon T. Stewart, *The American Response to Canada Since 1776* (East Lansing, Mich., 1992), 76–77.

13. Brown, *Canada's National Policy*, 389.

14. One of these provided for the creation of a panel of seven jurists, three from each side, with the last to be chosen by those six. Dyea and Skagway, meanwhile, would be explicitly reserved to the U.S. Ottawa objected that the same treatment ought to be applied to Pyramid Harbor, or, failing that, no such reservation should be made for either party. This, however, was unacceptable to the United States. The second proposal, floated in July, provided for Canada to receive a long-term lease to harbor facilities on the Lynn Canal and the right to link these up with the Yukon by rail. This would in no way be a Canadian port, however, and on those grounds Canada again demurred. For domestic political reasons, such provisions were also unacceptable south of the border. See Hay to Cushman Davis, August 4, 1899, JHP.

15. See Penlington, *Alaska Boundary Dispute*, 45.

16. In 1901 the Laurier government once again rejected reference of the issue to a tribunal composed of an equal number of members from each side.

17. The historian Charles S. Campbell, Jr. has suggested that, in addition to the pressure he felt from London, the prime minister worried that further delay over Alaska might permanently jeopardize other Canadian interests. He was particularly concerned that Washington might conclude agreements with Newfoundland (a self-governing colony still separate from the confederation) that would undermine the dominion's bargaining position on other issues (a United States-Newfoundland reciprocity treaty was signed in November 1902, but it ultimately failed of American ratification). Other historians have suggested that Laurier had begun to fear unilateral American action, especially if gold was discovered in any of the territory that was in dispute. A quick settlement of the controversy would avoid the dangers inherent in such a situation. See Campbell, *Anglo-American Understanding*, 259–64; Penlington, *Alaska Boundary Dispute*, 54–65.

18. Quoted in Penlington, *Alaska Boundary Dispute*, 47.

19. Theodore Roosevelt, *American Ideals and Other Essays* (New York,1897), 235.

20. Here see Granatstein and Hillmer, *For Better or Worse*, 22; Stewart, *American Response*, 61–95.

21. Brown, *Canada's National Policy*, 252–54; Thompson and Randall, *Canada and the United States*, 61–62.

22. Roosevelt to Wilson, July 12, 1899, *LTR*, 2: 1032.

23. Sir Michael Herbert was Pauncefote's successor.

24. Campbell, *Anglo-American Understanding*, 301–3; Howard K. Beale, *Theodore Roosevelt and the Rise of America to World Power* (Baltimore, 1984), 110–17.

25. Campbell, *Anglo-American Understanding*, 310–20; Penlington, *Alaska Boundary Dispute*, 70–81; Stacey, *Age of Conflict*,1: 95–96.

26. Beale, *Theodore Roosevelt*, 130; Penlington, *Alaska Boundary Dispute*, 88–89; Campbell, *Anglo-American Understanding*, 326.

27. Penlington, *Alaska Boundary Dispute*, 89–90; Campbell, *Anglo-American Understanding*, 326–28.

28. Quoted in Beale, *Theodore Roosevelt*, 127–28.

29. Penlington, *Alaska Boundary Dispute*, 90–120; Campbell, *Anglo-American Understanding*, 328–45; Stacey, *Age of Conflict*, 1: 96–100. Also see Thompson and Randall, *Canada and the United States*, 66–69; Granatstein and Hillmer, *For Better or Worse*, 30–34.

30. Penlington, *Alaska Boundary Dispute*, 66.

31. Kenneth Bourne, *Britain and the Balance of Power in North America, 1815–1908* (Berkeley, Calif., 1967), 313–51, 361–412; Friedberg, *Weary Titan*, 162–65, 169–74, 184–99.

32. Samuel F. Wells, Jr., "British Strategic Withdrawal from the Western Hemisphere, 1904–1906," *Canadian Historical Review* 49 (December 1968): 335–56; Stacey, *Age of Conflict*, 1: 125–26; Paul M. Kennedy, *The Rise and Fall of British Naval Mastery* (London, 1986), 208–12.

33. Excerpted at length in Bourne, *Balance of Power*, see pp. 380–83.

34. Alvin C. Gluek, Jr., "Pilgrimages to Ottawa: Canadian-American Diplomacy, 1903–13," Canadian Historical Association *Historical Papers* (1968): 65–75. The quotation is from James Bryce; see p. 1.

35. Gluek, "Pilgrimages," 75–83; Peter Neary, "Grey, Bryce, and the Settlement of Canadian-American Differences, 1905–1911," *Canadian Historical Review* 49 (December 1968): 357–80.

36. Philip C. Jessup, *Elihu Root*, 2 vols. (New York, 1938), 2: 88–89; Gluek, "Pilgrimages," 77–78.

37. "[I] speak the sentiment of millions of my own countrymen," he said, "in saying that we look upon the great material and spiritual progress of Canada with no feelings of jealousy, but with admiration, with hope, and with gratification." See Elihu Root, *Miscellaneous Addresses of Elihu Root*, ed. Robert Bacon and James Brown Scott (Cambridge, Mass., 1917), 157–61.

38. Jessup, *Root*, 2: 99.

39. Neary, "Settlement," 364. For their agenda, see Stacey, *Age of Conflict*, 1: 103–6.

40. See Thompson and Randall, *Canada and the United States*, 72.

41. Neary, "Settlement," 371. This agreement soon broke down, however, because of political opposition from affected interests in the United States. See Kurk Dorsey, "Scientists, Citizens, and Statesmen: U.S.-Canadian Wildlife Protection Treaties in the Progressive Era," *Diplomatic History* 19 (Summer 1995): 414–15.

42. Stacey, *Age of Conflict*, 1: 107–8; Thompson and Randall, *Canada and the United States*, 72–74.

43. Thompson and Randall, *Canada and the United States*, 74–76; Stacey, *Age of Conflict*, 1: 108–13; Granatstein and Hillmer, *For Better or Worse*, 40–42.

44. See Alvin C. Gluek, Jr., "Programmed Diplomacy: The Settlement of the North Atlantic Fisheries Question, 1907–1912," *Acadiensis* 6 (1976): 43–70.

45. Neary, "Settlement," 377–79; Dorsey, "Scientists," 416–22.

46. Quoted in Stacey, *Age of Conflict*, 1: 110–11.

47. For what follows, I have relied heavily on the discussions in Stacey, *Age of Conflict*, 113–17 and Charles E. Neu, *Uncertain Friendship: Theodore Roosevelt and Japan, 1906–1909* (Cambridge, Mass., 1967), 183–210.

48. Jessup, *Root*, 2: 89.

49. Quoted in Neu, *Uncertain Friendship*, 185–86.

50. See Stacey, *Age of Conflict*, 1: 115; also see Neu, *Uncertain Friendship*, 195–97.

51. Neu, *Uncertain Friendship*, 201–2.

52. Neu, *Uncertain Friendship*, 199, 207–8.

53. Alvin C. Gluek, "The Invisible Revision of the Rush-Bagot Agreement, 1898–1914," *Canadian Historical Review* 60 (December 1979): 466–84; Granatstein and Hillmer, *For Better or Worse*, 43–45; Thompson and Randall, *Canada and the United States*, 76–77.

54. Donald F. Warner, *The Idea of Continental Union: Agitation for the Annexation of Canada to the United States, 1849–1893* (Lexington, Ky., 1960), 9–32; John Bartlet Brebner, *North Atlantic Triangle: The Interplay of Canada, the United States, and Great Britain* (New Haven, Conn.,1945), 148–56; Orville John McDiarmid, *Commercial Policy in the Canadian Economy* (Cambridge, Mass., 1946), 67–71; Donald Creighton, *A History of Canada: Dominion of the North* (Boston, 1958), 256–68.

55. This despite rising sectional tensions in the U.S. Southern Democrats were won over by promises that a reciprocity treaty was the surest means of blocking

political union, while Northern politicians were drawn to Elgin's promises providing for extended American use of the fisheries and unrestricted navigation of the St. Lawrence system.

56. Brebner, *North Atlantic Triangle*, 156–64; Warner, *Continental Union*, 33–40; Lawrence H. Officer and Lawrence B. Smith, "The Canadian-American Reciprocity Treaty of 1855 to 1866, " *Journal of Economic History* 28 (1968): 598–623; Thompson and Randall, *Canada and the United States*, 32–37; Stewart, *American Response*, 49–71.

57. Warner, *Continental Union*, 40–42, 63–64, 71–72, 91–93, 151–60, 166, 179–89, 212–15, 220–26; McDiarmid, *Commercial Policy*, 131–35, 161, 167–74; Stacey, *Age of Conflict*, 1: 32–34; Stewart, *American Response*, 78–85.

58. Peter B. Waite, *Canada, 1874–1896: Arduous Destiny* (Toronto, 1971), 74–199, 240, 272–74; Brown, *Canada's National Policy*, 267–80, 350–51; Creighton, *History of Canada*, 345–94; Robert Craig Brown and Ramsay Cook, *Canada, 1896–1921: A Nation Transformed* (Toronto, 1974), 18–21; McDiarmid, *Commercial Policy*, 74–83, 155–79, 203–9; Stacey, *Age of Conflict*, 1: 89.

59. Some of the issues discussed here are developed at greater length in Robert E. Hannigan, "Reciprocity 1911: Continentalism and American Weltpolitik," *Diplomatic History* 4 (Winter 1980): 1–18. Also see Hannigan, "Continentalism and *Mitteleuropa* as Points of Departure for a Comparison of American and German Foreign Relations in the Early Twentieth Century," in *Confrontation and Cooperation: Germany and the United States in the Era of World War I, 1900–1924*, ed. Hans-Jürgen Schröder (Providence, R.I., 1993).

60. After 1905 the share of America's exports of such goods taken by its neighbors closely rivaled that sent to Europe (roughly 33 percent). Canada constituted the most lucrative of these markets. In 1909 the U.S. sent $207 million of merchandise (all categories) across the border, a figure more than double that of second place England and equivalent to almost 60 percent of Canada's import total. U.S. Department of Commerce, *American Manufactures in Foreign Markets*, Miscellaneous Series no. 11, 1913, 1–12; *CR 1909*, 418–19.

61. This played into concerns about conservation in this period as well.

62. Huntington-Wilson to Julius Kahn, July 6, 1911, HWP; Emory R. Johnson et al., *History of the Domestic and Foreign Commerce of the United States*, 2 vols. (New York, 1915), 2: 86–88; William C. Schluter, *The Pre-War Business Cycle, 1907–1914* (New York, 1923), 50; Stewart, *American Response*, 105; Dorsey, "Scientists," 407–8. On the connection with conservation, see especially Samuel P. Hays, *Conservation and the Gospel of Efficiency: The Progressive Conservation Movement, 1890–1920* (New York, 1974), 31, 122–48, 171. On Taft and conservation, see also Paolo E. Coletta, *The Presidency of William Howard Taft* (Lawrence, Kan., 1973), 80. Woodrow Wilson expressed similar concerns about the consumption of raw materials and foodstuffs, see Chapter 3.

63. Harold U. Faulkner, *The Decline of Laissez-Faire, 1897–1917* (New York, 1951), 73–75; Mira Wilkins, *The Emergence of Multinational Enterprise: American Business Abroad from the Colonial Era to 1914* (Cambridge, Mass., 1970), 113–76. In the case of Canada, there was also significant investment in branch plants of American companies. In addition to the above, see Thompson and Randall, *Canada and the United States*, 57–58, 81–82; Robert Bothwell, *Canada and the United States: The Politics of Partnership* (New York, 1992), 7, 11–12.

64. For Canada, see the tables presented in John Ball Osborne, "Commercial Relations of the United States with Canada," *Annals of the American Academy of Political and Social Science* 32 (1908): 330–42.

65. The reciprocity agreement was a "great step toward commercial union with Canada," wrote Taft to Sereno Payne on January 26, 1911, WHTP.

66. Osborne, "Commercial Relations," 330–42.

67. British industry presumably would be ensured of dominance of empire

markets and would control a more substantial base from which to meet its challengers. See Bernard Semmell, *Imperialism and Social Reform: English Social-Imperial Thought, 1895–1914* (Garden City, N.Y., 1968), 74–117, 150–56; Robert J. Scally, *The Origins of the Lloyd George Coalition: The Politics of Social Imperialism, 1900–1918* (Princeton, N.J., 1975), 96–145; Friedberg, *Weary Titan*, 21–134.

There were seen to be other implications as well. On his return from a trip to Canada in 1908, geopolitician and tariff reformer Halford Mackinder argued for British tariff changes that might halt Canada's growing involvement with its southern neighbor's economy, an involvement he feared would inevitably have political ramifications. "Canada," he argued, "was essential to the Empire. If all North America were a single Power, Britain would, indeed, be dwarfed. That great North American Power would, of necessity, take from us the command of the ocean." On the other hand, as he saw it, imperial preferences would promote imperial political consolidation. See W. H. Parker, *Mackinder: Geography as an Aid to Statecraft* (Oxford, 1982), 40, 68, 71. By contrast, Sir John Fisher, Britain's first sea lord, became an advocate of Canadian-American reciprocity, seeing it as a step toward closer relations between the British Empire and the U.S. In awe of America's rising power, Fisher saw a "great English-speaking [political] Federation," as the best way for Britain to ensure itself of a prominent position in the twentieth-century world. See Avner Offer, *The First World War: An Agrarian Interpretation* (Oxford, 1991), 253–54.

68. U.S. Consul Albert Halstead reported from Birmingham in 1907 that the Liberal Party was still strong, but "in the near future the American people will have to face the possibility, and even probability, of their best market being curtailed by the conversion of the United Kingdom into a tariff levying nation." Halstead to Department, November 21, 1907, SDNF.

69. Root to James H. Wilson, April 3, 1907, ERP.

70. Charles M. Pepper, "The Open Door to Canada," undated, PCKP; Taft to Pepper, July 12, 1909, WHTP.

71. "Memorandum Respecting the Tariff Act of the United States, Approved Aug. 5, 1909," PCKP. See also Frank W. Taussig, *The Tariff History of the United States* (New York, 1923), 403–4; Percy Bidwell, *The Tariff Policy of the United States* (New York, 1933), 49–50.

72. L. Ethan Ellis, *Reciprocity 1911: A Study in Canadian-American Relations* (New Haven, Conn., 1939), 7, 15, 35–36; McDiarmid, *Commercial Policy*, 220–24; Stacey, *Age of Conflict*, 1: 83–84.

73. Ellis, *Reciprocity*, 36–40.

74. Taft to Helen Taft, March 19, 1910, WHTP.

75. Ellis, *Reciprocity*, 44–45.

76. Davis and Pepper to Knox, May 24, 1910, PCKP; Davis and Pepper to Huntington-Wilson, May 24, 1910, PCKP; Pepper and Davis, "Trade Relations with Canada, Newfoundland, and Mexico," May 23, 1910, PCKP. The fate of these proposals with regard to Mexico is discussed in Friedrich Katz, *The Secret War in Mexico: Europe, the United States, and the Mexican Revolution* (Chicago, 1983), 80–84, and in Hannigan, "Continentalism and *Mitteleuropa*," 74–75.

77. See, in particular, "Minutes of Reciprocity Conference of January 7, 1911," PCKP. Gordon T. Stewart elaborates on Pepper's role in his *American Response*, 105–17.

78. Ellis, *Reciprocity*, 56. On Canadian opposition, see also note 87 below. The United States obtained reductions on some significant items, including motor vehicles, farm wagons, and agricultural machinery. But the negotiators had hoped to eliminate rates on the last of these and to obtain reductions on a host of other important commodities ranging from boots and shoes to electric motors. See U.S. Congress, Senate, *Canadian Reciprocity*, Sen. doc. 787, 61st Cong., 3d sess., 1911, 4–9;

Mack Davis, "Comments on the Confidential Reciprocity Lists, Free and Dutiable, Submitted by the Canadian Commissioners on January 9, 1911," undated, PCKP.

79. "Summary of Agreement Reached Jan. 16," PCKP; U.S. Congress, Senate, *Canadian Reciprocity*, 4–9.

80. "We have reached a stage in our own development," he asserted, "that calls for a statesmanlike and broad view of our future economic status and its requirements. We have drawn upon our natural resources in such a way as to invite attention to their necessary limit.... We have so increased in population and in our consumption of food products and the other necessities of life, hitherto supplied largely from our own country, that unless we materially increase our production we can see before us a change in our economic position, from that of a country selling to the world food and natural products ... to one consuming and importing them.... A far sighted policy requires that if we can enlarge our supply of natural resources, and especially food products and the necessities of life, without substantial injury to any of our producing and manufacturing classes, we should take steps to do so now." See U.S. Congress, Senate, *Canadian Reciprocity*, v–vi.

81. Taft to Roosevelt, January 10, 1911, WHTP.

82. U.S. Congress, Senate, *Canadian Reciprocity*, vi.

83. Address before the Associated Press and the American Newspaper Publishers Association, New York, April 27, 1911, in James D. Richardson, ed., *A Compilation of the Messages and Papers of the Presidents*, 20 vols. (New York, 1897–1914), 17: 7975.

84. Fielding to Knox, September 29, 1911, PCKP.

85. Ellis, *Reciprocity*, 88–186; Kenneth W. Hechler, *Insurgency: Personalities and Politics of the Taft Era* (New York, 1940), 178–92; Coletta, *Taft*, 143–49.

86. The Liberals had been in power since 1896. In Quebec there was also considerable dissatisfaction with Laurier's defense policy.

87. W. M. Baker, "A Case Study of Anti-Americanism in English-Speaking Canada: The Election Campaign of 1911," *Canadian Historical Review* 51 (1970): 426–49; Brown and Cook, *Canada, 1896–1921*, 180–85; Stacey, *Age of Conflict*, 1: 146–49; Granatstein and Hillmer, *For Better or Worse*, 49–53; Thompson and Randall, *Canada and the United States*, 89–92.

88. With the exception of one provision, enacted separately, designed to secure newsprint and wood pulp for the American publishing industry. Coletta, *Taft*, 151; Donald F. Anderson, *William Howard Taft: A Conservative's Conception of the Presidency* (Ithaca, N.Y., 1973), 221.

89. Quoted in Granatstein and Hillmer, *For Better or Worse*, 54.

90. Thompson and Randall, *Canada and the United States*, 92.

91. Thompson and Randall, *Canada and the United States*, 92.

92. Stacey, *Age of Conflict*, 1: 152–53; Taussig, *Tariff History*, 409–46.

93. Granatstein and Hillmer, *For Better or Worse*, 56–57.

94. Granatstein and Hillmer, *For Better or Worse*, 60; Thompson and Randall, *Canada and the United States*, 94.

95. Pepper and Davis, "Trade Relations with Canada, Newfoundland, and Mexico," May 23, 1910, PCKP.

96. Quoted in Katz, *Secret War*, 22.

97. *CR 1909*, 509–11; Ramón Eduardo Ruíz, *The Great Rebellion: Mexico, 1905–1924* (New York, 1980), 103; Alan Knight, *U.S.-Mexican Relations, 1910–1940: An Interpretation* (San Diego, 1987), 21.

98. For background, see W. Dirk Raat, *Mexico and the United States: Ambivalent Vistas* (Athens, Ga., 1992), 79–91; Lester Langley, *Mexico and the United States: The Fragile Relationship* (Boston, 1991), 7–8; John Mason Hart, *Revolutionary Mexico: The Coming and Process of the Mexican Revolution* (Berkeley, Calif., 1987), 19–162; Josefina Zoraida Vázquez and Lorenzo Meyer, *The United States and Mexico* (Chicago, 1985),

72–92; Karl M. Schmitt, *Mexico and the United States, 1821–1973: Conflict and Coexistence* (New York, 1974), 90–104; Robert Freeman Smith, *The United States and Revolutionary Nationalism in Mexico, 1916–1932* (Chicago, 1972); James D. Cockroft, "Social and Economic Structure of the Porfiriato: Mexico, 1877–1911," in Cockroft, André Gunder Frank, and Dale L. Johnson, *Dependence and Underdevelopment: Latin America's Political Economy* (New York 1972), 47–70.

99. Jessup, *Root,* 1: 515–16.

100. Katz, *Secret War,* 21–27; Hart, *Revolutionary Mexico,* 247–49.

101. Howard F. Cline, *The United States and Mexico* (New York, 1969), 115–16; Alan Knight, *The Mexican Revolution,* 2 vols. (Lincoln, Neb., 1990), 1: 48. Secretary Root, at the end of his term in office, opined that "when the strong, wise leadership of President Díaz is withdrawn there will be troublous times for Mexico for a period." See Jessup, *Root,* 1: 515.

102. Taft to H. Taft, October 17, 1909, WHTP.

103. On the Madero revolution, see especially Knight, *Mexican Revolution,* 1: 55–201. Also see Alan Knight, "The United States and the Mexican Peasantry, c.1880–1940," in *Rural Revolt in Mexico and U.S. Intervention,* ed. Daniel Nugent (San Diego, 1988), 28, 39–42.

104. P. Edward Haley, *Revolution and Intervention: The Diplomacy of Taft and Wilson in Mexico* (Cambridge, Mass., 1970), 25–26; Richard D. Challener, *Admirals, Generals, and American Foreign Policy, 1898–1914* (Princeton, N.J., 1973), 345.

105. Haley, *Revolution and Intervention,* 25–31; Challener, *Admirals,* 345–50; Walter V. Scholes and Marie V. Scholes, *The Foreign Policies of the Taft Administration* (Columbia, Mo., 1970), 84–88; Peter Calvert, *The Mexican Revolution, 1910–1914: The Diplomacy of Anglo-American Conflict* (Cambridge, 1968), 49–56; Anderson, *Taft,* 266–73; Archie Butt, *Taft and Roosevelt: The Intimate Letters of Archie Butt,* 2 vols. (Port Washington, N.Y., 1930), 2: 602. As it was, the president immediately faced criticism in the press, based on speculation that he had already decided to intervene and to do so without submitting the issue to Congress.

106. Quoted in Haley, *Revolution and Intervention,* 31.

107. Taft to Wood, March 12, 1911, WHTP.

108. Katz, *Secret War,* 39.

109. Ruíz, *Great Rebellion,* 388–90.

110. Knight, *Mexican Revolution,* 1: 201–4.

111. Scholes and Scholes, *Foreign Policies,* 89.

112. Katz, *Secret War,* 40–41; Calvert, *Mexican Revolution,* 61–67, 70–71, 95–100.

113. Knight, *Mexican Revolution,* 1: 248–322, 416–20; Katz, *Secret War,* 44–46; Ruiz, *Great Rebellion,* 139–52; Hart, *Revolutionary Mexico,* 253.

114. Scholes and Scholes, *Foreign Policies,* 90–93; Haley, *Revolution and Intervention,* 32–43; Challener, *Admirals,* 350–52; Calvert, *Mexican Revolution,* 111–13.

115. Knight, *Mexican Revolution,* 1: 322–67, 466–70.

116. See Challener, *Admirals,* 353.

117. Scholes and Scholes, *Foreign Policies,* 95; Haley, *Revolution and Intervention,* 44–49.

118. Haley, *Revolution and Intervention,* 49–50; Anderson, *Taft,* 272–74.

119. Knight, *Mexican Revolution,* 1: 473–77.

120. Knight, *Mexican Revolution,* 1: 477–78; Haley, *Revolution and Intervention,* 53–61; Scholes and Scholes, *Foreign Policies,* 96.

121. Knight, *Mexican Revolution,* 1: 481–90; Scholes and Scholes, *Foreign Policies,* 96–104; Haley, *Revolution and Intervention,* 53–73; Calvert, *Mexican Revolution,* 131–66; Anderson, *Taft,* 274; Kenneth J. Grieb, *The United States and Huerta* (Lincoln, Neb., 1969), 1–38.

122. At the same time, the administration also saw a return to constitutional

order as key to the long-term stabilization of Mexico. This whole approach can best be understood against the backdrop of U.S. Latin American policy as it had been evolving since the turn of the century. Root had lamented what he called "militarism and the condition of continual revolution" in the Caribbean. At the same time, he had, in Rio, praised the oligarchic regimes of South America for replacing the "forcible seizure of power" by "[p]eaceful succession." U.S. policy makers had repeatedly sought to use elections as a means of containing disorder and achieving such "peaceful succession" in the Caribbean. And the Wilson administration would do the same, for instance, in the case of the Dominican Republic.

In 1911 the Taft administration had indicated that this was the approach it would take in Mexico as well, if it felt compelled to occupy that country. But it was extremely anxious to promote stability without that action. For this reason, it seems likely that Taft, had he remained president, would eventually have recognized Huerta. See Elihu Root, *Addresses on Government and Citizenship by Elihu Root*, ed. Robert Bacon and James Brown Scott (Cambridge, Mass., 1917), 13–14; Root, *Latin America and the United States: Addresses by Elihu Root*, ed. Bacon and Scott (Cambridge, Mass., 1917), 7; Anderson, *Taft*, 274–75; Grieb, *United States and Huerta*, 36–37.

On coming to office, however, Wilson was presented with a vigorous critique of the logic of extending recognition to regimes that came to power by revolution. Professor Jacob H. Hollander of Johns Hopkins University, who had long experience in U.S.-Dominican affairs, argued that the effect was not only to countenance but reward political violence and upheaval." See Wilson to Bryan, April 8, 1913, *PWW*, 27: 272. Wilson's concern about the impact of Mexico on developments throughout the Caribbean has generally been neglected by historians, although it is given brief mention in Grieb, *United States and Huerta*, 44. This concern was, however, attested to repeatedly by the president and other policy makers throughout 1913–14.

123. Soon after it assumed power, Henry Lane Wilson urged the administration to recognize Huerta's government, on the grounds that that would promote stability in Mexico. The general was also, the ambassador reported, now willing to meet American wishes with regard to all the claims and other issues that had been raised by the Taft administration. The new administration declined to provide its representative with any instructions on this question. Haley, *Revolution and Intervention*, 85.

124. Knight, *Mexican Revolution*, 2: 11–62.

125. Josephus Daniels, *The Cabinet Diaries of Josephus Daniels, 1913–1921*, ed. E. David Cronon (Lincoln, Neb., 1963), 43–44.

126. "From the Diary of Colonel House," May 2, 1913, *PWW*, 27: 383.

127. "From Edward Mandell House," May 6, 1913, *PWW*, 27: 404; "From Delbert James Haff," May 12, 1913, *PWW*, 27: 419–25.

128. "Draft of Instruction to Henry Lane Wilson, May 15, 1913, *PWW*, 27: 435–36.

129. Wilson to Henry Lane Wilson, June 14, 1913, *PWW*, 27: 518.

130. "A Report by William Bayard Hale," June 18, 1913, *PWW*, 27: 536–52; "From William Bayard Hale," c. June 25, 1913, *PWW*, 28: 7–8; "A Report by William Bayard Hale," July 9, 1913, *PWW*, 28: 27–34; Larry D. Hill, *Emissaries to a Revolution: Woodrow Wilson's Executive Agents in Mexico* (Baton Rouge, La., 1973), 28–32, 35–38, 54–55. Meanwhile, the Wilson administration had also despatched another special agent, Reginald F. Del Valle, into the southern border region and northern Mexico. A wealthy Californian of Spanish-Mexican descent and a long-standing Democrat, Del Valle was asked to give his appraisal of the insurrection that was taking place in upper Mexico. Although he had good things to say about some of the leaders and partisans of that cause, such as the self-exiled Maderista governor of Sonora, José María Maytorena, Del Valle was harsh in his comments about the revolutionary

fighters. As he saw it, too many of these were "dangerous" people who constituted a threat to property and order. See Hill, *Emissaries*, 40–50, 56.

131. Grey to Spring-Rice, July 11, 1913, *PWW*, 28: 34.

132. Calvert, *Mexican Revolution*, 187, 198.

133. "Instructions to John Lind," August 4, 1913, *PWW*, 28: 110–11; Hill, *Emissaries*, 63–77.

134. Gamboa to Lind, August 16, 1913, *PWW*, 28: 168–75; Hill, *Emissaries*, 77–79; Grieb, *United States and Huerta*, 96–97; Haley, *Revolution and Intervention*, 99–100.

135. Wilson to E. A. Wilson, August 19, 1913, *PWW*, 28: 190–91.

136. "An Address on Mexican Affairs," August 27, 1913, *PWW*, 28: 227–31; Grieb, *United States and Huerta*, 100–101; Haley, *Revolution and Intervention*, 100–101.

137. O'Shaughnessy to Bryan, August 27, 1913, *PWW*, 28: 233–39; Hill, *Emissaries*, 82–84.

138. "From William Jennings Bryan," September 17, 1913, *PWW*, 28: 281–82; "Remarks at a Press Conference," September 25, 1913, *PWW*, 28: 322–23; "From William Jennings Bryan," September 25, 1913, *PWW*, 28: 324–25; Haley, *Revolution and Intervention*, 101–2; Hill, *Emissaries*, 94–95; Knight, *Mexican Revolution*, 2: 72–73.

139. "From William Bayard Hale," September 28, 1913, *PWW*, 28: 339–42; Hill, *Emissaries*, 95–96.

140. Wilson to Bryan, October 1, 1913, *PWW*, 28: 347–48.

141. Katz, *Secret War*, 168–69; Hill, *Emissaries*, 96–97; Wilson to E. A. Wilson, September 28, 1913, *PWW*, 28: 334–36.

142. Knight, *Mexican Revolution*, 2: 66–67, 73–75; Grieb, *United States and Huerta*, 104–6; Calvert, *Mexican Revolution*, 231–32.

143. Quoted in Haley, *Revolution and Intervention*, 106.

144. Bryan to O'Shaughnessy, October 13, 1913, *PWW*, 28: 399.

145. Katz, *Secret War*, 161–67, 170–73.

146. "A Draft of a Telegram to Walter Hines Page," October 11, 1913, *PWW*, 28: 388; Moore to Page, October 11, 1913, *PWW*, 28: 388–89.

147. "A Draft of a Circular Note to the Powers," October 24, 1913, *PWW*, 28: 431–33; "An Outline of a Circular Note to the Powers," c. October 24, 1913, *PWW*, 28: 434.

148. "From John Bassett Moore," October 28, 1913, *PWW*, 28: 458–64.

149. "An Address on Latin American Policy in Mobile, Alabama," October 27, 1913, *PWW*, 28: 448–53.

150. "A Note to the Powers," November 7, 1913, *PWW*, 28: 504–5.

151. Katz, *Secret War*, 173–80.

152. See Warren G. Kneer, *Great Britain and the Caribbean, 1901–1913: A Study in Anglo-American Relations* (East Lansing, Mich., 1975), 61–62, 110–15, 214–17, 156, 168–75, 179–80, 188–206; Katz, *Secret War*, 173–80.

153. "The British Embassy to Sir Edward Grey," November 14, 1913, *PWW*, 28: 543–45.

154. Grieb, *United States and Huerta*, 135–36; Arthur S. Link, *Wilson: The New Freedom* (Princeton, N.J., 1956), 304–14.

155. "From Sir William Tyrrell," November 21, 1913, *PWW*, 28: 573–74; Wilson to Tyrrell, November 22, 1913, *PWW*, 28: 574–75. Two days later, similar assurances, along with an explanation of U.S. policy (its purpose was to secure "peace and order in Central America"), were circulated to all powers with representatives in Mexico City. See Wilson to Bryan, November 23, 1913, *PWW*, 28: 585–86. Also see Grieb, *United States and Huerta*, 115–16.

156. Wilson to O'Shaughnessy, November 1, 1913, *PWW*, 28: 482–83; Wilson to O'Shaughnessy, November 14, 1913, *PWW*, 28: 539–40.

157. Quoted in Mark T. Gilderhus, *Diplomacy and Revolution: U.S.-Mexican Relations Under Wilson and Carranza* (Tucson, Ariz., 1977), 9.

158. Lind to Bryan, September 19, 1913, *PWW*, 28: 293–300; Lind to Bryan, October 9, 1913, *PWW*, 28: 382–83.

159. "From the Diary of Colonel House," October 30, 1913, *PWW*, 28: 476–78.

160. Wilson to Hale, c. November 11, 1913, *PWW*, 28: 525; Wilson to Hale, November 16, 1913, *PWW*, 28: 557; Link, *New Freedom*, 382–84; Haley, *Revolution and Intervention*, 114–18; Grieb, *United States and Huerta*, 112–13; Hill, *Emissaries*, 108–19.

161. Hale to Bryan, November 15, 1913, *PWW*, 28: 545–46; Hale to Bryan, November 17, 1913, *PWW*, 28: 561; Bryan to Lind, December 13, 1913, *PWW*, 29: 34.

162. Hill, *Emissaries*, 129–41; Haley, *Revolution and Intervention*, 125–29; Grieb, *United States and Huerta*, 121;Wilson to Page, January 29, 1914, *PWW*, 29: 196–97; "A Memorandum by Thomas Beaumont Hohler," February 11, 1914, *PWW*, 29: 255–61.

163. "I think our position before the world, our responsibility in the premises, and our interests demand that it be done," he wrote. See Lind to Bryan, February 24, 1914, *PWW*, 29: 286–87.

164. "From Walter Hines Page," February 24, 1914; *PWW*, 29: 285–86; Lind to Bryan, March 19, 1914, *PWW.*, 29: 357–60; Lind to Bryan, March 29, 1914, *PWW*, 29: 382–83.

165. The critical oil port was at that time becoming a focal point of the struggle between the Constitutionalist and Federal armies, and local guardsmen had been given orders to arrest any unauthorized personnel.

166. Grieb, *United States and Huerta*, 142–45; Lester Langley, *The Banana Wars: United States Intervention in the Caribbean, 1898–1934* (Lexington, Ky., 1985), 87–88; Challener, *Admirals*, 385–86; Robert E. Quirk, *An Affair of Honor: Woodrow Wilson and the Occupation of Vera Cruz* (New York, 1964), 1–28.

167. "From the Diary of Colonel House," April 15, 1914, *PWW*, 29: 448; "An Address to Congress on the Mexican Crisis," April 20, 1914, *PWW*, 29: 471–74; Grieb, *United States and Huerta*, 145–52; Langley, *Banana Wars*, 88–93; Challener, *Admirals*, 386–93; Quirk, *Affair of Honor*, 28–77.

168. Katz, *Secret War*, 195–96, 234–40; Challener, *Admirals*, 393–97; Langley, *Banana Wars*, 92–114; Grieb, *United States and Huerta*, 151–54; Quirk, *Affair of Honor*, 78–107.

169. Katz, *Secret War*, 197; Quirk, *Affair of Honor*, 107–17; Grieb, *United States and Huerta*, 154–58.

170. It was accepted by Huerta two days later, and an armistice went into effect on the thirtieth.

171. "An Interview," April 27, 1914, *PWW*, 29: 521; Katz, *Secret War*, 197; Quirk, *Affair of Honor*,107–17; Grieb, *United States and Huerta*, 154–60; Mark T. Gilderhus, *Pan American Visions: Woodrow Wilson in the Western Hemisphere, 1913–1921* (Tucson, Ariz., 1986), 32–33; Knight, *Mexican Revolution*, 2: 140–45.

172. "To the Diplomatic Representatives of Argentina, Brazil, and Chile," April 25, 1914, *PWW*, 29: 507–8.

173. He telegraphed the U.S. commissioners that, "The case lies in our mind thus: the success of the Constitutionalists is now inevitable. The only question we can now answer without armed intervention on the part of the United States is this, can the result be moderated, how can it be brought about without further bloodshed, what provisional arrangement can be made which will temper the whole process and lead to the elections in a way that will be hopeful of peace and permanent accommodation?" See "To the Special Commissioners," May 27, 1914, *PWW*, 30: 92.

174. Grieb, *United States and Huerta*, 159–77; Link, *New Freedom*, 405–13; Katz, *Secret War*, 199.

175. The president admonished Carranza to show "utmost care" in his treatment of foreigners, foreign interests, and the country's financial obligations, and also not to be vindictive in his treatment of opponents. See "To George C. Carothers and John Reid Silliman (for Villa and Carranza)," July 23, 1914, *PWW*, 30: 297–98.

176. The conflict now taking shape in Europe, he added, would also "make it impossible to obtain assistance anywhere on the other side of the water." See Haley, *Revolution and Intervention*, 149–50.

177. Knight, *Mexican Revolution*, 2: 109–29, 149, 167–71, 231–56, 270; Ruíz, *Great Rebellion*, 153–66, 199–212; Katz, *Secret War*, 123–55; Hart, *Revolutionary Mexico*, 268–80; John Womack, *Zapata and the Mexican Revolution* (New York, 1968); Friedrich Katz, *The Life and Times of Pancho Villa* (Stanford, Calif., 1998), 11–308, 330–36, 340–73.

178. Hill, *Emissaries*, 229–44.

179. The provisional president elected by the convention was Eulalio Gutiérrez. See Knight, *Mexican Revolution*, 2: 256–63; Hill, *Emissaries*, 263–66.

180. Friedrich Katz, "From Alliance to Dependency: The Formation and Deformation of an Alliance Between Francisco Villa and the United States," in, *Rural Revolt*, ed. Nugent, 229–49; Katz, *Pancho Villa*, 308–19; 336–38.

181. Hill, *Emissaries*, 132, 148, 158–59, 179, 189–90, 234, 260.

182. "From the Diary of Colonel House," August 30, 1914, *PWW*, 30: 463.

183. Quoted in Katz, "From Alliance to Dependency," 229. Also See Hill, *Emissaries*, 275.

184. Wilson to West, February 9, 1915, *PWW*, 30: 203–4; Hill, *Emissaries*, 309–13.

185. Hill, *Emissaries*, 271–78.

186. Hill, *Emissaries*, 314–21.

187. Knight, *Mexican Revolution*, 2: 309–27; Katz, *Pancho Villa*, 373–96, 437–98.

188. Hill, *Emissaries*, 334–39; Haley, *Revolution and Intervention*, 158–65.

189. Quoted in Haley, *Revolution and Intervention*, 163.

190. Haley, *Revolution and Intervention*, 165.

191. "From the Diary of Colonel House," June 24, 1915, *PWW*, 33: 449–50.

192. Haley, *Revolution and Intervention*, 163–82; Gilderhus, *Diplomacy and Revolution*, 25–31; Hill, *Emissaries*, 339–63.

193. He continued: "It comes down to this: Our possible relations with Germany must be our first consideration; and all our intercourse with Mexico must be regulated accordingly. It is the only rational and safe policy under present conditions." Quoted in Gilderhus, *Diplomacy and Revolution*, 31.

194. Katz, *Secret War*, 303–7; Katz, "From Alliance to Dependency," 238; Katz, *Pancho Villa*, 504–66; Knight, *Mexican Revolution*, 2: 343–45. George Carothers now reversed his opinion of Villa. "All the brutality of his nature has come to the front," he wrote in the wake of Columbus, "and he should be killed like a dog." See Hill, *Emissaries*, 370.

195. Gilderhus, *Diplomacy and Revolution*, 35; Haley, *Revolution and Intervention*, 188–90; Frederick S. Calhoun, *Power and Principle: Armed Intervention in Wilsonian Foreign Policy* (Kent, Ohio, 1986), 52–58.

196. Haley, *Revolution and Intervention*, 189–95; Gilderhus, *Diplomacy and Revolution*, 36–38; Katz, *Secret War*, 310.

197. Haley, *Revolution and Intervention*, 195–99; Gilderhus, *Diplomacy and Revolution*, 38–40.

198. Haley, *Revolution and Intervention*, 199–223, 227; Gilderhus, *Diplomacy and Revolution*, 40–48.

199. Katz, *Secret War*, 311.

200. Quoted in Katz, *Secret War*, 312. It was implied that American forces would not be removed from Mexico until these broader issues were satisfactorily addressed from Washington's standpoint. See Katz, *Secret War*, 311–12; Haley, *Revolution and Intervention*, 227–37; Smith, *Revolutionary Nationalism*, 55–59; Gilderhus, *Diplomacy and Revolution*, 48–50.

201. Quoted in Haley, *Revolution and Intervention*, 239.

202. Katz, *Secret War*, 314, 348–50.
203. Haley, *Revolution and Intervention*, 242–44; Gilderhus, *Diplomacy and Revolution*, 50–52.
204. Haley, *Revolution and Intervention*, 245–46; Smith, *Revolutionary Nationalism*, 71–92; Katz, *Secret War*, 497–503; Gilderhus, *Diplomacy and Revolution*, 53–58.
205. Haley, *Revolution and Intervention*, 253–55; Gilderhus, *Diplomacy and Revolution*, 63–64.
206. Katz, *Secret War*, 350–67; Gilderhus, *Diplomacy and Revolution*, 59–64. Also see Laura Garcés, "The German Challenge to the Monroe Doctrine in Mexico, 1917," in *Confrontation and Cooperation*, ed. Schröder, 281–313.
207. Haley, *Revolution and Intervention*, 255–57.
208. For subsequent developments, see Smith, *Revolutionary Nationalism*, 93–265 and Linda B. Hall, *Oil, Banks, and Politics: The United States and Postrevolutionary Mexico, 1917–1924* (Austin, Tex., 1995).

Chapter 6. World Order (to 1914)

1. As evidence for this, see for example Roosevelt's second annual message, December 2, 1902, *WTR*, 15: 151; Taft's speech before the American Peace and Arbitration League, March 22, 1910, WHTP; Root's speech in acceptance of the Nobel Peace Prize, 1912, in Root, *Addresses on International Subjects by Elihu Root*, ed. Robert Bacon and James Brown Scott (Cambridge, Mass., 1916), 155–73; Knox's speech before the Pennsylvania Society of New York, December 11, 1909, PCKP; and Wilson's first annual message, December 2, 1913, *PWW*, 29: 3.
2. Interestingly, American policy makers chafed against the restraints under which they themselves operated in international affairs in this period. They bemoaned the power of the Senate and the state of public opinion and strove to attain a much greater degree of independence for the executive. They had, of course, no doubt that in their case such independence would constitute the triumph of responsibility.
3. For more extensive discussions of this tradition, see Edward P. Crapol, *America for Americans: Economic Nationalism and Anglophobia in the Late Nineteenth Century* (Westport, Conn., 1973); Charles S. Campbell, *From Revolution to Rapprochement: The United States and Great Britain, 1783–1900* (New York, 1974); Bradford Perkins, *The Great Rapprochement: England and the United States, 1895–1914* (New York, 1968), 3–11.
4. Here see Stuart Anderson, *Race and Rapprochement: Anglo-Saxonism and Anglo-American Relations, 1895–1904* (Rutherford, N.J., 1981); Charles S. Campbell, Jr., *Anglo-American Understanding, 1898–1903* (Baltimore, 1957), 1–24; Paul F. Boller, Jr., *American Thought in Transition: The Impact of Evolutionary Naturalism, 1865–1900* (Chicago, 1969), 199–226.
5. See, for instance, Roosevelt to White, March 30, 1896, *LTR*, 1: 523.
6. "Memorandum for an Interview," c. December 18, 1895, *PWW*, 29: 365.
7. On the quality of Hay's Anglophilia, see Kenton J. Clymer, *John Hay: The Gentleman as Diplomat* (Ann Arbor, Mich.,1975), 104.
8. Summarized in Roosevelt to Meyer, April 12, 1901, TRP.
9. Also see, in this connection, Edward P. Crapol, "From Anglophobia to Fragile Rapprochement: Anglo-American Relations in the Early Twentieth Century," in *Confrontation and Cooperation: Germany and the United States in the Era of World War I, 1900–1924*, ed. Hans-Jürgen Schröder (Providence, R.I., 1993), 13–31.
10. See Holger Herwig, *The Politics of Frustration: The United States in German Naval Planning, 1889–1941* (Boston, 1976), 13–109; Nancy Mitchell, "The Height of the German Challenge: The Venezuela Blockade, 1902–1903," *Diplomatic History* 20 (Spring 1996): 185–209; Melvin Small, "The United States and the German 'Threat'

to the Hemisphere, 1905–1914," *Americas* 28 (January 1972): 252–70; David Healy, *Drive to Hegemony: The United States in the Caribbean, 1898–1917* (Madison, Wis., 1988), 4, 72–76; Ivo Nikolai Lambi, *The Navy and German Power Politics, 1862–1914* (Boston, 1984), 129–31, 226–31.

11. Robert Seager II, *Alfred Thayer Mahan: The Man and His Letters* (Annapolis, Md., 1977), 348–49, 500; Howard K. Beale, *Theodore Roosevelt and the Rise of America to World Power* (Baltimore, 1984), 390–95; Tyler Dennett, *John Hay: From Poetry to Politics* (New York, 1934), 384–94.

12. Quoted in Perkins, *Great Rapprochement*, 29.

13. Richard Olney, "International Isolation of the United States," *Atlantic Monthly* 81 (May 1898): 587–88.

14. Roosevelt to Mahan, May 3, 1897, *LTR* 1: 607–8.

15. Roosevelt to Francis Cruger Moore, February 5, 1898, *LTR*, 1: 768–69.

16. Perkins, *Great Rapprochement*, 33–47.

17. David F. Trask, *The War with Spain in 1898* (New York, 1981), 376–81; Perkins, *Great Rapprochement*, 46–47.

18. Roosevelt to Lee, November 25, 1898, *LTR*, 2: 889–90.

19. Quoted in Dennett, *John Hay*, 221.

20. For background and overview, see Norman Rich, *Great Power Diplomacy, 1814–1914* (New York, 1992), 278–99; Thomas Pakenham, *The Scramble for Africa, 1876–1912* (New York, 1991); Ronald Robinson and John Gallagher with Alice Denny, *Africa and the Victorians: The Climax of Imperialism* (Garden City, N.Y., 1968); Thomas J. Noer, *Briton, Boer, and Yankee: The United States and South Africa, 1870–1914* (Kent, Ohio, 1978).

21. Indeed, Secretary of State Hay had already become eager by September 1899 to see Britain deal decisively with the situation. "I hope, if it come to blows," he wrote Henry White, "that England will make quick work of Uncle Paul [Kruger]. Sooner or later, her influence must be dominant there, and the sooner the better." See Noer, *Briton, Boer, and Yankee*, 67.

22. Noer, *Briton, Boer, and Yankee*, 67–80; Perkins, *Great Rapprochement*, 89–97.

23. Noer, *Briton, Boer, and Yankee*, 19–58.

24. Quoted in Dennett, *John Hay*, 241.

25. Quoted in Noer, *Briton, Boer, and Yankee*, 71. Mahan opined that it would have been "imperial suicide" for London not to have taken the actions it did in South Africa. See his "The Merits of the Transvaal Dispute," *North American Review* 520 (March 1900): 312–26; also his *The War in South Africa* (New York, 1900) and Seager, *Mahan*, 425–27.

26. Roosevelt to White, March 30, 1896, *LTR*, 1: 523.

27. Quoted in Beale, *Theodore Roosevelt*, 95.

28. Quoted in Campbell, *Anglo-American Understanding*, 180.

29. Calvin DeArmond Davis, *The United States and the First Hague Peace Conference* (Ithaca, N.Y., 1962), 36–53; Norman E. Saul, *Concord and Conflict: The United States and Russia, 1867–1914* (Lawrence, Kan., 1996), 440–44. The tsar's rescript is reprinted in James Brown Scott, *The Hague Peace Conferences of 1899 and 1907*, 2 vols. (Baltimore, 1909), 2: 1–2.

30. Reprinted in Scott, *Hague Peace Conferences*, 2: 3–5.

31. The previous year the president had worried that the war with Spain and annexation of the Philippines might work to undermine that. This, at least in part, was what was behind his desire to "show that we had spared no effort to avert trouble" with Spain (see above, Chapter 2). McKinley seems also to have been concerned that the American acquisition of the Philippines might work to undermine other powers' commitment to the open door. See the undated, unsigned memorandum in WMP (series 5) that begins: "This Government does not propose a policy

of exclusion of foreign trade from the Islands which have come under the control of the United States." The administration probably also saw the conference at The Hague as an opportunity for the U.S. to make up for its unwillingness to arbitrate over Alaska.

32. Davis, *First Hague*, 64–93.

33. These instructions, dated April 18, 1899, are reprinted in James Brown Scott, ed., *Instructions to the American Delegates to the Hague Peace Conferences and Their Official Reports* (New York, 1916), 6–16. Its representatives several times found themselves in the minority, however, when discussion turned to limits on particular weapons. Adhering rigidly to their instructions, Crozier and Mahan, Washington's representatives on the arms limitation subcommittees, were determined to retain freedom of action for the U.S. with regard to weapons innovation as well. This led them to stand alone against a ban on the use of asphyxiating gas. Subsequently Crozier succeeded in getting limited to five years a ban on the dropping of explosive devices from balloons. Although the American army had yet to use them, he also sided with London's delegation in opposing a resolution condemning the use of dumdum bullets, which had been used by the British army in Africa and India. See Davis, *First Hague*, 110–24; Calvin DeArmond Davis, *The United States and the Second Hague Peace Conference: American Diplomacy and International Organization, 1899–1914* (Durham, N.C., 1975), 25–27. The McKinley administration adopted the position of its delegates and decided not to seek Senate approval of the conference's declarations against gas and dumdums. See Davis, *First Hague*, 196. There is some evidence to suggest that the latter were used in the Philippines. See Stuart Creighton Miller, *"Benevolent Assimilation": The American Conquest of the Philippines, 1899–1903* (New Haven, Conn., 1982), 241–42.

34. Davis, *First Hague*, 125–36. For ratification, see p. 202.

35. Davis, *First Hague*, 127–35.

36. See Scott, *Hague Peace Conferences*, 2: 4–5.

37. See Scott, ed., *Instructions*, 8.

38. It also laid out the steps by which this could be done. The convention is printed in Scott, *Hague Peace Conferences*, 2: 81–109.

39. See Scott, *Hague Peace Conferences*, 1: 260, 264.

40. See Scott, ed., *Instructions*, 14–16.

41. Quoted in Scott, *Hague Peace Conferences*, 1: 70.

42. Davis, *First Hague*, 137–51.

43. Andrew D. White, *The First Hague Conference* (Boston, 1912), 65.

44. White, *First Hague Conference*, 62.

45. White, *First Hague Conference*, 70–71.

46. White, *First Hague Conference*, 66–67.

47. Davis, *First Hague*, 151–61; Helen May Cory, *Compulsory Arbitration of International Disputes* (New York, 1932), 45–48; Margaret Robinson, *Arbitration and the Hague Peace Conferences, 1899 and 1907* (Philadelphia, 1936), 68–84.

48. See Scott, *Hague Peace Conferences*, 2: 91–93. As a further means of encouraging arbitration, Article 27 of the convention urged third parties to "consider it their duty, if a serious dispute threatens to break out," to remind the nations involved "that the Permanent Court is open to them." Even though this was construed as a moral, rather than a legal, duty, the American delegates, on reflection, became fearful that this might be attacked as an entangling obligation by members of the Senate. White subsequently drafted a declaration "stating that nothing contained in any part of the convention signed here should be considered as requiring us to intrude, mingle or entangle ourselves in European" affairs, and to this Low added wording "to the effect that nothing should be considered to require any abandonment of the traditional attitude of the United States toward questions purely

American." To the chagrin of the British delegation, this was then attached as a qualification to the United States' adherence to the final convention. See Davis, *First Hague*, 176–80; Robinson, *Arbitration*, 83–84; White, *First Hague Conference*, 104–6.

49. Davis, *First Hague*, 199–208. The president named ex-President Harrison, Justice Melville W. Fuller, Attorney-General John W. Griggs, and Judge George Gray as the first U.S. appointees to the court.

50. For background on the peace movement, see Charles DeBenedetti, *The Peace Reform in American History* (Bloomington, Ind., 1980), 3–85, here 80; David S. Patterson, *Toward a Warless World: The Travail of the American Peace Movement, 1887–1914* (Bloom-ington, Ind., 1976), 1–164; C. Roland Marchand, *The American Peace Movement and Social Reform, 1898–1918* (Princeton, 1972), 3–143; and Warren F. Kuehl, *Seeking World Order: The United States and International Organization to 1920* (Nashville, 1969), 3–171.

51. Roosevelt to Lodge, April 29, 1896, *LTR*, 1: 535–36.

52. Roosevelt to Burton, February 23, 1904, *LTR*, 4: 735–37.

53. Quoted in Beale, *Theodore Roosevelt*, 91. Also see Davis, *Second Hague*, 51–54.

54. Theodore Roosevelt, *The Strenuous Life: Essays and Addresses* (New York, 1905), 23. Also see his First Annual Message, December 3, 1901, *WTR*, 15: 115.

55. Davis, *Second Hague*, 57–61.

56. Second Annual Message, December 2, 1902, *WTR*, 15: 151.

57. Once arbitration had been raised as a means of resolving that affair, Hay, as well as many American newspaper editors, decided that this too would be an appropriate case to be sent to The Hague. Roosevelt hesitated, but agreed when he was certain that no decision could be rendered that would involve the acquisition by either Germany or England of Venezuelan territory. "There was one reason, and only one, which made it in my judgment better that I should arbitrate myself," he later wrote editor Albert Shaw. "This was the fact that in such case there would be no possibility of the court rendering a decision which might be in conflict with the Monroe Doctrine." "Of course I take it for granted," he continued, "that you would support me in refusing to acknowledge the power of the Hague court or of any other power to overrule us as regards our attitude on what I consider the cardinal feature of American foreign policy." See Roosevelt to Shaw, December 26, 1902, *LTR*, 3: 396–97; and Davis, *Second Hague*, 82–83.

58. Davis, *Second Hague*, 92–97.

59. For the text, see Scott, *Hague Peace Conferences*, 2: 89–91; also 1: 309.

60. See Scott, *Hague Peace Conferences*, 1: 328–30; Cory, *Compulsory Arbitration*, 51–52.

61. Davis, *Second Hague*, 97–101.

62. Quoted in Davis, *Second Hague*, 99.

63. Davis, *Second Hague*, 102–3, 112, 116.

64. The organization met in the U.S. for the first time in 1904, holding its conference at the Louisiana Purchase Exposition in St. Louis. Afterward the delegates traveled to Washington to meet with the president. See Davis, *Second Hague*, 103–10.

65. *Addresses of John Hay* (New York, 1906), 303; Davis, *Second Hague*, 111–12.

66. Davis, *Second Hague*, 116–18; Cory, *Compulsory Arbitration*, 35, 53–55; W. Stull Holt, *Treaties Defeated by the Senate* (Baltimore, 1933), 204–8; Shelby M. Cullom, *Fifty Years of Public Service* (Chicago, 1911) 396–401; Dorothy G. Fowler, *John Coit Spooner* (New York, 1961), 288–93; Patterson, *Toward a Warless World*, 126–27.

67. Roosevelt to Spooner, January 6, 1905, *LTR*, 4: 1092–93.

68. For general background, see James Joll, *The Origins of the First World War* (New York, 1984), 38–40; Rich, *Great Power Diplomacy*, 260–62; A. J. P. Taylor, *The Struggle for Mastery in Europe, 1848–1918* (Oxford, 1971), 325–45. Of special importance, see Christopher Andrew, *Théophile Delcassé and the Making of the Entente Cordiale: A Reappraisal of French Foreign Policy, 1898–1905* (New York, 1968), 4–21.

69. Andrew, *Delcassé*, 21–48.

70. Andrew, *Delcassé*, 48–52, 86–195.

71. Andrew, *Delcassé*, 87.

72. For background, see Aaron L. Friedberg, *The Weary Titan: Britain and the Experience of Relative Decline, 1895–1905* (Princeton, N.J., 1988); George Monger, *The End of Isolation: British Foreign Policy, 1900–1907* (London, 1963), 1–14; Zara S. Steiner, *Britain and the Origins of the First World War* (New York, 1977), 5–21; Paul Kennedy, *The Realities Behind Diplomacy: Background Influences on British External Policy, 1865–1980* (Glasgow, 1981), 17–109.

73. For an overview, see Kennedy, *Realities*, 109–27.

74. Friedberg, *Weary Titan*, 30–33, 46–48, 50–55, 62, 76–79; Bernard Semmel, *Imperialism and Social Reform: English Social-Imperial Thought, 1895–1914* (New York, 1968), 74–117; Robert Blake, *The Conservative Party from Peel to Churchill* (London, 1972), 167–84; Sydney H. Zebel, "Joseph Chamberlain and the Genesis of Tariff Reform," *Journal of British Studies* 7(1967): 131–57.

75. Friedberg, *Weary Titan*, 138.

76. Harold Sprout and Margaret Sprout, *Toward a New Order of Sea Power* (Princeton, N.J., 1943), 16.

77. Friedberg, *Weary Titan*, 98, 140, 146–47, 151, 168–69, 171–73, 179, 184, 191; Steiner, *Britain*, 25–29; Rhodri Williams, *Defending the Empire: The Conservative Party and British Defence Policy, 1899–1915* (New Haven, Conn., 1991), 6–40; Jon Tetsuro Sumida, *In Defence of Naval Supremacy: Finance, Technology, and British Naval Policy, 1889–1914* (Boston, 1989), 3–25; Paul Kennedy, *The Rise and Fall of British Naval Mastery* (Atlantic Highlands, N.J., 1980), 177–215; Paul Kennedy, *The Rise of the Anglo-German Antagonism, 1860–1914* (London, 1982), 3–266; Andrew, *Delcassé*, 195–215.

78. On the emergence of German *Weltpolitik*, see Imanuel Geiss, *German Foreign Policy, 1871–1914* (London, 1976), 73–95; V. R. Berghan, *Germany and the Approach of War in 1914* (London, 1973), 5–42; Lambi, *German Power Politics*, 1–178; Jonathan Steinberg, *Yesterday's Deterrent: Tirpitz and the Birth of the German Battle Fleet* (London, 1965); Holger H. Herwig, *'Luxury Fleet': The Imperial German Navy, 1888–1918* (Atlantic Highlands, N.J., 1987), 9–53; Fritz Fischer, *World Power or Decline: The Controversy over "Germany's Aims in the First World War"* (New York, 1974), 3–19; Kennedy, *Anglo-German Antagonism*, 205–50; and Paul Kennedy, *Strategy and Diplomacy, 1870–1945: Eight Studies* (Boston, 1983), 127–60.

79. Quoted in Lambi, *German Power Politics*, 146.

80. Lambi, *German Power Politics*, 178–79; Berghan, *Germany*, 46. Indeed, it was clear that Italy's ties to the Triple Alliance, entered into by Berlin, Vienna, and Rome in 1882, would be much less firm simply because of this Anglo-French agreement.

81. On Germany and the First Moroccan Crisis, see Lambi, *German Power Politics*, 241–64.

82. Andrew, *Delcassé*, 215–67.

83. Andrew, *Delcassé*, 268–73.

84. Andrew, *Delcassé*, 273–303.

85. Peter Larsen, "Theodore Roosevelt and the Moroccan Crisis, 1904–1906" (PhD dissertation, Princeton University, 1984), 1–141; Raymond A. Esthus, *Theodore Roosevelt and the International Rivalries* (Claremont, Calif., 1970), 66–83; Beale, *Theodore Roosevelt*, 354–70.

86. Roosevelt to White, August 23, 1905, *LTR*, 4: 1313.

87. Manfred Jonas, *The United States and Germany: A Diplomatic History* (Ithaca, N.Y., 1984), 67–87. Also see Frank Trommler, "Inventing the Enemy: German-American Cultural Relations, 1900–1917," in *Confrontation and Cooperation*, ed. Schröder, 99–125.

88. Roosevelt to Spring Rice, November 1, 1905, *LTR*, 5: 63.

89. See Beale, *Theodore Roosevelt*, 394.

90. Root to White, November 28, 1905, ERP.

91. Quoted in Philip C. Jessup, *Elihu Root*, 2 vols. (New York, 1938), 2: 58.

92. Larsen, "Moroccan Crisis," 217–23.

93. Esthus, *International Rivalries*, 83–111; Larsen, "Moroccan Crisis," 160–227.

94. Larsen, "Moroccan Crisis," 253–92.

95. Roosevelt to Reid, June 27, 1906, *LTR*, 5: 318–19.

96. Roosevelt to Grey, December 18, 1906, *LTR*, 5: 527. TR's complaints about Durand helped lead to his eventual replacement by James Bryce.

97. K. A. Hamilton, "Great Britain and France, 1905–1911," in *British Foreign Policy Under Sir Edward Grey*, ed. F. H. Hinsley (Cambridge, 1977), 113–32; Kennedy, *Anglo-German Antagonism*, 282–85; Steiner, *Britain*, 42–44; Samuel R. Williamson, *The Politics of Grand Strategy: Britain and France Prepare for War, 1904–1914* (Cambridge, Mass., 1969).

98. Beryl Williams, "Great Britain and Russia, 1905 to the 1907 Convention," in *British Foreign Policy*, ed. Hinsley (Cambridge, 1977), 133–47; Steiner, *Britain*, 79–83; David Gillard, *The Struggle for Asia, 1828–1914: A Study in British and Russian Imperialism* (London, 1977), 168–76; Joll, *Origins*, 41–56.

99. His circular, dated October 21, 1904, is reprinted in Scott, ed., *Instructions*, 59–63.

100. Davis, *Second Hague*, 112–16, 123–24.

101. Fifth Annual Message, December 5, 1905, *WTR*, 15: 296–300.

102. Roosevelt to Schurz, September 8, 1905, *LTR*, 5: 16–17

103. Davis, *Second Hague*, 125–28.

104. Davis, *Second Hague*, 129. This was so that there would be no conflict either with the Rio Conference or with another meeting scheduled in Geneva to revise the Red Cross conventions.

105. Davis, *Second Hague*, 135–37.

106. Sumida, *Naval Supremacy*, 24–61; Williams, *Defending the Empire*, 59–83; Kennedy, *British Naval Mastery*, 216–20; Kennedy, *Anglo-German Antagonism*, 331–35; Steiner, *Britain*, 48–49; D. W. Sweet, "Great Britain and Germany, 1905–1911," in *British Foreign Policy*, ed. Hinsley, 216–35, quote p. 218; Davis, *Second Hague*, 147–49.

107. Davis, *Second Hague*, 149–50.

108. Roosevelt to Reid, August 7, 1906, *LTR*, 5: 348–49.

109. Roosevelt to Carnegie, September 6, 1906, *LTR*, 5: 398.

110. Roosevelt to Grey, February 28, 1907, *LTR*, 5: 600–601; Davis, *Second Hague*, 150–61.

111. Patterson, *Toward a Warless World*, 129–30; Kuehl, *Seeking World Order*, 96–98; Davis, *Second Hague*, 163–64.

112. Roosevelt to Carnegie, April 5, 1907, *LTR*, 5: 638–42; Roosevelt to Eliot, September 22, 1906, *LTR*, 5: 420; Roosevelt to Spring Rice, July 1, 1907, *LTR*, 5: 699; Davis, *Second Hague*, 164–65.

113. Davis, *Second Hague*, 128, 170–73; "Meeting of the American Commission to the Second Hague Conference, Held April 20, 1907, in the Diplomatic Room of the Department of State," PCJP.

114. Dated May 31, 1907, these are reprinted in Scott, ed., *Instructions*, 69–85.

115. Scott, *Hague Peace Conferences*, 2: 289; Davis, *Second Hague*, 215–19.

116. Davis, *Second Hague*, 220–25; Bernard Semmel, *Liberalism and Naval Strategy: Ideology, Interest, and Sea Power During the Pax Britannica* (Boston, 1986), 108; Scott, *Hague Peace Conferences*, 1: 130–31, 465–511.

117. Joseph H. Choate, *The Two Hague Conferences* (Princeton, N.J., 1913), 65–74; Davis, *Second Hague*, 225–27; John W. Coogan, *The End of Neutrality: The United States, Britain, and Maritime Rights, 1899–1915* (Ithaca, N.Y., 1981), 93–94; Scott, *Hague Peace Conferences*, 2: 472–507; Scott, *Instructions*, 115.

118. Choate, *Two Hague Conferences*, 74–75.

119. The resolution is referred to, and quoted in its entirety, in Root's instructions, see Scott, ed., *Instructions*, 81.

120. Choate chose to champion this issue himself, and he campaigned hard for it even after it became clear that England, Russia, and Japan in particular were likely to withhold their support. Once debate ended, however, only Germany among the major maritime powers endorsed the proposal. Moreover, Berlin did so only after it was confident that defeat was certain. Berlin was principally interested in capitalizing on the differences that had emerged between Washington and London. Germany wanted to protect its trade. It did not, however, want to forfeit the right, as a belligerent, to engage in commerce raiding. Semmel, *Naval Strategy*, 106–8; Coogan, *End of Neutrality*, 92; Davis, *Second Hague*, 227–31; Scott, *Hague Peace Conferences*, 1: 699–704. Root expressed his doubts in a letter written to Ambassador Reid (and subsequently shared with Grey) the previous fall. See Root to Reid, October 24, 1906, ERP; Davis, *Second Hague*, 138–40, 171–72; Beale, *Theodore Roosevelt*, 348.

121. Seager, *Mahan*, 504–10; William E. Livezey, *Mahan on Sea Power* (Norman, Okla., 1981), 275–77; Richard W. Turk, *The Ambiguous Relationship: Theodore Roosevelt and Alfred Thayer Mahan* (Westport, Conn., 1987), 71, 77. Mahan had opposed the idea when he was a delegate to the first conference in 1899.

122. Quoted in Seager, *Mahan*, 507.

123. Quoted in Davis, *Second Hague*, 139.

124. "This 'doctrine of release,'" writes historian Bernard Semmel, "was of special importance to Great Britain and the United States whose navies could with greater facility bring a prize ship into their ports for adjudication by admiralty courts without running the risk of being captured in turn." No agreement could be reached on this question at the conference. See Semmel, *Naval Strategy*, 105; Davis, *Second Hague*, 172, 221.

125. In the end, although they got much of what they wanted, the British and American delegations refused to sign the convention that dealt with these matters. See Davis, *Second Hague*, 248–49.

126. The Declaration of Paris had established the principle that blockades had to be effective to be binding and the continental European powers insisted that this envisioned a close maritime siege, near to the enemy's coast. See Davis, *Second Hague*, 242.

127. Davis, *Second Hague*, 244–47; Semmel, *Naval Strategy*, 107–8.

128. Semmel, *Naval Strategy*, 102, 104.

129. Root had discussed the topic of contraband at his meeting with the American delegation in April. According to Scott's minutes, "The Secretary said that in this whole matter we must consider the American interest and that the catalogue of contraband should be enlarged or limited according to this interest. As a neutral and food producer we should be permitted to export necessities to either belligerent. Our interest, therefore, is to restrict the definition of contraband because it is not to be supposed that we will be participants in war and that we must as far as possible increase American trade. If nations declare war it is natural that the American merchant should take advantage of the belligerent market." In his formal instructions, Root noted a "recent tendency to extend widely the list of articles to be treated as contraband," and warned that "if the belligerents themselves are to determine at the beginning of a war what shall be contraband, this tendency will continue until the list … is made to include a large proportion of all the articles which are the subject of commerce, upon the ground that they will be useful to the enemy." "On the other hand," he continued, "resistance to this tendency … ought not to be left to the neutrals affected by it at the very moment when war exists, because that is the process by which neutrals become themselves involved in war.

You should do all in your power to bring about an agreement upon what is to constitute contraband; and it is very desirable that the list should be limited as narrowly as possible." Given these instructions, the U.S. might very well have been expected to welcome Britain's proposal. However, London simultaneously promoted the notion that neutral ships should be declared auxiliary warships if they carried either troops or supplies for the enemy, and on that basis be subject to capture or destruction. This idea reawakened in U.S. policy makers concern about the arbitrary treatment they felt the U.S. had suffered at the hands of the British navy in the nineteenth century. See "Meeting of the American Commission"; Scott, ed., *Instructions*, 84; Coogan, *End of Neutrality*, 94–95; Davis, *Second Hague*, 221, 233–42.

130. Davis, *Second Hague*, 242–43, 249–50.

131. Roosevelt to Grey, February 28, 1907, *LTR*, 5: 601.

132. Scott, ed., *Instructions*, 129; Choate, *Two Hague Conferences*, 80–81; Scott, *Hague Peace Conferences*, 1: 330–83; Davis, *Second Hague*, 277–84; Cory, *Compulsory Arbitration*, 69–75; Robinson, *Arbitration*, 52–67.

133. For the U.S. relationship to the court project, see Scott, ed., *Instructions*, 131; Choate, *Two Hague Conferences*, 77–80; Scott, *Hague Peace Conferences*, 1: 423–60; Davis, *Second Hague*, 260–76; Cory, *Compulsory Arbitration*, 75–81; Robinson, *Arbitration*, 89–101; David S. Patterson, "The United States and the Origins of the World Court," *Political Science Quarterly* 91 (Summer 1976): 279–83.

134. "Minutes of the American Commission." Also see Scott, ed., *Instructions*, 79; and Root's speech before the National Arbitration and Peace Congress in *Addresses on International Subjects*, 140–41.

135. Quoted in Scott, *Hague Peace Conferences*, 1: 427.

136. James Brown Scott, ed., *The Project Relative to a Court of Arbitral Justice: Draft Convention and Report Adopted by the Second Hague Peace Conference of 1907* (Washington, D.C., 1920), vi, 89–98.

137. Memorandum by James Brown Scott, "Mr. Choate's Various Proposals," April 22, 1909, PCKP.

138. James Brown Scott, ed., *Reports to the Hague Conferences of 1899 and 1907* (Oxford, 1917), 282–88. Also see Scott's discussion of the judges question in Scott to Knox, April 22, 1909, PCKP. At the last minute, in an effort to have the court established at the conference, the U.S.—banking clearly on its ability to command sufficient support from within the Americas—declared its willingness to stake its own membership on a process of election to the bench. However, this procedure proved unpopular among both small and large powers, and no such scheme was seriously proposed again. Choate claimed that "Germany and Great Britain turned against us on our plan of electing Judges by a vote of the nations, being afraid that it would result in their being left [out]." See Allen Hampton Kitchens, "Ambassador Extraordinary: The Diplomatic Career of Joseph Hodges Choate" (PhD dissertation, George Washington University, 1971), 435–37.

139. Burns, *Unwritten Alliance*, 121–26.

140. Davis, *Second Hague*, 294–302; Scott, ed., *Instructions*, 137. Also see U.S. Congress, Senate, *The Second Hague Peace Conference*, S.. Doc. 433, 60th Cong., 1st sess., 1908.

141. Root, *Addresses on International Subjects*, 3. For Root's ideas, discussed above, see especially "The Sanction of International Law," April 24, 1908, 25–32; "The Importance of Judicial Settlement," December 15, 1910, 146–48; and "Nobel Peace Prize Address," 1912, 155–73. Also see Sondra R. Herman, *Eleven Against War: Studies in American Internationalist Thought, 1898–1921* (Stanford, Calif., 1969), 22–53.

142. Root to Butler, December 24, 1906, ERP; Root, "The Need of Popular Understanding of International Law," in *Addresses on International Subjects*, 3–5; Marchand, *American Peace Movement*, 39–73; Patterson, *Toward a Warless World*, 143–63; DeBenedetti, *Peace Reform*, 84–85.

143. Jessup, *Root*, 1: 512.

144. Davis, *Second Hague*, 298–99; John Kenneth Kreider, "Diplomatic Relations Between Germany and the United States, 1906–1913" (PhD dissertation, Pennsylvania State University, 1969), 118–34, 148–53. The treaty, TR wrote William II, on May 6, 1908, "would confer a real benefit in the event of any sudden flurry both by providing the executives of the two countries with an excellent reason for demanding cool consideration of any question by their respective peoples, and also by enabling them to make a strong appeal under the sanction of a solemn treaty to both the peoples and their legislatures to accept an honorable arbitration." Furthermore, "the effect of such a treaty between Germany and the United States will be to furnish another evidence of the friendship between the two countries, while not to have the treaty, when such treaties have already been made with France, England, Japan … would I think invite comment." See *LTR*, 6: 1023.

145. See Root, *The Military and Colonial Policy of the United States: Addresses and Reports by Elihu Root*, ed. Robert Bacon and James Brown Scott (Cambridge, Mass., 1924), 127.

146. See "The Causes of War," February 26, 1908, in Root *Miscellaneous Addresses by Elihu Root*, ed. Robert Bacon and James Brown Scott (Cambridge, Mass., 1917), 275.

147. Davis, *Second Hague*, 300.

148. Davis, *Second Hague*, 306–8.

149. Davis, *Second Hague*, 308–12; Semmel, *Naval Strategy*, 108; Coogan, *End of Neutrality*, 105–24.

150. Scott to Knox, April 22, 1909, PCKP; James Brown Scott, *The Status of the International Court of Justice* (New York, 1916), 41–42; Davis, *Second Hague*, 312–13. Also see memoranda by J. R. Clark on arbitral court matters included in H. M. Hoyt to Huntington Wilson, September 17, 1910, PCKP.

151. After the inauguration, Knox was urged to take up the court project by Thomas Raeburn White, a representative of the Pennsylvania Arbitration and Peace Conference. White suggested that Washington move through diplomatic channels to establish the Court of Arbitral Justice simply as the project of a limited number of concurring great powers. Once established, he believed that "other nations would soon apply for admission to its deliberations." In a short time, it would "draw within the scope of its action the principal part of the international disputes of the world." James Brown Scott, the department solicitor, urged that Knox instead continue to try to constitute the new body by having its jurisdiction assigned to the prize court. To him, this seemed the easiest way of bringing the project to fruition. In the aftermath of the London Conference, moreover, Secretary Bacon had already suggested that such a U.S. initiative would be forthcoming. See White to Knox, March 31, 1909, PCKP; Scott to Knox, April 22, 1909, PCKP; Bacon to Reid, March 5, 1909, SDNF 12655.

152. See *FR 1910*, 597–605.

153. London had also come to feel that the draft convention for the new court offered too little to Britain's self-governing colonies. Reid to Knox, February 19, 1910, *FR 1910*, 608–11. France and Germany did not like the fact that the proposal relied on the unanimity of the signatories to the prize court treaty. They suggested that the new court be established instead through a supplementary or distinct agreement. See Hill to Knox, January 14, 1910, *FR 1910*, 606–7; Bacon to Knox, February 25, 1910, *FR 1910*, 611–13.

154. James Brown Scott, "Confidential Report to the Secretary of State in the Matter of the Negotiations of the Additional Protocol, the Prize Court Convention, and a Draft Convention to put into effect the Proposed Court of Arbitral Justice," memorandum dated March 31, 1911, PCKP.

155. Scott, "Confidential Report," PCKP; also see "Confidential Note on the Status of the Court of Arbitral Justice," March 31, 1911, PCKP.

156. "Confidential Note," PCKP.

157. See Semmel, *Naval Strategy*, 108–19; Coogan, *End of Neutrality*, 125–36; Clive Parry, "Foreign Policy and International Law," in *British Foreign Policy*, ed. Hinsley, 106–8; Avner Offner, *The First World War: An Agrarian Interpretation* (Oxford, 1991), 275–84.

158. See, for instance, Williams, *Defending the Empire*, 156–79; D. W. Sweet, "Great Britain and Germany, 1905–1911."

159. Quoted in Semmel, *Naval Strategy*, 115–16.

160. The government decided that it would not resubmit the measure until it had renegotiated with the other powers the wording of one section of the Declaration that it admitted was ambiguous. That was not accomplished until the fateful summer of 1914.

161. Patterson, "Origins of the World Court," 286.

162. Address in New York before the American Peace and Arbitration League, March 22, 1910, WHTP.

163. Address in Washington, D.C. before the American Society for the Judicial Settlement of International Disputes, December 17, 1910, WHTP.

164. Archibald Butt, *Taft and Roosevelt: The Intimate Letters of Archie Butt, Military Aide*, 2 vols. (Port Washington, N.Y., 1930), 2: 635.

165. Roosevelt to Taft, *LTR*, 5: 762; Harold Sprout and Margaret Sprout, *The Rise of American Naval Power, 1776–1918* (Princeton, N.J., 1967), 259–69; Charles E. Neu, *An Uncertain Friendship: Theodore Roosevelt and Japan, 1906–1909* (Cambridge, Mass., 1967), 110–12, 129, 211, 237–53; William R. Braisted, *The United States Navy in the Pacific, 1897–1909* (Austin, Tex., 1958), 180; Ronald Spector, *Admiral of the New Empire: The Life and Career of George Dewey* (Baton Rouge, La., 1974), 171–75.

166. Wilbur J. Carr, "Broad general arbitration treaties," undated memorandum, WJCP. The State Department, for instance, repeatedly pointed to arbitration during its campaign in 1910 designed to "bring out" the "altruism and unselfishness" of its diplomacy. See Knox to Huntington Wilson, May 20, 1910, PCKP; Huntington Wilson to Johnston, February 10, 1910, HWP; Huntington Wilson, "Strictly Confidential to Division of Latin American Affairs, the Diplomatic Bureau," memorandum dated May 21, 1910, HWP; Knox, "The Spirit and Purpose of American Diplomacy," June 15, 1910, commencement address at the University of Pennsylvania, reprinted in the *Congressional Record*, 61st Cong., 2d sess., Appendix, 470–74.

167. They were paired with the court, in part, because administration leaders hoped that the conclusion of such treaties might give a new boost to their campaign for that institution. See Knox's comments before the National Press Club, January 30, 1912, PCKP. Taft spoke in such terms before the Los Angeles Chamber of Commerce on October 16, 1911. At the same time, he revealed that he was beginning to think about the court in terms that went beyond Root's conception of it. "If we have such an arbitral court," the president told his audience, "the execution of its judgment will generally be through the force of international public opinion, but even if that is not enough, we may summon a police force to execute the decrees of that court." See WHTP.

168. See Bryce to Knox, April 12, 1911, with enclosures, PCKP.

169. Butt, *Taft and Roosevelt*, 2: 671–72; Kreider, "Germany and the United States," 165–70; Davis, *Second Hague*, 321–26. Numerous drafts exist in PCKP. For the treaties as signed, see U.S. Congress, Senate, *Arbitration with Great Britain*, S. Doc. 91, 62d Cong., 1st sess., 1911; U.S. Congress, Senate, *Arbitration with France*, S. Doc. 92, 62d Cong., 1st sess., 1911.

170. Their preamble therefore asserted that the signatories' purpose was, "to

conclude a treaty extending the scope and obligations of the policy of arbitration adopted in their present arbitration treaty ... so as to exclude certain exceptions contained in that treaty and to provide means for the peaceful solution of all questions of difference which it shall be found impossible in future to settle by diplomacy." U.S. Congress, Senate, *Arbitration with Great Britain*, 2. Also see Knox's handwritten notes of January 7, 1911, PCKP.

171. Knox, "International arbitrations have been in the past, as a rule diplomatic compromises," undated memorandum, PCKP; U.S. Congress, Senate, *Arbitration with Great Britain*, 3–4.

172. U.S. Congress, Senate, *Arbitration with Great Britain*, 2–3.

173. Knox, "A right in jurisprudence is an enforceable claim," undated memorandum, PCKP. Also see Knox's handwritten notes of January 7, 1911, PCKP.

174. U.S. Congress, Senate, *Arbitration with Great Britain*, 2–4.

175. John P. Campbell, "Taft, Roosevelt and the Arbitration Treaties of 1911," *Journal of American History* 53 (September 1966): 280–81; Herbert Erschkowitz, *The Attitude of Business Toward American Foreign Policy, 1900–1916* (University Park, Pa., 1967), 53; Kuehl, *Seeking World Order*, 136–43; Holt, *Treaties*, 230–31; clippings file in PCKP.

176. Theodore Roosevelt, "The Arbitration Treaty with Great Britain," *Outlook* 98 (May 20, 1911): 97–98; Roosevelt to Mahan, June 8, 1911, *LTR*, 7: 279–80; Roosevelt to Lodge, June 12, 1911, *LTR*, 7: 284; Roosevelt to Lodge, June 19, 1911, *LTR*, 7: 289–90; Roosevelt to Lodge, August 14, 1911, *LTR*, 7: 326–27; Roosevelt to Spring Rice, August 22, 1911, *LTR*, 7: 332–35; Roosevelt to Lee, August 22, 1911, *LTR*, 7: 337–39; Roosevelt to Lodge, October 3, 1911, *LTR*, 7: 400–401; Roosevelt to Bloomer, December 5, 1911, *LTR*, 7: 447–50.

177. U.S. Congress, Senate, *Report of the Committee on Foreign Relations together with the views of the minority upon the General Arbitration Treaties with Great Britain and France*, S. Doc. 98, 62d Cong., 1st sess., 1911, 3–7. Root's treaties had reflected demands from within the Senate for every case deemed arbitral by the executive to be submitted to that body for its advice and consent. Knox's treaties provided for the ratification of each *compromis*, but Lodge believed that the passage in question prohibited the Senate from amending or rejecting an agreement, after a Joint High Commission ruling had been obtained, "on the ground that in their opinion the question was not justiciable."

178. The leverage the treaties appeared to give the executive in its dealings with the Senate, meanwhile, greatly appealed to Root.

179. U.S. Congress, Senate, *Arbitration Treaties with Great Britain and France*, 9–10; Jessup, *Root*, 2: 271–76.

180. Carnegie to Taft, March 25, 1911, PCKP; U.S. Congress, Senate, *Arbitration Treaties with Great Britain and France*, 29.

181. The administration had hoped to defer the Senate Committee on Foreign Relations report as well. Taft to Knox, August 12, 1911, PCKP; Knox to Taft, August 12, 1911, PCKP.

182. Taft to Robert Taft, August 27, 1911, WHTP.

183. Taft to Knox, September 9, 1911, PCKP; Addresses of Taft at Marquette, Mich. (September 20, 1911), Denver, Col. (October 3, 1911), Boise, Idaho (October 6, 1911), and Sacramento, Calif. (October 13, 1911), all in WHTP. McKinley's campaign on behalf of reciprocity is discussed above, in Chapter 3. For his trip through the South on behalf of the Treaty of Paris, see Lewis L. Gould, *The Presidency of William McKinley* (Lawrence, Kan., 1980), 143; Robert C. Hilderbrand, *Power and the People: Executive Management of Public Opinion in Foreign Affairs, 1897–1921* (Chapel Hill, N.C., 1981), 28–42.

184. William Howard Taft, "The Dawn of World Peace," *Woman's Home Companion* (November 1911): 5–15. In discussions with its critics, the administration meanwhile

argued that qualifying the meaning of the treaties with the suggested lists of exemptions was unnecessary because the term "justiciable," as used in this case, ruled out arbitration of the questions senators had cited. To protect the third clause of Article 3, it asserted that the Senate could ratify the president's nominees to the Joint High Commission. And, with the same purpose in mind, its spokesmen also maintained that only the executive branch, not the senate, was bound by the findings of that committee. The opinions of international law expert John Bassett Moore and of State Department counselor Chandler P. Anderson were invoked to argue that the Senate's relationship to any *compromis* was the same whether it was submitted by the executive directly or after a commission ruling. Without violating the treaty, the Senate could reject arbitration of a question "which the special commission of inquiry had reported was within the scope of Article 1, if in the deliberate judgement of the Senate such question was not within the scope of that Article." See Chandler Anderson to Knox, November 2, 1911, PCKP; Notes for, and drafts of, Knox's Cincinnati address of November 8, 1911, PCKP. Also see Moore to Mahan, August 30, 1911, PCKP; and Moore to Clark, September 18, 1911, PCKP. Knox nevertheless believed the commission procedure could be valuable, as he added in a handwritten note: "Under present treaties the Senate retains power to defeat arbitration of the most general character. It can just refuse and give no reasons. In these treaties it must satisfy the world that the decision of commission is wrong."

185. U.S. Congress, Senate, *Arbitration Treaties with Great Britain and France*, 25; Knox to Taft, January 10, 1912, PCKP.

186. *Congressional Record*, 62d Cong., 2d sess., 2865–85, 2940–52.

187. *Congressional Record*, 62d Cong., 2d sess., 2953.

188. *Congressional Record*, 62d Cong., 2d sess., 2954–55.

189. *Congressional Record*, 62d Cong., 2d sess., 2955.

190. Davis, *Second Hague*, 335–37.

191. Patterson, "Origins of the World Court," 291.

192. See Davis, *Second Hague*, 332–33; Arthur S. Link, *The New Freedom* (Princeton, N.J., 1956), 280–83; Kendrick A. Clements, *William Jennings Bryan: Missionary Isolationist* (Knoxville, Tenn., 1982), 51–67; Paolo E. Coletta, *William Jennings Bryan*, 3 vols. (Lincoln, Neb., 1964–69), 2: 239–49.

193. Quoted in Josephus Daniels, *The Cabinet Diaries of Josephus Daniels, 1913–1921*, ed. E. David Cronon (Lincoln, Neb., 1963), 27.

194. For overviews, see Link, *New Freedom*, 314–18; Patrick Devlin, *Too Proud to Fight: Woodrow Wilson's Neutrality* (London, 1974), 220–25.

195. Regardless of the fact that the Wilson administration was in 1913 in the process of—temporarily—abandoning that approach in East Asia, both because it exaggerated the strength of the U.S. position there and because it had an overly simplified notion of the thrust of dollar diplomacy.

196. Address at Christiania, Norway, May 5, 1910, WTR, 16: 308–9; Taft to Otis, June 10, 1910, WHTP.

197. See Edward Mandell House, *The Intimate Papers of Colonel House: Arranged as a Narrative*, ed. Charles Seymour, 4 vols. (Boston, 1926–28), 1: 239–40, 246; "From the Diary of Colonel House," December 2, 1913, PWW, 29: 12–13; Burton J. Hendrick, *The Life and Letters of Walter H. Page*, 2 vols. (Garden City, N.Y., 1922), 1: 281.

198. See Seymour, *Intimate Papers*, 1: 240.

199. "From the Diary of Colonel House," May 2, 1913, PWW, 27: 383.

200. Seymour, *Intimate Papers*, 1: 240–41.

201. See Hendrick, *Page*, 1: 270–73.

202. "From the Diary of Colonel House," December 2, 1913, PWW, 29: 12–13.

203. Hendrick, *Page*, 1: 277–78; "From the Diary of Colonel House," December 12, 1913, PWW, 29: 33.

204. Seymour, *Intimate Papers*, 1: 246.

205. Seymour, to Wilson, May 29, 1914, *PWW*, 30: 109.

206. Seymour, *Intimate Papers*, 1: 255–56.

207. Seymour, to Wilson, June 3, 1914, *PWW*, 30: 140.

208. Seymour, *Intimate Papers*, 1: 260–61.

209. Seymour, *Intimate Papers*, 271. By the time he reached London, House had also added another component to his plan. This was to have the major creditor powers, after having reached an understanding, collaborate with regard to the promotion of conditions favorable to investment in the underdeveloped world, while at the same time ensuring that lending policies did not become subordinate to the narrow self-interest of bankers (as the Wilson administration felt had been the case with dollar diplomacy). See House to Wilson, July 4, 1914 (with enclosure, House to Wilson, June 26, 1914), *PWW*, 30: 255–57; House to Mezes, June 27, 1914, July 3, 1914, EMHP.

210. House to William II, July 8, 1914, enclosed in House to Wilson, July 9, 1914, *PWW*, 30: 265–67.

211. These issues are discussed in Kennedy, *Anglo-German Antagonism*; Steiner, *Britain*; Berghan, *Germany*; Jonathan Steinberg, "The German Background to Anglo-German Relations, 1905–1914," in *British Foreign Policy*, ed. Hinsley, 197–209; Konrad H. Jarausch, *The Enigmatic Chancellor: Bethmann Hollweg and the Hubris of Imperial Germany* (New Haven, Conn., 1973); Lambi, *German Power Politics*, 269–427.

Chapter 7. World Order (1914–17)

1. "Remarks at a Press Conference," August 3, 1914, *PWW*, 30: 332.

2. House to Wilson, August 22, 1914, *PWW*, 30: 432–33. Also see Wilson to House, August 25, 1914, *PWW*, 30: 450; "From the Diary of Colonel House," August 30, 1914, *PWW*, 30: 462, November 4, 1914, *PWW*, 31: 265–66, and November 25, 1914, *PWW*, 31: 354–55.

3. House told Wilson, for instance, that "Germany would never forgive us for the attitude we have taken in the war." "We have given them everything and they ever demand more," he later commented. He protested to Grey in 1916 that the "Allied Governments and press overlook the weight the President has thrown on their side at almost every turn." See "From the Diary of Colonel House," November 25, 1914, *PWW*, 31: 355; House to Wilson, May 14, 1916, *PWW*, 37: 42; House to Grey, June 8, 1916, *PWW*, 37: 178–80.

4. The maritime measures pursued by Britain had their origin in plans that had taken shape prior to the war in the minds of such navalists as Fisher and Maurice Hankey (at the Committee for Imperial Defense). While army leaders focused on the despatch of ground forces to the European continent, these figures still saw Britain's greatest strength as lying in its sea power. Particularly in the event of a long war with the Kaiserreich, they counted on it to ensure the volume of food and supplies that England and its army would need from overseas. Simultaneously they wanted to use Britain's naval power to deny as much of such trade as possible not just to Berlin's army but to the entire German economy and civilian population. See Avner Offer, *The First World War: An Agrarian Interpretation* (Oxford, 1991), 217–317; David French, *British Economic and Strategic Planning, 1905–1915* (London, 1982), 22–32.

5. See Page to Bryan, October 19, 1914, in *Policy of the United States Toward Maritime Commerce in War*, ed. Carlton Savage, 2 vols. (Washington, D.C., 1934–36), 2: 219–21 (this is an exceptionally useful collection of documents published by the State Department). On August 6 Washington had asked London and the other belligerent

governments if—provided its enemies did likewise—it was willing to adhere to the Declaration. But, seeking to enforce belligerent rights that extended beyond the compromises reached in 1909, London refused. Lansing subsequently sought to persuade the British that they could accept the Declaration and still achieve most of their objectives, and he even went so far as to suggest how this might be done—basically by stretching the definition of absolute contraband embodied in the Declaration and by getting neutral neighbors of Germany to agree to impose an "embargo on export of certain articles." Later he added that Washington was unlikely to object if Britain asserted a sweeping new belligerent right under which a neutral nation's port could be declared an enemy base. American policy on the Declaration can be traced through the many documents published in this work, 2: 185, 195–206, 219–21; and in House to Wilson, September 27, 1914, *PWW*, 31: 86–87; "From the Diary of Colonel House," September 28, 1914, *PWW*, 31: 92–93; "From Lansing, with enclosure," September 28, 1914, *PWW*, 31: 90–91; Lansing to Page, October 16, 1914, *PWW*, 31: 163–66; Lansing to Wilson, with enclosures, October 20, 1914, *PWW*, 31: 188–92; and Wilson to Lansing, October 21, 1914, *PWW*, 31: 198. In addition, see Marion C. Siney, *The Allied Blockade of Germany, 1914–1916* (Ann Arbor, Mich., 1957), 21–27; John W. Coogan, *The End of Neutrality: The United States, Britain, and Maritime Rights, 1899–1915* (Ithaca, N.Y., 1981), 172–74, 184–93.

6. Coogan, *End of Neutrality*, 193–253. Other useful discussions of the U.S. and the blockade are contained in Daniel M. Smith, *The Great Departure: The United States and World War I, 1914–1920* (New York, 1965), 29–49; Ernest R. May, *The World War and American Isolation, 1914–1917* (Chicago, 1966), 34–71, 305–29; Patrick Devlin, *Too Proud to Fight: Woodrow Wilson's Neutrality* (London, 1974), 157–210, 351–58.

7. Bryan to Gerard, February 10, 1915, in Savage, ed., *Policy*, 2: 267–69.

8. On the background to this effort, see House to Wilson, July 31, 1914, *PWW*, 30: 323–24; and "From the Diary of Colonel House," August 30, 1914, *PWW*, 30: 463; House to Wilson, September 6, 1914, *PWW*, 31: 5–6. Wilson made a pro forma tender of good offices, under Article 3 of the Hague convention during the first week in August. There had by this point also been an unsuccessful effort at mediation launched by Bryan in early September. He was subsequently kept from engaging in such activity. See "A Press Release," August 4, 1914, *PWW*, 30: 342; Smith, *Great Departure*, 17; C. M. Mason, "Anglo-American Relations: Mediation and 'Permanent Peace'," in *British Foreign Policy Under Sir Edward Grey*, ed. F. H. Hinsley (Cambridge, 1977), 468; Devlin, *Too Proud to Fight*, 229–30.

9. House to Wilson, September 18, 1914, *PWW*, 31: 45; Wilson to House, September 19, 1914, *PWW*, 31: 55; House to Wilson, September 19, 1914, *PWW*, 31: 55; House to Wilson, September 20, 1914, *PWW*, 31: 60–61; Spring Rice to Grey, September 20, 1914, *PWW*, 31: 62; Bryce to Wilson, September 24, 1914, *PWW*, 31: 82; "From the Diary of Colonel House," September 28, 1914, *PWW*, 31: 94–95; House to Wilson, October 8, 1914, *PWW*, 31: 137; Devlin, *Too Proud to Fight*, 228–33; Arthur S. Link, *Wilson: The Struggle for Neutrality, 1914–1915* (Princeton, 1960), 200–206.

10. Much in the way that Root had hoped the Central American court might constitute a model of broader relevance.

11. "From the Diary of Colonel House," December 3, 1914, *PWW*, 31: 385.

12. Quoted in Edward Mandell House, *The Intimate Papers of Colonel House: Arranged as a Narrative*, ed. Charles Seymour, 4 vols. (Boston, 1926–28), 1: 339–40.

13. Seymour, *Intimate Papers*, 1: 340.

14. "From the Diary of Colonel House," December 18, 1914, *PWW*, 31: 490.

15. See David Stevenson, *The First World War and International Politics* (Oxford, 1991), 91–94; Fritz Fischer, *Germany's Aims in the First World War* (New York, 1967), 110–113; Devlin, *Too Proud to Fight*, 242–45.

16. Stevenson, *First World War*, 106–10; V. H. Rothwell, *British War Aims and Peace*

Diplomacy, 1914–1918 (Oxford, 1971), 18–24; Mason, "Anglo-American Relations," 466–71; Devlin, *Too Proud to Fight*, 255–56.

17. "From the Diary of Colonel House," December 23, 1914, *PWW*, 31: 519.

18. For overviews and interpretations of his trip, see Seymour, *Intimate Papers*, 1: 359–471; Devlin, *Too Proud to Fight*, 264–82; Link, *Struggle for Neutrality*, 214–31; Mason, "Anglo-American Relations," 472–73; Lloyd E. Ambrosius, *Wilsonian Statecraft: The Theory and Practice of Liberal Internationalism During World War I* (Wilmington, Del.,1991), 36–39; May, *World War*, 87–89, 108–9; and Thomas J. Knock, *To End All Wars: Woodrow Wilson and the Quest for a New World Order* (Princeton, N.J., 1992), 44–47.

19. "From the Diary of Chandler Parsons Anderson," January 9, 1915, *PWW*, 32: 44–50.

20. Seymour, *Intimate Papers*, 1: 351.

21. Quoted in Link, *Struggle for Neutrality*, 219.

22. House to Wilson, February 9, 1915, *PWW*, 32: 205.

23. House to Wilson, February 9, 1915, *PWW*, 32: 205; House to Wilson, February 11, 1915, *PWW*, 32: 220–21; House to Wilson, February 15, 1915, *PWW*, 32: 237–38; Seymour, *Intimate Papers*, 1: 368–69.

24. House to Wilson, March 14, 1914, *PWW*, 32: 372–75.

25. See Seymour, *Intimate Papers*, 397.

26. Seymour, *Intimate Papers*, 369–70.

27. House to Wilson, February 23, 1915, *PWW*, 32: 278.

28. House to Wilson, March 20, 1915, *PWW*, 32: 402–3.

29. House to Wilson, March 20, 1915, *PWW*, 32: 402–3; House to Wilson, March 26, 1915, *PWW*, 32: 438–39; House to Wilson, March 27, 1915, *PWW*, 32: 441–43; House to Wilson, March 29, 1915, *PWW*, 32: 455–56; House to Wilson, April 11, 1915, *PWW*, 32: 504–7.

30. See House to Wilson, April 30, 1915, *PWW*, 33: 88–89; House to Wilson, May 3, 1915, *PWW*, 33: 100–101; House to Wilson, May 7, 1915, *PWW*, 33: 121–24.

31. For the text, see Savage, ed., *Policy*, 2: 265–66. Berlin, at this time, had in fact only a small number of submarines (as Britain was aware). Only two boats patrolled British waters in February 1915. See Holger H. Herwig, *"Luxury" Fleet: The Imperial Germany Navy, 1888–1918* (London, 1987), 219.

32. Bryan to Gerard, February 10, 1915, in Savage, ed., *Policy*, 2: 267–69.

33. See Karl E. Birnbaum, *Peace Moves and U-Boat Warfare: A Study of Imperial Germany's Policy Toward the United States, April 18, 1916–January 9, 1917* (Stockholm, 1958), 22–27; Devlin, *Too Proud to Fight*, 200–216; Link, *Struggle for Neutrality*, 309–67; Smith, *Great Departure*, 51–54; Savage, ed., *Policy*, 2: 52–56; Coogan, *End of Neutrality*, 221–36.

34. For overviews of the *Lusitania* and *Arabic* crises, see Birnbaum, *Peace Moves*, 27–38; Devlin, *Too Proud to Fight*, 283–334; Link, *Struggle for Neutrality*, 368–455, 551–87, 645–81; Smith, *Great Departure*, 54–63; Savage, ed., *Policy*, 2: 56–66.

35. House to Wilson, May 9, 1915, PWW, 33: 134; House to Wilson, May 11, 1915, *PWW*, 33: 158–59; Lansing to Bryan, May 10, 1915, *PWW*, 33: 144–45; Devlin, *Too Proud to Fight*, 289–91. Also see the important discussion in May, *World War*, 137–53, where he emphasizes, as I do below, the consideration of "prestige."

    Berlin had said it could not always adhere to the practice of giving passengers and crew the opportunity to first seek safety because of the fragility of submarines and their vulnerablity to ramming and light artillery fire.

36. See Kendrick A. Clements, *William Jennings Bryan: Missionary Isolationist* (Knoxville, Tenn., 1982), 106–9; Paolo E. Coletta, *William Jennings Bryan*, 3 vols. (Lincoln, Neb., 1964–69), 2: 301–20.

37. Quoted in Coletta, *Bryan*, 2: 317.

38. Bryan to Wilson, May 9, 1915, *PWW*, 33: 135.

39. Quoted in Coletta, *Bryan*, 2: 302.

40. House to Wilson, May 9, 1915, *PWW*, 33: 134.

41. Page to Wilson, May 8, 1915, *PWW*, 33: 130.

42. Wilson to Bryan, May 10, 1915, *PWW*, 33: 139.

43. Bryan to Gerard, May 13, 1915, in Savage, ed., *Policy*, 2: 315–18.

44. Gerard to Bryan, May 29, 1915, in Savage, ed., *Policy*, 2: 327–30.

45. Only the "actual resistance" of such merchant ships afforded submarine commanders "any justification for so much as putting the lives of those on board" in jeopardy, it said. See Lansing to Gerard, June 9, 1915, in Savage, ed., *Policy*, 2: 340–43.

46. Coletta, *Bryan*, 2: 329–44; Clements, *Missionary Isolationist*, 109–11; John Milton Cooper, Jr., *The Vanity of Power: American Isolationism and World War I, 1914–1917* (Westport, Conn., 1969), 41–43.

47. Kendrick A. Clements, *The Presidency of Woodrow Wilson* (Lawrence, Kan., 1992), 126.

48. Gerard to Lansing, July 8, 1911, in Savage, ed., *Policy*, 2: 351–55.

49. House to Wilson, July 10,1915, *PWW*, 33: 490–91.

50. Wilson to House, July 14, 1915, *PWW*, 33: 505–506.

51. Lansing to Gerard, July 21, 1915, in Savage, ed., *Policy*, 2: 361–63; Devlin, *Too Proud to Fight*, 309–12.

52. Devlin, *Too Proud to Fight*, 307–8.

53. Wilson to Galt, August 19, 1915, *PWW*, 34: 257–61; Wilson to Galt, August 27, 1915, *PWW*, 34: 304. Also see Wilson to House, August 21, 1915, *PWW*, 34: 271.

54. Wilson to Galt, August 9,1915, *PWW*, 34: 151.

55. House to Wilson, August 22, 1915, *PWW*, 34: 298–99; Lansing to Wilson, August 20, 1915, *PWW*, 34: 264–66.

56. Gerard to Lansing, August 24, 1915, *PWW*, 34: 320; Bernstorff to Lansing, September 1, 1915, in Savage, ed., *Policy*, 2: 378. Also see Birnbaum, *Peace Moves*, 34–35.

57. See Devlin, *Too Proud to Fight*, 327–34; Link, *Struggle for Neutrality*, 653–81; Birnbaum, *Peace Moves*, 35–37.

58. Grey to House, June 2, 1915, *PWW*, 33: 408; Grey to House, July 14, 1915, in Seymour, *Intimate Papers*, 2: 55–56; Grey to House, August 10, 1915, *PWW*, 34: 371–72; Devlin, *Too Proud to Fight*, 379–80.

59. For overviews and (a wide range of) interpretations of developments leading up to the House-Grey Memorandum, see Devlin, *Too Proud to Fight*, 376–453; Arthur S. Link, *Wilson: Confusions and Crises, 1915–1916* (Princeton, 1964), 101–41; Arthur S. Link, *Woodrow Wilson: Revolution, War, and Peace* (Arlington Heights, Ill., 1979); Smith, *Great Departure*, 67–70; Seymour, *Intimate Papers*, 2: 82–204; John Milton Cooper, Jr., *The Warrior and the Priest: Woodrow Wilson and Theodore Roosevelt* (Cambridge, Mass., 1983), 293–95; Ambrosius, *Wilsonian Statecraft*, 48–54; May, *World War*, 327–28, 347–56; N. Gordon Levin, Jr., *Woodrow Wilson and World Politics: America's Response to War and Revolution* (New York, 1970), 13–49; Knock, *To End All Wars*, 68–74; George W. Egerton, *Great Britain and the Creation of the League of Nations: Strategy, Politics, and International Organization, 1914–1919* (Chapel Hill, N.C., 1978), 25–29; Mason, "Anglo-American Relations," 473–77. Older historiographical debates in which the memorandum figured prominently are surveyed in Jerald A. Combs, *American Diplomatic History: Two Centuries of Changing Interpretations* (Berkeley, Calif., 1983), 140–42, 147–49.

60. "From the Diary of Colonel House," September 22, 1915, *PWW*, 34: 506.

61. "From the Diary of Colonel House," October 8, 1915, *PWW*, 35: 42–44.

62. Grey to House, September 22, 1915, *PWW*, 35: 71–72.

63. "From the Diary of Colonel House," October 15, 1915, *ibid.*, 35: 71.

64. House to Grey, October 17, 1915, *PWW*, 35: 81–82; Wilson to House, October 18, 1915, *PWW*, 35: 80.

65. Grey to House, November 9, 1915, *PWW*, 35: 186.

66. House to Wilson, November 10, 1915, *PWW*, 35: 186; Wilson to House, November 11, 1915, *PWW*, 35: 187.

67. House to Wilson, November 11, 1915, *PWW*, 35: 191.

68. Quoted in Seymour, *Intimate Papers*, 2: 98.

69. Seymour, *Intimate Papers*, 2: 98.

70. Bryce to House, November 26, 1915, *PWW*, 35: 347–48.

71. House to Wilson, January 7, 1916, *PWW*, 35: 454.

72. House to Wilson, January 11, 1916, *PWW*, 35: 466; Seymour, *Intimate Papers*, 2:129.

73. House to Wilson, January 11, 1916, *PWW*, 35: 466.

74. Seymour, *Intimate Papers*, 2: 117.

75. In his talks with Lloyd George, a good deal of attention was paid to Asia. Wilson's emissary urged Britain to turn its attention away from that continent in the future. "[I]f I were guiding the destinies of England, I would concentrate on Africa, Australia and her other colonies outside of Asia." India could not be held forever, he said. And House sought to warn Britain away from East Asia on the grounds that "China in the future might play the same rôle Turkey has in the past, and be the cause of innumerable bloody conflicts." House to Wilson, January 15, 1916, *PWW*, 35: 484–86; Seymour, *Intimate Papers*, 2: 129.

76. Seymour, *Intimate Papers*, 141–42; House to Wilson, February 3, 1916, *PWW*, 36: 122–24

77. House to Wilson, January 30, 1916, *PWW*, 36: 52.

78. House to Wilson, February 3, 1916, *PWW*, 36: 125. Briand was premier and foreign minister, Cambon the secretary-general of the Foreign Ministry.

79. House to Wilson, February 9, 1916, *PWW*, 36: 147.

80. Seymour, *Intimate Papers*, 2: 158.

81. Seymour, *Intimate Papers*, 2: 167–68; House to Wilson, February 9, 1911, *PWW*, 36: 150.

82. See Seymour, *Intimate Papers*, 2: 201–2. I would tend to agree with Devlin, *Too Proud to Fight*, 452–53, among others, that too much should not be made of Wilson's subsequent addition of a second "probably" to this document (in the second paragraph, between the words "would" and "leave"). Also see "From the Diary of Colonel House," March 7, 1916, *PWW*, 36: 266.

83. House to Grey, March 7, 1916, *PWW*, 36: 266.

84. Seymour, *Intimate Papers*, 2: 195; House to Wilson, February 10, 1916, *PWW*, 36: 166–68; House to Wilson, February 13, 1916, *PWW*, 36: 173; "From the Diary of Colonel House," March 6, 1916, *PWW*, 36: 262–63; House to Wilson, March 12, 1916, *PWW*, 36: 294.

85. Devlin, *Too Proud to Fight*, 450–51; House to Wilson, November 10, 1915, *PWW*, 35: 186. Wilson's relationship to Democrats in Congress in early 1916 is summarized in Cooper, *Warrior and the Priest*, 297–99.

86. See House to Wilson, December 24, 1915, *PWW*, 35: 388.

87. For overviews of the *Sussex* crisis, see Devlin, *Too Proud to Fight*, 473–82; Link, *Confusions and Crises*, 222–79; Birnbaum, *Peace Moves*, 70–92.

88. "From the Diary of Colonel House," March 30, 1916, *PWW*, 36: 388.

89. House to Wilson, April 3, 1916, *PWW*, 36: 405.

90. House to Grey, April 6, 1916, *PWW*, 36: 421.

91. Quoted in Link, *Confusions and Crises*, 238.

92. See "From the Diary of Colonel House," March 30, 1916, *PWW*, 36: 388.

93. House to Wilson, April 3, 1916, *PWW*, 36: 405.

94. Lansing to Gerard, April 18, 1916, in Savage, ed., *Policy*, 2: 476–80; Smith, *Great Departure*, 64–65. The next day, House wrote Wilson, enclosing a letter from Grey. "You will notice," House wrote, "that he makes the point that we saw was inevitable, that is if Germany is permitted to continue her submarine policy unrebuked,

we would lose the friendship and respect of the Allies to such an extent that they would not have confidence in our acting with a sufficiently strong hand in the peace councils." See House to Wilson, April 19, 1916, *PWW*, 36: 511–12.

95. Birnbaum, *Peace Moves*, 88–92; Stevenson, *First World War*, 71–72; Savage, ed., *Policy*, 2: 494–95.

96. "From the Diary of Colonel House," May 3, 1916, *PWW*, 36: 596–602.

97. "From the Diary of Colonel House," May 3, 1916, *PWW*, 36: 596–602.

98. House to Grey, May 7, 1916, *PWW*, 36: 652.

99. House to Wilson, May 7, 1916, *PWW*, 36: 631–32. Also see Wilson to House, May 8, 1916, *PWW*, 36: 652.

100. House to Grey, May 11, 1916, *PWW*, 37: 21.

101. Mason, "Anglo-American Relations," in Hinsley, ed., *Grey*, 477–80; Rothwell, *British War Aims*, 33–36; Paul Guinn, *British Strategy and Politics, 1914–1918* (Oxford, 1965), 124–25; Stevenson, *First World War*, 81.

102. Grey to House, May 12, 1916, *PWW*, 37: 43–44.

103. House to Wilson, May 14, 1916, *PWW*, 37: 42.

104. House to Wilson, with enclosure, May 17, 1916, *PWW*, 37: 62–64; Wilson to House, May 18, 1916, *PWW*, 37: 68; House to Grey, May 23, 1916, *PWW*, 37: 100.

105. Taft to Wilson, April 11, 1916, *PWW*, 36: 458–59. Wilson initially begged off. See Wilson to Taft, April 14, 1916, *PWW*, 36: 481. On the history of the League to Enforce Peace to this point see Warren F. Kuehl, *Seeking World Order: The United States and International Organization to 1920* (Nashville, Tenn., 1969), 184–92; and Ruhl J. Bartlett, *The League to Enforce Peace* (Chapel Hill, N.C., 1944), 3–56.

106. House to Wilson, May 9, 1911, *PWW*, 37: 6–7. Wilson's initial reaction to the League to Enforce Peace approach was less critical. See Wilson to House, May 18, 1916, *PWW*, 37: 68–69.

107. "An Address in Washington to the League to Enforce Peace," May 27, 1916, *PWW*, 37: 113–16.

108. Grey to House, May 29, 1916, *PWW*, 37: 11–32.

109. House to Grey, June 8, 1916, *PWW*, 37: 178–80.

110. Wilson to House, June 22, 1916, *PWW*, 37: 280–81.

111. House to Wilson, July 30, 1916, *PWW*, 37: 502.

112. "Remarks to the Associated Press in New York," April 20, 1915, *PWW*, 33: 38.

113. House to Wilson, January 16, 1916, *PWW*, 35: 488.

114. "An Unpublished Article," July 30, 1916, *PWW*, 37: 500–502.

115. These issues are referred to in Devlin, *Too Proud to Fight*, 140, 187–88, 490.

116. See, for instance, Seymour, *Intimate Papers*, 1: 458–59; and Jeffrey J. Safford, *Wilsonian Maritime Diplomacy, 1913–1921* (New Brunswick, N.J., 1978), 78–80.

117. For the U.S., see the discussion, in particular, of South American trade in Chapter 3. For England, see, for instance, Devlin, *Too Proud to Fight*, 351. Also see Bernard Semmel, *Liberalism and Naval Strategy: Ideology, Interest, and Sea Power During the Pax Britannica* (Boston, 1986), 163.

118. House to Wilson, December 7, 1915, *PWW*, 35: 311.

119. Seymour, *Intimate Papers*, 2: 284.

120. Gerd Hardach, *The First World War* (Berkeley, Calif., 1977), 238–40; Lansing to Wilson, June 23, 1916, *PWW*, 37: 287–88. Also see Siney, *Allied Blockade*, 177–79; Carl P. Parrini, *Heir to Empire: United States Economic Diplomacy, 1916–1923* (Pittsburgh, 1969), 15–16; and Safford, *Wilsonian Maritime Diplomacy*, 89.

121. Siney, *Allied Blockade*, 181–85; Devlin, *Too Proud to Fight*, 505–7.

122. Many in the U.S. voiced the belief that an objective was to steal American commercial secrets and information. See Kathleen Burk, *Britain, America and the Sinews of War, 1914–1918* (Boston, 1985), 41; Arthur Marsden, "The Blockade," in *British Foreign Policy*, ed. Hinsley, 511; Siney, *Allied Blockade*, 148–55.

123. British firms could not legally do business with such firms. Many Americans believed that the list was being used primarily to damage their trade. See Safford, *Wilsonian Maritime Diplomacy*, 90; Devlin, *Too Proud to Fight*, 505–14; Siney, *Allied Blockade*, 146.

124. And that good long-term relations between the two powers were necessary just in case Berlin sought to settle accounts with America after the war. See House to Wilson, May 14, 1915, *PWW*, 33: 197–98; House to Wilson, May 25, 1915, *PWW*, 33: 254; and "From the Diary of Colonel House," December 15, 1915, *PWW*, 33: 355–57.

125. See Lansing to Jusserand, May 24, 1916, in Savage, ed., *Policy*, 2: 498–504; and Polk to Page, July 26, 1916, 2: 505–7.

126. Wilson to House, July 23, 1916, *PWW*, 37: 467.

127. No similar analysis was applied though to U.S. behavior—to the contradictions that had recently been revealed in Mexico, for instance, in the meaning and practice of Pan-Americanism.

128. Seymour, *Intimate Papers*, 2: 319.

129. Quoted in Ross Gregory, *The Origins of American Intervention in the First World War* (New York, 1971), 110.

130. Devlin, *Too Proud to Fight*, 518. As historian Jeffrey Safford has noted, the administration's Shipping Act, which was enacted at this time and which gave the government emergency power to begin the construction of an American merchant marine, was also valued as a step which would allow the U.S. to thwart and challenge London's policies. See Safford, *Wilsonian Maritime Diplomacy*, 9–91.

131. Clements, *Wilson*, 128.

132. "An Annual Message to Congress," December 8, 1914, *PWW*, 31: 414–24.

133. See Link, *Confusions and Crises*, 15–54, 327–39; Cooper, *Vanity of Power*, 90–105.

134. House to Wilson, June 1, 1916, *PWW*, 37: 134.

135. House to Wilson, May 17, 1916, *PWW*, 37: 64. Also see House to Wilson, June 18, 1916, *PWW*, 37: 265; and House to Wilson, June 25, 1916, *PWW*, 37: 295.

136. Harold and Margaret Sprout, *The Rise of American Naval Power, 1776–1918* (Princeton, N.J., 1966), 334–46.

137. "From the Diary of Colonel House," September 24, 1916, *PWW*, 38: 258–59. Many in London now came to worry about Washington, as historian Bernard Semmel puts it, "seizing the trident," of naval supremacy. See his *Naval Strategy*, 167.

138. On the campaign, see especially Link, *Wilson: Campaigns for Progressivism and Peace, 1916–1917* (Princeton, N.J., 1965), 1–48, 93–164.

139. Link, *Campaigns*, 42–48, 106–112; Devlin, *Too Proud to Fight*, 527–28. Wilson also made some effort in 1916 to tie the theme of peace to his policy goals. The only guarantee of peace in the long-term, he asserted, was American participation in world affairs through its promotion of, and membership, in a league of nations. This would not constitute involvement in an "entangling alliance," the president argued, since its purpose would be to "disentangle the people of the world from those combinations in which they seek their own separate and private interests and unite the people of the world to preserve the peace of the world upon a basis of common right and justice." Quoted in Cooper, *Warrior and the Priest*, 301–2.

To Wilson, the U.S. had ever since the 1890s—when census takers reported that they could no longer draw a frontier line within the American West—"been caught inevitably in the net of the politics of the world." "We had a program for America in respect of its domestic life," he told one audience in October 1916. But, "we have never yet sufficiently formulated our program for America with regard to the part she is going to play in the world." See "An Address in Omaha," October 5, 1916, *PWW*, 38: 343–49.

140. Cooper, *Warrior and the Priest*, 304–308; Link, *Campaigns*, 111, 135.

141. See Gerard to Lansing, September 25,1916, *PWW*, 38: 313–14.

142. House to Wilson, with enclosures, October 20, 1916, *PWW*, 38: 494–96.

143. "From the Diary of Colonel House," November 14, 1916, *PWW*, 38: 646.

144. House to Wilson, November 20, 1916, *PWW*, 40: 5; House to Wilson, with enclosure, November 25, 1916, *PWW*, 40: 74–75.

145. "From the Diary of Colonel House," November 14, 1916, *PWW*, 38: 646–47; "From the Diary of Colonel House," November 15, 1916, *PWW*, 38: 656–59. House argued that such a move might also revive the prospects for a German victory. If Germany did accept, it would subsequently be more difficult for Washington to muster American public support for a firm line if Berlin decided to break with the *Sussex* pledge.

146. Wilson to House, November 24, 1916, *PWW*, 40: 62–63. House's subsequent letter was phrased in milder terms. See Link, *Campaigns*, 197.

147. See Bryan to J.P. Morgan and Co., August 15, 1916, in Savage, ed., *Policy*, 1: 194.

148. Lansing to Wilson, September 6, 1915, *PWW*, 34: 421–23. Also see Smith, *Great Departure*, 34–37; and Link, *Struggle for Neutrality*, 62–64, 132–36, 616–28.

149. See "News Report," November 21, 1916, *PWW*, 40: 19–20; Davison to Wilson, November 25, 1916, *PWW*, 40: 75–76; Wilson to Harding, with enclosure, November 26, 1916, *PWW*, 40: 77–80; and Burk, *Sinews of War*, 75–88.

150. Quoted in Burk, *Sinews of War*, 88.

151. Spring Rice to Foreign Office, December 3, 1916, *PWW*, 40: 136–37.

152. "A Draft of a Peace Note," c. November 25, 1916, *PWW*, 40: 70–74.

153. Enclosed in Wilson to Lansing, December 9, 1916, *PWW*, 40: 197–200. Also see "From the Diary of Colonel House," November 26, 1916, *PWW*, 40: 84–85; Devlin, *Too Proud to Fight*, 566; and Link, *Campaigns*, 199.

154. Enclosed with Lansing to Wilson, December 14, 1916, *PWW*, 40: 231–32.

155. Page to Lansing, December 15, 1916, *PWW*, 40: 247.

156. "From the Diary of Colonel House," December 14, 1916, *PWW*, 40: 238; Wilson to Lansing, with enclosure, December 15, 1916, *PWW*, 40: 241–43; Wilson to Lansing, December 17, 1916, *PWW*, 40: 256; Wilson to House, December 19, 1916, *PWW*, 40: 276.

157. "An Appeal for a Statement of War Aims," December 18, 1916, *PWW*, 40: 273–76. American representatives in the warring capitals were instructed to convey the impression "that it would be very hard for the Government of the United States to understand a negative reply."

158. Gerard to Lansing, December 26, 1918, *PWW*, 40: 331.

159. See, for instance, Wilson to House, with enclosures, November 21, 1916, *PWW*, 40: 20–24; Lansing to Wilson, with enclosure, December 4, 1916, *PWW*, 40: 141–46; Lansing to Wilson, with enclosure, December 5, 1916, *PWW*, 40: 160–61.

160. House to Wilson, December 27, 1916, *PWW*, 40: 337.

161. See Link, *Campaigns*, 221–25; Devlin, *Too Proud to Fight*, 580–83; Clements, *Wilson*, 135–36; Daniel M. Smith, *Robert Lansing and American Neutrality: 1914–1917* (Berkeley, Calif., 1958), 77–78; Robert Lansing, *War Memoirs of Robert Lansing, Secretary of State* (Indianapolis, 1935), 186–90. Also see "What Will the President Do?," memorandum dated December 3, 1916 in RLP. Lansing's remarks to the press almost resulted in Wilson asking for his resignation.

162. Guinn, *British Strategy and Politics*, 174–76; Stevenson, *First World War*, 110.

163. Here, in addition to the discussions in Guinn and Stevenson above, see Rothwell, *British War Aims*, 39–55, 59, 66.

164. Devlin, *Too Proud to Fight*, 544–47.

165. Guinn, *British Strategy and Politics*, 191–95; Stevenson, *First World War*, 111. Also see Robert J. Scally, *The Origins of the Lloyd George Coalition: The Politics of Social Imperialism, 1900–1918* (Princeton, N.J., 1975), 336–70.

166. Devlin, *Too Proud to Fight*, 548–51 (McKenna quote is on p. 551).

167. Page to Wilson, December 29, 1916, *PWW*, 40: 355–58; Rothwell, *British War Aims*, 60–61; Devlin, *Too Proud to Fight*, 587–88.

168. Sharp to Lansing, January 10, 1917, *PWW*, 40: 439–41.

169. Link, *Campaigns*, 238; Balfour to Spring Rice, January 13, 1917, *PWW*, 40: 500–503. Also see Rothwell, *British War Aims*, 64–65; Devlin, *Too Proud to Fight*, 591; Mason, "Anglo-American Relations," 486–87.

170. "From the Diary of Colonel House," January 3, 1917, *PWW*, 40: 403–5. Instead of this device, Wilson, in the end, simply asked to be allowed to address the senate. See Link, *Campaigns*, 264–65.

171. "From the Diary of Colonel House," January 11, 1917, *PWW*, 40: 445–46; "From the Diary of Colonel House," January 12, 1917, *PWW*, 40: 462–63. Although time was considered to be of "the essence," the speech could not be given earlier because it had to be transmitted, and transcribed into and out of code, so that it might simultaneously be reprinted and distributed throughout Europe.

172. See Link, *Campaigns*, 254–55.

173. "An Address to the Senate," January 22, 1917, *PWW*, 40: 533–39; "From the Diary of Colonel House," January 3, 1917, *PWW*, 40: 404.

174. House to Wilson, January 23, 1917, *PWW*, 40: 558.

175. Wilson to House, January 24, 1917, *PWW*, 41: 3–4.

176. House to Wilson, January 25, 1917, *PWW*, 41: 17–18; House to Wilson, January 26, 1917, *PWW*, 41: 24–26.

177. The above is based heavily on Birnbaum, *Peace Moves*, 20–21, 48–339. For German aims in this period, see Stevenson, *First World War*, 104–6; Fritz Fischer, *Germany's Aims*, 285–324; and Devlin, *Too Proud to Fight*, 570, 625–26.

178. Enclosed with Lansing to Wilson, January 31, 1917, *PWW*, 41: 71–79.

179. See Lansing to Wilson, with enclosure, February 2, 1917, *PWW*, 41: 96–99; Lansing to Wilson, February 2, 1917, *PWW*, 41: 99–100; "A Memorandum by Robert Lansing," February 4, 1917, *PWW*, 41: 118–25.

180. *PWW*, 41: 120.

181. "From the Diary of Colonel House," February 1, 1917, *PWW*, 41: 86–89.

182. *PWW*, 41: 87.

183. "A Memorandum by Robert Lansing," February 4, 1917, *PWW*, 41: 120. "We are the only one of the great White nations that is free from war today," he had told House several weeks earlier, "and it would be a crime against civilization for us to go in." See "From the Diary of Colonel House," January 4, 1917, *PWW*, 40: 409.

184. See Link, *Campaigns*, 296.

185. "A Memorandum by Robert Lansing," February 4, 1917, *PWW*, 41: 120–21; Lansing to Wilson, February 2, 1917, *PWW*, 41: 100; "From the Diary of Colonel House," February 1, 1917, *PWW*, 41: 87; Link, *Campaigns*, 298.

186. Link, *Campaigns*, 298–99.

187. If Berlin did, however, actually adopt the new policy announced with regard to the waters off the Allied nations, then Wilson would come back before Congress to "ask that authority be given me to use any means that may be necessary for the protection of our seamen and our people in the prosecution of their peaceful and legitimate errands on the high seas." See "An Address to a Joint Session of Congress," February 3, 1917, *PWW*, 41: 108–12.

188. Devlin, *Too Proud to Fight*, 642.

189. House to Wilson, January 27, 1917, *PWW*, 41: 39–40; "From the Diary of Colonel House," February 1, 1917, *PWW*, 41: 88–89; Penfield to Lansing, February

5, 1917, *PWW*, 41: 129–30. The British government had in late 1916 taken up the idea, as historian C.M Mason puts it, of trying to achieve a pacified postwar Europe by giving broad scope to the "principle of nationality." See Mason, "Anglo-American Relations," 485.

190. Lansing to Page, February 8, 1917, *PWW*, 41: 158–59.

191. Page to Lansing, February 11, 1917, *PWW*, 41: 211–14.

192. Page to Lansing, February 20, 1917, *PWW*, 41: 260.

193. Lansing to Wilson, with enclosure, February 21, 1917, *PWW*, 41: 267–68; Penfield to Lansing, February 27, 1917, *PWW*, 41: 297–300; Wilson to Lansing, with enclosure, March 3, 1917, *PWW*, 41: 313. Also see Link, *Campaigns*, 341–18, 385–86.

194. Link, *Campaigns*, 378–79; Devlin, *Too Proud to Fight*, 646.

195. Quoted in Devlin, *Too Proud to Fight*, 661. Also see Burk, *Sinews of War*, 93–95.

196. See Burk, *Sinews of War*, 310–13; 340–41; Devlin, *Too Proud to Fight*, 643–45.

197. Wilson may at first have even seen armed neutrality as a course that would allow him to keep his options open—as an effective means, in other words, of defending American trade with Britain if Germany did in fact attack. But, given the evident failure of such measures to protect Allied shipping, it is unlikely that he entertained that idea for long.

198. Link, *Campaigns*, 347–67, 372–77; Devlin, *Too Proud to Fight*, 652–63; Cooper, *Vanity of Power*, 158–60, 175–89.

199. Cooper, *Warrior and the Priest*, 320; Link, *Campaigns*, 399–400.

200. Quoted in *ibid.*, 398.

201. He appears to have made this decision by March 20. See Link, *Campaigns*, 390–419; and Devlin, *Too Proud to Fight*, 663–67, 671–88. Also see Lansing's memorandum of the cabinet meeting of March 20 in *PWW*, 41: 436–44.

202. "From the Diary of Colonel House," August 30, 1914, *PWW*, 30: 462.

Conclusion

1. Roosevelt to Spring Rice, March 16, 1901, *LTR*, 3: 16.

2. Some readers will immediately object that the broad patterns outlined here were reversed by a "return to isolation" in the 1920s. But the trend of scholarship for some time now has been sharply against the idea that foreign policy in that decade can appropriately be characterized in that way, and this study, I would argue, makes more clear than ever how continuous the 1920s were, in both goals and methodologies, with the fundamental trajectory of policy in the era from 1898 to World War I (continuity is also physically embodied in the presence of important figures such as Root and Stimson in the councils of what are now sometimes referred to as the "independent internationalist" administrations of the 1920s). Many of the postwar era's key emphases, on such things as dollar diplomacy, regional great-power arrangements for stability (like those provided for at the Washington Naval Conference), arbitration, and international law can all be better understood against this backdrop.

Central to the older, "isolationist" view of the 1920s was a misunderstanding of the attitudes of members of the Republican foreign policy establishment toward a league. At least until the issue became entwined with questions of intraparty and domestic politics (and with personality), the idea in fact had considerable support from prominent Republican policy influentials. Most "appreciated the value of a league in preserving order," as historian Frank Costigliola writes; to some extent this even includes "legalists" like Root who worried that such an organization might prove counterproductive. The policy debate between Republican influentials and Wilson was not about American involvement in the world or even necessarily a league. Rather it was more narrowly centered on the kind of commitment the U.S. would be making under Article 10 of the Covenant of Wilson's plan (under which each signatory would pledge "to respect and preserve as against external aggression the territorial integrity and existing political independence of all" members). Wilson asserted that the U.S. would be the "senior partner" in the institution, the "financial leadership will be ours," the "industrial primacy will be ours." But prominent Republicans were less sure how much power the U.S. would have within the organization and were worried that Article 10 might force it to act in instances where Washington's interests were not served.

Much important work has been done on the 1920s. For some of the more general studies, see Frank Costigliola, *Awkward Dominion: American Political and Cultural Relations with Europe, 1919–1933* (Ithaca, N.Y., 1987) (quotation p. 30); Joan Hoff Wilson, *American Business and Foreign Policy, 1920–1933* (Boston, 1971); Warren I. Cohen, *Empire Without Tears: America's Foreign Relations, 1921–1933* (New York, 1987); Robert Freeman Smith, "Republican Policy and the Pax Americana, 1921–1932," in *From Colony to Empire: Essays in the History of American Foreign Relations*, ed. William Appleman Williams (New York, 1972); and Williams's seminal essay, "The Legend of Isolationism in the 1920s," *Science and Society* 18 (1954): 1–20. On the Republicans and the League in 1919–20, see William C. Widenor, *Henry Cabot Lodge and the Search for an American Foreign Policy* (Berkeley, Calif., 1980), 300–348; Herbert F. Margulies, *The Mild Reservationists and the League of Nations Controversy in the Senate* (Columbia, Mo., 1989); Ralph Stone, *The Irreconcilables: The Fight Against the League of Nations* (New York, 1970); David S. Patterson, *Toward a Warless World: The Travail of the American Peace Movement, 1887–1914* (Bloomington, Ind., 1976), 250–55 (especially useful on Root); Richard W. Leopold, *Elihu Root and the Conservative Tradition* (Boston, 1954), 123–50; John Milton Cooper, Jr., *The Warrior and the Priest: Woodrow Wilson and Theodore Roosevelt* (Cambridge, Mass., 1983), 276–87, 301, 304–7, 311; Ruhl Bartlett, *The League to Enforce Peace* (Chapel Hill, N.C., 1944). The Wilson quotes above are from his "Address at Coliseum" in St. Louis on September 5, 1919, in *The Messages and Papers of Woodrow Wilson*, ed. Albert Shaw, 2 vols. (New York, 1924), 2: 767–77. For the Covenant, see U.S., Department of State, *The Treaty of Versailles and After: Annotations of the Text of the Treaty*, Conference Series 92, Pub. 2724 (1947), 69–122.

Index

Adee, Alvey A., 22, 38
Africa, 188, 189, 260, 344 n75; scramble for, xi, 57, 59, 200, 201. *See also* individual countries
Aguinaldo, Emilio, 13
Ailes, Milton, 75
Alaska: boundary dispute, 26, 137, 141–45, 148, 183–84, 188, 195, 199, 200, 318 n14; Seward and, 317 n12
Albert I (of Belgium), 248
Algeciras, conference at, 204–6, 207
Algeria, 200
Allied Economic Conference, 253
Allies (Entente), 207, 230, 236–38, 240, 245, 246, 248, 250, 251, 253, 256–57, 259, 261–66; U.S. economic leverage over, 252, 254, 257–58, 261. *See also* France; Great Britain; Russia
Alsop Company case, 78
Alverstone, Lord, 145
American Asiatic Association, 97
American Group (banking syndicate), 74, 119, 122, 123, 127–29, 135, 314 nn166, 168
American International Corporation, 88, 133, 317 n209
American Peace and Arbitration League, 220
American Peace Society, 196
American Society of International Law, 216
Amery, Leo, 260
Anderson, Chandler P., 216, 339 n184
Andrew, Christopher, 200
Anglo-German naval rivalry, 114, 219, 226–29
Anglo-Japanese alliance, 104, 106, 112
"anti-imperialists," 9, 304 n22
Antung-Mukden railway, 119, 313 n147
Arabic (British liner), 243–44, 245

arbitration, xii, 15, 33, 55, 65, 70, 78–79, 89, 116, 185–87, 196–97, 210, 218, 224–25, 236, 267, 270, 336 n144, 337 n166; over Alaska, 142, 143, 144, 199; and Anglo-French treaty of 1903; and Atlantic fisheries controversy, 148; and Central America, 35–38; and Hague conference of 1899, 192, 194–95; and Hague conference of 1907, 207, 210, 213–15; Hay treaties of 1904–5, 198–200; as method of settling domestic disputes, 12; and Mexico, 173; pact with England, 1896, 141, 189, 198–99; at Pan-American conference of 1889–90, 55–56; at Pan-American conference of 1901–2, 63; at Pan-American conference of 1906, 68; Root treaties of 1908, 216–17, 220, 224; "unlimited" treaties, 218, 220–24, 337 n170, 338 n184; and Venezuela boundary dispute, 58–60; and Venezuela claims confrontation, 30–31, 331 n57
Argentina (Buenos Aires), 56, 65, 67, 87, 88, 174–75, 179, 296 n31, 298 n79; bankers and, 73–74, 81, 299 n83; battleship sales to, 75–76, 79, 83; and Drago Doctrine, 63–64, 70–71; and Pan-American pact, 85–86
Armour and Company, 88
Armour, J. Ogden, 88
Army War College, 217
Arthur, Chester Alan, 55
Asquith, Herbert, 260
Atlantic Ocean, 17, 114, 115, 134, 146, 150, 187, 188, 205, 206
Australia, 149, 344 n75
Austria-Hungary (Vienna), 103, 199, 207, 215, 216, 219, 228, 265–66, 348 n189

Bacon, Augustus, 206, 223–24
Bacon, Robert, 39, 40, 75

Acknowledgments

I have incurred many debts in the process of writing this book. Early on, good friend Peter Weiler was extremely generous with his time. He let me talk through with him, in great detail, many of the key ideas I was seeking to develop. The points he raised, as well as the confidence he showed in this project, meant a very great deal.

I pulled together some of the central arguments presented here in two papers I was invited to present during the early 1990s. One was for the German-American Historical Symposium held in Krefeld, Germany in May 1990. The other was for the October 1991 meeting of the University of Connecticut Foreign Policy Seminar. In modified form, the latter paper has in fact become the first chapter of this book. I want to thank the organizers of those events—especially Hans-Jürgen Schröder in the former case and Tom Paterson and Ed Wehrle in the latter—for the opportunity each provided.

Many other people have also been generous listeners as well as encouraging and constructive critics. These include Herb Bix, John Cavanagh, Frank Costigliola, Tom Dublin, Paul Faler, Anne Foster, Bill Freund, Gerald Gill, Jim Green, Kristin Hoganson, Nian-Sheng Huang, David Hunt, Walter Licht, Doug Little, Elizabeth Mahan, Patrick Manning, Drew McCoy, Arnold Offner, Carol Petillo, Marty Sherwin, Ted Steinberg, and Peter Winn. During the many years of our friendship, I have frequently discussed early twentieth-century world affairs with Feroz Ahmad. I have gained enormously from his almost encyclopedic grasp of the history of Europe and Asia during that era. His encouragement and the enthusiasm he showed for this project were also deeply appreciated.

Early drafts of some chapters were read, to my very considerable profit, by Ken Greenberg and Jim O'Brien. At a later point, Cyrus Veeser provided me with equally valuable feedback on chapter one. I owe a special debt to several people who read and commented on the entire manuscript in its latter stages. Bob Van Meter provided precisely the sort of honest and useful criticism I needed, and was looking for, once I had assembled a complete draft. He generously spent many hours discussing with me how and where I might cut (a lot) and revise. Garry Clifford provided an extremely valuable critique of the manuscript as well. Possessed of a truly remarkable grasp of the historiography of twentieth-century American foreign relations, he was, in particular, able to help me see how I might present and situate my arguments more clearly. During the last round of revision, I also profited greatly from Grey Osterud's close and careful reading. She helped me to understand where I might still try to cut and clarify. No less important, she also showed me where I had perhaps made my case.

From this project's inception, Walter LaFeber has been enormously helpful and encouraging. On several occasions he very generously took the time to discuss and debate with me the arguments laid out here. He also read a number of outlines and drafts, including the first draft of the entire manuscript, finished early in 1999. His penetrating questions and criticisms, as well as extensive editorial advice, helped me to make this a much better book than would otherwise have been the case. For all this, I am most sincerely grateful.

The research on which this study is based extends back many years. It also took me through a number of libraries and archives. I very much want to thank, for their commitment and assistance, the staffs of the Library of Congress, the National Archives, Firestone Library at Princeton, Sterling Library at Yale, Butler Library at Columbia, and Widener Library at Harvard. I would like to thank the director of Myrin Library at Ursinus College for permission to quote from the Francis M. Huntington-Wilson Papers, the director of the Rare Book and Manuscript Library at Columbia University for permission to quote from the Frank A. Vanderlip Papers, and the curator of manuscripts at Houghton Library, Harvard University for permission to quote from the William Woodville Rockhill Papers. I would also like to thank Blackwell Publishers for permission to use passages drawn from an article I published in *Diplomatic History* (Winter 1980) entitled "Reciprocity 1911: Continentalism and American Weltpolitik."

It has been my great good fortune to work with Peter Agree and others at the University of Pennsylvania Press. I am extremely grateful for their professional and considerate treatment both of me and of this work. Over the years, numerous scholars have described Peter to me as one of the best social science-history editors in the business. From direct experience, I now understand why that characterization is appropriate. Others at the press who have been especially helpful include Alison Anderson, Audra Wolfe, Erica Ginsburg, Debra Liese, and Ramon Smith.

Finally, I want to thank my wife and son for being patient with a project that came to be far more involved than originally anticipated. Irene provided me with invaluable feedback when I first sought to conceptualize this book. An author herself, she has throughout also been an invaluable critic of my writing. I am most grateful for the fact that she understood from the start what this work meant to me and was unflagging in her insistence that—despite the dimensions it had assumed—I see it through. Ted only lately became aware of what exactly it was I was spending so much time on. No matter. His patience was no less real. He also, by the marvelous unfolding of his own inquiring mind, helped to stimulate and sustain my interest in the world, past, present, and future.